D0026229

Creating Games

Creating Games

Mechanics, Content, and Technology

Morgan McGuire
Odest Chadwicke Jenkins

A K Peters, Ltd.
Wellesley, Massachusetts

Editorial, Sales, and Customer Service Office

A K Peters, Ltd.
888 Worcester Street, Suite 230
Wellesley, MA 02482
www.akpeters.com

Library of Congress Cataloging-in-Publication Data

McGuire, Morgan, 1976–
Creating games : mechanics, content, technology / Morgan McGuire, Odest Chadwicke Jenkins
p. cm.
Includes bibliographical references and index.
ISBN 978-1-56881-305-9 (alk. paper)
1. Computer games–Design. 2. Computer games–Programming. 3. Game theory. I. Jenkins, Odest Chadwicke. II. Title.
QA76.76.C672M388 2008
794.8'1536–dc22

2008009564

The cover design is a Japanese *tomoe*, a kind of three-way yin-yang. It represents the trinity of game creation: mechanics (symbolized by the die), content (the artist's palette), and technology (the gear). It is a graphical introduction to the book's spiral organization through those topics. The *tomoe* is also a reference to the notion of Zen-like *balance* in game design between the three pillars fairness, stability, and engagement. It is a theme throughout the text, with related cyclic structures appearing in the main loop of software code, the art revision process, the rock-paper-scissors and air-land-sea game mechanics, and the plot-character-action cycle of narrative.

Printed in India
12 11 10 09 08 10 9 8 7 6 5 4 3 2 1

For our favorite game players (who have similar names):

Sarah & Sonya – Morgan

Sarah, Morgan, and Wesley – Chad

Contents

MANAGEMENT

2. Process of Development

3. Managing Innovation

4. Critique and Proposal

5. The Design Document

6. Game Technology

MECHANICS

7. Strategic Thought

8. Choice and Probability

9. Balance

10. Mechanics

CONTENT

11. Creating a World

12. Art Direction

13. 3D Modeling

TECHNOLOGY

14. Real-Time Rendering

15. Physical Simulation

16. Network Programming

17. User Input

18. Artificial Intelligence

19. Social Issues

Preface

Games Are an Art and a Science

Games contain *mechanics*, *content*, and *technology*. Games are inherently multidisciplinary and can be taught through the perspective of any discipline. Examples include the psychology of engagement and strategy, the anthropology of social interaction and play, the economics of strategic agents, and the mathematics of game mechanics.

This book touches on many disciplines, but it focuses on computer science and art. It is easy to see the part computer science plays in the *technology* of video games and the contribution of the *content* of board and video games. What is most exciting is how the two unite to form something unique in *game design*.

Computer Science

An entire computer science curriculum could be taught in the context of entertainment technology (as some schools have already shown!) because games incorporate ideas from all areas of CS:

- programming languages
- software development
- artificial intelligence
- low-level machine models
- machine vision
- control systems

- computer graphics
- networking
- brain and cognitive science
- scalable algorithms and computational complexity

Game design introduces the fundamental concepts of computation in a concrete way that appeals to a broad range of students. Board games introduce computation without programming. When you write the rules for a board game, you are writing an algorithm. The ideas in rule writing are state, specifications, post-conditions, determinism, conditionals, iteration, recursion, order of execution, probability, and computability. These exactly mirror algorithm specification and programming, but they use a context that is familiar to everyone. Game design even involves "debugging," which is both analytic and experimental. The variables (state) of a board game are also concrete: locations of pieces on the board, cards in the hand, and numbers on a score card become the analog of the computer's memory. If you can write game rules, you can write source code. The only difference is the implementation of the "computer" and the language it understands.

From a software engineering perspective, games are huge development projects with serious commercial impact. They belong in the computer science canon studied by all students, just as operating systems, compilers, and databases were previously incorporated when they rose to similar prominence. Some numbers give an idea of the scope of modern commercial games.

Most video games contain about 1,000,000 lines of C++ source code (including support libraries). Development budgets for top games are in the millions; for example, *Halo 2* had a $20 million development budget, with an additional $20 million marketing budget. Typical development teams contain tens of programmers and as many as one hundred artists working in closely coupled groups. Despite the large scale of development, the production cycle can be compressed to as short as six months (e.g., for *Karaoke Revolution*). "AAA" titles, like *Titan Quest*, can take as long as six years. Two years of development is a reasonable average. Complicating these development cycles are the needs for real-time constraints, robust simulators, network security, driver issues, and terabyte databases of art assets. The games industry as a whole reports about $12 billion in retail sales, which makes it larger than the film industry in terms of U.S. box office receipts. But there is a small side to the industry as well. Indie and casual games contain about 75,000 lines of C++, Java, or Flash source code. They're usually written by small teams who must produce several titles a year to be competitive.

To support this complex development, game developers use tools and strategies different from the rest of the software industry. They build their own compilers (*Jak and Daxter* team: Lisp; the *Unreal Engine* used UnrealScript; previous versions of the *Quake* engine used QuakeC; throughout the industry there are many graphics compilers and preprocessors). Game developers also build their own content management and project management systems, debuggers, and profilers. As a result, the games industry is a hotbed of rapid development tools and practices and are early adopters of new technologies.

Art

Games are a popular, commercial art. That popularity does not diminish their cultural or academic value. It is tempting to idealize artists of the past, but Michelangelo and Mozart worked from commission to commission, and organ recitals were the rock concerts of their day. An artist reflects on and engages the culture of his or her era. Games don't treat classic subjects in classic materials—they engage our culture with our medium: technology.

That the *content* of games is art is obvious from first glance. Games use the same concentration on form, composition, and technique as other artistic media. Game artists even employ the same range of materials as other artists, from modeling clay, paint, and brushes to Photoshop and 3DS Max. Game artists produce 3D models, character animations, video sequences, fonts, 2D textures, manual illustrations, box art, promotional art, and concept art. These are not intended as museum pieces of fine art, but no one can argue that images like those in Figure 1 were produced by anything but a talented and trained artist! In fact, traditionally trained artists are more in demand with game companies than "game artists." A company can easily train new employees on digital tools, but it is not in a position to teach art fundamentals.

Some of the best-known games are obscene, violent, and filled with sex. So are works by Bosch, Duchamp, Hirst, Kubrick, and Kerouac. Subjects that invoke powerful emotions can be used well or frivolously, and the merit of a work is not the choice of subject but how it is explored and employed. In the discussion of games as art it is also important to recognize that there are also games of high quality and games of low quality. For every exemplary game, there are thousands that are trash. Nobody is holding out *Manhunt*, *Heavenly Sword*, or *Bagman* as a work of cultural value worth much consideration, but that doesn't lessen the value of *World of Warcraft*, *Grand Theft Auto III*, *Psychonauts*, or *Fallout*.

Art communicates and engages. It creates dialogues among the piece, the audience, the artist, and other works. Art lives in a mainstream of thought and reference. It reflects and shapes its culture. Games do all of these

Figure 1. *World of Warcraft* promotional images. (© 2001 Blizzard Entertainment)

things, which is why we call them art. The most interesting artistic element of games is the *design* and not the *content*, based on traditional forms of narrative, image, or animation. Every medium is strong at communicating different kinds of ideas. Whereas films and books are great for telling stories, architecture, sculpture, and painting are ineffective. That's because they aren't about relationships in time but are instead about relationships in space. Games are also ill suited for communicating stories, and it is hard for the designer to control time and space in games. Player choice is the essence of games, and exerting control over plot and perspective destroys that choice.

The medium of games is best at communicating relationships among characters and their environment and expressing themes about relationships. They express ideas that are deep and transportable but hard to appreciate in words, like physical experience or Zen koans. The player must be free to experiment and engage with the game to discover these relationships.

Take a traditional arcade game like the Macintosh classic *Bubble Trouble*. The player first sees an underwater maze of bubbles. A maze is a limitation on movement, but these walls are revealed as malleable and thereby present their dual nature as an asset for both offense and defense, as well as a constriction. The gameplay is static but dynamic within the player's mind. A beginning player follows the explicit arcade goal of crushing opponent fish between bubble walls. Yet, in time, one realizes that this is a minor distraction and that significant scores can be achieved only by aligning gems and fish in specific configurations. Some bubbles bounce back and can kill the player. To the new player these might seem dangerous, but to the advanced player, they are a way to exploit rows of enemies and achieve large-score multipliers. The bubbles can be pushed, bounce like balls, or can hatch enemies like eggs. The game constantly reinforces the notion that nothing is inherently good or bad but can be turned either way by the situation and strategy.

The world of games is complete with its own experimental pieces. These don't necessarily succeed either as works or as commercial endeavors, but they do radically challenge our notions of what a game is and use interaction to express ideas that are inaccessible in other media. Five examples of experimental works that approach the notion of games as "high art" are:

- In *September 12th*, the families of civilians killed in the crossfire of a war on terror become terrorists, making the game unwinnable.
- In the dream world of *Cloud*, a hospitalized child can fly, and the goal is meditative peace.
- *Simmer Down Sprinter* players race—to relax, as measured by biofeedback sensors.

- *Flow* literally entrances the player in a three-dimensional world under a microscope without explicit rules or scores.
- *Defcon* delivers the nuclear message "Everybody dies" to a chromatic chorus of children and silent detonations that makes your own success seem horrifying.

Why We Study Games

We study games

1. to support the games industry,
2. as an educational vehicle and academic topic, and
3. as a research area with applications as diverse as economics and robotics.

The industry wants to improve its products. The games industry is complex and competitive. Today, entering it and succeeding in it as an individual require more knowledge than 20 years ago, when everyone was a novice. A software development company faces the same challenges as individuals. Margins are tight, expectations are high, and competition is fierce. Most small, independent developers go out of business before their product ever ships. Even large developers go out of business all the time.

In this environment, a deep understanding of the technology and theory of games gives the individual an edge. Understanding the methodology of the most successful companies gives a company an edge.

Although the advantages of studying games in the games industry may be obvious, what may be less obvious is the fact that games are a great teaching tool in academia. They are engaging, real-world applications with which most students are already familiar. The study of games is rewarding even for those who have no further interest in the entertainment industry. Strategic analysis and construction of game mechanisms are widely applicable life skills. They are a more in-depth version of the educational benefit of playing games. Modern games require players to see through the surface story of a game and analyze it as a mathematical system. Players must learn to create an abstract mental model of the game world and make timely strategic decisions based on that model. Players must learn to balance multiple developing situations while avoiding continual distractions. A game developer has both of these skills and the further insights from the ability to create such scenarios. In a business context, we'd value exactly these skills but call them by different names: *sorting* the important from the insignificant, *divining* and *manipulating* the underlying motivations of a person or an organization, and discovering the pressure points of a process. These serve a marketing director, manufacturing manager, politician, and investment banker as well as the game player and the creator. They are also skills that are not traditionally taught in schools.

Games also present important research challenges. Most simulation problems for virtual worlds have demands that are far beyond what most current methods can handle: real-time physics for entire worlds; creating stable political and economic systems for massive multiplayer games; balancing the gameplay for systems with thousands of interacting rules; software development and management, squeezing 1,000 mythical man-months into one calendar year; and the ultimate entertainment industry problem: reliably engineering engaging, approachable, and socially acceptable content.

Many books on games are available today. You are holding one of them, and we recommend several others throughout this text. Games have conferences and journals, both created by the industry and by academia. At the time of this writing, the preponderance of academic work on games is in the humanities and the narrow area of 3D rendering for the sciences. However, with dedicated games majors and tracks like those at C.M.U., U.C. Santa Cruz, R.P.I., U.S.C. Viterbi, Carleton University, and the MOVES Institute, we expect increasing emphasis on nongraphics technology and the science of gameplay.

How to Read This Book

Game development is a broad, multidisciplinary field. We wrote this book to help readers with minimal experience to understand the disciplines underlying the different roles of a game development team and how those roles interact. After reading the chapter on rendering, for example, you may not understand enough to program your own 3D graphics system, but you *will* understand enough to hold a technical conversation with a 3D programmer and to appreciate the impact of content and design on the rendering system. You'll know what the technical constraints of the game's vision are for graphics and how future technologies may have different limitations. We believe that it is essential for every member of a team to understand the other members' roles and to communicate clearly with experts in each discipline, using correct terminology.

This book provides several kinds of resources beyond the chapter text. *Exercises* at the end of most chapters combine comprehension tests with problems that help the reader to interact with the material. *Worksheet*

Exercises are creative activities that help project teams generate new ideas and then structure the best ideas in a lightweight version of a game industry design document. In addition to crediting sources for facts and concepts, *Resources* recommend further reading materials.

We wrote this book with three different audiences in mind: the college student in a comprehensive, multidisciplinary games course that has a game prototype as the final project; the indie game developer or hobbyist who spends late nights with a group of friends hacking out the next great independent title; and the aspiring or newly hired game developer in an established game company. We recommend a different approach for each audience.

The Student

The material in this book is organized first for students. As a student, you can benefit from reading the book cover to cover, performing all of the end-of-chapter exercises, and using the worksheet exercises to structure your final project. In an academic course, this book is the road map to each team member's responsibilities and the workflow between them.

By using an existing video game engine, starting with off-the-shelf assets, and bringing together a multidisciplinary team, you should be able to produce real video games in one semester. An alternative is to focus on board games, which let you spend more time on strategic and artistic design by entirely removing computers from the situation. We have taught one-semester games and graphics courses from this material at both graduate and introductory levels. We have even compressed the entire semester into an intensive four-week program that focuses exclusively on board games.

This book presents games foremost in a computer science context and secondly as a multidisciplinary study. We believe the essence of what makes games different from every other activity and art form is that they rely on strategic decision making, search, and information management—the elements of computation. Although computer science contains the core of games, computer science alone is not enough to build a game. The most successful students in our courses are those who create teams that consist of a variety of majors, including studio art, computer science, economics, mathematics, and English.

For the teacher of a games course, we recommend a particular assignment strategy. This book should be read by all students in parallel, while team members independently augment their knowledge with an introductory text corresponding to their area. We recommend several such introductory texts from different publishers throughout this book. The worksheet exercises directly become homework assignments.

The Indie Developer

Indie developers will probably want to read the chapters out of order. Cover the material for your own role first, although all the chapters will likely serve you in the end. As an indie developer, the worksheet exercises are the real focus of the book and where you should invest the most time.

Unlike the student who has only 12 weeks and a limited budget to produce a prototype, the indie team can extend to a 6- or 12-month development cycle. Here, the team members likely have art, audio, and programming expertise but have never worked on games specifically.

Because our worksheet exercises are drawn from the forms and proposal sheets used by commercial game developers, working through those exercises as a team is an excellent way to organize indie development. You may be tempted to skip some of the formalism and worksheets to spend more time implementing your project. Please don't! Indie games have longer development cycles and more team members than games developed in a class. Because of this, the discipline of software engineering, brainstorming and cooperation rules, and the design document are essential to keeping the team productive. For an indie developer, our worksheet exercises are even *more* important than they are for a student!

The New Professional

For the professional, we recommend using the text as a reference book. For example, before meeting with the design team, read the chapter on design. When a programmer comments that "specular highlights are blowing out the dynamic range," you can look up those terms in the chapter on rendering. Rely on the index to guide you through terminology and the diagrams in the introduction to help you quickly identify content areas.

As in any industry, communication and team skills are as important as domain skills. When first entering the industry, it is important to quickly gain a broad view of the company and field of development as a whole and not become exclusively focused on the demands of a particular role and product. Many game developers move fluidly between teams, assuming a new role with each project. It is perfectly normal to enter a company as a playtester, become a level artist, and then become a designer. Some artists find that the limited shader programming they experience while working in 3DS Max leads them to a programming career, and often the senior management team is drawn from people who were once the team leaders of individual areas.

This book gives the broad view that is needed to augment domain knowledge when interviewing for a game job, to communicate effectively in the industry after being hired, and to eventually manage others later in a career.

Acknowledgments

We'd like to thank the editorial staff at A K Peters, especially Alice Peters and Kevin Jackson-Mead, and to thank Sarah Jenkins for an amazing job of managing copyright permissions across many companies. We also thank the people from the game community who have taken the time to discuss game design and development with us over many years, and who made available the images and design documents to support this text.

These include Charlie Cleveland and Max McGuire (Unknown Worlds Entertainment); Eran Egozy and Mike Verrette (Harmonix); Chris McEvoy, Guha Bala, Jan-Erik Steel, Steve Derrick, and Rob Gallerani (Vicarious Visions); Jesper Juul (Singapore-MIT Gambit Game Lab); Kent and Kim Quirk (CogniToy); Al Reed (Demiurge); Aaron Orenstein (GrandVirtual); David Baszucki and Erik Cassel (ROBLOX, Inc.); Paul Chieffo, Brian Sullivan, and Arthur Bruno (Iron Lore Entertainment); Jeff Anderson (Turbine); Jesse Schell, Randy Pausch and John Buchanan (CMU); Colleen McCreary, Jim Hejl, Pawel Wrotek, and Corey Taylor (EA); Mike Zyda (U.S.C. Viterbi); Rémi Arnaud and Craig Reynolds (Sony); Jeff Foley (Atari); David Blythe, Andi Fein, and Mike Oneppo (Microsoft); Wei Wei and Jim Whitehead (U.C. Santa Cruz); Mike Macedonia (Forterra); and the members of the Northern Berkshire Games Group: Chris Warren, Nick Branstator, Seth Brown, Debbie Baker, Jay Sachs, and Josh Szmajda.

Williamstown, MA
Providence, RI

Morgan McGuire
Chad Jenkins
January 2008

CHAPTER 1

Minigame Design Exercise

We begin our exploration of professional game development with an exercise that takes about 55 minutes. This is the minigame exercise because you are making a miniature game. In the industry, the term "minigame" also means a game within a game. This is appropriate, because you might later find yourself incorporating the results of this exercise into a larger project.

The goals of this exercise are to stimulate creativity, experience game design, and learn how to incorporate playtester feedback. Diving right into this exercise will introduce the challenges of designing even a simple game and thereby prepare you to approach the rest of the book with the right frame of mind.

The first time you go through the exercise, it is fine to be casual with the format and not write anything down. The second time you perform the exercise, be more careful about actually writing down your rules clearly. This may be difficult because it forces you to be precise. That kind of precision, however, is an essential tool for designing and analyzing games.

Use a different set of materials for the second playtest. Almost anything can serve as play materials, and the more unusual the better for creativity. Some examples of materials are *Scrabble* tiles, Legos™, toothpicks, dominoes, foam, sand timers, M&M candy, and checkers.

On subsequent exercises, it is valuable to perform a shorter, 20-minute variation. We advise the short version as a daily or weekly warmup for both professional and student developers alike. It is described later in this chapter.

This exercise is structured for at least two people. If you have an odd number of people, make one group of three people, but that group should work slightly faster because they'll have to test more games. If you are performing the exercise by yourself, it will only take about half an hour. In

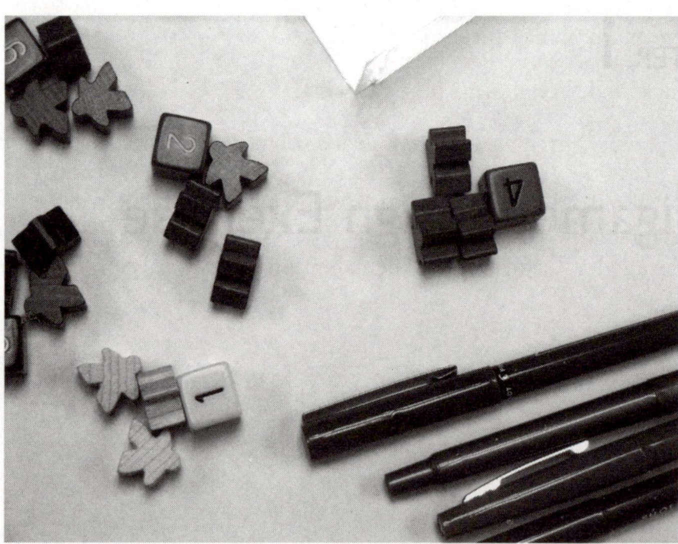

Figure 1.1. Pawns, dice, and pens for the minigame exercise. These *Carcassonne* pawns and dice were purchased on the Internet in bulk for a few cents each.

that case, try to create a single-player puzzle (which is much harder than a two-person game—alas!) and blend together the playtest and revision steps.

1.1 Design

(15 minutes) You have 15 minutes to design a board game that meets the following criteria, working by yourself.

1. Playable to completion in seven minutes or less.
2. Requires at most two players.
3. Completely explained on the provided rule sheet.
4. Contains at most seven rules.
5. Uses only the provided materials.

The following materials are provided to you (some of which are shown in Figure 1.1).

- A blank rules sheet (copied from Appendix A or our website).
- Five six-sided dice in red, green, blue, yellow, and black.

- Five blank white pieces of paper.
- Black, red, green, and blue markers.
- 15 pawns; three each of red, green, blue, yellow, and black.

You can use only these materials as raw materials and construction tools for crafting your game. However, you are not required to use them all, and you are encouraged to use them in unconventional ways.

1.1.1 Some Advice

Here are three pieces of advice for your design.

1. Start experimenting and writing immediately.
2. Your goal is to design *a* game, not a *great* game.
3. Leverage previous ideas.

The crazy limitations on both materials and time make it impossible to create a good game. They are, however, license to be creative and enjoy yourself. Some good advice for all projects is "git'r done," as in focus on *getting it done*, not on getting it done perfectly. There will be time later to perfect your completed solution.

Leveraging previous work is important in all endeavors. Creativity doesn't mean making up everything from scratch. You can approach the exercise by adapting an existing game, or rules from an existing game, to the pieces and limitations of the exercise format. Let the red pawns move like chess knights on a board of your own design, or play tic-tac-toe or shuffleboard with the dice and pawns.

1.2 Internal Playtest

(15 minutes) Partner up with one other person, and play each of your games in turn for no more than seven minutes each. When your game is being played, briefly explain the rules that you have written down or give a short demonstration. This time counts against your seven minutes, so be quick. As gameplay progresses, you'll find that you need to adjust the rules for clarity and fix unbalanced situations. Jot down brief notes to keep your rules sheet up to date without disrupting the flow of the game. You can discuss the quality of the game during play, but don't pause between games for a full review.

1.3 Revision

(5 minutes) Still working with your partner, choose the one of your two games that your intuition tells you will be the most successful (which one would you most want to play again?). Unless one game is obviously much better than the other, it doesn't really matter which game you choose to advance. Nobody's game will be very good at this stage, so keeping the flow of the exercise moving is the most important thing.

Quickly revise the chosen game as a team to improve it further, making changes to address specific issues observed during playtest. You may wish to incorporate ideas from the other game as well. Make a clean, legible copy of your rules sheet.

1.4 Kleenex™ Playtest

(15 minutes) Swap revised games with another two-person team. Designate one team as the Designers and the other team as the Players. The Players play the game they just received for no more than seven minutes, *based on the written-down rules.* Designers should avoid talking to the Players. When the game is complete, the teams switch roles and play the other game.

During a play session, the Designers evaluate the game based on the players' comprehension and play style, and the resulting game balance. See if Players understand the game as written (or described, if you are using the casual version of this exercise). Most of your experience in writing rules will come from watching people misunderstand your intent and learning to guard against confusion with precise language and examples. Once the Players understand the game, they likely won't play it in the style the Designers intended. Think about how you could change the game to make the Players' methods a viable and even better strategy or how you could change the rules so their approach is rechanneled if it destroys the balance. For balance, look for evidence that the game is (or is not) fair to all players, is stable against upsets, and is fun (engaging). Most minigames are not balanced, so what we're really seeking is an understanding of what wording in the current rules prevents the game from being balanced. This will help you to determine further changes.

The Players have never seen the game before. They are fresh and bring few expectations and zero experience to the game, accurately modeling the view of the real players who would buy your game. In the games industry, such testers are referred to as "Kleenex™" testers. Unlike in-house quality assurance and testing staff, a different team performs each Kleenex™ test to ensure a first-time player experience—you never use a tissue more than once.

1.5 Discussion

Think about what you observed in the playtests and what you learned about game design from the exercise. You are encouraged to revise your game (or one that you played) further after the exercise without any constraints on material, players, or time.

Most people find that the game they initially created is not much fun. The typical first-time game is one where you roll the dice and move the playing pieces according to the dice. If you find this dissatisfying compared to commercial games you've played, it is because a purely random game like this lacks strategy. The players do not have to make any decisions. In fact, the players are irrelevant, and we could just have robots play the game, or just flip a coin to determine the outcome of the game. If your game is like this, it doesn't mean that you're going to be a bad designer! It just means that you're starting from the same place as most people, which is having played many games but never made one yourself. You'll benefit from the ideas presented in this book, and you are already on your way to game development because you've just learned one of the first lessons about what makes a game engaging: meaningful choices for the players.

Most people also find that the game didn't play the way they expected it to. That's the value of the playtest. It is an experiment to determine both the qualitative human reaction and the quantitative effects of a complex combination of rules. The key to good game design is to begin that playtest process early and maintain it throughout development. When you worked with your partner to revise the game, you probably created a new game that was better than what either of you produced alone. You learned something from the playtest, and you benefited from having the effort and ideas of a team.

In the Kleenex™ playtest, you learned how to perform a playtest with outside parties. The Player's team had no prior knowledge of your game and had to figure it out from the rules. It might have been frustrating to watch them misinterpret your intentions, and maybe they even made fun of some features of your game. External playtests can be humbling experiences for these reasons. They are also very important for evaluating your work fairly. After you've seen how people interpret your rules for a few games, you will adapt the way you present and explain your game.

The basic format of the rules sheet that you created matches the rule book from a board game. Its critical elements are specifying the number of players, the materials, the play time, and the rules. The rules and the materials restrict what players can do, but they are also what makes it a game. An amazing fact about games is that they enable players to make choices by restricting what actions they can take. Without any rules, the players can do whatever they want, but people won't actually move play pieces around or find engagement without the constraints. The rules create a virtual world with different rules from those of the real world, and the materials represent the state of that world.

Although you have worked with board game materials, the process of specification, teamwork, playtesting, revision, and Kleenex^{TM} testing also applies to video games. The two critical differences between board and video games are:

- in a board game the players enforce the rules, but in a computer game a program enforces the rules, and
- in a video game, players generally don't know the real rules.

Instead, video game players are told an approximation of the real rules but are left to discover the boundaries of the virtual world on their own. Often they never understand the rules at a numeric level. For example, you may know that *Pac-Man* can't move through walls, but do you know how many pixels per second the character travels? Do you know how many points each pill is worth, or what algorithm the blue ghost uses for chasing the player?

The rules of a video game are embedded in the source code of the program, which also contains the implementation of enforcing the rules and creating images of the world. But the basic process of designing and setting down the rules is the same. The art design process is also essentially the same, just on a different scale. Furthermore, the process of writing source code—the technology difference between board and video games—feels very similar to the process of writing rules. Like the rules of a board game, computer programs must be unambiguous, quantitative, and explicit. The pieces of a program interact with one another in the same ways that rules interact with one another. And programs sometimes break or crash for, at least conceptually, the same reasons some rules contradict and don't make sense.

1.6 20-Minute Variation

After you've completed the full 55-minute version of the minigame exercise a few times, you can use this 20-minute variation to avoid cutting into the design time for your main game project. It is a good warmup at the beginning of the day and serves as the framework for other exercises. We recommend using an egg timer to restrict yourself to the time limits proscribed; it is easy to exceed time limits when you become wrapped up in your minigames. The following is a modified set of instructions for the 20-minute variation.

1.6.1 Design

(7 minutes) Design a game that can be played to completion by two players in about five minutes with, at most, seven rules. Follow the worksheet format rigorously.

1.6.2 Cleanup

(3 minutes) Clean up your written worksheet as much as possible so it can be read easily by others.

1.6.3 Playtest 1

(5 minutes) Team up with a partner. If you are working in a large group, choose someone you do not know or have not worked with very much. Exchange rules sheets and choose one game to go first. Have the designer explain the game very briefly and then play for the remainder of the five minutes. You will probably not complete the gaming session within the five minutes (and likely will not even want to). As rule changes are needed during the game, try to keep the worksheet up to date.

1.6.4 Playtest 2

(5 minutes) Now play the other person's game in the same manner as the first. At the end of the whole exercise, you can optionally discuss both games.

1.7 Exploration

Changing the materials available or the constraints on the game design lets you explore different aspects of game design within the quick warmup exercise. Here are some variations for designing a game that bring out particularly interesting design issues. Design a game where:

- There is no randomness. You can still use dice or cards, but they must not be used to create random outcomes.
- There are three players. This has different dynamics than a two-player game.
- Both players move the same pieces.

- There are two players, but the players have asymmetric in-game abilities.
- Players collaborate.
- Players have imperfect information (e.g., hidden cards or pieces like *Stratego*).
- There is only one player (i.e., a puzzle).
- There are no playing pieces at all! Charades, tag, and werewolf are three examples.
- An existing piece of art (e.g., a book, song, or painting) is a key structural element in the game.

CHAPTER 2

The Process of Development and Theory of Design

Terms Explained: *Game – Board Game – Video Game – Rules – Fiction – Abstract Game – Immersion – Mental Model – Mechanisms – Content – Developer – Game Design – Designer – Indie – Pod – Developer – Publisher – Team – Emergence – Progression*

Before you can create games, you must first learn to take them apart and appreciate their components. You can then innovate and combine your own variations. This chapter defines the term *game* and argues that it is helpful to consider that definition as flexible.

There are several methodologies for analyzing games. Levels of abstraction are models of gameplay at a cognitive level for the player. Emergence and progression are two different systems for giving rise to gameplay. Moving away from gameplay and towards the concrete artifact of the game itself, we can look at the major work products in a game: content, technology, and mechanisms. Each of those work products is created by a separate team within a game development company, leading to a developer-centric perspective. Finally, a process-based methodology considers the specifications between teams, the major steps in development, and the integration of work products.

This book discusses games in all their forms, specifically how to create both board games and video games. The concepts behind them are the same, and only the technology of implementation differs. Even if you are primarily interested in video game development, board games provide an approachable context for dealing with games early in an academic curriculum and for prototyping and thinking about mechanics in industry. One of the most profitable segments of the games industry is so-called casual gaming, with titles such as *Minesweeper*, *Tetris*, and online gambling. Most casual games closely resemble board games and are informed by them. Of course, video games require much more sophisticated technology than board games, and about one-third of this book is devoted to explaining that technology.

As described in the preface, this book has many paths. This chapter provides two different maps—one based on work products and one based on technology components—that guide you along those paths.

2.1 What Is a Game?

Consider this list of activities:

- chess
- *Monopoly*
- *Pac-Man*
- *Half-Life 2*
- *The Sims 2*
- *Dance Dance Revolution*
- *Chutes and Ladders* (*Snakes and Ladders*)
- hopscotch
- billiards
- ping-pong
- poker
- roulette
- pickup soccer
- professional soccer
- a professional flight simulator
- dolls
- dating

- peace treaty negotiation
- business meeting
- tending a fire
- a poetry course
- karaoke
- playing piano
- investing in the stock market
- the tax code
- a rock music concert
- reading a book
- hiking
- sleeping

Which of these activities are games? Everyone would probably agree that some of the activities near the top of the list are games. Classifying the activities at the bottom as games is questionable. The entries around the middle of the list are harder to classify as games or not games.

Think about the properties that the activities you would place in the *game* category have in common. Your list probably looks similar to Jesper Juul's definition [Juul 05] of a game: "A rule-based formal system, with variable and quantifiable outcomes, where different outcomes are assigned different values, where the player exerts effort to influence the outcome, the player feels emotionally attached to the outcome, and the real-world consequences are optional and negotiable."

Put more simply, Juul is saying that a game has these properties:

1. rules
2. players
3. goals (implies winning and losing)
4. choices that affect the outcome
5. consequences of winning or losing that are optional

This is a good working definition of a game. Let's look at its consequences. Under Juul's definition, roulette, or any gambling, is not a game because the consequences are not optional. You either win or lose real money. Likewise, professional sports (and professional chess) are not games because players' salaries and positions are determined by their performance. One could question whether any game's consequences are really optional, since personal satisfaction, group harmony, and prestige are subtly influenced by the outcome of a game. However, everyone is likely to agree that the consequences of a peace treaty negotiation are far more serious than those of a *Monopoly* game. More serious activities like negotiating a treaty, the stock market, paying taxes, attending a business meeting, and even dating are a lot like games in terms of strategy, but the "optional consequences" property rules them out. Note that there's no concept of "fun" in Juul's definition. It is implicit. If the consequences are truly optional, then the only reason one would play a game is for entertainment.

Under Juul's definition, *Chutes and Ladders* is also not a game because the players have no choices that affect the outcome. In a mathematical sense, this is another strike against roulette: although players can pick the number they are betting on, their choice is not informed, and the outcome is still random. A more surprising implication of the definition is that *The Sims 2* and other simulation software are not games because they have no explicit goals. The player chooses his or her own goals, but there is no objective winning condition. In the literature of game analysis, these activities are considered "toys" or "sandboxes" and are not proper games. Playing with dolls falls into the same category.

The computer science phenomena known as Conway's *Game of Life* is also not a game under Juul's definition (look for an online example of the *Game of Life* if you haven't seen it before). This is because, although it has rules and optional consequences, it has no players. Screensavers have similar properties.

The precise definition of *game* is of continuing debate in the field of ludology, or academic game studies. Ludology is a theoretical discipline of analysis, not game synthesis, and it draws its ranks primarily from the liberal arts, especially English, psychology, and sociology. Although this book contains many artistic and creative activities, it is ultimately written from an engineering and scientific viewpoint. We are less concerned with what a game is than with how to make *good* games. So we moderate Juul's definition for practical applications:

> Games are, generally, *entertainment* activities in which *players* make *choices* constrained by *rules* in pursuit of objective *goals* that they have a *fair* chance of achieving. These criteria can be relaxed; ultimately, if it feels like a game, then it is a game.

Many engaging activities such as gambling, children's games without strategy, and free-form simulations still intuitively feel like games. Game designers profitably create products for such activities, so all of our criteria are soft to admit a more general notion: "If it feels like a game, then it is a game." Feels like a game to whom? Although not useful as a theoretical definition, as a practical notion it is incredibly valuable to say "to most people" or "to the market," and since most people have similar ideas in this regard, "to me" is often sufficient. Although one can argue that almost any activity is a game (e.g., dreaming is a lot like playing a narrative simulation game), the point of defining games at all is so we can make meaningful statements about a class of activities. Expanding that class to include everything devalues the definition, so we ask the reader to draw a reasonable line between game and not game and avoid pedantry.

Although we exclude nonentertainment activities such as taxation strategy and warfare, we consider them closely related to games and recognize the advantages of sharing analysis and design tools among fields. Many of the analysis techniques in this book are drawn from economics and political science, where "games" are not entertainment at all. We are also less strict than Juul and allow that any significantly entertaining activity is a game, so poker and professional soccer are games, according to the popular conception.

It is interesting to look at the choices in certain activities that emphasize physical prowess, such as rhythm games (e.g., *Dance Dance Revolution*) and ancient sports (e.g., weightlifting). At first glance, these activities have no choices and no strategy. However, the weightlifter trains for years, employing a definite strategy in that training and in the preparation immediately before a meet. The game is also bigger than a single event. Choosing a weight class, an event schedule for the year, and when to push harder versus holding back to prepare for the next event during competition are all meaningful choices. During play of both video and physical games of pure physical skill, the player employs mental techniques to focus and get "in the zone," attempts to disturb the opponent's concentration, and makes strategic choices of body position and approach. So physical contests can be games, but the choices do not appear explicitly in the rules the way they do for other games. The same holds for mental contests akin to physical ones, such as a spelling bee or academic quiz bowl.

Games may be played on a computer, with real playing pieces, with pen and paper, or with words alone. For the sake of simplicity, we distinguish broadly between board games and video games. In *board games*, the rules are enforced by physical constraints (like a tavern puzzle) or by supervision by the other players. Even though they have no board, we casually refer to games like poker and *Carcassonne* as board games under this definition. In *video games*, the rules are enforced by a computer, so there is no opportunity for casual cheating or error in maintaining the game state. The computer might be a general-purpose machine, like a laptop or desktop, a handheld console like the Nintendo DS, a box that plugs into a television, or a dedicated one-game device like an arcade machine. Note that under this definition, a board game played on a computer becomes a computer game.

2.2 Levels of Abstraction

The world of a game operates at three levels of abstraction: fiction, the player's mental model, and the abstract game. The abstract game is the real set of rules, the fiction is the story that the designer tells the player, and the player forms his or her own mental model that is somewhere in between.

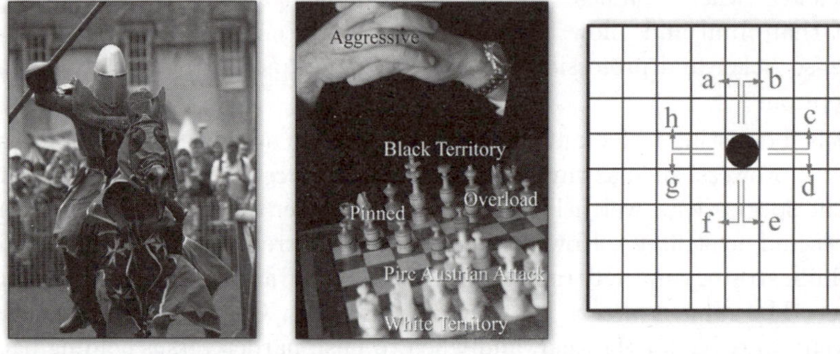

Figure 2.1. Fiction (left), a player's mental model (center), and the abstract game (right) in chess.

Fiction is the story the player is told; it is the rationale for the world of the game. In chess, the story is that two warring kingdoms face off across a plain. The foot soldiers, knights, and courtiers battle to capture the enemy king. In *Half-Life*, an MIT scientist in a government lab creates an interdimensional rift through which hostile aliens enter. The fiction also includes the explanations and justifications in a game. In chess, knights attack in an "L" shape because their lances hang off the side, as shown in Figure 2.1. Note that the gameplay is completely unaffected by the fiction. We could rewrite the fiction of chess by telling players that we're enacting a space battle and the piece attacking in an "L" has side-mounted phaser cannons. The shape of playing pieces, whether physical or 3D models, is part of the fiction. The sound effects, supporting artwork, box, plot, and dialogue are all fiction. Fiction draws the players into the game and helps them to form a mental model.

The *abstract game* is defined by the real rules, not the player's perception or fiction surrounding them. In contrast to video games, board games often tell players the rules and statistics outright. In some cases, such as poker, the rules we're told are accurate but obscure the underlying true mathematical rules of the system. A poker hand is just a complicated way of assigning nonuniform probabilities. That's because the rule description has a little bit of fiction in it; the rules of poker describe hands in exciting terms like "royal flush" and "aces high" instead of the more workmanlike concept of random numbers. In a game like chess, the rules are straightforward and clearly distinct from the fiction. The fiction—pawns are weak foot soldiers and castles shoot far-reaching arrows on straight lines—in modern chess is there only to help players remember the rules and lend gravitas to the act of moving markers around on a board. Some games have so little fiction that they are explicitly called *abstract*. These are usually puzzle games like go, *Yinsh*, *Maki*, *Hexen*, and *Tetris*.

The *mental model* is the set of rules and data that the player infers and uses to make decisions. This is the game that the player is really playing. Although most board games are closer to their abstract game than their fiction, some leverage so much storytelling that the fiction stays at the fore and the player's mental model drifts away from the abstract. *Dungeons & Dragons* and *Choose Your Own Adventure* books are examples where the story line and characterization encourage players to make decisions by role playing rather than pure strategy based on the rules.

Again, in *Half-Life*, for example, the player quickly learns that small "head crab" aliens are weak and easily killed, but if the head crab latches on, it can cause massive damage. Zombies are harder to take down. Zombies appear to have head crabs sitting on their heads (hence the crab's name), so surely if a head crab latches onto another scientist, he will become a zombie. What is interesting about the mental model is that it is often at least partially incorrect. In many games, the fiction is so compelling that it misleads the player. In *Half-Life*, head crabs can't really make new zombies. The zombies are actually completely separate enemies that have artwork that makes them look like scientists wearing head crabs. Because players are misled into forming a slightly incorrect mental model, they are likely to make suboptimal decisions from the point of view of winning the game. A player might meticulously clear the entire level of head crabs to save the scientists. Running past them is actually a better choice. Those scientists aren't real people who need saving, so attacking the crabs wastes bullets and offers no benefit. However, the subjective benefit of believing that the player has saved the scientists and the satisfaction of wiping out the enemy makes killing head crabs very engaging. So an incorrect mental model might make a game more attractive than a correct one. Often the goal of a game is not to win as efficiently as possible but to enjoy the process of playing.

By manipulating the fiction, the design team for a game influences the mental models the players build. Sometimes the goal is to help the players gain an intuitive grasp of a complex rules set. The players make their own simplified version of the rules and probabilities that helps them quickly make in-game decisions. This is how players approach complex games like *Puerto Rico*. In other cases, the abstract game is relatively simple, but the fiction creates a richer play experience by letting the player imagine complexity. The head crabs were one example of this; another is *The Sims*, where a relatively small set of rules simulates a wide range of human behaviors and lets the players pretend that in-game characters are alive.

We say that a game is *immersive* when the fiction meshes so well with the abstract game (as in *The Sims*) or the fiction is so compelling (e.g., the terrifying horror of *Resident Evil* or beauty of *Myst*) that the player's mental model follows the fiction instead of the abstract game. *Immersion* is a state of suspended disbelief, where the player effectively treats the game world as if it were real even though he or she knows at some higher level that it is not. Immersion is a very desirable quality for a progressive game or one that seeks to communicate at an emotional level. Not all games have to be immersive, however. The longest-lived games are abstract strategy board games like chess and go, which have zero immersion.

Sometimes the rules are simple and the player understands that but still forms a complex mental model. This is a way of coping with an explosive number of choices. This is the case for a game like go, which can be expressed in as few as four rules but presents hundreds of possible moves at each turn. Players know that the rules are simple and that the game has no fiction at all. However, the staggering number of choices makes the game too hard to approach based on just the rules. So players form a mental model based on "rules of thumb" or "heuristics" that guide their behavior. In go, these heuristics include "never play in an already-captured area," "divide territory early in the game," "form closed cycles," and a series of patterns. A good go player has hundreds of patterns memorized and is armed with about ten heuristics, even though the actual game rules don't reference these at all.

2.3 Emergence and Progression

You've heard the phrase "a minute to learn, a lifetime to master" applied to many games. It means that a game's rules are simple, but the strategy is complex. Complexity that arises from the combination of simple elements is called *emergence*. It is central to games. Every other form of entertainment is narrowly scripted. All of the complexity in a sonnet, a painting, or a symphony is there because the creator explicitly added it. Every word in a novel is written by the author. In a game, the developer builds the infrastructure and then allows the experience to emerge from interactions in the infrastructure. Not all games are emergent, although games like chess, *Counter-Strike*, and *Age of Empires* rely heavily on emergence for their gameplay.

Emergence is what makes games powerful, but it is also what makes them so hard to design. This is because games can surprise even their creators. One famous example of this is related by Warren Spector [Spector 07], the lead designer for *Deus Ex*. *Deus Ex* is a computer role-playing game played through the view of a first-person shooter. The player is a cyborg secret agent who is trying to unravel conspiracies in a dark science-fiction world. The game uses realistic physics and allows weapons to interact with the physics system. One weapon is a proximity mine, which can be glued to a surface and then explodes when an enemy (but not the player character) is nearby. Players discovered that the mine projects slightly from the surface it is on, and that as a result characters can stand on mines that have been applied to walls. The designers never added this ability explicitly; it just emerged from the rules for physics and the mine description built into the software code. By placing a series of mines on a wall, players built their own ladders and could reach areas of the game that the designers never intended them to see. This was a feature in the sense that it allowed players to creatively solve game problems in new ways. However, the designers didn't know about this feature ahead of time, so they built game levels in the typical way, where buildings are just facades and cities are only one block deep, even though they appear full from inside that block. When players climbed outside of the intended play area, they encountered a void. They expected to see more buildings and instead were stuck outside the game world. This result was a flaw, but whether the flaw was allowing emergence and player creativity to break the game (the publisher's business perspective) or not building the entire city to encourage this kind of behavior (Spector's design perspective) depends on your perspective—and your art budget.

Some games transfer control of the experience from the player to the designer. This is done by enforcing a *progression* through the game world, typically in the form of a plot. If you consider the entire history of gaming from primitive sports to medieval war games to modern video games, this is a relatively recent innovation. Only since the 1980s have computers been powerful enough to contain programs with the large amount of content to support a plot. And not until the 1990s were they able to display compelling graphics to support that plot in a cinematic style. Adventure games like *Adventure*, *Dungeons & Dragons*, *Diablo*, and *The Legend of Zelda* are examples of games with a strong progression.

The quest-style video games made famous by Tim Schafer and LucasArts, such as *Monkey Island*, *Full Throttle*, and *The Dig*, take progression to its logical conclusion. In those games, there is always exactly one correct action for the player at every point in time. Any other action results in a cycle back to the previous state or the end of the game. The positive aspect of this design is that these games can present beautifully complex stories because the designer has complete control. The drawback is that the players spend their time figuring out what the designer wants instead of solving in-game challenges their own way. Some players like the challenge, but others find it frustrating. Ultimately, it is important to keep in mind that in a progressive game, the player is playing against the designer, and in an emergent game, the player is playing against the environment.

Most games are not strictly progressive or emergent, but they have both kinds of elements. We've just discussed emergence in *Deus Ex*, but that game is also strongly progressive. Everyone who plays the game has essentially the same experience and sees essentially the same plot, although there are minor story arcs and alternative endings to unlock the progression a little. The large-scale strategy is progressive and locked down, but the small-scale tactics allow for emergence because simulation enables players to solve problems creatively.

Within the industry, many designers consider emergence to be elegant and progression to be a more prosaic form of design (this is our bias as well). This comes from trying to understand games and leverage them as a unique means of communication. Progressive elements are well understood from drama, literature, and music. In contrast, emergence is both unique among entertainment media and is also barely understood even in computer science and economics, which are the two fields that study it the most.

Progression is brute force in comparison. The game of go has a board, some stones, and about four rules, yet it has been one of the world's most popular games for many years. You can build your own go set out of pennies, dimes, and a board drawn on paper. Anyone can learn it in a few minutes, and it appeals to a wide range of people. That is emergence at its best. *Dreamfall* is an amazing progressive game, but it cost millions of dollars to create and about $50 for each player to buy (not counting the $2,000 computer you need to play it!). It appeals to a relatively small audience, and it is likely that nobody will be playing it ten years from now. You can see why many designers want to make games that are more emergent: it is both elegant and cost-effective to produce player enjoyment from very little content.

2.4 Development Roles

Games are complicated. Producing a board game requires the separate skills of drawing the box and board art, designing the pieces, designing the rules,

Figure 2.2. The development team for *Titan Quest.* (Image courtesy of Iron Lore Entertainment)

and writing the rules and other text in a clear and compelling fashion (ignoring the marketing and sales component, which is typically handled by a publisher). That easily requires three people; a video game development company typically contains between 5 and 80 people, with higher numbers common at large publisher-owned studios. Figure 2.2 shows a portion of the development team at Iron Lore Entertainment, a relatively large independent developer who was at the time working on their first title, *Titan Quest*. Lead designer Brian Sullivan (previously famous for design in *Age of Empires*) is fourth from the left in the back row.

The games business has four kinds of participants: the consumers who buy and play the games; the retail stores that sell the games; the publishers who fund the development, market the game to consumers, and distribute (sell) the games to the retail stores; and the developers who create the games. We'll discuss the relationship between these participants in Section 2.6. We begin with your role, the role of the developer who creates games.

It is common practice to call both the company as a whole and an employee of the company a *developer.* What is more confusing is that *developer* is also a short form of *software developer*, meaning the subset of employees who are programmers. We'll use *programmer* to explicitly identify those employees and minimize confusion.

The teams within a development company produce three distinct kinds of work products: mechanics, content, and technology. These three areas overlap. Mechanics are the mathematical machines that give rise to gameplay; they create the abstract game. Content is art, music, back story, dialog—the constituents of fiction. For a video game company, the technology is software, and it is produced by programmers. A board game's technology is the playing pieces and other physical components. Technology is the implementation of the abstract game rules and the enabler of content delivery. The

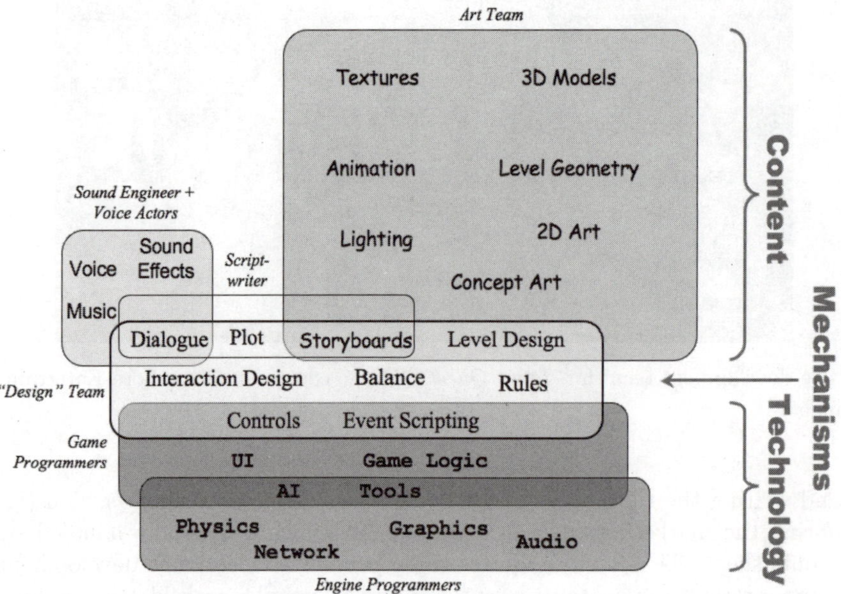

Figure 2.3. Teams and functional areas on a game project.

relationship between the mechanisms and the abstract game and between the content and the fiction is a bit like that between a recipe for a cake and the cake itself. Mechanics are concrete rule sets. The abstract game is a player's understanding that arises from those rules.

Figure 2.3 depicts the relationship among *teams* who work on a game within a development company and describes which kind of work product each creates. Each rounded box represents a team, with the name given in italics. Each team's areas of responsibility are written inside the boxes in fonts evocative of their domain (e.g., programming in Courier). Note that the teams overlap in many areas. This indicates an area where the members of two teams are likely to share responsibilities. In some companies, this means one person is a member of two teams. That happens very frequently at small developers. At a larger company, an overlap between teams means either that two teams will share responsibility for an area or that the responsibility might go to either team, depending on the nature of the specific game.

The size of each box is relative to the number of people on that team. Although specific numbers vary among projects, the content team is typically twice the size of the technology team, which is in turn about twice the size of the mechanism team. This was not always the case. Historically, board games were almost all mechanics. Early computer games like *Pong* and *M.U.L.E.* required equal parts technology and mechanics. As graphics improved to 256-color 2D and later to 3D, large art teams emerged and quickly began to dominate the size of the company.

Today we have reached a saturation point where larger art teams are too expensive. Thus, an interest in alternative content creation strategies developed. Player-created content is one way of achieving this, where the major challenge is finding and promoting the highest quality user content. The games *TrackMania*, *Second Life*, and *Spore* use this strategy. Other directions are procedural techniques and simulation, which leverage technology to synthesize content on the fly. Dynamic content synthesis has long been a staple of the "demo scene," which seeks to create tiny, gamelike demos that occupy the minimum disk space. Procedural content has recently gone mainstream with *Spore* and the *Pandromeda* engine.

For the "design" team, which is represented by the light box in the center, the word "design" is in quotation marks because although the term is used in the industry, it can be misleading to outsiders. The design team designs the game rules, layout, and concept—what we call the "mechanics" and "content" in this book. These make up the core of the game from a theoretical point of view. Most companies recognize the importance of that role and assign a high level of creative control and management responsibility to the lead designer. However, the design team does not design the structure of the software code, the character appearance, or details of the content, like lighting. Software design is called architecture and is performed by people called software architects or lead programmers. Art design is performed by the concept artist, the lead artist, or the art director (who might all be the same person).

Absent from the diagram are the management structure and the quality assurance (QA) team. These facilitate the game's development without directly producing elements that will appear in the final product. Each team has a lead, who is often the most senior member of the team. The lead is like a first-line manager in terms of priority setting, design oversight, and reporting but rarely has hiring and firing authority. The lead designer is often the manager of the team leads, although for a game that is particularly technology heavy the lead programmer may assume that role.

Producers and assistant producers work closely with the lead designer on specifications and scheduling. They have two major responsibilities: to keep the teams synchronized and delivering on schedule, and to maintain the relationship with the publisher. This means matching the specifications to the publisher's standards and often working with a direct counterpart producer at the publishing company. Traditional management roles in terms of budgeting, business negotiation, hiring and firing, legal issues, and basic company governance are handled by the general manager, president, chief technical officer, chief financial officer, chief executive officer, and so on. The management structure is often very flat and small within a game company because of the large ratio of product to business work. (The same often holds at a software start-up company, which has similar properties.)

The quality assurance team has both the roles of finding software errors in a video game company and of ensuring that the game is actually playable and engaging. Although playing games for a living sounds like fun, it is often one of the least desirable roles in a game company. Entry-level game QA involves the unenviable task of playing the same broken and incomplete game repeatedly, and then having to tell other developers the bad news that their work is broken. Playtests are an exciting time for the whole company, however. Internal playtests involve QA organizing the other developers to play the game and capturing their feedback for the designers. External (Kleenex™) playtests involve bringing in members of the public and observing how they play the game. This book proposes advanced analysis techniques that are just beginning to take hold in the industry for determining how a set of rules will play *without* the time and expense of observing actual gameplay for each rule change. However, today, playtesting is the industry's gold standard for evaluating a game before release. It will never be completely eliminated due to the ultimately human, and not mathematical, nature of entertainment.

The development teams can be used as a map of the chapters of this book. Each team's responsibility is primarily described in the chapters as follows.

Management. The Process of Development and Theory of Design (2), Game Technology (6), Managing Innovation (3), The Design Document (5), Social Issues (19).

Designers. The Design Document (5), Critique and Proposal (4), Mechanics (10), Strategic Thought (7), Choice and Probability (8), Level Design (11), Social Issues (19)

Artists. Art Direction (12), Creating a World (11), 3D Modeling (13), Technology (6).

Programmers. Technology (6), User Input (17), Artificial Intelligence (18), Physical Simulation (15), 3D Modeling (13), Real-Time Rendering (14), Network Programming (16).

This is not to say, for example, that a game programmer should read only the chapters on game programming. The teams need to communicate with one another. An artist must understand how a 3D model will be rendered to design it properly. The game designer must understand the technical limitations on the art and engine teams. This map of chapters helps you to identify areas describing your colleagues' roles so that you can have informed discussions with them.

2.5 Design as Theory

Although most game companies have similar operations, approaches, and corporate structures, their philosophies differ. As a result, there may be common ideas but no single accepted model of how to develop games in either the industry or academia. This book describes a workable model for taking games from concept through distributable product. Along the way, it discusses how the members of a game-development team interact and create their individual work products. We explain the generally accepted roles and issues involved in content and technology.

Mechanics are different. Outside of core industry design teams, few people even know how game mechanics are designed—even within the industry! Many people believe that game design is a black art or a free-for-all where designers face few creative restrictions. Others believe that all game designers are geniuses or that games spring fully formed from their minds.

Yet, game mechanic design is a discipline that can be approached in a principled way by anyone. We see the design team as a creative group working within the confines of a theory of mechanic design, whether or not they are consciously aware of that theory.

Consider an analogy to games. Music, literature, and visual art are creative, expressive disciplines. Yet, they are not completely dissimilar from engineering. Each has a long catalog of stock phrases that are combined with a few novel elements to create a new work. Each has a series of frameworks within which to innovate and a large body of previous work to build on. Each has an accepted process that leads to good results. And each has a theory field that can be used both to predict how engaging a work will be before it is ever performed and to guide the construction of works. For example, in music some stock terms are *arpeggios*, *scales*, and *chords*; some frameworks are *waltzes*, *verse-chorus-verse*, *operas*, and *lullabies*. Every new song is relative to hundreds of years of musical ideas, and music theory describes keys, rhythms, harmonies, and intervals.

We believe that games are a creative, expressive discipline and that a comprehensive theory of mechanism design for games is beginning to emerge. Games are fundamentally about players solving problems (making decisions) in the presence of opposing or confounding forces. The game designer's goal is to create rules that lead to interesting problems for players. A problem is interesting if it is neither too easy nor too hard, if it can be better solved with experience, and if the solution is personally gratifying (which often, but not always, means "fun"). The disciplines of economics, mathematics, political science, artificial intelligence, and psychology have long studied how decisions are made and which ones are gratifying. Industrial design and architecture are concerned with creating technology of artistic merit and maximal utility.

Today, a majority of games are not innovative because publishers cannot afford to risk a multimillion-dollar investment on a game that might not succeed. Even independent, student, and hobbyist games tend to minimize risk by remaking older commercial games like *Tetris* or *Quake*. For those developers, the critical resource is their time, and wasting that on a failed game is just as painful as losing money.

Working with a process for game development and a theory for game design removes much of the risk from game creation. When a framework and rules are in place for creativity, innovation can be pursued with less fear of creating a poor result. Less risk means less cost, which means more opportunity for creativity.

2.6 Industry Structure

The total annual value of the games market is somewhere between \$7 billion [Olson 06] and \$30 billion; estimates [Cassell and Jenkins 00, NPD Group 07] vary depending on whether hardware, used game sales, and domestic or international figures are included. Nevertheless, it is clearly on the same order as the film box office market and has been growing steadily for several years. Games are a big business managed by large publishing companies and organized from within. They present several interesting challenges in economics and business strategy.

The industry's professional organization is the International Game Developers Association (IGDA). It works in partnership with CMP Media, which publishes *Game Developer Magazine* and its online counterpart, the *Gamasutra.com* website. Local IGDA chapters have monthly meetings for talks and networking that are generally open to the public. CMP Media runs the annual Game Developers Conference (GDC), which focusses on business and technical content. Not affiliated with it or the IGDA, the Electronic Entertainment Expo (E^3) is primarily for marketing and business deals. It is where new games and game platforms are announced, and it is heavily covered by the press. In recent years, E^3 has gone from a massive tradeshow extravaganza to a more closed-door affair, in large part because advertisers have pulled out and thus reduced its budget.

Around the time of the scaling back of E^3, a number of other player-centric conferences were created by independent groups. Of these, the most significant is the Penny Arcade Expo (PAX). Created by the authors of the Penny Arcade blog and comic, this is an annual event that attracts thousands of attendees. It captures the "by players, for players" spirit. Thanks to the volunteers, community, and rules like "no booth babes," it is both more mature and more playful than comparable events. PAX avoids the comparatively heavy marketing overtones and commercial crassness of its competitors.

Like films, games are rated into age-appropriate categories based on violence, sexual content, and drug-use content. The rating systems and methods for preventing sales to minors vary among countries. In the United States, ratings are set by the independent Entertainment Software Rating Board (ESRB), based on information disclosed by developers. See Hyman's [Hyman 05b] article for a summary of the process in the United States and other countries.

Games are sold into several markets, which are differentiated by their platform: console (e.g., Sony PlayStation), portable (e.g., Nintendo DS), personal computer (PC), Web (e.g., PopCap, RealArcade), and cell phone. The largest market is consoles. Hit games in that space sell millions of units. The market is also segmented by the type of player. Casual players prefer puzzles (e.g., *Tetris* and *Bejeweled*) and other kinds of gameplay that have simple rules and require little time commitment. Hardcore players seek games with complex rule sets and skills that must be honed with repeated play. The emerging serious games sector targets education, public sector, social commentary, and training applications with video game technology (e.g., *Building Homes of Our Own*, *Virtual Iraq*).

The economics of game production are similar to those in the music and film industries because of the similar distribution schemes. There are both independent and publisher-owned studios. Independent development studios (developers) take a new game from the concept stage to a playable prototype. During this stage, external funding is rare, so most developers are funded from within or use royalties and advances from previous titles [Capps 06]. Using the prototype as proof of the game concept and the developer's abilities, the developer then submits a formal proposal [Ahearn 02] for the full game to publishers. If signed by a *publisher*, the developer then receives an advance on royalties, typically in the range of $500,000 to $5 million, to fund development of the full game over a period of months or years. The publisher receives the exclusive right to distribute and market the game and commonly also takes ownership of the source code, content, and intellectual property for the game franchise. Under an alternative model, many developers are wholly owned by their publishers, which directly funds development of new titles and reduces the cost of the relationship on the publisher side.

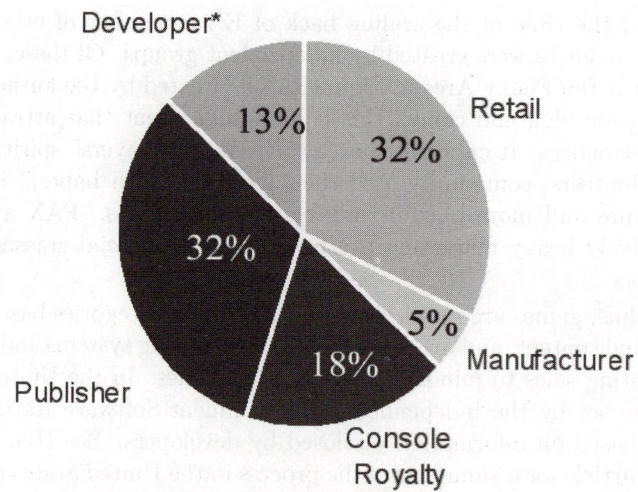

Figure 2.4. Typical division of revenue from a console game sale.

All but the smallest development companies work on multiple games simultaneously. This is necessary because of the 6- to 18-month time lag between when a game ships and when the royalty payments arrive. Without two games, being developed out of phase from each another, the developer would have no way to meet payroll demands. Small developers try to structure contracts with their publishers to avoid this lag. They either sell the whole game outright, receive advances on royalties, or use other methods such as shareware distribution, contractors, part-time employees, and stock grants to avoid salary compensation for employees after the game is completed.

When a game is sold at retail, the revenue is divided among the parties along the distribution chain, roughly as shown in Figure 2.4 (based on 2006 numbers from Games Investor Consulting [Games Investor Consulting Ltd. 06]). This chart is specifically for a console game; console manufacturers sell their hardware at a loss to gain market share and recoup the cost in part by charging a royalty on all titles sold for that console. Note that the developer only receives royalties after the publisher's advance is paid back. Thousands of games are published each year, but only tens of them are hits that recoup their development costs and lead to a profit. As a result, many developers fail to profit from their titles and ultimately go bankrupt. This is a source of agitation in the industry. It results in the common developer and player view of "controlling, money-grabbing" publishers and distributors exploiting their "creative, downtrodden" developers [Carless 06]. Such problems motivate the business problem of seeking more sustainable eco-

Figure 2.5. Indie games like *Darwinia* are often extremely creative but remain difficult to market under the publisher-driven economic model. The Steam Internet delivery platform was critical to the success of this game. (© 2005 Introversion Software)

nomic models, especially through Internet marketing and distribution channels that eliminate the manufacturer and retail, creating greater returns for the developer.

Small, independent (*indie*) game developers generally exist outside the conventional distribution scheme and rely exclusively on Internet distribution schemes. Many hobbyist indie developers also create modifications (mods) of existing games by replacing their content and portions of their gameplay programming, thus avoiding the costly technology phase of development. Indies are credited with some of the most creative new game ideas (e.g., *Darwinia*, *Gish*, *Weird Worlds*, *World of Goo*) and are encouraged through sessions such as the Independent Games Festival (http://igf.com/), Indie Game Jam (http://indiegamejam.com/), and Slamdance Guerilla Gamemaker Competition (http://slamdance.com/games/).[1] Indie development is also a strong motivating force among students who envision converting final projects and thesis work into their own game company.

Unfortunately, the current economic viability of indie development is questionable. According to Warren Spector, "You have a zero percent chance of success. The barrier to entry in terms of cost, quality required, access to a market ... forget it" [Olson 06]. John Carmack said, "In general, all the

[1]Slamdance may become a victim of its own artistic success. The culturally significant *Columbine* game, which explores a real-world high school massacre, stirred up so much controversy that the competition has been put in jeopardy.

technology progress has been essentially reducing the ability of a mod team to do something significant and competitive" [Dornan 06].

Yet, the last few years were an opportunity for renewed hope in the indie development scene. The Internet delivery platforms Xbox Live Arcade (XBLA) and Steam both delivered huge successes to indie games. In particular, indie developer Introversion's *Darwinia* (see Figure 2.5) and *Defcon* games sold incredibly well through Steam. Unknown Worlds Entertainment's sales of casual game *Zen of Sudoku* were reportedly sufficient to self-fund development of their major title, *Natural Selection 2*. Manifesto Games came online as a new developer-friendly Internet publisher for PC titles, and PopCap, RealArcade, and Yahoo! Games continued their huge successes in the casual indie market.

Finally, all major consoles (PS3, Wii, Xbox 360) and the Apple iPhone offer Internet delivery of games and microtransactions—the two pieces of infrastructure that have always been missing to make shareware/indie development a success. We believe that indie developers are one of the largest sources of innovation in the games industry and that a thriving indie scene is essential to the health of the games industry as a whole.

2.7 Exercises

1. What are the three components of game development?
2. What team usually has the most people on it in video game development?
3. What do game designers do?
4. Why are most games so similar?
5. Who receives most of the sale revenue per game in the traditional retail chain?
6. Choose two of the activities in the following list and discuss how they interact with our definition of *game*:
   (a) *God of War*
   (b) *Guitar Hero*
   (c) *Trivial Pursuit*
   (d) watching a baseball game on television
   (e) a foot race
   (f) recreationally bypassing a school computer's security

(g) surgery (for the surgeon)

(h) dating

7. Pick four of the following games that you have played (or research four of them on the Internet). For each of those games, give one or two sentences arguing why it is primarily progressive or emergent.

   (a) *Settlers of Catan*

   (b) a *Choose Your Own Adventure* book

   (c) *Bioshock*

   (d) *Guitar Hero 2*

   (e) *Super Mario Galaxy*

   (f) *Grand Theft Auto 4*

   (g) *Tetris*

   (h) *Mario Kart*

   (i) *Project Gotham Racing*

8. Differentiate between the fiction and abstract rules of a popular game with which you are familiar—for example, *Monopoly* or *Half-Life 2*. What do you expect a new player's mental model of the game to be? What about a veteran player? How does a maturing of the mental model affect the level of engagement and enjoyment that the player experiences?

9. It is important to stay current on the best work in the industry. Use the Internet to find the best video game, best indie video game, and best board game for each of the last three years. Make a list of those nine games, with their publishers, developers, year of publication, and platform.

   There are many ways to define *best*. You could research the best-selling games, the ones that won industry awards (e.g., from IGDA), or the games as rated by the end-of-year awards in magazines.

10. What is the salary budget for a high-quality commercial game? Make an estimate by assuming that a AAA game is in production for three years and has a total staff of 80 developers. Use *Game Developer Magazine*'s annual salary survey or other reasonable estimates to determine how much each team member is paid and Figure 2.3 or team

size information from published post-mortem articles to estimate the ratio of different teams at the developer.

2.8 Resources

2.8.1 Mainstream Thought

These are well-respected industry and academic resources for general games topics.

- *Gamasutra.com*
- *Game Developer Magazine*
- *The Journal of Game Studies*
- ACM Symposium on Interactive 3D Graphics and Games (I3D)
- ACM Video Game Symposium ("Sandbox")
- IGDA Education Summit
- The Game Developer's Conference (GDC)
- International Conference on Entertainment Computing
- FuturePlay conference
- DIGRA conference

Note that the popular gaming press magazines are generally useless for serious discussion. They pander to preteens and are biased, suspected to be corrupt, and driven by publishers' marketing efforts [MTV Networks 08].

2.8.2 Independent Thought

Many of the best resources for independent review and critical discussion of games are available online. These tend to combine the puerile, the brilliant, and the esoteric, but it is worth putting up with a little bit of sewer and a little bit of ivory tower for the insights. These are essential reading for those who want to stay current on games and the industry.

- *Penny Arcade* (http://www.penny-arcade.com/) comic and blog. This is one of the most successful online comics. It has millions of readers, and the creators are also behind the Penny Arcade Expo (PAX) and Child's Play gamer charity. Their reviews are unbiased, and comics tend to address real social issues in gaming. Be aware, however, that the comedy and writing frequently rely on obscenity for humor.

- *The Escapist* (http://www.escapistmagazine.com/) online magazine. Critical discussion of games by journalists; this is the *New York Times* of games journalism.

- *The Ludologist* (http://www.jesperjuul.net/ludologist/), Jesper Juul's blog, presents academic insights from one of the most significant ludologists.

- *Grand Text Auto* (http://grandtextauto.gatech.edu/), a group blog about procedural narrative, games, poetry, and art, is a collection of scholars debating what interactivity and technology means for art.

- Raph Koster's blog (http://www.raphkoster.com/), from the designer of *Star Wars Galaxies* and *Ultima Online*.

CHAPTER 3

Managing Innovation

Terms Explained: *Brainstorm* – *Innovation* – *Sunk Cost* – *Gantt Chart* – *Prototype* – *Hedge* – *Feedback* – *Time Estimate* – *Organization Chart*

Games are complex mathematical machines. To produce a good video game, your team must perform rigorous analysis, write thousands of lines of source code, maintain a large design document, and carefully model each of the scenes in 3D. To produce a good board game, your team must spend even more time on writing, analysis, and 2D art. But even all of this hard work is not enough to produce a *good* game.

Games are art that is evaluated subjectively by people. Technical proficiency at the fine arts is good enough to copy the masters but insufficient to produce a new masterwork. The same goes for games. Ultimately, your team needs innovation and creativity to create a unique vision. Their technical skills then will be directed to bring that vision to a playable title. Without the innovative vision, the team is all dressed up but has nowhere to go, and the game will not engage the player. So although most of the time and effort spent producing the game is of a quantitative, engineering nature, we must begin and always remain guided by a more qualitative approach.

To make a good game, you need to manage innovation. This is a constant cycle of encouraging creative thought and then paring down to the ideas that can actually be executed with the available resources. The management responsibility lies first with executives and team leads. However, every member of the team must also contribute to ensuring that creativity and engineering discipline work together. Innovation requires a supportive environment and process that can be achieved only as a team. In small indie teams, a team lead may not be clearly identified, which increases everyone else's responsibility because no one is in charge of discipline.

3.1 How Hard Can It Be?

A few hours of introspection, a serious look at your teammates' past work, and a few days of actually watching them work will give you a realistic evaluation of your team's abilities. For your first game, you won't have a good way to evaluate the difficulty of the project itself. However, a collaborative, positive working environment and an extremely conservative approach toward game development increases the chance of success. Even experienced developers can underestimate the work of new projects. On your first project, your ideas of what is possible will most likely be too optimistic. Whatever you think you can accomplish, try cutting back to one-tenth, or even one one-hundredth, of the initial idea. Seriously! Playing a game is fun, but *making* a game is work. The same is true of other creative endeavors. For example, it only takes about two hours and $15 to watch a movie, but it costs two years and $100 million to make one.

For many people, making a game is challenging, rewarding, and intellectually stimulating. But it is not the same as playing a game. Creating games requires a different skill set, huge amounts of time, and serious study. Video games are much harder to create than almost any other software application. The mechanics are as hard to design and balance as a tax code (and use many of the same techniques). The content—art, writing, and music—must succeed at both commercial and fine arts levels; the challenge is on par with industrial design.

Creating a game is a huge undertaking. Modern AAA video game (see Figures 3.1 and 3.2) budgets start at $5 million and involve at least 20 people working 60-hour weeks for several years. Huge games like *Assassin's Creed* or the *Madden* series have even larger budgets and may have hundreds of people on the development team [Cieslak 07]. Terabytes of art assets and millions of lines of code are needed. With huge teams, most of the budget, disk space, and head count is spent on art.

Even a board game like *Settlers of Catan* requires several experienced designers working for months, artists with professional training, thousands of person-hours of playtesting, and about $50,000 of investment to bring to even a first run to publication.

We hope you are impressed by these numbers, but don't let them discourage you. Instead, use them to set your expectations. The typical indie team consists of software developers working on the game as a personal project or unfunded start-up or students working for a class. Such teams have about four people and commit only a few thousand dollars and about six months of 20-hour weeks. Take a critical look at your team (critically evaluating yourself is an important skill we'll use often). If your team is like the one just described, you should not expect to produce a title comparable to those found in the boxes at the game store.

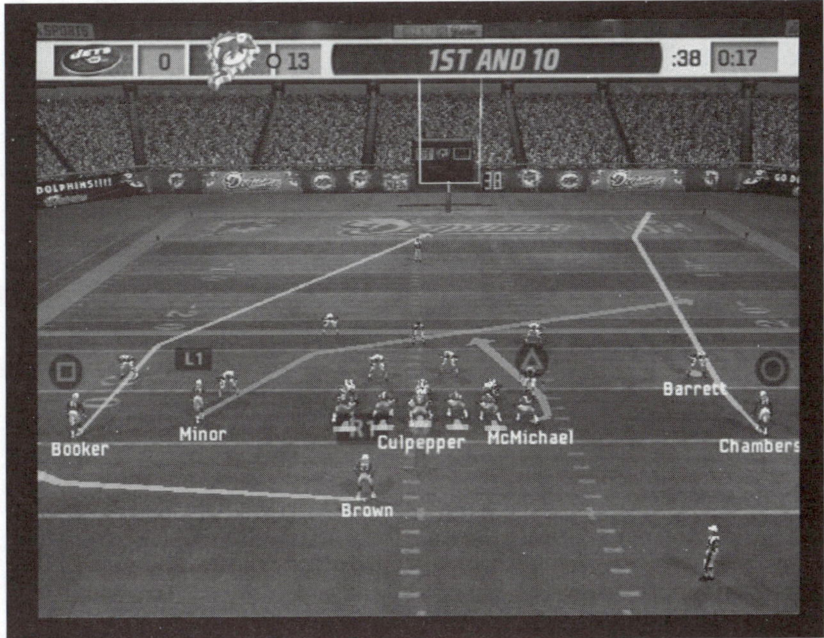

Figure 3.1. *Madden 2007*—tens of millions of dollars and person-centuries of work in the making. A small team is not going to create a game like this. (Image courtesy of Electronic Arts)

Figure 3.2. *Rock Band 2* contains pitch and beat recognition, real-time multi-track audio mixing, support for multiple custom input devices, and stylized 3D graphics—a small indie team is not going to produce a game like this. (Image courtesy of Harmonix Music Systems)

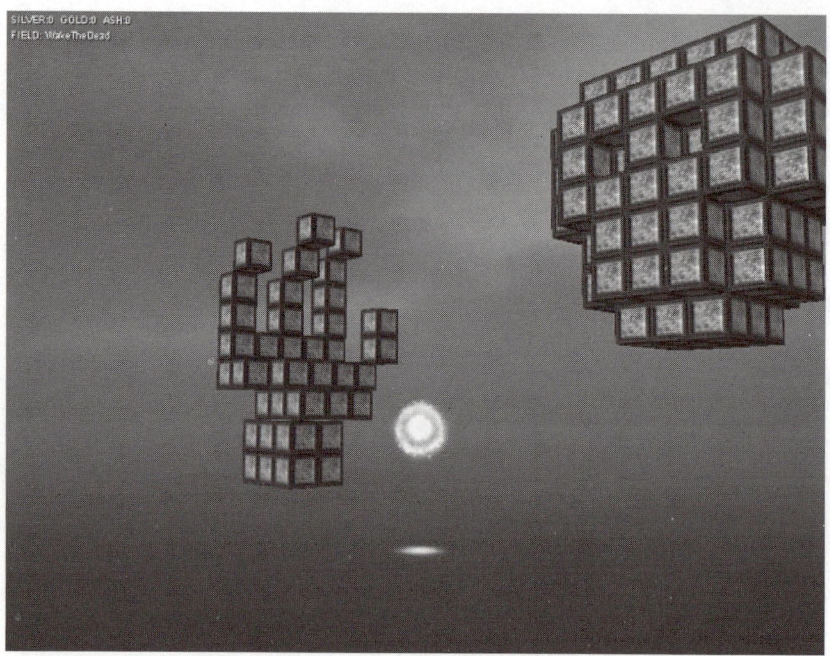

Figure 3.3. *Play with Fire* (shareware). A team of three programmers could make a puzzle game like this in two months. (Image courtesy of Manifesto Games)

Figure 3.4. *Cutthroat* (student final project). A team of two students made this board game in four weeks using purchased and hand-made materials.

Set your sights on something achievable. One person can make a solid and engaging computer or puzzle game in only a few months (see Figures 3.3 and 3.4). A team of four people with design, art, math, and writing skills can put together a board game in six weeks. A small but dedicated team can make a first-person shooter with one level and some innovative gameplay in 12 weeks if they work from an existing engine and 3D models. If that team tries to write a 3D game engine from scratch, they will end up with nothing but some buggy code and a model that won't load at the end of the time period.

One example of an impressive indie game is the *Natural Selection* mod for *Half-Life*. It completely reworks the underlying game engine into a hybrid RTS/FPS/RPG. The core of the game was created by a single programmer working around the clock for about two years. The models and maps were contributed by part-time artists. Your indie team can make something equally impressive if you have the opportunity to work full-time for a year and focus on the shortest path to your goal.

3.2 Attitude

Success at any creative endeavor requires a good attitude toward the work. You need a bold vision that is shared by the entire team, and you need to stick to it passionately. You must also accept that adjustments to that vision over time are both natural and necessary. Rarely does a successful game (or company, painting, song, movie, etc.) resemble the original concept. Yet, the heart of the vision will likely carry through the entire project. Here are the elements of a good attitude.

3.2.1 Champion Ideas

When a new idea is proposed, look for reasons to champion it, not to reject it. The reasons for rejection will usually be obvious to everyone or emerge naturally during the course of discussions. Of course, you don't have to artificially endorse something that you feel is a mistake, but you should look for gems in the rough. Even the worst suggestion either has some aspect of a good idea or at least has the potential to inspire a good idea, maybe by looking in exactly the opposite direction. By not immediately rejecting an idea, you are not implicitly accepting it. Good ideas will receive strong championship, and less good ideas will simply fall by the wayside as the good ideas attract all of the support. Often, after an idea has been aired, the original proposer will see flaws in it and drop the subject if it is truly inappropriate.

3.2.2 The Team Owns Ideas

Accepting changes means that you must be open to new ideas, regardless of their origin. When the shared vision grows to incorporate a new idea, that idea is "owned" by everyone. If the idea is eventually eliminated, don't accuse the team member who originally suggested it. Conversely, if the idea works out great, it is to everyone's credit for buying into it as a group. This is essential to creating a culture where every team member feels free to be creative. With group ownership, positive feelings are shared, and fear of embarrassment is avoided. Remember, your goal is to ship a game, not prove that you are smarter than your teammates. You all succeed or fail together.

3.2.3 Lead

Leadership means encouraging the rest of the team and setting a good example. This is true whether you are a formal leader, such as a team lead or manager; an informal leader, such as the senior member of a team of "equals"; or member of a team that has a leader, but a member who exhibits leadership qualities. As a leader, you aren't responsible for generating the best ideas. Instead, your role is to create an environment in which others can generate good ideas. Champion their work. Try to improve the process and environment, and make everyone feel valued. Even the weakest member of the team can have valuable contributions.

In the worst case, some members choose not to contribute or are unable to because of their environment. It is still important for them to feel valued and interact positively. As a member, it is important to treat them well, and as a team, a nonproductive member is better than an actively antiproductive member. Ultimately the good of the team and your personal reputation and relationships will outlast the project. The junior person whom you helped out may later become the CEO of another company and will remember your assistance early in his or her career. Many good teams have outlived their worst projects, especially if what made the project bad was beyond their control.

3.2.4 Understand Sunk Costs

Economists refer to the unrecoverable money already paid toward a goal as a *sunk cost.* Colloquially we might call this "water under the bridge." The key to sunk costs is that the value of something is what can be gained from it now, not how much it cost to obtain it in the first place. For game development, this means that the effort you put into a piece of code, a 3D model, or a design has no impact on its value. If you spent a week implementing a system for rendering spaceships, and the game vision changes to an ancient sea battle theme, the spaceship renderer is now worthless. This often means that you must be willing to toss out work that took a lot of effort if it isn't right for the project. This is difficult because we want to believe that our hard work is worth something. But the way to get the best value is to move forward and learn to let go if something is just not right.

This applies not only to work artifacts but to equipment, business deals, and hired employees, as well. Good game players know when to cut their losses, and game developers must apply the same dispassionate calculations to their own development process.

Of course, just because the sunk cost does not affect the value does not mean that other factors shouldn't be considered. Often, work products that are cut from one game can be modified to better suit the project or saved for another one. Rather than laying off an employee who was hired to work on a feature that was cut, look for ways to retasking him or her. Backing out of a business deal that turned sour may save money in the short run but hurt the team's reputation in the business world in the long run.

3.2.5 Eyes on the Prize

It is easy to get captivated with one specific element of a game and lose sight of the goal. Always keep the whole vision in mind. As negative examples, don't get so captivated with your vision of a particular sword-fighting scene that you lose sight of the entire pirate game. Don't get so engrossed on modeling the pirate king's parrot that you fail to create good models of all the other characters. Don't get so engrossed in optimizing the hash table that you fail to code up the rest of the game.

Remember that on any given task, the goal is not to get it perfect but to get it done. Game design is naturally iterative. It is always a good strategy to assemble an early version of the entire game before refining aspects of it. In the broader context, keeping your eyes on the prize means remembering to bury personal disagreements and cut anything nonessential in favor of shipping a great game.

3.2.6 Respect

Respect all aspects of development by evaluating them fairly and accurately. Respect previous games, which were also created by intelligent people, without worshiping them. Don't ridicule the flaws of another game, because your team is susceptible to exactly the same kinds of failures and must actively work to learn from others' mistakes. The best game designers have serious flops to their credit, as well. Study games that you enjoy, and try to imitate their systems and development processes. You are capable of similar results given the right resources, approach, and luck.

Likewise, there are no new ideas. Everything that you can possibly think of has been tried before. It may have failed or never gained popularity because other circumstances conspired against it. Seek out and study related work, whether in art galleries, research papers, designs, or whole games. Since your ideas are going to fall in line with previous ideas of others, you can give yourself a head start by looking at what they have done and figuring out how to use it to your advantage.

Respect your limitations and your team's limitations. A wise team targets goals just inside their capabilities and plays to their strengths.

3.2.7 Save It for the Expansion Pack

A culture that encourages creativity and innovation generates a lot of ideas. Most of those ideas are terrible, but some of them are good, and a few are both good *and* central to the vision. To succeed, the team must constantly cut out features and ideas to keep the core of the vision as focused as possible. If something isn't essential, it should be stripped.

Remember that anything that is cut is not ruled out for eternity. Any good idea that must be cut is a great candidate for an expansion pack, patch, or sequel. If you finish a project early or under budget, those ideas can even come back right away. Cuts don't mean "never," just "not now."

Target for the minimum feature set that will satisfy the contract, meet the market's expectations, or earn you an A in the class. Nobody was ever appreciated for failing to meet minimum expectations because he or she was trying to overdeliver.

3.2.8 Embrace Expression

You can wear a suit to work, sit in an immaculate cubicle, and make great games. But at most game companies, you'll find that the employees look more like rock stars than business people. This isn't a sign that they aren't professional; they just express their professionalism in different ways. Game developers work long hours for comparatively low pay, study their craft intensely, and speak at a high intellectual level about their roles. They wear expressive outfits (and hairstyles ... and piercings), decorate their work areas, and use "colorful" language as a way of embracing the creative endeavor. They surround themselves with art, games, and toys. This stimulates ideas and creates an environment that is comfortable for an often young and alternative culture workforce. You don't have to do these things if they aren't comfortable for you. But you may find that the pressure and creative drive of game development are best met with a more expressive environment than is appropriate for other jobs. Many studios provide recreation facilities and social spaces to encourage this kind of interaction, for example at the EA campuses in Figure 3.5.

Figure 3.5. Work hard, play hard. Electronic Arts studios around the world. The cafeteria at EA Madrid in Spain, with life-sized *Sims* characters (top). The arcade at EA Tiburon in Florida, USA (center). Soccer, basketball, and roof gardens at EAC (bottom). (Images courtesy of EA)

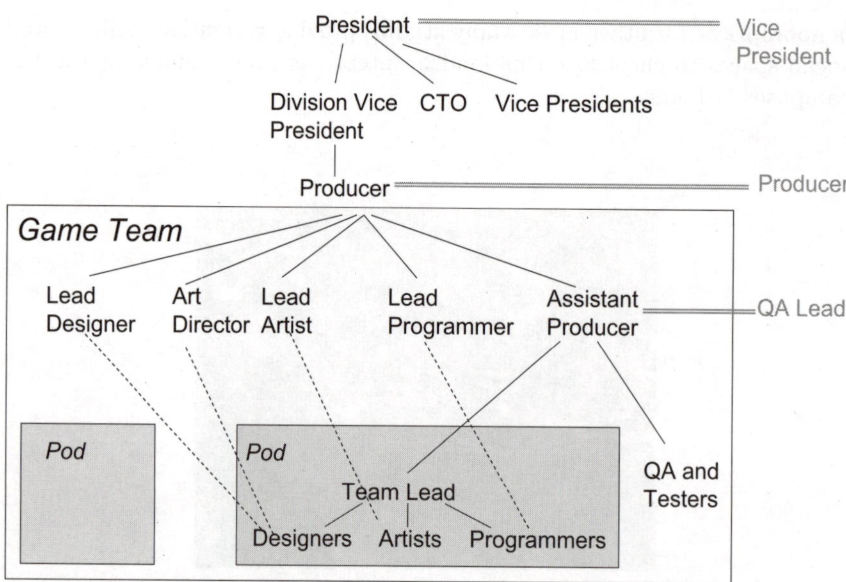

Figure 3.6. Organization chart for a medium- to large-size independent development company.

3.3 Organization Chart

For an indie, hobbyist, or student group, there is no need for an organization system. The team may have a leader, but everyone is essentially a peer. Larger and professional organizations need management structures. These vary from company to company but generally look something like Figure 3.6.

At the top of the reporting chain are the executives. They manage the day-to-day affairs of the company as a business enterprise and are rarely invested deeply in any one game. The producer is the executive who directly works with one or more games. He or she is responsible for that game and manages the relationship with the publishing company's counterpart producer. This involves regular meetings and demonstrations, as well as tracking of progress and bugs in the schedule. The game team has a lead developer in each area: content, mechanisms, and technology. These leads are responsible for overall operations but do not bear traditional managerial duties like scheduling, hiring and firing, and other human resources responsibilities. Feature areas, whether parts of the game like a level or overall aspects like an in-game inventory system, are assigned to teams called *pods* that consist of about five developers. Some pods will work on tools, others on core technology, and the remainder on the game itself. Pods have a team lead who usually does not have managerial responsibilities beyond representing the team at meetings and chairing podmeetings. Most game companies have a few internal quality assurance developers and a set of volunteer testers. The main quality assurance and testing role, however, is handled by the publisher.

No single organization chart fits all companies. It is common for several of these positions to be combined into one or for one person to hold multiple roles (e.g., producer/designers, CTO/lead programmers). Matrix reporting structures are also popular in game companies, where one person has a different reporting manager for different aspects of his or her job. The dotted lines in Figure 3.6 that indicates the relationships among area leads and developers in their area suggests this kind of relationship even within the strict hierarchy of the figure.

3.4 Consistency

It is important to maintain a consistent quality level throughout all aspects of a game. If one element looks spectacular, it can make everything else look worse, and if one element is weak it makes everything seem bad. If you have amazing art and average music, the music will sound comparatively worse than it really is, and the player will perceive that the game is bad. If you lower the art quality proportionally but do not improve the music, players will likely perceive the overall quality of the game as higher even though you have just *reduced* the net quality. They will also think that the music sounds better, even though the music hasn't changed at all.

The two places where video games tend to have severe quality issues are animation and plot. Realistic computer animation of human 3D characters is a difficult problem. In fact, it has proved much harder than realistic rendering, which is now possible in real time for many game scenes. This means that characters move like robots instead of like real people. As a result, players perceive the rendering as bad even though it is fantastic. Reducing the rendering and audio quality to match the animation gives a much better overall impression.

Video game plots and dialogue tend to be very weak, even by popular standards. This is partly because it is very hard to create interesting stories and dialogue within the gameplay of most game technology. It isn't that we can't tell good stories in games, but that we can't tell a good story while locked into a first-person shooter or RTS. Games like *Day of the Tentacle* and *Indigo Prophecy* set out to tell great stories and then built gameplay around that rather than bolting stories onto another mechanic that doesn't support them. In those games, the player ignores most of the rendering, audio, and other content and focuses on the story line. You can't play these games without paying close attention to the story.

Games like *Halo*, *DOOM*, and *Hard Boiled* are at their best when functioning as emergent combat games and at their worst when forcing a plot on the player. Given that, the avenues for improvement are to degrade the rendering, improve the plot (but since it is irrelevant to gameplay, players will largely ignore it and therefore have a hard time following an interesting plot), or drop the plot altogether, as *Unreal Tournament* and the *Quake* games did. If there is *no* plot, then there isn't a *bad* plot, and the overall level of quality becomes consistently high.

3.5 Inspiration

Working from a blank slate is hard. Instead, start your inspiration with some material, even if you later move away from it. One of the first questions in a game industry job interview is "What games are you playing?" That's because people who immerse themselves in games have a strong base of examples from which to draw inspiration. Many projects began with an existing game that the team then modified to make it better or simpler or to incorporate new ideas. You can start a project in other ways, too. Since mechanics, content, and technology are the three components of a game, those each can be a great starting point. We find that most successful teams start with a theme or story (content) and then add mechanics to fit them.

3.5.1 Mechanics

The largest room for innovation in game development today is in game design. To begin with mechanisms, choose a specific mechanic that you're interested in, such as a board game where players cooperate or combining FPS and RTS elements. Next, design abstract rules for this mechanic. Usually the process of balancing a small number of rules leads you to introduce additional rules. Those rules need a story to explain them and motivate the goal, which in turn leads you to a suitable theme.

3.5.2 Content

To begin with content, first select a 3D model, a set of sound effects, board-game playing pieces, or some concept art. Figure out what game would use this content. If these sound effects were from a movie, what movie would it be? What is the story behind this character? How would pieces like this move across a board? The critique process described in Chapter 4 is a good way to analyze an existing game and move forward with it. Another approach for content-based inspiration is to start with a theme. Here, the team selects a topic, like pirates or farming, and then brainstorms a list of all the words inspired by that theme. Then, they design mechanics to fit that theme (What is "walking the plank"? How does sailing work? What will gold represent?).

3.5.3 Technology

Technology can be either a good or bad source of inspiration for games. Designing a game around a rendering or physics technique generally fails to create a truly engaging experience. Technology showcase games like *DOOM* receive a lot of press attention but actually sell very few units and reach a small audience. The companies that do well with technology-centric games tend to succeed economically by licensing their technology, not by selling game units. The best-selling games are often not the most technologically advanced. For example, handheld games and cell phone games sell millions of units and have tremendous profit margins but generally have technology that is a decade behind the cutting edge.

3.5.4 Existing Ideas

Taking inspiration from technology is good if the technology fundamentally changes the way the player interacts with the game. The Nintendo DS and Wii use novel interaction schemes: touch, speech, and full-body movement. This leads to a new gaming experience, and developers are wise to explore ways to use these interaction methods. For example, consider a stylus and touch screen. The stylus can be a sword, an analog input device, a pen, a surgical scalpel, a water jet, Spider-Man's web slinger, or a conductor's baton. Brainstorming ways that a specific technology can be used leads to new mechanics and suggests themes.

Internet walkthroughs and strategy guides for other games are a great way to research them and get ideas. These provide offline reading material that will expose you to new gameplay ideas without the time investment of playing every game that is released. Often a game is no fun because of a bad implementation, but it still has ideas that can be put to good use.

3.6 Brainstorming

The attitude and inspiration guidelines come together formally during brainstorming sessions. Many of the exercises in this book and the processes that you will follow during development depend on the rapid generation of ideas.

Brainstorming is a process for leveraging a group's ability to generate those ideas. It is not a free-for-all. Brainstorming follows a specific set of rules designed to maximize creativity and collaboration.

1. **Write down every idea.**
2. **Do not criticize others' ideas.**
3. Set a time limit.
4. Warm up.
5. Seed the discussion.
6. Work on quantity, not quality.
7. Encourage others.
8. Build off and modify existing ideas.
9. Seek outrageous and humorous ideas.

The time limit (typically 10 to 30 minutes) adds just enough pressure to encourage the group to generate a lot of ideas quickly, instead of trying to generate a few perfect ones. It is hard to ask a group of people to instantly become creative in a meeting. To help get everyone in the right frame of mind, begin with a low-pressure social warmup like playing a short game, eating a snack, or sharing the names of your favorite songs. Then, to avoid starting with a blank slate, begin the session with a few seed ideas. The session needs a secretary who will write all suggestions on a board for everyone to see. He or she should come prepared with the seed ideas. After the seeds are out, everyone is welcome to contribute spontaneous ideas. The secretary should write down all the ideas, even if some of them were meant as jokes or are clearly inappropriate. The goal is to generate as many ideas as possible. Everyone else in the team should be similarly supportive. Do not say anything negative about ideas (there will be plenty of time for debate later), and encourage all suggestions by trying to build off what is already on the board. When the flow starts to slacken, reach for crazy ideas to get it restarted. It helps to brainstorm in a room with lots of distractions or decorations that act as idea generators.

3.7 Scheduling

For anything except a hobbyist team, you need a schedule to ensure that your commercial game will ship on time and budget or that your academic final project will complete before the course does.

A development schedule begins as a list of regularly spaced calendar milestones, either self-selected or imposed by a publisher. The team then works backward from milestones to a list of tasks that must be completed for each one.

The last milestone is obviously a completed game. Don't forget that *completed* means polished and tested. For a published game, it also means translated into multiple languages, advertised, and manufactured—factors that might double your technical development time estimate. The following discussion describes practices for making a good schedule and adhering to it. See Appendix E for sample schedules.

3.7.1 Build Early

A critical early milestone is the working *prototype.* For a short project (anything less than six months), you should have a playable prototype running in at most one-quarter of the total project time. This prototype must include every crucial feature. If it doesn't play well or can't be completed on time, you are not going to succeed with the current plan and must scrap it and restart with lower expectations. For a long project, limit this probationary period to six months at a maximum. For a video game, a playable prototype means a working "build"—code actually compiling and running. For a board game, it means that the essential rules are in place. In each case, the game design will still need huge amounts of work after the prototype—that's what the designer does for the other three-quarters of the project. The art will be either preliminary work by real artists, cubes-and-spheres "programmer art," or simply stock assets that have been dropped in as placeholders. But the mechanics have to work, and the play experience must be enjoyable.

It is important to get an early build working for several reasons. If your game is viable early on, it will be obvious what you need to do to perfect it. The team will play the game and be inspired to add the supporting features and to fix bugs quickly. The last quarter of a successful project will always be spent on polishing. During that phase, the design and features are locked down, and all changes are carefully scheduled refinements. Teams that don't have a polish phase find themselves releasing patches after the fact if they are lucky, and looking for new jobs if they are not.

The middle stretch of game development (half the total development time) is spent building out the prototype into a real system. Note that this assumes that building out an unpolished game takes (including the prototype time) three times as long as making a prototype! This is probably not conservative enough, but it is hard to get the early prototype out faster than six months or one-quarter of the total development time. First-time game developers often have a hard time believing that once the "real work" of the prototype is done, it's still a long way to shipping the product. The best evidence that building out is time consuming is the "Postmortem" series in *Game Developer Magazine.* Every month a new, professional team reports that it had to make huge feature cuts, shipped late, and went over budget because it underestimated the work of finishing a working prototype.

Finally, if you follow these guidelines and discover that your team was more productive than most and really did finish early, that means you'll get to spend more time on polish and add more features from your expansion pack wish list. This probably won't happen, but it is the upside of being conservative on scheduling.

3.7.2 Time Estimates

Three factors shape the schedule: external constraints, time estimates, and dependencies. *Time estimates* are each individual's, group's, or team's approximation of how long they think each feature will require to implement. *Dependencies* are cases where work on one feature cannot begin until another is completed. This can cause the schedule to push out even if the amount of work divided by the number of people otherwise looks achievable.

The *Gantt chart* shown in Figure 3.7 is one scheduling tool. It is a timeline on a grid where each developer has a row, and the columns represent days. Tasks appear in a developer's row. Obviously, no developer can be assigned multiple tasks in the same time slot. Tasks that depend on one another are linked by dependency arrows. If task B (e.g., implementing the

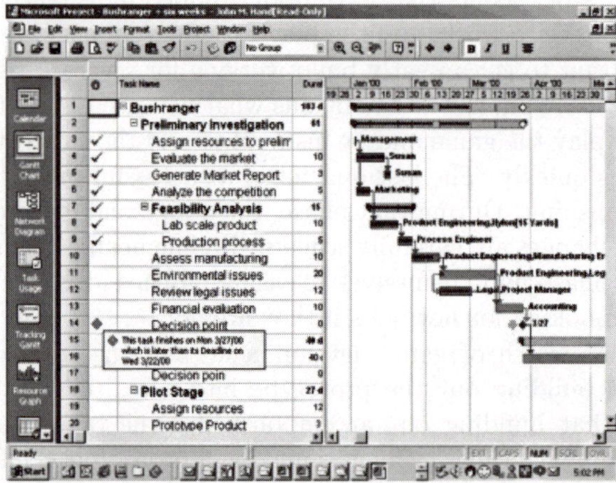

Figure 3.7. A development scheduled maintained in Microsoft Project, viewed as a Gantt chart. (Microsoft product screenshot reprinted with permission from Microsoft Corporation)

level geometry) depends on task A (e.g., writing the level editor tool), then an arrow stretches from the back of A to the front of B. Task B can never be dragged earlier in the schedule than the end of task A. When many complex dependencies are on the schedule, this tool makes it easier to ensure that no task is scheduled earlier than physically possible. The scheduling goal is to make the last task complete as soon as possible without ever violating a dependency. Blank spaces in the chart are areas where one person is stalled waiting for another and should be avoided.

Figure 3.8 shows the level of scheduling interdependence between the artists working on assets for *Spider-Man 3: The Game*. Each box represents part of an art asset—for example, a texture, a 3D mesh, or an animation. Those translate directly to boxes on the schedule. The edges between boxes are dependencies. An artist can't paint the texture for Spider-Man's suit

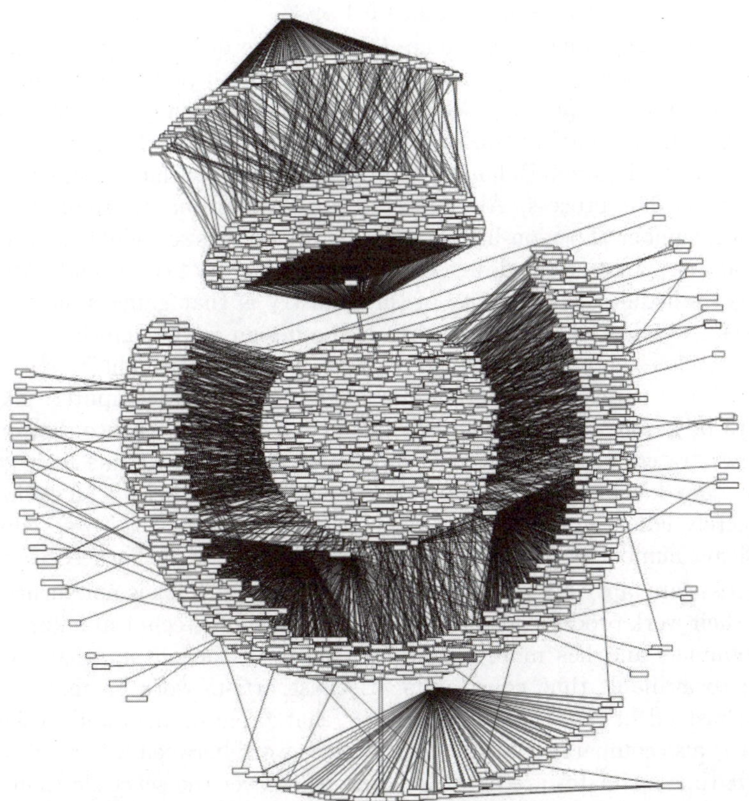

Figure 3.8. Dependence between artists for assets in *Spider-Man 3* for PS2. (Image courtesy of Vicarious Visions)

until the mesh has been modeled. The figure reveals a tremendous number of interdependent tasks that appear as the central ball. Many of those are related not to characters but to the level map, which is such a large task that many artists will collaborate on it.

Microsoft Project is one of the most popular scheduling tools and is built around a Gantt chart editor. Open-source solutions are available as well. Many developers simply choose to represent schedules as sums of time estimates in a spreadsheet, however, and trust the team to just keep an eye on dependencies as they create their own schedules.

The long path of the schedule is generally the engineering tasks, which have lots of internal dependencies that prevent them from being addressed in parallel by many programmers and also tend to be the tasks on which the other teams depend to begin their own work. Engineers also tend to have the worst time estimates, which makes it even more dangerous to have a long engineering path on the schedule. Before exploring this, let's see why design and art estimates are so much better.

The core of a game design comes together very quickly, especially if it is based on an existing game. Time estimates here don't really matter because it is so early in the project—with the notable exception of academic game projects, where spending two out of three weeks on just designing a game might lead to failure. Balancing the mechanics is a time-consuming and currently ad hoc process. Although balance time estimates are often poor, the total number of person-hours dedicated to design is so small compared to art that even inflating the design estimates by a factor of two wouldn't throw off most schedules. The reality of the industry is that game design today receives less effort than other areas. If the design isn't balanced on time, it still tends to ship and might be patched, or the rules might be amended later. Unlike patches to programming bugs that crash a computer, players tend to be happy about the release of gameplay patches because that opens up new strategies. Of course, an unplayably unbalanced game isn't going to have any loyal fans to download those patches, so this isn't an excuse to completely ignore game design on the schedule. The key is to schedule a significant number of playtests and start them early to gather feedback.

Artists are fairly accurate in their time estimates. This is not surprising, since their work product is less subject to catastrophic technical failure than programmers and has more subjective quality in the output that can be tuned to available time constraints. Because artists work on many small pieces instead of interconnected systems that programmers and designers use, it is also comparatively easy to rebalance work between artists. So even if their time estimates are off, it is easier to recover the schedule than it is for other groups.

Engineers are notorious for underestimating the amount of time it will take to accomplish their tasks. Most software products, including games, ship months late and, as a result, over budget. A large part of the problem is that engineers and managers mean different things by time estimates. When you ask a programmer how long it will take to accomplish a task, he or she will usually report the amount of time it will take to complete a proof of concept of the most technically interesting part of that task *if working full-time on just that task.* If you're a manager (or working as a group to make a schedule), that isn't the estimate you need. For scheduling purposes, you need to know how long it will take until that feature is completely done, tested, integrated into the system, and won't ever have to be touched again. Furthermore, you want an estimate that takes into account the fact that the programmer will be working on other tasks, attending meetings, interviewing candidates, responding to e-mails, fixing bugs in other code, and helping other team members.

Most programmers can write about 500 lines of code in a day if working on a brand-new project. Yet, on long-term projects, they average about 3 to 10 lines of code per day. That's because writing code is easy only if it doesn't interact with anything else. Once the project is under way, programmers produce many fewer new lines of code because they spend tremendous amounts of time maintaining old code.

A good way to estimate engineering time is to subdivide features into tasks that each take a few days. Any task that takes more than a week on the schedule probably hasn't been thought through well enough to give a good estimate. Unsurprisingly, when a task is subdivided, the individual estimates tend to add up to more than the original task estimate. This is because thinking through the software architecture for scheduling reveals new details that must be addressed. Schedule explicit testing and bug-fixing times. That way everyone is conscious of the difference between proof-of-concept and integrated-and-polished. It also ensures that everyone remembers to account for that extra time.

When working with a particularly complicated or bug-prone subsystem, most programmers want to rip out the subsystem and completely rewrite it. The argument usually is supported by claims that it will take longer to learn and work with the existing system than to just redo it the right way. This is almost always a scheduling disaster. The bugs in the existing system are at least known; if the code is rewritten, that process will introduce new, unknown bugs that have to be found and fixed. When patching an existing system, it is at least functioning at all times. With a new system, everything will be offline until it can be integrated, and the programmer can't be reassigned in the middle of the task if the priorities shift.

Examples of failure through "rewriting is faster" abound. *Duke Nukem Forever* is something of a game industry joke because, at the time of this writing, it has been in development for ten years. This is reportedly because the developers keep rewriting the game engine from scratch. The Netscape corporation used to produce the world's most popular Web browser. Then they decided to rewrite the codebase from scratch, and in the interim Internet Explorer swallowed their market share. Microsoft corporation rewrote their operating system from scratch between the Windows XP and Vista releases—and ended up shipping years late, with many features dropped. During almost the same time period, Apple shipped a major new version of its operating system and several point releases. Apple could do this because its OS was based on an existing system and incrementally improved instead of being rewritten from scratch.

3.7.3 Cut Features

When the tasks don't fit into the allotted time, the right response is usually to cut the feature set. This is sometimes wholly beneficial, because if features can be cut without compromising the game's viability, then they should be cut anyway. However, cutting features usually decreases the game's appeal in some way and is simply the least unpleasant of several undesirable options. Let's see why the other options are worse.

One response to a short schedule is to compromise on quality. Although small compromises like a one-color instead of four-color rule book are often acceptable, universally lowering production values usually lowers the entertainment and commercial values of the game proportionally.

Bringing in a bigger team is a dangerously attractive option that almost always ends in disaster. In software development this is known as the myth of the man-month. The scheduling myth is that work takes a certain number of person-(man-)months—that is, developers multiplied by time. If more time is not available, then more developers should improve progress. But this fails for many reasons. The first is that you probably started with a team of the best people you could bring together. Adding more (unplanned) people late in a project often means compromising on the quality of your developers, which means that you're saddling the entire process with less-efficient workers. Those workers need to be recruited, trained, and compensated, so they consume more time and cost than is initially shown on the schedule. The team also needs to communicate. A larger team takes longer to communicate because there are more combinations of people, more layers of management, and more people squeezed into each meeting. The overhead of hiring and managing a larger team often has a worse impact on the schedule and budget than the original problems.

A third poor response to an overloaded schedule is to increase the development time. This immediately puts the project at risk because the distance between the initial design mandate and the deliverable is longer. Your competition will release their products, the market will shift, and there is more opportunity for unanticipated disruptive events (like people leaving the team or the stock market crashing). If you are working with a publisher, you'll have to negotiate for a longer schedule, and that means giving up items you fought for in your initial contract. If you are a student working in a class, more time is either not an option or simply represents time that you aren't spending on your other work. For hobbyists, more time seems relatively inexpensive. But if you really want to complete a game, you need to keep the time frame short so it doesn't compete with other activities and so you don't become bored or distracted before it is finished.

3.7.4 Test Continually

Engineers and content creators have different approaches to work due to fundamental differences in the ways their workflow is affected by maintenance and revision. Good programmers are paranoid. They work very hard to avoid introducing bugs into their code and want to immediately drop everything to fix a bug when one is discovered. For game development, a routine that is too slow is a bug, so any routine that is inherently slow is something that should immediately be redesigned so that it is capable of executing more quickly. These good programmers annotate their code with assertions and internal documentation to prove and explain correctness, and they are obsessed with protocols for memory management and synchronization.

Programmers are paranoid because they know once a codebase is destabilized by bugs, it is very expensive to restabilize the system. Tracking down a single bug can be an enormous challenge. The process is a lot like a fictional detective tracking down the killer in a murder mystery. When many bugs are present, the process becomes disproportionally more complex. Imagine a detective trying to solve a murder when there are actually multiple murderers and victims within the same small social pool. Instead of clues ruling out suspects, they just confuse the situation because different clues apply to different murders, and the detective can't tell which is which. That's what happens when a programmer is trying to fix a bug in a system that has many interacting bugs. Even worse, many bugs (like memory leaks) will only create problems a small fraction of the time.

Finally, identified bugs that must be fixed and thus throw off the schedule are bad. Unknown bugs that slip through testing but crash a player's machine are much worse!

In contrast to programmers, good artists are not paranoid at all. They turn out multiple early drafts of everything, try from different approaches, and experiment freely. This is a successful approach because art is generally subjective, and it is best to get an early version for everyone to look at and compare to the rest of the game vision. For example, if the goblins are blue instead of green, the game won't crash, but it just might look a little strange. The first revision of a game character usually has a polygon count that is significantly too high or too low and has a very sketchy texture map. Game levels are often played as a simple collection of white boxes, with no lighting, texture, or even detail, until they are approved.

The "build early" guideline of scheduling reflects the artistic nature of game design as a whole, not just the graphic art component. Like an artist who seeks feedback on an early draft to make sure it is going in the right direction, the whole team should get an early version playable as soon as possible.

The "test continually" guideline reflects both the artist notion of continuous feedback and the engineer notion of keeping out bugs. For a video game, the code should always compile (from day one!) and pass basic low-level tests. When the source code is broken, the entire project is at risk. For both board and video games, it is essentially to keep the whole game playable because, like a programmer's concern, once the *design* moves away from engaging and balanced, it is hard to get it back there. The net advice is, therefore, "build and test, early and often" to ensure constant stability and feedback.

3.8 Managing Risk

Risk comes from factors that are unknown. For example: will the lead designer catch the flu? will the market turn away from sports games? Risk is bad. If we could completely eliminate risk, we wouldn't have to schedule conservatively and could accomplish more. However, driving a project to zero risk is actually not desirable because risk usually comes from innovation. By reducing the risk of bad things happening, we also reduce the chance of good things happening. A successful team decides what risks are acceptable given the potential rewards and then take further steps to minimize the risks that it has agreed to take on.

Some risks can be reduced by research. Playtesting, focus groups, prototypes, and market studies are all ways of gaining information about unknown quantities in the design, art, code, and market. Because research costs money and time and is subject to error, perfect information will never be practical. Nonetheless, making these unknowns *somewhat* known decreases the number of surprises that can occur during development.

Innovate in one area at a time. The more elements of a game that are new, the less likely players are to accept it and the more aspects that can go wrong during development. The standard formula in the entertainment industry is to bring together two proven ideas and then add an innovative twist. If you innovate on controller technology (such as using the Nintendo Wii controller), then use a relatively conventional story structure and setting.

If your visual style is new (such as *Jet Grind Radio*), then keep the basic gameplay familiar.

Beyond the market reasons, the idea behind innovating in one area at a time is also supported by failure analysis. It is a lot like a string of Christmas lights. Inexpensive Christmas lights are wired in "series," so the electricity must pass through each bulb to reach the next one. If one bulb is destroyed, the entire string goes out. Likewise if a game is to succeed, the whole game must work. If any element doesn't work, the entire game will be a failure. An alternative process is "parallel" failure modes. If you plug in a large number of night-lights separately, then breaking the bulb on one does not affect the others. To reduce risk (at added development cost), you can have two teams working on the same feature. One team works on the high-risk version and the other on the low-risk version. This way, even if one component fails, you still have a backup plan. On a broader scale, this is called *hedging.* There are many applications. Most game companies try to work on two games at once so they can withstand a market failure. Publishing companies produce tens or hundreds of games a year to minimize the chance of catastrophic failure. In these cases, the hedge has a real cost. The publisher might have been able to release one game that was exceptional and had a huge return, had it not hedged and published two average games that had only moderate returns. Hedging is a tradeoff between expected value and variance. We'll explore that tradeoff later in the probability chapter; it can be applied both to financial decisions like hedging and to random numbers in game design.

Buying assets and code instead of building them from scratch greatly reduces risk. Every task on the schedule carries an implicit risk that it will take more time than anticipated. Every stock model, sound effect, or code library that is purchased removes development tasks from the schedule. That brings in the schedule *and* removes risk. Although buying requires money, in many cases it reduces the total cost of specifying, developing, and refining. For example, a third party can sell you a game engine at a fraction of its development cost, because they amortize that cost over multiple clients. You don't have to pay either the initial development cost or the added risk of working with your own new technology.

There are two challenges to buying instead of building. The first is that buying can limit your designs to those similar to existing games. The solution here is to use preexisting technology and assets mainly for areas where your game is *not* innovative so that you can leverage your time and budget for those features that depart from what everyone else has created. The second challenge is that many developers want to build everything in-house. That makes them feel valuable and gives them additional experience. If your goal is to learn how to write a rendering engine or model a tree, then building everything in-house is fine. If your goal is to ship a game (or learn how to make a game) or to innovate on design, then "eyes on the prize" tells us that the right attitude is to outsource part of the job—buy as much as possible to get a head start. Even if the team ends up eventually replacing purchased components later in development, they are a way to get to a working build very early without growing the team size.

3.9 Exercises

1. What is a typical AAA game budget? How many person-hours are spent on such a game?
2. Why is it important to listen to even bad ideas?
3. Give an example of a sunk-cost evaluation from your own life (unrelated to games).
4. What is the difference between a team lead and a manager?
5. Briefly describe two games that you have recently played and what made them interesting. Do *not* use the words "I like" or "I don't like."
6. Make a list of the features from one of the games in the previous exercise. Remember to consider content, mechanisms, and technology. Give a wild estimate of how many person-weeks you think each one would take to create. Now imagine that you have to produce a similar game in half the time. How would you change the list to accomplish that goal?
7. Exercises 7–10 assume that you are a student or hobbyist who will work on a team project. If you are not, assume a four-week project to create a board game like *Settlers of Catan* or a video game like *Tetris* with four people on the team.

   Draw a timeline for your current or next major project. Label the points at which you should have the following.

   (a) A playable prototype

   (b) A stable nightly build (software projects only)

   (c) Feature-complete

   (d) A polished product
8. One member of your team is consistently behind schedule. How would you deal with the situation if that person seemed to be working his or her hardest? What if he or she seemed to be putting in less effort than

the rest of the team? What if he or she had an understandable external commitment, like an illness, a sports team, or a part-time job?

9. What steps will you take to keep the team creative over the length of the project?

10. If your prototype isn't engaging to play, what will you do? (Extending the length of the project is not an option.)

3.10 Resources

- Fisher, Ury, and Patton, *Getting to Yes* [Fisher et al. 92].
- *Game Developer Magazine* "Postmortem" series.
- Baty, *No Plot? No Problem!* [Baty 04].
- Brooks, *The Mythical Man-Month and Other Essays* [Brooks 95].
- McConnell, *Rapid Development* [McConnell 96].
- Maguire, *Debugging the Development Process* [Maguire 94].
- Spolsky, "Joel on Software" blog http://www.joelonsoftware.com/.

CHAPTER 4

Critique and Proposal

Terms Explained: *Critique* – *Genre* – *Key Experiences* – *Platform* – *Platformer* – *Proposal* – *Role-Playing Game* – *Shooter* – *Tagline*

Every game is proposed many times before it reaches production. One way that a game can begin is for an employee at a development company to have an idea and pitch it to other members on the same team. Together, they work out a common vision and present that to the design team or management. That proposal then is refined and researched into an early draft of a design document, which is then proposed to a publisher. This chapter describes the format of the initial proposals, from an individual to a team and from a team to management. The same format remains in the design document as the opening pages when it is sent to a publisher, providing a concise overview of the much longer document. An alternative model is that a publisher brings an idea (typically a licensed title) to a developer. There the project is essentially pre-approved. However, the specific design must still be taken back to the publisher for approval.

This chapter describes a two-page overview worksheet (Figure 4.1) that is designed to help you to format your proposal in a professional and compelling manner. For blank worksheet templates, see Appendix B and our website http://www.akpeters.com/mcguirejenkins/. The appendix provides two variations on the worksheet. The first, which is discussed in this chapter, includes information for marketing. This is closest to what is used in the games industry. The second removes the marketing points to make more room for an executive summary and mechanics diagram directly on the overview sheet. For discussion of these elements see executive summary in Chapter 5 and mechanics in Chapter 10.

The worksheet is intended for a number of different exercises:

- Brainstorming new game ideas as a team.
- Proposing ideas to management.
- Archiving ideas invented during work on one project for later explorations.
- Overview at the beginning of a full design document.
- Critiquing internal, newly created and externally published games.

When describing a new idea, writing the worksheet is a creative exercise that helps synthesize game designs and solidify a shared vision among the team members who are working on it. When completed, the worksheet is called a *proposal.* Proposals can quickly be evaluated by the whole team, upper management, and a publisher. Proposal worksheets are also used to archive good ideas for later work. A solid brainstorming session generates too many good game ideas, and the worksheet format is a way to wrap up the extra ideas and file them away for the next project. Proposals aren't just for designers. All members of the development team will have good ideas and should use this format to propose them internally.

When a student summarizes a preexisting game as homework using the overview worksheet format, the essence of the exercise is the same, but critical analysis replaces creative synthesis. Play the game for at least four hours to thoroughly familiarize yourself with it. Next, complete the worksheet as if you had just created the idea of the game yourself and were trying to describe it to your development team. Keep the game close at hand, as it is often necessary to experiment with it and closely read the instruction manual for analysis. Note that your goal is neither to review the game nor to record all of its detail, only to summarize the high-level essence.

Regardless of which exercise you are performing, plan on spending about 10 minutes for a cursory critique, 45 minutes for a good critique of a preexisting game, and at least two hours for a project proposal worksheet. Although you will take only minutes to generate the first draft of the proposal that ultimately begins your project, you'll look at several different ideas and then spend at least an hour polishing the one you like. You should expect it to take a few weeks to revise it as part of the design document.

The format of the proposal is relatively strict. Of course, if your game is exceptional in one area, then it is sometimes necessary to add a small amount of additional information. For example, if your game's narrative is the heart of gameplay, an additional paragraph beyond the "setting" field is in order. If you are using a major license (e.g., NFL, Michael Jackson songs, *Star Wars*), that should be explained. Another common area is an explanation of technological innovations like new graphics or online features that far surpass the technology of previous games. Your explanation here must defend several points: that your game is interesting because of this exceptional aspect, that your team can deliver on this, and that this feature is critical to the concept of the game.

4.1 Critique

Critique is a specific process used in art for evaluating the qualities of a work. In game design, we follow the same process for evaluating games. This is useful both to students and to designers in industry. The steps are:

1. describe
2. analyze
3. conclude

This process moves from objective qualities in the description to subjective ones in the conclusion. The analysis in the middle is the bridge in between them. Analysis interprets the objective qualities, deriving a larger result while maintaining objectivity.

One can perform either a casual, unstructured game critique or a formal, structured one. These have the same elements but different formats. The unstructured critique is an essay that addresses the three elements, whereas the structured critique follows the overview worksheet format and then appends a prose analysis and conclusion. The structured version is shorter and easier to read. However, it is actually more difficult to write concisely until you have experience critiquing games. This chapter covers the structure of the critique and the prose elements. The following section describes the overview worksheet elements, which are used both for a formal critique and when proposing your own games.

When writing a critique for an academic audience (e.g., as a research paper or homework assignment), begin the casual critique with a title. This is a thesis statement that puts forth an assertion you will defend. Some good examples are, "Camping stalemate is the Nash equilibrium in *Counter-Strike*," "Roads should be worth two points per tile in *Carcassonne*," and "Narrative creates tension in *Indigo Prophecy*." The best theses are those that are not immediately obvious, that go to the core of the game, and that can be well defended.

Critiques are more academic than industrial techniques. However, a well-written game review or paper on games follows the casual critique format. Game developers also will often follow the critique process—although perhaps with an even more informal write-up—when dissecting related games in their design documents and project proposals.

4.1.1 Describe

Begin the critique with an objective description of the game. Give the basic information about the title, publisher, developer, year of publication, number of players, genre, and so on. Descriptions should be unambiguous while avoiding subjective comments. For example, "The setting is a postnuclear war desert populated by mutants" is objective, whereas "The setting is stereotypical of a sci-fi B movie" is subjective and inappropriate at this stage. On the overview worksheet, the first page is primarily a form for objectively describing a game.

Because space is limited, in a casual critique you should focus your description down to about one paragraph and abstract elements of the game that will not be needed to support your thesis.

4.1.2 Analyze

Analysis is critical reasoning about a specific aspect of the game. One could easily write an entire book on almost any game, so when working with limited space, try to establish the scope of the game quickly and then focus on the key elements. Examples of aspects for analysis include the primary gameplay mechanic, the use of dynamic music, how elements of the narrative combine to create suspense, and how the art style serves the theme. If you have a thesis title, this aspect is the one from your thesis.

Analysis should rely on proven facts and reproducible experiments as much as possible. For example, you may want to argue that the card-trading mechanic is key to engaging players in *Settlers of Catan*. Although engagement is inherently personal and subjective, you can perform an experiment by running a series of game sessions with and without trading and asking players to rate their level of entertainment in the game after each session. Use numbers, equations, and charts as appropriate (see Chapter 10 for examples). Your goal is to construct an argument that is buttressed by facts, not persuasion. Avoid judgments like "good" and "bad" here. Reveal techniques and truths within the game. If there are facts that are counter to your thesis, you must also explore them to provide a fully disclosed argument (and if the vast majority of your facts do not support your thesis, your thesis needs work).

Quotations from independent player reports, such as those on BoardGameGeek, reviews on respected blogs, and quotations from articles by the developers in *Game Developer Magazine* and *Gamasutra* are good ways to present objective support for subjective factors. As with any sources, be sure to credit these, and select only the most respected ones. Avoid Internet forums and other locations where most of the information is based on rumor and personal opinion instead of fact and measured experience. Wherever possible, illustrate points with diagrams, equations, and screenshots from the game. These should not be decorative but instead provide support for a specific argument.

The Related Work section of the overview worksheet (do not confuse this with the References section described following) combines a small amount of description with a briefly defended analysis of the relation between previous games (or occasionally other forms of media) and the one being critiqued. For an unstructured critique, you can mention other games as needed, but you are not required to specifically enumerate related games unless it is necessary to support the analysis. Mentioning related games is important because many games implicitly reference the general body of games. For example, the *Bioshock* introduction tells the player to pick up a crowbar even though there is not one available; this is in reference to *Half-Life*'s famous melee weapon. The car ride at the beginning of the game is likewise a reference to *Half-Life*'s title sequence, and the art-deco world and storytelling style are based on the developer's previous title, *Fallout*.

4.1.3 Conclude

The conclusion of a critique makes a subjective conclusion based on previously presented facts. Here you can argue points such as the game is not fun, has social value, or is underrated. Your conclusion should follow from the analysis and description but need not be provable in the mathematical sense. It need not be long and should avoid restating the description or analysis. The best conclusions, and therefore the best theses, are those that focus on *how* elements of the game achieve a goal, such as balanced mechanics or effective narrative, rather than simply arguing that the mechanics are good or the narrative is effective.

4.2 Generating Ideas

Brainstorming is an effective way to generate good game ideas. Make many copies of the blank overview worksheet, and quickly fill them out with different ideas. Spend about ten minutes per sheet and more time for the ones you are really excited about. Bootstrap one idea from another, but never criticize or cut ideas.

With a series of proposal sheets before you, review them collectively. Choose the one that you like the best and spend about an hour honing it.

Don't feel constrained by your initial brainstorm sheet. In refining an idea, you can add or cut as much as you like.

It is good to riff off preexisting game ideas. So many games have been made that almost every good idea is already out there somewhere (which is a good reason to be familiar with previous work; see the Games Canon in Appendix F). Rather than inhibiting you, this fact should be liberating. Working already proven ideas into your new context is a recipe for success. The burden of originality is also lighter than it appears. Originality is a new combination of elements, not necessarily new elements themselves. In fact, in game design, as in other art forms, it is important to balance new ideas against proven conventions. A first-person shooter with onc new gameplay idea is considered brilliant (*Portal*), whereas too many new ideas put together can alienate the audience (*Amplitude*) or risk failure (*Trespasser*).

4.3 Format

The worksheet proscribes strict format and length limitations. In industry, these limitations vary between companies but are usually very similar. The

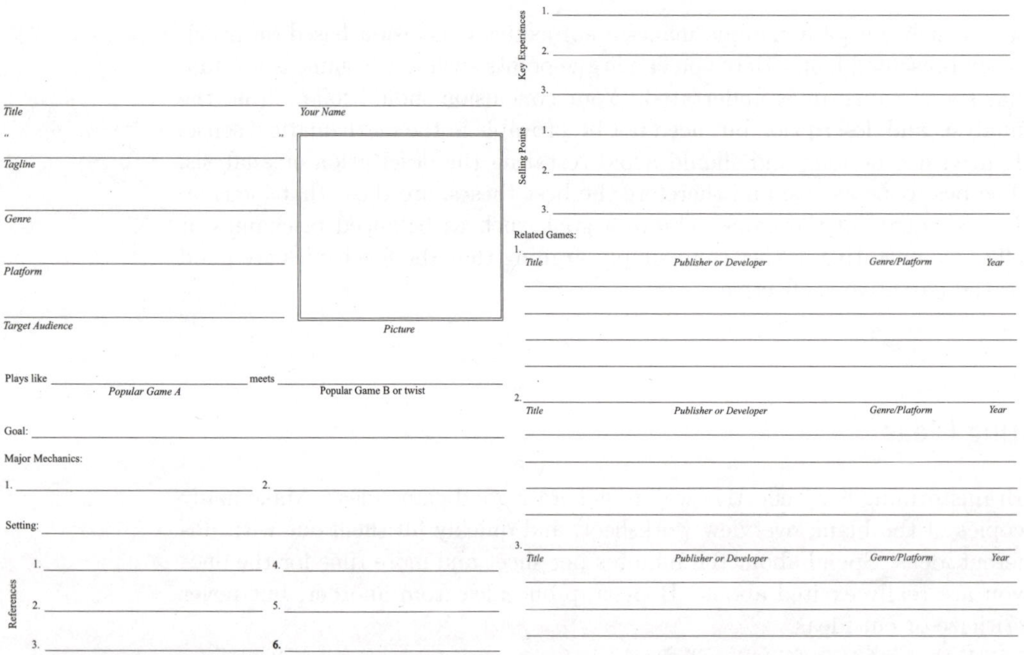
Title ____ *Your Name* ____

Tagline ____

Genre ____

Platform ____

Target Audience ____

Picture

Plays like ____ (*Popular Game A*) meets ____ (Popular Game B or twist)

Goal: ____

Major Mechanics:

1. ____ 2. ____

Setting: ____

References

1. ____ 4. ____
2. ____ 5. ____
3. ____ 6. ____

Key Experiences

1. ____
2. ____
3. ____

Selling Points

1. ____
2. ____
3. ____

Related Games:

1. *Title* *Publisher or Developer* *Genre/Platform* *Year*

2. *Title* *Publisher or Developer* *Genre/Platform* *Year*

3. *Title* *Publisher or Developer* *Genre/Platform* *Year*

Figure 4.1. Overview worksheet used for proposal and summary exercises.

The template for the worksheet in this book combines some of the most effective structures observed across multiple game companies.

The limitations on length are designed to force you to distill the core ideas. You will probably find that it requires hard work *because* it is so short and that it would be easier to write more than less.

You can start with more verbose sentences and ideas and shorten them to make room for more new ideas. That editing process naturally brings out the essence of your idea. Find the best words to express your idea concisely and compellingly. Here are some tips for concise, powerful writing.

- Write specific nouns (e.g., *coin, dragon, corvette, steel grate*) over generic ones (e.g., *bonus, thing, vehicle, barrier*).
- Write strong verbs (e.g., *soar, dash, anchor, pummel*) over weak ones (e.g., *fly, race, hold, hit*).
- Avoid adjectives and adverbs; they consume space and conceal weak nouns and verbs.
- Cut everything that isn't core to the idea. Watch out for the word "and," as in "My game is a first-person shooter, *and* you can fly planes *and* cast magic spells and..." Everything that is not part of the core dilutes the core.

Concise writing helps you fit the length limitations of the worksheet, but ultimately the importance of a tightly written document is that it takes less time for the rest of the team to read, presents a clearer vision of your game, and describes the game in a more compelling fashion to people who can approve it. The remainder of this chapter describes the specific fields of the worksheet and how to complete them. Two examples of completed sheets follow.

4.3.1 Title

When first brainstorming, the title is just a placeholder to give a convenient way to refer to the game. During polishing of a good proposal, the title is carefully crafted. It becomes a summary, a hook, and an aperture through which to view the game. It should immediately inspire the reader with the setting, primary game mechanic, and target audience. The title should be engaging, drawing the reader in.

Choose your words carefully in the title. Think about the difference between synonyms. For example, an espionage game could use the word spy in the title, but that is generic and boring. Some synonyms convey the same idea but have more descriptive flavor. "Secret agent" spices up the title and gives it a Cold War feel, *MI-6* (British Secret Service) lends a more debonair, James Bond approach, *undercover* emphasizes stealth, and *spook* implies a more goofy approach.

Don't be afraid to use made-up words, as long as they have clear connotations. In one of our example proposals, we combine the notions of a remote-control toy, daredevil stunts, and flying into the title: *R/C Airdevil.*

Leaning on previous works has both advantages and risks in the title. *Age of Empires* was a hit historical real-time strategy game that spawned many sequels and imitators. *Age of* is too generic to trademark, so the imitators are free to use *Age of Heroes*, *Age of Machines*, *Age of Warfare*, and so on. Using such a title immediately conveys to the target audience the type of gameplay, which is a huge advantage. The *Tycoon* and *Quest* game names have been similarly named. The risks of using variations on an established brand are running afoul of trademark law by being too similar (e.g., the Tetris Corporation aggressively pursues anyone who creates a falling-blocks game and gives it a name that ends in *-tris*) and of being associated with poor-quality imitations by others who also used a variation on a name brand.

During the final stages of game production, the title may be changed to respond to marketing demands, but a descriptive title is still important for communication and motivation throughout development.

4.3.2 Tagline

The *tagline* is an expanded title. It epitomizes the game in a single sentence instead of a single word. Taglines frequently employ double entendres to succinctly capture multiple ideas.

Unlike an advertising tagline for a product, don't try to be too clever or punchy with the game tagline. The proposal tagline borders on a mission statement for your team during development, and you want the mission to have content. You should always be able to judge later design decisions by whether they support the tagline. The "Get Ready to Rock!!" tagline for *Guitar Hero* was used to support the unity of design on the game; the developer reports that every design decision was subjected to the ultimate question "Does this rock?" [LoPiccolo and Sussman 06].

Here are some good examples of real game taglines.

- "The short word game," for *Quiddler*, a brief game about constructing words of three to seven letters. "Short" refers to both the words and the length of the game; "word" and "game" tell you the rest. A tagline with a double meaning is attractive to the word-game audience.

- "The game of outrageous fortune," for *Pirateer*, in which treasure-seeking pirates try their luck. "Outrageous" is an adjective, but it is a very strong one. "Fortune" is a strong noun and one that expresses both luck and wealth.

- "Evil has survived—an epic game of role-playing action and adventure," for *Diablo II*, a sequel involving questing and character building. "Survived" indicates the sequel, as well as telling players that their nemesis did not perish in the final battle of the first game, thus revealing the new plotline. The rest of the tagline succinctly explains the scope, genre, and mechanics to new players.

- "No man fights alone," for *Call of Duty*, a first-person war shooter ("fights") that emphasizes team tactics ("no ... alone").

- "Evil must be exterminated—but first it must be found," for *Metroid*, a platformer that involves searching ("found") underground lairs. "Evil" is misplaced, since the enemies in the game are more alien than intentional. However, "exterminated" is a strong verb that describes both the level-clearing nature of the game and the plotline of a spreading disease-like scourge.

- "Hell breaks loose," for *DOOM*, a game about a military base taken over by demons. "Hell" is of course eye-catching. It also conveys the satanic opponents and the mature content of the game. The use of a cliche is more theatrical than functional, but it works for a game that also has little subtlety.

- "Combat evolved," for *Halo*, which featured revolutionary ("evolved") gameplay and graphics in a first-person shooter ("combat"). As the only significant launch title and flagship game for the Xbox, "evolved" fit the branding message and escaping-X logo of the console as well as the game.

Make sure that your tagline expands on the title. It is important to avoid the temptation to just "say something cool." The tagline should accurately summarize the game, even at the expense of being a little boring. Like the title, it may be changed for marketing purposes before release, but during proposal and development, accuracy of description is paramount.

4.3.3 Genre

The concept of *genre* for games has more to do with where they sit on a store shelf than the underlying design. It blends together elements of game mechanics, setting, and target market; for board games it tends to conflate platform (play materials) with play mechanics. Nonetheless, a genre label is widely recognized as a quick way to summarize a game's basic play.

Genres emerged to group the variants of classic games with their canonical predecessor—for example, "falling blocks" summarizes all *Tetris*-like games and "first-person shooter" all *DOOM*-like games. Most games are, of course, hybrids—for example, *Counter-Strike* combines first-person shooter, real-time strategy, and role-playing (stat building) aspects. However, for the genre field to be useful, you should try to identify the single genre that best describes your game and optionally mark a second genre if combining two is the major innovation of the game.

Board game genres are often directly named after their mechanics and platform. The categories are both easy to understand and ad hoc as a result. Here are some common categories for board games (reading these genre lists should help inspire many ideas!).

Tabletop board. A generic term for games in which players move playing pieces on a board, draw cards, roll dice, and other activities associated with classic board games. Examples include *Settlers of Catan*, *Monopoly*, *Puerto Rico*, *Through the Desert*, chess, checkers, and go.

Tabletop miniature. War games involving strategic placement and movement of tens of units across tabletop terrain. Examples include *Hero Clix*, *Warhammer 40,000*, *Flames of War*, *Pirates of the Spanish Main*, *Battletech*, and *Axis and Allies*.

Puzzle. Generally single-player, physical or mathematical puzzles, also generally with no randomness. Examples include *Sudoku*, *Rush Hour*, *Tipover*, *Mastermind*, and *Subway*.

Tile. A game played primarily by building a map through constrained placement rules. Examples include *Carcassonne*, *Tongiaki*, dominoes, and *Scrabble* (which is also the canonical word game).

Card. Games played primarily through hands of cards, with no significant other state or source of randomness. Examples include poker, *Magic: The Gathering*, *Set*, hearts, solitaire, *Lunch Money*, and *Munchkin*.

Word. Emphasizes vocabulary and language skills, such as *Scrabble*, *Boggle*, crossword puzzles, and *Quiddler*.

Party. Light on strategy and heavy on player interaction. Examples include *Balderdash*, *Pictionary*, *Trivial Pursuit* and other trivia games, *Apples to Apples*, and charades. These grew out of the parlor games of the nineteenth century.

Alternate reality. Games that mix media and blur the line between reality and fiction by incorporating real-world phone numbers, advertisements, objects, locations, and websites in play. These can support hundreds of players, usually coordinated online, which makes it the board game analog of the MMORPG. Examples include *I Love Bees*, *Beast*, *Webrunner*, *Majestic*, *The Nokia Game*, and *PerplexCity*, as well as several "treasure hunt" puzzles and riddles historically put forth by artists and magicians.

Pen-and-paper role playing. Interactive storytelling games assisted by combat rules, often using multisided polyhedral dice. *Dungeons & Dragons* was the defining game of the genre. Others include *Top Secret*, *Shadowrun*, *Paranoia*, *GURPS*, and *Amber*. Live-action role playing (LARP) and interactive theater variants involve dressing in costume and directly acting out roles, usually with soft "weapons" to resolve combat.

The following are the classic genre categories for video games.

Adventure. Wandering through a storylike world, solving puzzles. These have minimal character building compared to a computer RPG (see following), although it is common to collect a handful of new weapons and abilities. Examples are *Adventure*, *King's Quest* series, *The Legend of Zelda* series, *Myst* series, *Tomb Raider*, *Indigo Prophecy*, and *Grand Theft Auto*. This is the closest computer analog of pen-and-paper role playing because it encourages you to really put yourself in the character's place and develop an emotional attachment to places and people in the game.

Strategy. Collect resources, build a civilization, research new technologies, and tactically control tens of units in battle. These are typically divided into real-time strategy (RTS), such as *StarCraft*, *Warcraft*, *Age of Empires* (see Figure 4.2), and *Defcon*, and turn-based strategy (TBS), such as *Civilization*, *Advance Wars*, *Master of Orion*, *X-COM*, *Age of Wonders*, *Heroes of Might and Magic*, *Weird Worlds: Return to Infinite Space*, and the open-source game *The Battle for Wesnoth*.

God games. A variant on strategy games, *god games* typically give the in-game characters more autonomy and make the battle more one of controlling the chracters in a semihostile environment than of battling against equal foes. The genre is exemplified by its first major title, *Populous*. Other notable god games include *Black and White*, *SimCity*, and *The Sims*.

Sports. Games simulating professional sports such as hockey or soccer, such as *Madden NFL*, *FIFA Soccer*, *Tiger Woods Golf*, and *Wii Sports*.

Figure 4.2. Real-time strategy game *Age of Empires III.* (Image courtesy of Microsoft Game Studios)

Rhythm. Beat-matching, usually music games that require the player to exactly match a series of joystick and button-pushing motions. Examples include *Guitar Hero*, *Dance Dance Revolution*, *PaRappa the Rapper*, and *Elite Beat Agents.*

Role-playing games (RPGs). Traditionally named after their improvisational acting form of play, *role-playing games* now are about building a character's statistics, skills, and inventory, such as *Diablo* series, *Final Fantasy*, *Titan Quest*, *Oblivion*, *Neverwinter Nights*, *Knights of the Old Republic*, and *Fallout.*

Massive multiplayer online role-playing games (MMORPGs) are virtual worlds where thousands of players use RPG mechanics simultaneously. Examples include *Ultima Online*, *World of Warcraft*, *RuneScape*, *EVE Online*, and *Star Wars Online.*

Action. Most real-time games without deep abstract strategy could be classified by the generic term *action game.* These feature the general mechanics of hordes of enemies, slow progression through a linear plot/world, and periodic boss battles (all common staples for any game genre). Examples include

God of War and *Gun Star Heroes.*

Figure 4.3. First-person shooter *Half-Life 2: Lost Coast Expansion.* (Image courtesy of Valve)

Shooter. An action game emphasizing reflexes, aim, and dodging, typically emphasizing gunplay or other violence. The actual shooting may be from a spaceship (e.g., *Space Invaders*, *Wing Commander* series, *Starfox*) or other vehicle, or by a character. 2D shooters are commonly called "shoot 'em ups."

First-person *shooters* (FPS) were hugely popular at the beginning of real-time 3D for games and have remained a staple of the gaming experience. Notable FPS games include *DOOM*, *Quake*, *Unreal Tournament*, *Half-Life* (Figure 4.3), *Fear*, *Far Cry*, *Crysis*, *Wolfenstein*, *Halo*, *GoldenEye*, *CounterStrike*, *Resistance: Fall of Man*, *Prey*, and *Portal.*

Third-person shooters are growing in popularity, with *Max Payne*, *Gears of War*, and some of the *Tomb Raider* games as notable examples.

Classic gameplay for 2D arcade shooters involved fighting hordes of enemies (usually from spaceships or jets) over long, scrolling, static backgrounds, so they are also known as "scrollers" The direction of the scrolling designated a game as a "side scroller" or "top scroller." Examples include *R-Type*, *Gradius*, *Spy Hunter*, *Raiden*, *Axelay*, *Desert Strike*, and *Defender.*

Platformer. Carefully timed jumping between vertical levels and avoiding foes, whether 2D or 3D. Examples include *Pitfall Harry*, many elements of *Half-Life*, *Super Mario Bros.* series, *Sonic*, *Contra*, and most 2D console games. *Platformers* tend to have little state associated with the character, which differentiates them from adventure and role-playing games.

Puzzle. Games devoted to primarily abstract puzzle-solving, either turn-based or real-time. Puzzles are considered the core of the casual games market, which greatly exceeds the size (in player base) of the hard-core traditional gamer market. Examples of puzzle games include *Minesweeper*, *Tetris*, *Bejeweled*, *Lumines*, *Meteos*, *Drod*, and *Sudoku*.

Despite its platformer appearance, *Lode Runner* is best classified as a puzzle game. Likewise for *Drod*, despite its adventure trappings.

Construction, Construct a virtual apparatus, typically to perform some role in a machine. Examples include *Incredible Machine*, *Bridge Builder*, and *Roblox*.

Race/driving. Race (usually cars) and beat opponents primarily by time through a fixed track. Examples include *Mario Kart*, *Project Gotham Racing*, *Podracer*, and *Need for Speed*.

Fighting. Opponents face off with a series of moves, typically one on one. *Street Fighter*, *Mortal Kombat*, *Smash Bros.*, *Soul Calibur*, and *Tekken* series.

"Brawler" games are the melee analog of a shoot 'em up and have the appearance of fighting games but with generally less complex moves. Examples include *Double Dragon*.

It is common to pair a literary or film genre with the mechanic when naming a genre for more specificity. *Sci-fi FPS* or *Mystery Adventure* are examples of such extended genre names.

4.3.4 Platform

Identify the hardware *platform* for a video game or major components for a board game. Be as broad as possible. If a specific platform doesn't matter, then make that clear—for example, "Xbox 360 or other next-gen console." Reasons for requiring a very specific platform are input features such as a keyboard or touch screen, an existing codebase for a platform, or a specific marketing deal.

Sample video-game platforms (and common abbreviations) grouped by broad categories include the following.

Figure 4.4. Nintendo DS handheld console. (Image courtesy of Nintendo)

PC. PC, Windows PC (Win, Win32), Macintosh PC (Mac, OS X), Linux PC, Windows PC on CD-ROM (PC-ROM), Windows PC on DVD (PC-DVD).

Web. Web browser (HTML, Flash, JavaScript, Shockwave; depending on technology).

Handheld. Nintendo DS (Figure 4.4), Nintendo Gameboy (GB), Nintendo Gameboy Advance (GBA), Sony PSP.

Console. Modern: Sony PlayStation 3 (PS3), Microsoft Xbox 360, Nintendo Wii. Historic: Sony PlayStation 2 (PS2), Sony PlayStation (PS1), Microsoft Xbox, Famicom/Nintendo Entertainment System (NES), Super Nintendo (SNES), Nintendo 64 (N64), Nintendo GameCube (GC), NEC TurboGrafx 16, Sega Master System, Sega Saturn, Sega Genesis, Sega Dreamcast (DC), Colecovision, Atari 2600, Atari 7800, Atari Jaguar, 3DO, Fairchild Channel F (VES), Magnavox Odyssey.

Other. Arcade console, Java phone, cell phone, watch, dedicated device, e-mail.

Sample non-video-game platforms include tile (e.g., *Carcassonne*), board (e.g., *Monopoly*), spoken word (e.g., riddles), card (e.g., poker), collectible card (e.g., *Magic*), pen-and-paper (e.g., *Dungeons & Dragons*), miniature (e.g., *Hero Clix*), physical puzzle (e.g., *Rush Hour*), field (e.g., soccer), dice (e.g., *Yahtzee*), and alternative reality (e.g., *I Love Bees*).

4.3.5 Picture

Games are a visual medium, and game developers are a visual group. Describe your game with an image as well as text. You need not be an artist (although this is a good opportunity for artists to excel). You can clip a picture from a magazine or use art found on the Internet.

The picture acts first as an icon to quickly grab the reader's attention and identify a specific game among many other proposals on the table. It is also a summary of the game. The picture could be representative of box art, a simulated screenshot, or simply evocative of the themes of the game. The picture is small on the sheet, so bold, simple images are more valuable than fine details that won't be seen by most viewers.

An image of the main character, the anticipated user interface, a simulated game board, or even simply clip art echoing the setting of the game are all good places to start with the picture.

4.3.6 Target Audience

Who will play this game? The age, gender, country, interests, and occupation of the target demographic drive many aspects of game design. Although it is usually desirable to address as wide a demographic as possible, having a specific core audience in mind gives the game focus. If you try to please everyone, you can easily end up with a game that appeals to no one. When marketing a game, a good strategy is to start with the core audience and then let a positive reception spread the game naturally to a wider audience.

Some examples of target audiences are casual gamers, teenage boys, teenage girls, Internet cafe users, football fans, "soccer moms," people who liked *Diablo*, affluent 20-somethings, secretaries, hard-core gamers, and fans of mystery novels.

4.3.7 Plays Like

Analogy and simile are powerful communication tools. The Plays Like section of the worksheet lets you convey your game idea as a combination of two games with which the reader is already familiar. The first game should be popular, with critical and hopefully commercial success (since imitating an obscure and unsuccessful game is not a good way to begin your career!). The second can be either another popular game or a twist on the original. An example of a game with a twist is *Lumines*, which could be pitched as "*Tetris*, where blocks rotate only on the ground" or "*Jewels* with squares."

The Plays Like section immediately starts the reader at a common reference point and establishes the direction in which you are expanding from the original game. It also constrains you to innovate within the bounds of mainstream taste. Using the ideas from two previous games as a starting point means you're beginning in a fertile area of design space.

The "A meets B" format is universal in all major game companies and is used extensively throughout the entertainment industry in film, music, and books. An example from the film industry is a series of films compared to *Die Hard*. *Die Hard* is an action movie where everyman Bruce Willis is trapped in a building with terrorists and must fight them and free hostages. After its phenomenal success, Hollywood writers crafted movies that seemed different to the public but had the same underlying mechanics. For example, *Speed* was pitched to executives as "*Die Hard* on a bus," and *Phone Booth* as the (seemingly ridiculous) "*Die Hard* in a phone booth."

4.3.8 Goal

How do you score points or win? For this field, write a single sentence that cuts to the core aspect of the game. Do not use the words "and" or "or" to pack multiple winning conditions or extraneous game detail into the sentence. A little detail, however, can help to differentiate otherwise generic winning conditions. For example, the goal of *Carcassonne* can be expressed as "Collect the most points by claiming features as tiles are placed," which is more illuminating than "Get the most points." The goal of *Half-Life* is literally to reach the end of the linear map/story, but it can be better described as "Battle aliens and marines to escape a laboratory under seige."

Note that the goal of the game might not be objective—for example, "Decorate a dollhouse so you're proud to show it to your friends"—although some would debate whether an activity without an objective winning condition is properly called a game.

4.3.9 Major Mechanics

Mechanics describe the abstract gameplay; they are the categories into which the specific game rules fall. Most games contain tens of different mechanics (see Chapter 10 for a detailed discussion).

The goal of this field is to identify the primary and secondary mechanics. For example, *Mario Kart* is primarily a racing game with limited shooter elements added. As is evident from that description, the line between a genre and a mechanic is blurry because the genre is often named after a mechanic.

For a board game, it is acceptable to describe up to four game mechanics, and in greater detail than for a video game, since board games are made or unmade by their mechanics alone.

When proposing a new game, you'll find that you want to share more of your vision than the proposal sheet accommodates. The mechanics and key experiences sections are where you will express most of your vision. They seem limiting (with only four mechanics and three experiences), but if you really hone your ideas, you will find that the major mechanics and content really can be expressed. Going beyond likely means you haven't sufficiently thought through your idea, which will be obvious to the people who evaluate your proposal. It is better to cut and focus up front and then expand the vision once it is accepted.

4.3.10 Setting

Where will the gameplay take place? Briefly describe the location, era, conditions, tone (e.g., comic, naturalistic, blockbuster) and scope of the game's fictional and thematic components. The setting drives art direction and often motivates the mechanics brought into play. It also is a strong factor in identifying the target audience.

This is a good place for evocative writing. Some sample settings are "Medieval England under a tyrannical king"; "Remote, broken-down starbase #12 on the eve of interstellar war in a comic, *Hitchhiker's Guide* universe"; and "Inside a human cell in a Jules Verne–era miniature submarine crewed by scientists."

References. The References section of the setting entry contains space for the titles of six previous books, games, and movies. Select works that will serve as reference and concept material. For example, the references of a pirate game might include *Pirates of the Caribbean* or *Treasure Island.* Choose recent works over older ones; recent works represent the popular conception of your setting and are likely to speak more directly to your target audience. For example, use the *Lord of the Rings* films instead of the original books. These aren't "references" in the bibliographical sense of citations or related work, but they are sources of inspiration for the style and appearance of the game. Try to find at least six.

It is often useful to write the setting as a "setup," describing the scenario in which the protagonist/player is compelled to enter the action of the game. For example, *Max Payne* begins with the terrifying murder of the protagonist's family that sends him on a quest for revenge. See Chapter 11 for more discussion of setting.

Key Experiences. List three *key experiences* the player will undergo that exemplify your setting and mechanics. For example, in *Guitar Hero*, the player holds a plastic guitar-shaped controller, can rip through the solo to rock anthem *Free Bird*, and watch the on-screen avatar perform stunts like playing guitar behind the head, smashing a guitar, and lighting a guitar on fire.

If your game were a theme park ride, what elements would appear along the ride? If it were a movie, what key scenes would remain in the viewer's mind? What would you tell a friend when describing a particularly exciting play session? These should be personal and cinematic. Another example is "jumping your dirt bike off the back of a trailer on the Golden Gate bridge as the camera swoops and silhouettes you against a sunset."

It may help to begin with the images you see when you think of the game. Describe level bosses, missions, characters, weapons, power-ups, and the cover art for the game box. What are the sounds and the graphic style? What are the bullet points that would go on the back of the box or in an advertisement? From these you can derive the key user experiences.

Another way to generate the key experiences list is to complete the sentence "This game is engaging because..."

Selling Points. Selling points are marketing arguments for why this is a good game to make. They may be a combination of financial, trend, and audience-driven concerns, and they will often overlap with or reference the key experiences. See the completed worksheets at the end of this chapter for examples of selling points.

4.3.11 Related Games

To understand a new game, it is important to research how it fits into the context of existing games. Select the three previous commercial titles closest to this one. For each, describe one interesting point—for example, how the related game differs, how it is similar, how it performed in the market, and what critics were positive and negative about. The references at the end of this chapter are good places to start your research. See the completed worksheets at the end of this chapter for examples of related game analysis.

When writing an overview worksheet for a preexisting game as a homework assignment, it is often most useful to look only at related games published before the one you are describing. This is because an older game will often not compare favorably with newer games. However, for recently published video games, comparisons against other recently published games are valid. Today's multiyear development cycles mean that both games were probably in development simultaneously and that their development teams were aware of each other's product through previews and beta releases.

The related games section is often not present in industry for initial proposals to a team, partly because developers in industry likely have passing knowledge of most significant related games and don't need explicit analysis for an early proposal. This section instead appears in a more significant form as a market analysis that will accompany the design document submitted to a publisher as a formal proposal.

In academia, the Related Works section is important on an initial proposal. It demonstrates scholarship and ensures that you have gained the background knowledge that might already be at the fingertips of an industry developer. It also shows what is innovative about your proposal, which is more critical in a noncommercial context.

4.4 Examples

4.4.1 Video Game Proposal

This is an example of a completed worksheet for a novel video game idea. It is intended for a team of one artist and one programmer to complete in a few months.

Title: *R/C Airdevil*

Figure 4.5. *R/C Airdevil.*

Tagline: "Miniature adventures in flying"

Genre: Side-scroller

Platform: Low power; Web, phone, or handheld console

Target Audience: Casual preteen gamer

Plays Like: *Choplifter* meets *Micromachines*

Goal: Rescue lost toys while avoiding hazards great and small

Major Mechanics:

1. Precision timing and dodging
2. Rescue

Setting: A toy's view of a suburban home and neighborhood, packed with angry pets, other toys, and environmental hazards

Setting References:

1. *Toy Story 2* film
2. *Nanochopter 3000* toy
3. *Army Men* game
4. *Lego Star Wars 2* game
5. Various cartoons

Key Experiences:

1. Helicopter automatically performs tricks like loops in appropriate circumstances
2. Slipping through narrow passages like windows and down a drainage vent
3. Snatching a teddy bear from a threatening alley cat

Selling Points:

1. Simple, two-button interface is easy to learn and ports to many different low-powered devices
2. Nonviolent, toy-oriented gameplay for preteen market
3. Casual; easy in, easy out

Related Games:

1. *Choplifter* for Commodore 64/Arcade; Broderbund, 1982

   The basic helicopter-rescue scenario is lifted from *Choplifter* but made more lighthearted (*Choplifter* was inspired by the 1981 Iran hostage crisis) and with drastically simplified controls. *Choplifter* has traditional video game controls, whereas *Airdevil* is more like a claw vending machine where timing is critical and control is limited.

2. *Army Men: Air Combat* for Game Cube; 3DO, 2004

   The poorly regarded *AM:AC* game previously featured toy helicopter antics but was essentially a by-the-numbers branding exercise with poor production values and uninteresting gameplay. Also, note the better-produced *Army Men: Turf Wars* for GBA; 3DO 2002, which more closely matches the platform target.

3. *Defender* arcade cabinet; Williams Electronics, 1980

   The limited controls and rescue mission are ultimately inherited from this arcade hit, where a spaceship defended civilians from invaders and had to catch falling humans in midair.

4.4.2 Board Game Proposal

This is an example of a completed worksheet proposing a new board game to be created in one month by a two-person team.

Title: *Cutthroat*

Figure 4.6. *Cutthroat.*

Tagline: "Treachery at sea"

Genre: Turn-based board game

Platform: Two-player board game

Target Audience: Ages 10+

Plays Like: *Pirateer* meets *Munchkin*

Goal: Sail captured treasure back to your secret lair

Major Mechanics:

1. Diamond-grid board naturally simulates the effect of wind direction on boat speed
2. Single-turn move-shoot-move sequence keeps sea battles constantly in motion
3. RPG cards create complex and entertaining encounters

Setting: Caribbean, 1670

Setting References:

1. *Pirates of the Caribbean* film
2. *Master and Commander* novels and films
3. *Pirateer* game
4. *Treasure Island* game and film
5. *Pirates of the Spanish Main* game

Key Experiences:

1. Master both wind and weapons in fast-paced sea battles, jockeying for a clear shot
2. Treachery: kidnapping crew, stacking cards for maximum impact, triggering mutiny on enemy ships
3. Plotting a successful course to slip your ships home through enemy fire

Selling Points:

1. Capitalize on the current popularity of pirates (due to the *Pirates of the Caribbean* films and *Sid Meier's Pirates* game) and dearth of solid strategic pirate board games
2. Engaging, high-quality game pieces: metal doubloons, glass gems, and wooden pirate storage chest
3. Manage an entire armada ... or craft one superdreadnaught

Related Games:

1. *Munchkin* card game; Steve Jackson Games, 2003

   Munchkin is a parody of the degenerate stat-building strategy of some pen-and-paper role-playing players couched in the mechanics of collectible card games like *Magic*, where cards add weapons and magic items to a character. Much of the enjoyment of *Cutthroat* derives from playing cards to fill out a ship's crew and inflict special attacks on opponents.

2. *Pirateer* board game; Mendicino Game Company, 1990

   The basic gameplay motivator is borrowed from *Pirateer*; players race ships across a grid to capture treasure. The actual interaction in *Cutthroat* is primarily naval battles, but there would be no conflict without the limited treasure resource.

3. *Pirates of the Spanish Main* tabletop miniature game; Wizards of the Coast, 2005

   Cutthroat (at least the prototype) will use ships and islands from this game and some of the basic war game ideas, but the gameplay is streamlined, and more strategy is added through cards.

4.4.3 Classic Game Summary

This is an example of a completed worksheet that summarizes a relatively old, preexisting game as if it had just been invented by the author. *Metroid Zero Mission* was developed and published by Nintendo for the Game Boy Advance in 2004 as a remake of the classic game *Metroid.* This summary is written relative to the original *Metroid* to show how to use historical context for related games.

Title: *Metroid Zero Mission* (Figure 4.7)

Tagline: "Evil must be exterminated—but first it must be discovered!"

Genre: Platformer

Platform: GameBoy Advance

Target Audience: Teenage boys; 30-something nostalgia-gamers

Plays Like: *Super Mario Bros.* meets *Duke Nukem*

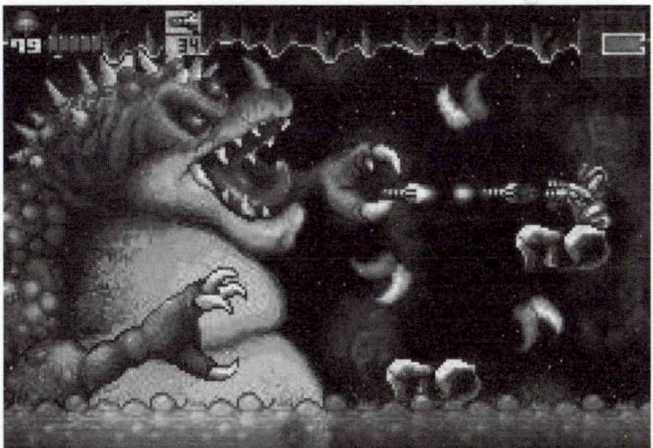

Figure 4.7. *Metroid Zero Mission.* (Image courtesy of Nintendo)

Goal: Exterminate an alien menace (Metroids) by collecting enough power-ups to reach its lair at the heart of a planet

Major Mechanics:

1. Arcade shooting
2. Upgrades to make areas reachable (lock and key)

Setting: The intergalactic bounty hunter revisits her home planet's ancient underground ruins, now infested by hostile aliens both miniature and gigantic

Setting References:

1. *Metroid* game
2. *Starship Troopers* film and novel
3. *DragonSlayer* film
4. *The Descent* film
5. *The Mummy* film
6. *Indiana Jones* films

Key Experiences:

1. Blasting missiles into a giant dragon while dangling over lava fields
2. Lifting the main character to secret platforms on carefully timed sequences of explosions
3. Discovering alterations of previously explored areas due to in-game events

Selling Points:

1. Nonlinear progression allows a sense of freedom a la *Grand Theft Auto* and other open-world games
2. Constant traversal over the same map with different power-ups extends the gameplay value of fixed art assets
3. Leverage the brand success and design of the *Metroid* series but add new levels and weapons to reinvigorate this remake

Related Games:

1. *Super Mario Bros.* for NES; Nintendo, 1985

   SMB set the stage for a platformer in a large scrolling world on the NES. *Metroid*'s darker graphics and more detailed weapons lead to a more mature game. *Metroid* emphasizes exploration.

2. *Gradius* for NES; Konami, 1985

   Although it is a side-scrolling shooter, certain elements are common: giant bosses, cave exploration, rapid gunfighting, a sci-fi setting, and significant power-ups. Should appeal to the same demographic.

3. *The Legend of Zelda* for NES; Nintendo, 1987

   Metroid leverages open exploration and power-ups from adventure games like *Zelda* but downplays the explicit story in favor of sci-fi mystery; *Metroid* has fewer puzzles and more action, which lead to more male-targeted gameplay.

4.4.4 Recent Game Summary

This is an example of a completed worksheet that summarizes a relatively new preexisting game as if it had just been invented by the author. *Half-Life 2* was developed by Valve and published in 2004 by Vivendi and Valve for Windows PC.

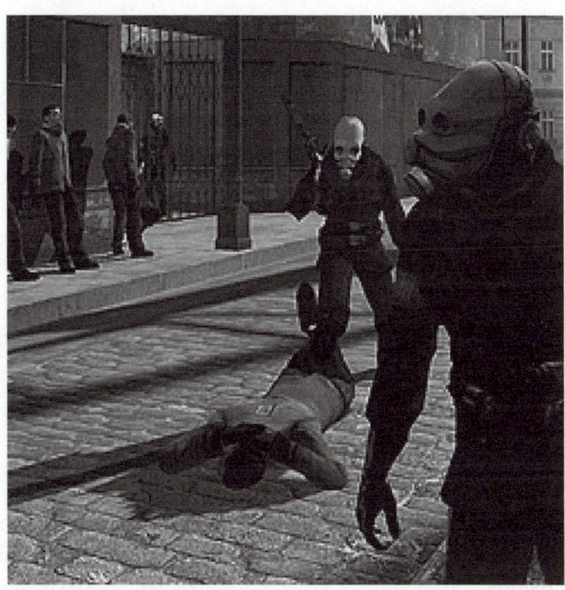

Figure 4.8. *Half-Life 2.* (Image courtesy of Valve)

Title: *Half-Life 2*

Tagline: "Run, Think, Shoot, Live. Again."

Genre: First-person shooter

Platform: PC or next-generation console

Target Audience: Men age 18–40; sci-fi fans

Plays Like: *Myst* meets *DOOM*

Goal: Battle for the resistance forces against fascist troops and aliens

Major Mechanics:

1. FPS combat

2. Physics puzzles

Setting: City 17: a near-future Eastern European police-state under siege from both a popular resistance and alien invaders who are malicious to all

Setting References:

1. *Half-Life 1* and expansion packs
2. *X-Files* TV series
3. *1984* novel
4. *Equilibrium* film
5. *Fahrenheit 451* novel
6. *Night of the Living Dead* (for gothic horror sequences)

Key Experiences:

1. Creativity with the gravity gun, a handheld tractor beam, including hurling saw blades, knocking over gun turrets, and righting vehicles after collisions
2. Holding the roof of a brownstone with a shotgun as zombies rattle up the drainpipes
3. Skimming along a drainage channel in a hovercraft, under fire from Apache helicopters and shore batteries

Selling Points:

1. Repeat the design and leverage the reputation of *Half-Life*, a critically acclaimed and a blockbuster (over 8 million copies sold) hit
2. Engine designed for mod creation so that *HL2* is a platform as well as a game, thus extending its effective market lifetime
3. First 3D game with effective, realistic physics puzzles

Related Games:

1. *DOOM 3*, PC; Activision/id Software, 2004

   Under development simultaneously with *HL2*. Both feature shader graphics, realistic physics, and FPS alien hunting. *D3* relies on superior technology and macho plot for tight, competitive FPS gameplay. *HL2* explores more beautiful locations, innovates with the gravity gun, and integrates detailed storytelling.

2. *Half-Life* for Windows PC; Sierra/Valve, 1998

   Stay true to the original *Half-Life* story line, adding more realistic physics and graphics and expanding the plot with real-world political issues. Increase the conspiracy aspects of the original and introduce new, younger characters.

3. *Tomb Raider: Legend*, Xbox 360; Eidos Interactive/Crystal Dynamics, 2006

   Also is story driven, with 3D platformer puzzles and action gameplay. *HL2* creates more interaction through the gravity gun and sidekick characters.

4.5 Exercises

1. Select a page at random from a novel. List all of the verbs on that page down one column of your answer sheet. Next to them write a second column of stronger verbs that have similar semantics.

2. Propose game titles based on the following game descriptions. Your titles should be names that are not already in use by some existing game and should be no more than three words in length.

   (a) A video game where you build machines from gears, pulleys, and other mechanical devices to solve physical puzzles.

   (b) A board game that matches part (a) but where the machines are simpler.

   (c) An RTS game of battles between microscopic single-celled organisms.

   (d) An adventure board game of arctic survival, where a nineteenth-century expedition with sled dogs and rifles seeks the North Pole. They must use their wits and resources to battle an environment filled with polar bears, glaciers, seals, storms, and crevasses.

   (e) Interplanetary privateers sailing old-fashioned boats with rocket engines trade and battle between the stars in a MMORPG.

   (f) A casual Web game where you design an organic garden, whose composition and layout must hold off various insect pests, rabbits, deer, and birds, as well as ensuring proper sun, water, nutrients, and space for each of the plants.

3. List the taglines for five major films from the previous summer. If you can't find their original taglines, write appropriate ones of your own (and state that you made them up).

4. Classify the genre and goal of each of the following games. You may need to invent new genre names or make hybrids. Research any of the games that you are not familiar with (you do not have to play them).

   (a) Poker
   (b) *Scrabble*
   (c) backgammon
   (d) *Frequency*
   (e) *Jak and Daxter*
   (f) *Halo*
   (g) *Burnout*
   (h) *Fight Night*
   (i) *The Sims*
   (j) *FIFA Soccer*
   (k) *Jet Grind Radio*

5. Write a casual critique that is no more than two pages long of one of the following games (or Web clones of them). You must actually play the game immediately before writing the critique, and you should have the game at hand while writing.

   (a) *Apples to Apples*
   (b) *Pit*
   (c) *Othello*
   (d) *Gears of War*
   (e) *Pac-Man*
   (f) *Breakout*
   (g) *Missile Command*

6. Play a game that is new to you, and complete the proposal sheet for it as if you were proposing it as a new game. When completing the related work section, pretend that you are proposing this at the time that the game was first published, so you should only reference *older* games.

7. Play a game (that does not have to be new to you) and write a formal critique of it.

8. Spend one hour with a small group of colleagues inventing and filling out proposal forms for three new games. The games do not have to be particularly good ideas. The point is to get experience using the format and allow yourself to be creative.

4.6 Resources

Many online sources have extensive information about video games and are useful for researching related games. These include:

- Wikipedia (http://wikipedia.com/)
- The Internet Movie Database (which also contains games) (http://imdb.com/)
- MobyGames (http://mobygames.com/)
- Review and enthusiast sites such as IGN, GameSpot, GameSpy, GameRankings, and FilePlanet

CHAPTER **5**

The Design Document

Terms Explained: *Choke Point – Design Document – Issue Tracking – Player Composite – Bugs – Plot Graph – Staffing Plan – Storyboard – Tags – Technology Plan*

The *design document* describes the development team's shared vision for all aspects of the game and the development process. It is considered a *working document* because it is continually revised, based on feedback and experience. The team begins writing the design document before the game, but the document is not finished until the game itself is finished!

The format of the design document is essential to its use as a reference document. Each chapter addresses a specific aspect of development, such as the user interface. The order and style of the chapters varies across companies, but any game-development project should contain most of the sections discussed in this book. When the developer works with a publisher, the developer proposes the game with an early version of the design document and later uses the design document to present the game's evolving specifications to the publisher. Some sections of the document resemble a business plan in order to meet these needs.

Design documents are often hundreds of pages and are maintained by the lead designer and producer, although other members of the team contribute a lot of the content. In the board game industry, design documents tend to be short and informal because board games are simpler than video games, and the development process is shorter and involves fewer people. A tightly-focused design document of about 20 pages is good for an indie game or classroom final project. As with any working document, controversy may arise about whether to write a long document (to create a full specification) or to write a short document (which is easier to keep up to date). We recommend keeping the design document on the short side and augmenting it with regular face-to-face communication between team members.

New document technology like webpages and wikis can make design documents up to date and more visible to the whole team. Online documents also have the advantage of hyperlinks between sections of the document and external concept art or supporting documents.

This chapter describes the basic content of the design document. Although all of the following features are presented in this chapter, later chapters discuss individual features in more detail.

1. Title page
2. Executive summary
3. Overview (see also Chapter 4, Appendix B)
4. Related games
5. Player composites
6. World (see also Chapter 11)
7. Characters (see also Chapter 11)
8. Progression graph
9. Art direction (see also Chapter 12)
10. User interface storyboards (see also Chapter 12)
11. Tags and dialogue
12. Technology plan (see also Chapter 6, Appendix C)
13. Software architecture
14. Controls (see also Chapter 17)
15. Level design (see also Chapter 11)
16. Mechanics analysis (see also Chapter 10)
17. Schedule (see also Chapter 3, Appendix E)
18. Budget (see also Appendix D)
19. Change log

5.1 Title Page

The title is on one page. It is graphically simple, like the frontispiece for a book. Yet it contains vital information. The title page should contain:

1. a picture (screenshot or box art);
2. the title of the game, and optionally, the tagline;
3. the name of the developer;
4. the date and revision number of the design document.

Larger companies or those working with publishers require legal statements on this page as well. For example, copyright information, "confidential/do not distribute" instructions, and the main office contact phone number and address.

5.2 Executive Summary

This one-page section describes the entire game in three sentences:[1]

1. a sentence about the basic setting;
2. a sentence that describes what makes the game interesting;
3. a sentence that will convince a publisher to approve or fund the game.

A game might be interesting and engaging because it contains a new technology, has an interesting story, contains a new mechanic, or can be marketed at a low price. There are many reasons a publisher might want to approve a game. These tend to focus on either novelty, e.g., "never before have RPG and puzzle games been combined" or "the first real-time Scrabble game," or (ironically) the complete absence of novelty, e.g., "this is a James Bond game, and all James Bond games sell 1M units." Often the text for the executive summary can be entirely drawn from other sections of the design document.

5.3 Overview

The overview consists of two or three pages that compactly describe the major qualities of the game. It follows the overview worksheet format from the previous chapter. It must pitch the core concept, review related games,

[1]An academic would call this the abstract for the document.

and present the reader with a mental image of the game as a whole. It is essentially a distilled version of the entire design document.

The overview is the first part of the design document that is written. Once accepted by an internal team, the proposal/overview then evolves into a proposal from the team to the company. The ideas from the overview are finally expanded into a full design document.

5.4 Related Games

This section reviews related games and serves as background research for both marketing and design purposes. Experience with previous work is important. You should extend the successes of previous games while avoiding their pitfalls. Rarely do truly original ideas emerge; usually someone has already come up with *your* great idea. So research previous work and then leverage it.

The related games section should devote about one page to each related game. The specific games chosen should be a superset of those described in the overview section.

Discuss existing games that resemble yours in any way (e.g., setting, mechanics, business model). Why do you feel that you can repeat the success of a previous game or avoid its failure?

Some previous work may be your competition. You need to address this head-on. Judge your own potential and account for competition in your design. Why will your game succeed if it is competing with an already established game?

A wise designer draws heavily from previous games. Most games companies have large libraries of games available for close study and reverse engineering during production (see Figure 5.1). Build such a library and plan on spending many hours perusing everything from menus to data files in other games.

5.5 Player Composites

This section creates a marketing model of the players who will purchase and play your game. These aren't the in-game characters but the real people who will playing the game. The characteristics of this group will help you create intuition for design decisions, as well as serve as a job description for the playtesters you will recruit.

Creating a *player composite* takes the player from being an ambiguous presence in the design (or, even more dangerous, a carbon copy of you!)

Figure 5.1. Library of related work games at Iron Lore Entertainment.

and makes him or her into a concrete person you want to make happy. For example, you may create the following profile:

"John Brooke, 27, accountant. Single. Graduate of Loyola College. Plays games alone about once a week, and with male friends on a next-generation console plugged into an HDTV in his living room on weekend afternoons. Focuses on competitive, action games like *Gears of War* and *Madden.* Watches football one day a week. Favorite TV shows are *Lost* and *Sopranos* reruns. Drives an Audi A4. Drinks imported beer."

The profile answers the following questions about this target player.

1. When and where does this person play games?
2. Who buys the games this person uses?
3. What platforms does this player use?
4. How much time does this person spend in each session, and how frequent are gaming sessions?
5. Who does he or she play with?
6. What does the player like about games?
7. What (non-game) brand images appeal to this player?
8. How much disposable income does this player have?

9. What licensed content would appeal to this player?

10. What competes with gaming time for this player?

Most games have both a primary market and a secondary market; for example, an *Asteroids* remake might target both preteens and nostalgic 40-somethings. Make a composite for each demographic you hope to target. When available, the composites can be based on actual market research. But even without such research, it is better to invent the composite than to have none at all. With a composite, the entire development team will explicitly agree, which is far better than having everyone independently make different personal assumptions.

5.6 World

For all but abstract games, like *Yinsh* and go, the setting and narrative are significant aspects of production. Most players never create a mental model more sophisticated than the fiction they are told and depend on a consistent virtual world for enjoyment.

In the world section, give the background. This may be the history of an entire civilization or just the conditions surrounding the main character. Record information about areas and events to keep the decisions made by various team members consistent. The *Halo* series is based on hundreds of pages of documents detailing several alien races, the main character, the rough geography of the universe, and the detailed geography of the ring world in which the game takes place. The amount of detail needed for your game depends on the scope of the setting and on the player's exploration ability. The only limiting factor is the time you can invest creating and maintaining this information.

Some of the world information will be revealed to players in the game manual or throughout the course of the game. Other aspects will never be revealed, but their consistency will be felt. Sequels and expansion packs are a great opportunity for revealing aspects that were kept secret in the initial game. Chapter 11 describes methods for building out your world.

5.7 Characters

Describe each character's background and motivation. This is especially important for the main character in a narrative-driven game, whose motivations will become the player's own. Include concept and in-game art for each character. List aspects including their:

1. motivation
2. physical description
3. likes and dislikes
4. family
5. friends and enemies
6. vital statistics
7. education
8. occupation
9. transportation
10. tools/weapons
11. clothing

For nonhuman characters, make sure their origins and race are well developed.

5.8 Plot Graphs

Create a flow chart to show the player's progression through the game. In a plot-driven video game with a strong narrative, this serves as the nonlinear map of the narrative. Figures 5.2 and 5.3 show plot diagrams for *Ultima VII* as drawn by player Urpo Lankinen.[2] Annotate your graph to show narrative arcs and different physical regions within which the player travels. For a *Choose Your Own Adventure* book, the progression graph essentially is the game; all that is missing is the flavor text (which, in that case, comprises all of the text that the player sees!).

For a game that lacks a strong narrative (e.g., an emergent instead of progressive game), the progression graph indicates the major stages through which gameplay changes occur. Strategy games like *Civilization* typically see an escalation of risk and power throughout the game that can be shown here.

[2](http://www.geocities.com/hoki_dragon/u7plot.png)

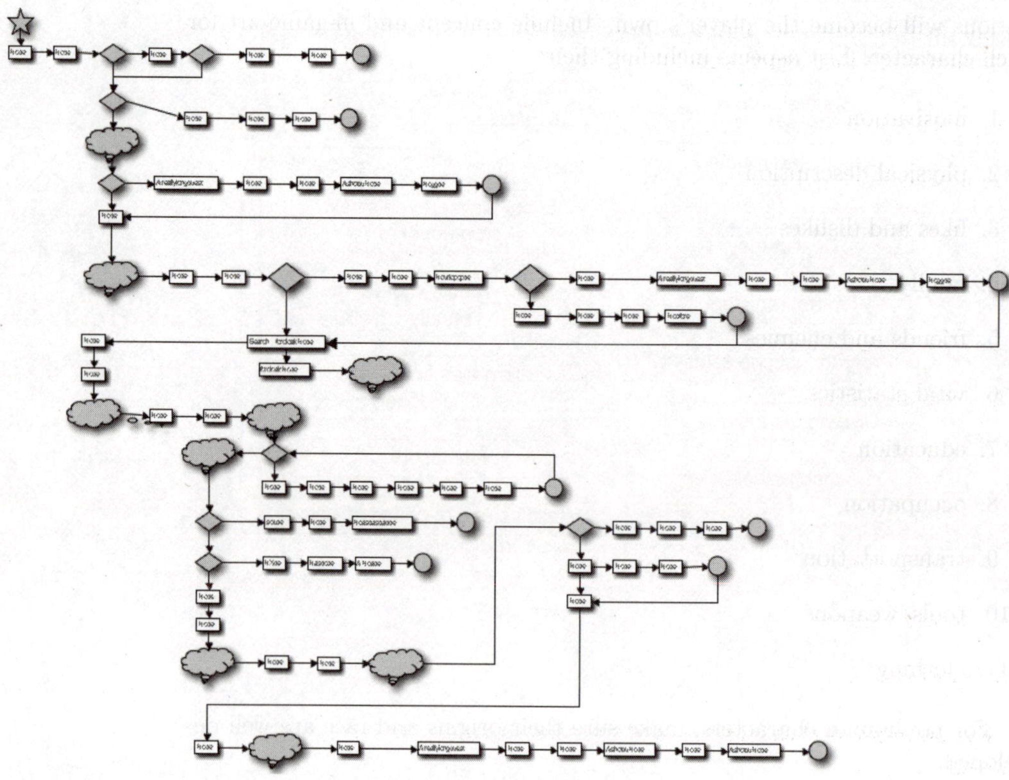

Figure 5.2. Plot graph for the main quest in *Ultima VII.*

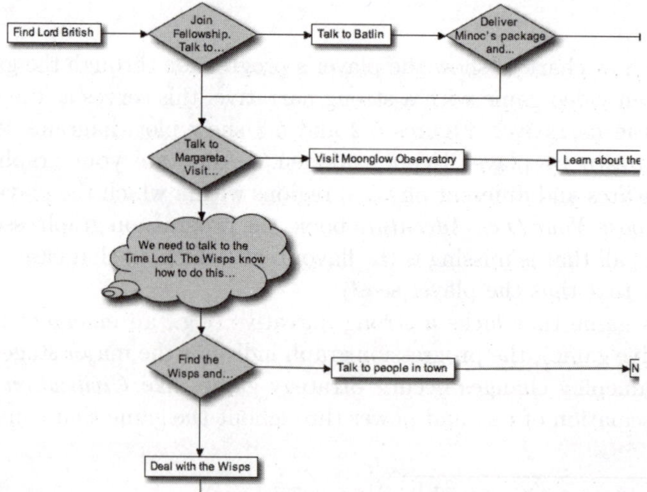

Figure 5.3. Detail from the progression graph for the main quest in *Ultima VII.*

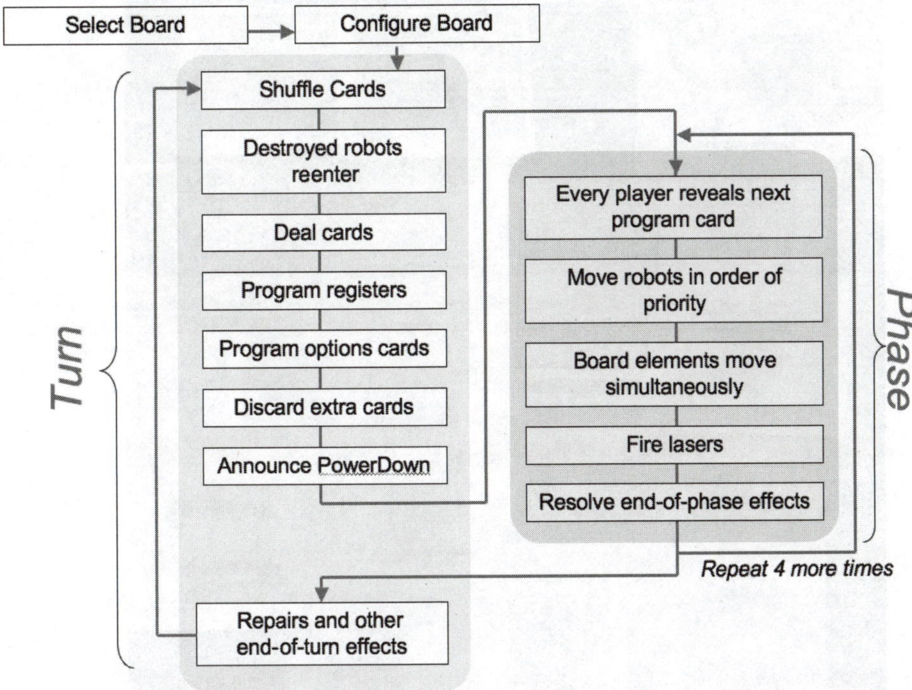

Figure 5.4. Progression graph for play in the board game *RoboRally*.

In a board game, the progression graph describes the setup and the states of the game. Most modern board games have several phases to each turn that can be clearly delineated on the turn progression graph. An example is shown in Figure 5.4 for *RoboRally*, a board game in which players "program" robots with cards and then have them fight on the factory floor.

5.8.1 Storyboards

For games with cutscenes and cinematics, label those scenes in the plot graph and provide additional material in the form of storyboards and scripts describing the scenes. See *Don Bluth's The Art of Storyboard* [Bluth and Goldman 04] for a good graphic introduction to these.

5.9 Art Direction

The art direction section is a combination of descriptive text and images that convey the graphic style of the game. It typically includes concept

Figure 5.5. Concept art for *Titan Quest.* (Image courtesy of ILE/THQ)

art (e.g., as shown in Figure 5.5), reference art from books to inspire the style, instructions on the use of lighting in a 3D game, font samples, and constraints specified by the underlying technology. See Chapters 13 and 14 for a discussion of some of the constraints that the graphics engine places on the artwork in a video game.

5.10 User Interface Storyboards

For a computer game, the user interface is the installer, the title screen, menus, dialogs, in-game heads-up display and information displays, options screens, and any other controls or text. Each of these must be storyboarded for both content and graphic style, although content is the primary purpose of this section. Storyboards can be simple sketches that show the GUI elements, with callout boxes and labels indicating the function of each element. Flow charts (state machines) are needed for each major GUI interaction showing the modes that the interface can be in and how the player's actions change modes.

User interface storyboards are simpler for a board game. In this case, they are essentially concept art for the layout of the play area, board, and pieces. The difference between the UI section and the concept art section is that UI focuses on functionality and concept art focuses on style.

5.11 Tags and Dialogue

This section is exclusive to video games. The tags and dialogue section is a database that maps descriptive labels (*tags*) used by the programmers and designers to actual text that the user will see and hear in game. For example, a button labeled "Launch Attack!" in the game might have the tag ATTACK. Later in the development cycle, the designers can decide that the button should instead say "Commence Firing." To make this change, the tag stays the same, but the value stored for that tag in the tag database changes. This way, the programmers don't have to update their source code for cosmetic changes, and the technology and design teams can work without interfering with one another. Tags are also used for dialogue lines. The tag HELLO_INKEEPER1 could map to "Salutations, weary traveler. Come in and rest yourself for a while."

Tags are critical for internationalization. Translators can work through the database without significant concern for where text appears in the game. Likewise for adjusting potentially offensive language to satisfy content ratings.

In games with spoken dialog, tags map not only to text but to audio files, although these are more difficult to change. However, like translators, voice actors can work through the database of script lines. Voice actors should be given some context and experience with the game so that their tone and inflection are appropriate.

5.12 Technology Plan

The *technology plan* is primarily for video games, but it can be adapted to board games in a useful way. A video game requires several major pieces of software. Some are part of the game itself, like the core engine (rendering, physics, and networking) and the gameplay code (user interface, artificial intelligence, and game logic). Other pieces are tools: the software used for maintaining the design document (e.g., Microsoft Word, wiki), the artist tools (e.g., 3DS Max, Photoshop), the programmer tools (e.g., Visual Studio,

VTune), the management tools (e.g., Project, Excel, Trac), asset management (e.g., AlienBrain, Subversion), level editors, art exporters, and so on. Hardware technology is also required for console development, development consoles, all development workstations and servers, and often special-purpose technology like motion capture and 3D scanners for artwork.

The technology plan enumerates all of the technology needed for producing the game and maintaining the company. It designates whether it will be bought or built in-house. For technology that can be bought, the specific solution selected should be explained and defended. For technology that must be built, the rationale for building in-house should be explained and the rough specifications for the project outlined. The buy/build decision is often easy except for core engine technology, where the company must decide if it can adapt an existing game engine or must build its own. For further discussion of core engine technology and this difficult decision, see Chapter 6.

Board games require some tools for production (usually 2D art programs and word processors) but not nearly as much as video games. However, board games have another technology requirement in terms of playing pieces and their manufacture. The technology plan for a board game should discuss how those pieces will be obtained and the costs associated with that plan. Generic pawns and dice can be purchased inexpensively, but custom pieces require a more significant investment. Playing boards and cards can be surprisingly expensive to produce, although there is great room for savings by altering the printing method or switching to lower-quality (sharp corner, monochrome, thinner) paper and cardboard components.

For students working on a class project, the technology plan is highly constrained by the materials available for the course. For a board game, reusing existing game pieces and boards is a fast and cost-effective alternative to producing custom pieces. For a video game, using open-source software or writing a mod for a game engine is a great alternative to buying or building. Students are often tempted to build most of their technology, but reusing existing technology allows you to focus more on design and innovation and less on reinventing the wheel!

5.13 Software Architecture

Video games require complex software design. The architecture documents describe the features of each programming module. This includes the major application interfaces (APIs), the algorithms that are used to implement them, and the design patterns behind them. In addition to text and tables of numbers, architecture typically contains many diagrams. These include inheritance diagrams, memory depictions of key data structures, and data file format diagrams. The two types of diagrams that always appear are the system module diagram and the data flow graph. The module diagram depicts the high-level control structure, and the data flow shows how information moves.

The system module diagram looks like a brick wall, where each brick is a software component. Components at the bottom are low-level libraries, such as DirectX and Havok. If we personify the components as people in a company, these are the laborers who will do the actual "heavy lifting." The components that rest on top of them direct the action of these lower libraries. Those themselves are managed by higher-level routines. In programmer terminology, higher boxes call into the boxes below them, creating a dependency. Components at the top of the module diagram are generally the most specific to the particular game, while those at the bottom are so generic that they may be provided by the platform manufacturer for use in all games.

The boxes in the data flow diagram are major software components (some of which are licensed), and the arrows show the kind of data that flow between them. The direction of arrows shows data dependence. Data generally flows in from pre-created art assets and real-time user input and out to the display. An example of the data flow diagram for a typical game appears in Figure 6.3.

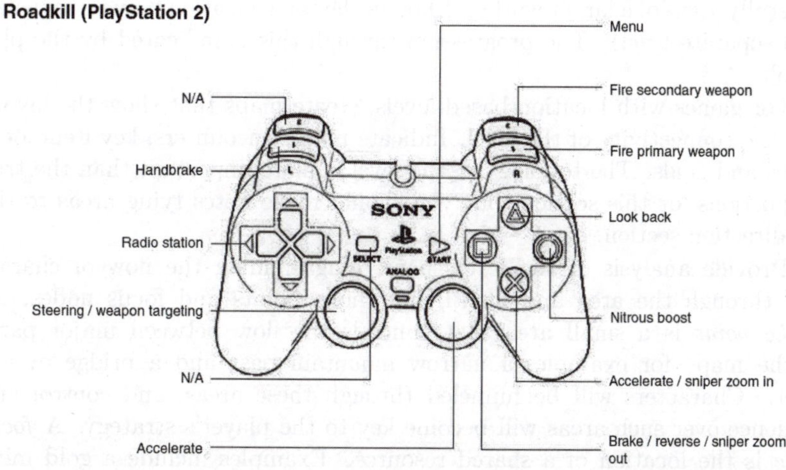

Figure 5.6. Controls for *Roadkill* on the PlayStation 2 by Red Octane. (Image courtesy of Red Octane/Activision)

5.14 Controls

Video games depend on their control schemes. An otherwise great game can fail because the input mechanic is too awkward or is targeted at the wrong audience. The controls section details both the mapping of buttons to in-game functions and the algorithms mapping analog inputs to actions.

This section contains images such as Figure 5.6 that show the explicit control layout for traditional input devices, as well as action diagrams for more recent innovations such as accelerometers (e.g., the Nintendo Wiimote), video cameras, and audio and gesture recognition. Chapter 17 explains the technology behind user input and theories of how to design effective input schemes.

5.15 Level Design

Most games are divided into *levels* that represent a discrete change in difficulty, such as different waves of aliens in *Space Invaders*. It can also be a scenario or map, such as the warehouse "Assault" map in *Counter-Strike* or the Joan of Arc battle in *Age of Empires*. In a classic emergent game like chess, levels become vague (although one could consider the opening, middle, and end games to be separate levels).

In a game that has a strong and primarily linear progression, levels are generally areas of a larger world (although the same location may be revisited as a separate level). The progression through this is indicated by the plot graph.

For games with location-based levels, create maps that show the layout and the connectivity of the level. Indicate major encounters, key item locations, and goals. The topology of the level is more important than the true proportions for this section, but you should make notes tying areas to the art direction section.

Provide analysis of the level space, diagramming the flow of characters through the area and identifying choke points and focus nodes. A *choke point* is a small area that controls the flow between major parts of the map—for example, a narrow mountain pass and a bridge over a river. Characters will be funneled through these areas, and control and influence over such areas will become key to the player's strategy. A *focus node* is the location of a shared resource. Examples include a gold mine in an RTS game, a key power-up in an FPS, a healing shrine in a fantasy game, the flags in a rally race, and a watering hole in an animal simulation. These areas increase player interaction by bringing them together.

Unlike choke points, they are not necessarily sources of contention because players may collaborate to use the resource and may share it if it is not limited.

Some games have randomly generated levels, like *Settlers of Catan* and the random maps in *StarCraft.* For these, discuss the kinds of features that will appear in the level and how the level-generation process ensures that they arise in the proper distribution.

5.16 Mechanics Analysis

The heart of the gameplay design in the document is the mechanics analysis section. It is equally important for video games, board games, major AAA titles, indie games, and class projects. Pen-and-paper RPG manuals, such as the *AD&D Player's Handbook*, give a good idea of what the mechanic descriptions in this section should look like. Economics textbooks give good examples of how to analyze, model, and balance mechanics.

Mechanics, also known as game mechanics, are small groups of rules that outline a strategic conflict, inspire a particular emotion in the player, or move the game forward. They are perhaps best understood through some examples.

Racing is a classic mechanic. Get to the finish line before your opponents. Racing puts time pressure on the player, creating stress and motivation. It is inherently both fair and balanced; the achievement scale is defined by the ratio of fastest to slowest racer. The racing mechanic need not be as explicit as cars on a track. For example, in a capture-the-flag game, a race mechanic begins as soon as a flag is taken and both sides are trying to reach the goal (or intercept the carrier) as fast as possible.

Shooting is a popular mechanic. It involves reflex actions, strategy in setting up a shot before the enemy appears, and leading the target when projectiles are slow. Shooting doesn't have to involve guns. Various games have used shooting mechanics to fire oneself out of a cannon, take pictures of wildlife, or successfully throw and catch a ball in sports.

Describe the mechanics in your game. Mechanics are typically shared between large numbers of games and are the primary definition of *genre.* Indicate what other games use similar mechanics and describe the differences. Motivate the gameplay reason for each mechanic. Does it prevent an undesirable strategy, simulate some aspect of the game's setting, or exist to deepen strategy in an otherwise too simple game? Explain alternative mechanics that could have been employed to address that need and why this one is better. What is the strategy that arises from the mechanic?

Give guidelines for making the mechanic balanced and useful for gameplay. Support these arguments in text, graphs and diagrams, and probability and mathematics.

Other common mathematical tools for evaluating and balancing mechanics are outcome matrices and unit databases. Outcome matrices are for evaluating competitive situations where one kind of unit is up against another kind. The matrix lists the first unit type along the rows and the second unit type along the columns. Each entry in the center describes the outcome for the combination of unit types (think of a multiplication table from school or a road map that shows the distance between cities). Unit databases are tables with the unit types listed down a column and adjacent columns describing their statistical properties, like hit points and movement speed.

For each measurable property of the game (e.g., points, gold, health), give a target graph of how it should ideally vary over time. See Chapters 7, 8, and 10 for further discussions of the mechanics analysis section.

5.17 Schedule and Related Elements

5.17.1 Schedule

The master development schedule describes the plan for producing the game on time. It is broken down into prototype releases and milestones, and those are divided into individual tasks assigned to developers. Milestones describe the features and user experience that will be available at distinct points in time. They should be monthly or bimonthly for a game that is in development for years, but for a month-long indie project, they may be weekly or every other day.

Tasks can be chained based on dependency in a Gantt chart to graphically indicate when a task has been inappropriately scheduled before another task it must build on. Figure 3.7 shows a project schedule maintained in Microsoft Project with both a Gantt view and a breakdown per milestone.

5.17.2 Staffing Plan

For a commercial game, the *staffing plan* describes how developers will be hired over time to meet the demands of the schedule. It can be expressed as hiring milestones or as a graph running along the bottom of the timeline. When designing it, remember that recruiting, interviewing, and training talent takes time from both the new hire and the existing team members. An indie team or a class project team generally has no hiring and needs no staffing plan.

5.17.3 Key Developers

Briefly describe the qualifications of team leads, producers, and managers. These are the people who should have proven track records and who will be held responsible for delivering a quality game product on time. Qualifications include education, previous job experience (especially games shipped), exceptional skills, and awards received.

In industry, this section is primarily to convince a publisher (or investor) that your team has the ability to deliver the game that it is promising to create. In academia, this is to convince your teacher that your team has the necessary skills.

5.17.4 Issue Tracking

Issue tracking is a more sophisticated version of maintaining a "to-do" list. Issues are known *bugs* (also: errors or drawbacks) of the game design or

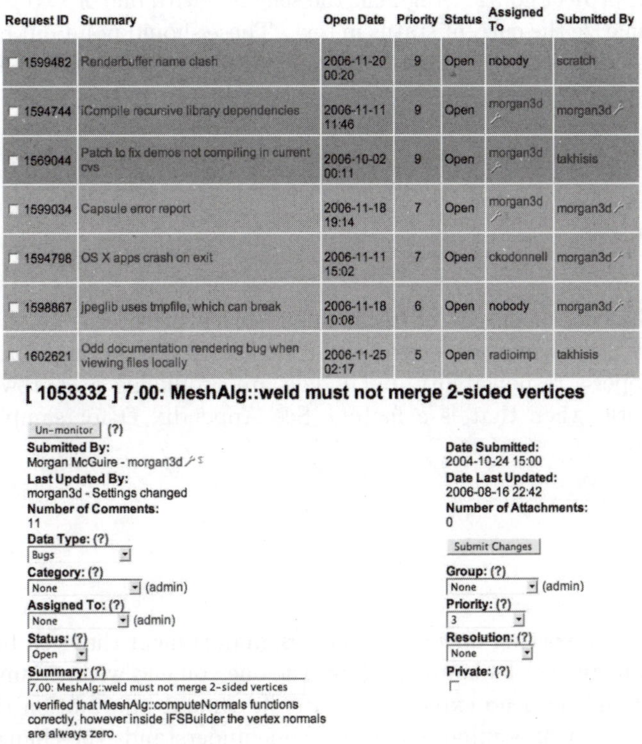

Request ID	Summary	Open Date	Priority	Status	Assigned To	Submitted By
1599482	Renderbuffer name clash	2006-11-20 00:20	9	Open	nobody	scratch
1594744	iCompile recursive library dependencies	2006-11-11 11:46	9	Open	morgan3d	morgan3d
1569044	Patch to fix demos not compiling in current cvs	2006-10-02 00:11	9	Open	morgan3d	takhisis
1599034	Capsule error report	2006-11-18 19:14	7	Open	morgan3d	morgan3d
1594798	OS X apps crash on exit	2006-11-11 15:02	7	Open	ckodonnell	morgan3d
1598867	jpeglib uses tmpfile, which can break	2006-11-18 10:08	6	Open	nobody	morgan3d
1602621	Odd documentation rendering bug when viewing files locally	2006-11-25 02:17	5	Open	radioimp	takhisis

[1053332] 7.00: MeshAlg::weld must not merge 2-sided vertices

Un-monitor (?)

Submitted By:
Morgan McGuire - morgan3d

Last Updated By:
morgan3d - Settings changed

Number of Comments:
11

Data Type: (?)
Bugs

Category: (?)
None (admin)

Assigned To: (?)
None (admin)

Status: (?)
Open

Summary: (?)
7.00: MeshAlg::weld must not merge 2-sided vertices

I verified that MeshAlg::computeNormals functions correctly, however inside IFSBuilder the vertex normals are always zero.

Date Submitted:
2004-10-24 15:00

Date Last Updated:
2006-08-16 22:42

Number of Attachments:
0

Submit Changes

Group: (?)
None (admin)

Priority: (?)
3

Resolution: (?)
None

Private: (?)

Figure 5.7. Sample bug list and a specific open ticket from the SourceForge issue tracking system for the *G3D* game engine.

implementation, customer support requests, and features that have been requested but not approved or scheduled. Issues are what you aim to eventually change into lines on the change log.

Issues are commonly owned by one developer, but they are stored in a format that is visible to management and the rest of the company. A video game has so many issues that they are usually stored in a database and not in the design document itself. For a board game or extremely simple (e.g., puzzle game) computer game, a bulleted list with some details at the bottom of the status section may suffice.

Figure 5.7 shows a screenshot from an issue-tracking system. The top of the screen is a table listing a small number of issues stored in the database. The table lists the developer who is assigned to resolve the issue, a summary, the date, and so on. The bottom is a detailed view of a single issue that has been selected.

5.17.5 Status

How is the project going? Augment the schedule with one or two paragraphs that summarize the current status in text. These should point out milestones that are at risk of slipping and major successes. Keep this up to date at all times.

5.18 Budget

The budget section describes the total cost of development. Line items include the cost of purchased technology, salary (according to the staffing plan), recruiting costs, art assets, and contractors. Marketing is not usually the developer's responsibility, but if you are producing a shareware/independent title, then that is a factor. See Appendix D for sample budget worksheets.

5.19 Change Log

Because it is a working document, the design document that you begin with might not might not look anything like the one you end with. Many changes are trivial and need no explanation. If you expand information that is already present or fix a minor error, everyone understands the change. When a major change is made, however, it is important to record that information. For example, if one mechanic is completely removed after a playtest, it should be noted on the design document, and everyone who will be reading it should be alerted. For such a change, add a line to the change log section briefly summarizing what happened—for example, "Removed time limit on water war stage because playtesters reported excessive tension on that level."

Developers frequently release rule changes (for board games) and patches (for video games) even after the game itself has been released. These are accompanied by change logs to let the players know what changed. Those change logs are edited versions of the ones that are in the design document.

Some designers call the change log the *revision history* and maintain it right after the title page. The back of the design document is another popular location. It is often useful to not only maintain a bulleted list but to designate build or version numbers between strings of changes. This is helpful when reviewing old playtesting information to see what set of changes were enacted before and after the test.

5.20 Exercises

1. Give one player composite for the core constituency of each of the following games.
   (a) *Pokemon*
   (b) chess
   (c) *Counter-Strike*
2. Draw a plot graph for your daily routine containing about 15 nodes. Use branches to indicate different ways your day plays out—for example, according to the day of the week or based on what you find in your e-mail.
3. Why are tags used in games instead of just putting the value of the tag directly into the game code?
4. What is the difference between the plot graph and level design?
5. List ten game mechanics—for example, racing, shooting, and rock-paper-scissors relationship.
6. What is the difference between the key developers section and the staffing plan?
7. Why is a change log useful?

8. Find the change log for a published game, and list a few of the major changes between versions.
9. Create a "blank" design document for your project. This should contain all of the sections that are relevant but need not have any content beyond the section titles and the cover page. You can do this by starting with one of the templates on our webpage and deleting unnecessary sections or by following the instructions in this chapter.

5.21 Resources

It is hard to obtain sample design documents for major titles because game developers and publishers consider them confidential internal documents. However, a few have been published. The following reading contains examples of design document templates or completed design documents.

- *Excalibur* design document in Chris Crawford, *The Art of Computer Game Design* [Crawford 84].
- Chris Crawford, *Chris Crawford on Game Design* [Crawford 03].
- The sample design documents in Andrew Rollings and Dave Morris, *Game Architecture and Design* [Rollings and Morris 99].
- Chris Taylor's design document template at http://www.designersnotebook.com/ctaylordesign.zip.
- Tzvi Freeman's article on design documents at http://www.gamasutra.com/features/19970912/design_doc.htm.

CHAPTER 6

Game Technology

Terms Explained: *Compiler – Database – Engine – Middleware – Mod – Revision Control – Tool – Visual Studio – Licensing – BSD – GPL – EULA*

Creating games requires technology in the form of tools for asset creation, code creation, and management. The games themselves are technology. For a video game, the technology includes real-time 3D graphics, audio, artificial intelligence, networking, and physics software. For a board game, the technology is comparatively modest: dice, boards, cards, and spinners.

This chapter introduces the computer technology needed to *produce* both board and video games and the technology for *playing* a video game. Materials for playing boards are presented in Chapter 8. This chapter includes both high-level descriptions of the kinds of technology involved in game development and lists of specific technologies that you may want to license (sometimes for free!) when developing your own games. When working on your game, use this chapter as a guide to the technology plan worksheet in Appendix C, which should appear in your design document.

The technology used to create a game is called a tool. Tools come in the form of computer software (e.g., Photoshop), computer hardware (e.g., a motion-capture rig), and traditional tools (e.g., scissors, paintbrushes). The technology that supports a video game at runtime is called an *engine*. Engines are relatively general purpose. For example, many first-person shooter games are based on the same *Unreal Engine*, even though they appear to be very different. That difference comes from additional game programming code that is layered over the engine and different content that is fed into it as data.

Both tools and engines can either be made by the development team (called "in-house"; the "build" decision) or purchased from a third party (called the "buy" decision). It is common to license a majority of tools for both board and video games and to license about half the underlying engine technology for video games. Despite licensing, for video game development some in-house tool development is typically required, although it may be as simple as writing your own build scripts or 2D-level editor.

6.1 Document Tools

Consider the technology requirements for supporting the design document. The design document is both read and modified by most of the team members. It is important that individual edits are correctly merged and that the latest version is continuously available. Since even electronic documents often end up on paper for reading on airplanes, incorporating into contracts, or handing in to teachers, a straightforward method for printing the document is also a common requirement.

In addition to editing, the design document must be internally distributed in a form that makes it easy for everyone to read and externally distributed to the publisher. For example, the internal format might be a private webpage and the external format PDF. Note that the internal and external versions might have slightly different contents, because the publisher and developers refer to different aspects of the specification.

There is currently no ideal solution to these problems. Instead, a range of different technologies is available, one of which will probably be best based on the size and composition of your development team.

The following are available technologies for editing the design document. A recurring theme in tools is the distinction between text and binary file formats. A *text*, human-readable, or ASCII format document is stored in a manner that is easy for programmers to access through add-on tools. This makes text format work with a large variety of external revision control systems and something that tools programmers can take advantage of. Some examples of text formats used in games are XML, RTF, HTML, CSV, MA, and ASE. A *binary* format document is stored in a (often proprietary) manner that makes it extremely difficult to combine with tools. Binary formats tend to be slightly smaller and faster but do not work with arbitrary revision management systems and may be hard for tools programmers to take advantage of. Some examples of binary formats used in games are JPG, 3DS, PSD, DOC, XLS, and PSF. Furthermore, extensible, encrypted, and plugin-based binary formats like MAX, ACC, and many MP4 files are protected by designs that make them effectively impossible for tools programmers and external systems to use.

6.1.1 Networked Files

The simplest technology for supporting the design document is to store the document as a set of text and image files in a networked computer folder that is accessible to everyone. This simple approach is viable for a one- or two-person team, but it has some drawbacks as the team size increases. If two people edit a file at the same time, the second one will either be locked out and unable to edit (which is particularly annoying when the first person opened the file and went home for the weekend), or one person's edits might be overwritten by the other. Also, it can be difficult to spot what has been changed recently or to roll back to an earlier version. The more separate files that the document is broken into, the lower the chance of two people editing the same file, but the harder it is to print or e-mail the whole document.

6.1.2 Multi-User Word Processors

An improvement over the shared directory method is using a revision control system with the networked files. Microsoft Word can track changes and merge edits from several people. It is easy to use, and it requires no server-side configuration. However, Word isn't always reliable for a large number of users, large files, and large number of edits. Programmers have long used revision control systems to solve essentially the same problems for source code. These have more recently been expanded into so-called asset or content management systems. Both are described in the following sections.

6.1.3 Source and Asset Management Systems

Source or asset management systems (which are described later in this chapter) can be applied to the document management problem, although the fit is not perfect. Source code management tools expect all data files to be plain text. They cannot properly merge edits in word-processing documents, spreadsheets, or images. One solution is to use a markup language like HTML or LaTeX for documents, which can be merged the same way as plain text by a source code management system. This is the solution that academics have long used for collaborative editing of large documents—in fact, this book was written collaboratively in Latex using the CVS revision control system.

The drawback with plain text revision control is that you lose the easy, what-you-see-is-what-you-get (WYSIWYG) editing capability of a word processor. For documents with lots of diagrams and nontechnical editors, that's a big drawback. Asset management systems tend to rely on external merge tools, which means going back to Microsoft Word, but with a little better revision control. Any of these management systems generally involves the overhead of configuring a management server, which is a fairly significant information technology undertaking that should be completed by a system administrator.

6.1.4 Wikis and Online Word Processors

A relatively new option that is very attractive for design documents is wiki technology or its more friendly recent cousin, Google Docs. A *wiki* document, like a blog, is simply a webpage that is easy to edit from within a Web browser. The Wikipedia user-edited encyclopedia is the most famous example of a collaborative document. It is maintained by thousands of mostly nontechnical writers using the MediaWiki software. A wiki can be run on an internal server by a system administrator or hosted on one of many external sites that provides private wikis (many of which are also free). Unlike Wikipedia, your document will not be visible to the rest of the world, only the members of your development team (assuming that you have configured it correctly). Like Wikipedia, multiple team members can simultaneously edit the document, and the whole team can interactively browse the latest version and see version histories. Because it is based on webpages, you can even put hyperlinks to quickly move through the document. The drawbacks of wikis are that there is no easy way to print the whole document, it is hard to maintain different simultaneous versions (e.g., an internal version and a version for the publisher), and it is still relatively clunky compared to a modern word processor.

Halfway in between a wiki and a word processor is Google Docs, which is Google's online word processor documents. (A spreadsheet version is available as well.) This allows an experience similar to Microsoft Word only in a web browser and with real-time collaboration support. These documents are private unless you explicitly share them publicly, and they are very easy to access and edit. Google Docs is relatively new. It offers fewer features than both wikis and word processors in terms of embedded content, control over edit and read permissions, and ways to create links between documents. Its reliability hasn't been demonstrated for very large files, and although the user interface is functional, it is not as good as a desktop word processor.

6.2 Asset Management Tools

Asset management tools are critical for maintaining source code, art, and other assets in video game development and are highly recommended for managing art resources in board-game development. Programmers produce source code, which is stored in text files. Artists produce textures, animations, and 3D models, which are binary files that require special programs to view, and audio technicians produce sound files. Just as the design team needs a document management tool to make revisions and changes to their document, the other teams need code and asset management tools (collectively called asset management here) for their work products.

Most asset management tools store all files on a central server. Team members download local copies of the files onto their workstations, change some of them, and then upload the changes to the server. Team members will also frequently download the latest version of each other's files to merge or overwrite the local copy.

Standard features in an asset management tool are: upload and download files, notify a user when some files do not match the latest copy on the server, merge changes from multiple users, and roll back to a previous version. Most asset management tools provide additional features like the ability to create a "branch" that allows a subset of users to merge changes with each other without affecting the rest of the development team. Terminal branches are created near release dates, and they make it possible to take the current copy of the system and modify it without having those changes ever go back into the main branch. For a risky project, it is common to make a short-lived branch for a group of users to work on and then merge that branch back into the main branch when their work is done. This way, the main build is working all the time, even when a small group needs to make radical changes that will temporarily break their own branch.

The major asset management tools used in game development are CVS, Subversion, Git, Perforce, SourceSafe, Vault, Accurev, and AlienBrain.

CVS and its more recent variation, Subversion (SVN), are source control systems that were created for programmers to manage code. Git is a similar tool that works distributed, without a central server. These products can manage binary files for art and audio assets, as well as binary document formats (like Microsoft Word). However, they cannot merge binary files, so if two artists edit the same Photoshop image, one of their changes will be lost. For images, this is not a major problem in practice because usually only one artist works on an image, but for binary documents, it is often unacceptable because many people edit them. The solution for documents is either to not use these tools for documents or to choose a document format like XML, HTML, RTF, or LaTeX that is text-based. Another disadvantage of applying CVS or Subversion is that because binary files are never merged, they take up a tremendous amount of space on the server. Every version of an image that has ever been made will reside on the server indefinitely, which could quickly build to terabytes of data for a typical game project. The major advantage of both CVS and Subversion is that they are are freely available on every major operating system. As a result, most hobbyist, academic, and open-source projects use these systems.

Perforce, Accurev, SourceSafe, and Vault are general-purpose asset management systems for software projects with per-user licensing fees in the hundreds of dollars. They tend to manage code and documents better than art and audio assets, but they are generally superior to the free tools in terms of features. SourceSafe requires a third-party add-on product called SourceOffsite to function across the Internet (instead of a LAN—for example, for working from home or another site), but all the other tools support both LAN and the Internet. At the time of this writing, Perforce is probably the most respected of these tools in the industry, and SourceSafe is the most widely used because it is closely integrated with Visual Studio.

AlienBrain is an asset management system specifically designed for 2D art asset management. It can correctly merge and store most image formats, including Photoshop (PSD) documents. Tools programmers can extend it to support 3D formats and other assets.

6.3 Art Tools

Art tools form a pipeline. For example, at many video game companies, textures are imported from a stock library into Photoshop, and then exported from there to 3DS Max for application to a model, and then exported into the game's proprietary model format. In addition to planning for the primary tools (Photoshop and 3DS Max in this example), the technology plan must encompass the importers and exporters. Different tools are used for 2D and 3D content.

6.3.1 2D

A lot of game art begins with natural media like paint, ink, and clay. These are then 2D or 3D scanned for easier management or as raw materials for digital refinement. A concept artist may work entirely with real-world tools, although concept artists are beginning to work more with virtual brushes in software. The first 2D art tools to consider are these real-world kinds (which are fortunately less expensive than their software counterparts) and a flatbed scanner or digital camera for moving assets into the digital realm.

There are two kinds of 2D assets: pixel and vector. *Pixel* artwork is stored as a grid of colored squares, like a digital photograph. Zooming in on pixel artwork reveals its underlying blocky nature. *Vector* artwork stores colored shapes. The colors here might be solid, or gradients and textures. Zooming in on vector artwork never reveals an underlying resolution—you can zoom forever and still see perfectly clean lines. This is important for art that must remain crisp when printed at large sizes (like a game board) or at varying resolutions. Most fonts are stored in vector format, for example. The drawback of vector formats is that most of the tools and filters artists use to adjust images cannot be applied to vector images.

Adobe's Photoshop image-editing software is the backbone of pixel-based art development for both board and video games. It runs on Windows and

Macintosh computers, works with every significant image file format, and interfaces with other tools and input devices like scanners and tablets. The user interface has a steep learning curve, but its excellent design makes it easy to use once you know your way around it. To help with that learning curve, hundreds of free and commercial tutorials are available in bookstores and online. Many artists use tablets, especially the Wacom Cintiq, to combine the feel of natural media with the features of paint programs.

Every game artist needs to be facile with Photoshop, even if his or her primary role is not 2D content production. Unfortunately for small teams, Photoshop can be expensive, and the alternatives are all inferior. One solution is to look for discounted copies—for example, students and faculty can purchase academic licenses at a fraction of the cost. Also, most new computers and digital cameras can be purchased with Photoshop bundled with them.

The (again, inferior) alternative tools are Adobe's ImageReady; the free GIMP, which also runs on Linux and FreeBSD operating systems; and Jasc's PaintShop Pro. Although it is free on every Windows computer, the Microsoft Paint program is not a viable alternative because it does not support most image formats, multiple layers, or image filters.

Adobe's allows the creation of 2D vector graphics. These look great no matter how high the resolution of the final output is and will never be pixelated. Vector tools are great for drawing iconic symbols and maps. For hobbyist and academic applications, a word processor's presentation graphics can often be used as a low-cost vector tool. Microsoft Word and PowerPoint, Apple's Keynote, and the open-source InkScape are viable alternatives that are either probably already on your computer or available to you for free.

6.3.2 3D

3D modeling and animation tools are used primarily for video games. Professional character models and props are generally created in Autodesk's 3DS Max or Maya; hobbyist and academic ones might be made in the open-source Blender and (for buildings) the low-cost SketchUp Pro. The free version of SketchUp can't export to useful formats for game development.

Game levels are either created using general-purpose modeling software or engine-specific level editor tools. Separate tools are often needed because levels contain more than just geometry and texture. Levels have invisible triggers that launch scripted sequences, spawn points where characters emerge, and item placement. They may also need additional hints like pathing for AI characters. Licensed game engines provide their own level editors. Developers who are working without a licensed editor and outside of 3D modeling tools either write their own level editors (often as plug-ins to a 3D modeling tool) or piggyback off an existing game file format. For example, the free Q3Radiant tool produces *Quake 3* format BSP maps that you can then load in your own games.

Also worth noting for video games, FlexPorter is a free and extensible exporter for 3DS Max. Most games that use a custom rendering engine use it to move data between the art tools and the runtime rendering components.

Large game developers often create scale models of key characters and objects in clay, or they hire actors and use 3D scanners, like the Cyberware system shown in Figure 6.1, to digitize them. The digital models are then retouched in 3D modeling software. This is a particularly effective method when working with licensed properties, where it is essential to exactly reproduce the likeness of a real actor. 3D scanners come in inexpensive forms that have less precision and very high-end models that reproduce individual

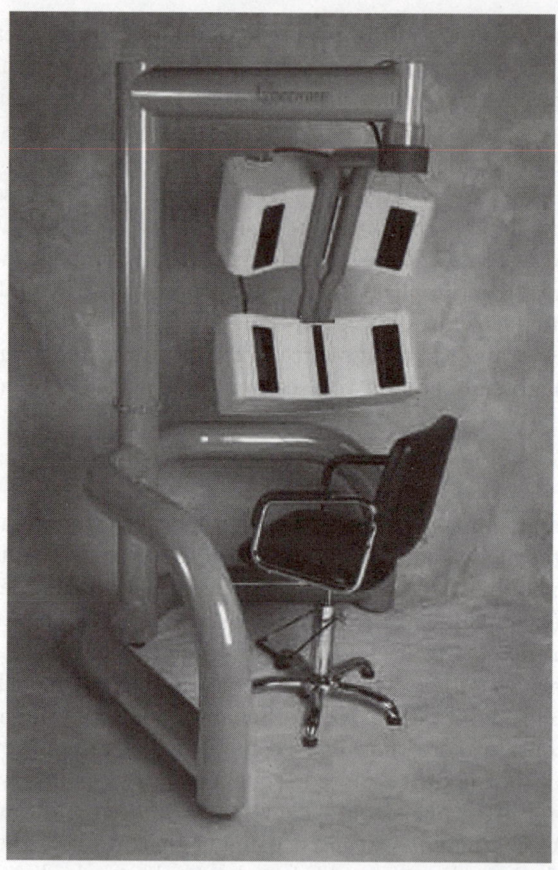

Figure 6.1. Cyberware's head and face scanner from http://www.cyberware.com/. (Image courtesy of Cyberware)

Figure 6.2. Actor in a Vicon motion-capture suit from http://um3d.dc.umich.edu/hardware/mocap/. (Image courtesy of Vicon)

pores and hairs as well as capturing color texture maps. The latter are so expensive that they are more generally rented than purchased.

Motion capture is a technique for "scanning" animation. An actor dons a special suit with regularly spaced markers, as shown in Figure 6.2 of a Vicon system. By filming the actor's performance through multiple cameras, the motion-capture system can track each marker and reassemble smooth animation data, which are then imported into a 3D modeling package for further cleanup. Newer systems also use inertial measurements from accelerometers to track motion without needing line of sight. Few companies own a motion-capture studio. Instead, they purchase pre-recorded motion or rent time at a dedicated studio.

6.4 Runtime Technology for Video Games

Figure 6.3 shows the major components of a video game engine and how they connect to one another, called a data flow diagram. The boxes are software components, and the arrows indicate communication at a high level. Data flow is not the same as a flowchart or progression graph. Think of it as a map of the telephone lines between different buildings in a city that tells you who can talk to whom.

In Figure 6.3, everything except the tools on the far left are components used at runtime on the player's computer. All of the boxes are technology. The Game Logic component implements the mechanics, Graphics and Audio implement the content, and the Database & File Loader feature brings previously created content into the game. The dashed arrows distinguish data from precreated content from the solid arrows of runtime data.

When a game is played, each of the different technology components is running and communicating data with the others. For example, note in Figure 6.3, that most other game components are connected to the Game Logic component and to the Database & File Loader. The components might run in parallel on separate threads of execution, or there might be a single thread of execution that switches round-robin between the different components in serial.

Parallel execution has the advantage that if there are multiple processors (as there are on the PlayStation 3, Xbox 360, and newer PCs), then the game can run faster. It has the disadvantage that communication between different components becomes complicated. Here's an analogy. Just as two

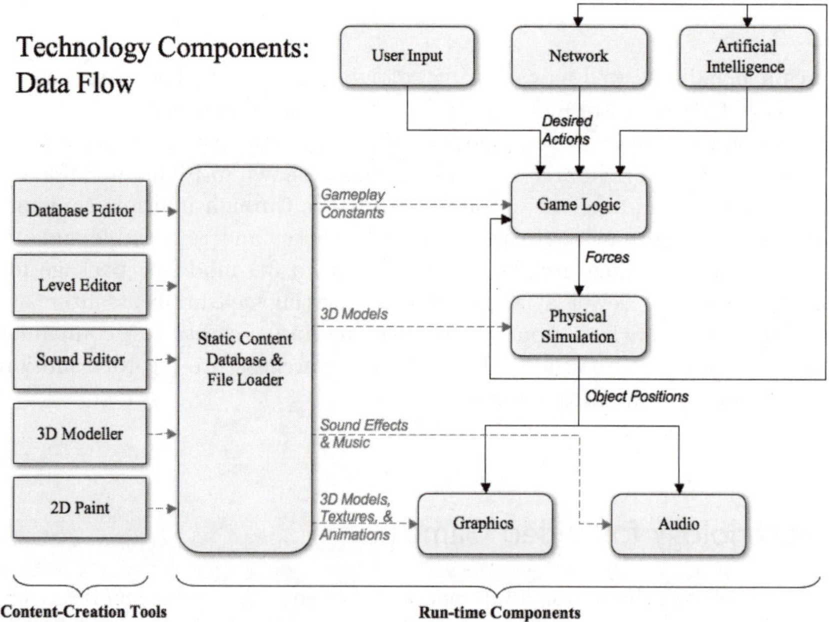

Figure 6.3. System diagram of game technology and assets.

spaceships must rotate to the same orientation and match speed to dock with each other, two game components must likewise be carefully synchronized to communicate. This usually means that one of them must be slowed down, reducing some of the benefit of parallel execution. Running in parallel is also harder for the programmers. If they fail to correctly synchronize all components, the results will be like those two spaceships meeting at incorrect angles: the data to be communicated can be smashed to bits and crash the entire game.

Note that the data flow arrows in Figure 6.3 form loops. Specifically, information about the current positions of objects in the world cycles out of Physical Simulation and back around to the Game Logic and Artificial Intelligence. In fact, many more loops appear in game technology that are too detailed to show here. The data loop is enabled by a control loop. The master part of the program that cycles between components when executing components in serial is called the main loop, which can appear in many different orders.

Figure 6.4 shows a control flow diagram, so the arrows tell you the order in which the operations occur (as in a flowchart or plot graph). The game makes it once around the loop for every frame rendered. Most games render at about 60 frames per second, so the loop executes in 1/60 of a second. That is faster than can be seen with the naked eye, so it appears to the

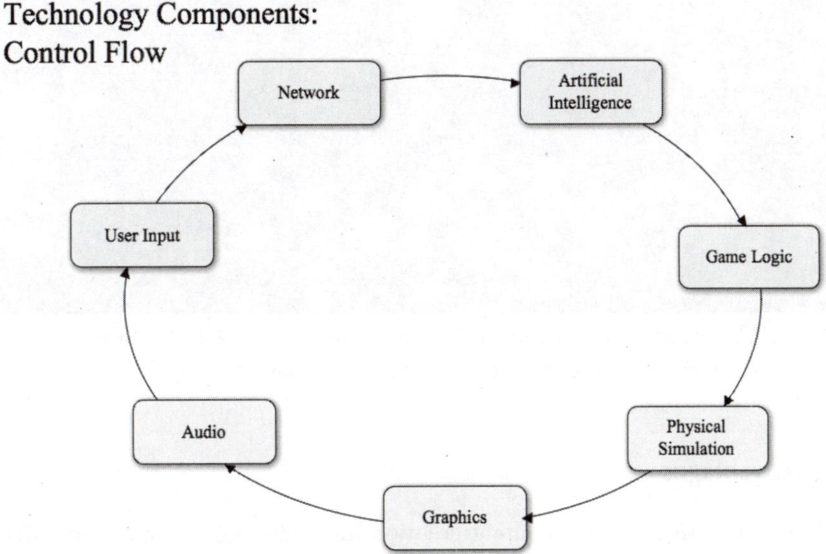

Figure 6.4. Main loop of a game (serial execution model).

player as if the graphics, physics, and controls in a game are continuously active even though they are only processed for a fraction of a second each and are run in discrete chunks.

6.5 Licensing

Technology components are packaged as entire games, engines, and libraries. The difference between an entire game and an engine is that a total conversion or modification (*mod*) of a game requires the original game at runtime and replaces mostly content and mechanics. An engine lets you create a standalone distribution.

Libraries are either part or all of one technology component. For example, Direct3D is a graphics library that covers about one third of the graphics component's functionality. Havok is a physics library that provides almost all of the physical simulation component that most 3D games would need (see Figure 6.5).

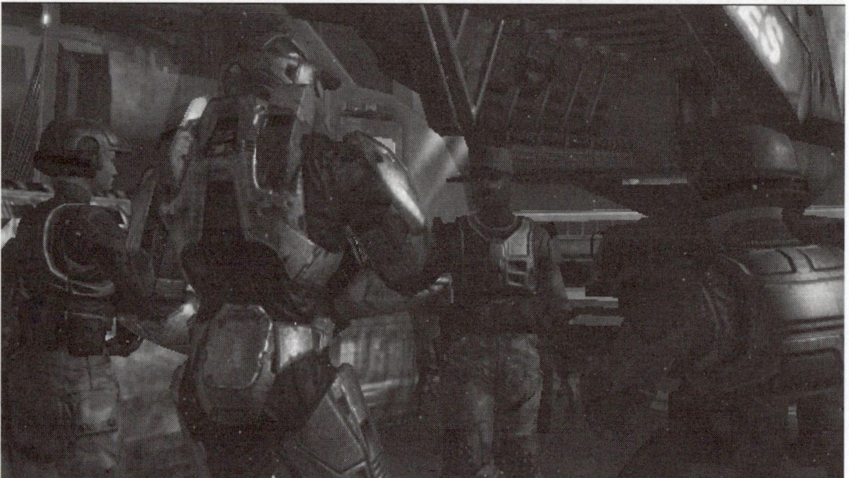

Figure 6.5. Microsoft's PC and Xbox game *Halo 2* uses the Havok Physics library for the physics component. (Image courtesy of Microsoft Game Studios)

6.5.1 Licensing Advantages

Just as one can outsource content creation by purchasing stock texture, 3D, and audio libraries, it is possible to outsource technology. In fact, outsourcing some technology, either by buying commercial solutions or leveraging free open-source ones, is necessary for producing even the simplest video games.

The advantage of leveraging such *middleware* is that it lets you shorten development time. If you started from scratch for even a simple single-player 2D game, it would take months to get to a playable version, and for a 3D or multiplayer game, it would probably take years.

The strongest argument in favor of licensing is the hidden cost of in-house technology. This comes in several forms: poor internal time estimates, maintenance cost, feature cost, and excessive freedom. Recall that programmers often estimate the time to prototype technology and fail to include the time to make it robust, general purpose, and well documented. When the programmer's initial estimate is expanded to include this time, and the programmer's time and salary are factored in, purchasing the licensed technology often costs less than producing it in-house.

The maintenance cost of licensed technology is low compared to technology developed in-house. Licensed technology has been used by many other developers, so the rough edges and likely bugs are already fixed. This is because if one licensee finds a bug or requests a feature, the vendor will resolve it and then propagate the feature to all licensees.

A technology is only as effective as the content that passes through it. A level editor is useless if artists and designers can't use it effectively or if the engine can't load its output. Similarly, an in-house rendering engine is useless if it can't communicate with the level editor. When deciding whether to buy or build a component, refer to Figure 6.3. What other components connect to this one? Who will use it? Because the components are highly connected in the figure, any licensed technology must be compatible with the other components to which it is connected. This is true for in-house technology as well. The development team may be less excited about writing their own rendering engine when they realize that they'll also have to write tools exporters and plug-ins to connect it to the physics engine to be as useful as a licensed product.

Of course, any licensed technology is less suited to your team's needs than a custom technology produced in-house. Limitations on licensed technology could, however, be a blessing in disguise. When a development team has complete control over the feature set of their tools and engine, they tend to constantly add to that feature set. Your goal is to produce a game, not just the technology for a game. Creating your own engine is therefore both a distraction from the primary mission and a source of risk. When the team can't alter a limitation, they will usually work around it and reach your goal faster.

Limitations also help define the goal and spark creativity. By analogy, it is hard to stare at a blank page and write a poem. Yet, it is easy to arrange words written on cards and create a poem, even though you are limited in your choice of words. Starting with licensed technology is a good way to avoid the "blank page" problem and get moving from day one, both creatively and in terms of execution.

6.5.2 Licensing Disadvantages

Middleware also comes with several disadvantages, which is why every game has some custom code and is not made exclusively from middleware. Commercial solutions cost money, and money is often the scarcest resource at the beginning of development. In the long run, middleware does save money compared to producing the code in-house (even unpaid programmers take *time* to write code, and they could be spending that time on something more productive!). However, saving money on technology over the long term is not useful if you can't afford to license technology in the first place.

There can be other disadvantages besides cost. Because your programmers are working with code written by someone else, time must be spent to train them on the new technology. It often seems easier (and more enjoyable) to just write the code than to learn someone else's interfaces, so junior programmers are frequently resistant to licensing technology. Another drawback of licensing technology is that it might constrain your gameplay or artistic style. If technology is licensed with source code, you can usually work around these limitations. If not, you may have to ask the original vendor for a new feature or simply change your game design to work within the limitations.

The maintenance downside of licensing is that if the vendor ceases to support the product or goes out of business, then your company is stuck with unmaintainable technology. One way to avoid this problem is to require the vendor to either provide source code or place the source code in escrow to be delivered in the event of product-support termination.

The external obligations of licensed technology might be unacceptable even if the feature set is a good fit. For example, an academic might be unwilling to license technology that prohibits distribution of the licensed source code, and a large company might be unwilling to license a tool that prohibits producing a competing product.

6.5.3 Legal Terms

Your use of licensed technology is limited by its license. Even when you buy a shrinkwrapped software box like Photoshop, you are not actually buying the software. Instead, you are licensing it from the vendor and are bound by an end-user license agreement (EULA). EULAs generally limit only the number of computers on which you can install the software and prevent you from reverse-engineering the product.

When working with a middleware engine or technology component, the license may be more complicated than a consumer EULA. Often, you must also be concerned with fees, the source, redistribution, and obligations.

Fees are structured as an up-front cost and a per-unit cost. The up-front cost may be either per project, per company, or per *seat* (i.e., number of developers or artists). The per-unit cost is based on the number of units of your game that are sold. It is common for the more expensive professional tools to carry a per-project cost in the tens or hundreds of thousands of dollars but have no per-unit cost. Tools produced by or intended for small developers tend to have a low up-front cost and a small per-unit royalty cost. That allows small developers to use the technology without initial funding but compensates the vendor if the game is a hit.

Licensed technology is most useful if it comes with source code. However, vendors are often reluctant to share their source code because if it became public, it would allow competitors to copy from it and undercut the product. Source code is important because it augments the documentation, allows programmers who are tracking bugs to follow the trail in and out of the licensed technology, and allows programmers to maintain the software independently of the vendor. From a managerial point of view, the difference between proprietary and open-source tools is up-front financial cost. However, the difference to a programmer is that the open-source tool ensures access to the source code. So although many open-source tools have inferior feature sets to the proprietary alternatives, they are very attractive from a maintenance (as well as financial cost!) perspective. Most proprietary game engines come with source code, but smaller components may not, and tools almost never provide source code. The fee structure may be different if source code is provided.

With a few exceptions, described following, licensed technology limits your ability to redistribute. In the case of a mod, for example, you can't redistribute the game engine, but you can release your modification. This means that you probably can't sell your modification without the original developer's consent, and you can't even give away a fully working copy. Components may come with multiple licenses. For example, one free license that gives no distribution rights and an alternative pay license that allows distribution. Usually you can distribute the compiled version of a licensed library or engine but not the source code or tools that the vendor provided.

Nontechnological obligations are often incurred when licensing technology. The most common is advertising. You may be required to display the vendor's logo in your product and credit them in the game. In some cases, vendors will actually pay *you* to have their logo in your game, even if you didn't use their technology. This is part of building brand awareness for them and is an important source of income for developers. The downside is that it misleads consumers. Often, a license will grant the vendor the right to use your company and product name when advertising their own technology.

Open-source technology comes in two major forms with regard to obligations. The BSD-style (originally Berkeley Standard Distribution) licenses are more like proprietary software licenses. You have to credit the vendor, but that's it! In fact, you can choose to distribute their source code if you want to, but you aren't obligated to. The other style is GNU GPL (GNU General Public License), which requires that you make *your own* source code available to end users. This is often called a "viral" license because its terms infect your own source code (like a virus). The latest draft of the GPL, version 3, also restricts the kinds of digital rights management (copy protection) and patent protection you can use.

Most companies determine that BSD-style licenses are acceptable but that GPL-style licenses are inappropriate for commercial game development because it forces trade secrets into the public. For academic and hobbyist development, however, the viral nature of the GPL may not be a problem.

6.5.4 Becoming a Vendor

You can profit by licensing your own technology as well. Because game companies augment licensed technology with their own tools and code, every developer has some in-house technology that adds value. It is common practice to offer that technology to others by becoming a vendor. Some game companies, like Epic and id Software, even make most of their income from technology licensing. The games produced by these companies have become showcases for their engines rather than primary revenue streams.

It is also practical to enter the industry not by making games but by making technology. This is both a great way to launch a company or gain publicity as an individual. For example, producing a single AI library is much easier than writing a whole game, but it can be just as satisfying and lucrative.

6.5.5 Moddable Games

Most successful (in terms of completion and distribution, not revenue) independent and academic games are modifications (*mods*), or "total conversions" of existing games. Most hobbyist and academic developers should target this level of technology because it can help them get up and running quickly, and it has a strong track record of success and broad development and player community. Plus, the license cost is cheap—just buy a copy of the game for each developer.

A mod requires that the player purchase the original game and then install the mod. Most mods leave the original game intact so the player can choose between them. The distinction between mod and total conversion is the extent of the changes. Some mods are small changes, like adding a new vehicle to an existing game. Others completely replace all content and gameplay and are occasionally called total conversions. Because they change an original game as an add-on, mods are almost exclusively the provence of PC gaming and are not popular for consoles and handhelds, which are very hard for independent developers to work on.

The most famous mod is *Counter-Strike* for *Half-Life*. Because you need *Half-Life* to play *Counter-Strike*, *Half-Life* continued to sell new copies for over a decade and probably made more money from *Counter-Strike* than from people who were playing the original game. It has consistently been the top non-MMORPG online game since its inception. Other popular mods for that engine include *Garry's Mod*, *Team Fortress*, and *Natural Selection*, all of which show the amazing degree to which a mod can change fundamental gameplay.

Most games today are intended to support some level of modification, although only a few have both a large enough installed base and flexible enough engine for creating an interesting game.

Here are the games to target today for mods (in order of suitability).

- *Unreal Tournament 2004*. Well-designed APIs and extensive modding support; provides custom tools.
- *Half-Life 2*. Works with/requires standard modeling and programming tools, extensive mod support (albeit with a suboptimal API design), giant user community, and a distribution channel through Steam.
- *Half-Life*. Primary platform for most of the previous generation of mods; extensive support and large installed base (despite *HL2*).
- *DOOM 3*. Extensive mod support and reasonably large user base but largely eclipsed in the mod community by the nearly simultaneous release of *HL2*.
- *Civilization 4*. Python scripting and level editor for creating similar games with custom content.
- *The Elder Scrolls IV: Oblivion*. Modify some game content, giant user community.
- *The Sims 2*. Allows creation of in-game objects with some scripting but not fundamental changes.
- *World of Warcraft*. Minimal support for modding, so most mods are only UI changes, but the largest user base of any game and great media coverage.

Of course, if your game design is very similar to an existing game, writing it as a mod for that game is more sensible than modding a very different game that has better mod support.

6.5.6 Engines

Game *engines* provide almost all the components and most of the tools needed for producing a game. The full-featured ones are expensive (hundreds of thousands of dollars) and complex, but they allow your team to get a prototype of your game playable in about a week and a full-scale commercial game completed in a year or two. These estimates assume that your team is already familiar with the technology. If not, the initial prototype will probably take closer to a month unless your gameplay is very simple.

A number of low-cost game engines are available. These generally provide rendering that is on par with their more expensive competitors but lack the rich tools, networking, physics, and system compatibility. For the indie team working with one of these budget engines, this is a good approach when the core game concept or distribution model won't work as a mod. In academia, the full-featured engines can usually be licensed at a steep discount (or even free in some cases, like the Unreal Engine, so the choice of budget versus full-featured engine depends on the learning curve, philosophy, and scope of the course or project more than the cost).

These are the full-featured commercial game engines (in order of suitability).

- **Unreal Engine.** Used in *Unreal Tournament.* Provides a scripting language, amazing level editor, particle systems, and support for every platform. The primary choice for AAA games.

- **Crytek Engine.** Used in *Crysis.* The most sophisticated rendering available, less widely used than the Unreal Engine and slightly less powerful tools.

- **Source.** Used in *Half-Life 2.* Great physics, easy to learn, and provides direct access to Steam networking. APIs and tools are less supportive than the Unreal Engine

- **DOOM 3.** A solid choice with great texturing for large outdoor environments and good networking but less emphasis on tools.

- **Gamebryo.** Primarily rendering component used in many major games including *Oblivion* and *Civilization IV.*

- **RenderWare.** Once the gem that powered *Grand Theft Auto III*, even owner Electronic Arts doesn't use this in-house for many new titles.

Many low-cost or free game engines are available that provide all of the runtime technology components, although the tools are usually less impressive. These are good choices for hobbyists and academics. The following "budget" game engines are, in rough order of popularity, for hobbyists.

- **Torque Game Engine.** \$150, PC (PC engines support Win32, Linux, and OS X but not consoles), http://www.garagegames.com/products/1, used in *Marble Blast Gold* and *TubeTwist*. Exceptional tools integration.

- **Ogre.** Free, open-source, PC, http://www.ogre3d.org/, used in *Heart of Osiris* and *Jack Keane* (Figure 6.6). Used extensively in academia and for hobbyist projects.

- **Panda3D.** Free, Windows/Unix, used in *Toontown*, used in the Carnegie Mellon ETC and other academic programs.

- **Nebula Device 2.** Free, open-source, PC and Xbox, http://nebula device. cubik.org/, developed mainly by commercial Radon Labs GmbH, sup-

Figure 6.6. Screenshot from commercial game *Jack Keane*, produced using the OGRE engine by Deck13 (http://www.deck13.com). (Image courtesy of Deck13)

ported by commercial 3DS Max and Maya tools, used on Radon Labs titles including *Genius*, *Nomads*, and *Sportfishing Pro*.

- **Quake 3**. Free, open-source (GPL), PC, http://www.idsoftware.com/business/techdownloads/, used in *Quake 3: Team Arena* and hundreds of other titles, relatively dated technology. Most of the source and scripting support from the actual game, supported by many tools.

- **G3D**. Free, open-source, PC, http://g3d-cpp.sf.net/, used in *Titan Quest* and *ROBLOX* games. Emphasis on sophisticated rendering. Used in courses at Brown, Williams, Harvard, and University of Texas. By the author of this book.

- **Delta3D**. Free, open-source, PC-only, assembly of other open-source projects (e.g., Lua, ODE) into a game engine.

- **C4**. $200/seat or higher, PC and PlayStation 3, http://www.terathon.com/c4engine/. By the author of *Mathematics for 3D Game Programming*.

- **Irrlicht**. Free, open-source, PC, http://irrlicht.sf.net/, used in *SlamSoccer2006* and *H-Craft Championship*.

Beware that searching the Internet for "game engine" returns thousands of web pages, mostly from hobbyists, that advertise rendering engines. These provide rendering and some networking but generally lack the tools and full gameplay support of a real engine. They may be free or extremely low cost, but that's because they don't offer much to the prospective developer. It is best to avoid these engines because they'll take more work to extend than they will save.

6.5.7 Components

The smallest level of licensing is components. You can assemble these individual pieces into a game engine of your own or add them to an existing engine. Components from both large and small vendors can be high quality because the specification is so focused that even a small open-source team or company can fill a niche and support it well.

The large commercial components cost tens of thousands of dollars and come with tools for additional content creation. Those produced by small companies may be a few hundred dollars, and there are plenty of free open-source components that are used in large commercial games.

6.5.8 Physics and Animation

There are two kinds of physics middleware: articulated dynamics and human motion. Articulated dynamics handles jointed bodies colliding with each other and the environment. This is good for dealing with explosions, robots, crates, and ragdolls (unconscious humans). Human motion deals with the much more complicated problem of moving a person in a plausible way. This means adjusting motion to take into account constraints, limited planning and foot placement, and a softening of all motion. Historically, most games used dynamics exclusively and simply hand-animated human characters to make them look lifelike. Newer games use human motion packages to synthesize human animation at runtime.

AGEIA's PhysX API provides full dynamics support. It has the ability to leverage custom physics processing unit (PPU) cards on PCs that have them, although at this time PPUs do not have a large installed base.

Havok's line of physics and animation components include event-driven AI, full dynamics, and animation. Their Havok FX product uses the graphics card to accelerate physics the same way that AGEIA works with custom hardware. The advantage of Havok's approach is that every game-playing PC (and console) has a GPU. The disadvantage is that that GPU is also a scarce resource for 3D rendering. Both AGEIA's and Havok's software libraries are expensive professional products suitable only for commercial deployment on well-funded games. However, they are also available to mod developers or engine licensees because most large games and game engines use one or the other. A free/trial version of Havok FX is available for hobbyist and academic development. However, it does not come with source and does not support all platforms.

ODE and Bullet are stable open-source projects that provide free alternatives for dynamics. They have been used in many commercial games and has a large user base. The primary difference between these and proprietary solutions is that like most open-source components, ODE and Bullet have little tools integration and require more in-house work to integrate into an engine. Of the two, Bullet is the newer open-source project. It provides continuous collision detection compared to ODE's static collision detection and penalty methods (see Chapter 15 for a discussion); however, it has received less testing and community support than ODE due to its relative youth.

NaturalMotion offers a series of large commercial solutions for animating humanoid characters using realistic physics. They also offer discounted academic editions of many of these. The Endorphin package integrates into 3D modeling tools to create precomputed animations. Its real-time cousin, Euphoria, performs similar animations based on dynamic data and supports PlayStation 3, Xbox 360, and PCs. Finally, their Morpheme product is a toolchain and runtime component designed to work with Endorphin.

RAD Game Tools' Granny is a widely used character animation package. It integrates into all major 3D modeling tools and provides a runtime library as well. It directly supports PhysX and is designed to retarget to other dynamics APIs.

6.5.9 Networking

Online and LAN games use the Internet or a LAN to connect multiple players. Adding networking to a game involves both a low-level technology and a fundamental set of design criteria. Unlike other areas of technology, it is hard to create high-level middleware for networking because the high level is intimately tied to the game design itself. So most network libraries focus on the low-level aspects. Be aware that although you can essentially bolt on a rendering or audio library, the same will not be true of networking, and even with a licensed low-level library, substantial development time will likely be spent on networking. The exception is the case where an entire engine is licensed that provides networking and where the game you are building is very close to what the engine provider envisioned.

Low-level networking provides several services. LAN discovery or matchmaking helps computers on a local network find each other so the players can join games together. WAN or Internet matchmaking does the same for worldwide networks. The challenge in the Internet case is that there might be thousands of servers and players and that matchmaking servers are popular targets for hackers. Voice chat enables players to communicate using microphones instead of typing, which is essential for fast-paced team games. Auto-update distributes patches to players across the network. It is more often considered part of the deployment, installer, and copy protection package than the network component. Encryption and authentication allows computers to communicate securely so players cannot cheat or be disrupted by intercepted messages. Messaging APIs make it easy to send information between machines, and synchronization is the high-level element that uses low-level messaging to ensure that the game state is the same on all machines. One of the crucial features a messaging API can provide for Internet gaming is NAT traversal, which allows them to bypass a system administration and security feature of network routers to provide connections to machines at schools, offices, and multicomputer homes.

Almost all network games use the built-in operating system socket (either Winsock or BSD Sockets) API at the lowest level. Making fast, reliable connections using sockets is tricky, however, so developers don't write directly to the socket APIs. Instead, they use either their console's network library (e.g., DirectPlay/Live on Xbox) or a third-party one for PC gaming. The major packages here are the free, open-source OpenSSL for authentication, the professional Quazal library for all low-level networking, or the hobbyist low-level packages TorqueNL and HawkNL. For matchmaking and NAT traversal, GameSpy is the current leader in the PC games space. Although their package is expensive and comes with logo requirements, GameSpy provides matchmaking servers as well as a software component, which saves on long-term maintenance complexity and expense. These are all relatively new packages with a constantly evolving feature set. It is important to research their current feature set and enter into network licensing with the understanding that in-house developers will probably still have to write substantial code over the network API.

6.5.10 Audio

Audio APIs primarily stream compressed background music (e.g., in MP3 format) from disk and play small sound effects. Some will manage real-time voice chat, although that functionality is also shared with network APIs. For a music game like *Guitar Hero* or *Karaoke Revolution*, the audio component must be more sophisticated and able to apply pitch shifts and effects such as reverb and manage multiple input or output channels simultaneously. Unlike graphics, dedicated audio hardware is less standardized and often emulated in software whenever sophisticated effects are needed. Positional or 3D audio allows systems with multiple speakers to simulate the location of an audio source and moving sources through Doppler effects. The most sophisticated APIs also allow a crude 3D model of the game world to be used for echo and damping effects.

The significant audio APIs include the folowing.

- **fMod.** http://fmod.org/
- **BASS.** http://www.un4seen.com/bass.html
- **DirectSound.**
- **OpenAL.** http://openal.org/
- **SDLMixer.** http://www.libsdl.org/projects/SDL_mixer/

fMod and BASS are the major PC audio APIs. They also support consoles, although many game developers use console-specific audio APIs as well. Both fMod and BASS offer free versions for personal use and a discounted shareware license. They include a number of sophisticated digital signal processor (DSP) effects and support hardware acceleration on most platforms, although DSP effects often revert to software.

DirectSound is a Microsoft Windows API that has effectively become a legacy API; it no longer supports hardware-accelerated audio. The analogous API for Xbox and Windows Vista is called Xaudio.

OpenAL is a nominally open-source (LGPL), low-level library for audio playback on multiple platforms. It is easy to use and supports many platforms in hardware, but it is sometimes difficult to find compiled libraries for platforms. In practice, development is dominated by Creative Labs, the hardware manufacturer, which does not release its Windows optimized drivers under the LGPL.

SDLMixer is an alternative LGPL project that is community supported and more open than OpenAL. It also supports basic audio playback on PC platforms, but, to work around licensing issues, most of the popular formats (like MP3) are only available through plug-ins that are somewhat complicated to install.

6.5.11 Scripting

Most game code is written in the C++ language, with Web games written in Flash and Java. C++ requires years of programming experience to use effectively and has undesirable workflow properties. In particular, it takes minutes to see the effect of changes, which means that developers are constantly restarting the game and waiting for their compilers to complete.

Scripting languages are more lightweight. They provide features that make them easier to learn and often allow changes to code while the game is running. Certain kinds of programmer errors are hidden, which makes the languages seem more friendly, and the tools are generally easier to use. They manage some of the more complicated aspects of programming, such as memory management, for the programmer and often ensure that even when a bug is present, the game won't crash.

These properties makes scripting languages great for prototyping. They also help team members who are not trained as programmers to create code. A lot of game logic and AI is programmed in scripting languages, which means that most designers today have at least some familiarity with them.

Although empowering to the design team and apparently easy and friendly, scripting languages have some long-term downsides compared to fully featured languages like C++ and Java. The code executes substantially slower than C++ (even 100 or 1000 times slower!), the tools are primitive, and it is much harder to find and fix bugs. These aspects aren't always experienced at first, and it is often months into a project when the team begins to see progress slow down due to the nature of the scripting language. Although using scripting languages is generally a good idea, it is important to plan their use carefully on projects that will take more than a month.

These are the key features to look for when selecting a scripting language (roughly in order of importance).

1. Learning curve and syntax.

2. Available tools, such as debuggers and editors.

3. Thread management (Can scripts be interrupted? What happens when they crash?).

4. Built-in features, such as string processing and search algorithms.

5. Ease of integration with the host language (usually C++).

6. Extensibility with new routines and language features.

7. Memory usage and execution speed.

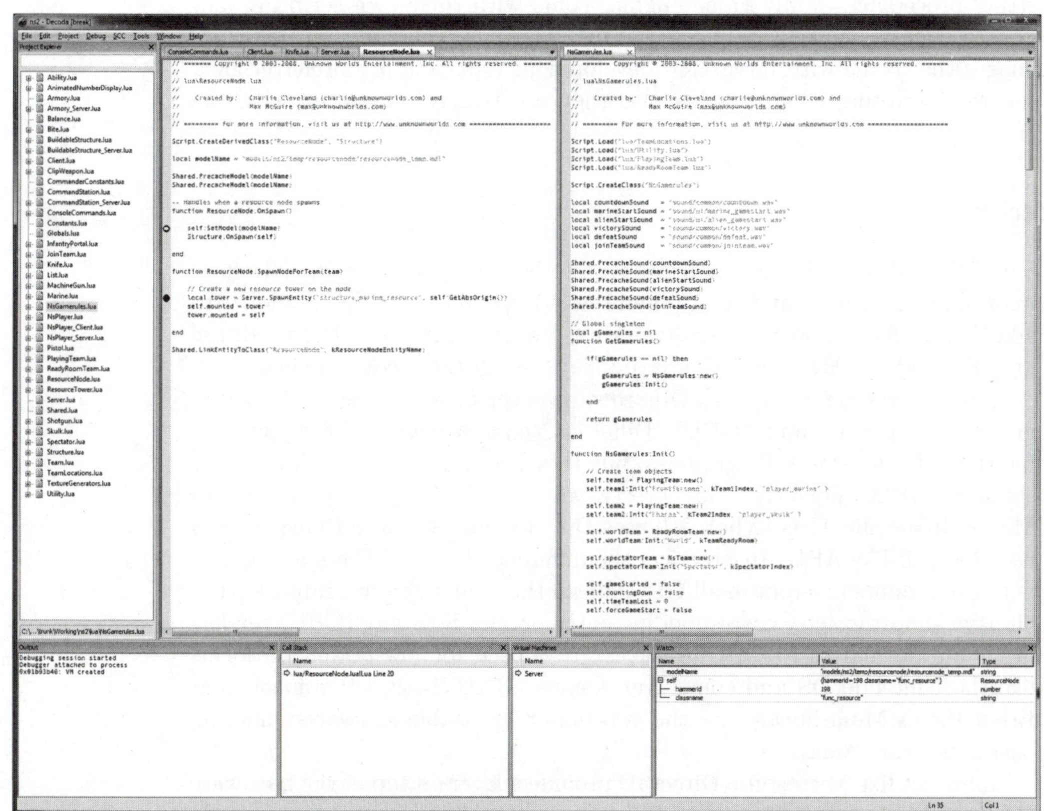

Figure 6.7. Decoda Lua debugger by Unknown Worlds. (Image courtesy of Unknown Worlds)

Scripting languages are mostly free open source. The most popular scripting language for games is Lua, which is extremely small and easy to integrate into a C++ project. It is primarily known for being easy to extend as well, but it comes with a relatively sparse feature set. The recently released Decoda debugger (Figure 6.7) for Lua makes the development experience comparable to that of a major language, however, and that is a strong argument for Lua development.

is a very popular Web-development scripting language that has seen increasing use in games as well. Python provides sufficient libraries to actually make a game entirely within the scripting language with no C++ at all. Python has a tremendous level of features in the built-in libraries, and even more is available from the online community. There are many implementations, but unfortunately, integration with a real-time game system can be tricky for many of them because of the way the internal threads are managed. Slightly older languages Perl and Tcl have seen less frequent use in games. They have extremely concise (i.e., cryptic) syntax and specialize in string processing. Many game engines come with their own scripting languages, such as QuakeC and UnrealScript. These are generally Java-like languages that come with integrated development tools and are preferred over separate scripting languages because they are tightly integrated with the engines.

6.5.12 Rendering

Sophisticated rendering components tend to be packaged as engines. In fact, many engines provide little more than rendering and expect the developer to add their own components for networking, physics, and tools. The hardware graphics and low-level rendering layers lie beneath these components.

Most rendering today is 3D-hardware accelerated, using a dedicated graphics processing unit (GPU). Different vendors have different internal interfaces for low-level 3D graphics, but they are exposed through industry standard APIs. OpenGL and DirectX are the platform-independent and Microsoft-specific APIs. Xbox 360 uses DirectX, and Wii and PlayStation 3 use OpenGL-like APIs. In practice, the difference between these are all minor. Constraints inherent in all GPUs mean that the different graphics APIs all have almost exactly corresponding entry points. Software (CPU) rendering is an alternative to GPU graphics. It is used for low-power platforms like the Nintendo DS and some Web games. RAD Tools's Pixomatic and Brian Paul's Mesa library are the two major licensable software-rendering packages in use today.

Libraries like Microsoft's Direct3D provide a layer on top of the hardware graphics that is very easy to use. These are somewhere between a very crude engine and a very sophisticated hardware layer. The platform-independent, open-source SDL library is widely used to abstract the minor differences between operating systems for PC gaming and has been used for hundreds of commercial and hobbyist games that run on Linux, OS X, and Windows. Most games need to load various image and model formats; lib3DS is one of the more popular libraries for loading 3DS files, and DevIL, libpng, libjpeg, and ImageMagick are commonly used to load image textures.

6.6 Exercises

1. What is an asset management system? How much data would you expect a major game (50-person team, two years in development) to store in one? Show some "back of the envelope" computations to support your numbers.

2. Draw a diagram in the style of a timeline showing how a nonterminal branch is used in an asset management system.

3. What business (i.e., nontechnical) factors do you think might influence a specific technology choice?

4. Explain why a vector-based or pixel-based 2D art tool would be better for creating each of the following kinds of images:

   (a) a photorealistic image of a modern soldier

   (b) a set of druidic symbols

   (c) an image in the style of an engraving

   (d) an image in the style of a watercolor painting of a barn

   (e) a Disney cartoon character

   (f) a technology architecture diagram

   (g) a program's icon

5. What documentation tool strategy would you recommend for a single person working alone on a video game? What about for two people working together? Why?

6. Imagine that you are making a hobbyist PC game for which you expect to sell 50,000 copies on the Internet and make $5 profit on each copy. Your development team has three people. How much are you willing to pay per copy sold for a royalty-based license if your other alternative is a per-developer seat license of $5,000? Show how you derived your solution.

7. Search the Internet for the key words "game engine." How many results does it return? List the names of the top 20 results. How many of these do you think are professional quality and how many are abandoned or hobbyist projects? Pay attention to the history of release dates, support systems, and documentation levels when investigating.

8. Complete the technology worksheet for your project.

9. Find the three engines that are best suited for your project (if your project is not a video game, choose the three engines best suited to re-implementing your favorite video game). Make a chart comparing their features and prices, and write a few sentences for each explaining how you would use each or change the game design if you had to use that engine.

CHAPTER 7

Strategic Thought

Terms Explained: *Algorithm* – *Complexity* – *Forced Win* – *Graph* – *Node* – *Vertex* – *Edge* – *Minimax* – *Pseudocode* – *Randomness* – *State* – *Strategy* – *Static Evaluation* – *Tactics* – *Tree* – *Zero-Sum*

Analysis of modern (a.k.a. German) board games and strategic computer games reveals some surprising results, including the following:

- The past is unimportant. It doesn't matter how game pieces got to their current positions.
- You can usually determine your opponent's next move.
- The game of chess has more possibilities than there are atoms in the universe.

These kinds of results arise from analysis of strategic thought, as compared to intuition of "seat of the pants" play and design. Designing equitable rules and creating artificial opponents for such games can be challenging. Developing such games requires concepts from computer science, economics, mathematics, and cognitive science. In computer science, these ideas are broadly called artificial intelligence (AI). In this chapter, we cover AI for strategic decision making. In Chapter 18, we cover AI more broadly in the context of nonplayer characters ("bots").

Although we focus on strategic play, games do not have to be complex or strategic to be engaging. Young children play games in a sort of sandbox mentality, where the game is a framework for storytelling, freeform play (abandoning the rules), and just seeing what happens. This is why many games for children (such as *Chutes and Ladders* and *Sorry*) are successful even though they lack the most crucial element of adult games: meaningful choices. You maybe believe that games for children are not real games and are insignificant, but it is important to recognize that the elements of these games—counting, manipulating pieces, following rules—are actually challenging skills for children. For a 40-year-old, learning to recognize and deploy patterns in go is challenging. To a vastly superior alien intelligence, go might be a trivial game. To the developing intelligence of a young child, counting out squares on a *Sorry* board is challenging.

We are primarily interested in making games for normal people of ages eight and up who have mastered basic skills, not for aliens or young children. Somewhere around middle school age, strategy becomes the decisive component of game playing. To understand strategic thought, we must strip away everything but the mechanics and then analyze them in a competitive framework.

Note that "competitive" doesn't mean player-versus-player. Computer games are ideally designed for collaborative human play against computer opponents, and some board games (e.g., *Shadows Over Camelot*, *Lord of the Rings*, pen-and-paper RPGs) allow collaborative play as well.

The heart of strategic thought is the notion that players are agents who seek to optimize their position. In a formal computer science context, this simply means they want to maximize their chance of winning. In an economic context (game theory), it means they want to maximize their utility.[1] These are equivalent and are the topic of this chapter. We assume mature, rational, and perfect opponents—that is, we do not play games thinking "I hope he or she doesn't notice," or "Maybe my opponent will make a stupid move." Instead, all players plan on their opponents knowing and choosing the best moves for themselves and choose accordingly for themselves.

The reality of game playing is more complex than the computer science and economic analysis. Players want to win, but they want to enjoy the process of playing even more. This often causes people to make suboptimal plays for the sake of excitement or social harmony. Also, in many video games, players don't even know the real rules of the game, so their decisions are more heuristic than those advocated by classic game-playing strategy. Designing games for real people instead of theoretical agents is addressed in the next chapter, which builds on the idea of strategic thought introduced here.

7.1 State

The *state* of a game is all the information needed to recreate a particular instant in the course of the game. In checkers, the game state is the position

[1] Utility is equivalent to financial value in economics, so you can think of maximizing utility as accumulating as much money as possible.

of each of the playing pieces, the information about which pieces are kings, and the knowledge of whose turn it is. If you write down all that information, you can pack up the game and then later resume playing where you left off. State is an important concept in game design and computer science. Conveniently, most board games are like checkers, in that the state consists primarily of the playing piece positions, so you can literally see the state of the game. In a video game, the state is stored inside the computer's memory and can't be seen.

The notion of writing down the state and resuming the game later is unusual for board games (with the notable exception of persistent pen-and-paper RPGs like *Dungeons & Dragons*). For a computer game, it is very common: saving the player's position in a game means writing all of the game state out to disk. In networked computer games, the network is used to keep the game state consistent between all of the players' computers while the game plays. Network computers effectively e-mail save games to each other 30 times per second.

Sometimes a board game has a state that isn't visible on the board but is instead in the players' heads—for example, whose turn it is. Many card games rely on players remembering who picked up which card in a previous hand. In small amounts, this can be interesting, but invisible state in board games is generally an undesirable design. It is hard for players to make good decisions when they risk forgetting something. In general, board game state should be physical and visible, since making players memorize information just adds difficulty without adding strategy. As an example, *Cartagena* suggests that players can either keep their hand open (visible) or closed. The instructions note that the open hand is the more strategic variation. This is because every player can play strategically regardless of how good their memory is. Many people report that this variation is also more fun because it removes the drudgery of memorizing the opponent's hand.

Strategically speaking, nothing *except* the game state matters when making decisions. Given a written description of the full state of a game, you can choose the best possible next move without knowing how the game reached that state. In a board game, it doesn't matter how the pieces reached their current locations, what your plan was, or what the other player's style is. All that matters is where the game is *now*. Of course, there are games where the direction of a piece affects its options, so how it reached a square is indirectly important. In that case, however, the direction is part of the game state. Since the game state is all that should affect rational decisions, identifying the state of a game is a critical skill for both a player who is exercising a strategy and a designer who is crafting the rules that support strategy.

Since only the game state matters in making decisions, we can evaluate any player's position for the remainder of game based purely on the current state. This is called *static evaluation*. The idea is that if we had enough time to consider all possible moves and to think through all possible outcomes, we could decide which player will win from the current state (assuming all players play perfectly). In games with randomness, we can't know for sure who will win, but we can compute the odds exactly. For tic-tac-toe, the game is so short and has so few possibilities that you can statically evaluate any board in your head in a few seconds. You can look at any paused game and identify whether X will win, O will win, or it will be a tie.

Static evaluation raises two interesting issues for design, one philosophical and one more pragmatic. You can statically evaluate a game from the starting position, so based solely on the rules of the game, you can immediately identify who will win. This is counter to typical notions about fairness in games. It means that for sufficiently good players, the outcome of a game is known *before* they even sit down to play. The rules determine whether the outcome for a two player game will be:

- The winner will be decided randomly due to randomness in the game.
- Player 1 will always win because the game is fixed.
- Player 2 will always win because the game is fixed.
- The game will always result in a draw.

Assuming wins are distributed uniformly, the random case is fair but makes playing the game irrelevant. We might as well flip a coin and skip the whole play session. The fixed-game cases are not only unfair, but also frustrating. Why play a game when you know who will win? The draw (a.k.a. "tie" or "cat game") case is fair yet pointless, since nobody can ever win. Yet, these are really the only four outcomes for any set of game rules in a two-player game.

We say that a player has a *forced win* if he or she can always win with perfect play from a given position. For the moment, let's limit our consideration to two-player competitive games where any points taken from one player are effectively added to the other player. In other words, the net effective score is always zero; such games are called *zero-sum* and comprise most of the two-player games that you have played. For such a game, the static evaluation of a game state produces a number between positive and negative infinity. The static evaluation of the game state is positive infinity (∞) if player 1 has a forced win, negative infinity ($-\infty$) if player 2 has a forced win, and zero if the game is definitely a tie. We say that player 1 is the maximizing player because he or she wants the static evaluation to be high and that player 2 is likewise the minimizing player.

For any game without randomness, we can immediately perform a static evaluation at the starting position to determine which player has a forced win. For tic-tac-toe, static evaluation of the starting board yields zero, telling us that the game will always be a draw (you probably agree with this statement; we'll explain how to prove it later). This is why few adults play that game. The reason that children will play, and the reason that the rest of us play any games at all, is the second, pragmatic point about static evaluation we referred to previously. Most games have so many possibilities that we can't statically evaluate them accurately.

Unlike tic-tac-toe, in chess, there are so many possibilities that even the fastest computers in the world today (and probably, even the fastest computers that will ever be made) can't perform a perfect static evaluation of the starting position and identify which player will win. We'll revisit how hard it is to statically evaluate a game, but you will certainly agree now that for most adult games, it is too hard to figure out the perfect set of moves from the start of the game. After all, if it *weren't* too hard, we wouldn't play these games. By "too hard" we mean that it is theoretically possible but practically unachievable because of the limitations of our brains and the speed of our computers. So strategic games have the odd property that what makes them interesting is that people are not very good at them!

Because we can't perform a perfect static evaluation of most games, when we refer to static evaluation, in practice we usually mean a heuristic (guess). If we cannot compute a definite evaluation in a reasonable amount of time, we assign some nonzero, noninfinite number based on who is more likely to win. For example, in chess, a checkmate position of player 1's king has static evaluation of negative infinity, but a midgame position where player 1 has half as many pieces as player 2 might only be rated –100—slanted toward player 2 winning but not yet decided. Likewise, in a game with randomness, we can assign some finite positive or negative number that is proportional to the probability of one or the other player winning.

7.2 Graphs

A *graph*, formally speaking, is a map that shows how different areas are connected. Instances of graphs in everyday life are subway maps, organization hierarchies, and airplane routing maps. Note that this differs from what we call a graph in everyday speech (Figure 7.1): a pair of axes with a curve on it or bars that show data like stock market returns or voting tallies. Those pictures of data are properly called charts or plots and are generally not what is being discussed in this book.

Graphs are used in many ways for game analysis. They allow us to look at the abstract properties of a game level without the distraction of content or details that are irrelevant to gameplay. For example, the connections between rooms in a first-person shooter are much more significant than the

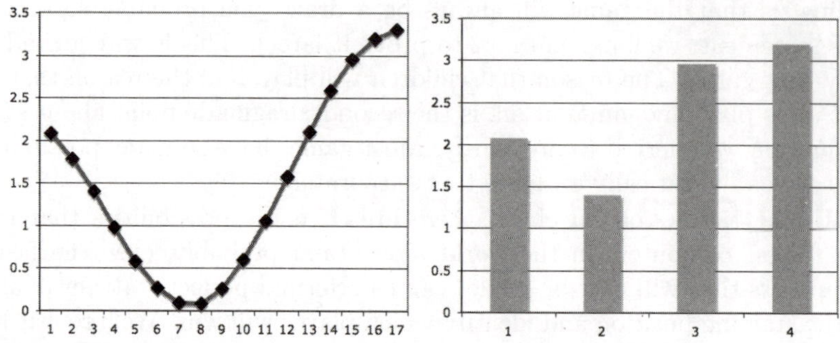

Figure 7.1. A plot (left) and a chart (right).

shape and volume of each room. The angles of the connections are almost completely irrelevant, and the textures on walls or small detail fixtures have no impact on gameplay. We use plot graphs to see the connections implicit in plot structure or within the rules governing a complex series of actions. Graphs can also represent thought processes of AI characters, the lines of communication between computers in a network, and the structure of an entire game board. This section describes the mathematical terminology for graphs and their properties that are used throughout this book.

Figure 7.2 shows a graph. The disks labeled with capital letters represent *vertices* (also called *nodes*), and the lines labeled with lowercase letters between them represent *edges*. The letters next to the vertices and edges are called *labels*. In general, only the connection topology matters, not the angles between edges or the size of the nodes. The length of the edges might be significant, depending on what is being represented by the graph. For example, if this is a graph of the hallway connections between rooms in a first-person shooter map, then the lengths of the edges are significant because they correspond to travel times and ranges.

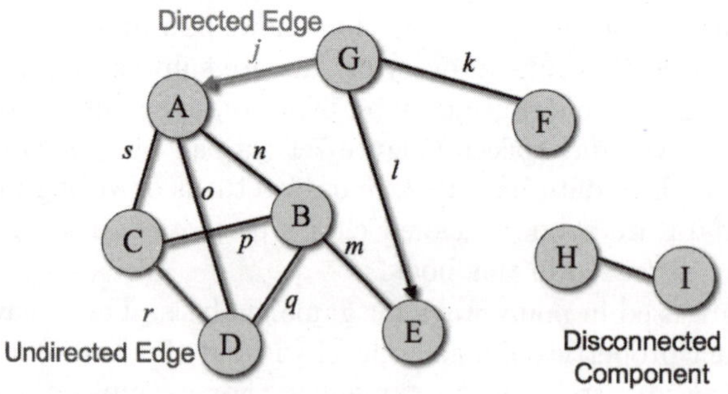

Figure 7.2. A graph.

Assume that edges can be traversed in both directions unless they are specifically directed. For example, edge r that connects vertices C and D is undirected. That means that one can travel from C to D or from D to C, like in a hallway. Edge j is directed from G to A. It is like a one-way door or a steep ramp. It is not legal to travel backward from A to G. The *degree* or valence of a vertex is the number of edges connected to it; the neighbors are the vertices at the end of those edges.

Vertices are not necessarily all connected to the main group. In this graph, there are two separate *components*. Because of disconnection and directed edges, it is not always possible to reach all vertices in a graph from all other vertices. For example, vertex F is not *reachable* from B in this graph because it is blocked by two directed edges. Also, vertex H is not reachable from E because those two vertices are on different components.

Some kinds of patterns in graphs are particularly interesting. Note that the set of vertices $\{A, B, C, D\}$ is fully connected. If you are at any vertex in that set, you can reach any other vertex in that set by traversing a single edge. We say that the set of vertices forms a *clique*, named after the (slightly pejorative) word for a tightly knit social group of people.

Vertices $\{A, B, C\}$ form a cycle (a closed loop) that is undirected. There are other cycles in this graph as well. When a graph has no cycles, it is called acyclic. A special case is the directed acyclic graph (DAG). Because there is no way to loop and no way to go backward, DAGs have the property that any traversal eventually gets stuck at some end vertex and that all traversals have finite lengths. Both of those are desirable properties in a plot graph—for example, they guarantee that the game will end.

An undirected acyclic graph with a single component is called a *tree* because it has the same branching structure as flora. By convention, we tend to draw our trees "upside down" with the single *root* vertex at the top of the page and the many leaf vertices at the bottom. They are drawn this way because trees are often used to describe the branching plot or dialogue paths that are available to a player, so time is increasing downward in the graph illustration. The word *tree* is also used to refer to graphs with this structure but all edges directed away from the root. At a vertex in the tree, we call the neighbors closer to the leaves its children, and the neighbor closer to the root its parent. Note that the leaves have no children and the root has no parent. Relationships like sibling, cousin, and so forth are occasionally referred to as well. We say that the *depth* (or height, depending on your perspective) of the tree is the longest root-to-leaf path that doesn't retrace its steps.

Graphs can have other styles in addition to the circle-and-line pictures shown in Figure 7.2. The outline that you'd prepare before writing a paper is actually a graph. The title is the root, and each of the bulleted topics is one of the root's children. The children of those bullets are the next level of the tree. A family genealogy tree is obviously a tree, and one in which the parent-child relationship is literal.

7.3 State Machine

A *state machine* or flow chart is a graph of how game state can change over time. Here, common speech trips us up again: the flow*chart* is in fact a graph and not a chart at all. Formalizing flowcharts is important because when we discuss them precisely, we can leverage a large body of computer science knowledge to lead directly to answers that might not be obvious just from looking at the graph.

In the state machine, each vertex describes a game state. Depending on what the state machine represents, this might be the state of the entire game, the state associated with an individual character, or the state of another game element such as a traffic light or gun turret. For diagramming purposes, vertices are typically labeled with a brief summary of what is interesting about that state. Edges are labeled with the conditions that cause the state to *transition* to another vertex. Edges are always directed, since they are one-way transitions.

As an example, Figure 7.3 shows a state machine for a traffic light. The traffic light has four states: red, yellow, green with a long wait, and green

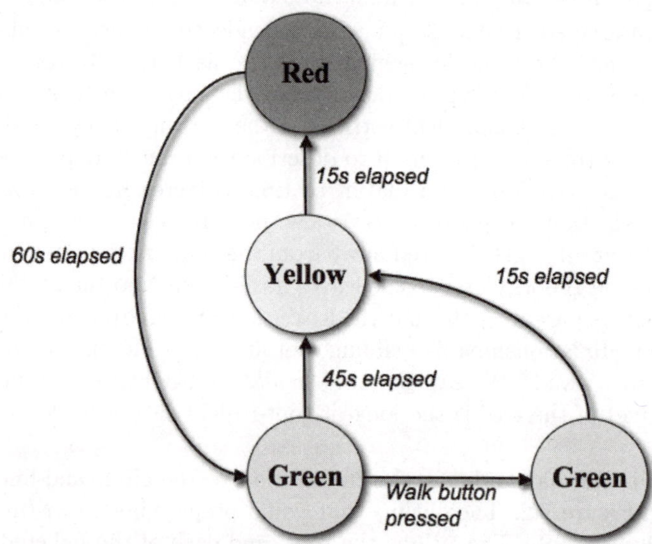

Figure 7.3. State machine for a traffic light.

with a short wait (the two greens are indistinguishable to an observer but important for the functioning of the light). Transitions between states are governed by elapsed time, except in the case where a pedestrian presses the walk button, which causes the green to switch to the short wait so the pedestrian will be able to cross the street soon. If implementing either a real traffic light controller or a traffic light in a video game, you would build a circuit or program that implements this state machine. If designing a board game for traffic control, you might actually have playing pieces and part of the board that look like this.

State machines are often used to control nonplayer characters. Figure 7.4 shows the state machine for an NPC soldier on guard duty whom a player wants to avoid. This guard can be in one of six states, where three of the states are safe for the player. If the guard is patrolling, the player has not yet been seen. A guard who patrols for a long time without incident gradually becomes more relaxed and might even stop walking to smoke a cigarette. If the guard hears a noise, however, he will then enter an agitated state where that guard actively looks for the player. Hearing a second noise panics the guard, who then calls for backup. Actually seeing the player will cause the guard to engage the player by attacking. This simple state machine controls the most relevant information about the NPC's mental state. It can produce the appearance of intelligence, even though the NPC is just transitioning around a graph with six nodes. Thinking of artificial intelligence as a state machine helps the designer plan NPC actions and analyze it for flaws.

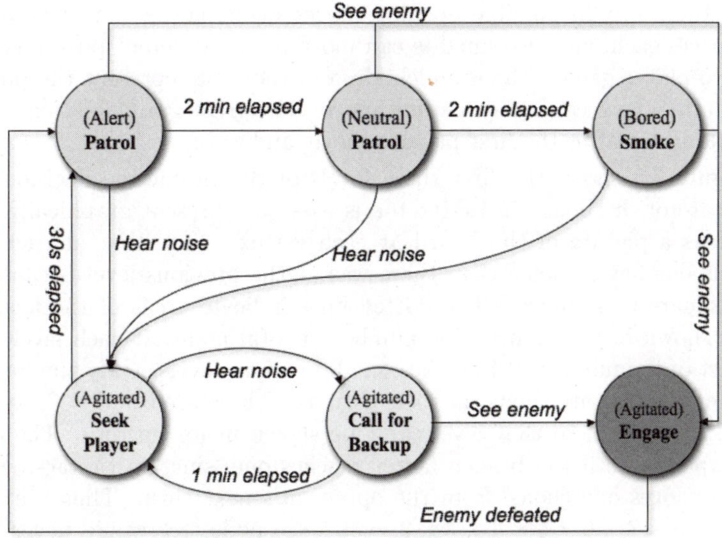

Figure 7.4. State machine for an NPC soldier on guard duty.

The state machine as shown contains a flaw. Every vertex should have an edge to the engage vertex in the lower right corner that is taken when the guard sees the player. But there is no such edge coming from the agitated/seek player vertex. This means that the NPC who has heard a single noise will ignore a player who walks right in front of him! This flaw might be hard to see in the source code and might not even be found during a playtest, but it is readily visible in the diagram.

For larger state machines, we can use established algorithms and proof techniques from computer science to verify that there are no undesirable states or transition patterns.

7.4 Decision Trees

One kind of tree that is very useful for strategic planning is the *decision tree*. In this tree, the vertices represent the game state at a point in time. The root of the tree is the start of the game, and the edges are transitions to different states. In most games, transitions are one-way, so this is a directed tree. A decision tree is a state machine for an entire game.

The edges exiting the root are all of the choices that the first player can make on his or her first turn. This means that the children of the root are the possible game states after each of those moves. For example, in tic-tac-toe, there are 9 possible starting moves, so the root has nine children. In chess, there are 20 possible opening moves–eight pawns can move one or two spaces each, and two knights can move to two different positions each. For two-player games, the grandchildren of the root represent the possible states after the second player's first move. The great-grandchildren are the possible states after the first player's move, and so on.

Figure 7.5 shows the first three levels of the tic-tac-toe decision tree. The state of the board in tic-tac-toe is easy to represent graphically. It is shown as a picture of the board at each vertex. Note that at each level there is one fewer choice than there was at the previous level because one more square is occupied. The dotted lines indicate areas of the tree that aren't shown in the figure. The number of total nodes at each level is the product of the number of branches on all previous levels. Only the first two levels of the tree are shown in their entirety. There are $9 \times 8 = 72$ vertices in the third level, so that level can't be shown in its entirety. The entire tree expands until the branch factor reaches one, since in tic-tac-toe each move removes one choice from the opponent's next turn. Thus the entire $9! = 9 \times 8 \times 7 \times 6 \times 5 \times 4 \times 3 \times 2 = 362,880$ node tree would never fit on this page.

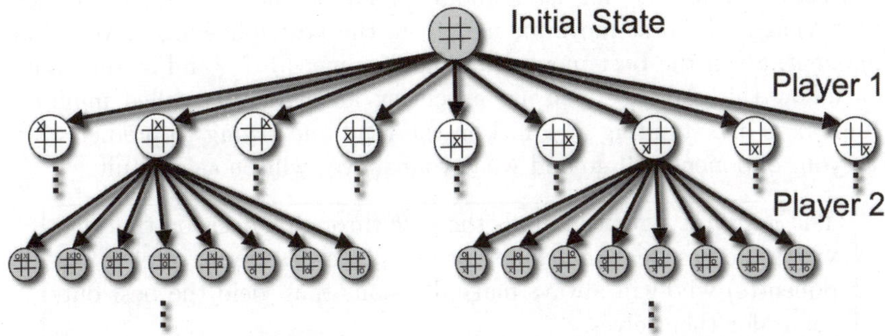

Figure 7.5. The first two levels of a decision tree for tic-tac-toe.

Decision trees can be made for games with any number of players. They can also be made for games where the choices are not discrete. Tic-tac-toe is discrete because we can enumerate each of the possible moves. In the real-time strategy game *Age of Empires*, there are effectively an infinite number of choices that the player can make for every frame that is rendered, since the player can direct any character to any pixel on the screen. This makes a continuum of choices—the space is continuous. For strategic purposes, however, we don't need to consider so many possibilities. In practice, the player has the initial high-level choices of rushing to attack an opponent, gathering wood, gathering food, creating more villagers, or creating a building. So there are really only five choices.

Even in discrete games, many choices are redundant. In tic-tac-toe, only three initial moves are unique under rotations of the board: center, corner, and side—so there is no reason to consider a tree with nine edges from the root.

7.5 Algorithms

7.5.1 Minimax

A surprising fact about most game playing is that you know what your opponent's next move is—at least in games where everyone has perfect information, because nothing is hidden in concealed cards or invisible units in that case. Assume that your opponent is smart, that he or she will always make a perfect play and take the "best" move. You know what move you are going to make now, so if you just put yourself in your opponent's place, given the new state of the board, you can decide what move you would make from his or her position. In fact, you can think ahead to decide what move you would make after that and then what move he or she would make next.

Strategic game playing isn't about "What is the best move for me?" but "What is the best move for me, given the best following move for my opponent, given the best move after that for me, ... ?" and so on. When you follow this strategy, you are executing an algorithm called minimax. Minimax is like standing at a fork in the road and trying to predict which way your opponent will go and what your moves will be as a result.

> The *minimax* algorithm finds the *path* through a decision tree that yields the best leaf (*outcome*) for one player, assuming perfect opponent(s) who will always make decisions that yield the best outcomes for themselves.

Minimax is the first example in this book of an algorithm in the strict computer science sense of that word. *Algorithm* is a formal term for a process, methodology, strategy, or a technique. What makes it formal is that for an algorithm, we can precisely describe the problem setup (the "inputs" or "givens") and the results ("outputs"). Algorithms must always give a correct answer; a process that usually, but not always, gives the correct answer is called a *heuristic*. Algorithms also technically have the property that they always finish (terminate). However, they are allowed to take an impractically long time, so that property is not useful for most game analysis and implementation.

7.5.2 Algorithms Are Rules

So far, our description of the minimax algorithm has been in English. The statement in the box describes the properties of the minimax algorithm, and the fork-in-the-road scenario describes the algorithm by example. We have not yet given a formal definition of *how* the algorithm works that you could use to actually execute this strategy. For a simple algorithm, a person can extrapolate how to execute it from informal discussion. For a more complicated algorithm, one might have a hard time figuring out how to follow the strategy without an explicit set of rules. In a video game, a nonplayer character can't follow even the simplest algorithm without an explicit set of rules. That's because today's computers can't think. Computers can't make inferences from a set of examples, use common sense, or apply intuition. Instead, all computers can do is follow rules. Being able to express an algorithm as a set of explicit instructions thus benefits a game developer in two ways. First, the developer can express it clearly for a player to execute in a board or video game, no matter how complicated the algorithm is. Second, we can express the algorithm for a computer to execute, which enables him or her to build AI players that follow strategies in computer games.

Expressing algorithms in an unambiguous set of instructions is important for games for another reason: it enables the player to follow rules. When you pick up a new board game, you probably appreciate a basic description of the rules that conveys the gist of the game. However, to actually play, you want to see an unambiguous set of rules—that is, an algorithm that distinguishes legal and illegal moves. For a video game, a computer enforces the rules. It relies exclusively on the rules expressed as algorithms.

A computer program is composed of algorithms even if the computer program isn't one that we would normally classify of as a video game. Since algorithms are rules and a set of rules is a game, this means that fundamentally all programs are games in some sense. They might not be particularly interesting games from a player's point of view, but what is important is that this duality lets us move between analysis of programs and analysis of games. That means you can leverage the understanding of games you've gained from this book to later understand computer science. It also means your study of games can benefit from decades of results in computer science and, indirectly, from thousands of years of results in mathematics.

7.5.3 Pseudocode

It is possible to describe an algorithm precisely using only prose, but it is easier to concisely express algorithms when the prose is combined with mathematical operators and formal structure. This format is called *pseudocode* because it is a combination of prose and computer code. Because pseudocode is written for people and not computers, the exact format varies. Certain concepts are useful and appear regardless of the format. These concepts also appear in real programming languages. To look at these in context, consider two pseudocode functions shown in Listing 7.1. The syntax chosen for the pseudocode in Listing 7.1 closely matches but is not exactly the same as the Python scripting language. Once you become comfortable with this format, you will also be able to read and write short programs in that language without much difficulty. That is a valuable skill for game designers, level designers, and artists.

Factorial is a mathematical function that generates the product of all numbers from 1 to n. We previously used it to compute the number of possible tic-tac-toe combinations, 9!. Listing 7.1 defines (using `def`) two different functions (also called procedures) that both compute factorial. These functions are named `factorialA` and `factorialB` and each takes as input a single parameter that is a positive integer.

In `factorialA`'s definition, there are two cases. If the argument n is less than or equal to 1, then the result is 1 because $0! = 1$ and $1! = 1$. The less-than-or-equal-to sign is written <= instead of the usual mathematical symbol $\leq$ because $\leq$ doesn't appear on a computer keyboard. In the second case, the argument n is greater than 1. Here, $n!$ can be reduced to $n \times (n-1)!$. This means that `factorialA` is defined in terms of itself, which is also how

```
def factorialA(n):

  if n <= 1:
    # 1! = 1
    return 1
  else:
    # make the problem 1 smaller
    return n * factorialA(n - 1)

def factorialB(n):

  total = 1
  for x from 1 to n:
      # put x into the product
      total = total * x

  return total
```

Listing 7.1. Factorial pseudocode.

a factorial is usually defined in a math class. This kind of definition is called *recursive*. Recursion is a powerful idea that appears frequently when dealing with decision trees because trees are made up of successively smaller versions of themselves. This means that many algorithms can be expressed (like factorial) by breaking the initial problem into one or more slightly smaller problems of the same basic form.

The second definition, `factorialB`, is called an *iterative* implementation. It defines a new variable, *total*, and assigns it the value 1. The function then repeatedly executes the multiplication instruction indented under the `for` for every integer value of x between 1 and n inclusive. This is more like the way a person computes a factorial: by writing down all of the numbers between 1 and n and taking their product.

Note that instructions are grouped by indenting in the listing. A series of indented instructions is considered a group. The indents tell us where the cases of the `if` and the repeating statements under the `for` begin and end, just like indenting in a document outline tells us where chapters, sections, and paragraphs begin and end. Lines beginning with # are comments; these are just notes to the reader and are not meant as instructions for execution.

These two definitions contain most of the constructs that appear in programming languages. The `def` denotes the beginning of a function *definition*. The lines of the form `total = ...` are *assignment* statements that bind the value on the right to the variable on the left. The `if` statements choose one of two paths for execution, allowing the function's execution to branch (much like a player's strategy branches in a game). The `for` loop iterates over a specific set of values and allows some work to be performed for each. Functions can *invoke* other functions, or even themselves, to delegate some of the computation, as is done in `factorialA`. The `return` statement specifies the value that will be returned when the function ends. Note that there can be multiple `return` statements in a function that uses `if` branches.

7.5.4 Minimax Pseudocode

A formal definition of the minimax algorithm is provided by the pseudocode in Listing 7.2. It is a recursive definition that evaluates the subtree at a vertex by in turn considering each of the subtrees of its children.

Listing 7.2 defines a function named `minimax` that takes two parameters, a vertex and the depth of that vertex from the root, and then computes the value of the vertex. There are two cases. If the vertex is a leaf in the decision tree—that is, it represents the end of the game—then the first branch of the `if` statement executes. In this case, the value of the node is computed by deferring to the static evaluator. Otherwise, the `else` part of the `if` statement executes. That case has two subcases: the depth from the root into the tree may be odd (indicating player 1's move) or even (indicating player 2's move). Player 1 is the maximizing player. If it is player 1's move,

```
def minimax(vertex, depth):

  if vertex is a leaf:

    value = staticEvaluation(vertex)

  else:

    if depth is odd:
         # player 1's move
         value = infinity
         for each child of vertex:
           value = min(value, minimax(child, depth + 1))

    else:
         # player 2's move
         value = -infinity
         for each child of vertex:
           value = max(value, minimax(child, depth + 1))

  return value
```

Listing 7.2. Minimax pseudocode.

then the value of each of the children of the vertex is the worst case—that is, the smallest possible final outcome—since that is the move that player 2 can be expected to follow with. Those final outcomes are themselves determined by minimax, so the algorithm invokes itself at each of the child vertices to compute final outcomes.

Minimax works its way up from the base case at the leaves back toward the root, or whichever vertex we started with. Minimax works by scoring all possible leaf vertices at a given depth m (assume that it is the minimizing player's turn at this depth). For vertices at depth $m-1$, the algorithm assumes the role of the maximizing player, selecting a single child at depth m with a maximal score. At depth $m-2$, the algorithm reverses roles and acts as the minimizing player, selecting children that minimize the score. The algorithm continually moves up, alternating minimizing and maximizing turns, until reaching the root vertex.

7.6 Search

The basic idea behind minimax is that players search the decision tree for the path that leads to the best outcome for themselves. Searching can be done in many ways. Say that you are looking for your car keys, and you know that they are somewhere in your house. You might go into each room of the house and perform a cursory check first. If you have not found your keys, then you will go back and search each room more carefully. If you still haven't found your keys, you will search each room extensively, looking everywhere. We call this process a *breadth-first search.* Consider the tree where the root is your house, each child of the root is a room, each child of a room represents the vicinity of a piece of furniture, and the children of a piece of furniture are the individual cushions, cracks, and so on. Your search took you into each room, covering the entire first level of the tree. Next, your search covered the second level of the tree. You continued through the tree level by level, covering the largest breadth first and then sinking to a lower depth.

Another way you might search for your keys is to go into your first room, walk over to a piece of furniture, and then search everywhere around it extensively. If you couldn't find your keys, you would then move to another piece of furniture in that room and continue. This search dives down the tree to a leaf and then progressively backs out, iterating across the leaves. We call this a *depth-first search.* Minimax follows this strategy. It immediately recurses toward a leaf and then later works back toward the root.

A hybrid approach is called a *best-first search.* This is probably how you would actually look for lost keys. In a best-first search, you extend the path through the tree that is most likely to lead to success. If you think that you lost your keys in the kitchen near the refrigerator, then you will first search in great depth near the refrigerator. If they aren't there, you will go to the most likely second place—say, a cursory check of the living room.

When searching a decision tree, the person or computer playing has limited time in which to choose a move. So they are unlikely to be able to actually follow the minimax algorithm to completion and choose the true best move. Instead, they will use a variation on minimax that replaces the line "if vertex is a leaf" with "if vertex is at depth *d*" and choose d to be the depth to which they reasonably expect to be able to search the tree without running out of time.

7.7 Complexity

A topic in theoretical computer science, the *complexity* of algorithm relates the running time (and memory requirements) of an algorithm to the size of its input data. This is a way of comparing algorithms independent of the computer (or person) executing them.

Time complexity is typically expressed using "Big O" notation as polynomial orders of magnitude with respect to the input size as it grows toward infinity. For example, finding the maximum value in an n-element list of integers requires on the order of n operations on the input data. This maximum value search is a linear time procedure, noted as $O(n)$. This means that input size in the worst case is related to running time by a linear order-1 polynomial. Examples of other time complexity orders include $O(\log(n))$ logarithmic time (e.g., binary search), $O(n^2)$ quadratic time (e.g., bubble sort), $O(n^3)$ cubic time, $O(2^n)$ exponential time (e.g., enumeration of all possible permutations of a binary array), and $O(n!)$ factorial time (e.g., solving the traveling salesman problem.) Exponential and factorial time algorithms are considered *superpolynomial* algorithms because their running time grows faster than any polynomial of n. Such algorithms fall in the class of *NP problems* that are often intractable to solve with standard computers.

The standard minimax algorithm, unfortunately, is an exponential time algorithm. The inputs into minimax can be considered the set of immediate actions available from the current state. The branching factor b is the expected (or average) number of player actions available from each state. Thus, the minimax algorithm must evaluate $O(b^m)$ leaf nodes, for search depth m, in a single turn. This $O(b^m)$ *game tree complexity* leads to an $O(mb^m)$ running time. Even for simple games, this superpolynomial growth can be overwheming. Tic-tac-toe, for instance, has $9! = 362,880$ possible game outcomes at maximal search depth. Slightly more complex games rapidly become more complex, such as game tree complexities of approximately 7.1×10^{13} for *Connect Four* (see http://www.connectfour.net/Files/connect4.pdf), 10^{58} for *Reversi*, 10^{120} for chess (as computed by Claude Shannon), and 10^{360} for go (as suggested by Victor Allis).

7.8 Heuristics

In the face of intractable complexity, *heuristic algorithms* are often used to find approximately good solutions with faster running times. Optimal algorithms have provable properties for the quality of their solutions and running times. This cost of proving quality and speed is that the properties must be guaranteed over all possible outcomes. In practice, however, significant numbers of outcomes can be summarily eliminated without evaluation because they are redundant, unlikely, or undesirable. This process is called *pruning* the decision tree. Without loss of optimality, many redundant or previously computed game situations can be pruned without explicit computation but not to within the range of tractability. Further pruning requires a heuristic for finding an approximation to the optimal solution within a narrowed set of possible outcomes.

The simplest minimax heuristic is to decrease the look-ahead search depth, ensuring optimality up to some fixed future horizon. A search depth of $m = 1$ is effectively a "greedy" heuristic that simply takes the action that results in the best immediate score. *Alpha-beta pruning* is one of the more popular heuristics for minimax search, where the search focuses on "more promising" subtrees at greater depth. This approach to pruning maintains an alpha-beta window storing the lowest (alpha) and highest (beta) scores at a particular depth for the maximizing and minimizing players, respectively. If this window is closed for a subtree (beta > alpha), then the subtree does not need to be explored because it will not represent the best play by both players. Various other heuristics for minimax extend alpha-beta notions for further pruning.

7.9 Game Theory

Game theory is an interdisciplinary field for studying the strategic interactions between players in a "game." A game in this sense goes beyond our common conceptions of board or video games to represent any social situation where the decision maker, or *agent*, acts to maximize his or her utility (or welfare). Game theory can be used to model various social and natural phenomena, such as the public stances of political candidates, the dynamics of negotiations, and the economics decisions of governments and individuals. Players are assumed to be *rational* in that they can judge the quality of a situation, understand the future consequences of taking actions, and when given a choice, will act to maximize their welfare. A *strategy* (or policy) is the collection of rules for guiding a player's decision making and is thus his or her manifestation of rational behavior.

Games can take a variety of forms based on the properties of the situation being modeled.

- Cooperative versus adversarial.
- Symmetric versus asymmetric: regarding the equivalence strategies regardless of the player's role in the game.
- Zero-sum versus non-zero-sum: the total welfare for all players sums to zero in zero-sum games.
- Simultaneous versus sequential taking of actions between players.
- Game duration.
- One-shot versus repeated.
- Player's ability to unambiguously perceive his situation.

To this point, we have explored minimax for adversarial, zero-sum, sequential, unlimited duration games with perfect perception.

Solutions to games are called *equilibria*. Equilibria describe the properties of a game when it has converged to a "stable state." Stability roughly refers to when the strategies of the players have reached a "status quo." This stability will remain unless some external intervention, outside the player's actions, is injected into the game. Equilibrium is not necessarily a positive or fun experience for any player. For example, a *forced win* is a form of equilibria where a certain player, with optimal play, is assured of winning the game despite the strategy of other players. The prisoner's dilemma is an example of where the rational strategy at equilibrium is to be selfish. The example consists of two criminal suspects arrested by the police. Each suspect is faced with a decision between two choices: confess or stay silent. If both suspects stay silent, they both serve a short penal sentence—let's say one year. If both confess, they both serve a medium (five-year) sentence. If one confesses and the other stays silent, the confessor goes free and other suspect serves a long (ten-year) sentence.

In these cases, there is no forced win for either player, but there is also no optimal simple strategy. In rock-paper-scissors, if you always choose rock, you will lose or tie two-thirds of the time in a single trial and all of the time in multiple trials if someone realizes your strategy. It turns out that choosing randomly between the three actions you will do much better. This is an example of a *mixed strategy*, where actions are chosen randomly, weighted by some probability distribution (for rock-paper-scissors, this distribution is uniform). In contrast, *pure strategies* are deterministic and choose the same action in a given situation with probability 1.

7.10 Exercises

1. List all of the states of the following games:

   (a) tic-tac-toe

   (b) chess

   (c) *Half-Life* (or another generic FPS) multiplayer death-match

   (d) blackjack (a.k.a. "21")

2. Consider a supermarket with one-way entrance and exit doors and the following locations: parking lot, meat counter, dairy aisle, fruit and vegetable aisle, housewares aisle, frozen foods aisle, fish counter, and checkout.

   (a) Draw a map of the grocery store, using a typical store layout.

   (b) Draw a graph of locations based on your map.

3. If an undirected graph with v vertices forms a clique, how many edges does it contain?

4. Draw a decision tree for the prisoner's dilemma.

5. The absolute value of x is x if $x \geq 0$ and $-x$ if $x < 0$. Write pseudocode for a function `abs(x)` that evaluates to the absolute value of x.

6. The "0th" Fibonacci number is $F(0) = 0$ and the "1st" Fibonacci number is $F(1) = 1$. All other Fibonacci numbers are given by $F(n) = F(n-1) + F(n-2)$, for $n > 1$. Thus, they form the sequence 0, 1, 1, 2, 3, 4, 8, 13, 21, 34, ...

   (a) Write pseudocode for a recursive implementation of `fibonacci(n)`.

   (b) Write pseudocode for an iterative implementation of `fibonacci(n)`.

7. How many nodes are there in the full decision tree for a game of *20 Questions* (assume all 20 questions are asked)?

8. Describe in text how to use minimax in a breadth-first fashion. Why would you want to do this?

9. Give static evaluation algorithms (in text, mathematics, or pseudocode) for the following games. Your static evaluations do not have to be particularly complex. Just include a few key heuristics that determine who is most likely to win.

   (a) *Pente*

   (b) a first-person shooter death match

   (c) soccer

   (d) *Age of Empires* or another RTS or TBS

   (e) *Mario Kart* or another racing game

10. For the minigame design exercise in Chapter 1, most people design a game that is essentially *Chutes and Ladders*. That is, they roll dice and move pieces along a board toward the finish line, but the outcome is random with no real choices for the players. Now that you are more experienced, read about strategic thought and try to create a more complicated game. In this game, you may not use dice rolling, card drawing, piece tossing, or any other source of randomness.

CHAPTER 8

Choice and Probability

Terms Explained: *Continuous – Dependent – Dice – Discrete – Expected Value – Playing Cards – Pseudorandom – Random Variable – Statistics – Variance*

All interesting games involve randomness at some level. It can take on different forms. In a board game with dice or shuffled cards, the randomness is explicit in the rules. For a computer, game attacks or opponent decisions can be explicitly made using random values that are not visible to the player. Even in a game with no explicit randomness, there must be implicit randomness for the game to be interesting. As described in Chapter 7, rock-paper-scissors is viable because the optimal strategy is a mixed one. The rules lead players to make random decisions because if they don't, their opponents will be able to predict their actions. Rock-paper-scissors is even considered a serious strategy game among some players in a similar, but simpler, way that poker is played at a strategic level because an opponent's failure to play in a purely statistical manner can be exploited over many iterations.

The good news about probability is that the most critical elements for game design and analysis can be easily understood and expressed in terms of accessible objects like dice. So if you can understand how dice and cards work, you can handle anything that you are likely to encounter in even the most sophisticated computer games. This is true partly because a little randomness goes a long way, and we don't need very detailed randomness schemes even in large games. It is more broadly true because anything other than extremely simple situations quickly become too complex to analyze. As soon as the complexity rises, even the best theoreticians will introduce approximations to bring the analysis back to something that can reasonably be handled. Approximations prevent us from reaching exact answers, but frequently we need only an approximate answer. This is especially true given the human factors involved in game design.

The bad news is that many results in probability are not intuitive, and it is important to trust the math instead of your instincts. The primary reason that gambling is not only successful but is the dominant part of the games industry is that people have terrible intuition for probability. Casual gamblers can afford to lose a little money in exchange for the entertainment of the game. However, game designers cannot afford to make probability errors that will unbalance their games and corrupt their analyses of mechanics. This chapter describes the most important aspects of probability analysis for games.

8.1 Statistics and Probability

Statistics is the study of past outcomes. When we talk about the batting average of a baseball player or the trend of a commodity in the stock market, we are quoting statistics. Those numbers are useful because we often assume that the past behavior is a good predictor of what will happen in the future. In this chapter, we represent events with capital letters, such as A and B. Each of these corresponds to and is shorthand for a sentence like A: "The batter hits a home run."

Probability is the likelihood that a specific event will happen in the future. As game players, we want to know probabilities because they help us make strategic decisions. As game designers, we want to control probabilities to change the way players make their decisions. We can do this by (1) assuming that previously gathered statistics are a good predictor and (2) computing facts about the systems involved.

Most people have poor intuition for probability. One reason that probability is nonintuitive is that it inherently deals with (and values change based on) notions of time and knowledge. Say that today is Tuesday and it rained for the last three days. The probability that it rained on Monday is 100 percent because the event happened in the past and we know the outcome. There is no uncertainty involved. Now, what is the probability that it will rain on Wednesday? It is less than 100 percent. Various estimates of that probability can be made with varying degrees of error. Knowing nothing else, you might guess that if it has been raining for three days, it is likely to rain tomorrow. If, based on your experience (i.e., gathered statistics), 50 percent of the time you noticed that it rains on the day after three consecutive days of rain, then you would estimate that the probability of it raining on Wednesday is 50 percent. But what if you did not collect that statistic and instead only noticed that it rains 10 percent of the time on any given day? Then you would estimate the probability of rain tomorrow at 10 percent. More information might also change the prediction. The meteorologist watching a severe storm pass through your area on radar might see that the clouds extend for some distance and estimate the probability of rain for tomorrow at 90 percent.

In each of the cases from this rain example, a different set of assumptions, knowledge, and statistics leads to a different estimate of the probability of it raining tomorrow. Ultimately, either it will rain or it won't. On Thursday we'll be able to say with 100 percent certainty what happened on Wednesday. Wednesday's weather is controlled by incredibly complex factors involving wind, pressure, humidity, and temperature that are beyond the ability of even the best computers to evaluate. Probability is a way of analyzing the future despite our lack of knowledge and ability to compute those complex factors.

Instead of saying "There is a 90 percent chance of rain tomorrow," it would be more accurate for the meteorologist to say, "There is a 90 percent chance of rain tomorrow, *given* statistics of cloud movement and the fact that I see continual storm cloud coverage and the predictive weather model and ..." In fact, in some cases these kinds of assumptions are so important that we will explicitly write them into equations. In this case, we say that the probability is *conditional* on our partial knowledge. In practice, many probabilities are conditioned on obvious assumptions like this and are not written down. It is important to keep in mind what the conditions are, however.

8.2 Random Variables

In algebra, you solve for the value of unknown variables like x and y. Constants represent known values. For example, to solve for the height x of a building with four floors, where each floor is h feet high, we simply write $x = 4h$.

Also in regular algebra, functions such as $f(x)$ are a convenient way to work with complex expressions without rewriting the entire expression at every step. They also are a way to create general formulas into which the specific function can later be inserted. For example, if $y = f(x)$ gives the height of the terrain at distance x from a reference position, then

$$\frac{\Delta y}{\Delta x} = \frac{\text{change in } f}{\text{change in } x} = \frac{f(x_0) + f(x_1)}{x_0 - x_1}$$

approximates the slope of the terrain between two positions, no matter what the height function actually is. When we later know a specific equation for f, we can insert it into that equation.

The algebra of probability uses these regular variables, constants, and functions, but it also extends them with a new concept—random variables—and functions of those random variables. Unlike a regular variable, a *random variable* is generally not something we want to solve for the value of something. In fact, a random variable does not even have a value that is a number that can be written down. It is a placeholder for all of the values that a variable *might* take on in the future.

Consider a coin that is labeled "1" on one side and "0" on the other side. We'll flip the coin five times. Let x_1 be the value, either 0 or 1, of the first coin flip; x_2 be the value of the second coin flip; and so on so that x_i is the value of the ith flip. In mathematical notation, the sum s of the five flips is given by the following:

$$s = x_1 + x_2 + x_3 + x_4 + x_5,$$

$$s = \sum_{i=1}^{5} x_i.$$

We know that the sum will be between $s = 0$ and $s = 5$, but before we actually run the experiment, we don't know the value. In this example, x is a random variable, and x_i is the actual value that the variable takes on after a specific trial (coin flip). Because s depends on x, it is also a random variable. We say that s is a *dependent* variable because once we know the values of some of the x's, we know something about the value of s. For example, if we have flipped the coin twice and got the results $x_1 = 1, x_2 = 0$, we know that after three more flips, s will be between 1 and 4. Random variable x is independent because, as we will see in a moment, past information tells us nothing about future values of x.

Since the whole point of probabilistic analysis is that we don't know the value that a random variable will assume, we need some way of characterizing those values. Several functions of random variables and events help us in this analysis. The simplest is the probability function, $P(A)$. This is the function that gives the likelihood of event A occurring. Events describe scenarios under which random variables assume specific values.

Returning to the coin example, if we flip the numbered coin once, we expect that $P(\text{"}x_1 = 0\text{"}) = 50\%$ and $P(x_1 = 1) = 50\%$. That is, the only two events that can occur are seeing a 1 and seeing a 0, and each is equally likely. We will write this for all events as $P(\text{"}x_i = 0\text{"}) = 0.5$, or just $P(x = 0) = 0.5$. We can also write events out in text, like P("two six-sided die rolls sum to 7") or P("it will rain on Wednesday"). When referring to the same event multiple times or in the abstract, we will often give it a name, such as A.

8.3 Generating Random Numbers

8.3.1 Board Games

When we flipped our numbered coin, we assumed that the coin was fair, not weighted. We also assumed that the physics of a coin leaving the hand, flipping through the air, and bouncing on a table are so complex that the flipper can't influence the outcome. When dealing with physical random number generators like cards, dice, and coins, we will always make these unstated assumptions. So a six-sided die comes up on each face with exactly the same probability, and because there are six faces, the probability of each number is equal to 1/6. For a deck of 52 cards, we assume that they are shuffled such that the probability of the top card being the ace of hearts (or any other specific card) is 1/52.

Cards provide a good example of the way probability interacts with time and knowledge. If you peek at the top card and see that it is the two of diamonds, then for you $P(\text{"the first card is the ace of hearts"}) = 0$, but for someone who has not peeked, $P(\text{"the first card is the ace of hearts"}) = 1/52$.

What is happening here is an implicit assumption. If we write out that assumption using conditional probability, it becomes clearer:

$$\begin{aligned}
\text{Let } A &= \text{"Card 1 is A}\heartsuit\text{"} \\
&\quad P(A|\text{no givens}) = 1/52 \\
&\quad P(A|\text{"I peeked and saw 2}\diamondsuit\text{"}) = 0 \\
&\quad P(A|\text{"I peeked and saw A}\heartsuit\text{"}) = 1 \\
&\quad P(A|\text{"I peeked and saw that the card was red"}) = 1/26.
\end{aligned}$$

In addition to cards, coins, and dice, we can also generate random numbers for board games using spinners or the outcome of simple minigames like rock-paper-scissors.

8.3.2 Video Games

Computers lack physical random number generators. A programmer can produce what is called a *pseudorandom* number by evaluating a function that gives the next term in a series of numbers with a nonobvious pattern. Such functions are built into most programming languages and are typically named `rand` or `random`. They can be thought of as just reading the next number out of a predetermined sequence, where the patterns in the sequence are so complex that it is hard to guess the next value.

For practical purposes, these pseudorandom values can be treated as if they were random numbers generated by die rolls. There are two important differences. The first is reproducibility. Because the numbers are in a predetermined sequence, we can run the program twice and receive exactly the same values. This is very useful when debugging a program that involves random numbers. It allows us to set up exactly the same scenario several times during testing despite the "randomness." This is also important for networked games where we need two computers to generate exactly the same random numbers in the same order so that the game states match across the network without communication.

The second case where true random versus pseudorandom is important is network security. Here, reproducibility is a drawback. Most encryption algorithms are based on the idea that a computer can generate a number that is hard for an attacker to guess. If the attacker figures out the equation that generated the pseudorandom sequence, that attacker will be able to guess each value in the sequence and hack into the game. Strategies are available for gathering hard-to-guess random numbers to defeat this. They generally involve sampling data like mouse movements or the number of processor cycles since the computer was turned on. These values are very sensitive to slight timing changes on the part of the user, so they are hard for an attacker to guess. Given one effectively true random number, we can then advance that number of values along the pseudorandom sequence and assume that the attacker will have a hard time figuring out where in the sequence we started. The same technique is often used for generating in-game random numbers, where it is important that they not be in the same sequence every time the game is played. The number of values that we advanced in the sequence is called the seed of the pseudorandom number generator.

8.3.3 Continuous versus Discrete

Dice and cards generate values from a fixed set. We call them *discrete* random numbers because each value is clearly distinguished. Consider an analog clock. The minute hand of the clock does not indicate a discrete value but a time value with infinite precision as it moves continuously around the face. This is called a *continuous* value. On a computer, we can generate random numbers that are either discrete (e.g., {1, 2, 3, ... }) or continuous (arbitrary fractions up to the ultimate precision of the computer). A board game spinner is effectively continuous, although most spinners are divided into discrete sections.

8.4 Cards and Dice

The examples in this chapter use dice and cards extensively to explain probability, and dice and cards are used in many board games. Game developers use a compact notation for expressing card values and die rolls. This notation is common even among video game developers who do not roll real dice.

Although not discussed further in this chapter, note that cards, dice, and coins can also be used as counters instead of random number generators. Many games use unlabeled coins (e.g., poker chips) to track points. A few games (e.g., *Shadows Over Camelot*) use the value on the face of a die to track scores instead of rolling them to generate numbers.

8.4.1 Playing Cards

A standard deck of playing cards contains 52 cards that are organized into four suits of two colors: red hearts ($\heartsuit$), red diamonds ($\diamondsuit$), black clubs ($\clubsuit$), and black spades ($\spadesuit$). Each suit contains 13 cards: the numbers 2 through 10 and four face cards: jack (J), queen (Q), king (K), and ace (A). Some games assign values to the face cards of J = 11, Q = 12, K = 13, and A = 14, or treat the ace as either A = 1 ("aces low") or A = 14 ("aces high") depending on the situation. It is also common to consider all face cards as having a value of 10. Some games also use an additional two cards called jokers or wild cards that typically assume any value that a player chooses. Cards are notated by a number (or letter) and the suit. For example, the ace of hearts is written as A$\heartsuit$ and the six of diamonds is 6$\diamondsuit$.

The set of cards that players select from is called a deck. The act of taking a card off the top is called drawing, and the process of mixing up the cards is called shuffling. The cards given to a player are called a hand (see Figure 8.1). The front of the cards is also called the face (not to be confused

Figure 8.1. A hand of five cards from a standard deck, as well as cards from *Settlers of Catan* and *Dungeoneer*.

with the face cards). Cards typically have printed back patterns that are the same for all cards. This ensures that when the cards are held concealed (a closed hand) or dealt facedown, other players will not be able to tell which card is which. It also makes the cards relatively hard to see through and disguises even cards that have telltale dirt marks on the back from frequent play. An open hand is one in which everyone can see the faces of the cards.

The benefits of the standard deck are its familiarity to most players, its ubiquity, and the fact that it is designed to be easily partitioned into two or four parts. Many card games use a standard deck with different images or numbers printed on the cards to add to the fiction of the game. For example, an *Uno* deck is a standard deck with different names for the face cards. It is also common to create custom card decks to alter the ratio of each kind of card or to use a different number of cards than 52.

8.4.2 Dice and Coins

Dice come in many shapes. The six-sided cube is familiar to almost everyone. It is either numbered with values 1 through 6 or with the equivalent number of pips (dots) on each face. Casino dice are always transparent and have filled-in pips so you can see that there are no weights or magnets hidden inside a die and that the different number of pips on each face does not affect its weight. Dice used for nongambling games have much less precision but are so nearly random that we can still ignore the effects of slightly different faces.

Dice come in many other shapes that are used in cases where a different range of numbers is desired. These are called polyhedral or role-playing dice (see Figure 8.2) and follow the Platonic solids: 4-sided (tetrahedron), 6-sided (cube), 8-sided (octahedron), 12-sided (dodecahedron), and 20-sided (icosahedron). The 4-sided die has a cluster of numbers at each point; whichever number is pointing up at the end is the value that was rolled. All the others have numbers printed on their faces, and most dice are labeled starting at 1. There is also a 10-sided die labeled 0 through 9. The 0 counts as a 10 except when rolling 1d100, as described later in this section.

In some games, dice are labeled with custom symbols instead of numbers; for example, a weather 6-sided die might have rain, snow, hail, lightning, wind, and sun on its faces. The symbols are just content, and we can treat these the same as numbers for mathematical analysis.

The Platonic solids all have the property that each edge and each face has the same shape, and the same angles are between the faces so we know the dice are fair. Because percentiles are so common in games, there are also 10-sided dice. These have asymmetric faces but are also fair. In fact, any even-sided die can be constructed fairly by making two faceted cones with half the number of faces and gluing them together. Relatively exotic 30- and

Figure 8.2. Polyhedral dice.

100-sided dice are also available. Most of the designs for these are also fair, but they are so nearly spherical that they are impractical to roll.

An individual die is denoted by a lowercase "d" and a number. For example, a 6-sided die is d6, and a 4-sided die is d4. In some cases, many of the same kind of die are rolled at the same time and their results added together. This is written as a number preceding the "d"—for example, rolling two 6-sided dice and adding their results is written as 2d6. If instead we wanted the player to roll one 6-sided die and then double the result, we would write it as $1d6 * 2$. It is also common to add to the die roll—for example, $2d4 + 3$ means "roll two 4-sided dice, sum the results, and add 3 to the total."

Occasionally, we need random numbers on unusual intervals. These are synthesized from existing dice. For example, 1d2 means either flip a coin or roll another die and count odd outcomes as 1 and even outcomes as 2. "Percentile dice" or 1d100 means take two different-colored d10's and designate one as the tens place and the other as the ones place. For example, a roll of "3" on the tens place die and "7" on the ones place die means 37, and a roll of "6" and "0" means 60. A roll of "0" on both dice is defined to mean 100. For odd die sizes like 1d3, we can roll the die with twice this many faces (in this case, 1d6) and divide the result by two and round up. Another way to generate an odd size is to roll any die with a higher face and reroll values that are higher than we were willing to accept. The next section explains why this is fair.

8.5 Outcome Tree

There is a simple strategy for computing the probability of any series of events: draw out all possible outcomes. If there were only one outcome per

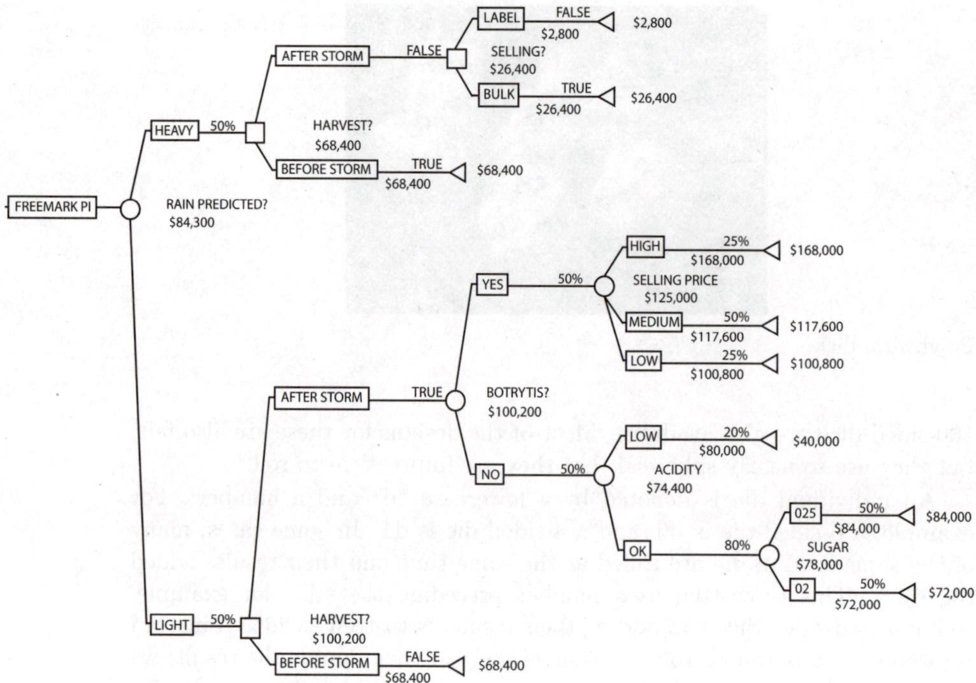

Figure 8.3. An exhaustive probability outcome tree.

event, the picture of the total set of outcomes would just be a timeline. When events have multiple possible outcomes, the timeline branches and forms a "tree." This outcome tree is similar to a decision tree, but in this case, "fate" is making the choices according to probabilities instead of a player making choices to gain advantage.

Figure 8.3 shows an outcome tree. Time begins on the left, and then the tree branches after each event. Edges are labeled with the probability of that outcome occurring. The probabilities of each branch emerging to the right of an event must sum to exactly 100 percent.

When the outcome tree is complete, the rightmost leaves are the final outcomes. To compute the probability of each outcome, simply take the product of all branch probabilities needed to reach that outcome, starting from the root on the far left. The final outcome probabilities must also sum to exactly 100 percent, since *some* outcome must always be the one that actually occurs.

Here's an example of how to use an outcome tree to solve a probability problem. Say we want to find the probability of rolling exactly two 4's when rolling two 4-sided dice and one 6-sided die. To begin, we draw the tree from Figure 8.4. The first two events correspond to the values that are rolled by

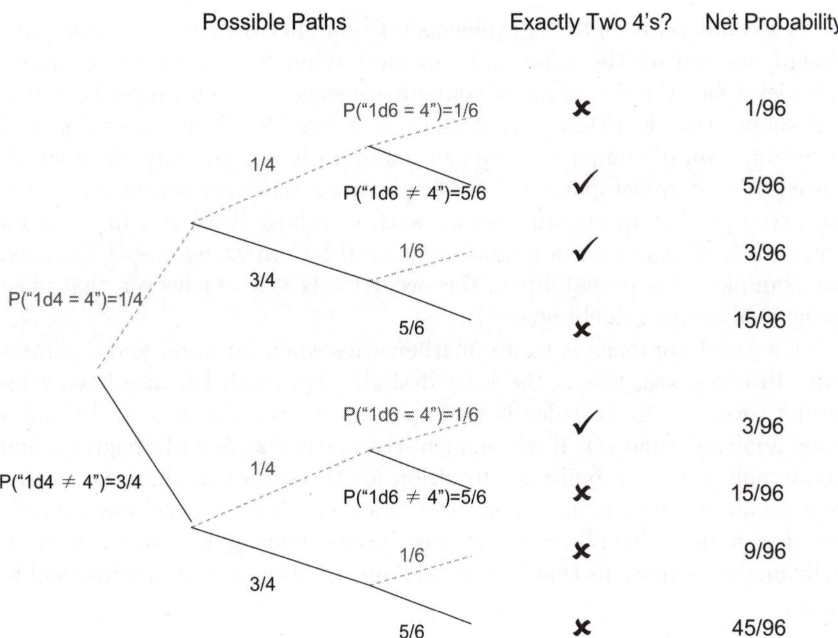

Figure 8.4. Solving a probability problem.

each of the 4-sided dice, and the third event is the result of the 6-sided die roll. Each 4-sided die has four outcomes, and each 6-sided die has six outcomes. In total, there are $4 * 4 * 6 = 96$ possible different sequences of rolls, each with a probability of 1/96. However, for this problem, we care only about rolling 4's, so at each event, there are only two relevant outcomes: "4" and "not 4." For the first two rolls of the 4-sided die, the probability of rolling a 4 is 1/4. For the third roll (of the 6-sided die), the probability of rolling a 4 is 1/6. In the figure, the center column contains a check if exactly two 4's were rolled. The right column is the probability of each case, computed by the product of branch probabilities. From this we can see that the cases where exactly two 4's are rolled occur with probabilities of 5/96, 3/96, and 3/96. These collectively add up to 11/96, or about an 11 percent chance of rolling exactly two 4's.

The outcome tree technique allows us to compute the probability of any outcome as long as we can draw the entire tree. Unfortunately, for some scenarios, so many cases are involved that the tree is too big to draw. This can be handled three ways. The first is to draw a representative tree and try to reason about it. For example, in the preceding situation, we did not draw out all 96 possible outcomes, only the 8 that we cared about. In situations with many events and many outcomes, this approach is often necessary.

A second approach to big problems is to simplify the situation. For game design, we control the rules and can alter them to make analysis easier. This is in fact the way a lot of computer science research proceeds. Often one shapes the algorithm so that analysis is feasible. When the rules need a certain level of complexity, we can maintain it but simplify the analysis instead. Many tabletop and video role-playing games have contingency rules for extremely low probability events, such as rolling three 20's in a row on three d20's (this is a certain kind of "critical hit" in *Dungeons & Dragons*, for example). The probability of this occurring is so low, however, that most game analyses can safely ignore it.

The third approach is to use mathematics when intuition and diagrams fail. In one sense, this is the least desirable approach because having intuition over the game rules is as important to the designer as having a good analysis. However, if we augment the mathematics with diagrams and continually stop to rebuild our intuition for the situation, then the mathematical approach gives incredible power for analyzing even the most complicated scenarios. The remainder of this chapter explains how to mathematically analyze situations that are beyond our intuition and are impractical to draw.

8.6 Combining Probabilities

Recall that $P(A)$ is shorthand for "the probability of event A occurring." Now, assume that events A and B are statistically independent. This means that if one of them occurs, that does not affect the probability of the other one occurring. The probabilities of combinations of the events are given by:

$$P(\text{not } A) = 1 - P(A),$$

$$P(A \text{ or } B) = P(A) + P(B),$$

$$P(A \text{ and } B) = P(A) * P(B).$$

We've seen examples of all three of these rules in the previous section. The probability of rolling a 4 on 1d4 is $P(\text{"1d4} = 4\text{"}) = 1/4$, so the probability of *not* rolling a 4 is $P(\text{"1d4} \neq 4\text{"}) = 1 - 1/4 = 3/4$. When computing the probability of fate taking a particular path through the outcome tree, we multiplied all the probabilities along that path, following the "and" rule. To compute the probability of any of the exactly two 4's outcomes, we added the individual outcome probabilities according to the "or" rule.

We say that a series of events are *collectively exhaustive* if they cover all possible outcomes. For two outcomes, they are collectively exhaustive if $P(A \text{ or } B) = P(A) + P(B) = 1$. If there are three possible outcomes, then to be collectively exhaustive, it must be true that $P(A \text{ or } B \text{ or } C) = 1$, and so on.

We say that events are *mutually exclusive* if only one of them can occur at a time. That is, if we know that one event has occurred, we also know that the other has *not* occurred. For two events, this means that $P(A \text{ and } B) = 0$; for three events,

$$\begin{aligned} P(A \text{ and } B) &= 0, \\ P(B \text{ and } C) &= 0, \\ P(C \text{ and } A) &= 0, \end{aligned}$$

and so on for higher numbers of events. When we looked at the outcome tree, the events at each fork were both mutually exclusive and collectively exhaustive—exactly one branch must be taken.

8.7 Expected Value

We can characterize the values a random variable is likely to take on in several ways. The first and most common way is to talk about its average value, which is also known as the *mean* or *expected value.*

An integer random variable can only take on values like 0, 1, 523, −100, and so on. For such a variable, the expected value is the weighted sum of the values that it can take on. Each value is weighted by the probability of that value occurring:

$$\begin{aligned} E(x) = &\quad \ldots \\ &+ (0 * P(\text{“}x = 0\text{''})) \\ &+ (1 * P(\text{“}x = 1\text{''})) \\ &+ (2 * P(\text{“}x = 2\text{''})) \\ &+ \ldots \\ E(x) = &\sum_{k=-\infty}^{\infty} (k * P(\text{“}x = k\text{''})) \,. \end{aligned}$$

This summation contains an infinite number of terms. The probability of x assuming most of those values is zero for most random variables (e.g., for 1d6, the probability of a value less than 1 or greater than 6 is zero), so we can usually sum over a smaller range.

The awkward part of calling $E(x)$ the *expected* value of x is that it is not necessarily a value that x will actually ever assume. For example, the expected value of 1d2 is as follows:

$$\begin{aligned}
E(x) &= \sum_{k=1}^{2} (k * P(\text{“}x = k\text{”})) \\
&= 1 * P(\text{“}x = 1\text{”}) + 2 * P(\text{“}x = 2\text{”}) \\
&= 1 * \frac{1}{2} + 2 * \frac{1}{2} \\
&= 1.5.
\end{aligned}$$

We know that a coin must land on either side 1 or side 2. We don't "expect" a value of 1.5 on any given flip, even though that is the "expected value," but we do expect the average of a large number of flips to be 1.5.

The 1d2 example brings up two other interesting points for game developers. The first is that the expected value of an n-sided die is not $n/2$, which is what most people initially guess. Instead, the expected value of 1dn is $(n + 1)/2$ because dice are numbered starting at one and not zero. The expected values of the standard dice are:

$$\begin{aligned}
E(1d4) &= 2.5, \\
E(1d6) &= 3.5, \\
E(1d8) &= 4.5, \\
E(1d10) &= 5.5, \\
E1d12) &= 6.5, \\
E(1d20) &= 10.5, \\
E(1d100) &= 55.5.
\end{aligned}$$

The second interesting point is that although we do not expect the real-life average of a *small* number of trials to necessarily match the mathematical expected value, we do expect the average of a large number of trials to be the expected value. This is called the Law of Large Numbers.

8.8 Variance

The amount of deviation between the expected value for a large number of trials and the actual average observed in practice is described by the *variance* of a random variable. This is important because expected value of a random variable does not tell its whole story. We also need to know how those values are distributed. Consider two groups of students. The first are in a course where everyone received a grade of B+. The second are in a course where half of the class received an A and the other half received a B. In both courses, the class average was B+; that is, the expected grade for any one student was B+. However, in the first course there was no variation, since everyone received a B+. In the second course, there was a high variation of grades. We could imagine other kinds of distributions. For example, distributions in which the individual grades are mostly near B+, but decreasing numbers are at increasing distances in a so-called bell-shaped curve or Gaussian curve, and distributions in which all grades are uniformly spread out between the highest and lowest values. See Figure 8.5 for examples of different distributions.

The variance of a random variable is a formal measure of how far the individual actual values are from their average. It captures only a small amount of information about the total shape of the distribution of values, but that information gives some idea of how much variation we can expect.

The variance function of a random variable is defined as

$$\operatorname{Var}(x) = E\left((x - E(x))^2\right). \tag{8.1}$$

In this equation, $E(x)$ is the expected value of the random variable, and $x - E(x)$ is the difference (or "distance," if we think of x as being a position) between the random variable and its average. Squaring and taking the expected value of that expression gives the variance, which is the average squared distance from the average value.

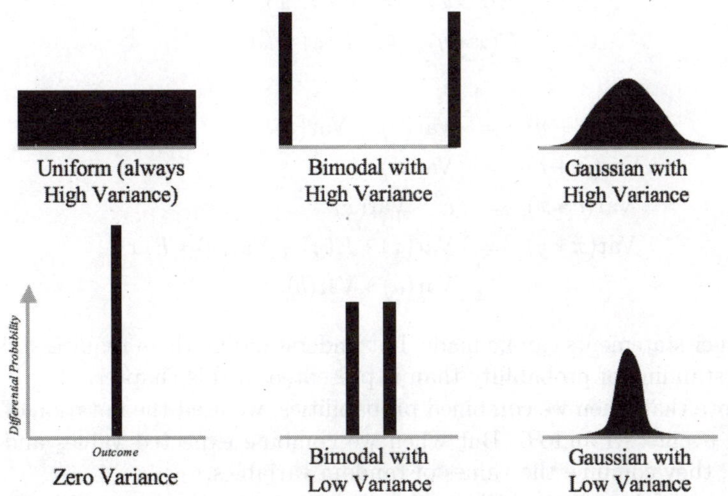

Figure 8.5. Changing distribution shape and variance.

If a random variable has zero variance, that indicates that it is always going to have a value equal to its expected value. If it has a very high variance, then the variable's values will usually be far away from the expected value. Of course, even in the high variance case, the value must be balanced equally on each side of the average; otherwise, it wouldn't *be* the average.

Equation (8.1) is mathematically equivalent to

$$\text{Var}(x) = E(x^2) - E(x)^2. \tag{8.2}$$

That is, the variance is the average of the squares minus the square of the average.

8.9 Compound Expressions

How are variance and expected value affected when the probability of multiple events is considered? For example, we know that if we roll 1d6, every value between 1 and 6 is equally likely, and the expected value is 3.5. But what is the expected value of 2d6? How much variance is there in 2d6?

For the simple case where x and y are independent random variables and c is a constant, the expected value and variance of various combinations are given by:

$$\begin{aligned} E(x+y) &= E(x) + E(y), \\ E(x+c) &= E(x) + c, \\ E(c * x) &= c * E(x), \\ E(x * y) &= E(y) * E(x), \end{aligned}$$

$$\begin{aligned} \text{Var}(x+y) &= \text{Var}(x) + \text{Var}(y), \\ \text{Var}(x+c) &= \text{Var}(x), \\ \text{Var}(c * x) &= c^2 * \text{Var}(x), \\ \text{Var}(x * y) &= \text{Var}(x) * E(y) + \text{Var}(y) * E(x) + \\ &\quad \text{Var}(a) * \text{Var}(b). \end{aligned}$$

Stronger statements can be made, but understanding them requires a deeper understanding of probability than is presented in this chapter.

Note that when we combined probabilities, we used the notation of combined events: A and B. But when we combine expected values and variances, they combine the values of random variables.

Be careful to distinguish independent variables in an equation. In particular, the results of separate die rolls (even of the same die) are different variables. For example, say a player rolls 1d10 on his or her turn in a game and gains one victory point if the result is a 10. How much variance does this player expect in their point total of 5 turns? Let $x =$ 1d10. Let $y = 1$ if "$x = 10$" and 0 otherwise. The variance of 5 turns is $\text{Var}(z)$, where $z = \sum_{i=1}^{5} y_i$, so $\text{Var}(z) = \text{Var}(y_1 + y_2 + y_3 + y_4 + y_5) = \sum_{i=1}^{5} \text{Var}(y_i) = 5\text{Var}(y) = 5\left(E(y^2) - E(y)^2\right)$. It is *not* $\text{Var}(5 * y) = 25\text{Var}(y)$!

8.10 Case Study: *Settlers of Catan*

We now examine the probabilistic properties of the popular board game *Settlers of Catan*. To simplify the analysis, we ignore certain aspects of the game, but the main results remain applicable to the actual full game.

In *Settlers*, players build towns at the vertices (corners) of a hexagonal grid representing land areas, like the one shown in Figure 8.6. Each land area is labeled with a number between 2 and 12 (except for 7), and each town is therefore adjacent to at most three different numbers. Each player rolls

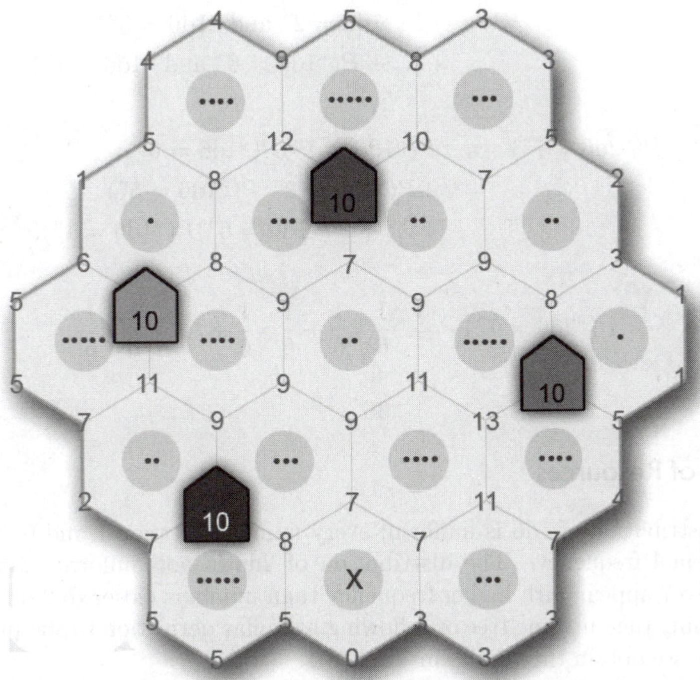

Figure 8.6. Abstraction of the game board for *Settlers of Catan*. The houses show several different ways of capturing a vertex with an expected resource production of 10/36.

2d6 at the start of his turn. All players who have towns on areas adjacent to hexes labeled with the resulting sum receive resources. However, if a 7 is rolled, then a robber moves throughout the land and allows the player who rolled to steal resources from another.

8.10.1 Probability of the Robber

The outcome tree for 2d6 has six branches from the root and each of those has six branches, giving a total of 36 outcomes. Six of those 36 outcomes are 7's, so the probability of rolling a 7 and moving the robber is $6/36 = 1/6$. Alternatively, we can follow the derivation explicitly to see that this is the case:

$$\begin{aligned} P(\text{"2d6 = 7"}) = P(& (\text{"1d6 = 1" and "1d6 = 6"}) \text{ or} \\ & (\text{"1d6 = 2" and "1d6 = 5"}) \text{ or ... or} \\ & (\text{"1d6 = 6" and "1d6 = 1"})), \end{aligned}$$

$$\begin{aligned} P(\text{"2d6 = 7"}) &= P(\text{"1d6 = 1" and "1d6 = 6"}) \\ &\quad + P(\text{"1d6 = 2" and "1d6 = 5"}) \\ &\quad + \ldots + P(\text{"1d6 = 6" and "1d6 = 1"}), \end{aligned}$$

$$\begin{aligned} P(\text{"2d6 = 7"}) &= P(\text{"1d6 = 1"})P(\text{"1d6 = 6"}) \\ &\quad + P(\text{"1d6 = 2"})P(\text{"1d6 = 5"}) \\ &\quad + \ldots + P(\text{"1d6 = 6"})P(\text{"1d6 = 1"}), \end{aligned}$$

$$\begin{aligned} P(\text{"2d6 = 7"}) &= \frac{1}{6} * \frac{1}{6} + \frac{1}{6} * \frac{1}{6} + \ldots + \frac{1}{6} * \frac{1}{6} \\ &= \frac{6}{36}. \end{aligned}$$

8.10.2 Probability of Resources

The distribution of 1d6 is uniform; every number between 1 and 6 appears with equal frequency. The distribution of 2d6 is not uniform. Numbers closer to 7 appear with higher frequency than numbers closer to 2 or 12. By examining the outcome tree or following a similar derivation to the previous section, we obtain the results in Table 8.1.

This distribution is shaped like a triangle. We can fit a function to this by inspection and derive the general expression for the probability of a given roll on 2d6 as:

$$
\begin{aligned}
P(\text{"2d6} = \text{2"}) &= 1/36\\
P(\text{"2d6} = \text{3"}) &= 2/36\\
P(\text{"2d6} = \text{4"}) &= 3/36\\
P(\text{"2d6} = \text{5"}) &= 4/36\\
P(\text{"2d6} = \text{6"}) &= 5/36\\
P(\text{"2d6} = \text{7"}) &= 6/36\\
P(\text{"2d6} = \text{8"}) &= 5/36\\
P(\text{"2d6} = \text{9"}) &= 4/36\\
P(\text{"2d6} = \text{10"}) &= 3/36\\
P(\text{"2d6} = \text{11"}) &= 2/36\\
P(\text{"2d6} = \text{12"}) &= 1/36
\end{aligned}
$$

Table 8.1. Probability distribution of 2d6.

$$P(\text{"2d6} = \text{c"}) = \frac{6 - |c - 7|}{36}. \tag{8.3}$$

8.10.3 Expected Production of a Town

Towns that are away from the ocean are adjacent to three hexes. Let r be the quantity of resources produced by a specific town in one turn. What is the value of $E(r)$, the expected quantity of resources that we expect a town to produce? This is an important question to answer when choosing where to build, since players want to maximize their resource income.

Let c_1, c_2, and c_3 be the labels on each of the adjacent three hexes. These are not random variables but some predetermined constants whose value is given by where we placed the town. The expected production value of the town is

$$E(r) = \sum_{i=1}^{3} P(\text{"2d6} = c_i\text{"}).$$

Using Equation (8.3),

$$
\begin{aligned}
E(r) &= \sum_{i=1}^{3} \frac{6 - |c_i - 7|}{36}\\
&= \frac{1}{2}\sum_{i=1}^{3} |c_i - 7|.
\end{aligned}
$$

For a concrete example, say that a vertex is surrounded by hexes labeled $c_1 = 4, c_2 = 6, c_3 = 11$. The expected value of a town at this location is

$$\begin{aligned} E(r) &= \frac{1}{2}(|c_1 - 7| + |c_2 - 7| + |c_3 - 7|) \\ &= \frac{1}{2}(|4 - 7| + |6 - 7| + |11 - 7|) \\ &= 4. \end{aligned}$$

A strategic player uses this formula to assess which locations are the most valuable. The value of a player's entire settlement, and therefore the player's resource production strength, is likewise the sum of the expected value over all of his existing towns. In the actual game, players also take other factors into account when evaluating locations such as expansion potential, seaside ports, and access to different kinds of resources. The last is less important than you might think. Except for cases where a player has a monopoly or is completely deprived of one kind of resource, resource diversity is important but not critical because the game features trading with other players and with the bank, making resources fungible.

8.10.4 Variance of Production

Depending on dice for resource production creates potentially high variance in *Settlers of Catan.* Players need resources to expand their civilizations. Maximizing the expected value of a town is only useful if the town actually happens to produce resources at the times when they are needed. A player can monopolize the valuable six and eight hexes but still have a difficult time if a number of turns pass before those numbers are actually rolled, leaving them without resources to trade in the interim.

Another rule in *Settlers of Catan* is that any player with more than seven resources in hand when the robber is moved loses half of his or her resources. Thus, receiving a huge boon on a six or eight that offsets the dry period between such rolls does not produce average wealth. Instead, it leaves the player with either no resources (because a six or eight wasn't rolled recently) or too many resources (between when a six or eight is rolled and when the player actually has the opportunity to spend the resources). A natural strategy is for players to avoid this by minimizing the variance of the resources that they will receive by seeking a mixture of different-numbered hexes. For example, a player with towns on all ten different numbers is guaranteed to collect a small number of resources on every roll (except for seven), thus avoiding both the boom and the bust.

8.11 Exercises

Use formal mathematical notation—for example, $P(\text{"1d6} = 1\text{"})$ or $E(3\text{d}6)$—to restate each problem, and show intermediate results or outcome trees. Show all work; the equations are more important than the answers.

1. Compute:
   (a) The average result (expected value) of rolling 1d6.
   (b) The average result of 3d6.
   (c) $E(kdn)$—that is, the average roll of k dice with n sides on each die.
   (d) $P(\text{"1d6} \geq 4\text{"})$, the chance of rolling a 4 or higher on 1d6.

2. Draw the distribution curves for 1d6, 2d6, and 3d6. What do you think the curve for 10d6 looks like?

3. (a) What is the chance of rolling 99 on 1d100?
   (b) What is the chance of rolling any number with two of the same digit on 1d100 (assume 1d100 is numbered 1...100)?

4. How can you simulate 1d5 in a fair way using only:
   (a) one 10-sided die?
   (b) one 6-sided die?
   (c) two 4-sided dice?

5. Consider a linear race game board that has 21 squares. In this game, four players start on square 1 and take turns moving forward by 1d6. The first player to the twenty-first square wins.
   (a) How long do you expect the game to take, measured in turns? (You need 20 "steps" to reach the twenty-first square. Note that it takes *four* turns for everyone to move once.)
   (b) How long do you expect the game to take, measured in seconds?

6. In a hypothetical role-playing game, you "hit" on an attack if you roll 15 or higher on 1d20. A hit inflicts $1\text{d}8 + 1$ points of damage, unless you rolled a 20 on your attack. A 20 on the attack is a "critical hit" that inflicts $(1\text{d}8 + 1) * 2$.
   (a) When you attack, how much damage do you expect to inflict (taking into account the fact that you might miss)?
   (b) How many attacks will it take to kill a troll with 20 hit points?

7. You are playing a poker variant with four people. A 52-card deck is shuffled, and then each player is dealt two cards face-up and three cards face-down. Each player (starting from you) in turn can then discard one of his or her face-down cards (after looking at it) and draw a new card. After the deal, these are the cards.

   Player 1 (you): K♡, A♠ showing, 2♣, A♢, A♠ hidden
   Player 2: Q♢, 9♣ showing
   Player 3: K♡, Q♡ showing, 4♡, J♣, 10♢ hidden
   Player 4: 5♠, 5♣ showing

   Assume that the events in each of the following exercise parts occur in order so the actions taken in one exercise impact subsequent ones.

   (a) Based on the cards that you can see, what do you think the chance that you will draw the A♡ if you discard your 2♣?

   (b) What does player 3 think that your chance of drawing the A♡ is immediately after the deal, based on the cards that he or she can see?

8. (a) Compute $E(\max(1\text{d}6, 1\text{d}6))$, the expected value of taking the maximum result from each of two 6-sided die rolls.

   (b) Compute $E(\min(1\text{d}6, 1\text{d}6))$, the expected value of taking the minimum result from each of two 6-sided die rolls.

9. (a) What is the chance of a hand of six cards drawn from a shuffled deck containing all four aces?

   (b) What is the chance of a hand of six cards drawn from a shuffled deck containing at least three aces?

10. Let's go back to the troll from Exercise 6. Say the troll's attack is a hit if it rolls 17 or higher on 1d20. Its attack inflicts 1d4 points of damage unless it rolls a 20, in which case it inflicts (1d4)*3 damage. Your health is 30. You attack first, and both you and the troll attack once per turn.

    (a) What is the chance that you will die (reach zero health) in this encounter?

    (b) How much health do you expect to have after the troll is dead (including cases where your character dies)?

8.12 Resources

- Drake, *Fundamentals of Applied Probability Theory* [Drake 67]
- Hogg and Ledolter, *Applied Statistics for Engineers and Physical Scientists* [Hogg and Ledolter 91].
- Moscovich, *Probability Games and Other Activities* [Moscovich 00].
- Mosteller, *Fifty Challenging Problems in Probability with Solutions* [Mosteller 65].
- Raiffa and Luce, *Games and Decisions: Introduction and Critical Survey* [Luce and Raiffa 57].

CHAPTER 9

Balance

Terms Explained: *Balance – Decision Tree – Engagement – Fairness – Feedback – Flow – Gameplay – Nash Equilibrium – Optical Outcome – Pattern – Randomness – Stability*

Mechanics make playing a game different from every other activity. Mechanics are the rules that motivate the players' strategies and decisions, and they provide both a rigid structure and freedom. Mechanics give rise to gameplay—the experience of the game—and are ultimately what will make a game succeed or fail. The true character of a game—what makes chess the game that it is whether the playing pieces are abstract marble shapes or *Star Wars* figurines—is in the mechanics and is separable from everything else.

Mechanics, the design team's most important responsibility, are usually handled by a group of developers who are fairly mathematically inclined. These designers must be extremely experienced with other games because that provides knowledge of what works and what does not. Most mechanics designers have played thousands of games and are very good at them. They are good at other games because they have trained themselves to immediately see through the fiction of a game. They perceive the underlying rules and perform small experiments in-game to determine the control structures and constants. For most people, game playing involves a lot of intuition, fantasy, and luck; it is qualitative. For a good game designer (or a professional game player), playing a game is a quantitative experience. It is a science where everything is reduced to hard facts. This can actually rob the game-playing experience of most of its enjoyment, or at least its traditional enjoyment, because this kind of playing is about perfection and winning, not the journey. This kind of ideal, optimizing play contrasts strongly with one of the points in this chapter, which is, what makes games enjoyable for "normal" people?

The process of designing and tuning mechanics is commonly called balancing. The goal of balancing is to make a game that is fair, stable, and engaging. Fairness means an equal chance of winning, stability limits runaway success or failure, and engagement measures entertainment value.[1] We will explore these technical terms in depth throughout this chapter. A game is balanced when all three are satisfactory. The process of balancing a game draws on computer science, economics, psychology, and theater. Computer science and economics provide the structures for analysis and solving for optimal constants in rule systems. They address the science of rational decision making. Psychology and theater address the motivations of players and how to influence them. These fields also introduce the notion that players often do not act in a manner that an economist would call "rational." That is, players often do not make the move that best increases their chance of winning.

By their nature, most mechanics are quantitative, and the most complex mechanisms revolve around combat and commerce. This is not necessarily because players prefer violent or capitalist games, but instead because combat and economies have historically been reduced to quantifiable elements by military strategists and economists. It is not surprising that many of the analysis tools and game strategies are drawn from military and economics methods. An interesting debate surrounds whether nonquantifiable activities are really games at all. *Electroplankton*, *Karaoke Revolution* in the nonscoring mode, and many aspects of Will Wright's simulation games seem to fit into this category of qualitative games. Under our definition of games, we include all of these but feel that the methods of strategic decision analysis may be better applied to *Age of Empires* than to *Karaoke Revolution.*

This chapter presents the ideals of fairness, stability, and engagement, and issues that make achieving them a challenge. The following chapter discusses how different mechanics affect each and recommends remedies for common design problems.

9.1 Our Methodology

The ideas and statements in this chapter were researched in a different manner from those in all the other chapters. Most of the chapters in this book describe accepted practices and theories. Each chapter distills wisdom

[1]Sometimes developers will refer to balance as just fair and stable and will call engagement the "fun" or "addictive" property of the game.

about which entire books are written, with the goal of giving you a complete overview of game design and development and the interactions among different aspects.

This chapter is different in that it presents ideas that you will not find as widely documented. Although they would probably agree with many of the ideas in this chapter, most game developers would also say that game mechanic design is a black art. Few people are explicitly trained in balancing mechanics the way that artists, programmers, and managers are trained by schools and books in their respective fields. Most game developers agree that this is a bad state of affairs, and this book is one attempt to improve the study and practice of mechanics.

Many of the ideas and terminology presented here are our own, based on significant research of both previous work in other fields and new analysis applied to games by us. Some we owe to hundreds of discussions with, and observations of, game developers. Other elements are from our experience with commercial games and artificial intelligence systems. Still other elements are in part adapted from general books on game design, economics, computer science, and psychology, some of which we explicitly recommend in the Resources section. We've personally tested this material in the classroom and in both professional and hobbyist game development. So although this material is new, we believe much of it encompasses and articulates others' ideas that may not have previously been presented in this context or brought together in this way.

9.2 Before Balance

Balance is not how you begin to design a game. When you start with a blank slate, you actually already have a game, albeit a ridiculously simple one. The simplest possible fair game is: everyone just agrees to a draw. That's it! There are no other rules, pieces, or decisions. That game is fair and stable but not engaging. Say we introduce some randomness by deciding the winner with a coin flip (or die roll for many players). Now the outcome of the game is at least not a foregone conclusion. Yet, the mechanics are still not interesting. Flipping a coin lacks meaningful choices, strategies, and interactions between players. And even if we implement the game on a computer and add 3D dragons, spaceships, and sound effects, the content still cannot make the underlying mechanic compelling.

The point is that although stability and fairness in mechanics are necessary properties of a good game design, they are not enough, and no amount of enjoyable content can overcome that. For a successful game, we need engagement that arises from the mechanics and is amplified by the content. Flipping a coin or playing tic-tac-toe is not interesting for an adult. We need more complexity to provoke engagement. Games aren't interesting unless they involve uncertainty about the winner.

The good news is that although balancing the mechanics that arise is difficult, generating engaging complexity that leads to those mechanics is easier. Building complexity is more of an art than a science. A game that is too complicated is frustrating. One that is not complex enough is boring. Adding complexity requires understanding the range of problems between what people find too hard and too easy. The choice of how to add complexity within that range is driven by artistic goals, which are what you want the game to express, the experiences you want to capture, and the ways you want players to think.

Emphasize creativity at the early stages of development. Then, during the balance process, apply analysis to reduce complexity and tune the mechanics. When building complexity, you should think first of expression, not computation.

Complexity can be added to a game in may ways. Three major ones are beginning with an existing game, beginning with a theme, and beginning with a combination of mechanics.

9.2.1 Modify an Existing Game

Starting with an existing game is a good idea for many reasons. It is how most professional video games and board games are created. *Half-Life* literally began as *Quake 2.* Developer Valve changed the content and introduced new mechanics to support the narrative. As another example, *No One Lives Forever* was created by the developers of *GoldenEye.* They wanted to make a sequel but no longer owned the rights to the James Bond license. So they transformed the James Bond theme to a sci-fi setting, kept the original mechanics, and added a few new ones appropriate for multiplayer and sci-fi. In board games, *Settlers of Catan* is essentially *Monopoly* developed with new mechanics to create more strategy and a new theme. Finally, chess and Chinese chess diverged from the same game over a thousand years ago. Each took a game that worked and then modified it in different ways.

Choose a game that you enjoy but feel is improperly balanced, meaning it lacks complexity (or has too much!), is too varied, takes too long to play, or fails to scale to a larger or smaller number of players. Occasionally, it is interesting to simply change the theme and then adjust the mechanics to fit the new theme. Most pen-and-paper RPGs arise from that approach.

A modification to an existing game can be presented as a mod, an expansion pack, or as an independent game where only the designer knows its derivation. The mod approach creates marketing opportunities because it is naturally targeted at owners of the original game who are looking for variation. Expansion packs generally build off an existing trademark and are produced solely by the original publisher.

The overview sheet asks you to describe a game as a hybrid of two well-known games, such as "*Rogue Squadron* meets *Splinter Cell*." This is also a good way to begin designing a game. Merge the aspects of two previous games, and then balance the resulting mechanics.

9.2.2 Work from a Theme

Starting with a theme is a great way to build a game. In this case, you try to capture the essence of the theme's inherent conflict with a set of mechanics that mimic the feel and strategy but simplify it. For example, in a farming game, conflicts arise between the farmer and nature and in the competition between farmers who produce the same commodity. From these conflicts, enumerate elements that affect each participant, such as farm equipment, weather, market conditions, plant combinations, fertilizer, pesticide, and diseases. This will lead to strategies—farm organically or target the highest yield? Invest in a larger combine or avoid debt? Underprice the competitor or change crops? You can then add mechanics that mediate the conflicts and balance them to control the viable strategies.

Begin by choosing the theme and then enumerating important elements on the theme worksheet (see Figure 11.4 for an example). Then build mechanics that simulate these elements.

Often the theme shifts as the game develops because the original theme was inconsistent with the final mechanics. For example, moving from gladiatorial combat to spaceship combat might reflect a change of pace, scope, and range in a game, yet starting with gladiatorial combat is what enabled work to begin in the first place.

9.2.3 Combine Mechanics

One of the more challenging ways to create a game is beginning with a set of mechanics. This is challenging because in the absence of a theme or guiding game, there is no natural context to inspire the imagination. You risk creating an abstract game that supports strategy but is not engaging. That said, many successful games have been created with mechanics and not theme as inspiration.

Here are some examples. *Set* and *Brawl* are real-time card games that one could imagine creating from the question "What would happen if we eliminated turns in a board game?" *Through the Desert* is essentially the encirclement mechanics of go combined with the expansion mechanics of *Settlers of Catan*. *Planetside* is a video game that merges FPS and MMORPG mechanics. Abstract video games like *Geometry Wars*, *Tetris*, *Flow*, and *Hexen* all arose out of mechanics.

The key when designing a game from mechanics is to choose a novel and possibly contradictory combination. Otherwise, you're just repeating an existing game and would be better served by trying to rebalance that game than to reinvent it. Cooperative, persistent, and real-time board/alternative reality games all challenged traditional mechanics combinations and have become the most interesting new ideas in games. In video games, three of the more radical recent mechanics ideas are sandboxes that have no objective goal, controller innovations (like *Guitar Hero* and Wii), and using simple controls for complex actions (like *God of War*, *Gears of War*, *Stranglehold*).

9.3 Fairness

For a classic two-player competitive game like go, players and designers value *fairness*. It is generally undesirable to play a game when the odds are against you. Systems like gambling and handicaps can make unfair games enjoyable, but they are only compensations for the underlying problem of the game being unfair. The straightforward test for fairness is:

> A game is *fair* if each of an evenly matched group of players has an a priori equal chance of winning for any given starting position.

This means that if two players are equally matched and play a game 100 times, we expect about 50 wins for each player if the game is fair. If the player who moves first wins 75 of the games, then we consider the game unfair because there is too large of an advantage to the first move.

Having both players subject to the same rules is not sufficient (or even necessary!) for fairness. For example, in most board and turn-based video games, making the first move is a slight advantage. Therefore, for two evenly matched players, the first player to move is slightly more likely to win. So the game is not fair, even though the rules are the same for both players. It is common to correct this by deciding the first player randomly, handicapping the first player with a restricted move set, or giving the first move to the weaker player. The weaker player might be identified as the loser from the previous round of the game or the younger player.

Our straightforward test for fairness is hard to apply because there are complicating factors such as human imperfection, alliances, and asymmetry. We now explore these factors at length but retain our simple and intuitive test as the practical measure of fairness.

9.3.1 Human Factors

Consider the human factors affecting fairness. Where will we find evenly matched players? Typically we say that two players are evenly matched at a game if they each win 50 percent of games. But if the game itself isn't yet known to be fair, then it isn't a valid way of evaluating the players. The phrase "evenly matched" implies that some players can be better than others. What does "better" mean? If players always made optimal, rational moves, then the only difference between two players would be randomness in the game. We know that real players do not always make optimal and rational moves, so a player's ability could be considered the number of mistakes that he or she does *not* make. This makes principled mathematical analysis of fairness difficult. The fairness of a game seems to depend on how it misleads players into making mistakes and whether it provokes equivalent mistakes among different people with otherwise "evenly matched" abilities. We can recover from this by abstracting the players as statistical entities, in the manner of AI characters who intentionally make random mistakes or limit their computation to avoid perfection. Consider the case of turn-based games. We can model one player as only able to concentrate two moves ahead in the game. That is, the player only has the time or mental ability to search two moves deep in the decision tree using the minimax algorithm. This player will make imperfect plays in situations that require more than two moves to resolve. We can model another player as having incorrect estimations of the odds of events (such as certain card hands) occurring and error in his or her memory of what events (such as played cards) have previously occurred. Most game-playing decisions are based on heuristics because completely evaluating a situation is either too complex or too boring. When we say that a person is good at certain types of games, we mean that her or she has a combination of good heuristics, the ability to search enough moves ahead, and a good mental model of the probabilities involved for the specific mechanics in that game.

9.3.2 Alliances: Beyond Zero-Sum

In a two-player, zero-sum game, we can talk about fairness as a mathematical experiment using minimax. What about less trivial configurations like multiplayer games and cooperative games? Here we do not have individual players in competition but whole alliances. What about single-player games? What about games where there is no winning condition, like *The Sims*?

In a multiplayer competitive game, the players who are not winning will naturally collude to bring down the leader. Even in a three-player game, this means that even with evenly matched players, the current leader is only half as powerful as his or her opponents. To combat this, it is necessary to give the current leader a temporary advantage, ensure that when the other players catch up they do not not bring the leader too far below their own level, or ensure that there can be multiple leaders at any point. We'll revisit these ideas later because they impact the stability and engagement

Figure 9.1. In *The Legend of Zelda: Twilight Princess* for the Wii, players will win 100 percent of the time ...with persistence and moderate action sequence ability. (Image courtesy of Nintendo)

of the game as well as fairness. Also, in a multiplayer game, certain players will naturally collude, based on both their strategic position in the game or their out-of-game relationships. The mechanics must be balanced to either minimize the advantage of collusion or to ensure that everyone has an equal opportunity to collude.

Single-player games like *Tetris* and cooperative multiplayer games like *Halo* co-op have the unusual property that the human players have no human opponents; *everyone* is allied. What does fairness mean in this context? One definition would be that the game itself wins (i.e., the players lose) 50 percent of the time. In this case, the game is modeling an equally matched human player. For example, in computer chess, the ideal opponent from a fairness perspective is one who possesses exactly your abilities. Of course, from an engagement perspective, this is dissatisfying. Most people like to win when they play against a computer.[2]

Another definition for fairness in the fully allied case is that the players should win 100 percent of the time, if they play perfectly rationally and with maximum physical ability. This specifically doesn't say anything about

[2]An exception is that a professional chess player probably wants to lose to the computer, so that he or she can learn something new.

how often they should win if they are playing poorly, and we know that players aren't perfect. However, this is a good guideline because people like to believe that they will win or lose a game based primarily on their own abilities. Most adventure games, such as *The Legend of Zelda* series (see Figure 9.1), ensure that players who have moderate ability with the controller and make about 80 percent of decisions rationally will win the game 100 percent of the time. Of course, the "Save" feature in such games artificially inflates the player's abilities, since the player can go back in time and make better decisions or replay an action sequence.

For games where there is no explicit winning condition, we can't define fairness in terms of winning. Instead, we can think about the alternative quantitative goals of the game. Every player should have chances proportional to their ability to reach every possible state in the game. No item or area in the game should be inaccessible from the start of the game or soon after. Massive multiplayer games such as the MMORPG *World of Warcraft* combine alliances and lack of winning condition. Players want to know that they can gain any ability of any other player, albeit possibly by creating a new character and playing with it for several hours. This leads to another complication of fairness in persistent worlds. What is the fair way of advancing oneself? Is it fair to gain relative to another player by playing more hours or by paying more real-world money? Persistent online worlds are still new enough that these are open questions. The current wisdom says that gaining an advantage by paying more real-world money is unfair, but it is still desirable from a sales and player perspective in certain circumstances.

The advantage of playing an MMORPG more hours seems to be considered fair by most players. However, that advantage should be sublinear so playing twice as long as another player does not grant twice the increase in character abilities. The closest board game analog is tabletop role playing, like *Dungeons & Dragons*. Such games tend to be balanced so that character advancement becomes more difficult as characters become more powerful. This allows new characters to gain abilities faster than existing ones and over time brings all the characters to approximately the same level. It also decreases the benefit for powerful characters to revisit low-level areas of the game to fight weak enemies for low-risk advancement.

9.4 Stability

A boat is stable if you can move about it freely without fear of tipping over, and it it unstable if the slightest motion sends you swimming. The stable boat has the property that it damps out small perturbations, whereas the unstable boat amplifies small perturbations.

A game can be stable or unstable in much the same way as a boat. Instead of the balance of the sailors, we consider the balance of power between players. A *stable* game is one in which no regular item or strategy will shift the balance of power substantially. To win, a player must consistently gain in power, not leverage a small or early upset. A stable game must have multiple viable strategies. Otherwise, all players will immediately execute the same strategy and deadlock. A precise definition of stability under these ideas is:

> A game is *stable* if:
>
> 1. feedback is negative at the opening, slightly positive in the midgame, and very positive at the endgame; and
> 2. it has multiple viable strategies (stable Nash equilibria).

We now explore feedback and strategies in more depth.

9.4.1 Feedback

In the context of stability, *feedback* means the impact of an event on the balance of power. An event has positive feedback if it encourages more events that are similar. An example of positive feedback are the player skills in *Neverwinter Nights*. A player successfully uses a skill, such as attacking with a sword, when a virtual die roll is lower than the skill value. On a success, the skill value increases, thus making the next attempt even easier. The high-pitched squeal you hear when a microphone is too close to its amplifier is a real-world example of positive feedback. The microphone senses the amplified version of the original sound, and it cycles back through the amplifier, building on itself.

Negative feedback discourages the same event from occurring. When a player scores a point in *YINSH*, one of his or her own pieces is removed from the board. The player thus has fewer pieces, which makes it harder to score again. An FM radio tuner uses a kind of negative feedback to aid the listener in tuning it precisely. As the frequency drifts away from a radio station and the signal becomes weaker, the radio automatically shifts back toward the stronger signal, decreasing the drift.

Figure 9.2 shows stable feedback curves for a two-player, zero-sum game. The horizontal axis represents the absolute score. When it is very negative (to the left), player 1 wins.[3] When the score is very positive (to the right),

[3]Note that here we are assuming that player 1 is the *minimizing* player.

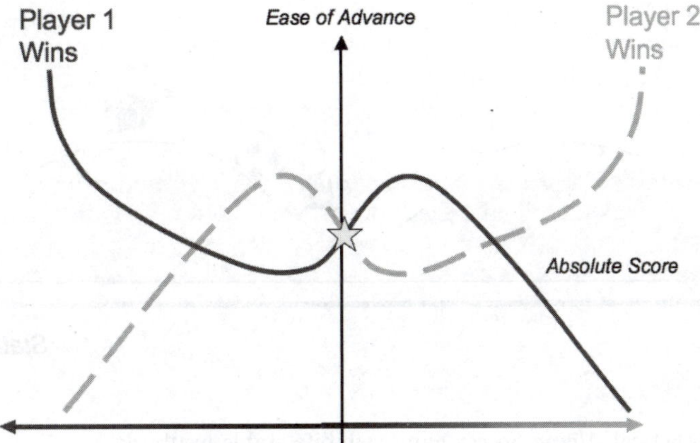

Figure 9.2. Stable feedback curve for a two-player game.

player 2 wins. The vertical axis represents the ease with which each player can advance the absolute score in his desired direction. Consider the solid curve of player 1 in the figure. At the beginning of the game, the score is zero, and we are at the origin of the graph in the center of the figure where the axes cross. Say that player 1 makes a good move (through luck or strategy), and the absolute score becomes slightly negative, moving us to the left of the graph. Note that player 1's ease of advance has decreased and player 2's ease of advance has increased. This means that although the score benefits player 1, player 2 has a slight advantage that will help him or her recover. This is *negative* feedback: player 1 performed well, so the game is raising the difficulty level for that player and aiding the opponent.

If player 1 continues to play very well, the score will become more negative and we move farther to the left in the graph. In the midgame, *positive* feedback begins, and player 1 gains a strategic advantage as well as a score advantage. Now performing well makes the game easier for player 1, pushing him toward victory. Player 2 can still recover, of course, but he or she is now facing an uphill battle instead of an advantage. In the endgame, the solid curve slopes steeply upward. This is strong positive feedback. Once the score has become very negative everyone knows that player 1 will win with reasonable play, and it is only a matter of time. An upset at this point would indicate that the game is unstable and the balance of power can be shifted too easily. Vice versa for player 2. The strong positive feedback both stabilizes the endgame and makes the game enjoyable (or at least not boring) by quickly bringing the foregone conclusion to fruition. Note that if player 2 recovered at some point early in the game, he or she would face exactly the opposite situation because the curves are symmetric (which appeals to our sense of fairness).

Figure 9.3. The hypothetical *Alpine Soccer* game exhibits stable feedback.

Figure 9.3 shows a simple, hypothetical game that demonstrates a stable feedback curve. The game is called *Alpine Soccer* because it is like a soccer game, but it is played on steep hills instead of a flat field. At each end of the field is a goal. A player wins by moving the soccer ball across the field and into his or her opponent's goal. The game is played to a single point, the ball is always kept on the ground, and the field has no width: players can only move back and forth between goals, not side to side.

The steepness curve of the field is critical. The goals and center of the field are in valleys with hills of equal heights between each goal and the center field. Play begins at center field. As a player begins to press toward his or her opponent's goal, the initial going is uphill, and the game aids the losing player. This causes the game to push players back toward center field. Once a player has made a significant advance, however, the playing field levels off and then begins to slope down toward the goal. When a player is close to achieving a goal, the field slopes downward so steeply that it is hard for the ball not to roll, on its own.

Limited or decreasing pieces with success is a mechanism employed in many games to prevent the positive feedback of the player with an early lead suddenly enjoying a disproportionate advantage. That is, it is used to balance the game against slight upsets. As previously mentioned, in *YINSH*, players need to complete three rows of five counters by deploying rings. But after a row is completed, the scoring player loses a ring and several counters. This gives an advantage to the losing player. Any game with nonrenewable resources or a limit on deployable assets inherently uses this mechanic. Examples include the limited number of followers in *Carcassonne*, and a dogfight simulation where ammunition cannot be replenished. As soon as a player uses resources offensively to gain an advantage, he or she also has the disadvantage of relatively fewer resources than the opponent.

9.4.2 Multiple Strategies

There should be more than one way to win the game. That is, there must be multiple paths through the decision tree to victory. It is not necessary to have different winning conditions, although that is one way to design multiple strategies into the game. But there must be different strategies—that is, sequences of choices and moves—that can win. Assume that each player is acting rationally and attempting to achieve the optimal in-game outcome for himself or herself.[4]

There are five relevant mathematical definitions of optimal outcomes, and it is important to understand the distinctions among them. Let each player have some objective and quantitative "utility" value, where it is better for that player to have a high utility than a low one. When economists consider utility, it typically represents money or resources with objective valuation. In a game, utility could be victory points, health, resources, or some combination. The following are the types of optimal outcomes, and what they mean from one player's perspective.

1. **Player optimal outcome.** My utility is as high as possible.
2. **Pareto optimal outcome.** My utility could not be increased without decreasing another player's.
3. **Equitable outcome.** Everyone's utility is the same, and as high as it can be without a disproportionate allocation.
4. **Efficient outcome.** The sum of everyone's utility is as high as it can be, even though mine might be low.
5. **Nash optimal outcome.** My utility is as high as it can be, given that other players acted in their own interests.

Note that some of these "optimal" outcomes are not reachable in a real game with ideal players, since players would have to act against their own interests (or make mistakes) for that outcome to arise. For example, in tic-tac-toe, the game is always a draw and the player optimal outcome of winning can never be realized unless the other player makes an error.

You can relate these definitions to forms of government. The player optimal outcome arises from a selfish monarchy, where everyone works for

[4]In-game rationality is a faulty assumption that we will revisit in the following section, but it is important for analyzing optimal play strategies, even if players choose not to play optimally for out-of-game reasons.

the benefit of the king. A Pareto optimal outcome arises from an efficient communist government that seeks to maximize the total allocation of value. Note that some players may have higher utility than others in this case; it is not necessarily an equitable distribution of utility. The equitable outcome arises from an ethical communist government, where everyone is treated the same even if that leaves some value untapped. A Nash optimal outcome arises from a capitalist democracy, where each player is selfish. In this case, a player's maximum utility is limited by his or her opponents' actions. This is why the Nash outcome is usually the one reached at the end of the game; it accurately models how rational in-game players make decisions.

At the beginning of the game, each player selects a strategy. Recall that by strategy we mean a potentially branching (and potentially randomized) set of decisions, not an explicit set of moves. Because each player is aware of the other's strategic choices, the player selects a strategy that leads to a Nash optimal outcome. If the game is fair, then the player has no advantage from doing so because his or her opponents have made similar choices for symmetric Nash optimal outcomes. As play progresses, each decision is made not by selecting the path that leads to the best player optimal outcome but by choosing the path that leads to the best Nash optimal outcome for that player. In board games, players sometimes even mumble out loud, "If I do this, then you do that, and then I do this...," thinking their way down the decision tree.

To be stable, a game design must have multiple Nash optimal outcomes for all players. It will therefore have multiple Nash equilibria, which are outcomes where each player does as well as possible, given the actions of the other players. Players never intentionally explore the part of the decision tree that leads to non–Nash optimal outcomes for themselves. Note that choices built into the game are worthless if players will never encounter them. So, for stability, we must have multiple viable strategies, arising from different paths to different Nash equilibria. A concrete example follows.

Figure 9.4 shows the full decision tree in a hypothetical two-turn, two-player game. Play begins at the top, with player 1 choosing one of the two solid paths. Player 2 then chooses a dashed path, and play proceeds until each player has made two choices. This game is zero-sum, so the outcomes can be represented by a single score representing the difference between the players.

A zero-sum game has the interesting property that every possible outcome is Pareto optimal; for one player to receive more utility, the other must receive less, so any outcome is the same from a Pareto perspective.

The only equitable outcome in a zero-sum game is a tie. Our game has two, and they are represented by zeros. The player optimal outcomes are +7 and −7. A naive player might try to make decisions that lead to his or

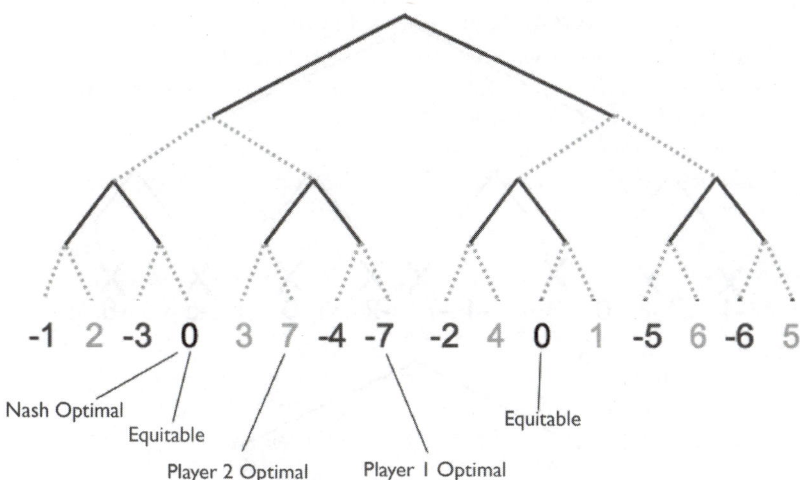

Figure 9.4. A decision tree for a hypothetical two-player game with two choices at each play.

her player-optimal outcome. A strategic thinker will realize that doing so is wishful thinking; the opponent will not collude and help reach that outcome, so there is no reason to strive for it.

For this particular game, there is a single Nash optimal outcome, and it is a tie. This makes the game unstable, and it collapses to degenerate play that will always proceed the same way. Analysis shows how we know there is only one Nash outcome and how we found it.

When thinking strategically in a game such as this, players work *backward* from the outcomes because they are applying minimax. This process is done in their heads, and then they select the forward move in the game that matches their analysis. Figure 9.5 shows this process. We begin at the final 8 branches that lead to the 16 outcomes. It is player 2's turn. Were the game to have come to any of these eight choices, player 2 would always choose the branch that leads to the most positive final score. This means that 8 of the 16 final outcomes are unreachable. The top row of the figure marks each choice that player 2 will *not* take with an "X." You can think of this as playing an inverse game, where instead of making forward choices each player can block a set of paths.

Moving backward through the game and down through the figure rows, it is now player 1's turn. There are 4 situations that player 1 might find himself or herself in, and 8 possible final outcomes (since player 2 has already ruled out the other 8 final outcomes). Note that player 1's player optimal outcome of -7 is already gone from consideration. Player 1 wants to make the final score as negative as possible, so he or she eliminates from consideration 4 of the paths that lead to higher scores.

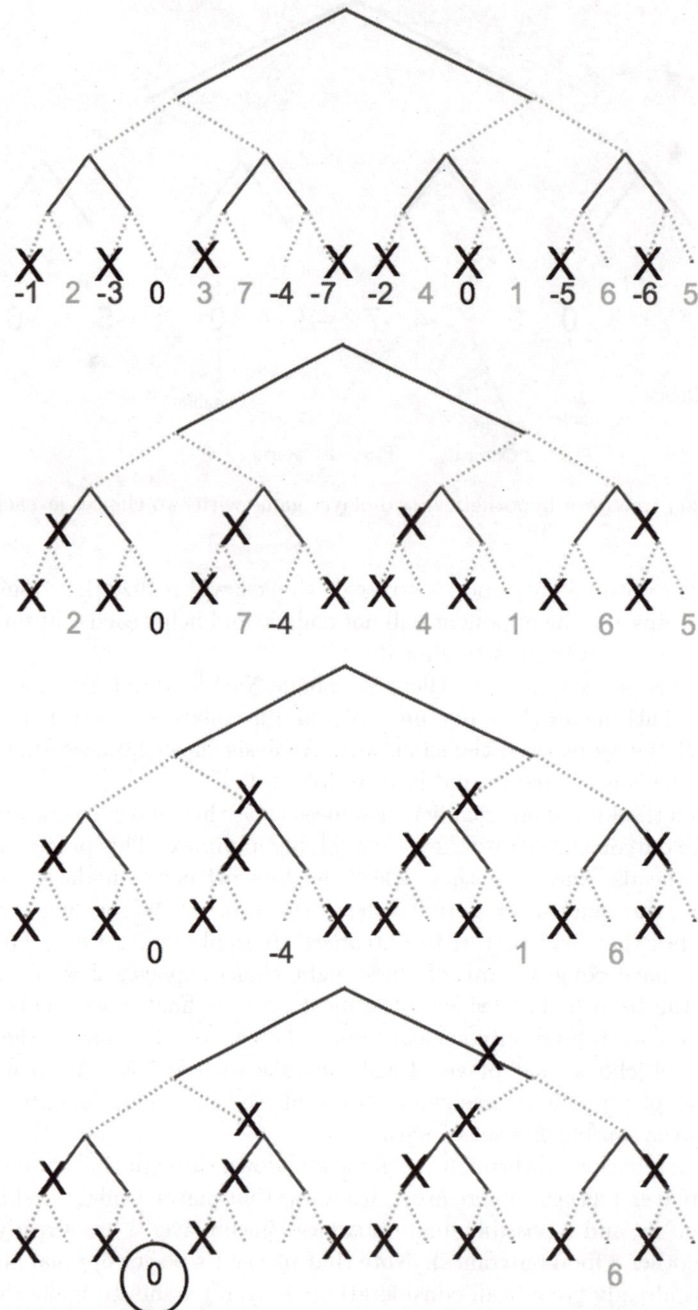

Figure 9.5. Optimal choices for each player, working backward from the outcomes.

This proceeds until the final row of the figure, when there are only two outcomes, 0 and 6, and player 1 chooses the initial path that forces the entire game to result in a tie. That is how we know the Nash equilibrium *and* that our game is unstable.

A final note on Nash equilibria: the equilibria themselves might be unstable. Most games either have a small amount of randomness or so much complexity that players can (effectively randomly) make suboptimal plays on minor decisions. We desire the Nash equilibria to be robust against small amounts of randomness like this. An equilibrium is itself stable, which is required for stable gameplay if it remains a Nash equilibrium even under randomness.

9.5 Engagement

Above and beyond stability and fairness, game mechanics must also be engaging, since *people do not play games to win.* Why don't people care about winning? One could distinguish games from real-life scenarios by the fact that it doesn't really matter if someone wins or loses the game. This must be the case for most games. As a demonstration, multiplayer games show that no rational person who wanted to win would play a game. In a four-person game, three people are going to lose. On average, why would you play a game if you knew that you had a 75 percent chance of losing? The answer is because playing itself is desirable as long as the outcome is uncertain. Likewise, nobody would play a game that you knew you would *always* win. Consider the game where we flip a coin and if it is heads, then you win, and it is tails, you win. Most people wouldn't play that game for enjoyment. Always losing is just as undesirable as always winning.

Games can be engaging without being fun. Like other forms of entertainment, games engage through frustration, anger, sadness, and terror, as well as humor, titillation, and joy. In the context of entertainment, even what are normally negative experiences can become pleasurable and rewarding. In fact, for most games, players spend their time feeling slightly anxious about falling behind, not satisfied about their performance. Games can engage players through tension and tragedy in the same way as plays like *Hamlet* or movies like *Titanic.*

A game that is extremely unfair or unstable will not be engaging. Nonetheless, it is often necessary to make changes for engagement that have the undesirable side-effect of decreasing fairness or stability.

We can learn to create engagement from psychology and the arts: theater, film, literature, and fine arts. Although traditional art elements like a good plot and impressive visuals do make a game more compelling, they should not be the heart of the game and are not necessary for a game to engage players. Games are not a narrative form. Every activity and art is a unique mode of communication, and they each have strengths and weaknesses. You do not expect good visuals from a book or good dialogue in a painting. Because they are interactive, games express ideas and compel emotions that are less accessible in other forms. They are not particularly good at telling stories, but they excel at expressing causality, relationships, and activating nonnarrative parts of the mind. We now look at specific ways that games can engage players.

9.5.1 Flow

Flow is a specific state of mind recognized by psychologists. You've experienced it many times in your life during activities that made you feel focused, creative, and fulfilled. People describe the sensation of flow as being "in the zone" or "losing track of time" and relate it especially to sports, but it can be experienced while working, reading, driving, or, of course, playing a game. Psychologist Mihaly Csikszentmihalyi defined flow as an action with the following eight properties:

1. a challenging activity
2. that requires skill and concentration,
3. with a well-defined goal
4. and a direct response (i.e, feedback, but not in the stability sense),
5. merging of action and awareness,
6. a sense of self-confidence,
7. a loss of self-consciousness, and
8. an altered sense of time.

The first four properties are a natural fit for a game. The second four properties should emerge from the first if the designer avoids elements that disrupt gameplay or demoralize the player. For a video game, responsive controls, minimal loading screens and confirmation dialogs, and an appropriate difficulty level achieve this. For a board game, the physical actions like card sorting and piece movement must be accomplished quickly, and the concentration level must not be excessive.

9.5.2 Pattern Recognition

Small children like to learn. They start as babies, experimenting with everything to try and learn what is food, what is soft, what makes parents happy (and often what makes parents unhappy), and so on. Then they learn to walk and talk, and they continue to learn by piecing together individual forms of evidence to recognize patterns. This is evidence of a deep-seated desire to experiment and find the patterns behind information: a desire to learn. Somewhere along the way to adulthood, we associate learning with undesirable activities, such as homework, tests, and sitting in a classroom. This is evidence that school is not always taught in a manner best suited to the way we learn (or that the topics addressed in schools are not ones that are natural to learn). It is not evidence that learning isn't engaging. Games are an example of where learning is engaging. Learning opportunities are a way to increase a player's enjoyment.

Learning can be narrative in a game, where the player pieces together plot clues. This is the weakest form of learning in a game, since it involves substantial progression and minimal emergence from the game rules.

Recognizing emergent properties is extremely rewarding. When a player recognizes the choke points of a multiplayer map in *Half-Life*, the right combination of units to deflect an attack in *Age of Empires*, or the underlying stone patterns of strength in go, they feel a sense of satisfaction. Just as our brain evolved to reward us with pleasure for eating fat, salt, and sugar (which are critical for life, although overabundant in the modern diet), it also evolved to experience pleasure from learning patterns (which is likely healthy, even in large doses!).

9.5.3 Adversity and Desire

Recognizing a pattern is one kind of achievement. It is overcoming chaos. Game players learn patterns to overcome other obstacles: passing a leader, defeating a boss, or completing a level. These challenges must be genuine and patterns sufficiently complex or obscured. If they are too easy, then players do not value defeating them (this is why the "heads you win, tails you win" game is not engaging). In fact, despite the economists' notion that the value of an object is what others will pay for it, psychologists have found that the value people perceive in an object or experience is based primarily on how hard it was to obtain. This is one of the reasons that fraternities and the military have such rigorous new member training (i.e., hazing): if getting in is challenging then recruits value membership more. Working hard for something makes it seem more valuable, and that increases desire.

Desire itself can provide more engagement than the actual acquisition. We have all had the experience of wanting something—window shopping for an outfit or saving up to buy a favorite toy—and then ignoring the object of our desire within a few days of obtaining it. The engagement of computer role-playing games is based on the fact that wanting is better than achieving. Players in RPGs spend their time planning out their upgrade path and fantasizing about objects and stats. When they actually achieve their next bonus or level up, they soon find themselves longing for the *next* upgrade, and after players reach the level cap, many quit or start the game over rather than play in a world where there is nothing to want.

9.5.4 Empowerment and Value

Games offer fantasy and empowerment. Even a person who has little power or opportunity in his or her real life can be a soldier, a fantasy hero, a rock star, or simply "a winner." This may seem like the primary source of engagement in games, but most of the empowering aspects of games, such as weapons and special abilities, are also engaging because they are part of problem solving and because the player desires them for so long in the game. So it is rarely empowerment alone that is engaging.

Empowerment is the ability to enforce one's will, to make meaningful changes, and to feel valued. Games are about decisions, so they are inherently empowering. They give players the opportunity to make choices. Empowerment is reduced when an opponent or situation decreases the number of choices that are available, so it is important to make players feel challenged without overly constraining them.

It is a basic human emotional need to feel appreciated, accepted, and necessary. Beyond that, there is great satisfaction in knowing that one made the right decision. In multiplayer games, it is important to make each player feel necessary. When there are alliances in the game, this can be accomplished by creating problems that can best (or only) be solved by a specific player. This is done frequently in *Lego Star Wars*, which has areas only reachable by certain characters. It is weak in that game when the necessity is explicit, for example a door with a picture of the unlocking character on it. It is strong when necessity is implicit. An example is a crevasse that is just slightly wider than the normal character's jump distance, so that only R2D2's hovering ability can span it.

Players can be differentiated by their in-game positions or by differing in-game abilities granted through items. This allows everyone to be the hero.

It is specifically *not* necessary to save the world or make other grandiose heroic gestures to feel valued and empowered. Many games use that B-movie plot because it is a convenient setup, but the players do not feel any satisfaction from being *told* that they are heros. Instead, satisfaction comes from having the power to defeat in-game challenges. Note that most good drama doesn't focus on saving-the-world plots but instead has characters resolving more personal struggles: getting into college, leaving a bad relationship, or conquering a personal fear. The journey is more important than the goal, and engaging journeys are all around us.

9.5.5 Dramatic Elements

The elements that make a novel, play, or film engaging are also good candidates for enhancing the inherent engagement of the mechanics. In a game with a strong narrative, these techniques relate directly. In a game that does not rely on narrative, dramatic elements are still possible, but they must emerge rather than being planted and are generally abstract.

A narrative game (or one in which exploration is a physical analog of narrative) must have interesting characters, conflict, and resolution. It might use a twist or revelation halfway through to reverse the conflict.

When working with conflict, or empowerment for that matter, it is important to periodically release tension. This prevents fatigue and allows the player to escape the need to endlessly escalate. It's the same as driving a car too fast or riding a roller coaster. If you move fast in a straight line with your eyes closed, it doesn't feel any different from moving slowly. In an airplane, you are moving about 900 km/h, but if you close your eyes, it feels like you are standing still. However, when the airplane takes off, you do feel a difference. Sports cars and amusement park rides depend on acceleration, not velocity, for the sensation of speed. If you are speeding up, slowing down, or turning, you feel the acceleration. When simply moving in a straight line at constant speed, you don't feel the same excitement. Remove powerful tools from the player or relieve narrative tension (e.g., with humor or resolving subplots) to decelerate conflict in the game. Then you can accelerate again by increasing the player's power or the plot suspense. Two acceleration periods feels faster than a long time at constant velocity.

People like attractive images and pleasant music. Both video and board games use these as rewards and ways to increase the aesthetic of the experience as a whole. Praise and reward your players when they make good decisions. Flavor text and creative names on in-game items, physical miniatures for board games, cutscenes, exciting in-game animations, and triumphant music all reward the player.

9.6 The Role of Randomness

Randomness can be a powerful tool for game development when carefully applied. It introduces mixed strategies, limits the how far players can (and, therefore, *must*) plan, and creates suspense through the possibility of an upset or comeback. Suspense is a major factor in engagement. The other two aspects impact fairness and stability.

It is important to note that randomness is not required in games. Plenty of games, from first-person shooters like *Crysis* to board games like checkers, have no mechanics that rely on randomness. Unless specifically designing a game where randomness is key to the central mechanic, it is best to start without randomness and then selectively introduce it to address balance problems that arise from the other mechanics in the game.

Recall from Chapter 7 that a strategy is a player's plan of action for the game and that a mixed strategy is one where the player himself or herself must choose randomly. For example, in the prisoner's dilemma, the optimal strategy is the mixed strategy of choose randomly between colluding and backstabbing. Choosing one action deterministically gives the other player an advantage because he or she can exploit the deterministic action. The same is true of video games. In *Age of Empires*, a player who consistently rushes will rarely win because other players will brace for the rush. But a player who is known to never rush will also rarely win, because his or her opponents will never hold back resources to hedge against a rush. In *Counter-Strike* most maps, like the warehouse-based "Assault," have two ways of approaching the goal. Consistently favoring one or the other is a losing strategy because it is predictable. The key is to choose the strategy randomly (and with probability proportional to its chance of success) so the other players cannot predict and exploit deterministic behavior. Employing a mixed strategy is a player's use of randomness, but it can arise in response to randomness in the game.

The key to randomness in design is controlling variance. When the variance is too low, players approximately know the outcome of random events, and the randomness may be an annoyance but has no impact on strategy. This arises sometimes in *Dungeons & Dragons* when a player need only roll a 2 or higher on 1d20 to score a hit because his or her attack modifier is large. Likewise, rolling 6d20 is silly because the outcome has a very high probability of being close to the expected value, $6 \times 11.5 = 69$.

When variance is too high, strategy is irrelevant, and players lose interest in the game because they have no control. A failure of randomness is evident in *Settlers of Catan.* There, a die roll determines who moves first. For good players, the game is largely decided by the first two moves, so the game is uninteresting because it is not fair. The outcome is determined by a die roll and not by the quality of a player's moves. Randomly choosing the first player isn't the real problem. The problem is that the first two moves are so crucial. This makes the game unfair and unstable. Fortunately, the rest of the gameplay is so engaging that the game has succeeded, although many advanced players abandon it for games without this problem.

It is easy for the strategy in a game to be too complex. In a completely deterministic game (that is, one that has no randomness), players can perfectly plan their moves all the way to the end of the game. Yet, few of us have either the cognitive ability or desire to play in such a mechanical style.

> *Randomness* is a way of relieving players of the burden of searching very far into the decision tree.

When random events can affect the game in a meaningful way, it is only worth planning a few steps ahead. This relieves players of choosing to play a winning versus an entertaining strategy. Classic abstract strategy games like chess and go require looking ahead five or even ten moves to play at a serious level. *Carcassonne*, *Dungeons & Dragons*, and *World of Warcraft* support tactical and strategic thought but limit its scope. As a result, the abstract strategy games like chess are treated much more like a professional sport (with rankings, tournaments, and ladders) or intellectual study, whereas the games with randomness are a pastime and social entertainment.

9.7 What Players Value

When considering fairness and stability, we took a strategic approach inspired by classic economic game theory. This was done with the caveat that players don't act in a rational way: players do not always make the best choices for winning. Understanding what players really value is the way to adapt that logical framework to the real world of players' complicated motivations.

If players don't value winning, then what do they value? A contractor playing golf with his or her client values the *client* enjoying the experience (and thus presumably signing off on a new project). A parent playing *Scrabble* with his or her child values the *child* enjoying the experience and the child learning strategy, spelling, and arithmetic. A group of college friends playing *Mario Kart* on a sofa values *everyone* enjoying the experience. Maybe one of those friends is possibly hoping another will find him attractive and want to go out to dinner afterward as well. He might intentionally throw the game to help her win, or try extra hard to win in order to impress her. When people play games face-to-face, the participants primarily value the entertainment experience. They also have secondary personal agendas, where one player might be willing to sacrifice his or her own satisfaction from the game itself to make another player's experience more satisfying.

When designing a game, it is important to avoid making players choose between an enjoyable play style and a successful play style. For example, consider a game like *Settlers of Catan*, where a player can track his or her opponents' hidden hand of cards by carefully monitoring and recording trades between them. Doing so is not particularly engaging because it is a menial task that brings the player out of flow and slows down the game. It is better with a mechanic like this to design the game with all cards public. In *Settlers* there isn't any true partial information, there are only natural limits on how much public information a player can practically retain. Likewise, if a player could win a game by a slow and tedious strategy, it is better to alter the rules so this strategy is not viable. That way, the player doesn't have to choose between boring play and risking losing. The targeted use of randomness to limit how far players can usefully think ahead is an example of avoiding the conflict between enjoyable and successful play.

Players experience a small entertainment value from leading or winning the game. However, making periodically rewarding good choices seems to be more satisfying than winning the entire game. So some aspect of their utility function is therefore related to selecting an objectively good strategy. It isn't whether they win or lose, but how they play the game that these players care about.

Players care much more about social harmony. It is important to ensure that everyone has a good time because the "metagame" of real life continues after play ends, and satisfaction or dissatisfaction—and agreements and arguments—experienced in the game will carry over not just into the next play session but into future social interactions. Given the choice of making a move that will greatly anger another player or a less strategic move that maintains social harmony, most players will choose the weaker move. Of course, everyone understands that they are opponents in the game and that competition there is socially acceptable. But making a move that increases your own chance of winning by robbing another player of enjoyment (e.g., kicking him or her out of a multiplayer game in the first few rounds) is usually unacceptable.

This is why cheating is rarely a problem in board games. If we consider cheating from a game theory perspective, it makes sense to cheat when you believe that the change to your chance of winning is greater than the chance of being caught and therefore forced to forfeit. In a social context where harmony is more important than winning, cheating is a bad strategy because it does not optimize the true utility.

The desire for social harmony, personal relation agendas, and for everyone to have equal enjoyment fades in the presence of online games between players who have no relationship outside the game. Here, winning is still rarely the player's true goal. Players want to maximize their own entertainment value. Empowerment seems to be a key motivating factor here, where players seek power even if not for the goal of winning and even if it substantially degrades the experience of other players. There is often a mischievous, or perhaps sadistic, desire to thwart other players. In an online game, this is not tempered by social relationships as in a face-to-face game. Thus, players may abandon their own team in multiplayer games (called "going Rambo") or choose an intentionally disruptive play style. Some online games introduce mechanics where players can eject those who go too far and seriously detract from group enjoyment.

Between face-to-face and anonymous online games lie online games with friends and clan games. Clans are teams that persist between sessions, analogous to sports teams. Online games with friends play much more like face-to-face games. Clan games play like professional sports, where engagement and personal enjoyment are irrelevant and the team is focused solely on winning.

9.8 Optimizing for Real People

We previously saw that a well-balanced game has multiple Nash equilibria. That analysis assumed that players cared about winning. If we step back to the metagame where players care about personal and group entertainment, the analysis becomes more complex. Here, a good game keeps everyone entertained. Part of that is still maintaining multiple Nash equilibria for the underlying strategy. But for the entire game, we actually want most of those Nash equilibria to also be Pareto (or ideally, egalitarian) optimal, taking entertainment into account. That is, we want the strategies that lead a player to winning to also be the strategies that result in all players being entertained and achieving social harmony.

Consider the case of "camping," which is where one player in an FPS holes up in a protected area with a sniper rifle and picks off other players. This is a good strategy for that player. He or she is exposed to little risk and exercises a lot of power. This is the reason military and police employ snipers in the real world: doing so is a winning strategy. If we consider the in-game outcome matrix where the strategic choice is to camp or not, it looks like this:

		Player 1's Choice	
		No Camp	Camp
Player 2's Choice	No Camp	Decided by other mechanics	1 Wins
	Camp	2 Wins	Stalemate

The choices here are similar to those in the prisoner's dilemma. If the players collude, then they both do well, but each player has an advantage for seeming to collude and then actually turning traitor. The Nash equilibria depend on the factors involved in the noncamping combat, and the optimal strategy is a mixed one. For many games, camping is the optimal Nash strategy, which makes the Nash equilbrium a stalemate.

However, taking engagement into account, we see that the true outcomes are different:

		Player 1's Choice	
		No Camp	Camp
Player 2's Choice	No Camp	Both Happy	1: Smug, 2: Mad
	Camp	1: Mad, 2: Smug	Both Bored

In each outcome box, player 1's emotional state is on the left, and player 2's emotional state is on the right. The box on the lower right is the Nash equilibrium. It is actually the worst possible outcome because it *minimizes* the sum of the players' utility. As game designers, we would like to drive players toward the equitable and Pareto optimal square in the top left, where both players are satisfied.

Complicating the analysis is that we must consider out-of-game decisions. Remember that players are not required to play the game. Their first decision is whether to play at all. Throughout the game, they continually reevaluate whether to keep playing. A player annoyed by a camper may simply quit the game session or quit playing the game altogether. When we take this out-of-game choice into account, we find that the outcome landscape has shifted to that in Figure 9.6. Here, the number of suboptimal equilbria has exploded, and they correspond to Nash equilibria.

It is therefore essential for engagment to introduce mechanisms that decrease the in-game effectiveness of camping. *Unreal Tournament 2004* altered its sniper rifle to cast a colored beam of light (matching *Quake*'s lightning gun) instead of an invisible bullet. This reveals the camper's location, decreasing his protection. Individual-level maps are designed so that there is no location from which it is safe to camp, which, combined with revealing

Optimal Equilibrium

	No Camp	Camp	No Play
No Camp	Happy, Happy	Mad, Smug	Bored, Bored
Camp	Smug, Mad	Bored, Bored	Bored, Bored
No Play	Bored, Bored	Bored, Bored	Bored, Bored

Sub optimal Equilibria

Figure 9.6. Camping analysis including out-of-game choices.

the camper's location, means that camping is no longer a player's optimal strategy. In *Medal of Honor* sniping is essential to the WW2 theme, so the designers kept it in the game but designed maps to offer few safe havens for snipers.

Other games have introduced in-game voting to ban players who camp or removed sniper rifles; several *Half-Life* mods like *Counter-Strike* offer both options to server administrators. An alternative is to drastically reduce the ammunition available to campers so they must leave their blinds to get more ammunition.

9.9 Exercises

1. What are the three elements to balance?
2. Name a (nonmod, nonexpansion pack) game that was probably designed by modifying an existing game, and why you think that was the process employed. (Please do not use examples listed in the chapter.)
3. Why do designers add randomness to their games?
4. What is utility (in the game-theory sense)?
5. Choose one of the games and briefly argue why it is or is not fair.
    - *Apples to Apples*
    - *Settlers of Catan*
    - *Puerto Rico*
    - *Halo* multiplayer
    - *Halo* single-player
    - *Halo* co-op
    - *Metroid*
    - *Meteos*
6. Briefly argue why poker is or is not stable.
7. In international tournament chess, a decisive game awards 1 point to the winner and 0 points to the loser. A draw awards 1/2 point to each. In contrast to this, the FIFA soccer rules for the World Cup award 3 points for a win, 1 point to each team for a draw, and 0 points for a loss. If chess tournaments were played using the soccer scoring rules, how would that affect the players' metastrategies for when to accept a draw?

8. Describe three games (or parts of games) that are engaging but not fun.

9. What are some nonviolent, nonfinancial ways to empower a player character?

10. Describe the effective use of dramatic elements in one progressive game.

11. Describe the effective use of dramatic elements in one abstract strategy game.

12. Consider the mechanic of trading and deal making, such as that used in *Settlers of Catan* and *Monopoloy.* Describe how it interacts with fairness, stability, and engagement.

13. Consider the mechanics of a specific superpowerful weapon, such as the air strike or Redeemer in *Unreal Tournament*, the Terran battle-cruiser in *StarCraft*, the Onos in *Natural Selection*, or the Cathedral tile in *Carcassonne.* Describe the mechanics that you chose as it interacts with fairness, stability, and engagement.

14. Choose one of the following games, and describe the factors in a typical player's utility function when playing it. Include both in-game and out-of-game elements.

    - *Shadows Over Camelot*
    - Chess
    - *Connect Four*
    - *Defcon*
    - *Counter-Strike*
    - *Karaoke Revolution*
    - Poker
    - *Twister*
    - *Elixir*
    - *Tetris*

15. (a) Describe a commercial game that creates tension between choices that are good in-game and choices that are good given the broader perspective of the world outside the game.

    (b) How would you balance this game to reconcile the in-game and out-of-game choices?

9.10 Resources

- Koster, *A Theory of Fun for Game Design* [Koster 04].
- Juul, *Half-Real* [Juul 05].
- Csikszentmihalyi, *Flow: The Psychology of Optimal Experience* [Csikszentmihalyi 90].
- Salen and Zimmerman, *Rules of Play: Game Design Fundamentals* [Salen and Zimmerman 03].
- Rollings and Morris, *Game Architecture and Design* [Rollings and Morris 99].
- Fullerton, Swain, and Hoffman, *Game Design Workshop* [Fullerton et al. 04].

CHAPTER 10

Mechanics

Terms Explained: *Character – Dialogue Tree – Handicap – Real-Time Strategy (RTS) – Role-Playing Game (RPG) – Technology Tree – Turn-Based Game*

Once the basis of the game has been established and is found to be engaging, it is time to fit mechanics to the fiction and start seeking balance. When working from fiction, the process of inserting mechanics may change the fiction substantially. Often it is necessary to reduce complexity or remove large fiction elements at this stage as well. For an abstract game, the designer may even begin the design at the mechanics stage and forgo fiction development entirely.

A game designer has two different intellectual toolboxes that he or she opens to fit mechanics into a game and achieve balance. The first toolbox is filled with common design patterns that appear in many games. These patterns are common mechanics, groups of mechanics, and parts of mechanics. The patterns are to the game designer what arpeggios, key signatures, chord progressions, and harmonies are to the composer. A designer combines these predesigned pieces. Each addresses specific kinds of problems that occur or simulates common ideas from fiction. By working from relatively large pieces of design and within common frameworks, the designer avoids some of the pitfalls of starting from scratch. He or she can also more clearly relate the new game to existing ones and thereby benefit from related work.

The designer's second toolbox contains analysis tools. We've already seen many of these. Chapter 7 introduced the decision tree (and its one-choice equivalent: the outcome matrix from Chapter 9), the plot graph, the state machine, and curves and tables. Chapter 8 explained how to use probability to analyze common game situations involving randomness, and Chapter 9 introduced various definitions of optimal outcomes. In this chapter, we'll introduce more methods for diagramming mechanics.

This chapter describes frequently employed mechanics and explains how they impact stability, fairness, and engagement. The importance here is not learning the ad hoc names of the mechanics but learning the technique of analyzing mechanics and how these common ones impact gameplay. You have probably observed most of these mechanics yourself but may not have considered their direct impact on the structure of the game. Some mechanics, like racing against time, are so straightforward that they need little explanation. The ones selected are therefore common, yet require a bit more explanation to appreciate some of the subtleties.

The primary message of this chapter is that there are no small decisions in mechanic design and balancing. The choice of how fast a button must be pressed, or the relative point values of corn and wheat can be the difference between success and failure of a game. This is not to say that most mechanics are terribly sensitive. Often there is a large range of values for which gameplay will still function. The issue is that if any one mechanic is outside of its balanced range, then the entire game will break. Think of the mechanics as links in an iron chain. Each link can take a lot of battery, but if one link breaks, the entire chain fails.

Throughout this chapter (and in many other places in this book), we say "character" to distinguish game pieces from the player controlling them. You could interpret this as a literal character—that is, a virtual person controlled by a player—but in almost all cases, "character" is meant in the general sense of the player's pieces. That is, it may also be an abstract piece, such as a chess pawn, or a set of pieces, such as an *Age of Empires* civilization, or even a *Magic: The Gathering* deck of cards.

10.1 Techniques for the First Move

Most turn-based games end immediately when a player reaches some goal. This creates a slight unfair advantage for the player who moves first at the beginning of the game. A number of mechanics are available for addressing this advantage.

10.1.1 Completing the Round

One remedy is to require that play completes the last round, even if one player has already reached the end condition. This gives another player a chance to tie. This last round is typically less engaging than the rest of the game because endgame upsets can be rare in a stable game where the players should not be that close together in score.

Puerto Rico and *Citadels* both have this mechanic. It is made viable by the inclusion of buildings (power-ups) in the game that grant points based on other properties, such as points proportional to the number of deployed workers. If a player has such a building, using his or her last turn to deploy new workers can create a meaningful point shift at the end. Such items must be carefully designed so a shift cannot destabilize and allow a player who is not close to the leader to suddenly win. These games also leverage another interesting mechanic. The end condition of the game is not the same as the victory condition. One player can cause the game to end, but another might win.

10.1.2 Explicit Handicaps

A disadvantage (handicap) applied to the player who moves first that exactly compensates for the advantage of moving first can rebalance a turn-based game. This also helps stabilize the game by not granting a double advantage to the player who makes a particularly good first move.

Many board games restrict the number of choices available on the first move. For example, *Pro Pente* forces the first player to play in the center of the board, and *Othello* restricts the first move to near the center of the board. Another approach is to explicitly grant points to the second player, as in go. This can also be used to make a game between unequal players more fair. The handicapping system in go grants players points according to their relative rankings as well as who moved first; the goal is that players should win about 50 percent of the time, despite differences in ability.

Having the weakest player move first is one way to make a differing-ability handicap act as a first-move disadvantage. It is poorly balanced but is simple and elegantly resolves the "who moves first?" dilemma. The weakest player can be identified heuristically as the loser from the previous play session or the youngest player. *Ticket to Ride: Europe* has the player who has visited the fewest European countries play first because a familiarity with European geography is a small advantage.

10.1.3 Implicit Handicaps

Under mechanics where revealing one's strategy early is a disadvantage, there is an implicit handicap to moving first that offsets the one-turn head start. This is also true in multiplayer games, where players are likely to form alliances against the leader. For example, in *Carcassonne*, the player who moves first is likely to be subverted by others who see his or her initial feature placement and either try to steal ownership of that feature or build the board in the opposite direction.

It is also possible to make the first move inherently undesirable. In *Cartegena*, players move by leapfrogging one another. The first player both has no other player to leapfrog and is establishing a path for the following players.

In *Scrabble*, the player with the first turn has no words to build from, so the player has both fewer points available and is forced to make an entire word from his or her letters. This is so significant of a disadvantage that the designer granted a compensating advantage in the form of double points for the first move.

10.1.4 Random

Choosing the first player randomly is unfair for a single game, but, on average, it is fair over a large number of games. In tournaments, it is therefore fair to play an even number of games with alternating first players (deciding the first randomly). In casual play, it is acceptable to choose the first player randomly if it is understood that the same group will play the game again in the future.

10.2 Character Building

Taking "character" in the broad view of a virtual person, a piece, an army, or any in-game manifestation of the player's force, character building is the process of building or customizing that force. Introducing this mechanic requires a system in which a great degree of customization is available to the player. It is used primarily in emergent games because few strongly progressive games can tolerate the variance introduced by customized characters. In an emergent system, objects in the world are defined by a set of properties. The properties of an object, such as weight, damage caused, cost, and physical appearance, implicitly define how that object interacts with other objects. Players collect these objects to empower themselves within the game. It is important that the rules are robust to objects being combined in unusual ways. This requirement makes character-building systems hard to balance.

The character-building mechanic turns simulations (of quests or combat) into extremely expressive puzzle games. Although players may technically be competing against one another or an in-game opponent, their strategies are in some ways against the game itself as they try to maximize their character's power, like a puzzle.

10.2.1 RPG

The strongest manifestation of character building is seen in role-playing games. Role-playing games (RPGs) originated as an interactive storytelling board game. These so-called tabletop (or pen-and-paper) RPGs evolved complicated mechanics primarily for combat, such as the statistical combat mechanic described later in this chapter. Computer RPGs (cRPGs) generally ignore the freeform storytelling aspect and focus on statistical combat, thus making the "role-playing" aspect minimal at best, but the name remains. Even for those without statistical combat, the core mechanic of an RPG is character building.

A fantasy game like *Neverwinter Nights* uses character building to influence constants in a statistical combat system. Collectible card games like *Pokemon* let players build a custom card deck that has varying properties. These systems generally need some notion of the value of an arbitrary configuration to ensure fairness. This is typically the number of points, cards, or in-game currency used to purchase the combination of objects and upgrades.

The primary engagement from a character-building mechanic is the craving or desire for items as puzzle-solving tools and the planning that this leads to. Players spend most of their time struggling to obtain new items. Games like *World of Warcraft* and *Diablo* are often called "addictive" because of the level of craving that they inspire in players. This is inherent in the mechanics and is what the game is really about at some level. The obstacles that the built character will encounter are typically there to motivate character building more than they are present to provide interesting gameplay in themselves. Put differently, character building is usually a strategic element of gameplay, and actually using the character is only tactical.

A second level of engagement comes from the fiction associated with items. *Diablo* is particularly famous for its item names, and most RPG card games like *Magic* and *Munchkin* are similarly well known for their flavor text. Wielding the Storm King's Death Hammer is just more attractive to most of us than arming our characters with a generic "+4 attack bonus." In many cases, this trumps the utility, but not the planning, from an engagement perspective. We can see that the fiction and planning are stronger than the deployment by considering games like *Little Big World* and *Karaoke Revolution*. These allow the players to highly customize their character's appearance and reward in-game success with new outfits and props. These capture most of the enjoyment of character building, even though the character's configuration lends no in-game advantage; it is purely cosmetic. This is not to say that character building is the primary mechanic in those games, and in fact, it is not. The point is that if character building were engaging primarily because of the deployment possibilities, then character building would not have been a popular element of games where there is no in-game advantage to character differences.

10.2.2 RTS and the Technology Tree

Real-time strategy (RTS) video games (and the now less popular turn-based games) extend character building to whole armies and civilizations. The basic mechanic is the same, but because of the scope of these games, it is difficult for a player to manage a wealth of individual statistics. Instead, these games tend to discretize upgrade choices along what is known as a technology or "tech" tree.

The tech tree represents the upgrades that a player has and those that are available. The player may only acquire new upgrades if the parent upgrade in the tech tree has already been obtained. Often there are multiple trees, or the player is allowed to upgrade multiple children of the same parent under certain circumstances. Otherwise, only a single upgrade path would be allowed per game, which limits the emergent capabilities of the system. However, to create strategic differentiation between players, many tree ver-

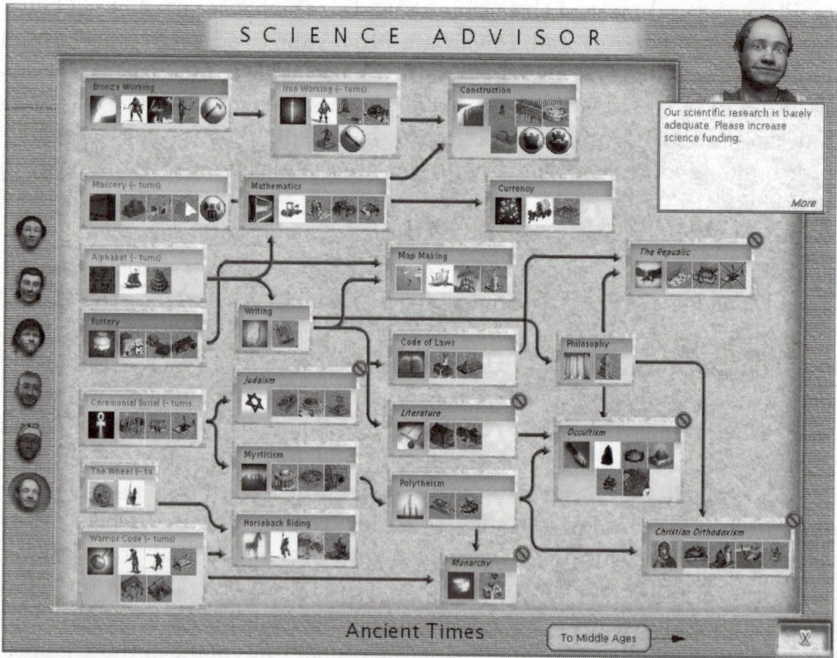

Figure 10.1. Ancient science technology tree in *Civilization*. (Image courtesy of 2K Games/Firaxis)

tices force a player to choose, at most, one of its children. This restricted choice might be explicit, as it is in *Natural Selection: Combat*, where the other children are not available after an upgrade. It might also be implicit, as it is in *Age of Empires*, where the player simply does not have enough resources to broadly acquire upgrades across the tree.

Figure 10.1 shows a small part of the very large tech tree from *Civilization*. In this figure, the root is on the left, and the leaves are on the right. This graph is not a tree in the strict mathematical sense. It is actually a DAG, where some vertices can be reached along multiple paths.

For engagement purposes, it is important to prevent players from either running out of upgrade levels or expanding too broadly in the tree. That is because the engagement of character building will be lost if the player's desire to explore new combinations or acquire many items is sated by a glut of upgrades. One way to prevent players from obtaining too many upgrades is to place a very powerful superunit at the leaves. If one player reaches the end of the tree, he or she will have so much power that he or she can quickly win the game. This prevents that player from exercising that power long enough for the novelty to wear off and also prevents him or her from broadening out in the other areas of the tree.

10.3 Action

Twitch, action, and arcade are different terms for a class of mechanics that depend on real-world agility to achieve in-game goals. Although there are a few real-time board games that reward some level of agility, action is primarily exercised in the domain of video games.

10.3.1 Avoidance

The simplest form of action is avoidance. From classic games like *Asteroids* to newer titles like *Fight Night*, defensively ducking and dodging requires the player to demonstrate both in-game environmental awareness of threats and correct timing to avoid them.

Driving games primarily combine obstacle avoidance with more fine-tuned vehicle control mechanics like controlled skids and shifting gears. Although a game like *Burnout* or *Mario Kart* essentially involves vehicles moving only small distances relative to one another, their interactions are made interesting by placing the action on a long track with obstacles. Obstacles are in the road or project from the curbs. One could also view the curbs themselves as obstacles. When negotiating a curve, from the car's reference frame, the vehicle is staying in place and the curb is swinging wildly in and must be avoided. In fact, older racing games represented the track in the program's state as a long obstacle that moved towards the car, instead of an area that the car moves around.

10.3.2 Shooting

Shooting takes many forms in games. The simplest is instant-hit (or "hit-scan") weapon simulation, where firing at the instant that the target crosses the line of fire ensures a hit. This is used for beam weapons like lasers and for fast-moving projectiles like sniper bullets. Instant-hit weapons are the easiest to simulate because they do not require additional state for tracking projectiles. Instant hit is also the simplest for players because it requires very little sophistication in planning the attack. Aiming slightly ahead of the target, known as "leading" the target, may be required to account for the player's reaction time, but otherwise the player simply lines up the crosshairs and presses the button. With slower projectile weapons, the lead distance must be significant to account for the particle's travel time. This requires more skill from the attacker and gives the target the opportunity for evasion.

Shooting is empowering, which is one component of engagement. It also acts as a ranged weapon, which allows attackers to avoid exposing themselves to direct counterattack if cover is available. When doing so is imbalancing because it allows the attacker too great of an advantage, the graphic representation of the attack can counter this. As mentioned in Chapter 9, *Unreal Tournament* switched from an invisible instant-hit sniper rifle attack to a visible-beam weapon (mimicking *Quake*'s lightning gun) for *Unreal Tournament 2004* to help prevent snipers from camping without defenders knowing the source of the attacks.

Ammunition can be used to balance different kinds of shooting attacks. Limiting ammunition is another way to force attackers to come into the open. Limiting the product of ammunition and damage caused by a weapon helps to balance the damage per clip that is available. In situations where ammunition is readily available, the expected damage per unit time from a weapon is as follows:

$$
\begin{aligned}
E[\text{dmg/attack}] &= P(\text{hit}) * (\text{single attack dmg}) \\
E[\text{dmg/time}] &= E[\text{dmg/attack}] * \frac{1 \text{ attack}}{\frac{(\text{clip size})}{(\text{rate of fire})} + (\text{reload time})},
\end{aligned}
$$

where $P(\text{hit})$ is the probability that a given attack will be successful due to the combination of the player's skill and situational factors. If this expected rate of damage dealt is constant across all weapons, then no one weapon will be universally the most powerful. Instead, players will make a strategic choice of weapon based on their own skills, the tactical layout, and factors such as ammunition availability, range (see Section 10.9), and extraordinary factors such as secondary weapon abilities. Beyond the strategic issues, designers can make shooting more engaging with bright muzzle flashes, ejecting shells, and sound effects that heighten the sense of empowerment.

Limitations, such as a long reload time, can become tension building and entertaining by well-scripted animations. The *DOOM* shotgun reload features the character's entire first-person arm reaching into the frame, slamming shells into the chamber, and cocking the weapon. This animation is generally seen as desirable by players because it is cinematic and makes the weapon feel powerful. This occurs even though the reload time is actually a significant drawback of using that weapon.

10.3.3 Jumping

Donkey Kong and *Mario Bros.* popularized jumping as an action mechanic. Jumping is used as a means of negotiating obstacles such as pits, as a method of locomotion, as a defense against incoming projectiles, and as an offense when enemies can be squished on landing. Although side-scrolling platformers remain a popular genre (particularly on handheld consoles), jumping in 3D games is frequently integrated into movement puzzles.

The *Half-Life* series is famous, or infamous, depending on the player's skill, for its jumping puzzles. These involve executing a series of well-timed jumps to reach difficult locations. Figure 10.2 shows one jumping sequence in *Half-Life 2* from the first-person perspective from a play guide on the Internet.

Jumping in most games is modeled with significantly different physics than in the real world. This is because real-world physics would be poorly balanced. They are hard to control (removing engagement) and operate too fast. In the real world, once a person has left the ground, his or her center of mass must move in a parabolic arc. The person's horizontal velocity will remain constant until landing, whereas the vertical velocity decreases at a constant rate until the apex and then increases again until (for landing on level ground) it is exactly opposite the take-off velocity. Video games tend to introduce some or all of the following unrealistic elements to motion.

Constant vertical velocity. Instead of a realistic arc, with constant vertical velocity the player's motion follows a straight line to the apex and then a straight line down. This keeps the player from accelerating too fast when falling, makes it easier for players to predict the path, and makes it (marginally) easier to simulate.

Running vertical jump. In the real world, a running jump achieves increased horizontal velocity and therefore increased travel distance. However, it does not increase vertical velocity. You can jump just as high from standing as when running at maximum speed, except for some small spring effects in the leg muscles. Yet, because many people believe that a running jump achieves greater height, games often allow a running character to jump higher than a character who is not running.

In some cases, the running jump also increases the tactical applications of jumping. For example, skating games like *Jet Grind Radio* and *Tony Hawk's Proving Ground* need to prevent players from simply hopping over key obstacles when immediately adjacent to them. If that were possible, the players could avoid the more complicated race paths that lead to key obstacles, which would shortcut the other skating mechanics. By increasing jump height with horizontal velocity, they force the player to approach such barriers at maximum speed.

Speed boost. FPS engines, particularly the *Half-Life* one, have historically allowed characters to move faster when in the air than on the ground. This

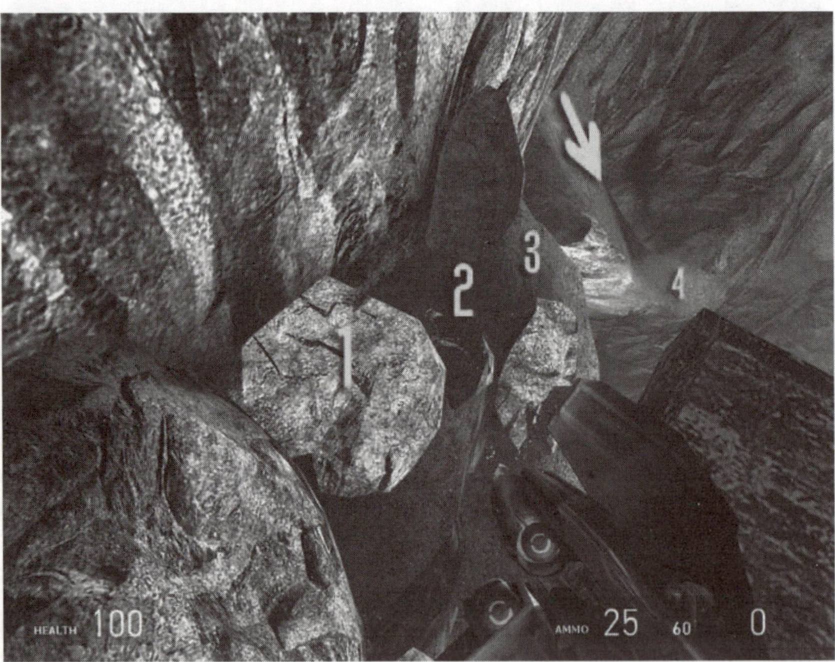

Figure 10.2. Walkthrough of the solution to a jumping puzzle in *Half-Life 2*. From http://www.visualwalkthroughs.com/halflife2/ourbenefactors/ourbenefactors.htm. (Image courtesy of Mike Mangold/Visual Walkthroughs)

is plausible because a jumping character can trade vertical elevation for increased distance by diving into the jump. This creates the tactic where in-game it makes sense to continually jump ("bunny hop") instead of run, since the maximum velocity stays high. This is a balance problem because the optimal strategy contradicts the fiction and thereby decreases engagement. For example, *Counter-Strike* matches are typically full of terrorist characters hopping their way to a bomb site, like bunny terrorists. In the real world, one cannot make a sequence of jumps like this because of the extreme stress on leg muscles and fatigue.

Game engines often mimic fatigue by slowing a player's initial movement after landing or limiting the speed boost to the first jump (which *Half-Life* actually does; the problem is that players have learned to exactly time the interval between jumps). Yet fatigue is frustrating in a virtual world because it feels like a loss of control, so there remains a tension between engagement and strategy.

Air control. Although in the real world you cannot change the arc of your center of mass while in the air, in many games, players have a small degree of control over their motion during a jump. This enables them to steer toward a safe landing or push away from an obstacle. Taking control away from the player dramatically reduces engagement, so this concession to balance is often satisfying. Many car-racing games (e.g., *Excite Truck*) allow air control as an unrealistic way of tilting the vehicle in preparation for landing to make the jumping action more complex and exciting.

An extreme example of the problems of removing air control can be seen in the few games that have entirely eliminated jumping. The original *DOOM* game had no way of jumping. As one of the first 3D games, that felt reasonable at the time but now is dated and feels unreasonable because the character cannot reach certain low ledges. The original *Rogue Spear* Tom Clancy game had no jumping because the SWAT and counterterrorist teams featured in it would never jump (or even run) in a real-world tactical situation. However, since jumping is ingrained in the gamer culture, this felt limiting to many players.

Air jump. Many fighting and some FPS games (e.g., *Lego Star Wars*, *Unreal Tournament 2004*) allow players to make a single additional jump while they are still in the air. There is no physical basis for this at all, but executing a double-jump correctly adds a level of skill and martial arts fiction above the basic jump mechanic.

Wall jump. In the real world, it is possible, but difficult, to jump from one vertical wall to another and continue to gain elevation as long as there is sufficient friction between the feet and the wall. Jackie Chan popularized this in his Hong Kong action films. Many games (e.g., *God of War*, *Super Mario 64*) added this to the basic jumping mechanic to match martial arts fiction and add additional skill moves to jumping puzzles.

10.4 Lock-and-Key

The core mechanic of adventure games is the locked door and the key that the player must find to open it. Although the locked door is sometimes literal, it is more often represented by alternative fiction to add narrative elements: the farmer whose chickens must be rounded up before he'll let you in his barn, the witch who requires a specific component for the potion you desire, the rubble-blocked passage that cannot be cleared without explosives, and so on.

These locks become more interesting when several are nested, chained, or interlaced. Players accumulate a stack of subquests that each need to be completed to return to the next-larger project. Locks allow a designer to reuse areas of the game world during play by changing what is available at different times. One interesting way to do this is with implicit locks. An example is *Metroid*, where some areas are inaccessible simply because they are too high to jump to or are beyond environmental hazards that can only be reached later, when new abilities are available. These implicit locks are more elegant than an explicit door because they allow the player to solve the puzzle instead of jumping through an explicit hoop; they lend a sense of discovery as well as achievement.

In a multiplayer cooperative game, new lock possibilities are available. For example, a door that remains open only while *another* player stands on a pedestal or nuclear-launch-style doors that open only when two panels are pressed simultaneously. The latter are used regularly in *Perfect Dark Zero* and *Lego Star Wars* to ensure that both player characters are in the same place before allowing them to advance to the next area.

Universal ("skeleton") keys create resource-allocation strategies and choice in an otherwise proscribed lock system. Say that a player has one red key, one blue key, and one universal key and is facing a yellow door, as occurs in an early *DOOM* level. The player can choose to search for the missing yellow key (perhaps behind the red or blue doors) or advance more quickly by using the universal key to pass the yellow door. If keys are consumed by use, then this is a strategic choice that might later lead to significant backtracking for an unlucky player.

Keys are dangerous for the designer in a competitive game (or a cooperative game with poor communication channels between players). Several failure modes are present. The first is that a losing or noncommunicative player can simply monopolize a key, preventing other players from advancing. This is powerful negative feedback, but it can be too powerful and is certainly undesirable in the endgame. A second problem is that players can accidentally reach that situation through deadlock. A correct minimax strategy on the part of each player might result in two players each holding one key when two are required for either to advance. Neither player can relinquish a key without giving it to the opponent, but neither player can advance.

Incidentally, something similar can also happen in the programming of a game, irrespective of the game design. If access to game state is synchronized between different parts of the program using locks (called mutual exclusion locks or mutexes by programmers), then two parts of the program can deadlock if they both need access to two different parts of the program state and each acquires a single part at the same time. Deadlock is one of the causes of games suddenly freezing, and it is likely to become an increasing problem in the future because consoles now have programs divided into many parts to take advantage of multiple processor cores.

10.5 Geometry

10.5.1 Matching

Abstract and puzzle games often build mechanics from geometric properties of groups of discrete pieces. The simple n-in-a-row winning mechanic appears in tic-tac-toe (three in a row), *Connect Four* (four in a row), and go moku (five in a row). *Tetris* made this into a single-player mechanic by assigning points for completing rows. From *Tetris*, the general idea of gaining points (and clearing accumulating pieces) by connecting n-in-a-row has led to a series of single-player games focused on aligning like pieces. *Maki*, *Bejeweled*, *Hexen*, and *Meteos* are among the most popular in this genre, which dominates Web and cell phone games.

10.5.2 Tile Placement

One could consider dominoes to be a series of two-in-a-row minigames. The constraint that played pieces must "match" in some geometric or set-based sense and fit the geometry of the board is central to tile-placement games that have evolved from dominoes. *Carcassonne* (Figure 10.3), *Tigris and Euphrates*, and *Ingenious* are among the best-known games with tile-placement mechanics, although hundreds of such games have been produced in the last decade. These games focus on players who are not so much moving pieces as

Figure 10.3. Tiles forming the board early in a game of *Carcassonne.* (Image courtesy of Elentin/Wikipedia)

building the board itself using domino-like mechanics as a constraint. The more complicated the kinds of properties that must be matched between tiles, the more opportunity for strategy and combination. (For interesting results on the tiling properties of square tiles, see "Wang Tiles" [Wang 61, Wang 65].)

10.5.3 Encirclement

Encircling an opponent's forces makes them fight on many fronts and at the same time cuts supply lines and retreat. Many games abstract the strategic value of encirclement by explicitly capturing encircled pieces. The classic game with this mechanic is go, in which a group of pieces with no open spaces ("liberties") adjacent to it is immediately captured and removed from the board. From go that mechanic has been transported to other abstract strategy games like *Pente* and *Othello*, both of which encircle by capping both ends of a row. *Cathedral* allows capture of board areas themselves that contain at most one opponent piece (which is then discarded); this is an explicit form of the implicit property in go that surrounded areas are rarely viable for the opponent to play into. *Cathedral* is relatively lightweight compared to go but typically has attractive wooden pieces that are shaped like medieval buildings. The more recent *Through the Desert* adds a charming set of pastel camel pieces for engagement but relies in part on the same mechanics as *Cathedral* for claiming territory. It hybridizes this mechanic with a way of capturing individual board locations by simply touching them.

10.6 Superunit

A superunit is a character or upgrade so powerful that it is practically invincible if a player can obtain it. This avoids actually playing out a position where it is obvious that one player will win by allowing him or her a quick and entertaining victory.

This would seem to make the superunit very enjoyable to deploy (for a short time), but also unbalanced because it is unfair. However, in a good game design superunits are only introduced in the endgame to provide overwhelming positive feedback to guide the winning player to victory. If introduced too early, they would indeed destabilize the game; in the endgame, they actually provide stability.

Examples of superunits abound. In *Natural Selection*, the Onos is a very powerful alien that can be achieved only late in the game. It is based on the *StarCraft* Terran Carriers, which have nuclear weapons that can blast an opponent if the player reaches the top of the tech tree. In chess and checkers, players who have enough control of the board to guide a unit to the opposite side are rewarded with the upgrade to superunit (queen in chess, king in checkers). Although the unit doesn't guarantee a win, it is sufficient positive feedback to widen that player's lead. *Age of Empires* allows the player with massive resources to create a Wonder of the World, which starts a timer that rewards that player with victory when it expires.

10.7 Rock-Paper-Scissors

Rock-paper-scissors (RPS) is a children's physical game where two players simultaneously choose one of the three objects represented by different hand gestures. The game is (somewhat) interesting because no single choice is most powerful. Rock smashes (beats) scissors, paper covers (beats) rock, and scissors cut (beat) paper. The three configurations of an object against itself are draws. RPS is used in game theory as a classic example of mixed strategies. The optimal strategy is to choose completely randomly among all three options. Players can win a disproportionate number of the times if they detect a pattern in their opponents' choices and exploit it.

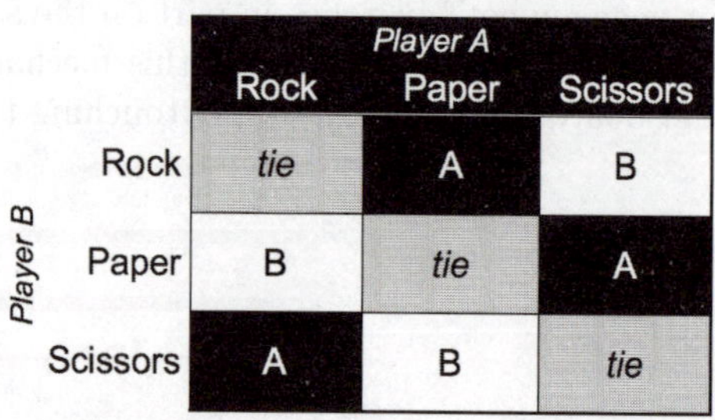

	Player A: Rock	Player A: Paper	Player A: Scissors
Player B: Rock	*tie*	A	B
Player B: Paper	B	*tie*	A
Player B: Scissors	A	B	*tie*

Figure 10.4. Outcome matrix for a one-turn game of rock-paper-scissors.

The circular relationship in RPS is very stable. Each choice is equally powerful, so several Nash equilibria are present, and the game is worth playing. More complex games, particularly strategy games, use this basic mechanic for the same purpose. It is a way to segment interactions into different realms and then make sure that at the few places where the realms interact, they are stable.

Figure 10.4 shows an outcome matrix for a one-turn game of rock-paper-scissors. In the figure, the columns represent player A's move, and the rows represent player B's (simultaneous) move. Each grid square shows the outcome of that combination of choices: either A wins, B wins, or the game is tied. Because the choices are simultaneous and each column/row gives the choosing player the same odds, every box is a Nash equilibrium.

10.8 Combat Simulation

Combat systems attempt to simulate the results of violence in a manner that balances realism against practicality for ease of play. The historical tradition is that these systems arose over hundreds of years from serious military war games, and the primary examples today exist in combat simulations for games. However, the same mechanics can be applied to noncombat tasks (e.g., *Harvest Moon* farming simulation), and that is an attractive direction for innovation.

Many board and video games use a statistical combat-resolution method popularized by *Dungeons & Dragons* and other tabletop role-playing games. In fact, many board and video games use precisely the open-source d20 rule set that today underlies *Dungeons & Dragons* (see Figure 10.5). Statistical combat is determined by three factors: skills/items that are purchased, randomness, and tactics. Of course, in some games, these factors are minimized or eliminated. *Amber* is a tabletop RPG with no explicitly random elements, yet it features sophisticated combat systems on par with other tabletop RPGs.

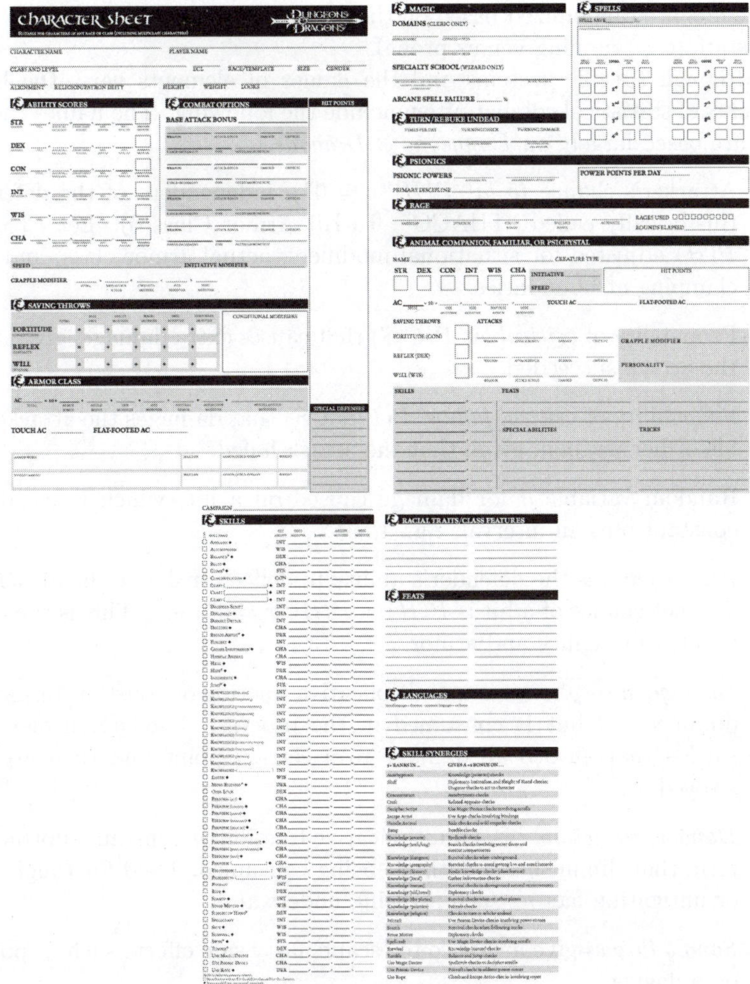
CHARACTER SHEET
DUNGEONS & DRAGONS
CHARACTER NAME
PLAYER NAME
CLASS AND LEVEL
ECL
RACE/TEMPLATE
SIZE
GENDER
ALIGNMENT
RELIGION/PATRON DEITY
HEIGHT
WEIGHT
LOOKS
ABILITY SCORES
STR
DEX
CON
INT
WIS
CHA
COMBAT OPTIONS
BASE ATTACK BONUS
HIT POINTS
SPEED
INITIATIVE MODIFIER
GRAPPLE MODIFIER
SAVING THROWS
CONDITIONAL MODIFIERS
FORTITUDE
REFLEX
WILL
ARMOR CLASS
AC
TOUCH AC
FLAT-FOOTED AC
SPECIAL DEFENSES
MAGIC
DOMAINS (CLERIC ONLY)
SPECIALTY SCHOOL (WIZARD ONLY)
ARCANE SPELL FAILURE
SPELLS
TURN/REBUKE UNDEAD
PSIONICS
PSIONIC POWERS
PRIMARY DISCIPLINE
POWER POINTS PER DAY
RAGE
RAGES USED
ROUNDS ELAPSED
ANIMAL COMPANION, FAMILIAR, OR PSICRYSTAL
NAME
CREATURE TYPE
STR DEX CON INT WIS CHA
INITIATIVE
SPEED
HIT POINTS
AC
TOUCH AC
FLAT-FOOTED AC
SAVING THROWS
ATTACKS
FORTITUDE (CON)
REFLEX (DEX)
WILL (WIS)
GRAPPLE MODIFIER
PERSONALITY
SKILLS
FEATS
SPECIAL ABILITIES
TRICKS
CAMPAIGN
SKILLS
RACIAL TRAITS/CLASS FEATURES
FEATS
LANGUAGES
SKILL SYNERGIES

Figure 10.5. Three of the four pages in the character sheet for maintaining state and computing statistical combat constants in *Advanced Dungeons & Dragons* version 3.5. (Images courtesy of Wizards of the Coast)

On one end of the statistical combat spectrum are more abstract and tactical games like *Axis & Allies* and *Risk*, and on the other are the RPGs like *Dungeons & Dragons.* Computer games tend to facilitate the more sophisticated methods because players don't have to manually manipulate the statistics. Obvious RPGs like *World of Warcraft* and *Knights of the Old Republic* all use these mechanics heavily, but so do games like *Counter-Strike,* where hits are randomized based on the particular weapon and player's current state (e.g., running versus prone).

Although specific systems and the names of elements vary, the basic elements of statistical combat often include the following. The names chosen here are based largely on *Dungeons & Dragons*.

- Attacker's chance *to hit* $P(H|\text{"}x = 0\text{"})$, independent of the defender (historically called "THACO": To Hit Armor Class 0). Let $P(S)$ be $P(H)$ adjusted for situational modifiers, actual armor class, and any clamping at boundaries.

- Probability of *critical hit* $P(C|S)$ that causes extra damage, given that the attack succeeded.

- Probability of *critical failure* $P(F|\text{not } S)$ that damages the attacker or his or her weapon, given that the attack failed.

- Random variable d for damage caused on a hit, which is usually a constant plus an interval, e.g., 1d4+2.

- *Armor class* is the defender's ability to deflect or dodge the attack, x. The net chance of a hit is $P(H) = P(H|\text{"}x = 0\text{"}) - x$. This is typically granted for agility and armor.

- *Damage absorption* a is a multiplicative fraction or constant term that diminishes d but is consumed in the process. Used for armor and shields that absorb all damage to a certain point and then are destroyed.

- *Damage reduction* r is a multiplicative fraction or constant subtractive term that diminishes d without being consumed. Used for tough skin or mitigating factors such as being underwater.

- *Saving throws* give a chance to escape nasty side effects such as poison on a dagger.

- *Hit points* (HP) represent a character's health.

- *Magic points* (MP) or "mana" represent a character's ability to deploy magical attacks.

- *Skill points* (SP) and *attributes* of a character adjust the above variables. For example, $P(H|\text{"}x = 0\text{"})$ may be proportional to a character's strength.

- *Situational modifiers* affect the above variables. Attacking from higher ground, while under the effect of a spell, or against a disabled opponent might all increase attack chance and damage. Attacking multiple targets or from great distance might decrease them.

In tactical games, situational modifiers are more significant than the underlying attributes. Common situational modifiers include:

- Direction of the attack.
- Number of units involved in attack and defense.
- Off-hand weapon.
- Wielding multiple weapons.
- Size difference between opponents.
- Who attacked first.
- The attack is a counter-attack.
- Racial or class vulnerabilities.
- Poor visibility conditions.
- Incapacitation level of defender.
- Elevation difference.
- Surprise.
- The attacker is taking other actions.
- The attacker is mounted.
- The defender is braced against the attack.
- The attack or defense relies on certain physical properties (e.g., piercing versus bludgeoning attack; magic versus conventional).
- Power difference between characters or players.

A statistical combat system is a lot like an economy. It must be balanced so that all elements have approximately the same value, taking their cost into account. Alternatively, the cost must be proportional to their value. Value is often the expected damage per turn dealt by an attack (or damage absorbed/deflected by a defense). Since attributes may affect both attack and defense, they must be addressed carefully. The actual equations used depend on the specific elements of the particular combat system and how they combine.

The following is a brief example of how to compute the expected damage of a weapon per attack. The example data is taken from the Wizards of the Coast *d20 Modern System Reference Document* [Slavicsek et al. 04].

The (abbreviated) statistics listed in the rule book, augmented with three columns of our analysis, are:

Weapon	Damage	Critical	Cost	Weight	Restrictions
crossbow	1d10	19-20	9	7 lb	none
Beretta 9mm	2d6	20	16	3 lb	license
M16A2 5.56mm	2d8	20	16	8 lb	restricted
frag. grenade	4d6	none	15	1 lb	military

Weapon	$E[D]$	Damage/Attack ($E[N]$) at $P(S)$= 15/20	Cost per Damage ($E[N]$/cost)
crossbow	5.5	5.8	0.64
Beretta 9mm	7.0	6.3	0.39
M16A2 5.56mm	9.0	8.1	0.51
frag. grenade	14.0	10.5	0.70

Note: $E[D], E[N]$ and $E[N]/cost$ are not listed in the rulebook.

This table assumes that players roll 1d20 to attack and that the "Critical" column indicates the range of values (either a 20 or 19 or 20) that cause double damage in the event of a hit. The expected damage, $E[D]$, values were computed according to the dice equations in Chapter 8. Assume that X is on the scale of a probability (0–1) and that there are no situational modifiers. For a specific, known $P(H)$, the attacker hits when

$$1\text{d}20 \geq \max(\min(\lceil 20 * (P(H) - X)\rceil, 20), 1),$$

because rolling a *natural* (without modifiers) 20 is a guaranteed hit and a natural 1 is a guaranteed miss. Ignoring the roundoff to the nearest integer, we can use this to express the net probability of a successful hit as

$$P(S) = \max((\min(P(H) - X, 1/20), 19/20).$$

The unconditional probabilities of critical hits are $P(C_{\text{xbow}}) = 2/20$ and $P(C_{\text{other}}) = 1/20$. The *conditional* probabilities of critical hits, $P(C|S)$ and expected net damage per attack, $E[N]$, depend on $P(S)$. There are three outcomes of an attack (ignoring critical failures, which do not damage the opponent): miss, noncritical hit, and critical hit. These are shown by the outcome tree in Figure 10.6.

The net damage is the sum of the outcome damage times the probability at each outcome leaf in the tree:

$$\begin{aligned} E[N] &= (P(S) * P(\text{not } C|S) * E[D]) + (P(S) * P(C|S) * 2E[D]) \\ &\quad +(P(\text{not } S) * 0) \\ &= P(S) * E[D] * (P(C|S) + 1). \end{aligned}$$

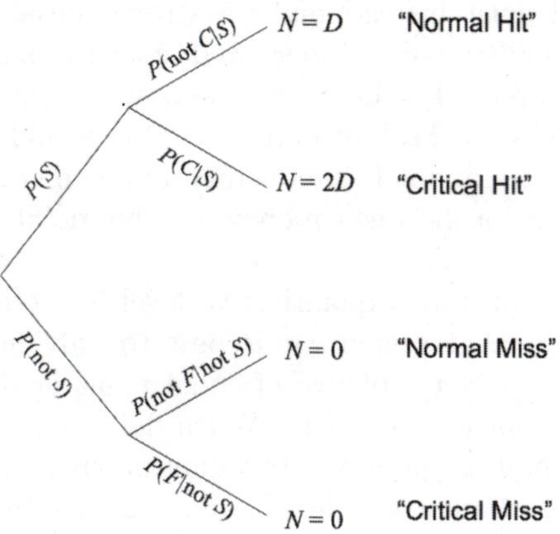

Figure 10.6. Possible outcomes of an attack in a statistical combat system.

Now let's compute the value of each weapon at $P(S) = 15/20 = 0.75$, which is a reasonable value to consider given the other rules in the d20 system. At that point, the critical hit probabilities given a successful hit are $P(C_{\text{xbow}}|S) = 2/5 = 0.40$ and $P(C_{\text{other}}|S) = 1/5 = 0.20$. From this we compute $E[N]$ for each weapon. For example, for the crossbow:

$$\begin{aligned} E[N_{\text{xbow}}] &= P(S) * E[D] * (P(C_{\text{xbow}}|S) + 1) \\ &= 0.75 * 5.5 * (0.40 + 1) \\ &= 5.8 \text{ (hit points / attack).} \end{aligned}$$

The $E[N]$ values for the other weapons are shown in the previous table. Given these $E[N]$ values, we can compute the dollar cost per point of damage inflicted on the enemy for each weapon. If these values are not all close (say, within 50%) of one another, then one weapon is clearly better and is therefore unbalanced.

The actual range of expected damage per cost for these weapons is from 0.39 to 0.70, so they are approximately balanced considering only cost and damage. In fact, they may be much better balanced than these numbers indicate. While players who choose the Beretta 9mm pay the least for each point of damage they inflict, economy might not be the only important factor. The Beretta requires a license to use in the game, so it might not be available to all players. It can make fewer attacks before loading than the M16A2, so the expected damage per turn will actually fall off if we consider battles that take many turns. Likewise, the most expensive weapon per damage is the fragmentation grenade. However, it causes such massive damage that the battle might not progress for many turns. When a character has little health left, he or she cannot afford to think about averages over the long term and must instead make a strong initial attack or retreat. Issues like concealability, noise, range, and splash damage will also affect the cost of each weapon. Furthermore, the cost of causing damage should be related to the cost of healing damage. One would hope that in this system it costs players about 0.5 monetary units to regain one hit point, otherwise the conversion between money and hit points breaks outside of combat.

Considering all issues at a quantitative level is prohibitive. Therefore, when balancing a combat system, it is best to only numerically balance equipment to within a factor of two of equal point or dollar cost to effectiveness ratios as we have shown here. When doing so, estimate the impact of other issues as best as possible, but continuously simplify and bound equations to keep them manageable. Then adjust the final attributes based on observations during playtests, including the players' engagement derived from the thematic value of each attribute and piece of equipment.

10.8.1 Combat Tables

Combat tables are like outcome matrices for individual game constants, such as tactical situation modifiers. Consider an example in the context of a hypothetical fantasy RTS game. In the game, there are three kinds of units: mounted knights called cavalry, foot soldiers carrying long spears called pikes that can be braced against a cavalry charge, and archers. An attacking unit causes 1d4 points of damage plus a bonus that depends on the combination of attacker and defender. That bonus is specified in a combat table. Figure 10.7 shows the attack bonus granted in our hypothetical game. In the table, pikes can prepare their spears against cavalry and cause significant (+1) damage. The pike grants no advantage over another pikeman (0) and actively gets in the way (−1) when attacking archers. Most games have significantly more rows and columns in their combat tables. Also, combat tables can represent

Defender \ Attacker	Cavalry	Pike	Archer
Cavalry	0	+1	−1
Pike	−1	0	+1
Archer	+1	−1	0

Figure 10.7. Attacker bonus combat table for a hypothetical fantasy RTS game that displays a rock-paper-scissors relationship.

any of the constants involved in the combat equations such as chance to hit, chance to defend, damage type, and damage reduction.

Although it is very simple, the example in Figure 10.7 does have something important in common with most real combat tables: it uses the rock-paper-scissors mechanic. Each row and each column sums to the same value (which happens to be zero). This means that no unit is strictly the best in this table. If some unit were the best, players would always use that unit, and there would be no strategic reason to have other units in the game.

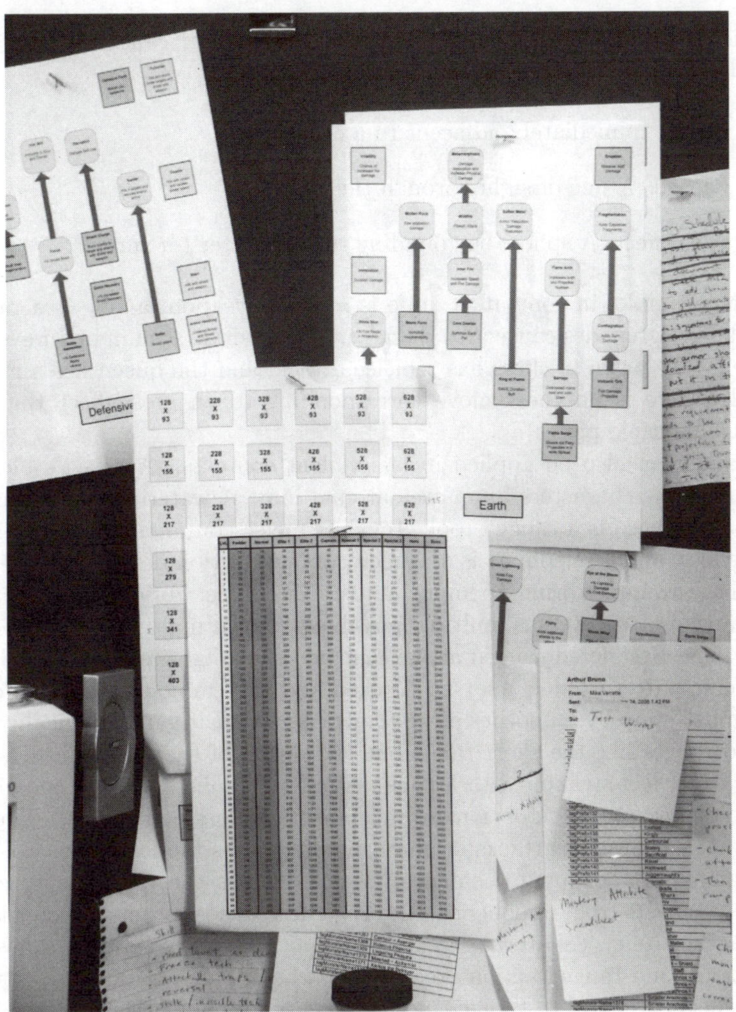

Figure 10.8. Combat tables, tech trees, and databases of combat constants posted inside game designer Arthur Bruno's office at Iron Lore Entertainment.

The table doesn't have to have constant row sums for the game to be balanced because there is more to the value of a unit than its attack bonus. Each unit might have noncombat abilities, a different creation cost, and a different maintenance cost. They probably have different movement speeds and sizes.

10.9 Effect Distance

Range is the maximum distance at which a character can affect the game world. The following are the three common ranges:

- **Melee.** Immediately adjacent to a character.
- **Ranged.** A line-of-sight through the world.
- **Area effect.** A sphere surrounding the character (or target).

For example, in combat, a knife is a melee weapon, a rifle is a ranged attack, and grenades cause area damage. They can be seen in other systems as well. The pawn in chess has a melee attack, and the queen has a ranged attack (there is no chess move corresponding to an area effect that can damage multiple pieces).

Range can also be applied in less-violent contexts. A priest's blessing can affect the characters in an area around him. A watering can is a melee tool, and a hose is a ranged tool. Touch is melee communication, speech is area effect, and a telephone is a ranged communication device.

These examples bring up important subcategories. For example, a single-line ranged attack versus multiple possible (or even multiple simultaneous) directions. Restricted ranged attacks include the knight in chess, which has a specific pattern but cannot be blocked and the cannon in Chinese chess that must jump over another piece to attack. Combat games typically offer hybrid ranges like the short range but wide blast of shotgun pellets, which is an area-effect weapon with a cone instead of a sphere area. The point is not to enumerate these options so much as to understand that altering the way that a character attacks dramatically affects its tactical value.

Range is important for balance. Melee exposes the character to countermelee effects from opponents. An area effect exposes the character to its own actions (e.g., collateral damage; you can't use explosives in a hostage situation), and ranged actions keep the character safe from counter-attack. Area effects are hard to target but can affect many units. Melee slows down interactions because it usually makes it hard to disengage; one's opponent is at close range and can retaliate if you try to retreat. Ranged effects tend to encourage camping out in a single location and sniping. Area effects allow access to characters who have concealed themselves from line of sight.

It is common to grant melee characters additional hit points, armor, or other immunities because they will be exposed to significant countereffects. Ranged characters are typically weak because they rely on distance to protect them. Melee, ranged, and area effect are often balanced as part of a rock-paper-scissors mechanic, with defenses correspondingly arranged to ensure that no one range is most powerful.

10.10 Rush Prevention

In many games, it is effective to "rush" by opening with an early attack before forces are built up for defense. For games with complex strategy, this is undesirable from an enjoyment point of view because it is unstable. The rusher will win or lose in the first few minutes, and it circumvents a majority of the game. In *Age of Empires*, players begin at the stone age with a handful of farmers. Creating a few soldiers and immediately attacking the other player is a rush strategy. The designers introduced wild animals such as wolves and lions to prevent such rushes. Early in the game, these animals are formidable and will kill would-be rushers. Later in the game, a lone wolf cannot affect a full army platoon. The wolves act as an antirush mechanism.

Rush prevention is important to stabilize a game by providing negative feedback at the start. Doing so also preserves engagement; it is no fun to be beaten by a cheap shot at the very beginning of the game.

10.11 Dialogue Trees

Artificial intelligence is not powerful enough today to handle natural language or qualitative interaction. Computers can present realistic combat opponents for chess and an FPS, but they are very poor at engaging in conversation. Dialogue trees are a way of simulating rudimentary conversations with an AI. The technique is sufficiently crude that it is more visible to the player as an explicit mechanic than a real conversation. Its use is limited to progressive games and progressions embedded within emergent games like *World of Warcraft*. Many adventure, quest, and role-playing games rely heavily on dialogue trees to advance the plot. *Choose Your Own Adventure* books essentially use the dialogue tree mechanic exclusively, although in many cases the choices aren't dialogue so much as actions in a deterministic world.

A dialogue tree is like a decision tree or outcome matrix. The AI makes a statement, and then the player is presented with a small menu of choices. Each of these choices corresponds to one response or question from the player. The player will only experience a single path from root to leaf in the tree and perceives it as a natural language conversation. Because the designer knows the entire tree, he or she can create responses for the AI that seem intelligent and natural.

When designing dialogue trees, it is advisable to limit the fan out while crafting choices to maintain engagement. The branching factor (number of choices) at any point should not be too large. If the number of choices is too small, then the player feels overly restricted and is forced to make a choice that he or she doesn't really like. If the number of choices is too large, the player can feel overwhelmed, and the designer is forced to contend with a gigantic tree. Remember that the designer must script every possible conversation, not just a single path. Three to five choices seems to feel about right for the player.

Give players meaningful choices rather than making a "right" choice and several wrong ones. When there are several meaningful choices, the player feels as if he or she can express himself or herself and solve problems creatively. This increases the player's trust in the game world and helps the player to suspend disbelief.

Giving a large number of choices but limiting the number of outcomes causes several paths to converge (perhaps after granting intermediate changes to game state to truly distinguish the paths). Introducing small amounts of nondeterminism through randomized responses or responses that are context sensitive allows the tree to feel fresh on replay of the whole game or if the player revisits the same scene at a later time in the same session. For example, *Deus Ex* characters are aware of the physical appearance of the player and alter their dialogue tree accordingly. A small boy will be frightened and run from a player police officer who engages in conversation with a gun drawn, but the boy is helpful if the player holsters his weapon and instead holds a candy bar.

Fahrenheit introduced a hybrid dialog-tree-action mechanic that smoothes the flow of conversation. While a nonplayer character is speaking, a small set of choices appears for the player to choose from. These are accessed using joystick gestures rather than a traditional menu. A timer bar across the screen shows the time until the AI finishes his speech. If the player has not chosen a response before time runs out, the conversation ends or takes a default path. When the player chooses a response in time, the actual player character speech is much more detailed than the placeholder menu text. This adds a real-time component to a traditionally turn-based mechanic and makes it feel more like an action game. The timer increases tension. To make that sense of time real, the dialogue trees in the game only allow about half of the paths to converge. So not only must players make permanent choices, but they must do it on the fly and under time pressure.

10.12 Economy

Most strategy games require the player to manage an economy. The commodities in the economy often include virtual money, points, attributes, resources, buildings, and characters. By presenting several commodities, they introduce risk management. Players must decide when to hold which kind of commodity. Often the value of a commodity changes over the course of the game, and players must recognize that and time their transactions appropriately. Economies naturally introduce positive feedback: the rich tend to get richer. This is good in small doses since it provides a reward system for successful management but cannot be allowed to dominate the entire game because it is unstable. Shifting values over the course of the game effectively resets the feedback loop, since dominating an early-game commodity is not valuable towards thc cndgame.

There are three broad steps in designing an economy. First, create the commodities. There are two kinds: liquid and frozen. *Liquid* commodities, such as cash, tend to exist in large quantities and are relatively easy to produce or trade. *Frozen* commodities, such as buildings, are rarer and cannot be converted into other forms. As a rule of thumb, you want about four classes of liquid commodities in order to provide sufficient complexity. Often there is only one class of frozen commodity, the elements of which are distinguished by different attributes such as armor, health, damage, cost, power, and lifetime. Here again you want about four attributes to provide sufficient, yet still manageable, complexity.

The second step in designing an economy is to create the *commodity flow graph*. This is a tool for visualizing how commodities are converted into one another. The vertices of this graph are commodity types. The directed edges show permitted transactions. Where multiple inputs are required to produce one output, link them using a "+" symbol. As an example, Figure 10.9 shows the commodity flow in the *Puerto Rico* board game. In that game, Goods and Doubloons are liquid commodities. At the start of the game, each player is given a Plantation and some Doubloons. Players strive to accumulate the most Victory Points. The ending condition is not the winning condition in this game. The game ends when the Colonists are exhausted or when a city is full of Buildings, but winning requires also capturing the most Victory Points. This is represented by dashed arrows from Colonists and Buildings to the Win box. In the game, there are multiple roles that a player may assume. Each of these enables one kind of transaction. Implicit

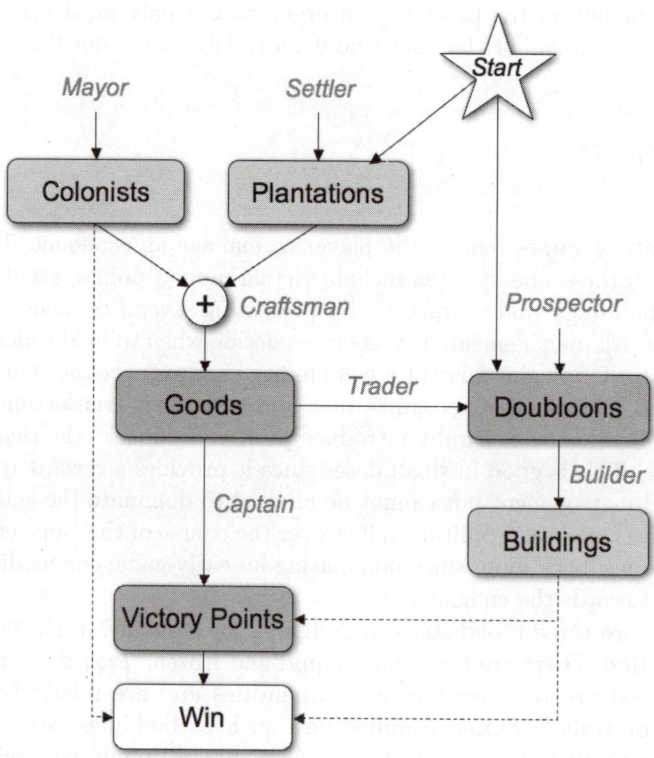

Figure 10.9. Commodity flow graph for *Puerto Rico*.

in the diagram is the fact that player turns (i.e., time) are a commodity as well. For example, one can convert a turn into Doubloons by choosing the Prospector role. Buildings are a frozen asset. Some yield victory points (indicated by the dashed line), but most offer other advantages not captured by the commodity graph.

Figure 10.10 shows the commodity flow graph for *Settlers of Catan*. Although the gameplay is simpler than *Puerto Rico*, the graph is more complicated because there are more liquid commodities: Wood, Brick, Wool, Grain, and Ore. To simplify the diagram, the starting allotment is not shown in the graph. The *Settlers* graph shows the combinations of liquid commodities that contribute to frozen ones. Note that the diagram does not attempt to quantify those elements. Doing so would add more information at the expense of our ability to quickly understand it. Often choosing what to leave out of a diagram is as important as choosing what to display. Note the cyclic relationship between Settlements/Cities and the liquid commodities. Liquid assets are required to build a Settlement, yet Settlements yield those com-

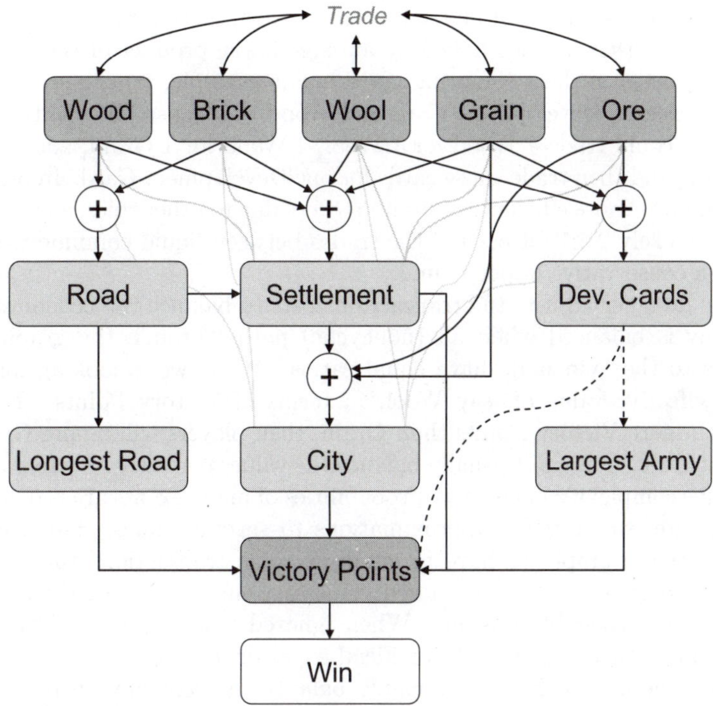

Figure 10.10. Commodity flow graph for *Settlers of Catan*.

modities. This is a positive feedback loop that allows players to advance. As you might expect from such a loop, advancement is exponential under such a system, and a player with a sufficient lead becomes unstoppable. The game is designed with several mechanics that limit the destabilizing influence of this loop. First, the game terminates after 10 points, which is just about when the lead player hits the steep (high payback) part of the exponential curve. Second, there is an effective hand limit of seven resource cards, which prevents hoarding. Third, the game has sufficient variance that it is possible to recover. The last point is interesting. Both high variance and positive feedback are destabilizing. Yet they can cancel each other's effects and provide a net stability.

The third step in designing an economy is balancing the value of each element. For commodities to be useful, the Win node must be reachable from all of them. Those edges might not all be shown in the diagram because the impact of a commodity (like a buildings in *Puerto Rico*) is indirect. Consider the conversion ratios between commodities, which occur at each edge. For example, in *Settlers*, any liquid commodity can be converted to any other at a 4:1 ratio or better. A Development Card costs 1 Wool, 1 Grain, and 1

Ore, so it is has a ratio of (1,1,1:1). The net transaction ratio between two commodities that are not linked by an edge is the product of the ratios on the path between them (ignoring cycles). For example, we can see that the ratio between a Development Card and Wood is at most 1:12. In the worst case, you could trade 4 Wood for 1 Wool, 4 Wood for 1 Grain, and 4 Wood for 1 Ore, and then trade those cards for one Development Card. In practice, one can make more efficient trades in *Settlers* due to other rules, so the ratios are more likely 2.5:1 for each of the trades between liquid commodities, but this is a conservative upper bound.

The designer adjusts the transaction costs to balance the economy. The economy is balanced when all (noncyclic) paths through the graph from sources to the Win node have equal ratios. What we're looking for here is the effective value of, say Wool, in terms of Victory Points. If Wool is worth more Victory Points than Grain, then players will ignore Grain in favor of Wool. One can't usually balance the values perfectly on paper due to explosive complexity. The exact probabilities of many events are too difficult to compute, so we make approximations to several values. Furthermore, in making the graph we have to suppress some transactions that are too complex to quantify. When ignored values are small, ignoring them should still give a reasonable answer. When ignored values are large, we must approximate their impact with artificial edges or sources.

The general practice is to roughly balance the economy on paper, and then playtest. In order to achieve stability, engagement, and fairness, one will generally adjust the economy at this stage of design anyway. Playtesting gives the designer a feel for how to approximate complex quantities. After the basic flow structure of the economy and other mechanics have firmed up in the design, the designer should then refine the transaction ratios on paper (or, more likely, in Excel) again. For casual board games, the economy need not be precisely balanced, and achieving that is often impossible because of the fixed ratios presented by small integers on cards and dice. For video games and hardcore board games, it is important to balance an economy as well as possible. There, players will exploit any slight value difference between commodities, since they will both study the transaction ratios carefully and likely put many more hours into play than casual players. When players identify and explore a difference, they render most of the choices in the game meaningless. That destroys engagement and makes the game undesirable.

10.13 Ensuring Entropy

Critical to nonpersistent games is the notion of a "ticking clock" so the game is guaranteed to end at some point. The universe actually has this property, which is called entropy or heat-death. Every action in the real world creates some disorder in the universe by dissipating energy. Although we can restore order, doing so consumes energy and creates other disorder, which, by the laws of thermodynamics, must exceed the energy that was put back in order. This means that a very long time from now, the entire universe will just be filled with ambient energy and gas, with no order or consumable energy. One could consider that the end of the universe.

Entropy is related to the halting problem, which is the problem of deciding whether a program terminates or runs forever on a given set of input data. The halting problem is famously an example of an undecidable problem in computer science, which means that it is impossible to solve it for an arbitrary program and input. That has interesting implications for game balance. It implies that we can't necessarily prove that a set of game rules has the termination property. Fortunately, it is possible to prove that *some* rule sets terminate; the problem is only undecidable if we are forced to face an arbitrary rule set. Entropy mechanics tend to be applied in a relatively heavy-handed way so that it is obvious the game will end.

Persistent worlds, like most MMORPGs and tabletop RPGs, must ensure that they do *not* have an entropy mechanic, or the world would cease to persist. *A Tale in the Desert* is a rare exception to this; it is an MMORPG where the world state advances until the game as a whole ends and the world is recreated to remove the entropy. For those games in which entropy is desirable, several classes of mechanics are available for ensuring it.

10.13.1 Relentless Entropy

Games that have a clear resource that is consumed in every turn, such as the tiles in *Carcassonne*, positions in cribbage, or squares in tic-tac-toe, clearly must end. This is the easiest mechanic to add that ensures termination. There is no way to avoid the end of the game, but there is no way to accelerate it, either. That precludes player strategies where a player turns a short-term lead into a win by terminating the game, as is possible in *Puerto Rico.*

Another factor to consider when using such relentless entropy is that players can predict when the end of the game will occur. This can cause the endgame to become too strategic, reducing the player's enjoyment of a more casual play experience by forcing him or her to choose between thinking of all of the ways to the end of the decision tree and playing in a more engaging, heuristic fashion.

A fixed number of points (e.g., gin rummy) or running countdown clock (e.g., *Super Mario Bros.*) are similarly heavy-handed ways of ensuring that the game does not run without end.

10.13.2 Player Entropy

In chess, capturing a piece increases entropy because when all the pieces are captured, the game ends. Unlike games with relentless entropy, capturing is a player-controlled mechanic. This means that the game end is not necessarily predictable. It also makes it hard to guarantee the play time of the game, and in fact, chess games can last anywhere between four moves and more than six hours. In practice, the capturing is only one kind of entropy in chess; there are also little-used rules that end the game in a draw after the same position is repeated three times, after 50 moves if no captures have occurred, or when insufficient pieces remain on the board for either player to win.

In *Bioshock* and most other first-person shooters, players constantly consume health and ammunition and are faced with hordes of enemies. These resources are consumed at a rate controlled (at least partially) by the player, but they ensure that the game cannot continue endlessly. Likewise, many RTS games have natural resources that become exhausted through the game, increasing conflict between players for the remaining resources and guaranteeing that expansion cannot continue indefinitely.

A classic example of infinite enemies as a mechanic for ensuring entropy is *Pac-Man*, where the ghosts can be delayed four times but never killed. What makes this example so interesting is that the game contains a flaw in the ghost's artificial intelligence that creates one location on the map where the player can hide and never be caught by the ghosts, thus defeating the entropy mechanic.

10.13.3 Optional Entropy

In more open-ended games, the entropy is completely under the player's control to the extent that the player can pause (but never reverse) it as long as desired. In all of the games in the *Grand Theft Auto III* series, the *The Elder Scrolls* series, and the *The Legend of Zelda* series, players are advancing through a unidirectional story. Progress in that story represents increasing entropy.

In these games, the player can abandon the story and explore the world for long periods of time without being forced to advance entropy. The absence of a mechanic restricting the player's style therefore leads to the lack of a game-ending guarantee. This is highly desirable for some players who want to explore, but ultimately it may be a double-edged sword for the players who become bored without the story constraints and abandon the game permanently instead of simply taking a break from the story.

10.14 Reward Cycles and Minigames

Games are not built from single mechanics or even from multiple mechanics at the same level. Instead, we see "games within the game" [Koster 07] (a.k.a. *minigames*). In other words, the full game contains mechanics built from other mechanics.

There are three reasons for this. Many games need to slow down the action and need tactics—even mundane tactics—to keep long-term strategy separate from individual decisions. If it were not, then the game would be too sensitive to individual moves and become unstable. Most games should tolerate one or two suboptimal moves without dooming the player who makes them.

Another reason for minigames is that the player must be trained to think about in-game problems in a certain way. This includes the controls for a video game or the rules for a board game. The first part of a play session ideally should lead the player though the mechanics in a way that makes him or her realize how to approach the rest of the game successfully.

The third, and perhaps the most critical, reason is that players need to make some kind of decision or action about every one to five seconds[1] to maintain flow and engagement. The time period should increase with the significance of the decision. Too little time between major actions leaves the player frustrated or anxious. Too much time leaves him bored. To maintain engagement without a monotone rate, it is important to add goals at multiple time scales. For example, have players continuously make trivial decisions, make minor decisions every two seconds, and make major ones every 30 seconds.

Scott Lewis gives an example of this structure in *Donkey Kong*, using actions instead of decisions. About once per second, the player must jump over a barrel. About once every five seconds, the player advances up the next vertical floor, and the player faces the boss and completes a level about once every 30 seconds. We see the same mechanic in *Tetris*, where players constantly try to avoid pieces stacking too high while also trying to complete rows on a longer time scale. *Age of Empires*, *Civilization*, and other strategy games offer differing end goals, where the player can win by cultural, economic, or violent means. This creates multiple layers of decisions at different time scales.

In a progressive game, overlapping goals on different time scales combine the game-long desire that drives the plot with per-chapter strategy and moment-to-moment tactics. This maintains the narrative structure while moving the action forward in a way that doesn't require extreme long-term planning for the player.

[1]According to veteran designer Will Wright.

In an emergent game, overlapping (explicit or implicit!) goals allow mastery of the game to continually deepen. New players focus on the shortest-term or primary goals. Once they have internalized those and can play the game almost unconsciously, they begin to play the game at another conceptual level and focus on the layered goal. We see this in *Bubble Trouble*, where new players follow the nominal goal of defeating enemies, but more advanced players focus on defeating enemies in a way that maximizes points. *Bubble Trouble* layers alignment puzzle mechanics over its low-level *Pac-Man* style of action; the puzzles offer significant point bonuses but must be completed in the midst of enemies. At the highest conceptual layer, players are solving the puzzles and fighting the enemies in a way that has become second nature.

10.15 Resources

- Bjork and Holopainen, *Patterns in Game Design* [Bjork and Holopainen 04].
- Falstein, *The 400 Project*, http://www.theinspiracy.com/400_project.htm.
- Board Game Geek's list of games by mechanic, http://www.boardgamegeek.com/browser.php?itemtype=game\&sortby=mechanic.
- Myerson, *Game Theory: Analysis of Conflict* [Myerson 97].
- Yee, *The Norrathian Scrolls: A Study of EverQuest (version 2.5)*, http://www.nickyee.com/eqt/home.html.
- Perla, *The Art of Wargaming* [Perla 90].

CHAPTER 11

Creating a World

Terms Explained: *Backstory* – *Characters* – *Conflict* – *Cutscene* – *Era* – *Plot* – *Profile* – *Setting* – *Theme* – *Tone*

Games create play experiences that inhabit a fictional space. For an abstract game, that space might be purely experiential. That is the case for many abstract strategy games, like with the Japanese teahouse feel of a thick wood go board and polished black and white stones. For a progressive story game, the fictional space is narrative, as is the case in *Grim Fandango*'s papier-mâché quest through the Mexican Day of the Dead. Emergent, nonabstract games are somewhere in between. Examples include the wacky *RoboRally* machine shop, *Portal*'s darkly comedic weapons-testing facility, *Magic: The Gathering*'s magical fantasy, and *Half-Life*'s alien-infested dystopia.

Early in the design process, the team creates the fiction of the world. The process is highly creative and is based on the initial vision for the game. The description of the world appears briefly as the setting on the overview worksheet and in great detail in the World, Character, and Progression Graph chapters of the design document. These sections must be maintained as the game moves forward. For example, during balancing, they will likely undergo several revisions to accommodate changes to the mechanics. The game world is described by its setting, characters, backstory, plot, and geography. Not all of these are appropriate for every game.

11.1 Setting

Designers craft their mechanics to achieve the desired gameplay and craft their content to create the desired setting. Technology enables both. The interaction between gameplay and setting is governed by three ideas.

> In a game with well-designed content
>
> - *setting* captivates the player,
> - *gameplay* brings the *setting* to life, and
> - the *setting* creates mnemonics for rules.

Setting helps us to immediately understand what is possible in the world. You would not expect to see a handgun in *Dungeons & Dragons* or a spell-casting wizard in the real-world Middle Ages, but you would expect to encounter a fighter plane in 1942 and a faster-than-light drive in science fiction.

The setting consists of an era, a tone, and a theme. From a high level, the era is the time, the theme is the place, and the tone is the feel. In addition, the setting is usually accompanied by a backstory that explains the current state of the world or justifies disparate elements of the setting.

11.1.1 Era

The *era* is the time period in which the game is set—for example, the age of dinosaurs, medieval, 1800s, and the year 1942. It doesn't have to be a time period from the real world or particularly specific with exact dates. However, it should immediately convey the level of technology, evolution, or important historical events that might affect the game. The following are some of the major historical eras from the real world.

- Age of Dinosaurs (Mesozoic/Jurassic Period; over 1 million years ago).
- Ice Age (circa 10,000 B.C.E.).
- Stone Age (circa 10,000–3000 B.C.E.).
- Bronze Age (3500–1100 B.C.E.).
- Iron Age (1000–500 B.C.E.).
- Greece/Rome: Antiquity (1000 B.C.E–500 C.E.).
- Chinese Imperial Era (220 B.C.E.–220 C.E.).
- Mayan Classical Era (300–900 C.E.).
- Middle Ages (includes Dark Ages) (400–1000 C.E.).
- Renaissance (1300–1600).
- Caribbean Piracy (circa 1560–1720).

- Spanish Armada (1588).
- Colonial Era (1700–1900).
- Napoleonic Wars (circa 1799–1815).
- American/French Revolutions (circa 1770–1800).
- American Civil War (1861–1865).
- Industrial Revolution (1700–1900).
- World War I (1914–1918).
- World War II (1937–1945).
- Cold War (circa 1945–1980).
- Modern Day.

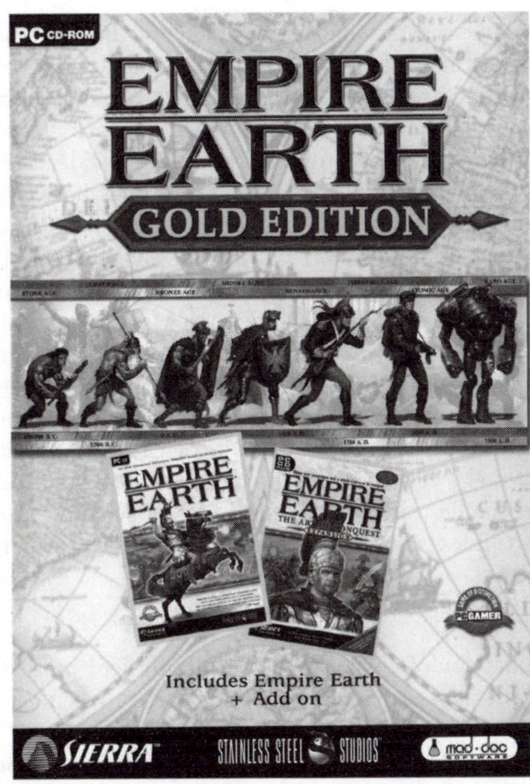

Figure 11.1. *Empire Earth* Gold box art shows the game's progression through varying historical eras. (Image courtesy of Sierra/Vivendi)

- Near Future.
- Far Future.

This list is useful for building progressive games through time (e.g., *Empire Earth*, shown in Figure 11.1, and other RTS games), as well as providing some inspiring settings.

Some fictitious eras imply their history, such as postnuclear holocaust. When setting a game in the future, one has tremendous possibilities to invent new technologies but also an obligation to decide what those are and to define what is not yet invented. Common future technologies include faster-than-light transportation and communication, robots with artificial intelligence, and contact with extraterrestrial civilizations. These are just some examples of what constitutes an *era* and what might make exciting games. Of course, this list isn't exhaustive and is not meant to influence your choice.

11.1.2 Tone

The *tone* of the game is somewhat like a film genre. Is the game about heroic action or personal drama? Is it comedy? If it is comedy, it could be animation (e.g., Bugs Bunny television show), slapstick (The Three Stooges films), ironic (*Hitchhiker's Guide to the Galaxy* books), or dark (*Brazil* movie). Often books and films make great tone references. Consider the gothic horror of Lovecraft's *Cthulhu*, which is similar to the *X-Files* horror mystery. Sherlock Holmes stories (see Figure 11.2) also have mystery and the arcane, but with a more Victorian and less-terrifying tone. Agatha Christie modernizes the mystery novel, downplaying some of Holmes's logic for more interpersonal and motivation-based drama and further reduces the horror aspect. Slasher films (e.g., *Texas Chainsaw Massacre*, *Hostel*) eliminate the logic and mystery in favor of a pure horror-survival tone. This has proven more commercially effective for games, perhaps because horror and survival are primitive elements that are easy to achieve with basic mechanics. Actual crime-solving mystery or subtle psychological horror requires more sophisticated game mechanics, and the handful of *Cthulhu* and *Sherlock Holmes* games have enjoyed less commercial success than their slasher brethren.

11.1.3 Theme

Theme is the collection of elements or overall physical context of the game. In the industry, theme is also referred to as flavor, and elements of the theme are often called flavor text or flavor elements.

Consider an amusement park like Disney World and you'll see many examples of themes. Some classics from Disney are Peter Pan, Pirates of the Caribbean, and the Snow White ride. These are essentially the same

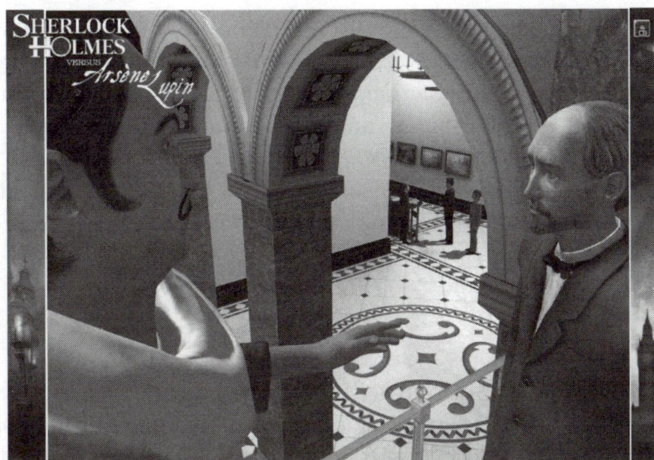

Figure 11.2. The Sherlock Holmes games, such as *Sherlock Holmes vs. Arsene Lupin*, combine mystery with the occult but limit terror in favor of logic. (Image courtesy of Focus Home Interactive)

(by analogy, they have similar mechanics and technology) but have different themes. Theme applies to both emergent and progressive games. The latter is obvious, since progressive games typically provide a narrative with a strong setting. The former is best served by some examples: themed chess sets, FPSs and RPGs without (useful) narrative but strong thematic control over weapons and art direction, strong Medieval theming in the otherwise abstract *Carcassonne*.

Be aware that the word *theme* is highly overloaded in game development. When discussing *flavor*, it has the same meaning that it has in *theme park*. It is also used to refer to the musical motif or line that accompanies the game or a character. Furthermore, *theme* has a literary meaning as the moral or meaning of a work. A game can and should have a theme in the literary sense. The literary theme is the most expressive aspect of the game. It should be a deep and concise idea that motivates you to create the game, not something that is engineered. In contrast to selecting a literary theme, creating the flavor theme is also a creative exercise, but it is one that is more amenable to process and structure. This section describes techniques for creating successful themes in the flavor sense.

11.2 Motivations for Setting

Most game designers advocate that a game should be engaging primarily because of the abstract game's mechanics. In the long run, strategic players ignore the setting and focus on the mechanics. A game with attractive content and boring mechanics ultimately fails to build a large player base. That is, mechanics and interaction are what make it a game. Great content can stand alone as a painting or music video, but it can't support a great game, book, or film alone.

If setting is subsidiary to mechanics, why worry about it at all? We'll examine one easy, short-term commercial answer and two deeper responses that go toward games as an art form.

11.2.1 Setting Sells

In the short view, *setting* is what sells the most games. The majority of game buyers (who, notably in the case of gifts and parents, aren't necessarily the game players) probably don't walk into a store or browse online to buy a game with RTS or bidding mechanics. Instead, they look for a *Harry Potter* game, a game with a female protagonist, a game with dinosaurs, or a *Star Wars* game. In other words, they shop by setting. The setting, the cover art, and the advertising campaign are what grabs the buyer. Commercial game developers have only a fraction of a second to convince that buyer before he or she moves on to the next game on the shelf. The best mechanics in the world are useless if no one buys the game to try it out. Even in the case of a free game download on the Internet, the player pays for every game with his or her time and must be selective. Setting helps a player to select. Of course, some savvy game consumers read detailed reviews and shop for games with certain mechanics or by specific publishers or developers. This kind of buyer isn't the majority. Furthermore, all branding is theme in a sense. Buying a game by designer Will Wright is buying a branded game—that is, buying according to a sort of simulation metasetting for which he is famous.

Some settings, especially theme brands, are so strong that they can sell a game despite lousy gameplay and bad reviews. Consider the previous examples. Any game with a *Harry Potter* or *Star Wars* theme can be expected to sell half a million units regardless of quality. At the time of this writing, there is no *Halo 4*, but you can expect one and expect players to buy it, regardless of the reviews and mechanics, based solely on the strength of the franchise.

As the number of games increases and revenue models switch from retail sales to MMO-style subscriptions and expansion pack sales, we can expect that the ability to deliver a great setting or licensed brand will no longer be sufficient to support a game. These new revenue models are long-tail methods that require a satisfied player base and positive word of mouth. *The Matrix Online* and *Star Wars Galaxies* were both strongly branded games with great settings that failed in the marketplace because they failed to deliver gameplay of the same quality as their settings. These MMO games simply weren't great games, and they couldn't sustain their early sales figures once players became dissatisfied (and largely transferred to *World of Warcraft*, which had exceptional mechanics). Recall that it is always critical to keep quality consistent across all aspects of the game. If the setting or branding is exceptional and the mechanics are lacking, the entire production will be perceived as worse than if the setting and mechanics were equally marginal. An exciting setting creates high expectations that some games cannot meet.

11.2.2 Experience

A well-chosen setting works with the mechanics and is inseparable from them. This speeds learning of the game and creates long-term player satisfaction. *Shadows Over Camelot* pits the knights of the round table against constant threats, including a potential traitor. The cooperative mechanics lead players to make noble sacrifices and bravely fight together against overwhelming odds. The competitive aspect encourages the traitor to play as deceptively as possible. The same mechanics could be presented with, say, a space battle or zookeeper setting, but the choice of Arthurian content leverages the mechanics. The mechanics lead to nobility and deceit, to magical exceptions and bloody battles. By using content that embodies those ideas, the game succeeds at an artistic level by making the players feel like a company of knights. *Gears of War* and *God of War* have brutal mechanics that favor all-out slaughter, and the mature content of those games is saturated with gore. *Mario Kart*'s weapon mechanics are cartoony, and the content is cartoony.

In contrast to these examples of well-chosen settings, *Meteos* has engaging puzzle gameplay with a cartoon alien setting forced on top of it. It would function identically with abstract play like *Tetris*. In fact, Nintendo subsequently rebranded *Meteos* with a Disney-character setting, demonstrating how irrelevant the original setting was.

As another example, the board game *Cartagena* has been criticized for pairing its pirate-jailbreak setting with abstract mechanics. Players have few piratical actions to take, and the pirate-themed elements of the game have no impact on gameplay. The major mechanics are leapfrogging and falling back to get ahead. The six different items in the game are indistinguishable: rum, pistols, hats, skulls, keys, and cutlasses are completely interchangeable and grant no distinct abilities.

11.2.3 Mnemonics

An ideal setting justifies the game's mechanics. In a video game with strong fiction, this is essential for immersion, allowing the player to suspend disbelief. That in turn allows the player to select strategies based on the fiction and not on the rules (i.e., create a mental model close to the fiction, not the abstract game). A flamethrower should not just cause damage but also make objects catch on fire. A flowerpot should break when dropped. The mechanics should make the world act the way that players expect. When mechanics fail to match the setting, the player mentally steps back and starts playing by the rules, ignoring the fiction. For example, it is very hard to play traditional adventure games like *King's Quest* or *Myst* by following the fiction because the game restricts player action by the mechanics. Players end up guessing what the designer wants them to do and solving puzzles rather than role-playing a character in the world. *Indigo Prophecy* and *Bioshock* perform better at this. Those games allow players to choose their own route and generally cause the world to react in a plausible manner.

In a board game or video game without strong fiction, the player's mental model is naturally closer to the abstract game. However, that abstract game may be very complicated. By rationalizing the mechanics, the setting helps the player to learn the rules and then recall them as needed. It isn't so much forming an alternate mental model as acting like a mnemonic. For example, in *Puerto Rico*, the players choose occupations in every turn. The Prospector receives gold directly, the Builder allows creation of new buildings, the Trader allows selling goods, and the Captain ships goods overseas. The players don't feel like a ship captain in the Captain phase and their character is not role-played, but the occupation names help players to remember the rules and choices.

In *Burnout 3*, large cars have high top speeds and lots of inertia in crashes. They also have poor acceleration and handling (the same is true of *Mario Kart*). There's engagement value in the fiction of driving a Formula-1 race car or a dump truck. More significantly, the thematic elements mesh with the mechanics by helping players to intuitively understand a vehicle's capabilities on sight.

One way to create this kind of mnemonic function and synergy between gameplay and theme is to begin design with content. Start your design with a strong setting, and introduce mechanics that simulate it. The mechanics are following the content, so they will naturally match. During balance, you will alter the mechanics. At that point, new explanations are required for the mechanics, which means that the setting must be modified to explain the new mechanics. This process also tends to take the game from a generic theme (e.g., pirates) to a unique, customized setting (e.g., interstellar ghost pirates).

There are many recurring themes for fictional elements in games. Some naturally follow from the theme—for example, an ice world should have slippery surfaces and loose controls. Some are counterintuitive; they grew from arcade conventions rather than natural thematic logic. Many games

Ice	Slippery, cold
Fire	Dangerous, hot
Water	Impassible or slows movement; in water, objects float/sink slowly
Wind	Gently pushes objects
Sand	Slows movement or quicksand
Sniper Rifle	Instant-hit, one-hit kill
Pits	Bottomless, instant death
Crates	Smash to receive upgrades
Barrel	Explodes on damage

Table 11.1. Simple thematic conventions.

expect players to smash every crate and vase they see to achieve upgrades, even though this is very strange behavior in real life. Table 11.1 lists some common fictional elements that act as mnemonics. These aren't necessarily things you have to include in your game, but they illustrate the way fiction helps the player to learn and recall the mechanics.

11.2.4 Backstory

The *backstory* of the setting is the explanation of how the world became the way it is. This may be a simple series of notes or an actual story. In some cases, you will reveal the story to the players, either piecemeal throughout the game or all at once in the exposition. In other cases, you will never tell players the story explicitly but instead will use the large body of descriptive material that you have generated to produce consistency throughout the content. Both *Star Wars* (the films, games, and books) and *Halo* series reportedly had huge backstories that were never entirely revealed to the players. Having everything in the world thought out provided consistency and allowed a large number of titles to inhabit those universes.

Later in this chapter, we discuss the plot, or story, of the game itself. Although this story flows out of the backstory, the backstory doesn't have to have the same narrative elements of a protagonist and a conflict. Think of the backstory as the fictional history of the world. In the case of an epic backstory, that history might not entirely predate the game's story itself. For example, in the *Star Wars* case, George Lucas reportedly planned out the backstory that preceded and followed the original sequence of three movies and then set them in the middle of his backstory.

A very effective way to develop and express the world in your design document is to accompany the backstory with a series of short stories or vignettes set in your world. These might become key scenes from the game's plot, but they could simply be exploratory creative writing that helps you to find and convey the boundaries of the setting and the overall tone of the game. The characters and locales need not match those of the game. Remember: the backstory and setting description are primarily for the development team. Whether or not you reveal them to the players depends on the choice of exposition method.

11.2.5 Brainstorming

Brainstorming is a good method both for generating a setting and then for generating elements of the setting or theme (see Chapter 3 for brainstorming rules). To select a setting, run a brainstorming session that begins with wacky or stereotypical settings. In the course of the session, you will hopefully veer into unique territory. Some classics (and examples of their use) to start you off are medieval (*Carcassonne*), space marines (*DOOM*), Arabia (*Through the Desert*), business (*Monopoly*), alien sci-fi (*Half-Life*), fantasy (*Warcraft*), and rock music (*Guitar Hero*). Many settings are the meeting of two others—for example, steampunk is science fiction using Jules Verne 1800's technology, and *Shadowrun* combines magical fantasy with science fiction (Figure 11.3).

When your team has selected a setting, record it on your overview sheet and then complete the theme worksheet. This begins with a brainstorming session that generates at least 200 words related to your game's theme. For example, if your theme is pirates, your list might look like the one in Figure 11.4. Include this in your design document.

After the brainstorming session, read over the entire list. Circle each of the elements that you feel a game with this theme absolutely must have.

Figure 11.3. Demon with a machine gun in *Shadowrun* by Fasa Studio, published by Microsoft for Xbox 360 and Windows. (Image courtesy of FASA/Microsoft Game Studios)

Pirates	**Spyglass**	Davey Jones	Spanish Main	Narwhale	**Boarding**	Gunpowder
Sailing	**First Mate**	Jolly Roger	Spanish Armada	Harpoon	Burning boat	Cannonball
Buccaneers	Aye, Matey	**Maroon**	South Seas	Tattoo	Nautilus	Ship's name
Cannon	Aargh	**Shipwreck**	Exploring	Maiden Voyage	Sea shell	Alongside
Swashbuckling	Yaar	Salvage	Windlass	Captives	Hideout	Ahoy
Sharks	HMS	**Walk the plank**	Compass	Brace of pistols	Cove	Hail
Peg leg	Royal Navy	Cat-o-nine-tails	Anchor	Rifle	Bay	Nautical flags
Kidnapped	Caribbean	Flogging	Crow's Nest	Knife	Inlet	Pirate flag
Shanghaied	Eye patch	Amputation	Curses	Three-cornered hat	Peninsula	**Skull-and-crossbones**
Pressgang	Sail	Surgeon	**Ghost ship**	Launch	Harbor	Secret codes
Mutiny	Cutter	Captain	**Derelict**	Rowing	Ocean	Writing in blood
Mutiny on the Bounty	Sloop	Cabin boy	Fishing	Oarsmen	Sea	Invisible writing
Parrots	Square-Rigger	Treasure Island	Albatross	Skipper	Fresh water	Ponytail
Monkeys	Mizzen mast	Captain Hook	Sea Monster	Whirlpool	Rum	Horses
Treasure map	Poop deck	Alligator	Sea Serpent	Neptune	Provisions	Scars
Bottle of Rum	Bowsprit	**Doubloon**	Kraken	Flying fish	Breadfruit	Homebound
Yardarm	Bow	Pieces of Eight	Giant Squid	Sting ray	Cargo	Mainsail
Keelhaul	Aft		White Whale	Man-o-War	Hold	Jib
	Abeam		Killer Whale	Ironsides	Ballast	Lines
	Thwart				**Stowaway**	
	Seven Seas				Barrel	

Halyard	Anchors aweigh	Tariff	Pilfer	Old English Font	Climbing rigging	Promotion
Clew	Docking	Taxes	**Plunder**	Blackletter	Rigging	Nailing things to the mast
Head	Waves	Smuggler	Pillage	Blackbeard	Soldier	Lost at sea
Tack	Typhoon	**Buried treasure**	Fort	Redbeard	Viceroy	**Desert island**
Point of sail	**Squall**	Pearls	Cliff	Bluebeard	Puerto Rico	Palm tree
Into the wind	Storm	Gems	Home base	Dread Pirate Roberts	**Port**	Sandy beach
Running	Becalmed	Sapphire	Pirates' Lair	Dreadnaught	Dock	Sandy spit
Reaching	In irons	Ruby	Alliances	Flotilla	Town	Spitting
Broad reach	**Brig**	Diamond	Deception	**Cannonade**	Buying things	Missing teeth
Beating	Trading	Emerald	**Double-cross**	Fleet	Equipment	Missing arm
Leeward shore	Hanging	**Gold**	**Cross current**	Admiral	Wine	One-armed pirate
Port	Bandanna	Silver	Current	Helmsman	Spices	Crutch
Starboard	Flag	Platinum	Sargasso Sea	Swab the decks	Rain	Wounds
Navigator	Country of origin flag	Bronze	**Reef**	Tar	Grog	Inn
Womenfolk	Inspection	Barometer	Fog bank	Bilge	Drunken sailor	Tavern
Breeches	Wages	Ship's bells	Pearl divers	Leaks	Killing your own crew	Brothel
Musket	**Divide treasure among crew**	Night watch	Gambling	**Sinking ships**	Poison	Cutting down trees
Sea chantey	**Bounty**	Cook	Slaves	Anchor line	Assassination	
Weigh anchor		Lie	**Fighting**			
		Swindle	Rations			
		Steal				

Figure 11.4. Thematic element brainstorming list for a pirate game.

In the example list, pirates would not be complete without ships, treasure, and islands. Remove elements that are not within the theme or don't match the tone that you have selected (remember, do this *after* brainstorming has completed—don't censor while generating ideas).

to make masts
Losing masts
Strategic combat
Shoot sideways
Ramming
Bomb
Treasure ships move slow
Row upwind
Broach
Tsunami
Black sand beach
Run aground
Commander
Ironwood
Coffin
Iron nails

Ropes
Hemp
Hawser
Spring line
Coiled rope
Snakes
Smoke
Smoke pots
Smoking pipe
Jig
Dancing
Bar maid
Ale
Salt
Old salt
Salt pork
Duff
Bread and water
Prison break
Fencing

Grappling hook
Towing boats
Repair
Carpenter
Musket shot
Wake
Plankton
Dolphin
Porpoise
Murder
Boxing
Evil eye
Diving bell
Salvage
Legend
Pirateer
Privateer
Penalty
Trade winds
Zephyr

Equator
Tropic of Cancer
Tropic of Capricorn
Tropics
Jungle
Spanish
Treasure chest
Earring
Anchor
Maelstrom
Whirlpool
Cutthroat
Voyage
Seas
Rob
Raid
Ravage
Lost-at-sea
Breakers
Coral

Adventure
Brine
Surf
Swell
Ocean
Drogue
Seafarer
Barnacle
Backstab
Betray
Cheat
Barge
Yacht
Schooner
Bark
Sloop
Dory
Lifeboat
Boom
Mast
Cunning
Devious

Carpenter
Gunner
Boatswain
Corsair

Figure 11.4. (cont.)

When you add a mechanic to the game, find the most appropriate fictional justification (e.g., trailing pirate ships are slowed because their wind is blocked). Then put a checkmark next to it, or boldface it if working with a word processor so you don't accidentally reuse the same element for a different mechanic. Try to use the circled elements first because you have already identified them as the most important. Maintain this theme worksheet throughout the design process. It allows the team to combine the mathematical creativity of mechanics with the artistic creativity of theme without having to switch thinking modes between them. You can always return to your stockpile of theme ideas when working on mechanics later.

11.2.6 Application

Setting manifests implicitly and pervasively through music and art direction in a game. It appears on the box art, on the board and card decorations of a board game, on the user interface of a video game, and, of course, on the characters, environment, and pieces in the game.

Backstory and in-game text explicitly bring out details. The backstory is conveyed in video games through text in the manual and through scripted *cutscenes*. These are dramatic scenes that are either prerendered to video, rendered live in-engine, or actually played interactively by the player. Prerendered scenes are just little movies. The *Final Fantasy* and *Diablo* series are famous for these. They have the best appearance and are the most cinematic of the three options, but they jolt the viewer out of the game and can make the game appear graphically poor in comparison. Rendering cutscenes live using the game's own rendering engine, as done by *Deus Ex*, *DOOM 3*, and *No One Lives Forever*, maintains a consistent level of graphical quality. This is more immersive and even allows the cutscene to be customized to a particular player's avatar. It still removes control from the player. The *Half-Life* series is famous for interactive cutscenes. In that series, the player never loses control of the character, and that character never speaks (thus never saying something that the player would not choose to). This is much more immersive and integrates story into the game. However, it is still limited compared to true interaction. The ideal cutscene is not perceived as a cutscene at all; the player should simply move through the world and participate in the story at the level of a pen-and-paper RPG, where players can take any action they wish and discover the story organically. As described in the technology chapters in this book, computer animation, dynamic sound generation, and artificial intelligence present major challenges that must be solved before we can create that kind of experience.

In-game text, called flavor text, appears as the names and descriptions of items, characters, and abilities. The card game *Magic: The Gathering*

Figure 11.5. Pearled Unicorn card from *Magic: The Gathering.* (Image courtesy of Wizards of the Coast)

and video game series *Diablo* are both famous for their use of flavor text to convey theme, which then increases the engagement of otherwise abstract combat mechanics. For example, two *Diablo* swords are distinguished in game terms by "Damage 1d9 + 4 / Durability 50" and "Damage 1d10 + 5 / Durability 60." But the game calls these swords "Gibbous Moon" and "Doombringer," in keeping with the epic fantasy theme. One *Magic* card that costs 2 and summons a creature with 2 power and 2 toughness is named "Pearled Unicorn/Summon Unicorn" and is labeled with the following text (see http://ww2.wizards.com/gatherer/CardDetails.aspx?\&id=261).

> *"Do you know, I always thought Unicorns were fabulous monsters, too? I never saw one alive before!" "Well, now that we have seen each other," said the Unicorn, "if you'll believe in me, I'll believe in you."*
> *–Lewis Carroll*

This flavor text, naming, and artwork (Figure 11.5) help the player to remember this particular card (e.g., "the unicorn is weaker than the griffin") and express the magic fantasy theme of the game.

11.3 Characters and Plot

There are two kinds of *characters*: those that serve as thematic mnemonics (and commonly, in this case, stereotypes) for a set of attributes and those

Figure 11.6. Character archetypes from *Team Fortress 2*. (Image courtesy of Valve)

that participate in a plot. Mnemonic characters are common in emergent games. For example, characters have no gameplay-affecting personality in *Team Fortress 2*, but, from the room-clearing Heavy to the sneaking Spy, the artistic and flavor design of the characters shown in Figure 11.6 helps players to understand each one's abilities.

Characters that participate in the *plot* are like literary characters; they must drive the story. The remainder of this subsection describes some aspects important in designing these "real" characters and the plot.

11.3.1 Protagonist and Antagonist

Characters that further plot are progressive game-design elements borrowed from literature and film. As with theme, these elements are most effective when they are integral to the narrative and when that narrative is integral to gameplay. When the story is *not* integral to gameplay, a good choice is to use a B-(bad)-movie plot. Although critics are harsh with games that have weak plots, there is no reason for an emergent game to have a strong plot. A strong plot and characters in an emergent game just disguise the underlying mechanics, which are what the player wants to get at in an emergent game. If the plot isn't part of the gameplay, it can remain for thematic reasons but should not distract and confuse the player. Of course, when the game is

Figure 11.7. Protagonist Lucas Kane in *Indigo Prophecy*. (Image courtesy of Atari)

progressive, a weak plot means a weak game. We now focus on progressive games.

One special character is the protagonist, who is usually controlled by the player. That protagonist might also have a foil nonplayer character—the antagonist—who creates conflict for the player and must be defeated in some way. Sometimes there are multiple player-controlled protagonists that can be rotated through. For example, in the *Knights of the Old Republic* game, the player controls a group of three characters. *Indigo Prophecy* is a relatively unique game in that the player controls both the protagonist (a sympathetic murderer, shown in Figure 11.7) and antagonists (the police) in a strongly progressive mystery (although about midway through the game, the police begin to side with the protagonist, and a new antagonist is introduced for them to collectively battle).

A story is not just a series of events that happen. It is a journey with an overarching message that introduces and then resolves a conflict. Typically, the protagonist must resolve the conflict and is changed by the process. Along the way, minor conflicts will arise and resolve, mirroring the larger structure. To quote the famous comic artist Scott McCloud, "The protagonist's desire is the engine of a story." Without the protagonist, the conflict, and his desire to resolve that conflict, we just have a bunch of characters sitting around.

Plot is the manifestation of the actions of a set of characters. It is important to consider each character's motivations separately from the designer's goal of creating a specific plot. As far as each character is concerned, he or she is the star of his or her *own* story. The protagonist is the character whose story the player is following directly, but many of the stories revolving around it are only glimpsed by the player. A character's actions must not be in service of the protagonist's plot. Within the game world, an antagonist does not appear to give the protagonist something to do. The antagonist as a fleshed-out character must have his or her own motivations to act. For each character, consider his or her motivations and the constraints on his or her actions.

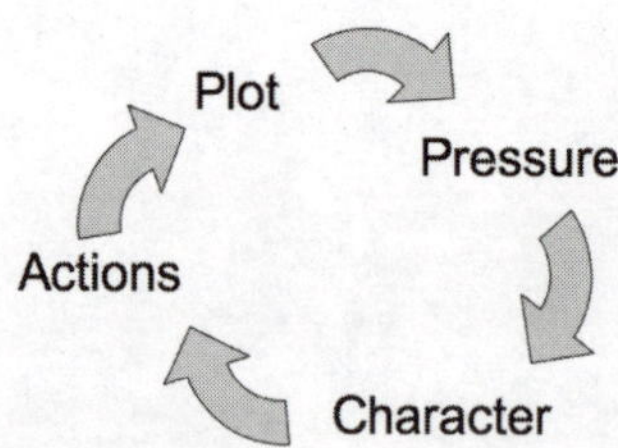

Figure 11.8. The driving relationship between character and plot. (Adapted from [Glassner 04])

Viewed this way, a cycle of actions drives the story forward, as illustrated in Figure 11.8. Each character experiences pressures that drive him or her to take actions. The result of these actions is the plot, which then puts pressure on the characters, and the story advances. When the plot turns so the driving pressure on the protagonist is resolved, the story (and the game) ends.

11.3.2 Profile

Each character in the game requires a *profile.* More important characters, like the protagonist and sidekicks, deserve a page or more of detail, whereas minor characters might be sketched out with only a paragraph or a name and one-sentence description. The more complete the description of a character, the closer the shared vision will be for everyone on the team. The following are some descriptive elements that can help flesh out your characters.

- name
- concept sketch
- personal backstory
- relations with other characters (perhaps expressed as a graph)
- primary desire
- role in the story
- occupation
- dwelling
- transportation
- weapons or artifacts
- physical description
  - gender
  - ethnicity/species
  - age
  - height, weight, build
  - injuries
  - wardrobe
  - pets

- positions on in-game controversies
- group/guild memberships
- musical theme
- color scheme

11.3.3 Conflict

Aristotle classified stories into three types, based on the form of their *conflict*. Our understanding of story hasn't changed much since then; stories are a fundamental form of human communication. Updating Aristotle's classification with modern language, the choice is merely one of who is the antagonist.

Person versus environment. Here, the antagonist is the world itself and fate. For example, *Tomb Raider: Legend* pits the player primarily against the game's level geometry and puzzles, and animals within the environment. Few other humans are in the game. All puzzle games could be considered environmental conflicts, but the categorization is best applied to progressive, narrative games.

Person versus person. The antagonist is a villain with greater power or resources than the protagonist. That power disparity gives the player sympathy for the protagonist and creates tension. How will the protagonist prevail? Most video games are a struggle between the player and an evildoer main boss who must be defeated.

Person versus self. In potentially the most sophisticated form of drama, the protagonist's own nature is the antagonist. It cannot be defeated explicitly. Instead, the character must change as a person to resolve this conflict. Typically, a visible external conflict arises from the internal conflict. *Deus Ex* plays with the notion of the protagonist as an ethical traitor. *Prince of Persia: The Two Thrones* has a rather explicit Jekyll-and-Hyde conflict between the protagonist's own natures. More true to the literary tradition, *Shadow of the Colossus* presents an external conflict between the player and giants that is later subtly revealed as an internal conflict between the player's desire to win the game and to act in an ethical manner. That game succeeds at a high-art (if not commercial) level because the player himself or herself begins to experience that conflict even more than the character; the characters in the game do not speak and have no explicit backstory.

Considering Maslow's hierarchy of human psychological needs, the protagonist, like anyone else, needs a base level of safety, health, and belonging (survival and community). Above those needs are desires for beauty and thought (culture: art and entertainment). At the highest level of psychological needs are self-actualization and transcendence (faith and ethics). Person-versus-environment conflict attacks the protagonist's survival. Interpersonal conflict begins to move into the more abstract realm of addressing not only survival but attacking the roots of the protagonist's culture. Internal conflict with one's self goes to the highest level of the protagonist's own identity.

11.4 Geography

Every world needs a map. When creating a map for your world, consider both the backstory geography and the areas that are actually observed in the game. Usually a world is designed with more area than the player actually experiences. This conveys the scope of a large and continuous world without the expense of actually building it to show to the player.

Maps can be both geometric and topological. A geometric map represents the true scale of the world (at least, within the limits of the map's projection). Note that the playable world, and even the backstory's larger world, need not be a planet. For a story that takes place on a single city block, the city might be the extent of the encompassing world. For a science fiction game, the "world" may be an entire galaxy. For an ant-themed game, the world might exist only within the confines of an ant hill.

A topological map is a graph. Like most subway maps, it shows how different locations are connected. Details other than connectivity are abstracted, and lengths and angles are adjusted to make a convenient layout of the graph. The topological map of the world is a meta-level. It shows how the major areas are connected. It is often used to explain the geography of the plot to the design team. In a progressive game, it shows how key characters move through the world during the story. In an emergent game, it shows the pathways between major areas that the player can follow.

Geography and maps need not be literally restricted to describing space. In a game with a major psychological element, it might be useful to map a character's mental space. For a time-travel game, locations on the map are placed both in time and space.

11.5 Exercises

1. What are the elements of setting?

2. Is an airline route map (the kind with lots of arcs into major airport hubs) topological or geographic? Why?

3. Extend Table 11.1 with more thematic conventions from games.
4. Create a list of ten interesting settings, describing each in one sentence that includes era, theme, and tone.
5. Write a profile for a famous character from literature.
6. Characters need not be intelligent, living creatures. For example, the camera (i.e., the audience) can be a character in a film if the other characters react or talk to it. In the film *The Red Balloon*, the balloon is a character. Describe a nonanimated character from a film, game, play, or book.
7. Draw a progression graph for the plot of a *Choose Your Own Adventure* or other game book.
8. Draw topological and geographic maps for a novel with varying locations, such as the *Lord of the Rings* books.

11.6 Resources

Wizards of the Coast makes available their role-playing game "system reference documents" under an open content license. These are a good source of elements for the theme worksheet:

- http://www.wizards.com/d20/files/SRD.pdf; *D&D* 4.0; fantasy theme, without statistics.
- http://www.wizards.com/default.asp?x=d20/article/srd35; *D&D* 3.5; fantasy theme, with statistics.
- http://www.wizards.com/default.asp?x=d20/article/msrd; modern military theme, with statistics.

The following texts discuss all aspects of creating a world, including narrative and setting.

- Todd, *Game Design: From Blue Sky to Green Light* [Todd 07].
- Rollings and Adams, *Andrew Rollings and Ernest Adams on Game Design* [Rollings and Adams 03].
- Isbister, *Better Game Characters by Design* [Isbister 06].
- Schutyema, *Game Design: A Practical Approach* [Schutyema 06].

- Baty, *No Plot? No Problem!* [Baty 04].
- Booker, *The Seven Basic Plots: Why We Tell Stories* [Booker 05].
- Glassner, *Interactive Storytelling* [Glassner 04].
- Despain, *Professional Techniques for Video Game Writing* [Despain 08].

CHAPTER 12

Art Direction

Terms Explained: *Art Director* – *Color Palette* – *Concept Art* – *Depth* – *Lighting* – *Reference Art* – *Shape Silhouette* – *Orientation* – *Visual Language*

The art director for a game establishes how the setting manifests through visual presentation. He or she creates guidelines for the materials, style, and technical properties of all artwork, including animation and lighting, throughout the game. For a small indie team, the art director may be the project lead or the primary artist. A large professional team usually has an explicit art director who specifies and approves all visual elements.

This chapter begins with a description of the visual language of art and design, which draws heavily from the fine arts. In fact, most game companies exclusively recruit artists with fine arts degrees and experience, even if they are less experienced with the tools of digital art creation. Learning a new tool like Photoshop or 3DS Max is easy compared to learning the skills of composition, design, and expression. Although the ability to draft, sketch, and paint with natural media is not required for all game art positions, few artists acquire the necessary talents without also learning those classic skills.

The art team begins working from collected reference artwork. From those, they produce concept art sketches that drive the production work. These preproduction and production stages involve artists with a number of specialized skills. Those roles and the interactions within the content team are presented in this chapter. The following chapters then address interaction between the content and technology teams, especially in the context of 3D games.

12.1 Visual Language

The art for any game must be both internally consistent and complementary to the setting and mechanics. It must also be properly supported by the technology. The art director establishes a *visual language* for the game that satisfies these constraints. Just as the setting establishes what kinds of events and objects can exist in the game world, the visual language establishes how objects appear.

The key idea of a visual language is to first establish the overall feel of the world and then to differentiate as much as possible within those constraints. In *Team Fortress 2*, all the characters are smooth and rounded, and all the buildings are angular. However, within these proscribed shapes, proportion radically differentiates the characters. The Heavy is squat, with an enormous torso and arms. The Spy and Medic are tall and thin, with gangly limbs that imply intelligence and facility over strength. A card game should use color, shape, font, and layout to distinguish each card so that it is immediately recognizable at a Gestalt level. However, all cards must fit within a common visual language so they appear to be from the same game and are not visually jarring.

The vocabulary of a visual language is specified by selecting choices for each of the elements of traditional artistic design and composition, described in the following subsections.

12.1.1 Shape and Silhouette

The *shape* of objects in the world might be organic and curvy or mechanical and angular. What are the geometric primitives of the world? How much complexity is there to the shapes? Smooth, simple shapes are friendly, whereas complex, jagged shapes are aggressive. The level of complexity implies complexity of mechanics or narrative. For Pixar's film (and games) *Cars*, the shape language of the entire world is that of cars. Beyond the cars themselves, the mountains of that world are shaped like the fins and hoods of 1920s American cars. The buildings, trees, and clouds echo the curves of cars. All elements of the world also reflect vehicles, not people: this is a world built and operated by cars. Early 3D games were limited to angular shapes made from few polygons because computers were too slow to draw more detailed models. Today, the limits are our imaginations and not our technology. Board games must balance the cost of manufacturing complex board and piece shapes against their artistic value.

The most important shape cue is the *silhouette* (outline). Every object—whether weapon, character, environment piece, or vehicle—should be recognizable from its silhouette alone. All other elements, such as color, shading, and texture, are subsidiary and should not be addressed until silhouettes

Figure 12.1. Silhouettes from *The Champions* comic. (Image courtesy of Marvel)

are strong and unique. The silhouette must not only be recognizable as belonging to a specific object, but the player must be able to read more information from it. For character, this information includes the facing direction, action, intentions, currently equipped objects, and even the level of health or power-ups.

Figure 12.1 shows a set of Marvel superheroes from *The Champions* drawn by Barry Kitson (see http://forum.newsarama.com/showthread.php?t=102650). Note that, even though reduced to partial silhouettes, each is unique and recognizable.

12.1.2 Proportion

Proportion controls both the perceived weight and the reality of objects. Tall, thin objects look fast, brittle, and light. Squat ones appear heavy and solid. An object also has proportions. Many games, particularly those influenced by anime and other Japanese aesthetics, use caricature, which is an exaggerated deviation from the average. A muscular character will bulge with muscles, a short character is half the height of an average person, and weapons become enlarged in proportion to their threat. The anime aesthetic also dictates childlike proportions, with enlarged heads and eyes and small noses and mouths. Those proportions appear in both human children and baby animals and are perceived as cute. For games, they also have the advantage of making the face, the expressive part of a character, large enough to see even when the character is small on the screen. Even in games that do not appear overly exaggerated, heads are often slightly larger than they should be. Many games also exaggerate a character's features to make them appear more heroic and attractive. For example, a superhero will have: large muscles, fists, and breasts; small waists and thin ankles; long legs; broad shoulders; angular jaws; and long hair.

The proportion between characters and objects in the world is important. In FPS games, the spaces between objects in the world are typically enlarged to aid navigation. Likewise, most props are about three-quarters of the size they should be. In *Deus Ex*, the main character's apartment has a relatively low, small couch and coffee table that are placed far apart to facilitate movement through the environment. In third-person games, this exaggeration is closer to half size, as can be observed in games like *The Legend of Zelda* series. Even in games with a realistic aesthetic like *Diablo II* and *Titan Quest*, buildings are barely taller than a character when seen from the outside. This is done to emphasize the importance of the characters, shrink the distances the player must travel between interesting areas, and give a topological graph quality to the world outside buildings. Buildings are the nodes that we travel between, and all the activity at a building is contained inside that node.

12.1.3 Orientation

The orientation of objects in the environment affects the player's perception of space. Cartoony games often use simplified shapes with slightly off-kilter orientations. The *Star Wars* universe contrasts technological, urban, vertical spaces like the Death Star with rural, horizontal spaces like the planet Tatooine. In those games, the orientation of the level geometry expresses the kind of level that the player is in. *Half-Life 2* not only uses vertical and horizontal elements to convey the tone of the setting, but it involves them deeply in gameplay. When a player is working his way up a steep mountain switchback, the first-person view limits his ability to perceive threats from above and below. This raises the tension and surprise of those levels. In contrast, a traditional building-layout level allows the player to see potential enemies and their hiding spaces at a greater distance, thus emphasizing tactics over quick reactions.

12.1.4 Color Palette

Every fictional world has its own *color palette*, and every character and level has its own subset of that palette. Colors are described by hue, value, and saturation. Hue is what we casually call "color." It varies around a color wheel, passing through red, orange, yellow, green, cyan, blue, purple, and then back to red. Colors near red are called warm colors. Although interpretation is partly cultural, warm colors invoke excitement, action, danger, heat, warmth, daytime, and affection. Colors in the blues and greens are called cool colors and are associated with cold, nature, distance, nighttime, and calm.

Value is also called brightness, luminance, shade, and intensity. A painter would say it is the amount of color pigment versus black in the color. Yellow and brown have the same hue, but brown is much darker. When drawing with charcoal or pencil, you are reducing the value of white paper with each stroke. Value is primarily perceived through contrast. A (bright) high-value object stands out against a (dark) low-value background, whereas a low-value object blends into that background.

Saturation is the amount of color versus white; it is also known as tint. A desaturated color is a pastel; a saturated color is bold and pure. Saturating colors makes them appear stronger but also more comic. Desaturating makes them seem softer and more realistic but weaker.

Just as the silhouette carries the bulk of shape information, the value of a color carries most of its information. To have art communicate clearly and intensely, it should work just as well in grayscale. It often helps to perform art direction purely in grayscale at first and add hue later to avoid weakening visual communication by overreliance on hue. This is especially important given that one out of every ten males is color blind to some extent and cannot distinguish some hues. Having a boost or a curse distinguished in a game by only red or green and not by value and shape means that a color-blind person will be unable to play your game.

Game developer Epic provides examples of good and bad color use, shown in Figure 12.2. They have come a long way since their first megahit, *Unreal*, in 1998. That game was flooded with red, green, and blue lights and saturated characters. By 2004, the current game in that series, *Unreal Tournament 2004*, had begun to rely much more heavily on value than hue. Their latest blockbuster games as of 2008, *Unreal Tournament 3* and *Gears of War*, are mostly desaturated, with information conveyed almost exclusively through value and not hue. The hues are restricted to a primary color with accents and are used in more sophisticated ways than they were back in 1998.

Color palette selection depends on the medium. Most mass-produced display methods blend a set of primary colors. Computer screens use red, green, and blue primaries. Printers often use cyan, magenta, yellow, and black primaries. It is not possible to generate all colors just by mixing primary colors. The set of colors that can be achieved by mixing is called the gamut of the medium. When selecting a palette, it is important to

Figure 12.2. The *Unreal* series games from 1998, 2004, and 2008. (© 1998–2008 Epic Games, Inc.)

consider both the tools that will be used to create images for the game and the final display process's gamut, since the actual colors available will be limited by both. For example, computers display very nice reds and greens, but they tend to have limited ability to reproduce shades of orange. This isn't to say that you can't show orange in a computer game, only that the exact color desired may be harder to achieve and nuance than for a printed board game.

The field of color theory proscribes many ways of selecting good color combinations to form a palette or scheme. This field is a mixture of aesthetics, psychology, and neurophysiology. As a result, it is highly subjective and is sensitive to cultural trends. Most palette theories are based on the notion of a color wheel, which is itself subjective. The ideal color wheel divides all hues according to a perceptually uniform distribution, but that distribution is subject to the saturation and value of the chosen colors as well as the physiology and psychology of the observer.

The following are some common schemes.

- **Complementary.** Choose opposing, saturated hues from a color wheel for maximum hue contrast. Such colors tend to visually vibrate against each other, so this is best when both colors are not observed at the same time. Christmas colors of red and green are used for traffic lights for this reason.

- **Analogous.** Use a small number of distinct hues that are adjacent on the color wheel. These are typically augmented by neutral (completely desaturated) colors. This produces low hue contrast but harmonious color.

- **Triad.** Use three equally spaced hues around the wheel. Rely most heavily on one, and let the others act as accents. A variation on triad is split-complementary, which brings the accent hues closer to each other. Two legs of the triad are often used to select strong colors that are attractive together. For example, red and yellow is a common action color combination.

- **Square.** Use four equally spaced hues. This is good for board games where you need a number of distinct shades to represent players.

- **Saturation gradient.** Choose primary and accent hues, using one of the preceding schemes, and then vary saturation to generate distinct colors. Varying saturation lends sophistication and denotes maturity, complexity, and elegance. Most fine clothing and wallpaper patterns have a single hue and vary saturation.

The easiest way for new artists to choose colors is to mimic existing schemes rather than synthesize new ones from first principles. Look at clothes, websites, printed materials, vehicles, and buildings. For each, identify the primary and accent hues. Note how saturation and value are varied to create additional colors. Observe the level of saturation. In some schemes, nothing is ever fully saturated, whereas in others, nothing is ever desaturated. Value shifts according to lighting on 3D objects, so it is less carefully controlled than hue and saturation.

12.1.5 Motion

For video games, how objects move is a key part of how they are perceived by players. Like the silhouette, a character's animation conveys his or her mental state, intentions, age, speed, and abilities. Animations are obviously customized to the practical constraints of a character and a scene, but the overall art direction should specify the bounds on motion and overall feel of motion in the game. Characters, particularly the player character, should have a signature move or set of moves that align well with the key experiences of the game. For example, in *Gears of War*, mantling and pressing flat against walls are signature moves that relate to the importance of cover in that game. In *Splinter Cell*, the signature move is the wall split, where the spy holds himself above enemies in narrow passages. Mario's signature move is his jump, with one fist held high. In fighting games, the signature move is often the finishing move or special attack.

12.1.6 Depth

Because of the dense clustering of information in both video games and board games, it is important that art uses *depth* cues to help separate foreground and background elements. In a 3D game, foreground and background literally are 3D distances. For 2D video games and board art, background tends to be decoration and foreground is information. Here are the major cues for helping to visually separate foreground and background elements.

- The foreground occludes (covers) background.
- Black or white outlines around foreground isolate it.
- Drop shadows visually lift foreground above background.
- Ambient occlusion shadows lift foreground without an explicit light source.
- Defocusing the background keeps attention on the foreground.
- Desaturating the background (i.e., "fogging" it) keeps attention on the foreground.
- The foreground/background values are adjusted to create contrast.

Figure 12.3 shows several examples of combining these techniques. Outlines offset data without creating much perceived depth. Soft or ambient shadows have recently become popular for making foreground elements pop out without the hard, two-plane look of traditional drop shadows. The choice between depth cues depends on the setting, types of background artwork, and amount of foreground data.

12.2 Reference Art

Preproduction begins with collecting tens or hundreds of *reference art* materials, which are the inspiration for the art style of the game. Combined with textural descriptions, these establish a shared artistic vision for the game. Reference art is chosen to demonstrate all the elements of visual language, including palettes, scales, and interactions between objects.

It is important to understand not only the subjects within reference art but how they are composed and presented to the viewer. For example, when creating a a football game like *Madden*, just having good character and stadium 3D models isn't enough. You also have to copy the camera angles used in TV coverage, the style of the information placed over the images, the background sounds, and the pacing of camera cuts.

Some good sources of concept art are the Google image search website, stock image libraries such as iStockPhoto, nature magazines such as National Geographic, and large-format art books.

Work with reference art from both academic and popular sources. There is a fine line between reality and fiction; sometimes illustrations and films

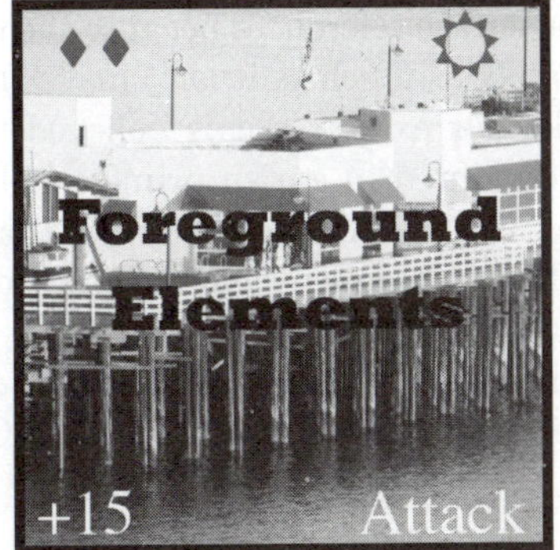

Poor initial design due to competing foreground and background.

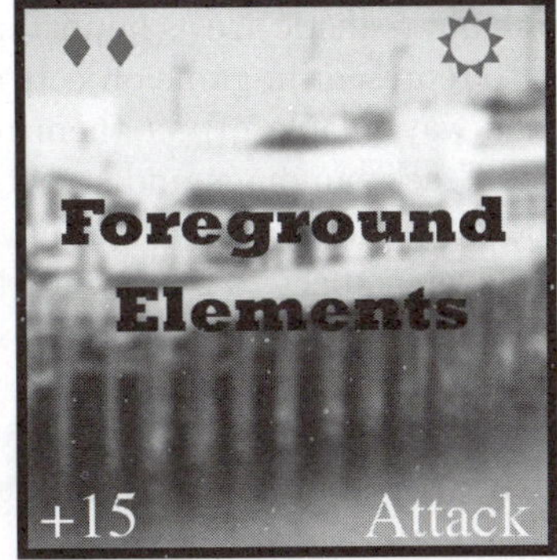

Defocusing and increasing the value of the background shifts attention to the foreground.

A white scrim behind the foreground increases value contrast, and ambient shadows on text subtly but effectively control interest.

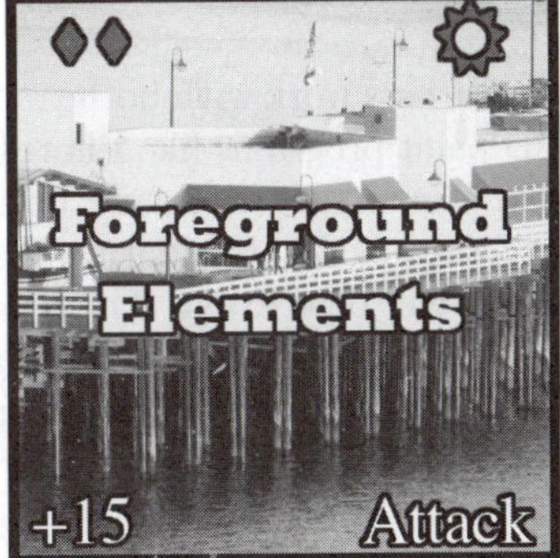

Desaturating the background and adding black outlines create bold contrast. Note that outlines appear to darken foreground colors.

Desaturation with thin outlines and ambient shadows is more subtle than thick outlines but maintains most of the intent.

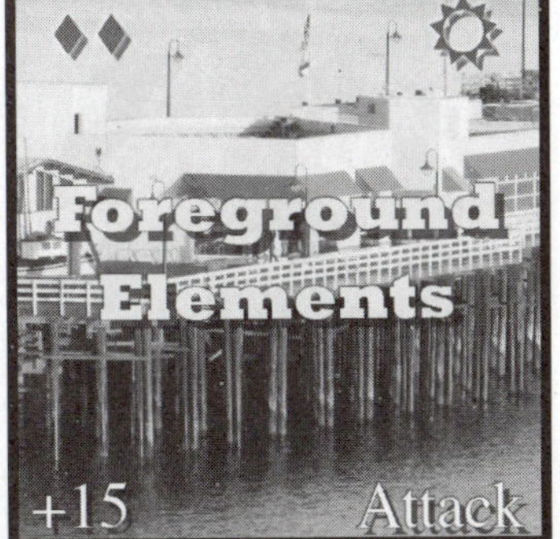

Sharp drop shadows create two distinct planes of depth, offsetting the foreground in a very conscious manner.

Figure 12.3. Leveraging depth cues in 2D art.

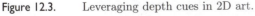

that are not realistic are as important as accurate references because the goal is not to represent in-game objects accurately as much as it is to make them look the way people *expect* them to look. For example, it is believed that ancient Greek buildings and statues were painted in garish primary colors. But because the modern ruins have been washed to white marble, that is what players expect to see, even when playing a game set in ancient times. This often means making objects larger or smaller than they actually are or adding decorative touches that would never be found in reality: a drill sergeant's beard and cigar, wings on an interstellar spaceship, or a 3D GUI on a hacker's programming terminal.

12.3 Concept Art

Concept artists work with both traditional media like pen and paper and clay and 2D paint programs like Photoshop. They create concept art images like those in Figure 12.4 that show both full-color paintings intended to give the sense of an object and blueprint-like front, side, and top views from which the 3D model will be created. Those detailed views often show zoomed-in areas or have additional notes that explain proportions, coloring, and important features. Concept artists will also produce paintings of full scenes that help the team visualize what the game will feel like when played. Occasionally,

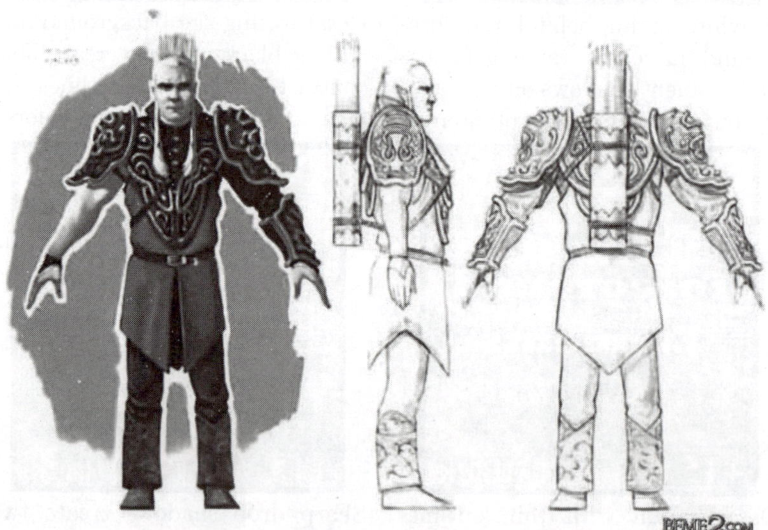

Figure 12.4. Concept art from *The Battle for Middle Earth 2.* (© 2006 Electronic Arts)

a concept artist will produce a full 3D sculpture that can then be digitized and act as a starting point for a digital 3D model. Concept artists often compile large libraries of reference material. For example, an artist working on a game set in the ancient world would work from Egyptian, Greek, and Roman history illustrations; pictures and maps of the region; documents describing clothing of the period; archeology texts; and fantasy works with the same setting.

12.4 3D Art Roles

Because 3D graphics are so integral to games, members of the content, technology, and design teams all participate in graphics and need some basic knowledge of the process. Artists on the content team produce the 3D models using tools created by the tools team and following the direction and goals of the design team. The core technology team spends a majority of its effort creating systems to render those 3D models in either a realistic or stylized fashion. The concept artist and art director discussed previously are of course present on the content team for 3D art production in addition to the roles discussed following.

12.4.1 Tools Team

In game development, the tools team produces in-house applications for modeling 3D worlds and the objects that inhabit them. Often, they will extend existing modeling packages like 3DS Max, Maya, Lightwave, Poser, and Blender to work with the rest of the game's technology. A word processor has an intermediate file format (like ".doc" files for Microsoft Word) used for editing the document and a final format (like ".pdf," ".ps," or ".html") for distributing polished read-only copies. Similarly, 3D modeling packages have intermediate formats (some common ones are ".obj," ".max," ".3ds," and ".lwo"). The tools team is responsible for creating exporters and plug-ins that can convert these intermediate formats to a custom read-only format that will be used by the game when a model is complete.

12.4.2 Content Team

Artists on the content team create animated 3D models as well as 2D art used for user interfaces, title screens, and marketing. The art roles are broken down into a lead artist or art director, concept artist, modeler, texture artist, animator, lighting artist, and level artists. Depending on the team size and type of project, one person may take on more than one of these roles. The art director controls the visual style for the entire game, ensuring that it is self-consistent and implements the aesthetic of the project. In doing so, the art director works most closely with the concept artists and the effects programmers.

12.4.3 Modeling Artist

When the concept art has been approved, a modeler uses the software supported by the tools team to create a 3D model from it. Often, modelers will load scanned concept art reference drawings into their 3D software and align the model's silhouette to the original image, and then finally add details on the interior. Modelers must balance the artistic vision of the concept art against practical concerns of a video game. For example, narrow features like spikes might disappear between the pixels at low resolutions, so enlarging them can improve the appearance of a character. Lots of small features produce a 3D model that has a lot of geometry, which might slow down the game. Likewise, making smooth curves requires lots of geometry because most games can only represent models made out of polygonal meshes. Smooth curves are approximated with many small polygons, so the modeler tries to keep the polygon count as low as possible without making the character too angular or losing too many details.

Historically, polygon counts as low as 500 were required for in-game characters. Today, 10,000 polygons is reasonable for a character on a PC or Xbox 360, and scenes that contain as many as a million polygons can be rendered in real time. However, it is still easy to waste geometry and create models with too many polygons, so conserving geometry remains an important skill. One new technology that helps with this is normal maps, which are one of many forms of "displacement mapping." Normal maps, which are described

Figure 12.5. Characters from *Spider-Man 3: The Game* in the rest pose. (Image courtesy of Vicarious Visions)

in Chapter 13, allow a relatively coarse character to appear more detailed when it is rendered on the screen. Most modeling software now includes utilities for automatically reducing a high-polygon character to a low-polygon character with a normal map.

Figure 12.5 shows two characters from *Spider-Man 3: The Game* after the modeling artist and texture artist have finished their work. The characters are in a neutral rest pose that helps the texture artist to see all parts of their surface. The animator will then create lifelike poses for them. These characters are about 1500 polygons each. The relatively low polygon counts are for two reasons. First, these characters are rendered on the Wii and PS2, which are relatively low-power consoles. Second, these are enemy characters. Many of them will appear on screen at once, so each one must be simplified in order to render all simultaneously.

12.4.4 Texture Artist

If a modeling artist's plain 3D model were inserted into the game, it would probably look like a plaster statue because the modeler is responsible for creating the shape of each object but not the materials and colors on its surface. It is the texture artist's job to paint those details. Either the modeler or the texture artist assigns texture coordinates, or "U-V's," to the 3D model that map every point in 3D to a point on a 2D image. This 2D image is called a texture map (hence the title *texture artist*). As shown in Figure 12.6, the texture map looks like an unrolled and flattened version of the 3D model—sort of like an orange peel or a bearskin rug. The texture artist paints the texture map in a 2D art program like Photoshop.

Figure 12.6. 2D texture map as painted by the artist and its in-game appearance applied to a 3D model from *Natural Selection*. (© 2004 Unknown Worlds)

Many materials have interesting properties that can't be represented by a single texture map. For example, a knight has shiny armor, a velvet cape, and a little exposed skin on his face, and each of these materials interacts with light in a different way. The texture artist can use one map to describe the base color of these materials and additional maps to mark areas that should reflect (like the armor), be softly shaded (the velvet), or receive special rendering attention for realism (like the skin). In science fiction and fantasy settings, many materials even glow in the dark, so that glow can be painted into still another map.

12.4.5 Animator

Once a model is textured, it appears realistic—but only for a single frame. Machines and characters are constantly in motion. Even trees sway in the breeze. The animator's job is to use a separate modeling program or modeling plug-in like Character Studio or Natural Motion to create animations for the models. Animation can be done in two ways: key frames and skeletal animation. Key frames use completely separate models for every frame of animation. The animator typically produces them by modifying a base model (which is often a character with arms outstretched in a standard T-shape). Key framing gives the animator great control, but it is laborious, creates large amounts of data to distribute with the game, and limits the ways that animations can be combined with each other. Skeletal animation is largely preferred today. In this method, the animator rigs the 3D model with a skeleton that has bones and joints. For a human character, this skeleton might look similar to a real-world skeleton, but it will likely contain many fewer bones and a few extra joints to work around peculiarities in the animation software. The animator attaches the polygon skin to the skeleton by assigning different scaling factors, called weights, at each vertex (point) on the polygons. Moving the underlying skeleton then moves the model. One advantage of skeletal animation is that the same animation can be transferred between multiple models provided they all have compatible skeletons. Conversely, the skeleton can be fitted with different models to represent an aging or damaged character. This flexibility leads to the animation and skeleton sometimes being considered the real character and the model the "skin" that it wears. There are many methods of incorporating real-world data, simulated physics, and hand-created animations at runtime. These are discussed at length in Chapter 15.

12.4.6 Level Artist

Some models are so large and complex that manipulating them is an entirely different skill set. The environment, or "level," in a game, which typically consists of either terrain with buildings on it or a large interior area like an office building, is created in level-editing software by a level artist. Because the design of game levels is very specific to a particular game, the technology team will usually create a level-editing program that is tailored to the specific game. These programs include the ability to place precreated models; label the locations for power-ups, enemies, and spawn points; and place limits on where the players may travel.

The level artist works with (or often *is*) a level designer who plans the floor map of a level. Once the basic areas of interest have been identified, the level artist makes a mockup of the level that will be playtested. Based on the designer's observations during the playtest, the level artist modifies the 3D geometry to increase flow, adjust sight lines, or steer the player in the right direction. When the level geometry has been approved, the level artist textures the level.

Figure 12.7 shows the level artist's view of a typical game level in 3DS Max. Each area is color coded. Note that the space between buildings is filled with geometric primitives like squares and cubes. These are triggers and flags that are invisible to players. There are many applications for these. They cause events to occur when the character enters a certain area. Some are spawn points for characters and items. Some indicate parameters for the

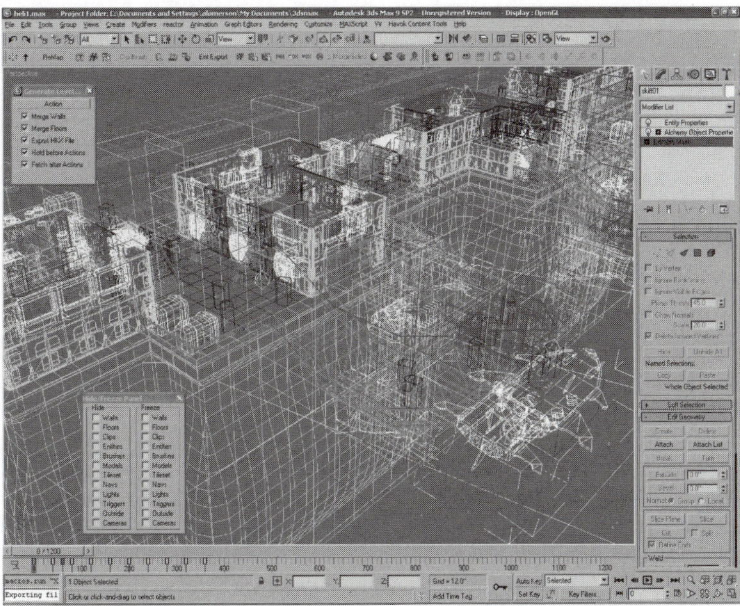

Figure 12.7. Level geometry from *Marvel Ultimate Alliance* in 3DS Max. (Image courtesy of Vicarious Visions)

lighting system. Finally, certain nodes help AI characters navigate through the level.

12.4.7 Lighting Director

Beginning during the process of level design and carrying on to the final versions, the lighting artist or lighting director (who is often the art director or a level artist) adds illumination to the world. In-game lighting does not accurately model real-world lighting, which is both an advantage and a disadvantage. It is convenient to be able to create lights that don't cast shadows, for example, but it can also be frustrating to work with computer graphics lights that rarely produce realistic-looking shading.

12.4.8 Core Technology Team

In parallel with content development, the technology team either writes a rendering engine from scratch or, more likely, customizes an existing licensed engine. Without this technology, there would be no way to actually view the 3D models in the game. The remainder of this book describes the issues involved in creating a rendering engine, which in turn impact how content must be created for that engine.

CHAPTER 13

3D Modeling

Terms Explained: *Alpha – Billboard – Bump Map – Normal Map – Particle System – T-Junction – Texture Coordinate (UV) – Texture Map – Triangle Mesh*

Modeling is the process by which artists create 3D shapes and assign them materials and animations. In other words, it is what happens when the game is being created. Another part of modeling is the technology perspective: how those shapes are represented within the game and what tools are needed to facilitate their development. Rendering is the process of creating a 2D image on the screen from a 3D world—what happens when the game runs (although writing the code for rendering is, of course, part of the production process). Because rendering brings together content and code, it is essential for the content creation team to understand what makes a model slow or fast to render and how the controls they see in their modeling programs impact the final image.

This chapter describes the team interactions and workflow surrounding 3D content creation in tools like 3DS Max and Maya. Detailed artistic methodology and how to use specific modeling packages is not covered, but a list of recommended resources for artists is presented at the end of the chapter.

13.1 Triangle Mesh

In the real world, we describe shapes using a variety of primitives such as spheres, cylinders, cubes, lines, polygons. For example, you might describe a stop sign as an octagon atop a thin cylinder pole. Most modeling software uses similar primitives, as well as curved patches with less familiar names like NURBS, splines, and subdivision surfaces. But rendering software, especially for games, works exclusively with a single primitive called a *triangle mesh.* All of the other primitives are converted to triangle meshes at some point during the modeling process to conform to the rendering constraint. Most modelers choose to perform that conversion fairly early in the modeling process so they will have detailed control over the modeled surface.

A triangle mesh is a set of triangles that approximates the desired surface. The triangles touch each other at their vertices—their corners—and at their edges—the shared side of two triangles. It is usually essential to ensure that triangles only meet at these locations. Failing to ensure this property leads to rendering artifacts.

13.1.1 Avoiding Artifacts with Watertight Meshes

If triangles in the mesh *interpenetrate* by passing through one another at their faces, as in Figure 13.1, then the intersection may appear to vibrate when it is rendered. Also, shading could be incorrect on the interpenetrating surfaces, especially if they are translucent. Many special effects such as shadows and outlining depend on triangles only meeting at their edges.

Another situation to avoid is the *T-junction*, an example of which is shown in Figure 13.2. If the vertex of one triangle lies on the edge of another, then small roundoffs inside the graphics card during rendering can cause the vertex to run off the edge. This creates a small gap through which the background can be seen. To correct a T-junction, subdivide the triangle so that triangles share entire edges and are completely tessellated at vertices.

Another way gaps can appear in a mesh is when two vertices are so close that they appear to be identical but are in fact at slightly different locations. Unless the surface texture or color changes across an edge, or the edge represents a sharp crease like the edge of a cube, multiple vertices should never be located in the same location ("colocated").

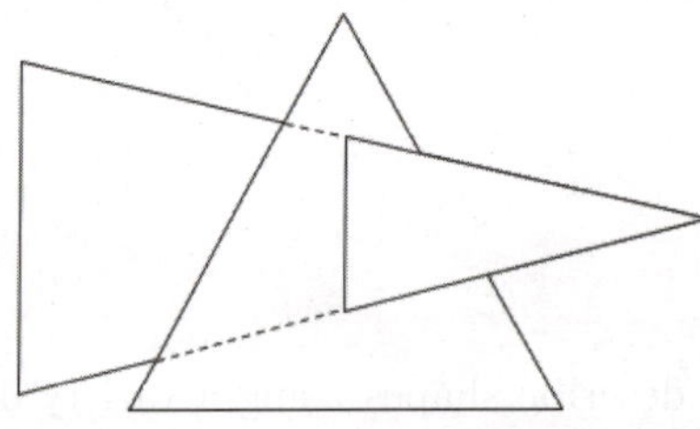

Figure 13.1. Interpenetration (dotted line) leads to artifacts when rendering.

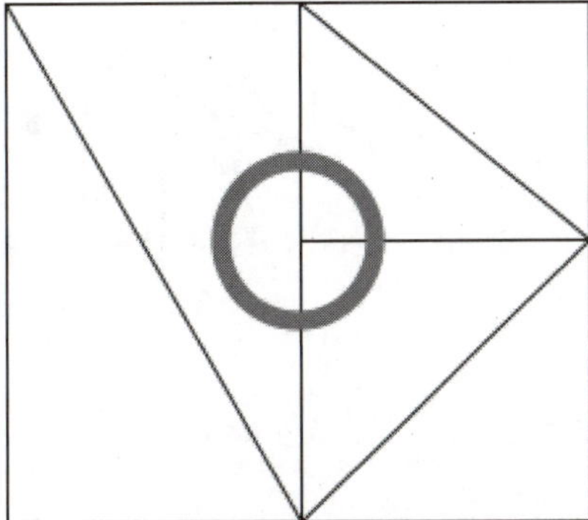

Figure 13.2. A T-junction (encircled center vertex) creates a crack during rendering. The mesh can be fixed by subdividing the triangle whose edge it intersects.

A nonintuitive fact of 3D rendering is that triangles are generally one-sided. That means that when viewed from the front, they appear to be a solid surface but are invisible when viewed from the back. This is done because triangles viewed from the back are necessarily on the back of a volume, and since the viewer sees the front of the volume, the back is not visible and need not be rendered. Of course, a gap in the front allows the back to be seen, which is why it is important to avoid gaps. This also means that every edge should be between exactly two triangles. An edge attached to only one triangle is a boundary of the surface and represents a location where the surface may disappear if seen from the wrong side. Such edges are called *broken* or *dangling* edges and should be eliminated by adding additional triangles to close the surface. When representing an extremely thin surface like paper, you must either match each triangle with one oppositely oriented on the back or disable the default back-is-invisible behavior on the graphics card.

When all triangles meet at shared vertices and have no gaps or dangling edges, and the mesh has no T-junctions, the mesh is said to be *watertight*, meaning that *if* the mesh were filled with water, it would not leak. Watertightness is required for several rendering algorithms and is often a necessity for the graphics engine.

13.1.2 Why Triangles?

Why must game models be reduced to triangle meshes when quadrilaterals ("quads"), spheres, and other more complex shapes are available? The answer is that triangles are the universal atoms of the polygon world and have desirable properties. They are atoms in that every other polygon can

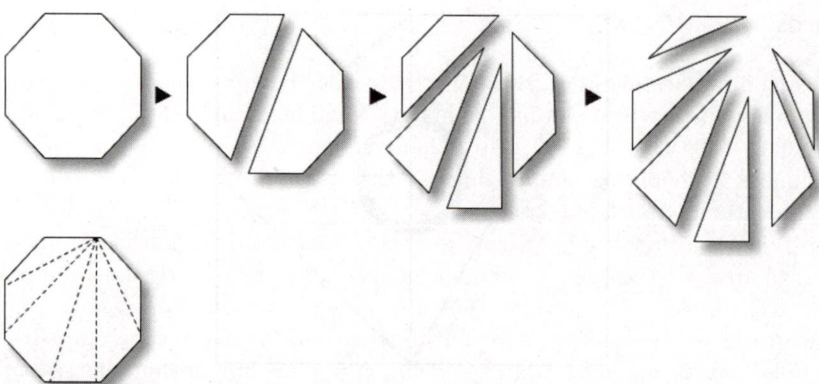

Figure 13.3. All larger polygons can be subdivided into triangles. This octagon can be subdivided into seven smaller pieces as shown. The exploded view is for clarity; an actual tessellation would look like the bottom row.

be subdivided into polygons with fewer sides, but there is nothing simpler than a triangle. For example, an octagon can be divided into two irregular five-sided polygons. Those five-sided polygons can each be subdivided into a quadrilateral and a triangle, and then that quadrilateral can be divided into two triangles. The top row of Figure 13.3 shows this progression. The bottom row shows that we also could have created six triangles directly from the octagon. The triangles, however, can't be subdivided into simpler shapes. We could subdivide them into more triangles, but those wouldn't be any simpler. So one reason triangles are good is that they are as simple as possible. Another is that given enough triangles, we can exactly represent any other polygonal shape.

Another advantage of triangles is that they are are guaranteed to be planar. Consider the full octagon in Figure 13.3 again. The octagon appears to be flat, but each vertex could be moved in and out of the page to create a complex three-dimensional shape. Even if we know the exact three-dimensional position of each vertex, the exact shape of the surface between them is ambiguous. For a triangle, the three vertices define exactly one flat plane.

In part because triangles are guaranteed to be planar, they are comparatively easy for the rendering system to draw on a screen. The rendering system contains an algorithm (usually built into the graphics card) that knows how to find all pixels inside a triangle. It is possible to draw shapes like spheres without first turning them into triangles, but doing so is much slower. For games, we want the fastest rendering possible and are willing to accept the limitations of converting all shapes to triangles first.

13.1.3 Billboards

Triangle meshes are the fastest way to render complex shapes on modern graphics cards, which can handle about 1 million triangles at 60 frames per second. But what is even faster than rendering complex shapes made of triangles is rendering simple shapes—that is, approximating the complex shapes using fewer triangles.

When an object is far from the viewer, most of the triangles cover less screen area than one pixel. So modelers typically create several detail levels for each model. At runtime, the most-detailed model is used only when the object is very nearby. As it falls farther into the distance, progressively simpler models are used. Many modeling programs support automatic detail reduction. When using these, the artist creates the most-detailed version of a model and lets the software automatically simplify it to reduce the polygon count. Since the automated version is rarely ideal, the artist then adjusts vertices on the simplified mesh so that it has the best shape possible given the reduced number of triangles.

Sometimes an object can be modeled with as few as two triangles covered with an image of the complex shape. So-called *billboards* or *impostors* are single quadrilaterals painted with an image. The rendering system can automatically rotate them to always face toward the viewer so they never appear edge-on, which would ruin the illusion. Historically, in old games, *all* objects were billboards called *sprites*. For 2D games, it is obvious that in-game objects can be represented by images, since they never rotate. *Wing Commander* was the first game to popularize the use of sprites for creating illusion of 3D objects. Each spaceship in the game was drawn from several angles during the modeling process, and the correct image was then displayed at runtime to give the appearance of flying through 3D battles. Even today many games use billboards for foliage, power-ups, bullets, and distant objects.

13.1.4 Reducing Polygon Counts

One important polygon savings comes from modeling only the outer shell of objects. Most of the time, an object is represented only by its surface, and all of the internal detail, like the engine of an automobile, is removed to reduce the polygon count. When buildings the player cannot enter are part of the game, for example, they are typically modeled as empty facades that are only a few centimeters thick and have no interior. It is common for buildings to be simple facades with no internals or even a back.

The shading across the surface of a model will look relatively good no matter how low the polygon count. Polygons are most useful, therefore, along the silhouette of an object. If you know your object will be viewed primarily from one direction, only use polygons that tessellate the silhouette when it is viewed from that direction. If your object will be viewed from many directions, it is still possible to optimize for the silhouette. For example, a character's breast and back are rarely in silhouette, but the sides of the chest and the limbs are. Any thin projection, like horns or fingers, needs special consideration.

13.2 Particle System

Amorphous animated objects such as fire, smoke, rain, and sparks can be represented by a *particle system.* The particle system tracks the position of hundreds of individual-point particles. Those are animated according to relatively simple equations such as ballistic motion. Each particle is graphically modeled by a billboard, usually one that is translucent so the many particles blend together into the appearance of a large cloud or at least several layers of rain.

Modeling a particle system is very different from modeling a triangle mesh. Most particle systems are created using in-house editors that are specific to the rendering system used for the game, but they tend to have the same properties (see Figure 13.4). Each system can contain multiple kinds of particles. A particle is parameterized by its billboard image, the rate at which it is generated (spawned), how long it lives before being removed from the system, how it is blended with other particles if translucent, and

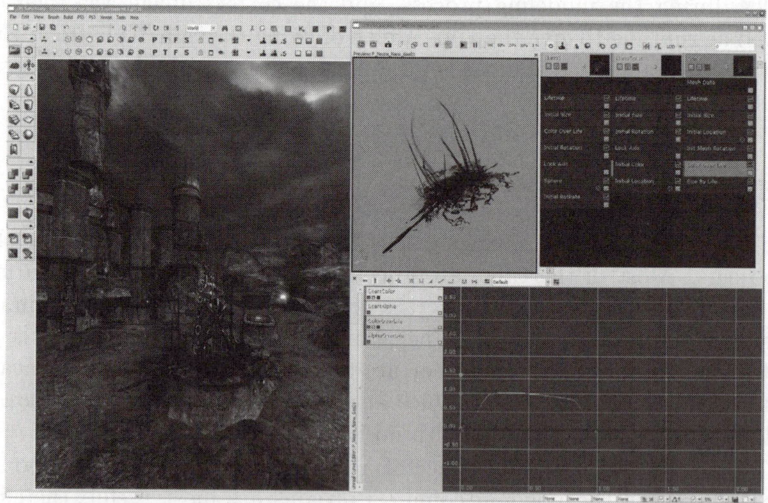

Figure 13.4. The UnrealCascade particle system editor. (© 1998–2008 Epic Games, Inc.)

motion parameters. Motion parameters typically involve gravity, dispersion, and noise. Each property is driven by a curve on a graph that can be edited by dragging control points.

Complex effects are simulated by combining many kinds of particles. For example, a supernova might have an exploding core of white particles that fade to blue and radiate outward from the center. Outside these, large dim blue streaks jet outward more slowly to simulate escaping gasses, and black shapes silhouetted against the gasses are the chunks of atomized planets.

13.3 Texture Map

13.3.1 Textures are Images

Figure 12.6 showed a *texture map* for a space marine that was handpainted by a texture artist. It is called a "texture" map for historical reasons. "Material property map" would be a more accurate name, since texture maps are images that encode a map of the varying light-reflectance properties of a 3D model. The figure showed the diffuse color texture map; other properties of a surface, like transparency, can also be painted into a texture map. Those material properties are described later in this chapter. Images can be used to map any value across the surface of a model. They are even used to map small height deviations like ridges and dents from the flat triangles, encoding what a layperson would call "texture." Since the word texture was already used to describe colors, those images are called *bump maps.*

Textures are typically authored using Photoshop because they are images. Photoshop supports multiple layers for editing. Each layer is like a separate transparent canvas that can be painted on. The image observed is the composite of all the layers. A texture artist will commonly paint different material properties onto different layers. Different elements of the same material might also be on a group of related layers. For editing, the entire image file is saved on Photoshop's PSD file format, which is extremely large but can encode all the pixels exactly as well as all the layers.

When the texture assets are ready to be applied to a 3D model in the modeling program or in a game, they must be exported to a more convenient and typically smaller file format than PSD. To do this, the artist isolates the layers for each material property and flattens them into a single image. That image is then saved out, commonly as a JPG, PNG, or DDS file. Some companies have their own proprietary texture formats to which Photoshop plug-ins can export. It is important to retain the original PSD file so changes to the texture can be made later.

The exported files are compressed to save space. JPG-compressed files are particularly small, but they are comparatively slow to load and may have visual artifacts if compressed too much. These artifacts appear as blurring, noise pixels, and occasionally the appearance of superimposed 8×8 pixel boxes. PNG files are compressed losslessly, which makes them larger than JPG files but enables them to exactly represent the original data. DDS files (which, despite being named DirectDraw Surfaces, can be used with both OpenGL and DirectX graphics APIs) are compressed in a special way. DDS compression is neither lossless nor particularly efficient. However, DDS files remain compressed when they are stored on the graphics card. Since graphics cards have limited memory, using DDS or related texture-compression methods allow a game to either have higher-resolution textures, have more textures, or run on older graphics cards. Saving space on a graphics card also equates to running slightly faster in many cases because less data must be moved around inside the card in every frame.

Textures usually have power-of-two-sized dimensions, and before the year 2004, this was a graphics card requirement. Today, it is not required, but it offers several subtle technical advantages and is likely to be requested by the graphics programmers. The powers of two are numbers produced by multiplying two by itself multiple times (i.e., raising it to powers)—that is, 4, 8, 16, 32, 64, 128, 256, 1024, 2048, 4096, 8192. Most graphics cards do not support textures larger than 4096×4096, and many do not support larger than 2048×2048. Note that even with the power-of-two guideline, textures do not have to be squares; 128×1024 works fine.

13.3.2 Texture Coordinate

To apply the texture map to the model, a mapping from the flat 2D image to the 3D shape is needed. For a billboard, this mapping is obvious, since each corner of the image corresponds to a corner of the quadrilateral. For a complex shape like the space marine, the mapping is not so obvious. It is controlled by an artist explicitly identifying the location in the texture map that corresponds to each vertex. The texture map location of a vertex is called the *texture coordinate*, or *UV*. The first term is used by programmers, and the second term is used by artists and refers to the fact that since (x, y, z) is the 3D position of a vertex, it is natural to use different variables (u, v) to represent its 2D texture coordinate. Another common choice for texture coordinate notation is (s, t).

The process of assigning texture coordinates can be somewhat automated. Most modeling tools can generate an arrangement that projects each triangle from the mesh to a different location in the texture map. A good mapping keeps triangles that are next to each other in 3D adjacent on the texture map so the texture varies smoothly across them. A good mapping also keeps each triangle's area in the texture map proportional to its 3D area so there is little distortion. But those two criteria conflict with efficient texture usage. Larger, unbroken pieces of the mesh create irregular shapes in the texture map that are hard to efficiently pack together into the larger square. In the space marine example, note how the different parts of the body are packed together like jigsaw pieces to avoid wasting space, although some unused gray area is still visible. Modeling programs can make decent mappings, but they always need to be fine-tuned by the artist to trade off these properties.

In everyday experience, we are used to images having a top, a left, a bottom, and a right. Textures can be used in this mode, but a programmer can also tell the rendering system to treat a texture as an infinite tiled plane, where the image provided is one tile of that plane. This makes it convenient to texture a large area using a small texture map. For example, an entire desert could be textured with a single 1024×1024 patch of sand that just repeats. Of course, it is important to create repeating textures in such a way that their repeating nature does not become visually distracting. In the case of sand, the artist must ensure that there are no patterns in the seemingly random sand variation that jump out visually when tiled.

Texture coordinates for a single tile are expressed as fractions of the texture resolution. This makes them independent of the resolution of the texture that is applied, which is convenient because it allows the texture artist to work independently of the 3D modeling artist. It also allows the programmer to write code to dynamically change the resolution of textures at runtime. So each of the (u, v) values is on the range 0 to 1. For tiling textures, values less than 0 and greater than 1 are allowed. These values are assumed to wrap around, so 1.5 is the same ordinate as 0.5 and -1.5.

13.3.3 Conserving Space

It is a good idea to pack textures for different parts of a model as closely together as possible in a texture to conserve space. Any unused pixels in the texture map are a wasted resource. One way to get the most use out of each pixel is to only draw half of the texture for symmetric objects. A texture map for a human character might have only the left side of the body drawn into it. The right side is produced by assigning the same texture coordinates to the model in the opposite orientation so that the left texture becomes mirrored. One exception is the person's face. Because real faces are not perfectly symmetrical, it looks strange for game characters to have perfect texture mirroring on a human face. As a result, an artist usually will reserve enough space to draw both sides of the face.

Because the act of switching textures during rendering can dramatically slow down a game, each model is generally textured using a single texture map. In fact, it is a good idea to pack the textures from multiple models into a texture map, which reduces the number of texture switches. Some games are able to pack as much as 75 percent of the textures used in the entire game into a single texture map, although as models become increasingly detailed, this will become harder to achieve in the future.

Two limitations on how closely textures can be packed arise from the way that they are used at runtime when the pixels of the texture don't align perfectly with the pixels on the screen. When the model is close to the camera, each texture pixel is much bigger than a screen pixel. So the pixel boundaries of the texture are not visible on the screen as blocks of color, and the rendering system will blend smoothly between texture pixels. This bilinear (i.e., in both s and t directions) interpolation of nearby values means that areas just next to a triangle in the texture map may influence the triangle's color around the edges. So at least one pixel of padding around each triangle is needed to prevent the texture background color from bleeding into the edges. Of course, where many triangles that are adjacent in the mesh project to adjacent locations in the texture map, no padding is needed *between* those triangles: padding is only needed at the boundary of projected triangles where their texture touches unused space or texture for a different part of the model.

When a model is far from the viewer, many texture pixels lie inside each screen pixel. If only one texture pixel were used to color the screen, then as the object moved relative to the viewer, its surface would appear to shimmer, because different-colored texture pixels might correspond to apparently the same object location at different frames. To prevent this, the rendering system creates different levels of detail for the texture. The texture provided by the artist is the highest level of detail. Subsequent versions are smaller, blurred versions (the blurring is necessary to avoid the shimmering problem). The set of all detail levels is called a *MIP-map* (see Figure 13.5). Creating multiple-detail (also known as *MIP-*) *levels* approximately doubles the size of the texture in memory. When rendering, *trilinear filtering* is used to blend simultaneously across (bilinearly) the pixels in a given detail level and across the two detail levels nearest to the resolution needed (making another linear interpolation).

The combination of MIP-mapping and trilinear filtering affects texture packing because each detail level is half the size of the previous detail level along each dimension. So a 1024×1024 source texture leads to detail levels of sizes 512×512, $256 \times 256, \ldots 2 \times 2, 1 \times 1$. When packing different parts of the model's texture into nearby locations in the texture, it is still necessary to maintain a 1-pixel boundary for bilinear interpolation *at each MIP-level.* Obviously 1-pixel padding in the 1×1 level will not work, so graphics programmers clamp the minimum-detail resolution. Say that 128×128 is the minimum resolution. That is $\frac{1}{8}$ the resolution of the original 1024×1024 tex-

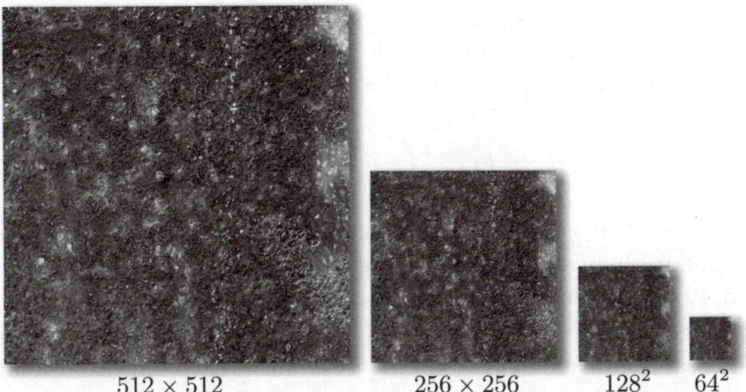

Figure 13.5. MIP-maps contain multiple-detail levels of the same texture. Four resolutions of a rusted metal texture are shown here. Smaller versions are used on faraway objects.

ture. So 1-pixel padding at 128×128 becomes 8-pixel padding at 1024×1024. Thus, in practice, several pixels of padding are needed around each section of the model's texture map to ensure that when the object is far from the viewer, its texture areas do not bleed into one another in the low-resolution MIP-levels.

13.3.4 Normal Mapping

Textures create the illusion of additional geometric detail on a model without requiring additional polygons. However, that illusion breaks down in the presence of strong directional lighting because it is obvious that the shading on the surface of the mesh is based on the underlying flat triangles and not on the detail depicted in the texture map. Several forms of *bump mapping* can adjust both the shading and the color to help preserve the illusion of real displacement.

Normal mapping or *bump mapping* specifies the relative displacement of the textured surface from the true flat triangle using a *bump map*. This is a grayscale texture map where white areas are "high" and black areas are "low." The bump map can either be painted explicitly in a tool like Photoshop, roughly captured by photographing a rough surface with a headlamp, or computed from a high-polygon version of the model. The last method is by far the most popular and successful for creating convincing bump maps, but it requires a very high-polygon model to start with, and constructing such models can take a significant amount of time. From the bump map, the rendering system computes a normal map, which stores a 3D vector that describes the slope of the surface at each point as another texture map. Because each pixel in the normal map has a 3D value, it is encoded using color so the RGB values correspond to (x, y, z) directions. Those directions must be packed from the range -1 to $+1$ along each axis into RGB values between 0 and 1, which is accomplished by the following mapping:

$$(r, g, b) = \frac{1}{2}(x + 1, y + 1, z + 1).$$

As a result of this coloring, most normal maps appear to have, on average, a chalky blue color, since the vector $(x, y, z) = (0, 0, 1) => (r, g, b) = (0.5, 0.5, 1.0)$ represents a flat surface.

Although normal mapping distorts the apparent slope of the surface and in turn creates convincing shading, it does not create self-occlusion or parallax. A more sophisticated method called *parallax bump mapping* actually distorts the texture coordinates based on the viewer's perspective and the relative height of the bump map so the surfaces appear to have real 3D depth as well as 3D shading.

13.4 Materials

In real life, a camera records the light that enters the lens from objects in a scene. Except for light sources (e.g., the sun, glowing hot magma, a car's

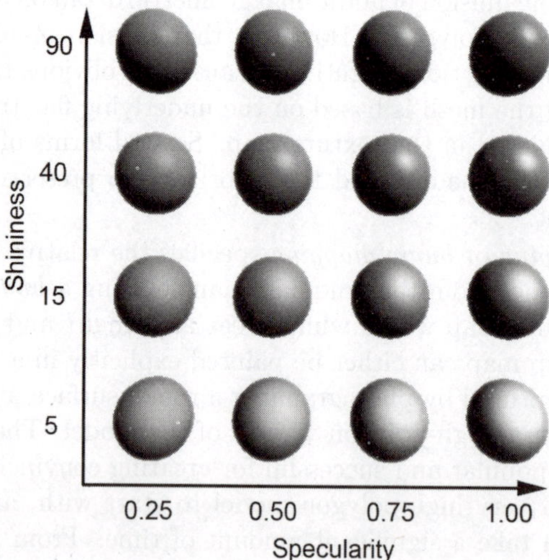

Figure 13.6. Models rendered with different shininess and specularity. Specularity increases to the right, shininess increase from bottom to top.

taillight, LEDs), objects don't have their own light; they just reflect the light that comes from somewhere else. Sometimes the surface's appearance changes as the camera moves, even if the object and the light are held steady. To see this, hold a shiny coffee cup still and move your head. The highlight appears to move over the surface so it is always pointed at you. So simulating the appearance of a surface involves not just the surface itself but also the camera position and the sources of light in the scene.

Although real materials can have complex interactions with lighting, real-time graphics tend to simplify material descriptions into simple terms [McGuire 05]. These terms are used by designers, especially the art director and lighting designer, when talking about surfaces. They are also used by the programmers when implementing the pixel and vertex shader programs. A graphical overview of these terms is shown in Figure 13.6.

13.4.1 Emissive

The *emissive* color of an object is the (dim) light that it gives off but that doesn't affect nearby surfaces. For example, a glow-in-the-dark sticker has an emissive color that is green. It will appear bright even in a dark room, but it doesn't produce enough light to see by or to cast shadows. Most objects have a diffuse color of black, which means they don't glow.

13.4.2 Diffuse

The *diffuse* color of an object describes its matte appearance, which is technically how much light it reflects independent of the viewer. The diffuse color is usually what we mean when we talk about the color of an opaque real-life object.

13.4.3 Specular

The *specular* color of an object describes how bright its highlights are and whether they are tinted. An object like a red apple has white highlights, not red highlights, so its specular color is white and not red. Some surfaces, like clay, have little or no specular highlights, and their specular color is dark gray or black. Most objects with specular highlights have a white specular color, meaning that highlights assume the color of the light source. An exception is metals, which have the same specular and diffuse color. If you look at the highlights on a brass doorknob, for example, you will find that they are yellowish and not white.

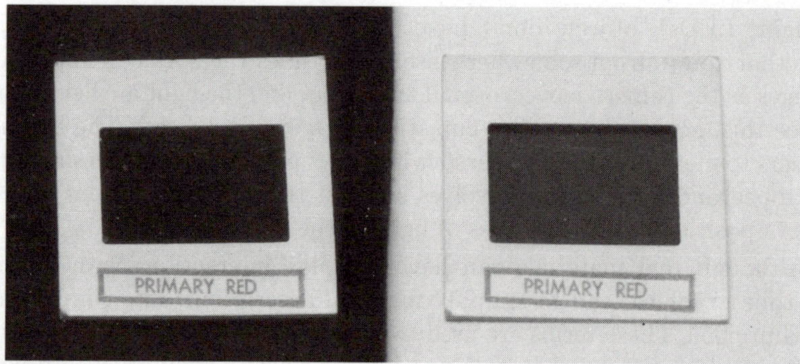

Figure 13.7. Photographs of colored glass against white and black backgrounds. Note that when no light is coming through from the back, the glass reveals that its diffuse color is black.

13.4.4 Shiny

The *shininess* of an object is how focused its specular highlight is. In general, smooth surfaces tend to be more reflective and shinier. "Shining" an apple by rubbing it on your shirt smooths out the surface and rubs wax into its pores, making it shinier. Roughly sanding a piece of plastic will coarsen the surface, reducing its shininess.

13.4.5 Translucent

The *translucent* color of a surface describes the amount of light that passes through it. This can be nonintuitive. A red gel actually has a black diffuse color and a red transparent color. You can see this by holding the gel against a black background so no light is passing through it and the only color observed is the diffuse and specular light bouncing off the surface. Translucent colors are used for modeling glass, gel, and liquids and are implemented in the GPU's output merger by multiplying the old frame buffer color by the color of the translucent surface. As with other terms, a translucent color of black means that there is no glasslike translucency (see Figure 13.7).

13.4.6 Alpha

Glassy transparency isn't the only kind of translucency. Fog, smoke, and thin hair are all partly transparent, but they don't filter the color of the object behind them like glass does. Instead, the diffuse color of the fog blends with the color of the object behind it. This kind of translucency is modeled with an *alpha* channel on the diffuse color and the corresponding blend operation in the output merger. Fog typically has a translucent color of black but an alpha value around one-half, indicating that it is not glassy but is not opaque either.

"Binary" alpha values of either completely opaque (1) or completely invisible (0) can also be used to cut irregular shapes out of triangles. When modeling a tree, it is common to make entire leafy branches from single quadrilaterals but use the alpha channel of the diffuse texture map to cut out the individual branch and leaf shapes. (This is discussed more in Chapter 14.)

13.4.7 Reflective

Finally, the *reflective* color of an object is another specular term, but it is applied to mirror reflections and not just highlights. Because light sources are so much brighter than the rest of the scene, it is essential to always show their reflections (which are what we call specular highlights). In reality, everything in the scene is actually reflected by every object, but usually those reflections are so dim or dull that they can't be seen. For some objects, like mirrors and glass at glancing angles, the reflections are bright enough to be seen and must be rendered as well. Using reflective color as a tinting term for "mirror" reflections and reserving the specular color for just light reflections allows artists flexibility to specify which surfaces need the increased computational demands of reflections.

Reflections rendered in a game have several limitations. First, reflections will generally be very sharp and focused. If you look closely at a dark real-life piece of dishware or at the glossy cover of a magazine, you will see a reflection of the room around you. But that reflection is blurry, not sharp like in a mirror. Unfortunately, the process of blurring out a reflection is slow, so most games use only sharp reflections. Most of the time, the reflections in games are also rendered using a precomputed cube texture map. Because this cube map is not updated in real-time, objects aren't reflecting their actual 3D environment but some idealized static version of it. Of course, when the player comes to a large body of reflecting water or looks at the mirror in a bathroom, it would be obvious if this trick were used. In those special cases, it is common to render dynamic reflections. This is done by running the whole graphics pipeline twice per frame. The first pass through the scene renders the mirror's view of the world to a texture map. The second pass renders the camera's view, and where the mirror appears in the scene, it appears as the reflection texture map multiplied by the mirror's reflective color. This render-to-texture trick is slow and can be used only for a few surfaces at a time.

13.5 Exercises

1. Draw a set of flowcharts (or dependency diagrams) for the art-modeling process of a game containing animal characters and a large world of rolling hills dotted with labrynthine ancient temples. Label boxes in the flowchart with the work product (e.g., "3DS Max Model Exporter"), the person responsible for producing that work product (e.g., "tools programmer"), and the tools they will use (e.g., "Visual C++").

2. Why are T-junctions bad? Why are triangles good for modeling?

3. How many pixels of padding are needed around texture areas for a 2048×1024 texture if the smallest MIP-map level has a resolution of 256×128?

4. How many triangles are required to model a 3D-extruded block letter "W" that has no texture maps and is watertight? Draw a diagram showing the construction of your model from an isometric (45-degree) view.

5. What is the difference between "shiny," "specular," and "reflective"?

6. What experiments could you perform while playing someone else's game to determine how the reflections are rendered?

7. What tools can the technology team introduce to aid the art team? Go beyond the specific tools mentioned in the text.

8. Tessellate the following polygons so they contain only triangles and form watertight meshes (except at the external boundary). The circles represent the vertices.

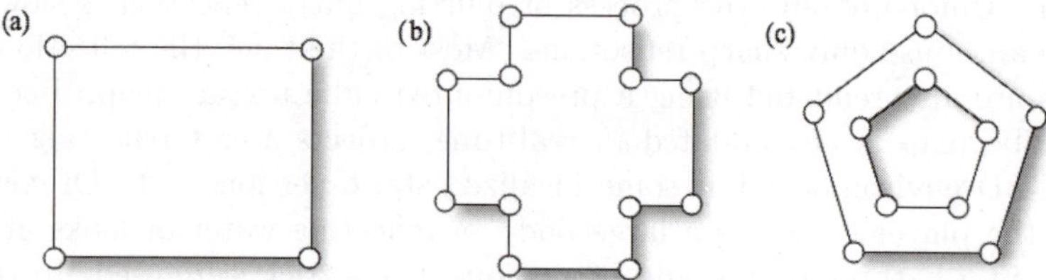

9. Give reasonable RGB triplets (on a scale of 0 to 1, or color names like "dark blue") for the transparent, reflective, emissive, and diffuse colors of the following materials: brushed aluminum, wood, a blue LED backlight, heavily rusted iron, red wine, black smoke, unoxidized copper, and green-tinted sunglasses.

13.6 Resources

Because computer graphics is such a popular area, most bookstores have entire sections devoted to the topic. To help you select from among the many titles, we list some of the resources that we consider the most valuable and that are used by many professional game developers.

- Walker and Walker, *Game Modeling Using Low Polygon Techniques* [Walker and Walker 01].
- Steed, *Animating Real-Time Game Characters* [Steed 02].
- Steed, *Modeling a Character in 3DS Max* [Steed 01].
- Derakhshani, *Introducing Maya 6: 3D for Beginners* [Derakhshani 04].
- Omernick, *Creating the Art of the Game* [Omerick 04].
- Ahearn, *3D Game Textures: Create Professional Game Art Using Photoshop* [Ahearn 06].

CHAPTER 14

Real-Time Rendering

Terms Explained: *Diffuse* – *Graphics Processor (GPU)* – *Cache* – *Output Merger* – *Rasterizer* – *Z-buffer* – *Pipeline* – *Parallelism* – *Shader* – *Diffuse* – *Specular* – *Z-fighting* – *Depth, Alpha, Stencil Test* – *Local, Global Illumination* – *Surface Normal*

Real-time 3D rendering immerses players in virtual worlds. The majority of the budget, time, staff, and code in a modern game is invested in modeling and rendering 3D scenes. The ideas and technology for game rendering are not limited to games alone. They are a part of the broad scientific, engineering, and industrial field of computer graphics. That covers disciplines as diverse as creating product images for billboards, movie special effects, robot vision, and MRI images for doctors.

Console, portable, PC, and even cell phone games all rely on hardware acceleration, which is typically accessed through the Direct3D (also known as XNA, WGA, and DirectX) and OpenGL interfaces. From a technical perspective, both interfaces provide essentially identical functionality, since they connect to the same underlying graphics hardware. Likewise, most graphics hardware at the same price point is equivalent, with the vendors attaching different marketing terms to the same features. No vendor can veer too far from the common path, since game developers are unlikely to support hardware that is not widely installed or is hard to port to and from. The graphics processing unit (GPU) sections of this chapter explain the basic architecture of all modern hardware graphics, including consoles like Microsoft's Xbox 360, Sony's PS3, and the Nintendo Wii. This architecture dictates what kinds of real-time 3D rendering are possible and what features are visible in Direct3D, OpenGL, and console-specific APIs. If you understand the GPU architecture, then you understand the constraints and abilities of Direct3D and OpenGL.

This chapter explains the kinds of challenges that programmers working on the rendering system face and how they are likely to solve them. The lighting section progresses as far as the basic math used in lighting that describes how colored surfaces interact. This is not only useful to programmers. Artists and designers need to understand how illumination operates to predict the effects of the lights and textures they introduce. Increasingly, from within 3D modeling programs such as Maya and previsualization software such as RenderMonkey, 3D artists also directly edit the source code of "shaders"—small programs that run on the graphics card. So artists need a background in the mathematics and algorithms of 3D rendering. Full details of 3D algorithms and programming can be found in the books recommended at the end of the chapter.

14.1 Graphics Processor (GPU)

14.1.1 Why GPUs Are Fast

Most nongame software executes computations in the central processing unit (CPU) of a computer and stores its data in random-access memory (RAM) accessible to that processor. The CPU is designed to run most programs at a reasonable speed. It has a general-purpose architecture that can't favor one kind of program (such as spreadsheets) over another (such as word processing), since computer users run all kinds of applications and expect them to all run well.

The amount of computation and memory needed for 3D rendering is much larger than that needed for other consumer computing tasks such as e-mail, Web browsing, word processing, and even spreadsheets. The general-purpose architecture of the CPU just can't handle the processing load of computer graphics in real-time.

The graphics processing unit (GPU) is a separate processor and memory on a card, as shown in Figure 14.1. The GPU is designed specifically for running computer graphics at incredible speeds—often as much as 100 times faster than the CPU could. However, this performance comes at a price. Compared to the CPU, the GPU has very limited functionality. Some of these limitations are that the GPU can only access its memory in specific ways, it can't communicate at all with devices such as the network adapter or disk, and it must be programmed using special tools. Although it is theoretically possible to run, say, an e-mail program on a GPU, doing so would take tremendous amounts of programming effort and would have little benefit.

Because the GPU has limited functionality, it can be specially tailored to run graphics algorithms at high speed. The details of the GPU architecture

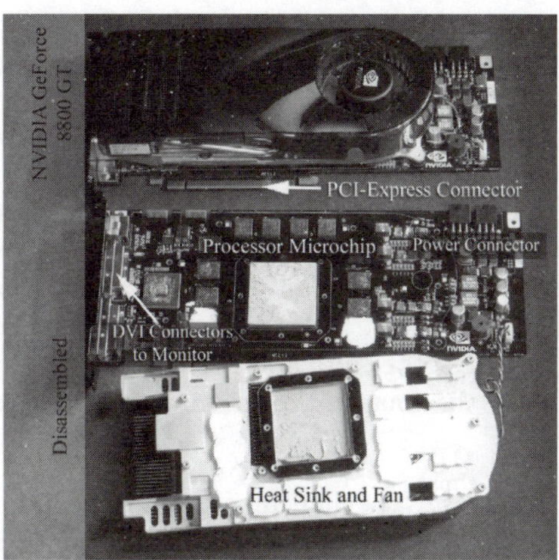

Figure 14.1. An NVIDIA GPU expansion card for a PC. Similar components are built permanently into consoles.

change with every hardware generation. However, the reasons the GPU is so fast for rendering tasks have been consistent since the first hardware renderers were introduced in the 1970s by Evans and Sutherland, although not all GPUs have taken full advantage of all of these.

- **Most graphics tasks can be executed in parallel across pixels.** Instead of a handful of general-purpose units like CPU cores, a GPU contains tens or hundreds of identical special-purpose units. These allow GPUs to execute thousands of independent threads of execution—typically one for each pixel. By processing multiple pixels independently, the GPU can run more computations in less clock time. The downside of parallelism is that some graphics algorithms can't be spread over multiple processors because the processors would have to communicate too frequently.

- **Fixed-function rasterization and output merger.** The need to quickly find all pixels inside a triangle is common to all graphics programs, because most 3D models are triangle meshes. The GPU contains a special unit called the rasterizer, whose only job is to turn triangles into pixels at high speed. Using a special highly optimized unit for this task and restricting that unit to have no programmable features enables it to perform the task much faster than a CPU. The output merger is a unit that processes pixels immediately before they become visible on the screen. It has a specific set of functions detailed at the end of this chapter. Because its task is confined mostly to computer graphics and is well-defined, having a special-purpose circuit for that task allows the GPU to outperform similar operations on other processor architectures.

- **High memory bandwidth.** The GPU to GPU-memory transfers are both in larger chunks and faster than the CPU to CPU-memory ones. A CPU trying to run graphics code is often forced to sit idle while it waits for data to be read from a texture map, but the GPU can often read and write data faster than it can process it and tends to be slowed by computation, not memory. Since rendering a single image can involve processing gigabytes of texture and geometry data as well as the frame buffer that holds the final image, fast memory access is essential for fast graphics.

- **Fast context switches.** The line of program execution for each pixel is called a *thread.* Even though the GPU memory is fast, it still is not as fast as the GPU's processor. This means that a thread reading from memory is temporarily stalled. Its processing unit is available but cannot proceed until the memory access returns. GPUs are designed to quickly swap threads that are stalling on memory access with ones that are waiting for an available processor. This process is called a *context switch.* Because of massive parallelism, there are often thousands of threads executing at the same time on only about a hundred processing unit. Fast context switching allows the GPU to hide the cost of memory operations. No processor will actually go unused—while one thread is waiting for memory, another thread will be swapped in. In contrast, CPUs have slow context switches, so they do not swap threads out and actually stall the processor while waiting for memory accesses to complete.

14.1.2 Architecture

The GPU is composed of the smaller units shown in Figure 14.2. The processing units (tessellation, vertex, geometry, rasterizer, pixel, output merger) and texture cache are combined into a single microchip, and the GPU memory is usually a series of separate microchips located nearby. These GPU components can be mounted either on an expansion card like a PCI-express card or directly on the motherboard near the CPU. GPUs also have a limited ability to access the CPU's memory by sending data across the PCI-express bus. Although this is often necessary when moving data from the CPU to the GPU, reading CPU memory is comparatively slow, and programmers try to avoid it.

Although in Figure 14.2 it appears there is one tessellation shader, one vertex shader, and so on, there are actually many copies of each unit. This is the parallelism in the graphics card. In the latest hardware, there aren't

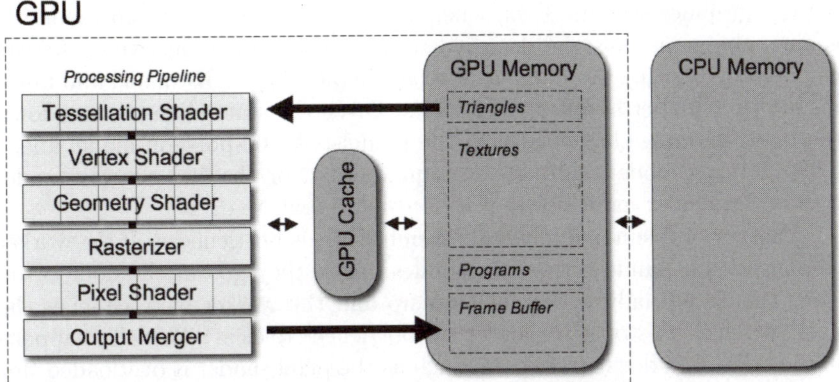

Figure 14.2. The GPU processing pipeline (left) and GPU/CPU memory hierarchy (right).

even dedicated units; there are generic "graphics units" that turn into, say, pixel or geometry shaders as needed. So when the rasterizer feeds pixels down the pipeline to the pixel shader, it is really dumping all of the pixels to a pile in memory, and many different pixel shaders are picking up those pixels and processing them at the same time. And although a single triangle takes a while (in computer terms; it's really only a fraction of a millisecond) to move through the entire pipeline and emerge as an image at the bottom, the units near the top of the pipeline do not sit idle once they've processed that triangle. Like an assembly line or a physical pipeline, all parts of the hardware graphics pipeline are constantly in motion. Thus, there are two kinds of parallelism: each box in Figure 14.2 is replicated many times ("horizontally"), *and* all parts of the vertical pipeline are working simultaneously.

The GPU suffers the same weakness as a physical assembly line. In an automotive construction assembly line, if a worker near the beginning of the line takes a break and is not replaced then soon the downstream workers will "starve" for work and have to stop because they are not being "fed" jobs fast enough. This kind of stall occurs in the graphics pipeline when an upstream unit such as the vertex shader is running too slowly. The upstream unit might run slowly because it is executing a program that is too complex. More commonly, it will run slowly because it is reading too much data or data that is spread out too much on a texture map, which is causing the memory to work inefficiently. This is explained in more detail in the next section.

State changes are another major cause of pipeline stalls. When the programmer directs the graphics card to load a new program, or changes which 3D model is being rendered, no data can enter the pipeline until the new state has been fully transferred. This leaves the GPU with no work to do. Identifying stalls is a major part of the graphics programmer's job in optimizing the graphics system. Even when using a completely licensed rendering engine, the game must be designed to use that engine effectively. Artists can help by limiting the number of separate pieces on a 3D model and minimizing the number of different textures. Often the state changes slow down the program more than rendering the models. A 500-polygon model and a 5,000-polygon model might render equally fast, or the 500-polygon model could even render more slowly if it used more texture data.

Another problem in a physical assembly line is bottlenecks. If the worker responsible for painting the automobiles before they go out the door is too slow, then eventually work will back up and the worker who attaches the doors will have to stop and wait for the bottleneck to clear. This also happens in the GPU. If a downstream unit such as the pixel shader is overloaded (for the same reasons that an upstream unit might stall), then the upstream units will have to wait for the bottleneck to clear. This can even back up so far that the CPU, which ultimately issues commands to the GPU, is forced to wait. Many programmers have found while optimizing performance that all of their CPU time is spent just waiting for the GPU to finish processing. Obviously it is better to avoid this situation by balancing GPU load, but when the load has already been reduced or balanced as much as possible, an alternative is to run CPU code like physics and audio while waiting for the GPU to catch up so processing cycles are not wasted.

14.1.3 Hierarchical Memory Model

The GPU memory stores triangle meshes, texture maps for those meshes, shader programs that execute on the graphics processor, and the output buffers used in rendering. The output buffers include the color buffer that is shown on the screen, the depth buffer, and some auxiliary buffers that may be used for postprocessing and special effects. Of all this data, the texture maps commonly occupy the most memory. GPU memory is very fast, often allowing data access at up to ten times the rate of CPU memory. But to reach the necessary gigabytes-per-frame memory rates, an additional memory unit is needed.

The GPU's cache is a small memory (see Figure 14.2) that is even faster than the GPU memory. It gains its additional speed in part from residing on the same microchip as the GPU processing units. Since physical layout space is limited on a single chip, the cache is a fraction of the size of the GPU memory (megabytes instead of gigabytes). To achieve fast access to data, it is therefore ideal to store the most-frequently-accessed data in the cache and the less-frequently-accessed data in the GPU memory. In fact, we can look at memory as a hierarchy where data that are seldom accessed can be offloaded to CPU memory, and data that are frequently accessed can be stored in really slow locations like the disk or across the network.

Moving data between disk, CPU memory, and GPU memory is explicitly controlled by the programmer, based on his or her understanding of how the game as a whole operates. For example, say the player is running down the street toward the entrance to a building. This is a good time to move the geometry describing the inside of the building from disk through the CPU memory and up onto the GPU. By doing so, when the player enters the building, that data will be ready for rendering, and the game will not hitch. The GPU cache operates differently. The programmer does not explicitly move data into it. Instead, the cache automatically keeps track of the data most recently used by the processing units and makes the assumption that in the future, the processing units will access either that data again or data that is very nearby in memory. This is a good assumption because if one unit is coloring a pixel, other units are probably coloring adjacent pixels, using nearby locations on the same texture map and the same geometry. When the most-recently-used assumption does not hold (usually because the programmer read so much data that it wouldn't all fit in the cache), the processing units may stall while waiting for data to be transferred from the GPU memory, slowing down rendering substantially.

14.1.4 Shaders

The nonmemory units inside the GPU are divided between shader units and fixed-function units. The name *shader* indicates a unit that is capable of executing code; it is an independent miniature processor inside the GPU. Shader is a historical term that arose when computing light and shading was the primary function of programmability inside the GPU. Today, processing unit would be a better term.

Because the GPU is specialized for graphics, writing a shader program is different from writing CPU code, even though the shader programming languages HLSL, GLSL, and Cg are designed to look similar to regular C++. Shader programs cannot support most modern development techniques such as object-oriented and event-driven programming. In fact, they are limited to a more limited programming style dating back to the 1950's and owe a lot to the original scientific programming language, FORTRAN [IEEE 84]. This restricted execution environment greatly simplifies the hardware implementation so it can run extremely fast. Unfortunately, it also makes shader development time-consuming, a process that is exacerbated by the limited tools available for finding errors (bugs) in shader programs. CPU programs are comparatively easy to debug because both the program being edited and the programmer's development tools execute on the same processor. With a shader, the development tools are still executing on the CPU, but the shader program is running on the GPU, and there are no facilities for inspecting the running shader program to discover why it is running incorrectly. Furthermore, even if it were possible to inspect a running shader program, there would be too much data for the programmer to interpret. A single shader program might easily execute over 30 million times a second. Today, many companies are creating GPU emulators that run (slowly) on the CPU, allowing some level of debugging. Until such tools become widespread, most shader debugging involves intentionally rendering a series of experimental images on screen and inferring the source of the problem from the final image.

14.1.5 Tessellation Shader

Although at the time of this writing, no GPU contains a hardware tessellation shader, it is expected [Bleiweiss 05] that the next generation of hardware will offer this feature. The processing units inside the GPU are arranged in a pipeline where geometry enters at the top through the tessellation shader and then flows down through the other units until it ends as pixels on the frame buffer. Tessellation shader programs increase detail in the triangle mesh. This can be done either by subdividing some triangles to make smoother curves or by adding additional triangles that represent more detail (usually from a bump map). Why don't we just create a more detailed mesh in the first place? The advantage of the tessellation shader over a high-polygon mesh is that we don't need more detail everywhere, only in areas close to the player or along the silhouette of an object. So the tessellation shader can selectively increase detail, maintaining an overall low polygon count with additional polygons only where they'll be seen. Of course, as with every shader unit, the tessellation shader isn't restricted to its intended role. Programmers can find clever ways to perform other applications for it. One example is Havok FX, a library that uses the GPU to perform physics calculations for games as well as graphics.

14.1.6 Vertex Shader

For each vertex of each triangle that is rendered, the vertex shader executes a program once. Its primary role is to transform vertices from the object space reference frame of the model to the local reference frame of the camera and then prepare them for projection from the 3D to the 2D screen (the actual projection, which is just a division operation, technically occurs in the rasterizer pipeline unit that follows). Vertex shaders can also be used to perform lighting calculations at the vertices. Because the result of per-vertex lighting will be interpolated (blended) over the entire triangle, per-vertex lighting is not common in today's games. It misses sharp highlights that occur on the inside of a triangle and not at the vertices.

Morphing a model based on its animated skeleton is a common secondary role for the vertex shader. This is called matrix skinning, bone blending, or skin-and-bones animation. Be aware that skinning is a confusing term because a texture artist's role of painting the model surface is also called skinning.

14.1.7 Geometry Shader

The output of the vertex shader is a stream of vertices, every three of which represent one of the original triangles in the mesh. The geometry shader reassembles these into triangles and can either prevent those triangles from progressing farther down the pipeline (for example, if it determines that they cannot be seen), pass them along as is, or subdivide those triangles in a similar manner to the tessellation shader.

Subdivision is used to turn individual triangles into smooth curves or to increase detail. It is also used to make duplicate copies of a triangle when rendering multiple views simultaneously. For example, in a driving simulator, both the view out the windshield and the images seen in the rear- and side-view mirrors might be rendered simultaneously by making copies of all geometry. The geometry shader also has applications for rendering particle systems, shadows, and effects like fur and grass efficiently. In each case, a single object like a point or a triangle creates some more complicated geometry near it, and a geometry shader program is where the programmer expresses that transformation.

14.1.8 Rasterizer

The *rasterizer* is the first fixed-function unit in the hardware graphics pipeline. This means that unlike the shader units, it is not programmable. As with the other limitations on the GPU, the rasterizer is limited to a fixed function so it can run extremely fast. The rasterizer performs the final step in the process of transforming 3D triangles into 2D triangles that the vertex shader began. It then finds all the pixels that lie within the 2D triangles and blends the texture coordinates, depth, lighting, and any other per-vertex data across the face of the triangle so that each pixel is associated with a set of attributes that will be used to compute the final shading. These pixels queue up for the pixel shader to process.

Since the in-game camera typically has about a 90-degree field of view both horizontally and vertically, only about one-eighth of the 3D world is ever visible at one time. The edges of the frame define whole planes that extend out into the 3D world, dividing geometry into what can be seen and what can't. Sometimes the plane crosses midway through a triangle because the triangle is partly on-screen and partly off. These planes are called clipping planes because they clip geometry down to only what is on the screen. The rasterizer is responsible for clipping all geometry before converting it to pixels, since there are no pixels that match off-screen geometry.

In addition to the side-clipping planes, near and far clipping planes also exist. The near plane clips geometry that is too close to the camera, and the far plane clips geometry that is too distant. The near and far planes have many functions. Obviously, any geometry that is clipped is not rendered, so clipping faraway geometry reduces the load on the downstream pixel processor and makes graphics run faster. Less obvious is that near and far clipping increase the accuracy of rendering. Computers have finite precision and memory, so there is no way to efficiently represent the coordinates of triangles over the potentially infinite distance that the camera can see. By reducing the range to something small (like a kilometer), more precision is available.

Due to the way numbers are stored in the depth buffer, precision increases rapidly if it does not have to store very small depths. So moving out the near-clipping plane can make the depth buffer more precise. This increase of precision is visible in the final image as crisper intersections between penetrating surfaces, like where a wall sinks into the ground. It also reduces a visual artifact called *z-fighting*, which is shown in Figure 14.3. Z-fighting occurs when two surfaces are parallel with very little gap between them, like a tapestry hanging on a wall. If the z-buffer precision is too low, both the z (depth) coordinate of the tapestry and the wall will round off to the same value. When that happens, it is impossible for the GPU to tell which surface was supposed to appear in front of the other, and the wall will appear to poke through the tapestry, often in a zigzag pattern arising from the rasterization algorithm.

Unfortunately, it is not always practical to push the near-clipping plane out to avoid z-fighting. In a first-person game, a near-clipping plane at a

Figure 14.3. Z-fighting artifacts occur at overlapping surfaces when the clipping planes are configured poorly. They can be corrected by a polygon offset or moving the near plane.

distance of one meter would cause any nearby object, like another character participating in a conversation, to disappear. When the near-clipping plane has to be close, it can be difficult to avoid z-fighting. One way is to increase the number of bits allocated to the z-buffer. Using 16-, 24-, and 32-bits per pixel are common alternatives. However, increasing the bit count also increases the amount of GPU memory that is required, which makes the cache less effective and reduces the data traffic and storage space available for textures. Another solution is to modify the underlying models to guarantee that no objects are so close that they z-fight. Finally, the hardware has an option to allow the programmer to add a z-offset to triangles after they have been projected. By offsetting decal objects such as tapestries toward the viewer, z-fighting is avoided when viewed head-on while still appearing flush when viewed from the side. Introducing offsets may require making other changes that slow down the graphics pipeline, however, so it is usually reserved for objects that are particularly problematic.

The clipping planes collectively define a volume of space called the view frustum. It looks like a pyramid with the top lopped off that projects out from the camera.

14.1.9 Pixel Shader

The pixel shader consumes the majority of the GPU's processing power, and graphics programmers spend most of their GPU programming time working on pixel shader programs. Yet, this most important unit is also the simplest to understand: it decides the color of a single pixel at a time.

A pixel shader program transforms the raw pixel data produced by the rasterizer into the final colors that are seen on the screen (almost—the final output merger unit can change them slightly). The pixel shader operates on a single pixel at a time and cannot use data on adjacent pixels in computing its result. The simplest pixel shader programs just read the appropriate pixels from a texture map and color them by the per-vertex lighting that the rasterizer interpolated across the triangle.

More sophisticated pixel shader programs compute separate lighting at each pixel and combine multiple texture maps to simulate interesting materials such as metal, glass, and skin. The pixel shader program is also where the programmer implements normal mapping and other kinds of per-pixel displacement mapping solutions to create the illusion of added detail. Because the target pixel is identified in the frame buffer before the shader program executes, per-pixel displacement mapping can never create real detail; normal-mapped objects may appear rough head-on, but their silhouettes will be smooth. Only the vertex, geometry, and tessellation shaders can actually move silhouette geometry.

The pixels produced by the pixel shader contain more than just a color. They have additional invisible values that include their z-depth into the scene relative to the camera and the so-called alpha channel, which is often used as a measure of opacity for translucent materials such as glass and smoke.

14.1.10 Output Merger

The *output merger* is the last processing unit in the graphics pipeline. It has a fixed set of functions, but they can be modified slightly by the programmer. Its overall role is to combine the pixel color produced by the pixel shader at a specific location on the screen with the value already stored in the frame buffer at that location. Although each frame begins empty, there is no reason that two triangles won't overlap the same pixel at different depths. The output merger is then responsible for either combining their colors or deciding which one will be visible.

For a pixel produced to be written to the frame buffer, it must pass three tests. The *depth test* decides whether a pixel is allowed to overwrite a previous one at the same location by comparing their z-values. It is commonly set to allow pixels to pass only when they are closer to the camera than the current frame buffer value, a process that correctly hides surfaces that cannot be seen since they are behind another object. It is occasionally useful to reverse that test when implementing specific algorithms or to disable the depth test entirely when rendering translucent objects that allow multiple depths to color the same pixel.

The *alpha test* allows pixels to pass only if their invisible alpha value is greater than a constant. It can also be reversed. The alpha test is commonly used to cut irregular shapes out of triangles. For example, an oak tree leaf is a complex shape that would require many triangles to model. But the same leaf can be modeled as a triangle larger than the entire leaf and a texture map with an alpha channel that is zero outside the leaf shape. When rendered, the pixel shader applies that texture map to the pixels, and the output merger rejects pixels that are not on the leaf body. This way, they do not color the frame buffer, and more important, those off-the-leaf pixels do not set the z-buffer and occlude objects that should be seen through them.

The *stencil test* is similar to the alpha test in that it allows pixels to pass only if an invisible value is greater than a constant. But the stencil test can also be paired with other operations in the output merger to update a per-pixel count of the number of times the frame buffer is written to a certain location. This is used by specific algorithms to cut holes in the geometry—for example, to see inside the roof of a house when the character walks inside—and also for some kinds of shadow casting.

When a pixel passes all of the depth, alpha, and stencil tests, it is ready to be combined with the current frame buffer. The frame buffer contains many

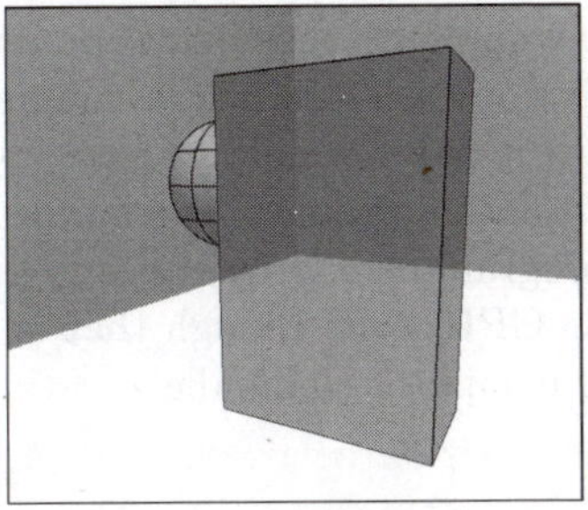 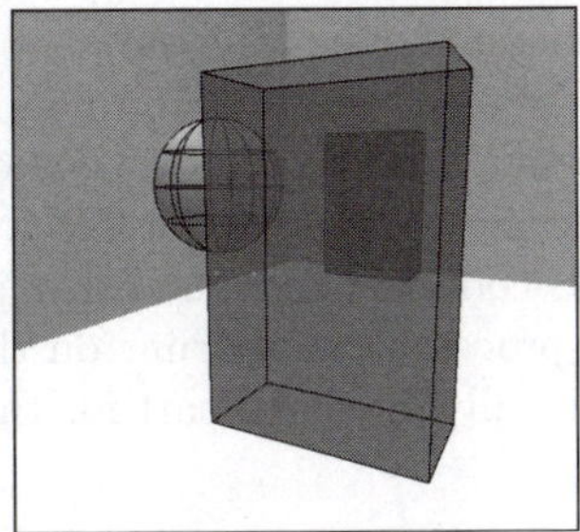

Figure 14.4. Left: incorrectly sorted translucent triangles create artifacts. Right: correctly sorted triangles provide a more realistic appearance.

separate buffers, or images: the RGB color buffer that will be displayed on the screen to the user; the alpha buffer, which is only useful when the image rendered is to be later sent back down the graphics pipeline as a texture instead of immediately shown to the user; and the z- or depth-buffer, which records the depth of each pixel from the camera. We have already seen that it is used to ensure that only the closest surface is seen at each pixel. Finally, the stencil buffer has its special applications.

The output merger overrides the current depth value with the new one (unless explicitly configured not to), updates the stencil buffer according to the configuration, and then blends the color and alpha values of the new pixel and the current buffer according to the blending mode. The simplest blending mode is to just overwrite the old color and alpha with the new one. When rendering translucent surfaces, more complex blending modes are used. For example, when looking through a piece of red glass, everything behind the glass should have a red tint. This can be accomplished by first rendering the opaque surfaces to the frame buffer and then rendering the glass with a blending mode that multiplies the red glass color by the colors already in the buffer.

When multiple translucent surfaces are present in the scene, all translucent surfaces must be sorted so that the farthest back from the camera is rendered immediately after the opaque surfaces, and then the next farthest back, and so on. Artifacts like those shown in Figure 14.4 will occur when this depth sorting is not performed. In the figure, it appears as though the ball and box in the background disappear when viewed through the glass box in the foreground. This is a result of the glass rendering too early and setting the z-buffer, so the objects behind it fail the z-test. The right side of the figure shows a correctly sorted rendering of the same scene.

Depth sorting is a good example of a graphics algorithm that is not run on the GPU. Sorting involves comparing many different values. The GPU's parallelism makes it hard to compare different values because if those values are on different copies of the same processing unit, then extra communication is needed to synchronize the different copies. That extra communication ability doesn't exist on the GPU, and if it did, it would be slow anyway. So sorting is typically run on the CPU. In fact, graphics programmers write a lot of CPU code just like any other programmer. Only the very end of the rendering process actually runs on the GPU, even though that is the most computationally intensive part for the computer to handle.

14.2 Lighting

A lighting artist studies how lights interact with the scene to intelligently choose good colors and values, and a programmer studies the same phenomena to simulate them.

Rendering breaks lighting into three components: emissive light from glowing objects, direct illumination from a source straight onto a surface, and indirect or "global" illumination that reflects around the scene before lighting objects. Emissive lights are painted directly into emissive texture maps and are read directly in a pixel shader program. Direct illumination is more complex. It is simulated in the pixel or vertex shader by combining material properties painted into the texture maps with lights placed by the lighting artist. The programmer controls the algorithm that combines these; the following subsections explain the basics of that algorithm. Indirect illumination is significantly more complicated to simulate. In fact, it is so hard to simulate that most games use precomputed lighting stored on

Variable	Meaning
D	Surface diffuse color
S	Surface specular color
N	Surface normal
k	Shininess of material
C	Light color
L	Direction to light
R	Direction light is reflected off surface
V	Direction to viewer
I_{emissive}	
I_{ambient}	
I_{diffuse}	Diffuse illumination reflected toward viewer
I_{specular}	Specular illumination reflected toward viewer
I_{reflect}	
I_{refract}	

Table 14.1. Defines the variables we use in this section.

special textures called light maps. Computing the light maps takes hours, but that is done once during game development, and then the light maps are distributed with the game content just like any other texture maps. At runtime, that precomputed lighting is painted onto the scene. This gives the appearance of complex lighting without the cost. It also lacks some of the realism; for example, lights and large objects such as walls cannot be moved or destroyed when the lighting is precomputed. Table 14.1 lists the variables used in the remainder of this section.

14.2.1 Direct Illumination

Real lights interact with surfaces by multiplication. Shine a single colored light straight down on a perfectly diffuse (no specular highlights) white surface, and you'll see the color of the light. Shine the same light on a colored surface, and the result is the product of the light color and the color of the surface. Mathematically, if the light color is $C = (C_r, C_g, C_b)$ in terms of red, green, and blue values, and the diffuse surface color is $D = (D_r, D_g, D_b)$, then the color intensity observed is

$$(D_r * C_r, D_g * C_g, D_b * C_b), \tag{14.1}$$

which can be written compactly as $C * D$. As in real shader code, this notation uses an asterisk ($*$) for multiplication instead of the $\times$ symbol because (1) $\times$ looks too much like the letter "x," (2) there is no $\times$ on the keyboard, and (3) $\times$ is used for a special kind of multiplication in 3D graphics called the cross product.

From the formula in Equation (14.1), you can also see why a colored light shining on a white surface produces the color of the light—for a white surface, $D = (1, 1, 1)$. Note that diffuse surfaces have the same effect on incoming light as translucent glass has on light passing through it from behind: they filter the light that is observed by the camera.

Real lights interact with each other by addition. Shine two lights with colors C_1 and C_2 straight down on a perfectly diffuse surface with color D, and the result is the sum of the light that would be observed for each independently. Light 1 contributes $D * C_1$, and light 2 contributes $D * C_2$, so the total light is $D * C_1 + D * C_2$. With more than two lights, we just continue to add their contributions: $D * (C_1 + C_2 + ... + C_n)$.

In the sample situations of lights shining straight down on a surface, "straight down" was critical to the equations. If the light shines at an angle to the surface, then it appears less bright. This is the same as the notion of a glancing blow. When a car hits a wall head on, it causes a lot of damage, but when it scrapes by at an angle, the impact is much less serve. The same thing happens with light. Light shining straight down on a surface has full intensity, but as it rotates toward a glancing blow, it loses its impact. The geometry of the situation determines that the intensity falls off at the same rate as a rotating door appears to get thinner when it spins, which is mathematically the cosine of the angle between the surface and the light direction (it falls off at this rate for the same reason that the spinning door appears to get smaller, just as you see less of the door, the light sees less of the surface). This means that to compute the intensity of the light, you must know the cosine of the angle between the light and the surface.

For real-time lighting, games work with light sources that are either very far away, such as the sun, or fairly small, such as a lightbulb. Both are mathematically convenient because when shading the point on a surface that colors a single pixel, all the light (from one source) comes from a single direction. This makes it possible to compute the cosine of the angle, which is needed to shade the surface.

Faraway lights are often called "directional" lights because everywhere in the game world the direction to the light is the same. For instance, at noon, the sun is straight up from every location within several kilometers. Small lights are often called point sources because they are approximated by a single 3D point.

The direction from a surface point toward the light is represented by a 3D vector $L = (L_x, L_y, L_z)$. This is a direction because it has the following length:

$$\sqrt{L_x^2 + L_y^2 + L_z^2} = 1.$$

This length equation might look familiar. It is just the three-dimensional version of the Pythagorean theorem for finding the length of a diagonal in a triangle.

The surface orientation at a point is represented by a 3D normal vector $N = (N_x, N_y, N_z)$ that points straight out of the surface. To help visualize a surface normal, consider a porcupine. The porcupine's skin underneath all the quills is the surface mesh. The normals are the quills, which stick out at right angles to the skin everywhere. Figure 14.5 shows a visualization of a human face with the surface normals rendered as thin arrows. Of course, normals are just a mathematical idea, not something that is actually seen in the final image. The normal vector can be the vector pointing out at a right angle to the actual triangle, but that would make objects appear faceted like a gem because every triangle has a single normal over the whole surface, and then the next adjacent triangle has a completely different normal. Instead, the true triangle normal is usually discarded and replaced either by an artist-specified per-vertex normal that is smoothed over the surface of the mesh or, more commonly, by the normals painted directly into the normal map. Given the direction to the light L and the surface normal direction N, the cosine of the angle between them is the sum of their components. This expression

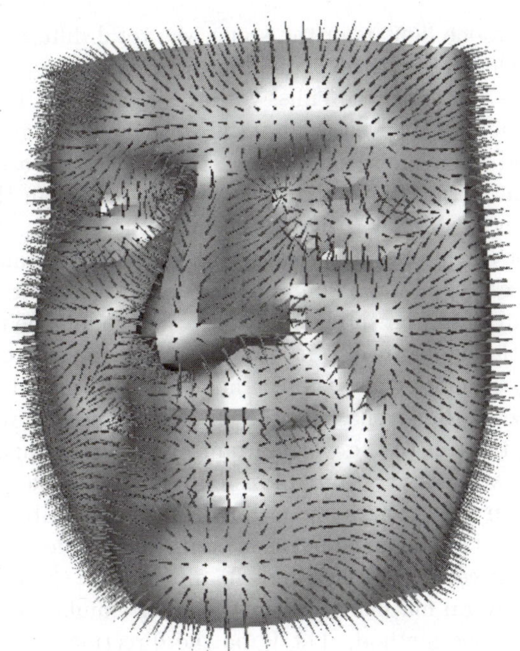

Figure 14.5. Surface normals are vectors that point directly out from a surface, like this human face. They are not normally drawn like this but are instead used to compute the shading of points on the surface.

is so common in computer graphics that it is given a special name, the dot product, and written as follows:

$$\begin{aligned} N \cdot L &= \cos(\text{angle between } N \text{ and } L) \\ &= N_x * L_x + N_y * L_y + N_z * L_z. \end{aligned}$$

Note that on the left side of the equation, the operator is a dot $(\cdot)$ for dot product, not an asterisk for multiplication. This measure of how glancing the light is on the surface is combined with the equation for the color of the result, giving the entire diffuse illumination amount:

$$I_{\text{diffuse}} = \max(0, N \cdot L) * C * D.$$

The "max" function prevents $N \cdot L$ from ever being negative; it means that the back side of a surface receives no light. We've followed the math in such detail up to this point because this exact equation appears in the pixel or vertex shader responsible for illumination. So you now understand a piece of the real code and mathematics running on a graphics card.

If more than one light is in the scene, the total diffuse term is the sum of the diffuse shading for each individual light. Likewise, when the surface has an emissive material, the emissive term is added to the diffuse terms. When the surface has a specular material, specular highlights are computed and added, and when the surface is reflective, reflections are added.

The specular term is only slightly more complex than the diffuse term. Specular highlights vary with the position of the viewer. Here's a mental experiment (or a real one, if it is a nice day outside). Stand near a glossy surface, like a car hood, on a sunny day. Look at the position of the bright highlight from the sun on the hood. Now walk around the car. Notice how as you move, the highlight also moves, appearing to swim over the surface. The highlight is more or less the car hood acting like a dark mirror for a very bright scene. It is reflecting the sunlight directly into your eye, and it is reflecting the rest of the world around you, but, compared to the sun, the rest of the world is very dim and is only barely visible in the reflection. Because specular reflection is like a mirror, it is primarily visible when the surface is oriented so the angle between your eye and the surface is the same as the angle between the surface and the direction to the light.

There are several mathematical methods for simulating specular illumination. Here is one method. Let V be the direction from a point on the surface to the viewer, called the view vector. Like the surface normal and the light vector, it has a length of one. Let the reflection vector R be the direction that a perfectly reflected ray from the light source would be traveling if it bounced off the surface:

$$\begin{aligned} R' &= 2(N \cdot L)N - L, \\ R &= \frac{R'}{||R'||}. \end{aligned}$$

The equation for R has two parts because the first line calculates the direction and the second line ensures that it has a length of one.

When the view vector is close to the reflection vector, the light source is being reflected toward the viewer and is visible in the surface as a highlight. When the view vector is far from the reflection vector, the light from the source is reflected somewhere other than toward the viewer, so it isn't seen and no highlight appears. Figure 14.6 shows the geometry of the situation. Note that in Figure 14.6, R and L are at the same angles (on opposite sides) with respect to N.

The full equation for the specular illumination under this model takes into account both the angles and the colors of the surface and the light. In the modeling chapter, we described a surface as having both a diffuse color (which is what you would casually call the color of the surface) and a specular color. The specular color of nonmetals is a shade of gray, and

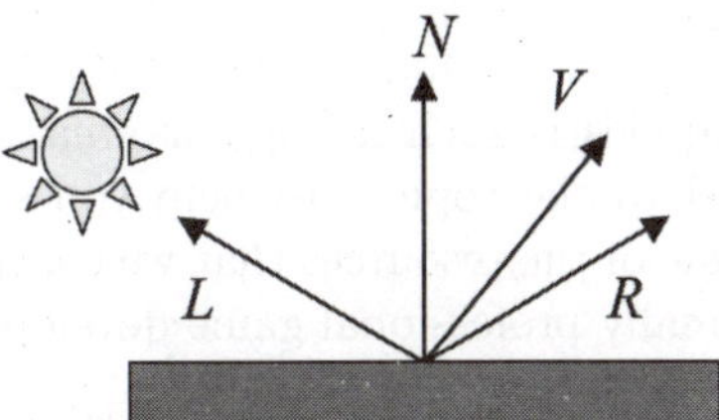

Figure 14.6. A specular highlight is visible in a shiny object when the reflection vector (R) is nearly identical to the view vector (V). In this figure, they are not identical, and no visible highlight appears until the light moves up or the viewer moves down relative to the surface.

the lighter the shade, the brighter the highlight. Because the specular color has no hue, the color of the highlight is the color of the light source. The intensity of illumination due to specular highlights is

$$I_{\text{specular}} = \max(0, (V \cdot R)^k) * C * S,$$

where C is the color of the light, S is the specular color of the surface, and k is the shininess of the surface, which is generally a number much bigger than 1, like 100. As the shininess increases, the radius of the specular highlight shrinks, and it becomes visible only when it is very close to the reflection vector. When the shininess is low, like 1, the highlight is visible from a wider angle and appears to be more blurred out.

14.3 Exercises

1. This chapter described how a CPU and a GPU work together to render 3D graphics. Some computers use multiple GPUs (e.g., through SLI or CrossFire) that together produce a single image for each frame. Speculate on how two GPUs can effectively divide up the work of rendering a 3D scene.

2. How much energy does a diffuse white surface lit at a 45-degree angle by a light reflect toward the camera compared to the same surface hit head on by the same light? Hint: It isn't 50 percent!

3. Can you tell the difference between a diffuse yellow surface lit by a green light and a diffuse green surface lit by a yellow light? What colors will each surface appear?

14.4 Resources

Because computer graphics is such a popular area, most bookstores have entire sections devoted to the topic. To help you select from among the many titles, we list some of the resources that we consider the most valuable and that are used by many professional game developers.

- Akenine-Möller, Haines, and Hoffman, *Real-Time Rendering*, Third Edition [Akenine-Möller et al. 08].
- Lengyel, *Mathematics for 3D Game Programming & Computer Graphics* [Lengyel 02].
- Shirley et al., *Fundamentals of Computer Graphics*, Second Edition [Shirley et al. 05].
- Foley, van Dam, Feiner, and Hughes, *Computer Graphics: Principles and Practice* [Foley et al. 96].
- Eberly, *3D Game Engine Design* [Eberly 00]
- Stroustrup, *The C++ Programming Language* [Stroustrup 00].
- Read, "How to Be a Programmer" [Read 02]

The ShaderX and GPU Gems series of books present cutting-edge programmable hardware techniques in a reference format.

DirectX/Direct3D is documented through Microsoft's online reference material at http://microsoft.com/directx and through the official books:

- Gray, *The Microsoft DirectX 9 Programmable Graphics Pipeline* [Gray 03].
- Turcan and Wasson, *Fundamentals of Audio and Video Programming for Games* [Turcan and Wasson 03].

OpenGL is documented through the OpenGL website (http://opengl.org) and a series of reference books, the two most important of which are the following:

- Shreiner et al., *The OpenGL Programming Guide: The Official Guide to Learning OpenGL Version 2 ("The Red Book")* [Shreiner et al. 05].
- *The OpenGL Shading Language,* 2nd Edition (*"The Orange Book"*) [Rost 05].

Many practical papers describing graphics techniques can be found in the proceedings of the scientific conferences SIGGRAPH, Eurographics, EGSR, I3D, and NPAR and in the *Transactions on Graphics* and *journal of graphics tools* journals.

CHAPTER 15

Physical Simulation

Terms Explained: *Dynamics* – *Force* – *Impulse* – *Integration* – *Constraint* – *Rigid Body* – *Particle* – *Mass* – *Acceleration* – *Newton's Laws*

Most games intend to give their player a sense of immersion in a virtual, although physically plausible, world. That is, a player's common-sense expectations from our physical world about how objects move and interact should roughly hold in the virtual game world. Implausible physical interactions,[1] such as when your weapon hits an enemy but is not recognized or when your *Breakout* ball bounces in the wrong direction, can lead to big user frustration. Obviously, completely faithful modeling of our physical world might complicate gameplay or interfere with the progress of a game's story. Game players, first and foremost, are engaging in some degree of escapism.

Regardless, a game must have some rules and procedures that govern how its world evolves from one instant of time to the next.[2] A developer could certainly make up their rules about how objects should move in the game world. This approach, typically using some creative combination of triggers and scripting, has been the most common since the dawn of video games. However, ensuring plausible and consistent physical rules over all possible game situations can be difficult and tedious. As a result, gameplay can become overly structured toward a fixed story line rather than promoting *emergent gameplay*, where unexpected events can occur beyond a designer's intent. For instance, animation of human characters can be performed by

[1]Not including intended physical implausibilities, such as super-human jumping or cartoon stretching and squashing, that are consistent within a game's story and gameplay.

[2]*Procedural animation* is the formal term for animations generated automatically from algorithmic rules and models.

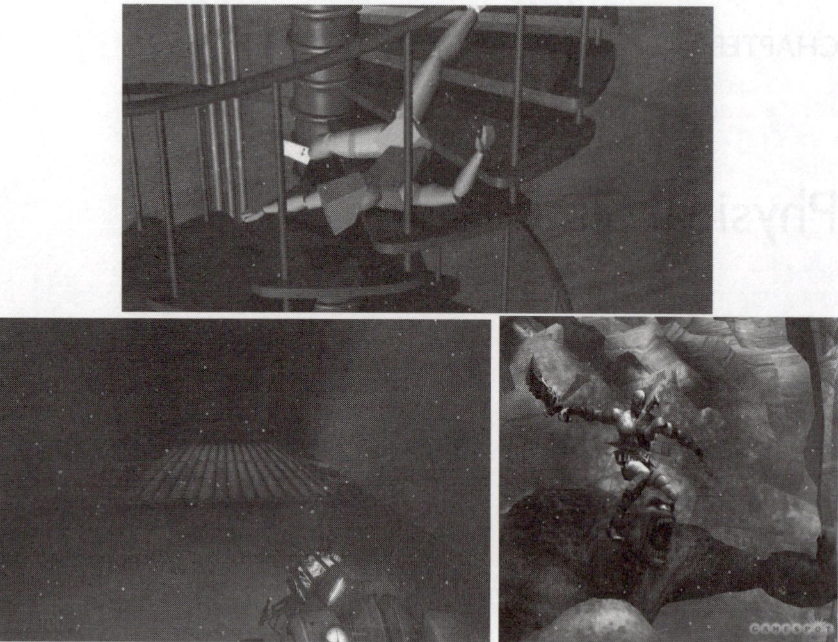

Figure 15.1. Physical simulation is often used for ragdoll effects (top) to produce the passive falling motion of an unconscious character. *Half-Life 2* (bottom left) uses physics within its gameplay with features such as a gravity gun for manipulating objects to make cover, solve puzzles, or whatever the player can conceive. Although both are good options, the emergent gameplay aided by physics in *Half-Life 2* is contrasted by *God of War* (bottom right), which features more structured interactions in its combat system. (Bottom-left image courtesy of Vivendi Universal; bottom-right image used with permission from CNET Networks, Inc., Copyright 2008, All rights reserved)

blending between a database of motion capture clips[3] or keyframe animations. While the result will be highly aesthetic and reliable, the character animation will have limited ability to adapt to game situations, such as adapting to the stature of opponents in fighting games or the (now ubiquitous) ragdoll effects in shooters.

Why not use what is known from the study of real physics to simulate physics in the game world? Fortunately, there is a continually growing

[3]Motion capture is a static snapshot of a human's dynamics over a specific window of time that captures only partial information (bone and joint motion) of the physical interactions that occurred to produce the data. This data is analogous to video, which is a static snapshot of the physics of light that occurred over some period of time.

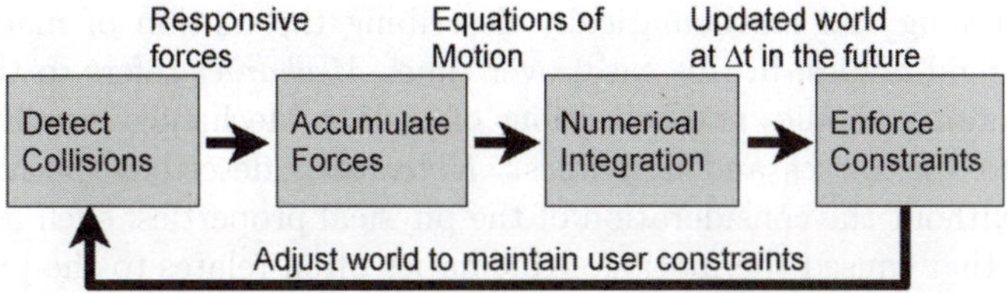

Figure 15.2. The job of a physical simulation engine is to continually update the state (position and velocity) of each rigid object over time. At a given time, this process roughly follows four steps: 1) detection of objects in collision; 2) accounting of forces due to contacts, gravity, motors, etc.; 3) using Newtonian equations of motion to update state one step ahead in time; and 4) adjusting state to conform with specified constraints, such as making sure bones stay connected in a skeletal hierarchy.

number of libraries (such as the Open Dynamics Library and Havoc) and hardware (such as Aegia's PhysX Physics Processing Unit) that allow you to incorporate physical simulation into your game. Further, games such as Valve's *Half-Life 2* have demonstrated that gameplay can be greatly enhanced when physics is properly incorporated into a game. At the core of these implementations, you will find formulations of basic mechanics, principles, and mathematical laws governing the motion of bodies, particularly with respect to Newton's laws of motion. Understanding of such mechanics will aid you in both using existing physics packages but also the development of your own systems.

This chapter provides an overview of some basic principles and techniques used in simulating physics for games (see Figure 15.2). While not a guide for thorough computational implementation, our coverage is meant to give some insight into how physical simulation works, coverage over commonly used techniques, and some tangents into physics in the greater picture. We outline the basic principles for animating articulated characters (such as humanoids) using rigid body dynamics to (approximately) simulate real-world physics. This chapter covers the basic principles and computation of Newtonian physics from a particle to a rigid body, collision handling for rigid bodies, and enforcing articulation constraints to produce ragdolls and motor-controlled humanoids. We will briefly touch upon Newtonian simulation of natural phenomenon using particle systems and finite element methods.

15.1 Newtonian Mechanics

We start with some big-picture perspective and definitions. Physics in games often refers to *Newtonian mechanics* (or classical mechanics), the physical laws governing and mathematically describing the motion of macroscopic objects (rigid bodies, in this case) over time. *Mechanics* refers to the study of the motion of bodies and collections of bodies. Mechanics roughly breaks down into kinematics and dynamics. *Kinematics* describes the motion of objects without the consideration of the physical properties, such as masses or forces that caused the motion. Kinematics often relates to the properties of a body's configuration, such as position, velocity, and acceleration. In contrast, *dynamics* pertains to forces and interactions that produce or affect motion.

Rigid body dynamics refers to the *equations of motion* for a set of bodies based on Newtonian mechanics and applied in a computational setting. Based on Newton's second law, equations of motion give us the math to deterministically predict what the state of the physical world will be at some future time given the current world state. Thus, simulating physics is really about making good predictions about the future. The quality of your simulation's predictions will require proper translation of physical equations into computational procedures, some finessing of differential equations, and reasonable guesswork on the physical properties of each rigid body.

Newtonian mechanics is only a particular subset of mechanics, which is a subset of physics as a field of study. Generally speaking, physics is the branch of science concerned with the discovery and characterization of universal laws that govern matter, energy, space, and time. Physics strives to understand and mathematically explain the true nature of the universe, giving us a logically ordered picture of nature in agreement with our collective experience. Other areas of physics include electromagnetism (the motion of charged particles), thermodynamics (the action of heat and conversions between forms of energy), the theory of relativity, and quantum mechanics.

15.1.1 Brief Tangent: Quantum Mechanics

Quantum mechanics is another major sub-field of mechanics that offers an alternative view of how bodies move at the atomic level. Newtonian mechanics focuses on the motion of macroscopic objects, such as projectiles, machine parts, and planets. Further, predictions made through Newtonian mechanics are deterministic in that a single state at a future instant of time is predicted with 100% certainty. In contrast, quantum mechanics focuses on the behavior of particles at the atomic level. Such particle behavior is governed by the propagation of waves that are *probabilistic* in nature. That is, there is no single future state prediction that results from a current state, but rather an infinite set of possible future states that are weighted based on

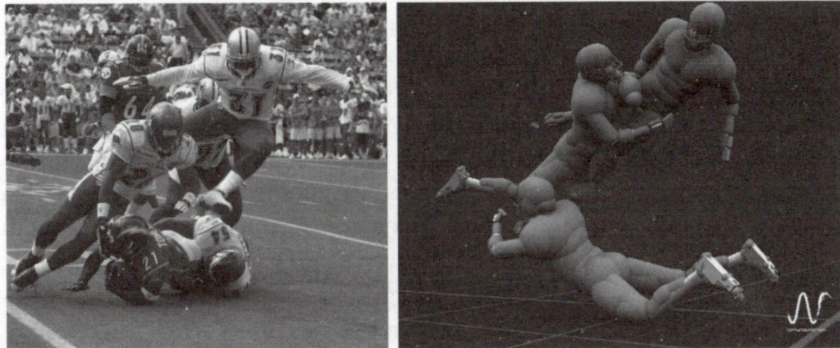

Figure 15.3. Physics studies the laws of how the universe behaves. Mechanics is a subfield of physics for modeling the motion of collections of bodies. Newtonian mechanics provides the ability to model and predict outcomes for real-world physical interactions, such as professional football players tackling each other (left), and physically plausible interactions for virtual characters, such as in Natural Motion's Endorphin system (right). (Right image courtesy of Natural Motion)

how likely they are to occur.[4] For instance, when you drop an oblong object (like an American football) onto a floor, there are many different types of bounces it could take, each of them having some probability of occurring. The probability of the object bouncing 10 meters into the air, however, is extremely low.

While quantum mechanics could be argued to be more accurate and precise than Newtonian mechanics, Newtonian mechanics is often sufficient for predicting physical outcomes of common phenomena. The reconciliation between the deterministic versus probabilistic views of physics can be philosophically contentious. Albert Einstein, for instance, remarked "God does not play dice with the universe" about the nondeterminism of quantum mechanics. Mechanics based on the theory of relativity, useful for modeling black holes and their interactions, is needed when bodies are moving very fast, at magnitudes comparable to the speed of light. Computationally, however, there is no question that Newtonian mechanics is much faster and amenable to digital representation than quantum mechanics. Just remember that game physics is about immersing the player with plausible physics, not understanding the true nature of the universe. Thus, sacrificing the accuracy and precision of quantum mechanics for the speed and certainty of Newtonian mechanics is currently a must given the limited CPU cycles that can be allocated for physics. Some day, if we succeed in building quantum computers, these roles might reverse.

Now, let's dive into some details about Newtonian mechanics.

[4]It should also be noted that a particle has no certain location, rather a wave function that is a probability distribution indicating where the particle could be.

15.2 Newton's Laws of Motion for a Particle

The essence of Newtonian mechanics comes from Newton's Three Laws of Motion. We consider the example of a volumeless 3D particle as a simple body for illustrating how these laws are used to state dynamical equations of motion. Equations of motion express a dynamics function that relates a particle's new state in the future given its current state in the form of a first-order differential equation.[5] As we discuss in the next section, this differential equation is numerically integrated over an interval of time to yield the actual prediction about the particle's future state.

Newton's Three Laws of Motion are stated briefly as:

- **First law.** An object in motion will remain in motion unless acted upon by external force.
- **Second law.** Force equals mass multiplied by acceleration ($F = ma$).
- **Third law.** For every action, there is an opposite and equal reaction.

We are principally interested in the Newton's Second Law because it allows us to predict the particle's new state. In its basic form, this law expresses acceleration $\ddot{x}$ as a function f of forces that depend only on the particle's position x, velocity $\dot{x}$, and time t:

$$\ddot{x} = f(x, \dot{x}, t)/m.$$

This equation is a second-order differential equation because acceleration depends on the change in velocity which depends on the change in position. Because second-order differential equations can be difficult to work with, it is better to rephrase this equation into two coupled first-order differential equations, using velocity $v = \dot{x}$ as an explicit intermediary:

$$\dot{v} = F/m,$$
$$\dot{x} = v.$$

Given the forces acting on the particle, the particle's new velocity and position can then be determined at some time Δt by solving these differential equations numerically (discussed in the next section). The particle's state is then represented as a 6D vector, concatenating position and velocity. The result is a single first-order differential equation:

$$\frac{d}{dt}\begin{bmatrix} \dot{x} \\ \dot{v} \end{bmatrix} = \begin{bmatrix} F/m \\ v \end{bmatrix}.$$

[5] Differential equations involve continuously changing variables and their rates of change.

Note that although we present the dynamics with respect to a single particle, multiple particles can be simulated at the same time within the same system by simply maintaining multiple instances of state variables. If particles need to interact, procedures for collision detection and response must be present, which we discuss in the context of rigid bodies.

To better understand what these variables mean, let's break down Newton's Second Law into its respective parts, considering mass m first. The mass of the body is simply a scalar number indicating how much matter is in an object, or more intuitively, the "heaviness" of the object.[6] Because our particle is simply a single point, it can be assigned some arbitrary but reasonable value. A more general formulation of mass is given as $m = pV$, density p times volume V, to which we give more attention later in this chapter.

A particle's acceleration $a = \ddot{x}$ is derived from the rates of change in its velocity $v = \dot{x}$ and position x.[7] Velocity is generally defined as the speed of something in a given direction. For our particle, velocity refers to the change in the particle's position over some unit of time dt, or the first derivative of position $\dot{x}$:

$$v = \dot{x} = \frac{dx}{dt} \approx \frac{x_t - x_{t+\Delta t}}{\Delta t}.$$

Δt is a scalar length of time, and x_t is the position of the particle at time t. Computationally, for our 3D particle, x and v are 3×1 vectors. Variable x is the *global* position of the particle in some external coordinate system, or world space. The vector v indicates both the particle's direction of movement and its magnitude (or speed). Note that as Δt gets increasingly small, the discrete approximation of v, $\frac{x_t - x_{t+\Delta t}}{\Delta t}$, becomes closer to the true instantaneous velocity $\frac{dx}{dt}$.

Similarly, acceleration is the first derivative of velocity $\dot{v}$, referring to the change in the particle's velocity over time as a 3×1 vector:

$$a = \dot{v} = \frac{dv}{dt} \approx \frac{v_t - v_{t+\Delta t}}{\Delta t}.$$

Further, acceleration is the second derivative of position $\ddot{x}$:

$$a = \dot{v} = \frac{dv}{dt} = \frac{d}{dt}\frac{dx}{dt} = \frac{d^2x}{dt^2}.$$

---

[6] Weight is not equivalent to mass. Weight is mass under the effects of gravity.

[7] Also, variables for acceleration, force, velocity, and position are expressed as vectors and, thus, can be added, subtracted, multiplied by scalars, etc.

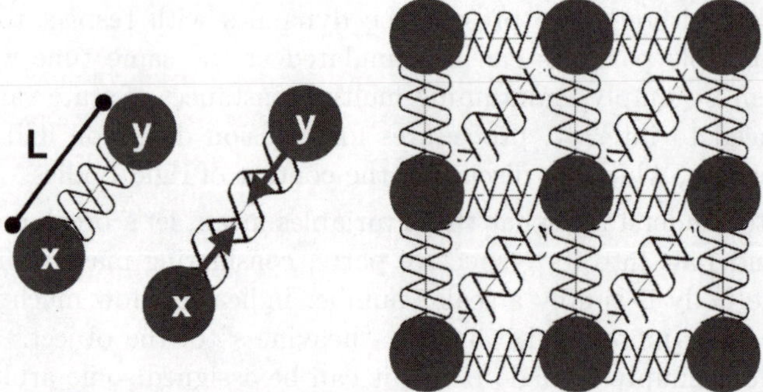

Figure 15.4. Two particles, x and y, can be connected by a spring to constrain their distance to l. When the particles' distance is greater than l, the spring applies opposite corrective (or penalty) forces on each particle to bring them closer to their equilibrium distance l. Spring-mass systems are constructed by connecting particles together with a network of springs.

Newton's Second Law restated as $a = F/m$ allows us to rephrase and determine the particle's change in velocity with respect to force and mass:

$$a = \dot{v} = F/m.$$

Just as with acceleration, F is a 3×1 vector referring to the *net force* (or resultant force) as the sum of all externally imposed forces f_i (also 3×1 vectors) acting on the particle:

$$F = \sum_i f_i.$$

Individual forces are linear and represent the acceleration of the particle along a particular direction that could result from gravity ($f_i = mG$), interactions with another particle y connected by a spring of equilibrium length l, stiffness k_s, and damping k_d (see Figure 15.4),

$$f_i = k_s(||x - y|| - l) + k_d v, \tag{15.1}$$

collisions with other objects (as indicated by Newton's Third Law), or artificial forces generated by a user, artificial intelligence procedure, or from a method of your choosing. Discussed later, multiple particles connected by springs can be used to simulate various types of articulated and deformable systems.

15.3 Solving Equations of Motion

Newton's laws provide only a mathematical description of how our particle should move, in the form of equations of motion. Equations of motion alone, however, provide no specific procedure for updating the particle's state forward in time. This responsibility falls upon a *numerical integrator*[8] to accumulate the effects of the equations of motion, expressed in a dynamics function $f(x, v, t)$, from time t to predict the particle's future state at time $t + \Delta t$. This process is often referred to as *solving the equations of motion*, referring to this integration as an *initial value problem.* That is, restating $s_t = [x_t \text{ and } v_t]$, given an initial state s_t and a *velocity field*[9] $\dot{s} = f(s_t)$, predict the future state $s_{t+\Delta t}$, which is equivalent to evaluating the integral

$$\int_t^{t+\Delta t} f(s_t) ds_t.$$

Note that the state variable s could refer to any type of time-evolving phenomenon, not just a 3D particle. Several numerical integration techniques exist, as discussed in Baraff and Witkin's course notes [Baraff and Witkin 97] and *Numerical Recipes in C* by Press et al. [Press et al. 92]. We discuss two of these techniques, Euler integration and Verlet integration, although the Runge-Kutta and backward Euler methods are notable omissions.

15.3.1 Euler Integration

Euler's method is the simplest approach to this numerical integration. Euler's method prescribes simply adding the derivative from the velocity field $f(s_t)$ weighted by the time step duration Δt to the current state s_t:

$$s_{t+\Delta t} = s_t + \Delta t f(s_t). \tag{15.2}$$

The problem with using Euler's method is finding the proper time step length Δt that yields optimal performance. For infinitely small time steps, Euler's method will perform accurately, yielding the proper physical evolution of the particle's state. However, each update of the state variable costs time and computation, and small time steps mean many updates will be performed. Games are especially time-critical applications where computationally expensive procedures are not looked upon favorably. In many situations, a single update with a larger step length will suitably approximate the accuracy of multiple updates with a smaller step size. While easing the

[8]In specific situations, however, analytical closed-form solutions to the equations of motion could be formulated instead of a numerical approximation.

[9]A velocity field outputs state derivatives given any state. This velocity field represents a first-order ordinary differential equation.

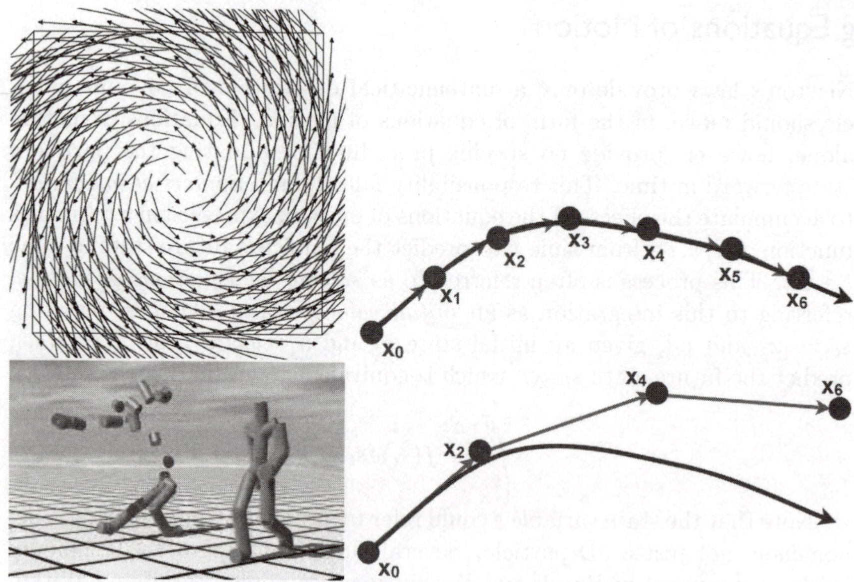

Figure 15.5. Top left: from any state s_t, the dynamics $f(s_t)$ output a state velocity direction, forming a vector field. Top right: proper numerical integration will accurately predict the proper state trajectory by iterating over multiple discrete time steps. If the step length is too long, simulations tend to "blow up" (such as the humanoid in the bottom left) due to divergence from the proper state trajectory (bottom right).

computational burden, however, this approximation breaks down as the step length increases (see Figure 15.5). If the step size is too large, the integrator can overshoot the proper state trajectory, causing crude approximations or instability (i.e., divergence from the proper state trajectory). These artifacts will appear in a particle's motion as jittering or, at worst, complete disappearance from the screen. In humanoids, integrator instability is often responsible for the character "exploding," where body parts violently fly apart from each other. Players of your games will not be happy with such unintended behavior.

One reason why Euler's method often fails is due to treating the change in state from $f(s_t)$ as a linear translation[10] when the actual dynamics may be nonlinear. Consider the case where the dynamics follow a set of concentric circles, or rings of increasingly larger radius with the same center. When starting directly on one of these rings, $f(s_t)$ will output a vector that is

[10]Remember that state dynamics $f(s_t)$ is a first-order system because position and velocity were concatenated into the particle's state. These dynamics are still second-order systems with respect to the particle's position x_t.

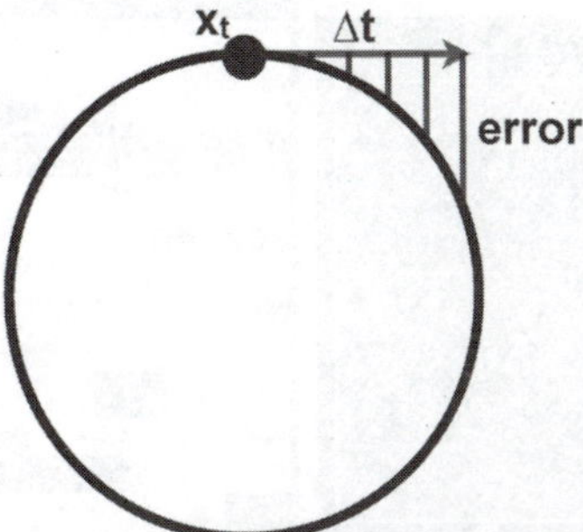

Figure 15.6. The dynamics velocity field provides a linear direction along which to step the simulation forward, much like the tangent vector of a circle. However, the system dynamics may actually be nonlinear, causing the predicted linear dynamics at state x to drift away from the actual nonlinear dynamics. In the case of the circle, as the step length Δt increases, divergence between linear prediction and the circle's parabolic curvature increase to introduce greater error in the step.

tangent to the ring. Even for a small Δt, integrating using Equation (15.2) will diverge from the ring[11] due to the ring's nonlinear curvature. This divergence gets worse in a single step as Δt increases and, over multiple steps, accumulates to drifting further and further away from the initial ring (see Figure 15.6).

Euler integration divergence raises two important points. First, Newtonian mechanics is primarily suited to a world with continuous time. Time, in reality, is not broken up into large discrete steps and is more naturally modeled as Δt, allowing for faithful second-order computation. Second, to get the benefit of unnaturally large time steps, better prediction is needed to avoid divergence. One approach, as taken in the Verlet and Runge-Kutta methods, is to increase the scope of time derivatives by expanding to higher-order differential equations.

15.4 Verlet Integration

Made popular by IO Interactive's *Hitman: Codename 47*, *Verlet integration* has become a standard for stable and extensible dynamical integration. Hitman: Codename 47 used Verlet-integrated physics to simulate a variety of phenomena such as cloth, plants, rigid bodies, and ragdoll humanoids. As West recently covered in *Game Developer Magazine* [West 06], Verlet inte-

[11]Unless Δt is infintesimally small.

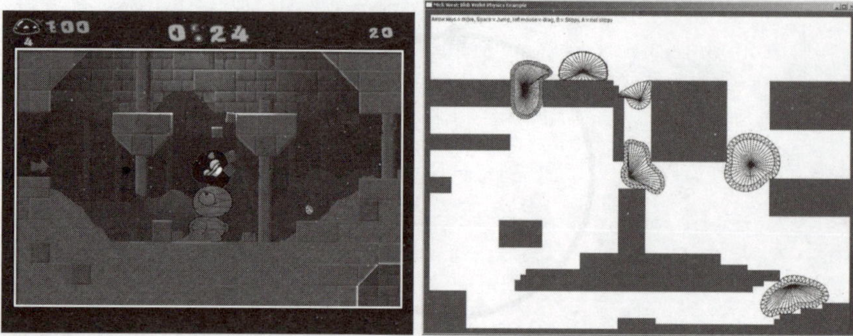

Figure 15.7. Particle systems composed of infinitely stiff springs are examples of structures created with with Verlet integrators. With a little creativity, such particle systems can be arranged to provide blob physics, where the system has fluid-like movement when interacting with the environment. *Gish* (left) and *LocoRoco* are games that use blob physics as a central game element. West explored creating simple Verlet-based blobs (right) in a recent issue of *Game Developer Magazine* [West 06]. (Images courtesy of Chronic Logic, LLC and Mick West of *Game Developer Magazine*)

gration is not much more difficult than the Euler approach and is useful for blob physics, such as in *Gish* or *LocoRoco* (see Figure 15.7).

The basic approach to Verlet integration examines the position of the particle one step ahead, $x_{t+\Delta t}$, and before, $x_{t-\Delta t}$, the current moment t. These positions are expanded to third-order equations using the *Taylor expansion*:

$$x_{t+\Delta t} = x_t + v_t \Delta t + \frac{a_t \Delta t^2}{2} + \frac{b_t \Delta t^3}{6} + O(\Delta t^4),$$
$$x_{t-\Delta t} = x_t - v_t \Delta t + \frac{a_t \Delta t^2}{2} - \frac{b_t \Delta t^3}{6} + O(\Delta t^4),$$

where a_t and b_t are the particle's acceleration and third derivative with respect to time and $O(\Delta t^4)$ is a bound on the error introduced by Taylor expansion terms higher than the third order. Adding these two equations together and simplifying yields the following update equation:

$$x_{t+\Delta t} = 2x_t - x_{t+\Delta t} a_t \Delta t^2 + O(\Delta t^4).$$

Note, this basic approach to Verlet integration does not directly incorporate velocity, although velocity can be computed after updating position. For this reason, the *velocity Verlet* (outlined in the following) is often the preferred for integration:

1. Update: $x_{t+\Delta t} = x_t + v_t \Delta t + 0.5 a_t \Delta t^2$.

2. Update: $v_{t+\frac{\Delta t}{2}} = v_t + 0.5 a_t \Delta t$.

3. Update: $a_{t+\Delta t}$ as the net external force on the particle.

4. Update: $v_{t+\Delta t} = v_{t+\frac{\Delta t}{2}} + 0.5 a_{t+\Delta t} \Delta t$.

15.5 Rigid Body Dynamics

We now turn our single volumeless particle into a full-fleged 3D rigid body by including rotational and volumetric information into the body's state.[12] We also need to generalize some of the particle's notation, such as mass computation, for our rigid body dynamics.

Jumping right into it, the state vector for a rigid body is

$$\begin{bmatrix} x_t \\ R_t \\ P_t \\ L_t \end{bmatrix},$$

and the equation of motion is

$$\frac{d}{dt}\begin{bmatrix} x_t \\ R_t \\ P_t \\ L_t \end{bmatrix} = \begin{bmatrix} v_t \\ \omega_t * \cdot R_t \\ F_t \\ \tau_t \end{bmatrix}.$$

Whoa! There are a lot of new variables here. Let's attach some definitions to these variables, starting with the state vector. x_t and R_t are, respectively, the position vector and orientation matrix (or, alternatively, quaternion vector) of the body in global coordinates. P_t and L_t are the linear and angular momentum, respectively. F_t and τ_t are, respectively, the net linear force and torque (i.e., rotational forces) acting on the body.

The variable x_t looks like our familiar position for the particle but is now the location of the body's *center of mass.* Because our body now has volume, mass m (simply stated as density times volume) is determined by integrating over each location r inside the body's geometry V weighted by that location's density, given by the density function $\rho(r)$:

[12] A rigid body actually has no geometric information in its definition, but some notion of body shape is needed for some precomputations.

$$m = \int_V \rho(r)dV,$$

and the center of mass is the average location inside the body's volume weighted by density:

$$x_t = \frac{\int_V r\rho(r)dV}{\int_V \rho(r)dV}.$$

Center of mass is a precomputation that often involves approximating the body's volume in a cubic grid. For simple geometries, however, there are standard formulations of volume that allow for closed-form determination of mass. One example is the volume of a sphere as $4/3\pi r_s^3$, where r_s is the sphere radius. which can be multiplied by some chosen density.

The variables x_t and R_t define the transformation to global coordinates from *body coordinates*, where x_t is the origin. A body space point p_b is translated into global coordinates p_w by first rotating by R_t and translating it by x_t:

$$p_w = R_t p_b + x_t.$$

The linear velocity v from particle notation is now folded into a linear momentum term P, which is mass times velocity $P_t = mv_t$. Newton's Second Law still holds as the conservation of momentum $\dot{P}_t = F_t$.

Angular momentum L_t has analogous relationships with inertia I_t (intuitively "mass for rotation"), angular velocity ω_t, and the net torque τ_t (or rotational force) imposed on the body. Specifically, angular momentum is inertia times angular velocity, $L_t = I_t\omega_t$. Angular momentum is conserved, $\dot{L}_t = \tau_t$, similar to conservation of linear momentum. These angular properties, however, are less intuitive being that they are rotations occurring along axes that are themselves continually moving in global coordinates. So, we will keep the discussion limited to what is needed without diving into too many details. References such as and Baraff and Witkin's course notes [Baraff and Witkin 97] are a good reference for further details.

Inertia is the angular equivalent of mass, specifying a body's resistance to rotate about a particular linear axis. For 3D rigid bodies, inertia I is expressed as a symmetric matrix, or *moment of inertia tensor:*[13]

$$\begin{bmatrix} I_{xx} & I_{xy} & I_{xz} \\ I_{yx} & I_{yy} & I_{yz} \\ I_{zx} & I_{zy} & I_{zz} \end{bmatrix},$$

[13]Moments of inertia are the set of second-order statistical moments for a 3D distribution, similar to the 2D image moments described in Chapter 17.

where, assuming each position r has coordinates[14] $\{x, y, z\}$:

$$\begin{aligned}
I_{xx} &= m\int_V (y^2+z^2)\rho(r)dV, \\
I_{yy} &= m\int_V (x^2+z^2)\rho(r)dV, \\
I_{zz} &= m\int_V (x^2+y^2)\rho(r)dV, \\
I_{xy} &= -m\int_V xy\rho(r)dV, \\
I_{xz} &= -m\int_V xz\rho(r)dV, \\
I_{yz} &= -m\int_V yz\rho(r)dV.
\end{aligned}$$

It is best to precompute I as I_b in the coordinates of the rigid body. Otherwise, computationally costly evaluation of these integrals will need to be performed at every time step due to the rotation of the body in global coordinates. A body-centric inertia matrix allows for determination of global space inertia at a given time t through simple rotational transforms:

$$I_t = R_t I_b R_t^T.$$

Angular velocity ω_t is a vector that specifies how the rotational axes of the body (or the columns of R_t) move. ω_t contains both the body-centric axis around which the body is spinning (given by the direction of ω_t) and the speed of the body's spin (given by the magnitude of ω_t). Through some mathematical trickery, angular velocity can also be represented as a matrix ω_t^*, allowing for updating R_t as

$$\dot{R}_t = \omega_t^* R_t = \begin{bmatrix} 0 & -\omega_{z,t} & I_{xz} \\ \omega_{z,t} & 0 & -\omega_{x,t} \\ -\omega_{y,t} & \omega_{x,t} & 0 \end{bmatrix} R_t,$$

where $\omega_{x,t}$, $\omega_{y,t}$, and $\omega_{z,t}$ are the scalar components of the angular velocity vector. It is important to note that linear and angular velocity are distinctly separate variables that update the body's translation and spinning independent of each other.

Individual external torques $\tau_{i,t}$ (represented as vectors and illustrated in Figure 15.8) are related to individual external linear forces $f_{i,t}$ as

$$\tau_{i,t} = (r_{i,t} - x_t) \times f_{i,t},$$

[14]We use x both to denote the position of the body and the horizontal coordinate of a particular location. Our use of x as a coordinate is only with respect to inertia matrix computation.

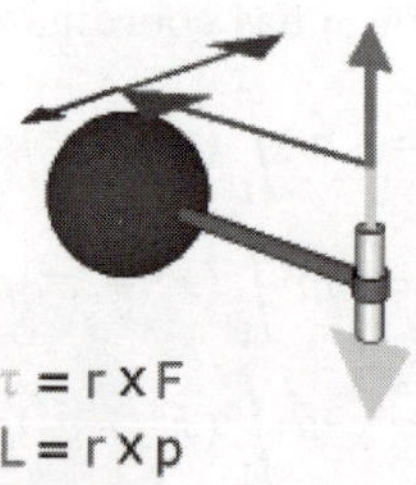

Figure 15.8. Shown for a mass rotating around a pole, torque τ represents rotational force about some axis. Torque is the cross product of the mass's relative position with respect to the rotation axis r and a linear force acting directly on the particle F. Angular and linear momentum, L and P, have a similar relationship.

where $r_{i,t}$ is the location in body coordinates where force $f_{i,t}$ is applied. Just as the net linear force is the sum of individual forces, the net external torque τ_t is the sum of individual torques:

$$\tau_t = \sum \tau_{i,\iota}.$$

At this point, you have the basics for understanding how rigid body dynamics work. Because the topics related to simulating physical dynamics can delve so deep,[15], the remainder of this chapter will be discussed with a relatively high level of "handwaving."

15.6 Collision Detection, Response, and Friction

Up to this point, we have expressed the dynamics of physical rigid bodies in 3D without respect to interactions between bodies, i.e., collisions. Collision detection and response procedures[16] give us the ability to determine when and where inter-body interactions occur (see Figure 15.9) and how to generate appropriate forces in response to produce proper interaction behavior. During collisions, we must also consider lower-level issues such as friction, avoiding large interpenetrations, and finding specific points of contact when generating response forces.[17]

[15]If you decide to take the red pill, you can follow the chapter references to see how deep the rabbit-hole goes.

[16]It is often best to start with an existing collision detection library, such as RAPID or OPCODE, rather than implement your own.

[17]Although applying forces to bodies can be very fun, it is important to remember Newton's Third Law. Interaction forces applied to one body must be applied (with negative magnitude) to the other body in contact.

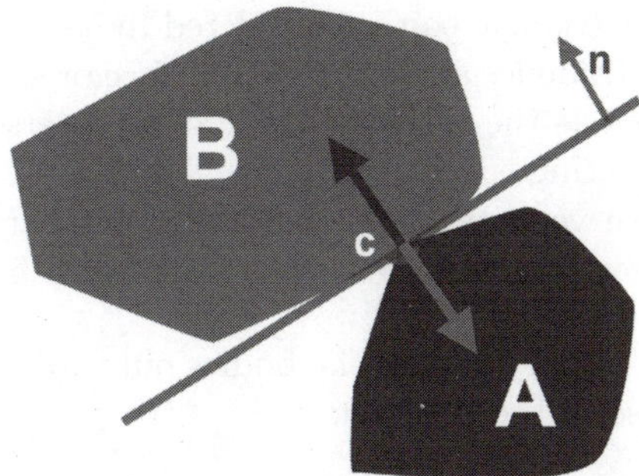

Figure 15.9. When a collision occurs between two geometrical bodies A and B, both bodies apply equal and opposite response forces to each other, according to Newton's Third Law. These response forces occur at a contact c and along a contact normal n defining a separating plane between the bodies.

From an input-output viewpoint, a collision-handling mechanism is given each body's geometry[18] and (through queries) configuration at any point in time.[19] Remember that a numerical integrator only uses variables about "physical" properties (position, mass, etc.) and does not use information about geometry to solve equations of motion. Rigid body geometry is "additional" information that is used primarily for collision detection.[20] From this information, collision handling produces:

- points and normals of contact between pairs of bodies and times when these contacts occur;
- response forces or impulses for each contact.

Let's look at the outputs one-by-one in a simplified approach, starting with determining points of contact. The simplest approach to finding such contact points would be finding the intersection of every triangle on each body with all triangles on all other bodies. Such intersection tests would be performed during each time step of the simulator. A "separating plane" test is a simple means to determine if two triangles (and their respective bodies) intersect. This test attempts to find a plane (defined by any three of the six vertices in the triangle pair) that separates the vertices into their respective objects. The possible separating planes can be enumerated into a finite number of cases and quickly evaluated geometrically. If there is no

[18]Geometry is assumed to be the ubiquitous polyhedra as a 3D polygonal mesh composed of triangular faces.

[19]That is, we evaluate the states of every body by integrating to an arbitrary time t.

[20]Although there are some recent research efforts that attempt to include collisions in the integration of a time step.

separating plane, the triangle pair is considered to be intersecting. The contacts between these triangles are either vertex/face or edge/edge.[21] Contact normals can be taken as the surface normal of an intersecting face or cross product of two contacting edges.

From the relative velocity of the contact point between the bodies,[22] three cases emerge for generating response forces with friction:

- if the relative velocity pushes the bodies outward, no response force is required to resolve the collision;

- if the relative velocity pushes the bodies inward, the contact is colliding or sliding with Coulomb friction forces along the contact normal and tangential against the relative velocity;

- if the relative velocity is zero, the contact is resting with Coulomb friction forces along the contact normal and tangential within some tolerance.

There are several problems with this simplistic approach to collision handling.

First, intersection tests between all pairs of triangles is $O(N^2)$, for N triangles. This needlessly wastes precision computation cycles, especially given the large numbers of triangles used in modern games. Pruning is typically used to eliminate unnecessary tests using a hierarchy of bounding volumes of increasing resolution. This hierarchy allows coarse collision testing over large collections of bodies to occur cheaply. These low-resolution tests can then determine where more expensive higher-resolution intersection testing is required. Hierarchies can be formed by collections of various simple geometric primitives, such as axis-aligned bounding boxes, oriented bounding boxes, or spheres. A variety of techniques also exist for quickly intersecting these simple geometries, such as *hash space* or *sweep-and-prune* procedures (see Figure 15.10).

A second problem is that large simulation step lengths can result in stepping over the occurrence of a contact; stated differently, collisions may not be detected until large interpenetrations between objects occur. These interpenetrations can be avoided by essentially performing a "do over" with a smaller time step. The simulator is restarted from the current state with increasingly smaller time steps until the time of contact is found, within some tolerance. Verlet integrators avoid interpenetrations by enforcing collision constraints that project an invalid solution into the space of valid solutions.

[21]Vertex/vertex, vertex/edge, and collinear edge/edge contacts are non-standard cases that need to be handled separately.

[22]The relative velocity $\dot{c_{AB}} = n(\dot{c_A} - \dot{c_B})$ is based on the velocity of the contact c with respect to bodies A and B and the contact normal n.

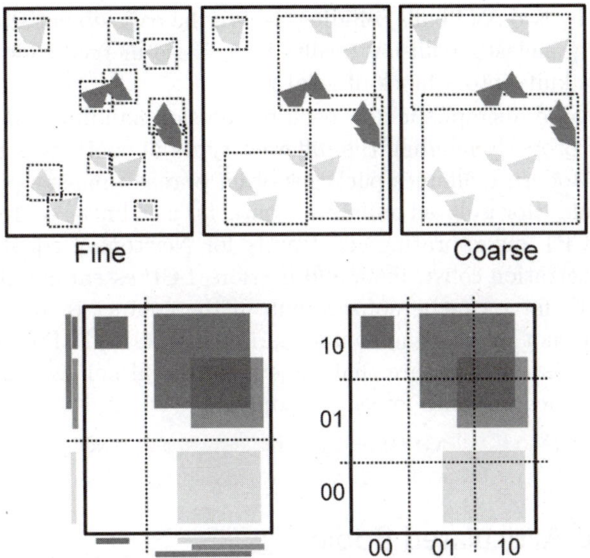

Figure 15.10. (Top) Hierarchies of axis-aligned bounding boxes, from coarser to finer resolution, allow for collision detection to prune away pairs of polygons that do not require precise intersection testing. In the illustrated example, only two pairs of polygons are intersecting (dark gray). Axis-aligned bounding boxes can be tested for intersection by a sweep-and-prune procedure (bottom left), by intersecting projections along each axis, or hash spaces (bottom right). Hash spaces encode each box as associated with a set of binary string tags based on regions of space they occupy.

A third problem is that forces generated for colliding contacts do not immediately change relative velocity, and, thus, large interpenetrations could occur. The problem is that a responsive force, no matter how large, needs the simulator to advance in time before the object's velocities change. By the time the response is applied, the object pair will be penetrating. The solution to addressing this delayed-response issue is through applying *impulses.* An impulse is a large force applied over an infinitesimally small duration. An impulse $J = F\Delta t$ allows for increasing force F while decreasing the duration of the force Δt. It is is used to produce the same behavior as properly applying a responsive force but without taking a forward simulation step. Although impulses are frictionless, their magnitude can be determined in closed form (a big equation for finding J) and incorporates a coefficient of restitution. The coefficient of restitution $\epsilon = \frac{\dot{c}_{AB}^{+}}{\dot{c}_{AB}^{-}}$ is the ratio of the velocity after the collision over the velocity before the collision. It is used for specifying the elasticity or "bounciness" of a collision. Elasticity in this case is the degree to which colliding objects stick together. An elastic collision is exemplified by two pool balls colliding, where the balls do not stick together. A completely inelastic collision results in a single merged rigid body, such as sticking a knife into a block of gelatin.

Even beyond a simplistic approach to collision handling, addressing the problems of properly handing the different types of contacts is a significant challenge. Modern dynamics packages often phrase time-stepping for rigid body dynamics (for isolated unilateral contacts) as a linear complementarity problem (LCP), incorporating constraints for Newtonian equations of motion, nonpenetration constraints, and friction. LCP essentially dictates that each contact's force can be nonzero only if the contact is maintained, and its force may not exist if the contact is not maintained. Solutions arising from these constraints ensure that penetrations will not increase at any of the contacts once response forces are applied.

15.7 Constraints and Articulated Bodies

In order to build articulated bodies, we need to enforce constraints that specify how rigid bodies are connected in a larger mechanism. A humanoid character, for instance, is a collection of rigid bodies connected by joints. Each joint is a constraint that connects two rigid bodies and restricts the relative position and orientation. Joints can take several forms, such as a hinge joint that revolves around a single axis, a ball-and-socket joint that has three axes of rotation, or a prismatic joint that slides along a single translational axis. The dimensionality, or number of free parameters, used to express the configuration of a joint are called *degrees of freedom (DOFs)*. By only enforcing joint constraints, our humanoid will be a *ragdoll* that will go limp and fall down. In the next section, we will cover how to make the humanoid move by computing motor torques.

Using what we know up to this point, we may be inclined to enforce joint constraints with spring forces. Such springs would attach two bodies at their relative locations for the joint center and have an equilibrium at length zero. This spring is considered a *penalty constraint* because it produces forces that penalize any nonzero spring distance towards equilibrium. Because penalty forces react to violations of constraints, our humanoid will be a wobbly mess with rigid bodies that continually oscillate around their joint centers.

Approaches to formulating constrained dynamics that allow for the expression of articulated characters typically have either implicit or explicit constraints. Explicit constraints are inherently and rigidly connected as a single entity, analogous to steel links connected in a chain. Implicit constraints treat each rigid body as an independent entity where the constraints dictate how bodies work together, analogous to how magnetism connects Ge-

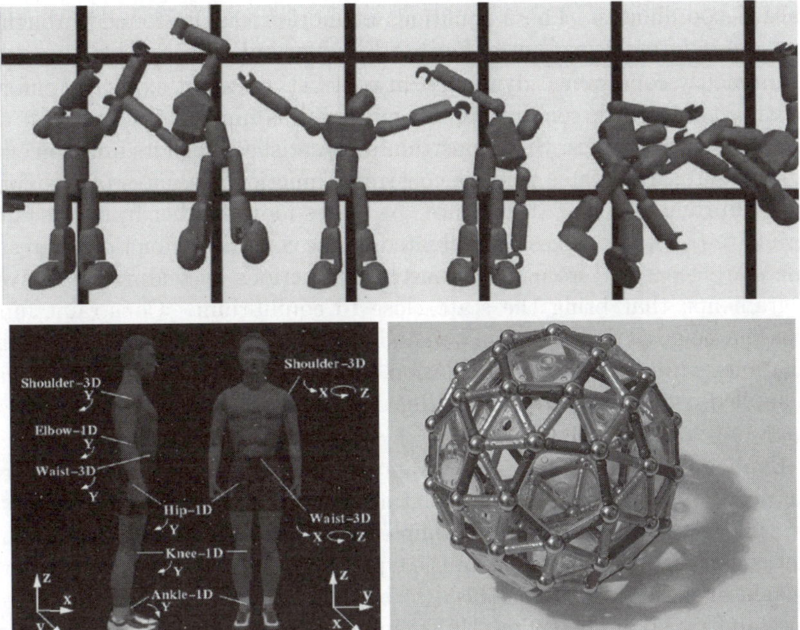

Figure 15.11. Humanoid characters are composed of rigid bodies connected by joints. Rotations about joints allow the character to pose in a variety of configurations (top). The character's kinematics define degrees of freedom, specifying how joints can rotate. Early research into physics-based animation by Hodgins et al. used dynamics that explicitly held the bones of humanoid characters together (bottom left). However, most dynamics engines used in modern games have independent rigid bodies that are held together by constraints, similar to how magnetism holds Geomag structures together (bottom right). (Bottom-left image courtesy of Jessica Hodgins; bottom-right image courtesy of Geomag SA)

omag or Magnetix balls and sticks (see Figure 15.11). Typically, implicitly constrained dynamics are favored by game developers because they allow for greater control over entities and their interaction with a virtual environment, whereas explicit constraints are favored by engineers and roboticists seeking to model the interaction of a single device with a real environment.

Explicit constraints formulate a new set of coordinates, or *generalized coordinates*, where the constraints are always met. For humanoids, these generalized coordinates define physical state as a set of angles formed between connected bodies, or joint angles, and their velocities.[23] The equations of motion in this case define the torques necessary to update state in gen-

[23]Note that the root of the humanoid either needs to be fixed or simulated as a free body.

eralized coordinates. These equations of motion can be found through a *Lagrangian* formulation[24] or a *Newton-Euler* formulation.[25]

Implicitly constrained dynamics, in contrast, does not explicitly enforce constraints. Instead, constraints are expressed as implicit functions on the state of the rigid bodies. Such constraints are satisfied when its function evaluates to zero. The states where a constraint function evaluates to zero form an equilibrium region of state space. As states move further from this equilibrium region, their values, as evaluated by the constraint function, increase. Forces are generated from these constraint functions by finding derivatives, or gradients, that bring the state close to equilibrium. Constraint functions can be analytically formulated and solved to quickly correct constraint violations without constant oscillation. Further, multiple constraints can be applied concurrently by taking linear combinations (a weighted sum) of constraint gradients.

Explicit constraints have the advantage of having fewer free parameters that need to be solved and never violating the intrinsic constraints of the system. Implicit constraints are not completely faithful at properly maintaining joint constraints. For example, in the Open Dynamics Engine, there are two scalar user parameters[26] that need to be manually tuned to get functional constraint satisfying behavior. Unlike implicit constraints, however, explicit constraints are difficult to specify and cannot be easily combined. Implicit constraints provide a much cleaner means to express various constraints dynamically without completely reworking the entire expression of generalized coordinates.

15.7.1 Verlet Constraints

Verlet integrators are prone to enforce constraints by simply moving, or projecting, a particle in violation of a constraint into the closest nonviolating location. Such constraints are used to enforce collisions and interparticle distance, and to form articulated structures, such as plants, humanoids, and cloth as in *Hitman: Codename 47*. These constraints are enforced after an integration step to rectify violations that occurred during update. For instance, if a particle travels outside of a bounding region during update, a collision constraint would project the particle back in bounds before continuing to the next timestep. Articulated bodies can be formed by connecting particles together with constraints representing infinitely rigid springs. For

[24]The temporal derivative of the partial derivative of kinetic minus potential energy with respect to each generalized coordinate.

[25]At each time step, velocities and accelerations are propagated "forward" from the root to outboard bodies and corrected "backward" to the root with forces and torques backward.

[26]The Error Reduction Parameter and the Constraint Force Mixing.

example, two particles at locations x and y with spring equilibrium length l can be enforced with the following constraints:

$$d_1 = x - y, \tag{15.3}$$

$$d_2 = \sqrt{d_1^2}, \tag{15.4}$$

$$d_3 = \frac{d_2 - l}{d_2}, \tag{15.5}$$

$$x = x + 0.5 d_1 d_3, \tag{15.6}$$

$$y = y - 0.5 d_1 d_3, \tag{15.7}$$

Note that when x and y are equilibrium length, d_3 is zero, and the points are not displaced. When not at equilibrium, x and y are moved along their difference vector d_1 into the proper distance. However, there is little to stop one[27] from replacing the last two constraints for x and y with $x = x + d_1 d_3$. Thus, just moving a particle for convenience is different than applying physical forces. Physical fidelity requires that momentum is conserved and prescribes a specific outcome. Rest assured, however, that the Verlet integrator will seamlessly update the motion of these particles in future timesteps, providing enough continuity to be plausible in a game. There is one additional hitch: what happens when there are multiple constraints that could interfere with each other? Fortunately, multiple constraints are easily dealt with by *relaxation*, that is, continually iterating through enforcing each single constraint until all of them are (reasonably) met.[28]

15.8 Articulated Kinematics and Motion Control

Motor forces for our artificial rigid body humanoid are analogous to muscle forces in natural biomechanical humans. Motor forces are torques applied at each joint to achieve and maintain a desired relative configuration[29] for the two bodies attached to the joint. While motor forces are subject to Newton's laws, they are not specified by Newton's laws. Instead, motor forces are based on some control mechanism that determines what state the system should be in and what forces should be applied to reach that state. Such questions get to larger notions of artificial intelligence. For now, let's consider the simple *motion control* problem: given a desired configuration and a current configuration for an articulated body, how do we generate motor forces from the current state to the desired state.

[27] Maybe except for the spirit of Newton's Third Law.

[28] Another case of the simplest answer making the most sense.

[29] For this section, we consider only rotational joints in generating motor forces.

Motion control forces us to rethink our basic formulation of the physics differential equation $\dot{s_t} = f(s_t)$. Because motor forces, which we specify as u_t, are not generated in the simulator, they are a parameter that must be specified externally. This brings a new motor-inclusive statement of physics as $\dot{s_t} = f(s_t, u_t)$. Note that these motor forces u_t are a subset of forces that contribute to the overall net force exerted on each rigid body.[30]

The simplest approach to motion control is to phrase control constraints that will move specific bodies or particles to particular world space locations. This type of constraint simply attempts to minimize the distance between a point on a body and a given target location. The management of articulation constraints and other interactions while executing control constraints falls upon the numerical integrator or the application of user forces. A *meathook* is one application of these constraints that is attached to a character to keep them standing upright. Such constraints are external forces not generated by the character, analogous to how a marionette does not generate internal forces to produce its motion. This marionette analogy is particulary relevant to games such as *Rag Doll Kung Fu*, where the player controls a ragdoll character by moving its constraints (see Figure 15.12). As a consequence, implausible superhuman motion can result if new target locations outside the character's reachable space are abruptly introduced. Further, too many control constraints applied to a body can cause articulation constraints to be violated and result in the body pulling apart.

While control constraints are by far the preferred method, true motor forces are generated internally within the character's embodiment, using muscles or motors to produce actuation. Motor forces are applied in an equal-and-opposite manner between two bodies connected by a joint. Locomotion and other global movement can only realistically occur when interacting with an external object, such as pushing off of a ground plane. Before we can consider how to generate internal motor forces, however, we must consider how desired configurations are represented and expressed. This brings us to the topic of *forward kinematics* for articulated collections of rigid bodies. Forward kinematics is about specifying and transforming between a set of body-centric coordinate spaces related by a hierarchy. Essentially, forward kinematics is equivalent to a *scene graph hierarchy*, differing only by adding consideration of motor-powered joints. Such hierarchies are typically considered to be trees (thus, contain no cycles) and have a root that is fixed to a particular world space location or is a free rigid body. Forward kinematics allow us to specify the world space location of any point in space with respect to the coordinates of any body in the hierarchy. Conversely, *inverse kinematics (IK)* is about estimating the configuration of bodies in a

[30] Although they cancel out over the entire articulated structure if they are internally generated.

Figure 15.12. Without control forces, humanoid characters are passive ragdolls that can only fall down or serve as crash test dummies, such as in *Truck Dismount* (top left). Humanoids in *Rag Doll Kung Fu* move and are held upright using external forces for user control of characters similar to marionettes. To be true to physics, control forces should be generated internally, the way muscles apply equal and opposite forces to bones connected by a joint. van de Panne's *Ski Stunt Simulator* uses PD-servos to generate internal motor forces for executing skiing maneuvers. Users can control the pose of the skier, but reaction forces from the ground actually produce the character's motion. (Images courtesy of Jetro Lauha (top left), Mark Healey (top right), and Michiel van de Panne (bottom))

hierarchy that would result in a point on a particular body being in a specific world space location.

In such hierarchies, a motor-powered joint connects a parent (or inboard) body to a child (or outboard) body. The coordinates of a joint have an origin at some user-selected joint center. This joint center relates the location of the joint to the center of mass of each connected body in the respective body's coordinates. Traditionally, the joint's rotational axes are aligned with the orientation of the parent body.[31] The joint angles representing the relative configuration of the child to the parent body are expressed with respect to these axes. Transformations from a parent joint to child joint are expressed as matrices[32] and can be chained through multiplication to traverse the hierarchy.

At a given moment in time, we will have current and desired joint angles specifying the desired angular displacement about the rotational axis of each joint. The current joint angles are the angles formed by bodies relative to each joint rotation axis in the current state of the simulation. We would like to move this simulation state such that desired angles at each joint axis are formed. One could try to compute these torques directly through inverting the equations of motion and solving for force. Such a move to a desired joint angle state will not necessarily occur in a small number of time steps due to issues such as limitations on torque. This could be in place to enforce constraints similar to human biomechanics.

For each individual joint axis, the generation of motor forces often is phrased as a *feedback* process where torques serve to continually minimize the error between desired and current joint angles. For explicitly constrained rotational joints, this is accomplished using the proportional-derivative (PD) servo. About the jth-axis of rotation, motor force

$$\tau_j = k_p(\theta_{j,c} - \theta_{j,d}) + k_d(\dot{\theta_{j,c}} - \dot{\theta_{j,d}})$$

is a penalty force generated from the current $\theta_{j,c}$ and desired $\theta_{j,d}$ joint angles. For implicitly constrained joints, motor forces can be expressed as an additional constraint expressed as an implicit function, or at the very least, use IK procedures to find reasonable target locations.

Maintaining constraints using only internally generated motor forces can be problematic. Humanoid balance can be a particularly difficult problem because the quantity that needs to be controlled, the character's center of mass, cannot be directly manipulated. Static balance requires the center of mass to remain over a *support polygon*, or "footprint," as the convex hull of the character's contact with the ground. The situation becomes further complicated for motion requiring *dynamic balance*, such as running and jumping, where there are flight phases with no support polygon. While there are algorithms to address balancing, they will not necessarily provide the level of control to grab a player's attention. This further highlights that some solutions are more suited for the real world (and for engineers and

[31]Parent space alignment of rotational axes is typically the default approach for simplicity, but other rotational axes can also be used.

[32]This matrix is a multiplication of matrices for rotating the rotational axes by the joint angles and translating to the child's joint center. Additionally, the transformation from a child to a parent is the inverse of this matrix.

roboticists) and less of a good match for your game. The difference between RoboCup and EA's *FIFA* can be worlds apart.

15.9 Particle Systems and Natural Phenomena

Coming back to simulating particles, we now explore multiple particle simulations, or *particle systems* (see Figure 15.13). Particle systems simulate the collective effect of multiple particles running in parallel, often providing some noticeable "macroscopic" behavior from many smaller "microscopic" interactions. These systems are well suited to simulating natural phenomena (e.g., smoke, snow, water), simple biological collectives (e.g., swarms of insects), and collections of small and passive objects (e.g., human hair, cloth). In its simplest form, a particle system just adds more particles to a system without concern for their interactions. These systems are a small extension of the particle simulator we covered previously to maintain and update the states of multiple particles. The motion of falling snow, rising smoke, or exploding fireworks can be simulated separately for non-interacting individual particles. Such phenomena assume the programmer applies appropriate external forces to each particle that approximate factors such as wind, air resistance, buoyancy, and viscous drag in addition to gravity. Further, incorporating response forces from collisions allows for particles to interact with each other or environment geometries, such as with water in a fountain or waterfall.

External forces can also be applied to individual particles to simulate the motion of simple biological creatures, such as insects in a swarm or birds in a flock. Unlike natural phenomena, biological control does not necessarily follow equations found in a physics text as it requires information outside

Figure 15.13. Particle systems are useful for simulating effects such as hair (left) and explosions (middle), although finite element methods using Navier-Stokes equations are more appropriate for fluid, such as water in a cup (right).

the state of the particle. For instance, an insect in a swarm may want to stay close to its neighbors and avoid fast-moving swatting objects. Discussed in more detail in Chapter 18, a simulated insect will generate *control* forces to react to these environmental situations as well as be subject to natural external forces.

Using springs to constrain interparticle distance, *spring-mass systems* can be constructed to create deformable objects, such as cloth or hair. As we have previously discussed, a spring can constrain the distance between two particles to a fixed equilibrium length through the application of forces, as in Equation (15.1), or formulated constraints, such as the infinitely stiff spring in Equations (15.3)–(15.7). Springs allow particles to be chained together to form larger structures. For instance, a strand of hair could be modeled as a set of particles connected in sequence by springs. Cloth is often modeled as a spring-mass system in a rectangular grid arrangement. The choice of numerical integrator will have a strong impact on the behavior of a spring-mass system. Consider a spring-mass system in equilibrium at a moment when one particle is suddenly moved in some direction. With a basic Euler integrator, the system will lack stability and, in the best cases, produce noticeable oscillations over several time steps to regain equilibrium. The culprit for this instability is the use of discrete time steps to propagate spring effects. Specifically, the effect of moving one particle requires a time step for the spring to affect its immediate neighbors and another time step to affect the neighbors of its neighbors, and so on.[33] The infinitely stiff springs used in Verlet schemes avoid this propagation problem by always ensuring the springs are at equilibrium at each time step. The result is that the springs actually behave like rigid rods. While this produces fast and stable motion, the system cannot stretch or shear, which is very natural behavior for cloth.

Although the simplest approach, particle systems are not necessarily the right choice for simulating the motion of fluids. Fluid dynamics typically produce better results as *finite element methods*, where the volume of the region being simulated is chopped up into a rectangular grid. The dynamics of fluid particles in the grid are governed by *Navier-Stokes equations*, an application of Newtonian mechanics to fluids. Navier-Stokes equations define velocity and pressure fields across elements of the grid to direct the motion of fluid particles. Instead of representing each particle individually, however, grid elements store *particle density* to approximate the amount of particles currently at a particular location. This density representation both avoids expensive modeling of every particle and provides a macroscopic view of the phenomenon at each volume element. At every time step, density is exchanged by neighboring cells of the grid based on factors for diffusion,

[33]The originally displaced particle itself will also be subject to a feedback effect once its neighbors are displaced.

advection, and external forces with consideration of kinematic viscosity and resulting updates to the velocity and pressure fields for future time steps. We refer to Stam's tutorial on real-time fluid dynamics [Stam 03] for further details.

15.10 Resources

- Bourg, *Physics for Game Developers* [Bourg 01].
- Hecker, "Rigid Body Dynamics" series, *Game Developer Magazine*, October/November 1996–June 1997 [Hecker 97].
- West, "Using Verlet Physics to Simulate Blobs", *Game Developer Magazine*, May 2006 [West 06].
- Jakobsen, "Advanced Character Physics", *Game Developers Conference*, 2001 [Jakobsen 01].
- West, "Practical Fluid Dynamics", *Game Developer Magazine*, March/April 2007 [West 07].
- Stam, "Real-Time Fluid Dynamics for Games", *Game Developers Conference*, 2003 [Stam 03].
- Terdiman, "OPCODE: Optimized Collision Detection", 2003 [Terdiman 03].
- Gottschalk et al., "OBBTree: A Hierarchical Structure for Rapid Interference Detection", *SIGGRAPH 1996 Proceedings* [Gottschalk et al. 96].
- Baraff and Witkin, "Physically Based Modeling", *SIGGRAPH 1997 Course Notes* [Baraff and Witkin 97].
- Baraff and Witkin, "Large Steps in Cloth Simulation", *SIGGRAPH 1998 Proceedings* [Baraff and Witkin 98].
- Press et al., *Numerical Recipies in C: The Art of Scientific Computing* [Press et al. 92].
- Ward et al., "A Survey on Hair Modeling: Styling, Simulation, and Rendering", *IEEE Trans. on Visualization and Computer Graphics*, March/April 2007 [Ward et al. 07].
- Eberly, *Game Physics* [Eberly 03].

- Craig, *Introduction to Robotics* [Craig 04].
- Spong et al., *Robot Modeling and Control* [Spong et al. 05].
- Halliday et al., *Fundamentals of Physics* [Halliday et al. 07].

15.11 Exercises

1. Implement a physical simulation for a single 3D particle using Euler integration. Collision detection and response should keep the particle within a 3 m × 3 m × 3 m box. The particle should be initialized with a position at the center of the box and a small horizontal velocity. A gravitational force of −9.81 m/s along the upward-facing vertical axis should always be applied to the particle.

2. Add a second particle to your Eulerian particle simulator. Attach the two particles together 0.2 m apart using spring forces to enforce this equilibrium length. Be sure to choose appropriate spring k_s and damper k_d coefficients. How stable is this system?

3. Replace your simulator's Euler integrator with a velocity Verlet integrator. Phrase constraints to enforce collision detection with the box and equilibrium for an infinitely stiff spring to maintain interparticle distance. How can these two constraints be satisfied together?

4. Try to make a simple cloth consisting of 9 particles in a 3 × 3 arrangement. Constrain one of the particles to be fixed in a single location. Can this arrangement be extended to a blob or humanoid figure?

CHAPTER 16

Network Programming

Terms Explained: *Bandwidth – Bit – Discovery – Ethernet – Fully Connected Network – Lag – Latency – Network Address Translation (NAT) – Protocol – Router – Star Network – Transmission Control Protocol (TCP) – User Datagram Protocol (UDP)*

Computer networks are how computers communicate with each other for multiplayer games. The physical network is built from wires and radio (wireless) transmissions, but more significant is the virtual network of software protocols built on top of the physical network. The primary responsibility of game networking is helping players find each other and then keeping the state of their games synchronized. Unfortunately, it takes time for information to travel through a network, so by the time one machine has communicated its state to the other one, that state is already out of date. When players perceive this delay, they call it *lag*.

The challenge of game networking is to hide lag from the players while establishing a reliable and secure communication infrastructure. Compared to other areas of game programming, the algorithms in networking are not particularly complex. As a result, they tend to represent only a small portion of the game's code base. However, networks are susceptible to an uncontrolled environment, including radio interference, congestion on the Internet, and malicious hackers. These situations are unpredictable and occur infrequently, which makes them hard to test. This makes network programming a thorny problem. Undesirable situations that have only a small chance of arising *will* eventually occur in a shipped title with millions of users, so programmers need to defend against potential failure in almost every line of code.

Networking is further complicated by the fact that it interacts with all the other code in a game. Because the game must synchronize all game state between multiple computers, the network model indirectly affects everything that touches that state—in other words, all of the code. This is why there is also no one-size-fits-all model for network architecture. The network design must be specifically chosen for the design and interaction model of the game at hand and how it represents its state. This also means that the network design must be part of the game's architecture from the beginning. Effective network infrastructure cannot be added to an existing game without rewriting major portions of it. Adding networking late in the design process usually leads to limited interaction and large amounts of lag because the state synchronization will be too constrained to be efficient.

Networks enable communication between programs running on different computers. In some cases, the programs communicating are two different copies of the same software, although different parts of those programs may be communicating on different ends. This is the case for Nintendo DS games: everyone is running the same game, but one machine is "hosting" the game. PC titles with small numbers of players, such as *Counter-Strike*, also run in this mode. For added performance, the hosting player can choose to run a dedicated host. The dedicated host does not allow anyone to play on that machine but instead enables communication only between other machines. We often call a dedicated host a server. In some cases players are not allowed host their own games—for example in *World of Warcraft*. In this case, the server is usually a completely different program that is part of the same game. It solely functions to enable communication and store information about the game world. The server is optimized for this role and may not contain very much code in common with the player machines, which are called clients in networking terminology.

16.1 An Extended Analogy

An analogy makes the central problems of computer networking intuitive. Say you want to play a board game, like chess, with a friend who lives on the other side of the world. The example works even better for a multiplayer game, so instead of chess, let's have the game be *Settlers of Catan* and have the players be a group of far-flung friends in Australia, Japan, Egypt, Germany, and the United States. If you haven't played *Settlers*, all you need to know for now is that it is a multiplayer turn-based game that takes place on a board and has additional secret information maintained in a hand of cards. Note that *Settlers* has been implemented as both a board game, card game, and as a computer game on Xbox Live, so it is a good example of how real-world communication translates into computer communication on a network.

Assume that the friends each have their own copy of *Settlers*, which they set up in an identical manner at the beginning of the game. The first problem is that you will need to keep everyone's copy in synchrony as the moves are made. So everyone connects to a mutual friend via instant messenger. Let's call the mutual friend "the server."

For this example, the server won't be playing the game himself, and we'll call everyone who is playing the game a client. Also, the server has a lot of instant messenger windows. Everyone is going to talk directly to the server in a separate session instead of using one big chat room. That way, you don't have to read any messages that weren't intended for you, and it is impossible to cheat by reading private information that the server sent to another client.

Play proceeds with each player sending the server his or her desired action and the server telling the player the result of card draws, die rolls, and movements. When the state of the board changes, the server must send everyone the same message on how to update the board. The server can send either a large message saying where every object on the board now sits or a small message that describes how to update the board from its previous state, since everyone should be looking at the same setup. Note that the boards the clients are looking at are like ghosts of the real board that is maintained by the server. The actual game state advances solely on the server's copy (e.g., the server rolls dice for you), and a short time later, the client boards are updated to match whatever the server says the state is. The server, of course, will refuse to let you request an action that is illegal to prevent cheating.

After a few moves, the clients will get tired of typing full sentences like "Please trade these four cards for a town marker and place it at the intersection of the tile that is six over and three down from the corner of the board." Instead, the group will probably establish a tight protocol for messages. In one such protocol, the previous move might be the more terse message "New Town @ (6, 3)" or even "T6,3." The latter wouldn't make much sense to someone who didn't know the protocol, but for someone who does, it allows efficient communication. Cheating and disruption are ever-present dangers when playing games remotely. To combat this, the group might extend the protocol further to ensure that even if one of the clients or a third party were to somehow intercept another's messages, then that malicious party couldn't disrupt the game. One way to do this would be to include a password at the end of each message. If the password became known, that scheme would break down. It would be better to use a scheme like adding an extra number at the end that is the last digit of the sum of a secret value and the letters in the message. This would help both the clients and the server to authenticate one another's messages and detect if they had been modified. Another layer of subterfuge would be necessary, however, if we also wanted to prevent someone from reading them at all.

Now imagine that instead of *Settlers*, you and your friends want to play soccer—not a board or video game but an actual game with a ball on grass. The server brings together a group of neighborhood kids to represent the clients in his or her own yard. All of the clients round up their own neighborhood gangs of kids to represent the same state for themselves. Once again, everyone instant messages the server what they would like to do, and the server sends back messages telling you how each of the players has moved. Compared to the turn-based game of *Settlers*, the real-time, timing-sensitive nature of soccer is harder to successfully implement using messages. The server is going to have a hard time keeping up with the steady stream of messages (i.e., he has limited bandwidth). Even if the server manages to furiously type out messages fast enough, there's still some delay when the "instant" message has to travel around the world. Computer messages travel no faster, and often are slower, than voices on a telephone. If you called a friend on the other side of the world, you'd experience a one-second delay during the conversation, and the same thing happens to computer messages.

Because of the delays (called latency) and limited bandwidth involved, the kids in your backyard are always out of position compared to where the corresponding kids are in the server's yard. This means that every client experiences his or her own version of reality and is making decisions based on a slightly different world. Even considering just the server and one client, three versions of the game state are present:

1. The server's game state.
2. The client's slightly old knowledge of #1.
3. The client's view of #2.

In our now somewhat silly example of instant messenger soccer, the reason that the client's view doesn't match his knowledge is that it takes a little while for the local kids to move to their new locations even after the client has been notified of the updated game state. A real video game mimics this, even though it could instantly move characters to their updated locations. Players expect to see characters move smoothly on the screen, so it is better to show characters in the slightly wrong position (but moving to correct that) than it is to show them in more accurate positions but warping around the screen.

The client's gang of kids won't really dash to new positions and then stand there doing nothing while waiting for the next update from the server. Instead, the client's gang of kids will *predict* the next message and keep running in the same direction as their last message. This keeps the game moving smoothly. Sometimes they'll anticipate incorrectly and look a little silly backtracking, but most of the time this client-side prediction will hide the fact that their movements are being remotely controlled. Now, consider the fact that you yourself are one of the players located in your yard. Since you know exactly where the server is going to tell you to move yourself (which is wherever you'll request to move, assuming it is legal), you can exactly predict your own movements on the client side.

Client-side prediction works well for a player's view of movement, but it would be unfair to use client-side prediction to change state. At first, it seems attractive to simulate on the client. If you shoot for a goal, your game state has more accurate information about your position and the ball's position than anyone else and can be used to decide if you scored. The first problem here, however, is that nobody is going to trust you not to cheat and say that you always scored. Even ignoring that major problem, the client's idea of the opposing goalie's position might be out of date. So although the client's view of the local player is more accurate, the client's view of everyone else is less accurate compared to the server's. So, again, it is most fair and trustworthy to have all state changes decided on the server.

The issues involved in this example of playing games over instant messenger are the same in a networked video game.

- Protocols
  - Some matchmaking method is needed for gathering the group of clients in the first place.
  - The format of messages between clients and servers must be mechanical and agreed on ahead of time.
- Synchronization
  - Communication occurs in a set of discrete electronic messages.
  - Communication is limited by both the rate of messages (bandwidth) and the delay of sending a message (latency).
  - The clients must maintain a copy of the server's state.
  - State updates can describe the small change from the previous state or the large listing of all the current state.
  - Three realities: the player's view of the world is an artificially smoothed version of the client's actual state, which is slightly out of date from the server's state.
  - Client-side prediction can conceal some network delays; it is very accurate for the local player but problematic for resolving key simulation points.

- Cheating
  - All authoritative simulation and state changes must occur first on the server.
  - The server must reject illegal move requests.
  - Authentication schemes help prevent malicious parties from changing messages in transit.
  - Encryption streams help prevent malicious parties from reading intercepted messages.

16.2 Protocols

For interactions between people, a *protocol* is a set of rules that guides each side's behavior. For example, the protocol when a meeting of strangers convenes is to shake each person's hand, introduce yourself, and then have everyone sit down. We usually think of protocols for diplomats or high-level businesspeople, but most social interactions are governed by protocols. For example, this is the protocol for a telephone call.

1. Caller dials the recipient's phone number.
2. Recipient picks up the phone and says, "Hello, this is *recipient name.*"
3. Caller says "Hello, this is *caller name.*"

Then a conversation takes place and concludes with both parties saying, "Goodbye."

Computer network protocols are a lot like telephone protocol. They establish a communication conduit, identify the parties involved, allow for exchange of information, and then terminate the conduit. The protocols are just a set of rules (published as a specification) that programmers agree to follow in their code. If one program veers away from the rules and violates the protocol, then the program it is talking to will get confused and typically terminate the connection. In the previous section's *Settlers* example, we used messages like "T6,3" to express positions. If you understand the protocol, then you know that this message means: "place a new town at coordinate (6,3)." Without the protocol, the message is meaningless. For example, under a different protocol, that same message might indicate a chat statement that contains the letter T six times, followed by the , symbol repeated three times.

Communication between computers has many standard protocols identified by acronyms that end in P, such as TCP (Transmission Control Protocol), IP (Internet Protocol), and SMTP (Simple Mail Transfer Protocol).

Most protocols are layered on top of each other. The web's HTTP (Hypertext Transfer Protocol), which you have used many times when typing URLs (http://www...), is built on TCP. TCP is itself is layered on IP.

Each game has its own custom protocol that is invented specifically to communicate between clients and servers of that game. Before we look at the design decisions involved in high-level game protocols, we need to build our way up from the lowest-level protocol: Ethernet.

16.3 Ethernet

Although older low-level network protocols still exist, most wired networks run on *Ethernet* today. The cable that connects your PC to the wall is an Ethernet cable, and your cable modem or DSL router gives you a local Ethernet. When you use wireless networking (WiFi), it is a different but closely related protocol. Both Ethernet and WiFi are physical networks, and they have real computers and wires (or at least radio transmissions). Later we will discuss virtual networks, which are implemented in software and use underlying physical networks.

An Ethernet consists of a small number (fewer than 255) of computers, all connected by a wire. Because these computers can only communicate with others on that wire, they form a local-area network (LAN), but they

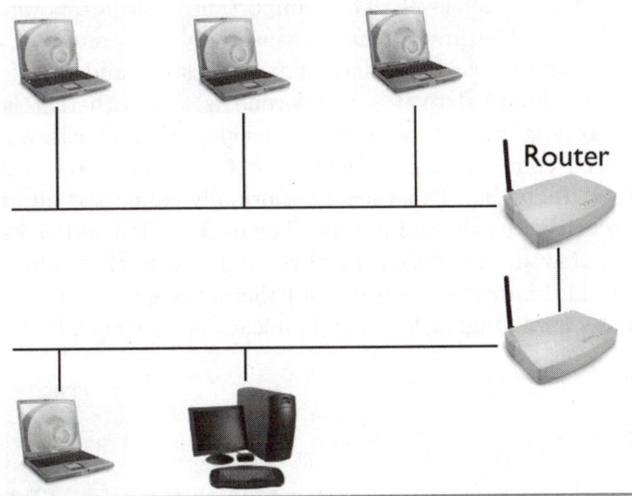

Figure 16.1. Physical network topology.

do not have access to the Internet. The LAN can be connected to another LAN by a router. A *router* is just a special computer, like a game console, that does not have a keyboard or monitor but otherwise has all of the same processing power.

Figure 16.1 shows three Ethernet LANs. The top row of three laptops and one router are on one Ethernet. The two routers are on a second Ethernet (note that one computer can be on multiple physical networks!). The bottom row of one desktop, one laptop, and one router is a third Ethernet. The laptops are just representative of any computer; they could be game consoles or handhelds as well as laptops.

Consider the single Ethernet of the top row for a moment. The four computers on it are connected to a shared wire. In practice, that wire might loop in and out of the router or a similar device called a hub so it looks like a number of separate wires, but all of those cables are really connected together into a single wire. To send a signal, a computer changes the electric potential along the shared wire, which propagates in both directions away from it like ripples when you throw a stone into a pond. As the signal (the electric wave) passes other computers, they see it and receive the message it encodes. Note that all the computers on the same Ethernet can see one another's messages. Also, if two computers were to transmit at the same time, their messages would interfere with each other. That scenario is called a collision. The Ethernet protocol ensures that each receiver knows which messages are for it and prevents two computers from transmitting at the same time.

The further details of how the Ethernet protocol resolves collisions and addresses computers are not important for games because game networking operates at a higher level. Three important concepts, however, should be kept in mind. The first is that because only one computer can transmit at a time, the network becomes more congested (and therefore slower) as computers are added to it. The second is that Ethernet is based on real wires, so it is limited in range. A single Ethernet can only support a few hundred computers, and they must be within about 1,000 meters of each other. Individual Ethernets are normally connected into the virtual metanetwork that we call the Internet. The next section addresses how communications are routed between the physical networks that comprise the Internet. The third important concept of Ethernet is serialized packets, which form the basis for all higher-level communication; they encode the bytes of a message.

16.3.1 Bits and Bytes

To understand how packets are constructed and the units of measurement for them, we must first discuss how computers represent state at the lowest level. If you send a postcard to a friend, you write a message using words in natural language. Each word is composed of letters. The English language has 26 letters, ten digits, punctuation, and many types of symbols. These comprise an extended alphabet for English. In contrast to the relatively small English alphabet, the Chinese alphabet has thousands of individual characters. Computers use the smallest possible alphabet internally. It contains only two digits: 0 and 1. A single letter in this computer alphabet is called a *bit*, which is a contraction of "binary digit." Depending on the protocol, it can be considered to store either the integer 0 or 1 or another binary value, such as true or false.

A single bit doesn't encode much information. To store larger numbers, computers use bits strung together. A byte—an 8-digit binary number—contains 8 bits. If we count integers starting from 0, a byte can store the numbers 0 through 255, inclusive. To see why, consider decimal numbers—that is, the kinds of numbers you're used to, using digits 0 through 9. A single decimal digit can count from 0 to 9. After 9, we need two decimal digits, which allow us to count up to 99. The largest decimal value that can be stored in d digits is $10^d - 1$; the -1 is there because we started counting at zero. Decimal has 10 digits and binary has only two, so the largest binary value that can be stored in d binary digits is $2^d - 1$. That is why a byte can encode integers up to $2^8 - 1 = 255$.

Even more important, d binary digits can store 2^d distinct patterns of 1's and 0's. Whether we choose to interpret those patterns as integers between 0 and $2^d - 1$ or some other set of values depends on how the program operates. To store text, most computer programs assign an encoding from each English letter (in the extended sense, including lowercase and symbols into the alphabet) to one of the 256 patterns possible in a byte. That encoding is called ASCII.

To store numbers, most programs use 32 bits. When storing nonnegative (unsigned) integers, we can represent values from 0 to $2^{32}-1$ in those 32 bits. Signed integers are commonly stored as ranging from $-2^{31}+1$ to 2^{31} (the + 1 is because we don't need to count zero twice). Real numbers are stored in a format that allows the decimal point to "float" its position based on the magnitude of the number. This so-called floating-point format can store a much larger range of values than the integers and can also store fractional values, but it has varying precision. Thus, not all numbers can be represented accurately in floating-point representation. This is why typing "10 / 3 * 3" into a computer calculator gives back 9.99999 and not 10; floating-point representation couldn't accurately represent the intermediate 10/3 fraction. There are, of course, other number formats (some of which can store 10/3 accurately) and some that use larger numbers of bits. You might hear about 64-bit or even 128-bit integers or "double-precision" floating-point numbers with 64 bits.

Medium	Incoming "Download"	Outgoing "Upload" (if different)
Analog Modem	28.8 to 56 kb/s	
ISDN	128 kb/s	
DSL	128 kb/s to 3 Mb/s	128 kb/s to 1 Mb/s
Cable Modem	1 to 6 Mb/s	128 kb/s to 1 Mb/s
T1/DS1	1.5 Mb/s	
Ethernet 10	10 Mb/s	
T3/DS3	44 Mb/s	
Ethernet 100	100 Mb/s	
Gigabit Ethernet	125 MB/s	
IEEE 1394 (Firewire 800)	8 MB/s	
USB 2.0	40 MB/s	
IEEE 1394B (Firewire)	100 MB/s	
IDE (Hard drive) ATA133	133 MB/s	
32× PCI-E (GPU connector)	8 GB/s	
Video RAM (GPU internal)	64 GB/s	
Register (CPU internal)	4 TB/s	

Table 16.1. Typical transmission rates for common media.

Data structures within a computer typically contain many individual values. They quickly grow to thousands of bytes. A kilobyte is 1,024 bytes (2^{10} bytes or $8*2^{10}$ bits); a kilo*bit* is 1,024 *bits*. A megabyte is 1,024 kilobytes, and a gigabyte is 1,024 megabytes.

Bandwidth, the data transmission rate for a network, is expressed in bits per second, bytes per second, or scaled versions of these. For example, a typical cable modem uploads data at 768 kilobits per second (kb/s) and downloads data at about 3 megabits per second (Mb/s). Data rates for other popular transmission media are shown in Table 16.1. For comparison, the table shows both network and nonnetwork media. Note that the networks are remarkably slow compared to the speed of other computer components. This is why it is important to minimize the size of messages sent across the network.

Table 16.1 can be useful when considering the amount of data that must be sent between computers to synchronize game state. If you expect some of your players to be on ISDN lines, you would use much smaller messages than if you believe all players will have cable modems. Note the change from megabits (Mb) to megabytes (MB) as the numbers grow.

As discussed later in the routing section, a network's speed is limited by its slowest link. Many companies have 100 Mb/s Ethernet LANs but only a 1.5 Mb/s T1 connection to the Internet, so the effective bandwidth available to a game is 1.5 Mb/s. Also, that bandwidth must be divided over all the computers that are using it. If ten machines on that network are all playing

PREAMBLE	TO	FROM	LENGTH /TYPE	DATA	ERROR CHECK
64 bits	48	48	16	variable	32

Figure 16.2. Ethernet packet format. The numbers indicate the bit length of each field.

the same game on an Internet server, each will only see 0.15 Mb/s of usable bandwidth, not the 100 Mb/s of their Ethernet.

16.3.2 Packets

A *packet* is a sequence of bytes to be sent on the network. It is a message whose format is defined by the protocol. Most packets are only a few kilobytes, so long communications must be subdivided into separate packets by the sender and reconstructed by the receiver. Ethernet doesn't handle messages that are split across packets. A higher-level protocol, like TCP, must do that.

Just as you'd send a postal mail letter inside an envelope with an address written on the outside, the data payload of the packet is adorned with address information. The Ethernet packet format is shown in Figure 16.2 (all packet diagrams in this chapter courtesy of Thomas Murtagh). It contains the Ethernet (also known as MAC or hardware) address of the sender and receiver, a field indicating how much data are present, and the actual data that the sender wants to transmit. The front of the packet contains a preamble that helps the receiver to detect the beginning of the transmission, and the end of the packet is a 32-bit error check value to detect small amounts of corruption during transmission.

The receiver will extract the data and discard the header information, just as you'd discard the envelope when receiving a letter. The process of wrapping and unwrapping the data is entirely handled by the operating system and network adapter card and is invisible to the programmer. The exact format of the Ethernet packet isn't important, but for our discussion, it is important to understand that the packet contains both header information and data and that every communication between computers must be made in distinct pieces.

16.4 Routing

Computers on an Ethernet or WiFi can only communicate with other computers on that physical network. To send a message between computers on different computers, that message must be routed across multiple networks. This is the job of the router.

To route messages between networks, they must contain address information about the ultimate destination. Because the Ethernet (or WiFi) packet header with addresses is removed when it is received by a router, that ultimate address information can't be stored in the Ethernet header. Instead, a different protocol called Internet Protocol (IP) contains the Internet address of the true destination.

16.4.1 Internet Protocol

Figure 16.3 shows the format of an IP packet. It is drawn as a 2D table in the figure to fit it on the page, but like the Ethernet packet format, it is just a long 1D string of bits. The format contains various information fields. As expected, it has from and to addresses that are IP addresses. They are four bytes (32 bits) long and are commonly written as four numbers separated by periods, like 192.168.1.100. Because each number is one byte, the numbers between the periods must be between 0 and 255.

The IP network (i.e., the Internet) is not a physical network like Ethernet but a virtual network constructed by software. To actually send an IP packet, a computer must place the data inside the IP packet, fill out the IP address information, *and then wrap the IP packet with an Ethernet packet.* The IP packet is placed inside the Ethernet packet's data field. The Ethernet packet contains the addressing information of the first router en route to the final destination.

When a router receives an Ethernet packet, it removes the Ethernet packet and reads the IP header inside the Ethernet packet's data field. It then places the same identical IP packet inside a new Ethernet packet, addresses that packet to the next router en route to the final destination, and

4 bytes	4	8	16
IP version	Hdr len	Service class	Packet Length
Packet Number			Fragment Number
TTL		Protocol	Error Check
From Addr			
To Addr			
DATA (up to 65516 bytes)			

Figure 16.3. Internet protocol (IP) packet format.

sends it on the next network. When a router receives an IP packet for a computer on its LAN, it wraps that packet with an Ethernet packet that is addressed to the actual recipient.

When it reaches the recipient, the operating system removes the Ethernet header and extracts its data payload. It then removes the IP header from that and extracts its data payload. That payload typically contains a TCP or UDP packet (described in the following section), which also has a header. That header is removed, and the final data inside is delivered to the high-level application protocol. The game receives this innermost data and processes it according to the game's own protocol.

16.4.2 Sources of Error

Physical Ethernets and WiFi are fairly reliable. They manage interference from collisions and generally deliver the packets that they are tasked with reliably, albeit after multiple attempts in some cases.

Although it is built out of reliable networks, the virtual IP network is not so reliable. Individual network wires can be cut or unplugged, routers can crash or lose power, and while crossing the many individual networks of the Internet, the chance of bit errors due to electrical interference or cosmic rays increases with every kilometer covered. These problems are real and can be observed when transmitting large amounts of data. However, another more mundane problem causes IP networks to drop a large fraction of their packets even when the underlying physical networks are flawless.

When a router receives packets faster than it can send them, the packets begin to back up at the router. This is increased latency caused by limited outgoing bandwidth. If too many IP packets back up, the router runs out of memory to store them. In this case, the router simply deletes some of the packets. As many as 80 percent of the packets going through a router could be lost under normal operation if it is managing the connection to a very popular server. In some cases, nearly 100 percent are lost—for example, when trying to reach a news service web server during a disaster.

Because of dropped packets, IP networks are unreliable. Higher-level protocols must manage transmissions to ensure that reliable communication can be reestablished on top of this unreliable layer.

16.5 Transmission Protocols

User Datagram Protocol (UDP) and Transmission Control Protocol (TCP) add features to the underlying IP network. Like IP, they operate on virtual networks and are handled by the operating system. Game programmers write their network code to the UDP and TCP level using "sockets" or similar APIs. That is, programmers never see the UDP and TCP headers, but those packets are wrapped directly around the data that the programmer creates.

Most commercial games use UDP but build TCP-like features on top of it. Many indie games use TCP to avoid the performance overhead and programmer time of building their own protocol. The preference for UDP has to do with a technicality of routing on the Internet and is discussed in the following NAT section. For a game developer, the only advantage of UDP is that it makes it easier to host an Internet game from a home network. The advantage of TCP is that it provides a reliable baseline for networking and therefore requires less work on the game developer's part.

16.5.1 UDP

Figure 16.4 shows the UDP packet format, which does not carry much information. The value of the UDP packet is in the source and destination ports. These are 16-bit numbers that designate which virtual network connection the data is for. Consider a PC playing *Unreal Tournament* while downloading a movie in the background and sharing music across the LAN. Packets coming into that computer all have the same Ethernet address and the same IP address. But the operating system has to deliver those packets to different programs. *Unreal Tournament* won't know what to do with packets from the movie, and the music-sharing program won't know what to do with state updates for the game.

When sending a UDP packet, the sender designates what program it is for by specifying the port number. Ports are preassigned for specific programs. For example, *Unreal Tournament* primarily uses port 7777 for communication, and a web server uses port 80 (lower numbers are reserved for more standard programs). As long as the client and server agree, any port number can be used, but using the number assigned to another program will prevent the other program from working correctly. The ports used by some common games and other programs can be found at http://kbserver.netgear.com/kb_web_files/N100495.asp.

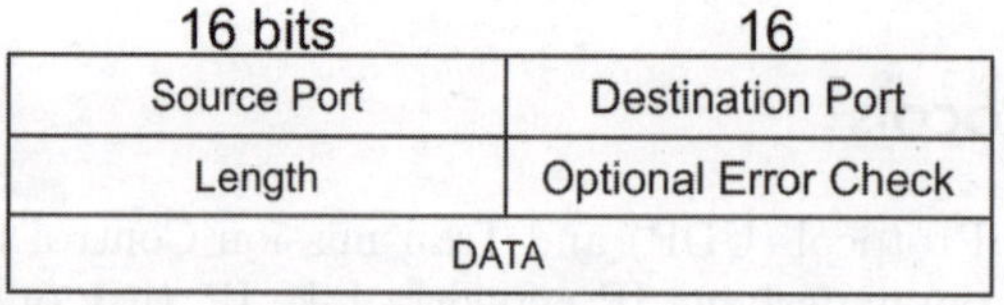

16 bits	16
Source Port	Destination Port
Length	Optional Error Check
DATA	

Figure 16.4. User Datagram Protocol (UDP) packet format.

UDP is unreliable. It does not guarantee that two messages will arrive in the same order that they were sent, that messages will arrive at all, or even that a message won't be duplicated. In practice, UDP on a LAN is fairly reliable and acts as you might expect. On the Internet, UDP's unreliability is a serious liability, and all games that use it build their own higher-level protocols for correcting delivery errors with UDP packets. Those protocols are network code, but they do not have anything to do with the operating system, network, or network adapter. That code is purely inside the game (or engine) and acts by reordering, requesting resends, or discarding data from inside the UDP data field.

16.5.2 TCP

All the protocols discussed so far are designed for discrete messages. We talk about "connections" in the network, but the software has no notion of a persistent connection with Ethernet, WiFi, IP, or UDP. This means that when sending a sequence of messages in separate packets, there is no guarantee that the messages will arrive in order. In fact, there isn't even a guarantee that the messages will arrive at all with those protocols.

Instead of providing a message-based interface, TCP allows a program to create a persistent connection between two computers on an IP network, addressed by IP address and port numbers. Once established, that connection guarantees that bytes sent along the connection will arrive exactly once and in the same order that they were sent. TCP decides when to break the stream of bytes into separate packets, and that division is not seen by the programmer.

Most games that use TCP build a packet-based model on top of its streaming connection-based model. An important consideration when doing so is to disable "Nagel's Algorithm" in TCP, which delays sending any packets for a short period of time. The algorithm is on by default for nongame programs that don't want to send small packets and are willing to accumu-

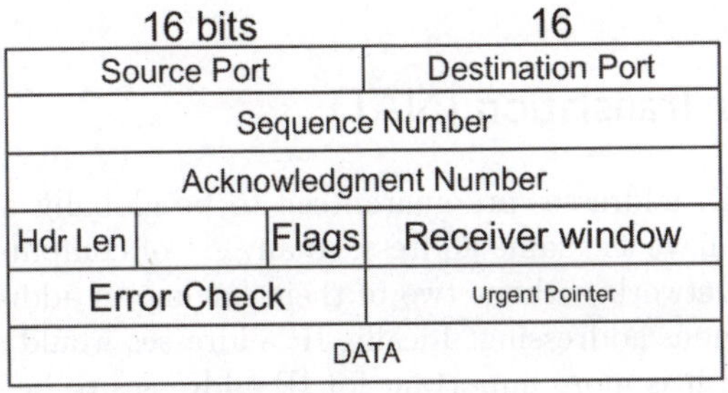

16 bits	16
Source Port	Destination Port
Sequence Number	
Acknowledgment Number	
Hdr Len / Flags	Receiver window
Error Check	Urgent Pointer
DATA	

Figure 16.5. Transmission Control Protocol (TCP) packet format.

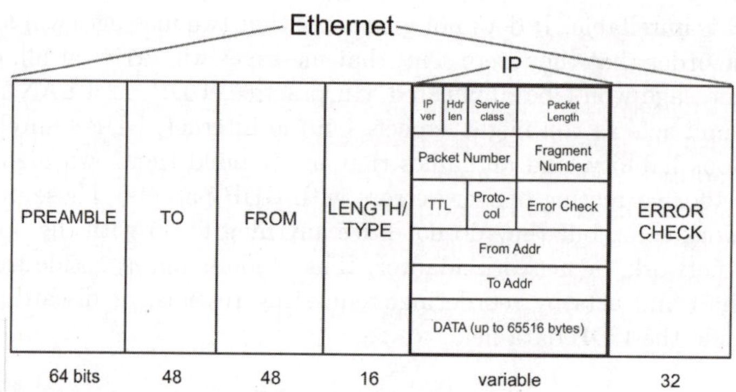

Figure 16.6. TCP packet inside IP packet inside Ethernet packet.

late larger pieces of the stream over time before sending. For games, this would cause an unacceptable lag; we want to send packets as soon as they are ready to go. Another catch with TCP is that one game-level packet might be split over multiple TCP packets. So it is important for the receiving code to carefully manage the input buffer and divide/reunite the incoming TCP packets to form correct game packets.

Figure 16.5 shows the TCP packet format. Note that it contains not just ports but other fields that are used by TCP to keep track of the order of packets and acknowledge packets when they are received.

Just as with UDP packets, TCP packets are embedded within IP packets, which are in turn embedded within Ethernet packets. Figure 16.6 shows what this whole structure looks like. The actual data from the game are inside that DATA field, behind all of the headers. If this looks like a lot of overhead, it is! Games tend to send relatively small data messages, about 1 kB or smaller. In that case, the headers might double the effective size of each message, which means that half of the bandwidth of a physical network connection is used sending header information, not actual data.

16.6 Network Address Translation (NAT)

Ethernet (MAC) addresses are guaranteed to be globally unique. No two Ethernet cards have the same address, so any set of computers can join the same physical network without two of them having an address conflict and creating ambiguous addressing. Ideally, IP addresses would also be globally unique. In fact, it is more important for IP addresses to be unique because they are used on a global Internet scale, whereas if two computers did have the same Ethernet address, unless they were physically close to one another, the conflict would never be noticed.

Unfortunately, IP addresses are not unique. Every company, school, and even household manages its own LAN that connects to the Internet and assigns IP addresses locally. Large service providers like Verizon and Comcast register specific blocks of IP addresses with ICANN, the international committee that oversees the Internet. They in turn lease specific IP addresses to companies that run servers—for example, the Blizzard servers that host *World of Warcraft.* Those servers have unique IP addresses, guaranteed by ICANN.

If you are running three computers at home off a cable modem connection, however, your local computers do not have specifically assigned IP addresses. They are probably assigned by the Dynamic Host Configuration Protocol (DHCP) running on your combined cable modem/router/firewall server and are unique on your LAN. But your neighbor probably has the same model of server box, and it probably assigned the same IP addresses on his or her LAN.

Network address translation (NAT) is a process that some routers perform that allows local networks to have nonunique IP addresses without creating addressing confusion on the Internet. Unfortunately, a by-product of NAT is that it makes it hard to host an Internet game from behind a NAT router, and it makes it very difficult for certain kinds of connections to cross from the rest of the Internet onto the LAN for gaming.

The idea of NAT is that a router (like the one built into your cable modem) keeps a table that maps internal-source IP addresses to external-target IP addresses. The router then impersonates computers from the LAN. When a machine on the LAN sends a packet to a server on the Internet, the NAT router modifies that packet so the "from" address on the IP packet matches the router and not the LAN machine that it actually came from. This causes the Internet server to believe that the packet came from the router. The router must have a globally unique address for the server to respond to it, but the original sender on the LAN no longer needs a unique address, since the Internet server won't see the LAN machine's IP address.

When the server responds, it will send a packet to the router and not to the LAN machine that it is not aware of. The router accepts that packet and then looks up the server's address in its NAT table. It finds the entry that tells it which LAN machine was communicating with this server and then alters the incoming IP packet so the "to" address is not the router but the LAN machine. It then forwards that packet onto the LAN, where it is correctly delivered. Neither the Internet sever nor the LAN machine notices that the router has been changing addresses in the middle.

Since there may have been more than one LAN machine communicating with the same server, the router actually changes both the IP address and the

TCP or UDP port, tracking both in its NAT table. This system works well for most kinds of applications, such as Web browsers and e-mail programs. For games, however, it causes some problems that developers must work around.

If using TCP, the address translation works great when the client is on the LAN and the game server is on the Internet. In this case, the client connects out to the server, the NAT router creates a table entry, and communication continues across the TCP connection. The problem with TCP is that if a player wants to host a game from behind a NAT router, other clients cannot connect in across the Internet. This is because the server does not have an address that is visible on the Internet; only the router has such an address. Clients that try to connect to the router's IP address will not be forwarded to the server because the server has not yet made an outgoing connection, so the NAT table is empty. There are a few solutions to this problem, but they require the server administrator to make changes; the game itself is powerless to fix the problem. The most common solution is for the server administrator to configure the NAT router to explicitly forward incoming connections on the game's port to the server on the LAN. Most routers make this relatively easy to do, but that doesn't mean that the average game player is aware of it or comfortable making the changes.

UDP initially seems like it won't work with NAT. Since UDP does not use connections, there is no reason for the NAT router to expect a UDP reply from outside the LAN and therefore no reason for it to maintain a NAT table entry. In practice, UDP actually works better with NAT than TCP does, although it requires some tricks that abuse the protocol and the help of a separate Internet server.

In practice, a NAT router might simply guess that outgoing UDP traffic will lead to incoming UDP traffic and make the appropriate table entries and forwarding as if the UDP traffic were TCP traffic. Most routers, in fact, will do this, which means that once packets have been sent out of the LAN, UDP responses will be allowed into that machine. This means that a client behind a NAT can connect out to an Internet server and receive responses, functioning much like TCP (although, in this case, depending on the router to understand what is going on, which is likely but not guaranteed).

Even if the NAT router can guess that UDP packets will have responses, that does not solve the problem of running a server behind a NAT because that server still has no unique IP address and does not have an entry in the NAT table. The trick here is to fool the router into creating such an entry, which can be done in a variety of ways such as traversal using relay NAT (TURN) and simple traversal of UDP through NAT (STUN). A game can either follow one of those methods explicitly or use its own equivalent method. The idea here is that the game server behind the NAT regularly sends UDP packets out to a known Internet server, thus causing the NAT router to create a table entry for the server on the LAN. Since that game server wants to be listed somewhere for discovery purposes, the Internet server is typically the listing server, and the packets are advertising the game.

When a client wants to connect to the game server, it connects to the listing server and asks it to mediate the connection. If the client is not behind (another) NAT, then the listing server simply tells the game server about the client, the game server sends a packet to the client, and the NAT router creates a table entry that will link the client and game server. If the client is behind a NAT as well, there are two options: the listing server can either continue to forward traffic between the client and server, acting as a middleman for the entire game duration, or it can send a set of packets with intentionally incorrect from addresses that make the client and server think they are receiving packets from each other. They then take over the addresses that were being used to individually connect to the listing server, effectively creating a direct communication channel.

16.7 Lag

Networks are limited by two factors: latency and bandwidth. *Latency* is the amount of time it takes the first byte to travel from the sender to the receiver. So, if the network was a road, latency would be the length of the road. *Bandwidth* is the rate at which bytes can be transmitted, so, bandwidth would be the width of the road. There is rarely enough bandwidth available for any game, so clever techniques are used to squeeze as much information into as few bytes as possible. Ultimately, latency is the more significant problem because it introduces delay between one player's action and another player's perception of that action.

Gamers refer to latency as "ping time" or "lag." Ping is a network debugging utility that measures the round-trip time to send a packet between two computers. Although games do not use ping itself, the terminology has stuck, and many network games report the so-called ping time, which usually means half the round-trip latency. For the following discussion, assume we are considering games with a client and a server that are connected to each other through the Internet. We will consider alternative network structures in the following section.

For games where both the client and the server are on wired Ethernet within the same country and have at least cable modems, latency on the order of 100 ms is common and a good average when estimating normal conditions. Latencies as large as 1,000 ms (1 second) are not unusual, however, and latencies are rarely lower than 50 ms unless both computers are on the same physical Ethernet.

A 100 ms latency on a client-server (star) network means that it is at least 200 ms between one player's action and another player's perception of that action. At 60 fps, that is more than ten rendering frames of delay! For action games that involve racing or shooting, this delay would be maddening if players actually perceived it. And since a player's own character would wait 200 ms for a server round-trip packet before moving, the local input and character would seem decoupled. For a first-person view, this makes most players physically ill as well as confused. For 1,000 ms ping times, the perceived lag would be absurd, and even in the ideal case of a 50 ms ping time, the latency is too high to tolerate if not abated.

No amount of clever coding can substantially reduce the network latency because it is limited by the physical propagation rate of the medium. When you shout across a large sports field, a person on the other side hears the sound slightly later because the sound waves have to travel across the field. That time is the latency or propagation delay. Electric fields, radio waves, and light travel faster than sound does through air, but they all take measurable amounts of time to cover large distances. Light is the fastest; it travels in a vacuum at about 3×10^8 m/s. No physical object or even information can propagate faster than this. A fiber-optic cable can approach transmission at the speed of light because it uses light (although not in a vacuum). Wireless networks also approach the speed of light for propagation. A wired network like Ethernet usually propagates signals at about half the speed of light in a vacuum.

Since we can't make the network actually go faster, the next best approach is to hide the latency so even though it exists, players don't notice it in most cases. The drawback of trying to hide latency is that when it breaks down, players will not only notice the latency but will also see additional artifacts of the scheme that were supposed to hide it, which might be worse than just observing latency artifacts alone.

16.7.1 Design Around Latency

The first attack on latency is to plan for it from the beginning as part of the gameplay. Many games aren't based on direct control of the characters. For example, in popular fantasy games *Diablo* and *Age of Empires*, players control characters by clicking on the destination with the mouse. The player-controlled characters use artificial intelligence algorithms to search for paths between their current locations and the destinations. This hides both limited bandwidth and high latency in the network. Little bandwidth is needed because the server only transmits character destinations. The frame-by-frame positions of characters are computed on each client deterministically and in lockstep, so the same positions are generated on each machine. Because the characters aren't directly controlled by the player, the delay between when the player clicks on the mouse and when the character begins to move is seldom noticed. The character moves smoothly after its path has been computed, so no further latency is observed past the original click.

A second way to design around latency is to not show fast-moving objects such as projectiles. Before networked multiplayer games, most shooter games explicitly rendered bullets and missiles. As the speed of bullets in games increased (to the point where dodging them was impossible) and network games (with high latency modems) were introduced, the speed and rate of projectiles became a limiting factor. Games ceased to show individual projectiles and either rendered a beam or nothing at all to represent weapon fire. This avoids the rendering cost and much of the synchronization cost (in both bandwidth and latency) and hides any synchronization errors.

16.7.2 Local View

Players are most sensitive to latency in the control of their own character. Fortunately, this is the character for which it is easiest to hide the latency. Rather than sending the local character's input to the server and then waiting for the server to send back that information, a game can simulate the local character on the client side. This means that the local character responds instantly to input.

The drawback of this method is that the client-side simulation uses slightly older data than the server-side simulation, since the client is slightly behind the server in synchronization. Occasionally, the server and client will produce different results from simulation, and the client state for the local character must then be adjusted to match the server's data. This might happen, for example, if a character moves through a doorway during a period of high latency. On the client side, the door might appear open, so the client-side simulation allows the character to move forward. On the server side, the door may have since been closed and block the character. From the player's perspective, he or she will see the character move through the door and then suddenly jerk back behind it when the client synchronizes with the server.

16.7.3 Dead Reckoning

Consider a car racing game, where the state of each car includes its position. If the client and server synchronize 10 times per second and the clients render 60 times per second, then cars will appear to move only once every six frames. This will cause their motion to appear jerky, despite the high rendering frame rate. To hide relatively low synchronization rates, most games use dead reckoning to simulate objects forward in time on the client side.

If we consider the velocity of each object as part of the synchronization state, then the client has enough information to predict ("dead reckon") the path of each object forward in time between synchronization steps. If the objects accelerate by speeding up, slowing down, or turning, then this prediction will diverge from the actual position. However, in many cases it gives a better prediction than assuming objects stay in place between synchronization steps.

For a powerful client machine, we can even simulate limited forms of acceleration. For example, a game with a realistic physics system might perform collision detection and response on the client to predict the path of bouncing objects and those under the influence of gravity as well as those moving in a straight line across the ground.

16.7.4 Hiding Error Corrections

At some point, the client will synchronize with the server and have substantial error to resolve. If the client immediately snaps all objects to match the state specified by the server, the player will see objects warp to new positions, orientations, and animations. Although this gives the player the most up-to-date view of the world, it is visually jarring and breaks the illusion of a realistic game world.

A better alternative is to remove error slowly over time—that is, slide objects to their new position from the current one rather than snapping them. For objects such as people and cars that move the way they are facing, this might mean using high-level planning to actually turn the object before moving it.

Sometimes the error is large enough that a player would notice an object moving to its synchronized position but small enough that the exact position is irrelevant for gameplay. For example, a character in *Diablo* can be anywhere within a few meters of its actual position without changing gameplay, since the player must explicitly click on a character to attack it instead of having to aim at it like in an FPS. In cases like this, it makes sense to define an error tolerance in the synchronization routines. If an object is within an acceptable error tolerance, it is left at the current position to avoid the jarring effect of having it suddenly move just to resolve synchronization error. This avoids having characters make complicated movements to change position slightly, as well as much of the warping if sliding is not used.

16.8 Synchronization and Topology

Network code in a game synchronizes state between instances of the game running on different computers. The high-level network design provides answers to two critical questions.

1. Which computer owns the authoritative state of the game?

2. How is that state synchronized with the other computers?

Physical networks, such as Ethernet and WiFi, are composed of real computers and wires, fiber-optic cables, and radio waves. Virtual networks, such as the Internet and Xbox Live, exist only as algorithmic concepts. They use underlying physical networks to transport packets but hide those networks from the network code. Whether two computers are connected in a physical network is independent of whether they are connected in a virtual network because the virtual network's connections are established by routing between physical networks and virtual addresses.

It is important to understand how physical networks and routing work because they are the source of latency, failures, and constraints on the virtual network. However, games never interact directly with the physical network. Instead, they are built on top of virtual network protocols such as TCP and UDP. Game engines abstract those protocols to even higher-level synchronization and messaging APIs.

The topology of a network is a description of the connections within it. Any network can be considered as a graph, where the vertices are computers and the edges are connections. Topology specifically ignores the geometry of that graph, so lengths, which might indicate physical distance, transmission time, or bandwidth, are unimportant here. We can refer to the topology of a physical network, a virtual network, or the game's own subset of the virtual network. The first two are out of the game designer's control. This section therefore focuses on the game's own communication topology, which is built on top of the virtual network.

16.8.1 Fully Connected

In *fully connected* topology, the following is true.

1. *Every computer* maintains state for its *own player*.

2. *Every computer* sends its *own state* to *all others*.

The simplest way to maintain distributed game state is to require each computer to manage state associated with its own player. In an FPS, this would include the player's health, the players's current position and facing direction, the player's animation pose, and any projectiles that the player had launched. The simplest way to synchronize is to then have each computer send a message to every other computer, relaying the information about the player. This must be done frequently to keep the state close on all machines, so those messages must travel every synchronization step. For a turn-based game, synchronization steps might be separated by seconds. For a real-time game such as an FPS, a synchronization step is a fraction of a second, maybe equivalent to a rendering frame or simulation step.

This design is called a *fully connected network.* A diagram of such a network for four computers is shown in Figure 16.7. The latency of this network (at least, if the physical network underlying it looks similar) is low. Every computer receives full-state updates directly from the computers that maintain that state, so information propagates very quickly from the source to the machines that are trying to synchronize. This presents a problem about how to deal with state that doesn't belong to a particular player, such as the position of AI players (bots) or pieces of the environment such as a movable drawbridge. Such a state, however, can be divided equally among the players.

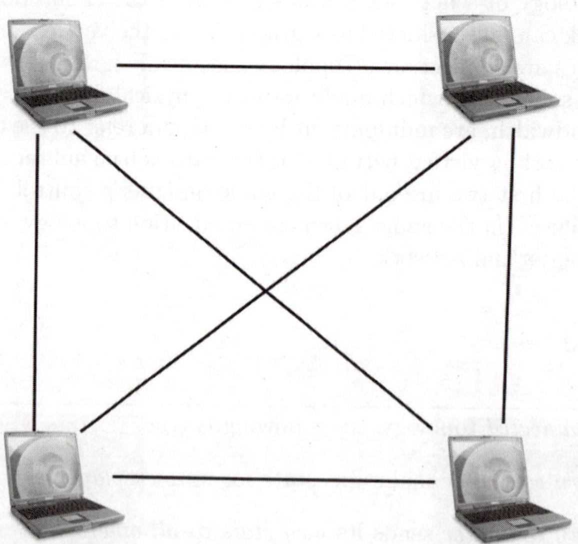

Figure 16.7. A fully connected network.

If the physical network does not look like the virtual network, the latency might actually be higher. Say that each computer in the physical network has a single connection rather than the three shown in Figure 16.7. In that case, the three messages sent and received by each on every synchronization step cannot all travel simultaneously and will back up at routers, driving up the latency—in this case, by a factor of three.

The cost of the simplicity of a fully connected network is that it requires a tremendous number of pairwise connections, which becomes apparent from Figure 16.7. Two computers require only a single edge between them. Three computers need three edges, and four computers (shown) need six edges. This is like the number of possible pairwise handshakes in a crowded room of people. For a small number of people, there aren't many, but the count quickly grows larger than the number of people. As in any fully connected graph, the fully connected network with N computers requires $N(N-1)/2$ edges. Ignoring the constant factors, it grows like $O(N^2)$. That means that doubling the number of players in the game *quadruples* the number of network connections required. Each network connection is susceptible to the usual problems of dropped packets, NAT traversal, security, and transaction overhead. Thus, the number of potential network problems grows like $O(N^2)$. Because of this, fully connected networks are rarely used for games with more than two or three players.

16.8.2 Star

In *star* topology, the following is true.

1. The *server* maintains the state for the entire network.
2. Each client is *directly connected* to the server. It uploads input and downloads state.

The *star network* differentiates between clients and the server. The server runs the primary simulation of the game world and maintains all of the state. The clients display the game for each player and receive the player's input. This divides the game's architecture into two pieces: rendering, input, and audio are on the clients, and simulation executes on the server. The network, which connects the two pieces, is called a star because placing the server in the center of a diagram, as shown in Figure 16.8, creates a star or asterisk pattern. One could also think of the server as a star or the sun, and the clients the planets orbiting around it.

In the star network, each computer maintains a single network connection instead of the $N-1$ connections required by the fully connected network. Although it must download state about the entire game every step, it sends

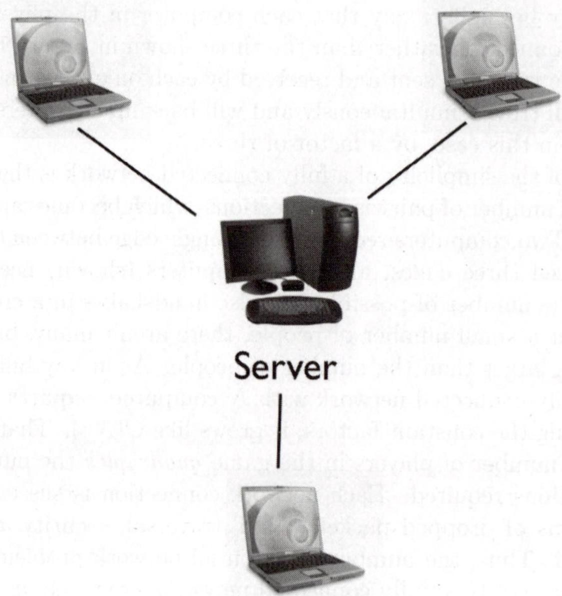

Figure 16.8. Star network topology.

very little information back to the server—just the local player's current input.

This means that the bandwidth requirement at the client is about half of that in the fully connected network, where every computer had to send and receive $N - 1$ pieces of data. In the star network, each computer sends 1 piece of data and receives N pieces back. This asymmetry is important. Many home network solutions, such as cable modems, have much higher download bandwidth than upload bandwidth. This makes the star network well suited to home networks, which are the primary physical networks used by games.

The latency in a star network is twice that of a fully connected network because to update the state at a client, the server must first receive information from that client. Thus, the current synchronization step uses inputs from the previous one, doubling the lag observed on a fully connected network.

The cost of low-client bandwidth is that the server's bandwidth must be very high. The server sends state about every computer to every other computer, so its outgoing bandwidth requirement is $O(N^2)$. In the fully connected network, that load was shared, with every computer bearing an $O(N)$ bandwidth requirement. The same is true of processing power. The

Topology	Bandwidth			Latency	Connections
	Client In	Client Out	Server		
fully connected	$b(N-1)$	$b(N-1)$	none	t	$O(N^2)$
star	$b(N-1)$	b	$2bN$	$2t$	$O(N)$

Table 16.2. Comparison of fully connected and star topologies.

server must compute physics and other simulation data for every player, whereas in the fully connected network, the processing was distributed.

The star network is well suited to situations where the client computers have varying specifications but the server is controlled. It is the most common network configuration for small (64 or fewer player) games, where a powerful hosted computer is connected to a high-bandwidth network connection and a variety of clients connect in.

Table 16.8.2 summarizes the properties of fully connected and star networks. Let the bandwidth required to transmit state for one player be b bits/second, the latency of each transmission be t seconds, and N be the number of players. In the table, the client bandwidth is separated into incoming (download) and outgoing (upload) bandwidth. The server number represents the combined up/download bandwidth for the server. In each case, the total bandwidth consumed across the network is $bN(N-1)$. This is a measure of how the game is consuming network resources shared with other games and applications.

16.8.3 Regions and Multiple Servers

Both the fully connected and star network topologies require client bandwidth proportional to the number of players in the game. For massive multiplayer games with thousands or millions of simultaneous players, that kind of growth is impossible.

Even for smaller games, it is often desirable to not inform every client of every player's state. A client does not need state information for players that are far from the location of the current player within the game world because faraway players are not visible. If the game does not synchronize state for distant players, then it can both save bandwidth and decrease client-side cheating. For example, if a client has full information about the game world, then it can be hacked to show opponents who are behind the walls, giving an advantage to the local player. If distant or invisible players are simply not synchronized, then the client machine has no more information than the local player and cannot be abused for cheating.

Synchronization regions are a way to reduce the amount of state synchronized with each machine. Several schemes are possible. The basic idea of each is to divide the geography in the virtual world into regions and then

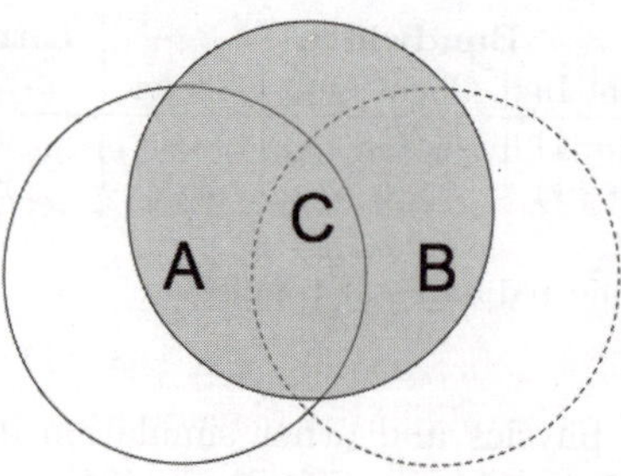

Figure 16.9. Circular synchronization regions.

only share information with a player about other players in that region (the same idea is also used to make physics simulation faster; only nearby players can affect one another).

Figure 16.9 shows a circular update region—a top-down view of the locations of three players, A, B, and C, within the virtual world. An imaginary circle around each shows the area those players can see. For a third-person or top view, it makes sense that the player can see an area both in front of and behind the character. Circles are also useful for first-person views, however, because players can turn relatively quickly. The client machine should be able to show the new view as fast as the player can turn, even if that exceeds the network synchronization time.

In Figure 16.9, player C receives updates about both A and B because they are in view. Likewise, both A and B receive state updates regarding C. However, A and B are too far apart, so they do not receive state updates about each other.

For games with indoor settings, distance is a poor metric for visibility. Rather than being circular, the visibility region is likely to be divided into a polygon by walls and doorways when indoors. Games such as *Counter-Strike* therefore use a synchronization region based on true line of sight.

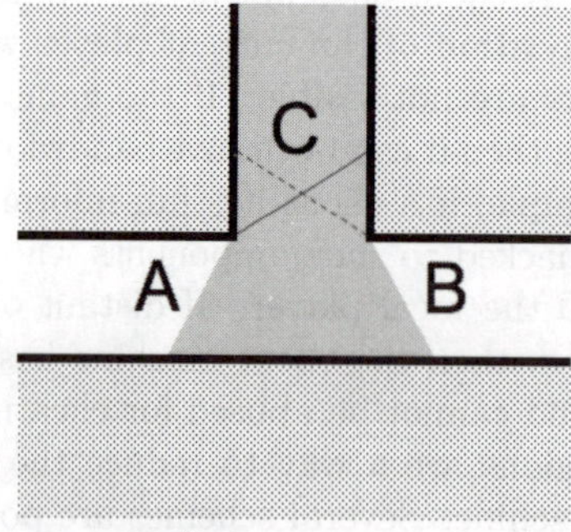

Figure 16.10. Line-of-sight synchronization regions.

Figure 16.10 shows three players in a T-shaped hallway. Here, players A and B can see each other because nothing obstructs their view. Player C is back up the connecting hallway and cannot see either player A or player B. Thus, no one receives state updates from C, and C receives no state updates about any other player.

Circular and line-of-sight synchronization regions reduce the network bandwidth required for synchronization. By themselves, they cannot solve the problem of thousands or millions of players simultaneously inside a game because one server must still handle all of those players and determine which are close to each other. To make a game truly scale to a large number of players, such as those in *World of Warcraft*, we must divide the players across multiple servers. For a continuous world that runs on multiple servers, we say that each server manages a geographic zone.

Figure 16.11 shows a world divided into grid-based zones. Each square is a separate zone simulated by one server. A client is synchronized with the zone that its player is in and all eight adjacent zones. In the figure, C receives information about A and B (and vice versa) because their nine-square neighborhoods overlap. A and B are outside of each other's neighborhoods, so they do not receive updates.

This kind of grid-based zone is typically used with a star network for each zone. There is a limit on the number of clients that any one server will have to communicate with because only so many players can fit within a certain region of the game world. Each player is simultaneously logged in to nine servers, but the actual servers involved change continuously. This can be hidden from the player by having each player connect into a single server that then manages the connections for the client behind the scenes within the hosting organization's local network.

The zones need not be small compared to the update regions. For example, in many games, a zone covers an entire village or dungeon, and players could not possibly see all of the way across it. Figure 16.12 shows large zones. The numbers in each represent the number of the server that simulates that

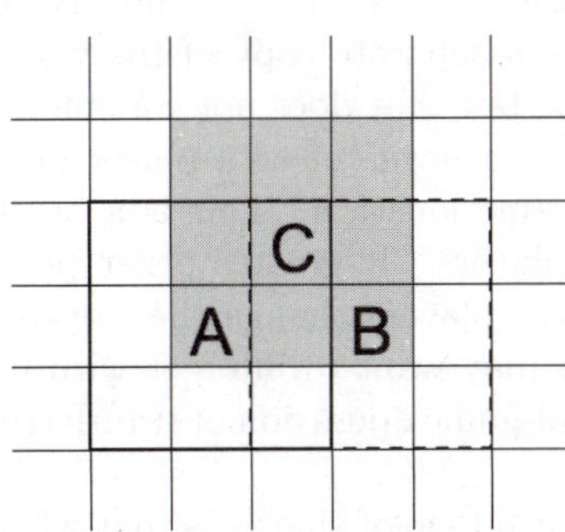

Figure 16.11. Grid-based synchronization regions for small zones.

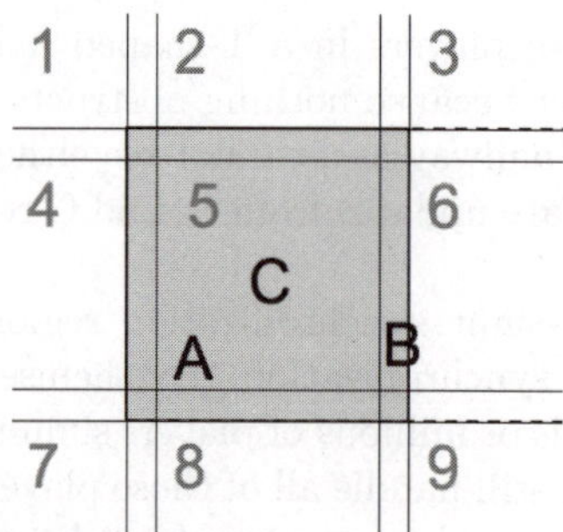

Figure 16.12. Grid-based synchronization regions for large zones.

zone. The thin areas between zones are boundaries. A client receives information about the zone that it is in and the boundary. A client whose player is in a boundary region receives information about both adjacent zones. The boundary regions may be simulated on both adjacent servers, or there can be a scheme for allocating them among servers. This is just a generalization of the grid-based scheme.

For the example in Figure 16.12, players A and C are both on server 5. That server may use a circle update region to determine whether they receive state updates about one another, but at the very least they are both connected to server 5's star network. Player B is in the boundary between servers 5 and 6. It synchronizes against both of those servers. This is less efficient than the situation players A and C are in, but relatively few players will be in the boundary regions because the boundaries are small.

When a game reaches about 1 million players, even zones may not be sufficient to handle the load. Zones must become smaller as the number of players increases, and when many players are present, the shrinking zones may no longer correspond to sensible geographic divisions of the world. The solution most game companies use at this point is to create multiple copies of the whole game world, called shards. Shards are like parallel dimensions, and each shard is a separate copy of the world, with the same locations and zone divisions, but that does not communicate with other shards. A player on one shard can never meet a player on another shard, even if they are in the exact same location. This is a brute-force solution to the problem of too many players. It creates other problems, of course, since the shards can diverge as players change the worlds within them in different ways. Also, players may want to interact with friends on other shards, which requires the out-of-game operation of transferring a character between servers.

A major business advantage of shards is that when a zone server for one shard crashes, only that shard is affected. In a game without shards, a zone server that is down means that the entire game may have to go offline to keep adjacent areas from becoming desynchronized.

16.8.4 Reducing Bandwidth

When the server synchronizes state with a client, it does not have to send all of the game state. If the transport protocol is reliable and guarantees ordered deliveries, the server can send only the *changes* ("deltas") since the last state update. Since most of the game state is unchanged, this means that a much smaller amount of data must be transmitted. This saves bandwidth.

For example, consider an FPS. If players turn on average twice per second and the game synchronizes at 10 fps, then only one out of every five synchronization messages carries information about a specific player. For the other 80 percent of the messages, that player is still moving with constant velocity (the position has changed, but the server can rely on the client's dead reckoning to update the position correctly under constant velocity). The 80 percent figure is actually a good rule of thumb. With dead reckoning and careful selection of which state to synchronize, usually 80 percent of the naive synchronization data can be eliminated for proportional bandwidth savings.

One way to reduce bandwidth (and hide latency) is to perform extensive reliable simulation on the client side. For example, rather than running AI on the server and sending the position of every AI entity in the world to the client, the server and client can run the identical AI code. This is a very advanced version of dead reckoning. If the code is *exactly* the same, it will produce the same outputs, and there is no need to communicate the AI player's position to the client, since the client will already know it. The catch is that the timing, "random" numbers, and interaction with the local player must be identical on the client and server. Ensuring that these are identical requires careful bookkeeping when writing the network code—for example, to ensure that the client isn't using client player inputs during the current frame before they would have propagated out to the server.

16.8.5 Peer-to-Peer (P2P)

The phrase *peer-to-peer* (P2P) network means two things in the context of games, both of which are interesting and neither of which is currently used much (although that may change in the near future).

The first meaning of P2P is a fully-connected synchronization scheme where there is no server. No single client is authoritative. Instead, each maintains a part of the game state and all clients share data with all other clients continuously. This spreads the computation and communication load across all machines. When properly designed, it also allows machines to enter and leave the network without the game itself ending. The reasons that this is not a popular scheme are that it creates many opportunities for cheating by altering data on the client, that it requires additional network code to manage the addition and removal of machines during the game, that it creates a potentially huge (i.e., $O(n^2)$) number of interconnections as the number of machines rises, and that the server environment is neither controlled nor more capable than the clients (since there is no server!). The reason that it may become popular soon is that portable platforms such as the Nintendo DS and Apple iPhone are well-suited for forming ad-hoc networks. A small group of machines may need to support a game without connection to an external server, and they may need to adapt to players entering and leaving.

The second meaning of P2P is as a physical network topology. We are generally concerned with the virtual network topology and assume that any two computers can communicate if desired by our virtual topology. However, there are many cases where there is no physical link between machines (or a virtual link cannot be created to simulate it). For example, consider a set of wireless portables stretched out along a subway. Each sequential pair of portables is close enough to communicate with one another, but the farthest apart two are out of range of each other. If the central portables perform the service of passing along data, however, they can form a chain (or a "bucket brigade") that allows even the farthest two portables to communicate. This creates a mechanism for virtual connectivity that exceeds physical connectivity. That is independent of the choice of synchronization scheme. We can run a client-server system, a fully-connected network, or anything else on top of this P2P network. Outside of games, in the context of file sharing, "P2P" means this kind of virtual connectivity. It is attractive for portable games but is not used much on PCs and consoles today. That is because machines with a stable or wired network connection tend to also have metered bandwidth, which the owners do not want to use to pass packets for others. Doing so would also create latency as packets are retransmitted.

However, if we step back and look at the Internet as a whole, P2P is very popular. Most computers are not in fact connected by physical wires, but by chains of network connections and routers. The routers are computers. They are nothing more than "peers" that pass packets on behalf of the two computers at either end of the network connection.

16.9 Matchmaking

Thus far, we have considered the problem of synchronizing state between the computers playing a game. But how did those players enter the game in the first place? When you play a massive multiplayer game, your shard server is assigned, and the game can automatically connect to that server on start-up. But for smaller multiplayer games such as *Halo*, you must first browse and connect to a server. Matchmaking systems ensure that players can locate servers and help them choose the one they will find most satisfying. Let us first consider the problem of how to find all the available servers and then how to choose among them.

16.9.1 Discovery

The process of finding servers is called *discovery*, and both the local-area network (LAN) and the Internet can be searched. LAN discovery involves the server broadcasting an advertisement for its game across the entire network. This obviously wouldn't work for the Internet, since a game server should not waste bandwidth telling everyone in the world about itself (and in practice there is no protocol for broadcasting to the entire Internet). On a small network with at most a few hundred machines, broadcasting is simple and efficient. To avoid even the small bandwidth waste of the server continuously broadcasting on the LAN, the process can be improved by having new clients broadcast a request for servers and then having the servers only respond to those requests.

Internet discovery is typically managed through a centralized server listing. Here, clients connect into a special designated server that does not run the game. Instead, it maintains a list of all known game servers. When a client connects to the listing server, it sends back a list of all game servers. When a game server starts up, it immediately tells the listing server about itself. When a game server shuts down, it also tells the listing server to remove itself from the list. There are three problems with centralized server listings. The first is that they are a single point of failure. If the centralized server is down, then no Internet games can be played, even though both clients and game servers may be working. The second problem is that because it is a single point of failure, it becomes an attractive target for hackers. Popular game servers are under constant attacks. The third problem is that even though a game server and client may both be able to communicate with the listing server, they may not be able to communicate with each other. So a client may receive a list including servers that it cannot contact directly itself.

16.9.2 Selection

Once the client has discovered compatible game servers, it must select which one to join. The simplest method of resolving this is to show the player a list of all the servers and require him or her to choose one. The player will choose a server based on what map is currently in play, the number of other players, what modifications the server is using, the server's bandwidth, the ping time to the server, and the server's name, so all of those must be displayed for the player. Since that information is constantly changing, this means that a server browser must either request information from each game server directly at a regular interval (a kind of limited fully connected network) or must refresh its list from the central server (more like a star network).

Some browsing tools can provide a better user experience than a flat list. Giving players the ability to filter out certain servers reduces the number of choices they must consider. Common filters are to exclude empty servers, exclude full servers, and exclude servers with high ping or low bandwidth. Play is most satisfying when players are close together in ability. A sophisticated server browser could track player statistics, friends, and favorite maps, and then select a server with good network performance that has players of comparable ability and other characteristics that are appealing to a player. Sophisticated server browsing and automatic matchmaking are especially important on handhelds and consoles, where limited user-interface control from joysticks makes it difficult to navigate a more traditional browser.

16.10 Security

Network security for games falls into three categories: preventing disruption of the game, preventing attacks against other software, and preventing cheating.

16.10.1 Disruption

A game can be disrupted if the network creates a vulnerability that allows an attacker to bring down a server or client. In this case, the players are aware of the attack, and gameplay remains correct until it ceases. Downtime can cost the developer directly for subscription games, where refunds must be issued, and indirectly for all games because players are less likely to purchase a game that is known to have lots of downtime. The two types of disruptive attacks are denial of service and exploits.

A denial of service (DoS) attack is one in which the attacker floods a computer with information in an attempt to consume all of its processing capability or network bandwidth. For example, 1,000 computers all repeatedly sending network requests to a server might overload its capability and cause it to be nonresponsive to real players. DoS attacks can never be prevented, but they can be limited by careful server administration. This includes installing a firewall to block everything except the game ports and denying access to known DoS sources. Many servers allow the game administrator to ban certain IP addresses or player IDs, as well.

Game protocols and servers can also be designed to be resistant to DoS attacks—for example, by ignoring multiple requests from the same source and by limiting the amount of bandwidth that can be consumed by an individual request.

An exploit attack uses a flaw in the game software to crash the game. If a particular build of a game is known to have a bug where it runs out of memory when a player fires a weapon in a certain location, an exploit attack might create a client-side bot that immediately runs to that location and begins shooting. Certain programming practices can reduce the chance of bugs like this in production code, but some will likely always slip through. The best defense against exploit bugs, beyond good programming and testing in the first place, is to release patches as they are discovered.

16.10.2 Attacks Against Other Software

Preventing attacks against other software is important because a game should not create a vulnerability that allows an attacker to gain control of information on a computer outside the game. For example, imagine a bug that allows a player to send a certain chat message that causes credit card information on your local computer to be transmitted back. These attacks are almost always in the form of exploits of bugs in the game.

The most common exploit for these attacks in games, as well as in other software, is the buffer overflow. Games written in C++ frequently exhibit the flaw that if a longer piece of text than was expected is sent across the network, part of it overflows the buffer that was allocated and writes to a different part of the memory. If the text is carefully constructed and the bug has a certain form, that can allow an attacker to place new code in memory that will then execute. That code gives the attacker control over the client computer and can be used to install a virus, to install a back door for later control, or to send sensitive information to the attacker.

As with exploits that are used to crash computers, there is little beyond good initial programming and testing practices that can be done to prevent this kind of attack. These attacks are relatively rare against games compared to the number of attacks seen against Web browsers and e-mail programs, but it is a vulnerability that game developers must be prepared to test against and patch after shipping if discovered.

16.10.3 Cheating

Most of the effort in network security for games is to prevent cheating. Network-based cheating can occur if an attacker can either see game state they should not or modify game state as it is transmitted between a server and a client. Encryption technology is a way of making messages unreadable to third parties as they are transmitted across the network. It ensures that an attacker cannot read information that is intended for a different client. Authentication technology is a way of electronically signing a message that cannot be forged. It ensures that the server or client can trust that the contents of a packet came from the correct source and was not forged or modified by an attacker. Authentication and encryption are often combined to prevent attackers from either reading or writing messages. These are collectively called cryptography methods.

Ancient cryptography relied on obscurity. One classic method of coding messages was to add a certain offset to each letter. For example, say the offset was 3. To send the letter A, the sender would actually send the letter $A + 3 = D$. The receiver must already know that the offset is 3 and then subtracts the appropriate amount from each letter. The problem with security through obscurity is that if the attacker figures out the method, the cryptography is broken, and the attacker can then send and receive messages freely.

Modern security methods are based on the idea that a cryptography method should remain secure *even if the attacker knows the encryption algorithm.* They primarily rely on a single secret piece of information, called a key, that is maintained at both the client and the server. Given that key, an algorithm encodes a message in a way that can be undone quickly if the key is known but takes a tremendous amount of time if the key is not known.

Most of these encodings depend on the products of large prime numbers. A prime number, such as 7, 103, or 241, has no factors (other than itself and 1). The product of two large prime numbers has exactly two factors—the two primes. Finding the factors of a number takes substantial time if the number is large, but if one factor is known, then the other can be obtained quickly, so this is a good basis for building encryption. For encryption purposes, "large" means 512- or 1024-bit numbers. Those are inconceivably large for practical purposes; they can count to values much higher than the number of atoms in the universe.

It is difficult to design good algorithms for encryption, authentication, and securely exchanging the encryption keys in the first place, although once the algorithm is designed, it is usually easy to implement it in code. These algorithms are hard to design because they rely on specific number theory properties. Slight changes may break those properties and create a scheme that is easy to attack, even though the algorithm looks almost identical.

OpenSSL is one secure network package that includes many popular protocols known to be secure. It can either be used as a library or, because it is open source, sections of the code can be combined into the game code directly. See Bruce Schneier's book [Schneier 96] or the *Secure Programming Cookbook* [Viega et al. 03] for additional cryptography algorithms in a form suited to incorporation into a game.

16.11 APIs

TCP and UDP are available on all platforms through the Berkeley Sockets API or the equivalent Winsock API. This is accessible from essentially all programming languages, including C++ and Java. The only other low-level alternative is DirectX's DirectPlay API, an improved version of sockets for Windows and Xbox that is also integrated with Microsoft's Live service. The advantage of regular sockets is that they work on all platforms, making code highly portable.

Most games use their own TCP-like protocols built directly on UDP because this allows them to work through NAT routers. This is necessary because TCP requires the server either to not be on a NAT or to be on a NAT that is configured to pass traffic to the server, effectively exposing it to the Internet. Note that under TCP, the client can be behind a NAT, but the server cannot without a special router configuration (such as dynamic DNS or port forwarding).

Many relatively low-level gaming middleware products provide TCP-like guarantees and messaging protocols appropriate for games. The most popular of these are Xbox Live, Powered by GameSpy/GameSpy Arcade, TorqueNL, Quazal, and Rakarsoft. Xbox Live and Powered by GameSpy provide Internet discovery, NAT traversal, and messaging. Xbox Live is used on Xbox 360 and Windows Vista titles. GameSpy is used on Windows, Wii, Nintendo DS, and PlayStation games.

The smaller packages from Torque, Quazal, and Rakarsoft provide varying levels of messaging and voice APIs. None of these packages provides full-blown synchronization, which is so game-specific that it can only be provided by a genre-specific game engine such as Source or the Unreal Engine. Many PC and indie developers simply write their own network APIs. Console developers are likely to use the networking already provided by their platform API or engine.

16.12 Exercises

1. What is the topology of an Ethernet?
2. Why would a large company use more than one Ethernet?

3. What is the primary source of dropped packets on the Internet?
4. If you were on a team that had two weeks to write a demo of a networked game to show in-house on your LAN, starting from scratch, which protocol would you use: UDP, TCP, or Ethernet?
5. If you ship a 500-gigabyte drive across the United States, and it takes exactly two days (48 hours) to arrive, what is the effective bandwidth of that transaction? How does that compare to a cable modem?
6. After the first synchronization step, both the server and client agree that an airplane has velocity $(300, 15, 100)$ km/h and position $(100, 100, 0)$ m. If there is no further synchronization, what position will a client compute 0.1 s later if dead reckoning is used? What if dead reckoning is not used?
7. Why is discovery different on a LAN than on the Internet?
8. What properties would a player want to know for matchmaking before joining a server for an online version of *Monopoly*.
9. Why is network address translation problematic for games?
10. Say that the position of each unit in an RTS is stored as two numbers (x, y), each of which takes 32 bits (equivalent to 4 bytes). There are 100 units in the game, and all of their positions must be sent from the dedicated server to each of six clients every synchronization step. Synchronization runs ten times per second, and the header overhead of the transport protocol is 64 bytes. Assume that all positions fit in the same packet. What is the bandwidth consumed
    (a) incoming (downloading) at each client?
    (b) outgoing from the server?
11. Why would a four-player game use zones?
12. Some in-game download accelerators can connect to multiple servers and download different parts of the same map at the same time.
    (a) Using the terms from this chapter, explain why this might be faster than downloading from a single server.
    (b) In what situation would the multiple-download method not be faster than downloading from a single server?
13. Earth is about 40,000 km in circumference. What is the *minimum* latency for any transmission protocol, routing method, or type of network when sending a message between Auckland, New Zealand, and Malaga, Spain, which are exactly opposite each other on Earth?

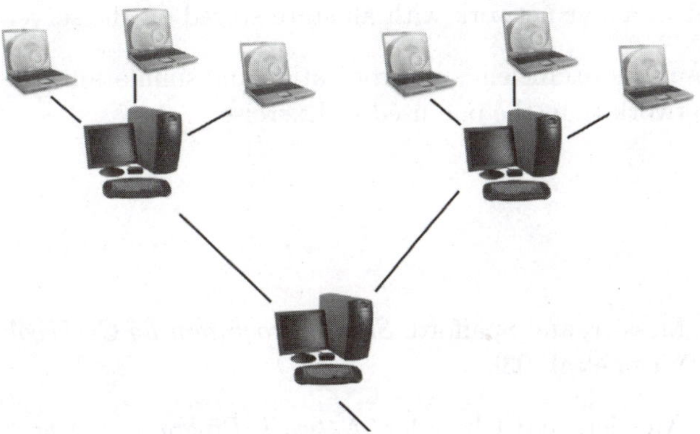

Figure 16.13. Tree network topology.

The remaining exercises refer to the tree network topology described in the following paragraph.

Figure 16.13 shows an alternative game network topology called a tree. In this network, the servers from separate star networks are themselves connected as if they were clients in a star network with a master server. The servers connected to the real clients are called first-level servers. The master of those servers is a second-level server; it is connected to a third-level server, and so on.

For the following exercises, let the number of clients for the first-level servers be M (the figure shows $M = 3$). Let the number of "client" servers connected to each other master server be S, and let there be k levels of servers.

14. Consider the case of $M = 3$, $k = 3$, and $S = 2$. How many network connections are involved in the *best* case of transferring a piece of state between two clients? The latency will be proportional to this number.

15. Consider the case of $M = 3$, $k = 3$, and $S = 2$. How many network connections are involved in the *worst* case of transferring a piece of state between two clients?

16. How many clients are supported by the network in terms of M, S, and k?

17. Say that all state is maintained on the single level-k server. The synchronization step sends input from the clients to that server and authoritative state back from it (passing through the intermediate servers

both ways). How do latency and bandwidth in this network compare to that in a star network with all state stored on the server?

18. Propose a more efficient synchronization and simulation scheme for the tree network than the one used in Exercise 17.

16.13 Resources

- Viega, Messier, and Spafford, *Secure Programming Cookbook for C and C++* [Viega et al. 03].
- Viega, Messier, and Chandler, *Network Programming with OpenSSL* [Viega et al. 02].
- Snader, *Effective TCP/IP Programming* [Snader 00].
- Stevens, *Unix Network Programming* [Stevens 97].
- Mulholland and Hakala, *Programming Multiplayer Games* [Mulholland and Hakala 04].
- Barron, *Multiplayer Game Programming* [Barron 01].
- Schneier, *Applied Cryptography* [Schneier 96].
- Cisco whitepapers at http://www.cisco.com/en/US/tech/tk652/tk701/tech_white_papers_list.html.

CHAPTER 17

User Input

Terms Explained: *Analog Potentiometer – Blobfinding – Inertial Measurement Unit (IMU) – Optical Character Recognition (OCR) – Shape Descriptor – Touch-Based Input – Touch Surface – Triangulation*

In the context of the overall user interface, user input is about translating a player's physical motion into actions in the game world. A user interface is the player's entry point into the game world. It governs how a player experiences the virtual environment, game dynamics, and underlying story put forth in a game. This forms a continual feedback loop: the player observes the game world through the rendering of some display and, based on these observations, makes a decision that is expressed through some form of user input and has an effect in the game world. We further break down the user input process into two parts: (1) the sensing of the player's physical motion into detectable events and (2) how sensed events are translated into effects in the game. Although the second part can vary depending on the nature of a game, the sensing of the player's motion events (through a game pad, accelerometers/Wiimote, or camera/EyeToy) is a relatively game-independent issue, which we focus on in this chapter.

We roughly categorize user input devices for games into touch-based, inertial-based, sound-based, camera-based, and "advanced sensing." We examine devices in these categories, including game pads, analog controls, light guns, Wiimotes, EyeToys, and electromagnetic markers for sensing user motion, and discuss the basic mechanisms for how they work. For cases where the sensed signals are noisy or ambiguous, we discuss more general concepts of state estimation for perceiving user events using the general framework of the Bayesian filter. Advanced sensing refers to technologies that offer richer input modalities but are (often) cost-prohibitive for real-time input into current console systems. Such technologies include motion capture, time-of-flight depth cameras, RFID tags, laser rangefinding, and stereo and multiview computer vision. Although advanced sensing is outside the scope of this chapter, many resources are available through commercial vendors and research papers that describe such devices and how they can be used.

17.1 Touch-Based Input

We roughly categorize *touch-based input* devices as those that use physical contact to sense user input. These devices include keyboards with button contact, mice with trackball contacts, and touch surfaces with stylus and finger contacts. Many of these devices are based on an electrical circuit where the user's contact varies the flow of current on the circuit. The computer keyboard is arguably the most ubiquitous user interface. The keyboard is essentially a collection of digital buttons, or pushbuttons. A digital button functions as a binary switch that modulates the current of an electrical circuit between two distinguishable states. When the button is pressed, the circuit is completed by the switch to yield "high" voltage. When the button is "unpressed," "low" voltage results. These voltages are reliable indicators of user keystrokes. To minimize the number of erroneous button presses, soft material is often placed between the contact to provide a slight but significant

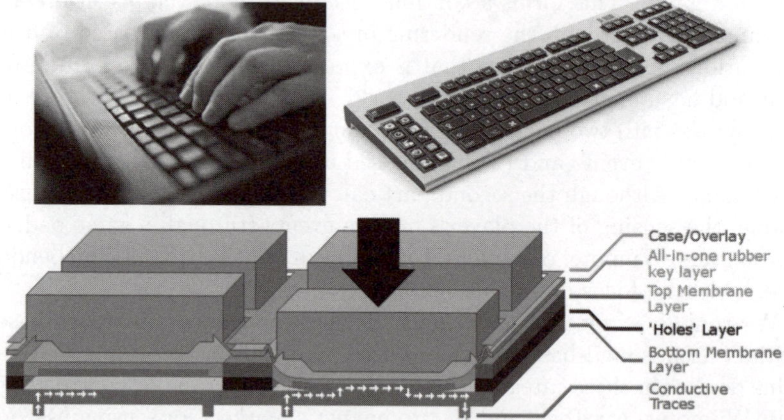

Figure 17.1. A keyboard remains the standard device for user input, typically involving user events related to touching two electrically conductive materials. OLED keyboards offer small displays on each key that could make for easier association between key presses and game events.

amount of resistance. For example, dome switches form a rubber dome over a contact that a user must collapse to press a key. As an interesting tangent, buttons on a keyboard are typically associated with a specific label such as a letter, a number, and so forth. With new OLED (organic light-emitting diode) technology, small image displays can be inserted within each physical key, allowing for dynamic visual relabeling of keyboard buttons (see Figure 17.1).

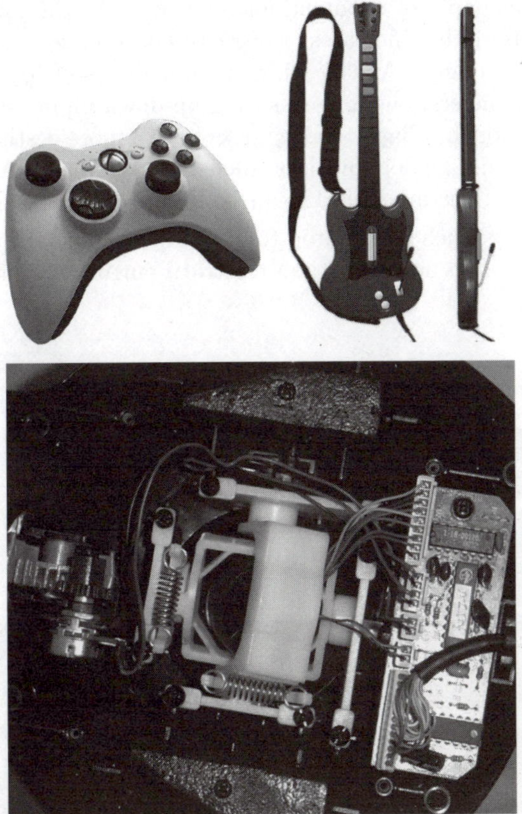

Figure 17.2. Game pads (such as an Xbox 360 or *Guitar Hero* controller) often use a combination of digital keys and analog joysticks. Analog joysticks typically associate the stick's position with an angular sensor, such as a potentiometer or optical encoder, along each axis of movement. The bottom image shows the inside of an analog joystick through its bottom, showing two white parts that can rotate along the separate axes. As these parts turn, they also turn an associated potentiometer, causing its electrical resistance to vary in direct proportion to the joystick's position. (Image courtesy of Wikimedia and Piotr Jaworski)

Game pads and joysticks often use some combination of digital buttons and *analog potentiometers.* For example, a *Guitar Hero* controller has mostly digital buttons for sensing fret presses and strumming, but it also has an analog whammy bar for fine modulation of long notes. (*Guitar Hero* guitars also use a mercury switch—an old-fashioned 1-bit accelerometer!). Unlike the "on/off" nature of a binary switch, a potentiometer allows for continuous resistance variability to the amount of current permitted to travel over an electrical circuit. Potentiometers are often used to measure rotation as the amount of current allowed to pass over a circuit. A volume control knob is a canonical example of a potentiometer's use. As the knob is rotated, the potentiometer either increases or decreases current resistance, providing fine control over volume. Analog sticks on game pads or joysticks typically use two potentiometers, one for measuring up-down input and one for left-right input. Although today's analog sticks have a more aesthetic "ball-and-socket" design, older analog joysticks, such as those for the Apple II, give a clearer picture of their inner workings (see Figure 17.2).

Touch surfaces, such as a laptop touch pad, Wacom tablet, or Nintendo DS touch screen, also use changes in electrical current to detect the move-

Figure 17.3. Touch surfaces include touch pads, typically used with personal computers, and see-through touch screens, popular for portable gaming and media devices such as the Nintendo DS and Apple iPhone. (Images courtesy of Tobias Rtten and Greg Lipscomb)

ment of a stylus or human finger over a (typically) flat surface. These devices form some baseline electrical state over the touch surface when there is no user interaction. This baseline state is noticably affected or sensed when the user interacts with the surface. Based on the properties of the electrical interference or electromagnetism, the location (and sometimes area) of user contact with the surface can be determined through various forms of signal processing (see Figure 17.3). A Wacom tablet is a common form of touch surface that uses a stylus with an electromagnetic pad. The pad emits a specific electromagnetic field that allows the tip of the stylus to determine its 2D location with respect to the pad. Contact of the stylus pressed against the pad is sensed by a digital switch or analog sensor. Wacom tablets are often used like mice for cursor control. Unlike mice that only control relative movement, however, touch surfaces allow for absolute placement of the cursor on the screen through the placement of the stylus on the surface.

Touch screens allow for a graphical display to be viewed through the touch surface. Many touch-screen technologies are available for use, with resistive and capacitive being among the most common (see Figure 17.4). A Nintendo DS touch screen is an example of a resistive touch technology. Resistive touch screens run current between two conductive, thin metallic layers separated by small spacers. When the user touches the surface, these two layers are brought into contact over a single area. The result is a change in the electrical field that is translated into the contact location. In contrast, a capacitive touch surface, such as a laptop touch pad or tablet PC screen,

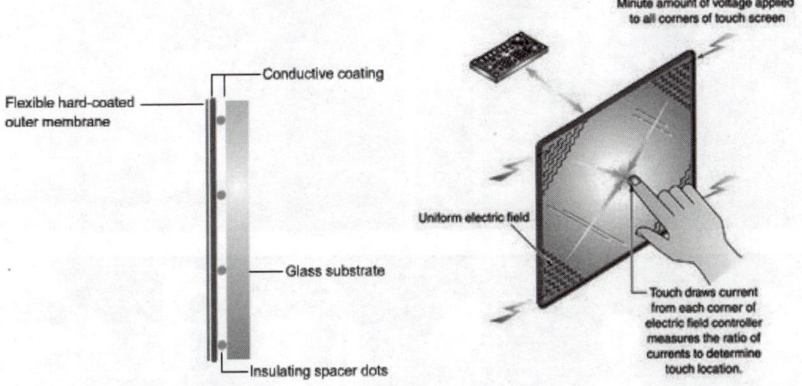

Figure 17.4. Resistive and capacitive are two of the most popular types of touch-screen technology. Resistive screens (left) sense touch information based on the change in an electrical field between two metallic layers when in contact. Capacitive screens (right) rely on absorption of electricity by the human body from a set of electrical sources with known locations. (Images courtesy of touchscreenguide.com)

uses capacitors to store electrical charge at or near the touch surface. Because the human body conducts electricity, current is discharged from these capacitors to the user upon contact with the surface. The relative discharge of capacitors in known locations can be used to localize the point of contact. Capacitive surfaces often are more expensive than resistive surfaces, but typically they are more robust to damage and yield clearer pictures by allowing more display light to pass through the touch surface. Newer devices, such as Apple's iPhone, use multitouch screens that allow users to establish multiple points of contact. Multitouch extends the space of possible direct interface controls beyond cursor movement to operations such as rotation and scaling.

17.2 Optical Character Recognition

Often used for "typing" into a personal digital assistant, *optical character recognition (OCR)* can be a useful tool for incorporating mouse/stylus gestures, such as for spell casting in *Swordplay* (Figure 17.5), into a game. In its general form, optical character recognition is the process of converting various forms of text (handwritten, typed, or printed) into sequences of elec-

Figure 17.5. Optical character recognition was used for spell casting in *Swordplay*, a student game project by Ignatoff, Katzourin, and Quirk, where the objective is to fight off increasing swarms of simple enemies. The user held a 6D electromagnetic tracker as his sword and, while pressing a button, drew symbols to initiate a spell.

tronic characters (often as ASCII text). OCR has many open problems for interpreting handwritten, especially cursive, text due to the lack of spacing between characters and variance in the writing of individuals. Fortunately, many of these problems can be avoided in typical gameplay by using a mouse click while a symbol is being drawn and selecting an alphabet of characters that are clearly distinct.

OCR is essentially a classification problem. That is, given examples of characters in an alphabet (or a training set), determine where these characters appear in an image. Let's assume only one character is drawn at a time to produce an input binary image of a white symbol on a black background. Each of our training examples is assumed to be a binary image of this form. In this case, we can determine the similarity between an input and training image as their intersection—the number of overlapping white pixels. However, this approach to matching will fail if input and training images are not the same size and orientation or are separated by some translational offset. When differences in translation, scaling, and orientation occur, it is possible to compute statistics, or *shape descriptors*, for each image such that comparison between images becomes invariant to relative offsets, size, and rotations. Statistical moments, or image moments, are one form of shape descriptor useful for describing both coarse "low-order" properties, such as area, mean, and variance, as a well as fine "high-order" detail. For a given image, moments are computed at different orders (roughly meaning levels of detail) to form a feature vector. The *pq*-order moment invariant to translation (or centralized moment M_{pq}) is computed as

$$M_{pq} = \sum_{x}\sum_{y}(x - \bar{x})^p (y - \bar{y})^q I(x, y),$$

where $I(x, y)$ is the value of the image at location x, y, and $(\bar{x}, \bar{y})$ is the average white pixel location (which is also M_{11}). The similarity between two images can be computed as the Euclidean distance between their feature vectors. Although OCR with moments is not foolproof, it can provide relatively high accuracy with sufficient image resolution and high-order feature vectors.

Of course, OCR does not need training examples to work effectively. Simple gestures, such as lines and circles, can be effectively recognized with simple hand-coded models describing their shape. Further, we need not treat the input as a static image but rather a trajectory of 2D positions. Such trajectories are called time-series because they refer to something changing over time. Time-series in this case is a position moving over time, but it could also refer to audio as amplitude moving over time. As we will see later when we discuss speech recognition, hidden Markov models is often the computational tool of choice to perform recognition with time-series data, although neural networks or dynamic time warping could also be used.

Figure 17.6. The mechanical mouse is the standard input modality for user pointing. This mouse works by measuring the rotation of horizontal and vertical rollers, whose motion results from user movement of the mouse against a surface. Mice need not take this standard mechanical form, such as the Nintendo Wiimote's use of inertial and infrared information.

17.3 Mice

Mechanical mice and trackballs are ball-and-socket devices that sense the relative movement of a contact (see Figure 17.6). Contact is established by a spherical ball that sits within the device but is partially exposed. The ball sits on two wheels whose rotations can be counted using optical encoders to measure forward and sideways movements of the ball. Optical encoders use discs with patterns along their edges to determine the relative rotation of a wheel. Movement of the ball is caused by physical movement of the mouse against a surface, which then forces the mouse wheels to rotate. The amount of rotation of the mouse wheels is sensed by the optical encoders to determine how much the user moved the mouse both horizontally and vertically. Mechanical mice and trackballs are upside-down versions of each other. Trackballs expose the ball upward, sitting on the wheels, for direct user contact. Mice expose the ball downward for contact with a ground surface.

Mice are not restricted to the standard mechanical form often used with most personal computers. The standard definition of *mouse* is a device for detecting two-dimensional relative movement on some supporting plane, regardless of its internal mechanics. For example, optical mice use the visual perception of a color texture on a surface to measure relative movement. However, the connotation of mice has expanded to commonly refer to any pointing device. Devices capable of sensing absolute position, such as an accelerometer-based Wiimote or an electromagnetic "mouse," are considered mice.

17.4 Inertial-Based Input and Global Positioning

Inertial sensors, or *inertial measurement units (IMUs)*, use their own movement and other natural phenomenon, such as Earth's gravitational and magnetic fields, to estimate the orientation of an input device. Inertial sensors are mostly mechanical devices that measure the effect of various phenomenon on a physical mass. IMUs have long been used in robotics and virtual reality. However, recent advances in microelectromechanical systems (MEMS) have led to increasingly smaller inertial sensors that are now often the size of your pinky fingernail. Common MEMS inertial sensors have the following features.

- **An *accelerometer* for sensing the direction of acceleration and gravitational forces about a single axis.** An accelerometer allows a small mass to rotate around a bar. Gravity pulls the mass toward a particular angle about the bar's axis that can be sensed. (This assumes that the accelerometer's axis is not aligned with the gravitational vector.)

- **A *magnetometer*, a compass for sensing the direction of Earth's magnetic north.** A compass contains a mass coated with magnetically sensitive material that is guided by Earth's magnetic field, absent the presence of nearby metallic objects.

- **A *gyroscope* for sensing angular velocity.** A gyroscope uses a mass spinning around an axis to resist changes in orientation. This mass is allowed to pivot around its center of mass, allowing the mass to rotate when angular velocities occur that can be sensed.

The Nintendo Wiimote is a common example that has managed to leverage the small form factor and decreasing cost of MEMS inertial sensing. By itself, the Wiimote uses two accelerometers for measuring its pitch (up-and-down rotation) and roll (twist rotations) in Earth's global coordinates. Figure 17.7 demonstrates how the accelerometer operates. When the object

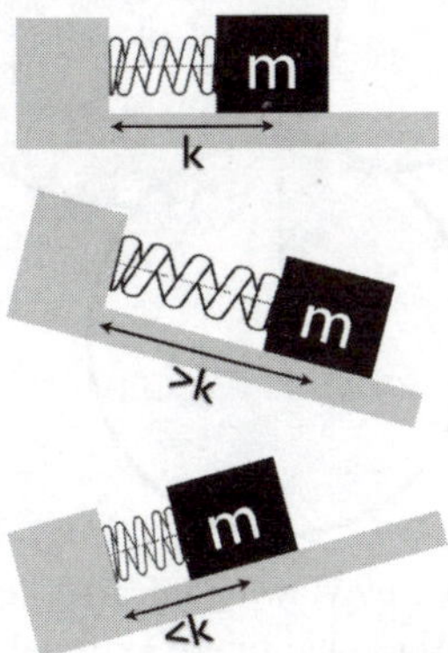

Figure 17.7. Illustration of the spring-mass accelerometer concept for sensing orientation based on the length of a spring.

is flat, gravity has no effect, and the spring will rest at its equilibrium at some distance k. When tipped downward, gravity will pull the mass downward and stretch the spring. When tipped upward, the spring will compress. This information is communicated over Bluetooth to a Wii console, or any Bluetooth-enabled device programmed to interact with a Wiimote. To fully localize (i.e., measure its position and orientation), the Wiimote requires an external reference called a sensor bar. The infrared lights of the sensor bar are analogous to the satellite signals in a global positioning system (GPS), allowing the Wiimote to infer its pose in a "local" coordinate system about the sensor bar.

Common GPS receivers (ubiquitously used for vehicle navigation) typically require signals from four or more satellites orbiting Earth to determine its position, using a geometric procedure called trilateration (see Figure 17.8). Trilateration calculates a location B given at least three reference

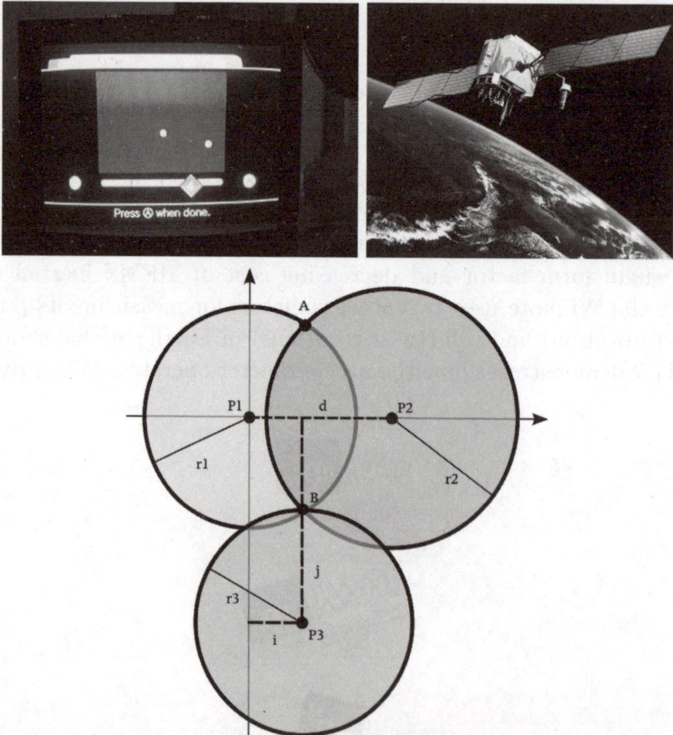

Figure 17.8. A Wiimote can localize its pose by viewing infrared lights in known locations. Similar to GPS satellite signals, these lights are external references used in geometric calculations, such as triangulation or trilateration (bottom). (Top-left image courtesy of Kenneth Lu)

points (P1, P2, P3) and their distances (r1, r2, r3) to B. Each GPS satellite continually transmits signals containing its current time (maintained by its atomic clock) and position (calculated from its orbital model) at the moment of transmission. Assuming satellite signals are transmitted at a constant speed (the speed of light), a GPS receiver estimates its distance from a satellite using the difference between a signal's time of transmission and the current time at the receiver.

Briefly delving into device specifics, Wiimote localization follows a similar but scaled-down process compared to GPS, typically using *triangulation* instead of trilateration. Unlike a GPS receiver that performs its own calculations, the Wiimote only provides information sensed by the device and leaves processing of the information up to individual Wii applications or any program with access to Bluetooth. Information sensed by the Wiimote could be processed in a variety ways in addition to or in place of localization to facilitate successful incorporation into a game, with tradeoffs for and against. In its most general usage, the Wiimote can see two to four infrared light sources[1] from a small infrared camera on the front of the device. These sources appear as "blobs" to the Wiimote, whose size in the image indicates the distance between the Wiimote and the light source (where larger blobs indicate a closer light source). As with GPS, trilateration can be used to localize the Wiimote, assuming the light sources are placed in a known configuration and are within the Wiimote's field of view. In its typical usage, the light sources are arranged as two sources on a fixed sensor bar. In this case, the geometric relationship between the Wiimote and two light sources forms a triangle, allowing the Wiimote's position to be determined through triangulation. Triangulation calculates a location B given two reference points (P1 and P2) and distances between all three locations, forming the geometry of a triangle. Wiimote orientation information (roll, pitch, yaw) can additionally be determined by analyzing the line formed by the two light sources through its slope and midpoint position (along vertical and horizontal axes). Triangulation in this manner, however, assumes a known calibration between blob size and depth and that the user keeps the light sources in the Wiimote's field of view. Although calibration can be relatively straightforward, there are no guarantees the light sources will remain visible. In such circumstances of unreliability, you can either use Wiimote sensing some other way or consider a more general approach to tracking, as we explore next.

17.4.1 Noisy Sensing and State Estimation

One downside to Wiimote and inertial sensing is that they lack the reliability and precision of common devices such as keyboards and mice. Users

[1]You may not be able to see this infrared light, but your digital camera probably can.

are often accustomed to the near-deterministic reliability of standard but limited input devices. Standard devices offer both high degrees of accuracy (correctly sensing specific user events, such as keystrokes) and precision (sensing user events as they occur without delay or randomness in timing). Although inertial-based systems offer exciting and more natural forms of user input, Wiimote sensors often are burdened by various quirks, such as saturation at fairly low acceleration (about 2.5 g), periods of occlusion (when the sensor bar signals are blocked), and ambiguity (where two different Wiimote poses could be inferred from the same reference signals). Most commercial GPS systems are restricted to relatively coarse timing and satellite orbit information, limiting their accuracy to approximately 5–20 meters.

For games, such uncertainty can cause a prohibitive amount of user frustration if not masked during gameplay or countered through more sophisticated computation. In particular, localization through trilateration or triangulation is a deterministic calculation that requires perfect or near-perfect information about distances to and positions of reference points. Imperfect information can be accounted for directly if the form of the error is known. For instance, if reference signals are mostly correct but have high-frequency "jitter" or occasional missing information, a low-pass filter (i.e., a simple average over a window in time) can smooth out the signal. When errors are caused by a small number of "outlier" references, increasing the number of references provides additional robustness through redundancy. Redundancy can enforce consistency through least squares fitting or finding consensus in localizing with different subsets of reference signals—for example, in a random sample consensus (RANSAC) algorithm. While such error correction procedures can improve accuracy, the result of these procedures is a single answer, which could be vastly incorrect.

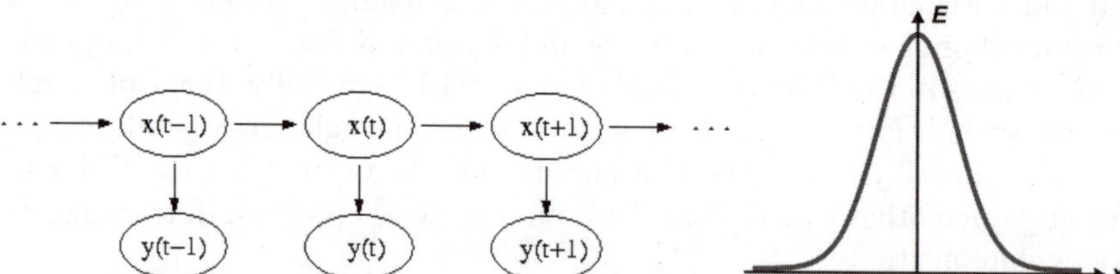

Figure 17.9. To account for noise and uncertainty, tracking a user input device can be treated as a state estimation problem. Shown as a graph (left), state estimation distinguishes known observation variables y from unknown variables of the device's state x at each moment in time. Further, unknown variables are treated as "soft" probability distributions, such as a Gaussian (right), instead of providing a single "hard" answer.

More broadly, state estimation is the general problem for tracking an object (or any form of user input) while accounting for various forms of uncertainty (see Figure 17.9). State estimation divides information at any moment in time t into two types of variables: *observations* $y(t)$, which are directly sensed, and *state* $x(t)$, unseen information that describes the object being tracked. It is assumed that an object's state at a given time both determines how it is observed and affects the object's state at the next moment in time $x(t+1)$. This flow of information can be shown graphically as a Bayesian graphical model that is similar to Bayesian procedures that filter your e-mail spam, where each node is information and arrows indicate a "caused by" relationship. This model used to be called a Bayes filter, and it takes the following form:

$$p(x(t)|y(1..t)) \propto p(y(t)|x(t)) \sum_{x(t)} p(x(t)|x(t-1))p(x(t-1)|y(1..t-1)),$$

where state variables are actually probability distributions over all possible poses of an object rather than a single pose at time t. Such probability distributions have two main constraints: each state must have a positive nonzero probability, and the sum over the probability of all states must equal one. That is, $p(x)$ notes the probability of being in any state x, all other things being equal. State estimation provides the *conditional probability* $p(x(t)|y(1..t))$, indicating how probable a particular pose $x(t)$ is given all the observations from some start time up to the current time. Note that the Bayes filter assumes that we only need to know about the current time t to predict what will happen next at time $t+1$. This property is referred to as "Markovian dynamics" and allows the procedure to run recursively over time by replacing $p(x(t-1)|y(1..t-1))$ with $p(x(t)|y(1..t))$ at each timestep.

Such distributions allow multiple different "hypotheses" about the object's state to be maintained in case no single answer makes sense. Different state estimation algorithms use different approaches to represent probability distributions. The Kalman filter, for instance, assumes state variable distributions are unimodal or Gaussian. Such distributions have a single most-probable state (or "peak"), with the probability of other states decreasing (at an exponential rate based on the width of the distribution) as the distance from the peak increases. The width of this probability distribution is small when the observations are accurate and large when the observations contain uncertainty. The particle filter, in contrast, is multimodal and maintains peaks at multiple states. The multimodal approach allows for multiple disparate state possibilities to be maintained when ambiguity is present (such as during occlusion) and resolved to a single state when observations are more trustworthy.

17.5 Light and Positional Guns

Light guns, such as the NES Zapper or those used in the *House of the Dead* series, are distinctly different from positional guns used by arcade games such as SEGA's *Gunblade NY* (see Figure 17.10). Positional guns are essentially analog sticks mounted in a fixed location with respect to the screen. Light guns, in contrast, have no fixed a priori relationship with a display. Instead, light guns rely on the quick, unperceptible flash of a pattern on the screen to localize the gun. When the trigger of the gun is squeezed, a specific pattern is flashed on the screen and viewed by a camera in the barrel of the light

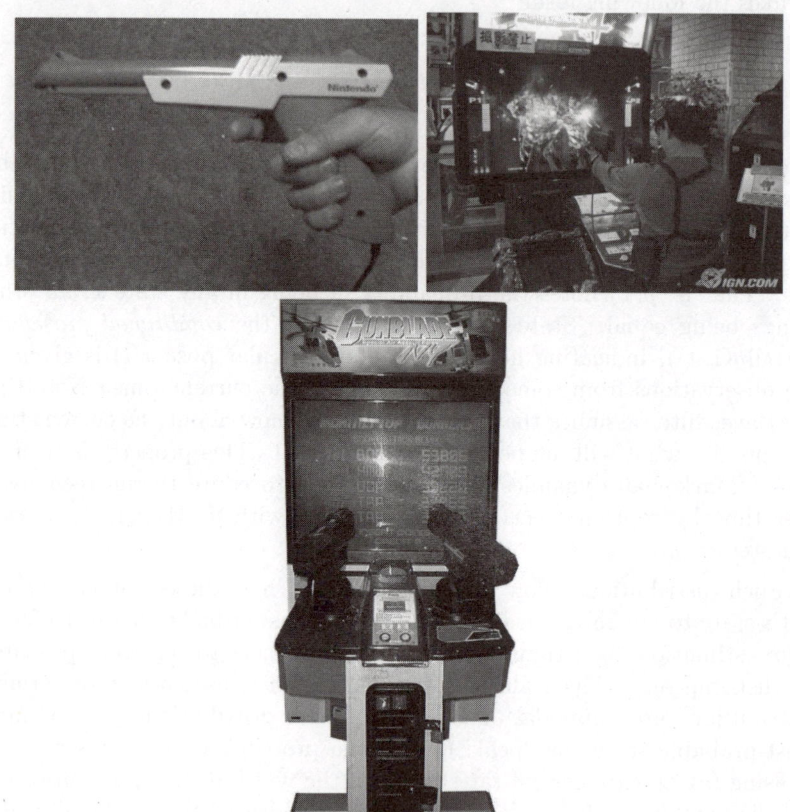

Figure 17.10. Light guns, such as the NES Zapper (left) and *House of the Dead* gun (right), sense where the user is pointing by quickly displaying reference signals when the trigger is pressed. Light guns differ from positional guns, such as in *Gunblade NY* (bottom), that are essentially analog joysticks. (Images courtesy of Sega and KLOV.com)

gun. Like the Wiimote infrared sensor, this pattern is used to triangulate the position and orientation of the gun with respect to the screen. Once localized, a ray in 3D can be cast from the gun through the screen into the virtual world to determine what objects have been hit. Other methods, such as cathode ray timing, provide more accurate results by leveraging the specific properties of a display device.

17.6 Sound-Based Input

The microphone is the traditional input device of choice for sound-based input. It is used to provide voice-chat between remote players of online games. Ideally, the game should be able to perform speech recognition—recognizing a player's speech commands (see Figure 17.11). This task may seem like a

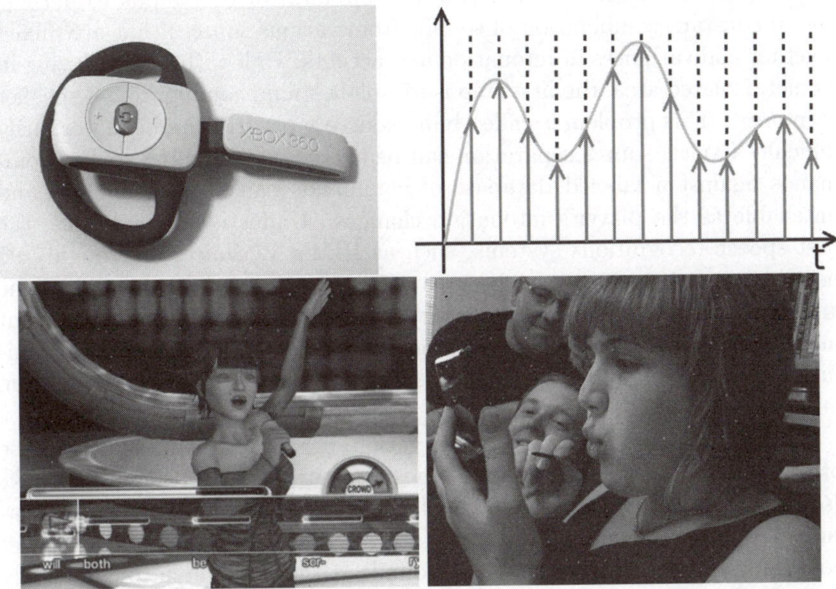

Figure 17.11. Microphone devices such as the Xbox 360 headset (top left) allow for sound to be captured from a user. Sound is represented as a digital signal (top right) where a sequence of samples captures the amplitude of sound over time. Although recognizing spoken words is difficult, games such as *Karaoke Revolution* (bottom left) use pitch information to determine if a user is roughly hitting the right notes. Nintendo DS games often involve blowing into a microphone (bottom right). (Bottom-left image courtesy of Harmonix Music Systems, Inc.)

simple matching operation. When the user presses a button, simply find the best match from a set of prerecorded commands spoken by that user. In its simplest form, matching involves computing the similarity, as Euclidean distance, between an input audio clip (a time-series represented as a vector of amplitude samples over time) and each audio clip in a training set. Euclidean distance computation assumes the input clip is scaled in time to match the length of each training clip. This time scaling is often a linear transform that speeds up or slows down the speed of the input clip by some constant. More generally, this matching refers to the registration (or sequence alignment) problem, where one time vector is warped to look like another vector to determine their similarity. Dynamic time warping was historically the approach to sequence alignment, using dynamic programming to variably adjust the speed of an input clip to best match a training clip. Modern speech-recognition systems, however, use hidden Markov models trained on each command to perform with greater robustness to time variations and audio noise. Hidden Markov models and dynamic time warping are not limited to audio signals and can be used to match any time-varying vectors.

Like vision, however, sound is a difficult form of user input to harness due to constant combination of sounds from various sources that are mixed together and variances in intonation and accents. Unless they are playing in a quiet, isolated area, the first step is to isolate sound coming from a speaker of interest. This problem is called blind source separation and is notoriously difficult. Even if source separation can be overcome, matching spoken commands against a labeled database of commands can also be difficult and unreliable as the player's intonation changes. Under ideal conditions, the best speech-recognitions systems, such as IBM's ViaVoice, are roughly 95 percent accurate, which may be great for dictation and automated phone answering. However, this accuracy often decreases to around 60–75 percent in common console gaming environments. Again, such technological limitations can be countered by creative gameplay devices to mask recognition failures.[2]

Given the difficulty of speech recognition, it is often advantageous to use other properties, such as amplitude and pitch, in the sound signal. *Karaoke Revolution* cleverly uses the pitch of the incoming sound signal to measure the player's accuracy for singing a given song. (Of course, the player could sing the wrong words or other sounds at the right pitch to completely fool the game.) Pitch is the fundamental frequency of a sound. A sound signal, sensed in the time domain, can be thought of as a combination of sine waves—specifically, a weighted additive sum of sine waves with various frequencies (see Figure 17.12). These weights allow a sound signal to be alternatively expressed in the frequency domain as the coefficient weights of

[2]Such as through humorously insulting the player, as presented in a guest lecture by Mac Doc Software at Brown University during Spring 2006.

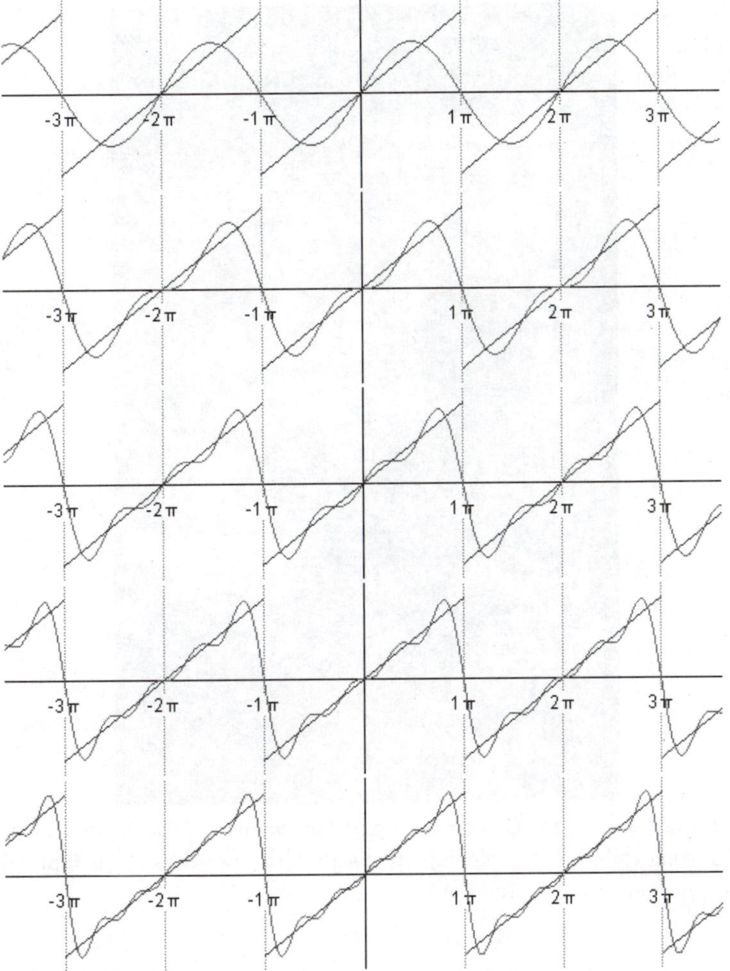

Figure 17.12. The extraction pitch from sound relies on sound signals being a weighted sum of sine waves at different frequencies. In this example, the "sawtooth" function is approximated as the straight-line function by successively adding sine waves of higher frequency.

each frequency that can reconstruct the original sound signal through addition. Once in the frequency domain, it is simply a matter of checking that the right pitch frequencies have coefficients above a threshold. Algorithms, such as the Fourier transform, can convert sound signals into the frequency domain. Further, the Nyquist-Shannon sampling theorem roughly states that to exactly recover all frequency/Fourier components, the input device must collect amplitude samples (meaning the "sampling rate" at which the

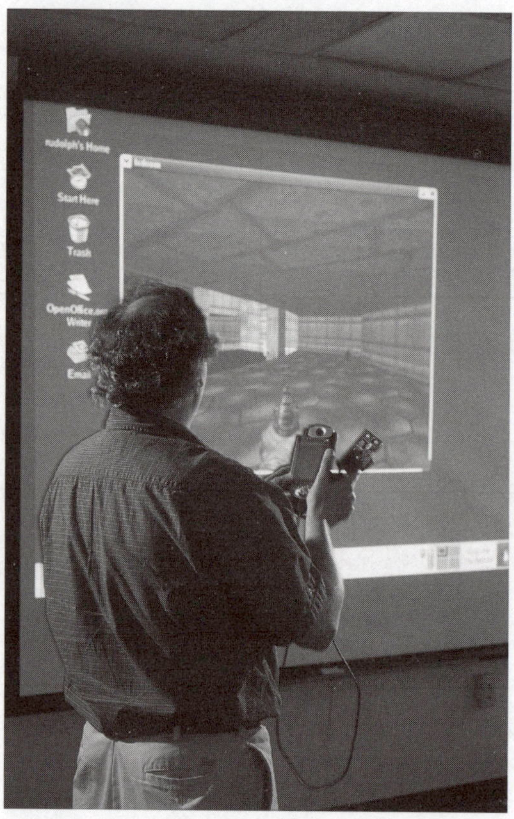

Figure 17.13. Sonar devices, such as the Crossbow Cricket for playing *DOOM* in an MIT project, use ultrasonic "chirps" as reference to localize the position of an input device. (Image courtesy of Larry Rudolph)

sound is converted into digital samples) of the sound hitting the microphone at twice the highest frequency. Given that the human vocal range spans roughly 80–1100 Hz, sampling at the Nyquist frequency is not a concern.

Various games for the Nintendo DS use the amplitude of the sound signal to control a single real-valued input variable. Although any sound could have been used for this form of input, the input was cast in the form of "blowing" to engage the user's sense of imagination. In *The Legend of Zelda: Phantom Hourglass*, for example, the user is required to blow through the game microphone to extinguish fires or defeat enemies.

Sonar (sound navigation and ranging) is another form of sound-based input that is used as a ranging device. Sonar works by emitting sound and then sensing the time it takes for the sound to return. Given the speed of sound, this travel time can be used to calculate the distance to nearby objects. Although sonar-based ranging has not been used extensively in games, interesting prototypes that use sonar-based devices have been developed, such as MIT's use of Crossbow Cricket sensor networks to play *DOOM* (see Figure 17.13).

17.7 Camera-Based Input

Like sound input, camera-based input is a formidable challenge for computational perception that has been struggled with for decades. Cameras sense many visual artifacts that may be easy for a human to perceive but extremely difficult for computational algorithms to recognize. Environmental issues such as shadows, lighting (or lack thereof), textures (or lack thereof), surface contours, occlusion, camera resolution, and so on, in addition to issues for computational complexity, create a perfect storm of difficulties that have yet to yield out-of-the-box computational perception (see Figure 17.14). However, products such as Sony's EyeToy (Figure 17.15) have revealed a few vision techniques that can work well enough to yield fun gameplay.

Arguably, the simplest approach to vision processing is color *blobfinding* (see Figure 17.16 (top)). In this scenario, the user wears or holds (typically fluorescent) color markers. The blobfinder then scans through the image, identifying pixels with those specific colors. Adjacent pixels with the same color identification are grouped together to form "blobs" in the image. The

Figure 17.14. Interpreting images from cameras presents a multitude of problems for handling visual artifacts, such as shadows, textures, contours, lighting, and reflections.

Figure 17.15. Sony's EyeToy (top) is a small, low-resolution camera used to play specially designed games for the PS2, such as *Groove* (bottom left) and Sega's *Nights* (bottom right), solely through body movement. *Groove* is a rhythm game where the user must wave his or her hand over certain locations at specific times in the camera image. In *Nights*, the user guides the flight of his or her character by using his or her arms as a differential drive. (Images courtesy of Sony (SCEA) and Sega)

location and size of the blobs can then be used as user input. For example, a marker could be used to drive a car with a vertical position related to acceleration and a horizontal position tied to steering. Unfortunately, color blobfinding is very difficult to use reliably in common environments, due to problems with color calibration. Blobfinding is highly sensitive to lighting conditions. Subtle changes in lighting, due to a slight tilt of a marker or uneven lighting in the environment, can yield drastic changes in pixel color values. Consequently, calibrating the colors and thresholds of a blobfinder is a very tedious and brittle process. Overly conservative blobfinders are unable to consistently detect markers, and overly liberal blobfinders yield too many false positives for spotting markers.

Background subtraction is another simple vision technique where foreground silhouettes of moving users are extracted from the image (see Figure 17.16 (bottom)). Background subtraction works by taking the difference at each pixel between a background image model—typically a picture with no one in the camera's view—and images collected during gameplay. The

Figure 17.16. Color blobfinding and background subtraction are relatively simple techniques for processing images. Color blobfinding classifies each pixel into one of a set of known colors (or an unknown label), such as processing a robot soccer field (top) with the CMVision software library. Background subtraction (bottom, shown for human movement tracking) essentially extracts a foreground silhouette, similar to using a "blue screen," using either a solid background color or an arbitrary background image. (Top images courtesy of Bruce et al., CMVision, Carnegie Mellon University, 2000)

resulting image difference is thresholded to find silhouette pixels. Silhouettes can then be used to push or strike objects, touch virtual on-screen markers, or perform differential drive such as in Sega's *Super Monkey Ball* and *Nights.*

Similarly, optical flow techniques extract the motion of objects in the foreground of an image stream. *Optical flow* refers to a vector field in the image that relates the displacement of each pixel from one instant of time to the next. More specifically, the window around each pixel—say, a 5×5 pixel window—must find a corresponding window with a similar visual appearance in the next frame (see Figure 17.17). A naive correspondence search for images with n pixels will be $O(n^2)$, which is too slow for interactive-time games. More sophisticated algorithms, such as the Lucas-Kanade method, can efficiently solve for such correspondences as a linear system of equations. In practice, however, many EyeToy games simply take the difference between two subsequent frames as a crude but effective motion estimate. Through image differencing with static background, areas of an image where a person is moving can be easily isolated and used in a similar manner as a button click. Menuing systems for EyeToy games typically use this mechanism for selection. It just goes to show the value of the KISS principle (Keep It Simple, Stupid!).

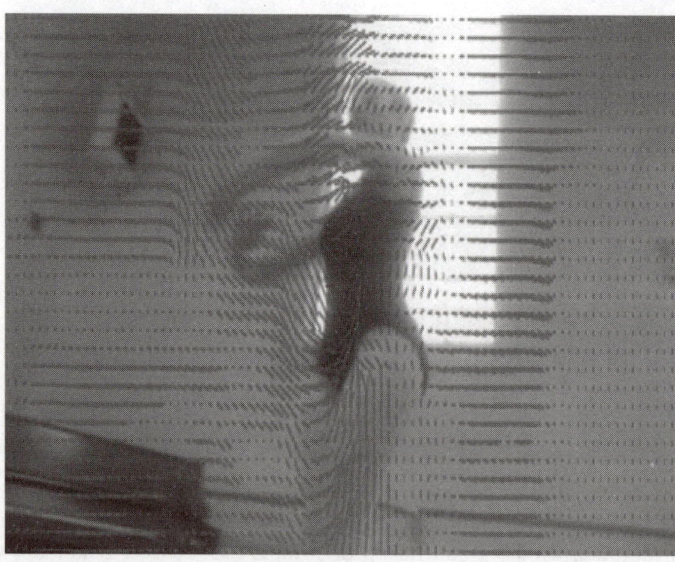

Figure 17.17. Optical flow of a dancer generated by the BorisFX Avid plug-in. Optical flow computes the "movement" of each pixel from one frame to the next. The result is a velocity field over the image that indicates where each pixel's color was in the previous frame. (Image courtesy of BoisFX)

As evidenced in games such as *AntiGrav*, face tracking has demonstrated reliable and fun results for using a player's appearance for user input. Face tracking works by initially acquiring a picture of the player's face, called a template. The player's face should be in a frontal view, centered, and covering most of the template image. At runtime during the game, template matching is performed on each frame to find the best match of the player's face in the current image. Template matching scans all possible locations and scalings of the template with a simple sum-of-squares image-difference, image-matching criteria. The best match is found in each frame, providing a user input similar to a blob in color blobfinding. In *AntiGrav*, the location of the face is used to control the steering of a hoverboard with horizontal movement, and ducking and jumping with vertical face movement (see Figure 17.18).

An emerging technology for vision-based games is object recognition, which is about defining features unique to a given object with the ability to recognize the object in the future. That is, given a prespecified object, recognition is the ability to know when the object is in view and the relative pose of the object to the camera. Unlike color blobfinding, object recognition explicitly expects objects to have an intricate and identifiable texture that is distinct. Different types of objects are suited to different types of recognition algorithms. 2D objects, such as relatively generic black-and-white block

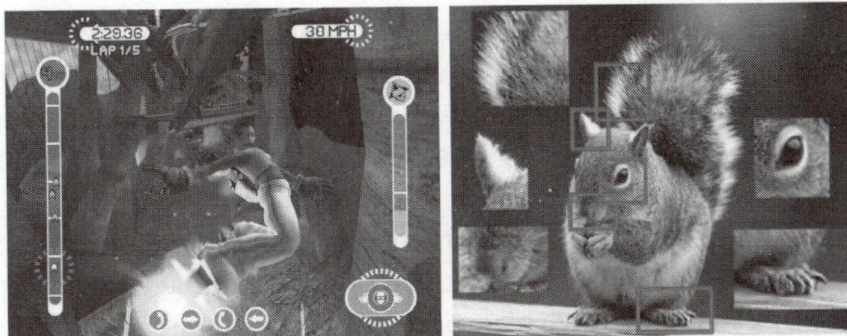

Figure 17.18. *AntiGrav* (left) uses face tracking in the form of template matching as an input for controlling a hoverboard. Template matching (right), scans an image for smaller template images that are representative of some important feature. (Images courtesy of Harmonix Music Systems, Inc. and societyofrobots.com)

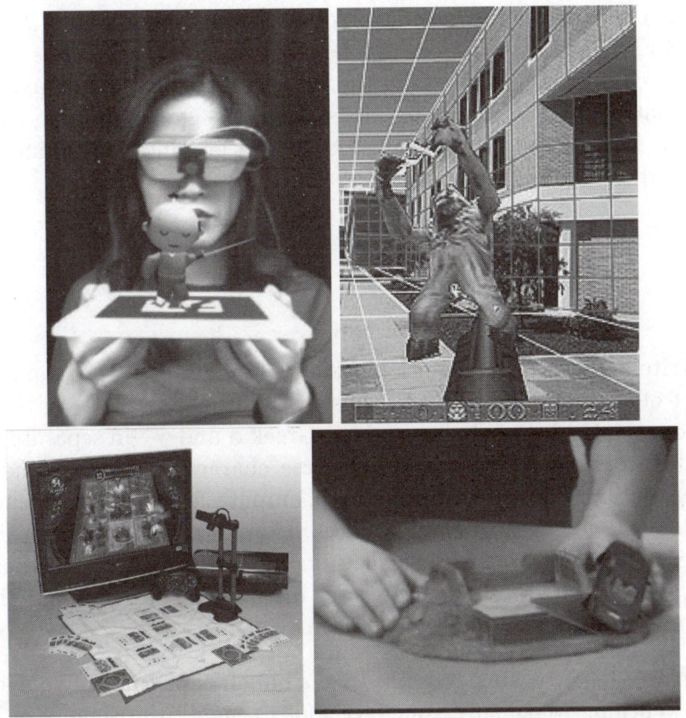

Figure 17.19. The ARToolkit library (top left) is commonly used to place virtual objects for augmented reality through recognizing objects with specific visual patterns. Games such as *ARQuake* (top right) and Sony's *Eye of Judgement* card battle (bottom left) use augmented reality to bridge real and virtual worlds. Particularly compelling are applications that combine physically simulated and real objects, such as the virtual car driving up on the real hill object (bottom right). (Images courtesy of Human Interface Technology Laboratory, ARQuake (Dr. Bruce Thomas), Sony (SCEA), and Total Immersion)

patterns and more elaborate *Magic*-like cards, could use template matching. 3D objects in cluttered environments, however, require recognition with more sophisticated types of features, such as scale invariant feature transforms (SIFT), which has demonstrated utility for image stitching and robot localization.

One compelling application of object recognition is augmented reality, which overlays graphical elements on top of camera images. If the pose of a recognized object is known with respect to the camera, then the real object can be visually replaced or modified (assuming the object is not occluded) by a virtual object in the augmented view. Software libraries such as ARTag and ARToolkit (Figure 17.19) can recognize specific types of black-and-white checkerboard-style patterns in video streams to support virtual object placement. Although game-based augmented reality has been around for several years, such as in prototypes such as *ARQuake*, Sony's new *Eye of Judgement* system for the PS3 EyeToy could take it to the next level. *Eye of Judgement* is a card battle game where the camera recognizes cards placed on a "battle mat." The PS3 maintains the state of the game, allowing players to play against a computer opponent and special graphics and animations to be overlaid on the camera image.

17.8 Exercises

1. Write a character-recognition system. Using a paint program, draw a set of examples for an arbitrary set of characters—let's say ten letters from the English alphabet and the Greek α and γ—in separate images. Also draw an additional set of these characters (that are not exact replications) to separate images. Compute feature-vector centralized moments for each of these images. Compute the Euclidean distance between each pair of feature-vectors. For each image, what other image produced the lowest feature-vector distance? Can you make this into an interactive character-recognition system?

2. Write a face-tracking system. Take a bunch of pictures of yourself with a webcam. Make sure your face looks roughly the same size in each of these images. Create a template image by cropping out a tight box from one of these images that shows only your face. Write a template matching system that scans each of these images for the template. Draw a box around where your face has been found in each image. Can you get this system to work interactively with a video stream?

3. Localize your Wiimote. Using one of the existing Wiimote libraries (WiiRemote for OS X, GlovePie for Windows, or CWiid for Linux),

write a program to access accelerometer and infrared information from the Wiimote. Just for fun, you may also want to try making the LED light up and vibrate the Wiimote. Assuming the dimensions of the sensor bar, write a trilateration routine to estimate the pose of the Wiimote when the sensor bar is in view. Try creating new types of sensor bars using candles or other LEDs. How accurate are your pose estimates? Try the character-recognition exercise again, using the Wiimote for input.

4. Drop balls on yourself through background subtraction. Using a camera in a fixed position (preferably on a tripod), take two pictures of a stationary environment: one with you in the picture (the foreground) and one without (the background). At each pixel, calculate the difference between the two images to produce a difference image. Compute a silhouette image by thresholding the difference image by some value of your choice. Using this silhouette to matte, write a program that displays only foreground pixels within the silhouette. Within this program, create balls that drop from the top and bounce off this silhouette.

CHAPTER 18

Artificial Intelligence

Terms Explained: *Classification – Closed Loop – Decision Making – Decision Tree – Feedback Control Loop – Open Loop – Pathfinding – Regression – Reinforcement Learning – State Space – Turing Test*

What makes nonplayer characters (NPCs) smart? How do enemies decide to take certain actions to navigate the game world or to hurt the player? How do friendly NPCs help the player? Do NPCs learn from their past experiences? What distinguishes a human player from an NPC? The answers to these questions lie in the application of artificial intelligence to game development.

Artificial intelligence (AI) for games is mostly about making good decisions based on knowledge from the game environment. In this chapter, we take a whirlwind tour through a variety of AI techniques for topics such as pathfinding, learning with neural networks, and theorem proving. We particularly emphasize decision making for nonplayer characters (NPCs), complementing our description of strategic AI in Chapter 7. Decision making alone, however, is only part of the story. AI also deals with how characters perceive the game environment, learn from past experience, and generally affect the game state. We use the notion of a feedback control loop to put the various AI techniques into context to realize different forms of intelligence.

18.1 What Is AI?

Artificial intelligence (AI) is the science and engineering of endowing man-made machines with "intelligence" (to paraphrase John McCarthy; see http://www-formal.stanford.edu/jmc/whatisai/node1.html). AI is a confluence of many fields, often combining the algorithmic thinking of computer science, the understanding of biological entities from the cognitive sciences, and the physical expertise of engineering. At its core, AI poses the incredibly difficult problem of answering "What is intelligence?" Like physics searching for the true nature of the universe, the science of AI attempts to understand the true nature of human cognition and the mind through building artificial minds. AI is often used to denote both the field of artificial intelligence and a specific artificial system with decision-making abilities. Consequently, the path to such deep understanding often poses more problems than answers, as evidenced by continual debates about intelligence in academic circles.

Fortunately, creating AI engines for sufficiently "smart" characters does not require full understanding of intelligence. For example, the *Turing Test* argues that a true human-level AI controls an NPC such that human players believe they are playing with another human. More generally, the Turing Test is based on the perception of a human user that a given AI (e.g., automated game players, conversational "chatterbots," movie characters, airplane autopilots, traffic control systems) is believed to be a human. A common example illustrating the Turing Test is Joseph Weizenbaum's ELIZA conversational program. ELIZA acts as psychotherapist that attempts (through a chat terminal) to help a human user work through his or her problems. In actuality, however, ELIZA is simply a parody of a therapist that simply rephrases key words from a user's statements into questions it reflects back to the user. Although ELIZA has no sophisticated algorithms or "intelligence," it has been able to illicit serious and heartfelt conversations with humans (Figure 18.1). Over time, though, ELIZA fails the Turing Test as users realize its simple conversational trick. To this date, no AI system has been able to pass the Turing Test.

It is important to note that an AI capable of passing a Turing Test need not be intelligent and AI need not pass the Turing Test to be engaging enough for games. For example, many modern commercial aircraft are controlled mostly by automated programs with little intervention by human pilots. As a passenger, you might not realize that you have a computer as your pilot because flights follow a very specific and tightly controlled procedure. If a problem were to occur on the flight, however, the differences between the human and computer pilots would be clear. Similarly, an NPC could be narrowly engineered to pass the Turing Test for a specific game for a limited amount of time. Such systems will likely perform ineffectually for other games and will not adapt over time. It is difficult say whether NPCs in modern games pass the Turing Test, but is clear that most are customized for individual games. It would likely be difficult to adapt an AI from a soccer game to play a first-person shooter at the level of a customized NPC bot. There exist many efforts to build AI engines that exhibit more general

Young woman: Men are all alike.

ELIZA: In what way?

Young woman: They're always bugging us about something specific or other.

ELIZA: Can you think of a specific example?

Young woman: Well, my boyfriend made me come here.

ELIZA: Your boyfriend made you come here?

Young woman: He says I'm depressed much of the time.

ELIZA: I am sorry to hear you are depressed.

Young woman: It's true. I'm unhappy.

ELIZA: Do you think coming here will help you not to be unhappy?

Young woman: I need some help; that much seems certain.

ELIZA: What would it mean to you if you got some help?

Young woman: Perhaps I could learn to get along with my mother.

ELIZA: Tell me more about your family.

Young woman: My mother takes care of me.

ELIZA: Who else in your family takes care of you?

Young woman: My father.

ELIZA: Your father.

Young woman: You are like my father in some ways.

ELIZA: What resemblance do you see?

Young woman: You are not very aggressive, but I think you don't want me to notice that.

ELIZA: What makes you think I am not very aggressive?

Young woman: You don't argue with me.

ELIZA: Why do you think I don't argue with you?

Young woman: You are afraid of me.

ELIZA: Does it please you to believe I am afraid of you?

Young woman: My father is afraid of everybody.

ELIZA: What else comes to mind when you think of your father?

Young woman: Bullies.

ELIZA: Does that have anything to do with the fact that your boyfriend made you come here?

Figure 18.1. Excerpt of conversation between ELIZA and a young woman, taken from "dialogues with colorful personalities of early ai" by Güven Güzeldere and Stefano Franci. (Stanford Electronic Humanities Review, vol. 4, issue 2: "Constructions of the Mind".)

notions of intelligence, such as automatic learning, improved performance from experience, and the ability to adapt to new tasks and games. *Cognitive architectures*, such as Soar and Massive, and *machine learning* techniques, such as Q-Learning and genetic algorithms, aim to realize general AI systems, while *AI middleware* packages provide reusable libraries of useful routines for programming AI systems.

In pursuit of its loftier goals, the field of AI has produced a large set of algorithmic tools and conceptual devices suited for NPCs and, more generally, any sort of autonomous behavior. Before diving into the toolbox, we cover some concepts that combine these techniques for intelligent characters. Conceptually, an NPC is an embodied autonomous agent whose interactions with a game are modeled by a feedback control loop. We use these concepts to form a unified framework for grounding our presentation of AI in this chapter.

18.2 How Smart Does My AI *Really* Need to Be?

Not that smart. *Really*! Players typically use games to have a fun experience, to escape into a world where they can be someone else or have an interesting adventure. In many cases, having a "smart" or "intelligent" adversary can get in the way of having fun. Consider AI systems that play Reversi (or Othello). These systems are not overly complex and are often implemented as an assignment for undergraduate AI classes. However, human players often fare very badly against these players. It would not be an understatement that computer Reversi players "mop the floor" with human players. As a result, Reversi can prove frustrating and unentertaining for casual gamers who are looking for a fun diversion from reality (see Figure 18.2). (Serious

Figure 18.2. Reversi is a common case where an AI can be unbeatable by human players and, thus, not fun. Games such as *Mario Kart* and *NBA Jam* often adjust the strength of their AI to provide human players just enough of a challenge to have an enjoyable gameplay. (Images courtesy of Nintendo and Midway)

games are another matter because they are often training for a serious purpose. In these cases, we really do want these people to improve by facing the toughest challenges possible.) Playing on an easy difficulty setting can provide the right level of challenge to yield an enjoyable experience but can be a significant blow to a player's ego.

A good AI game should make the player feel confident and be capable of encouraging fun gameplay. Typically, AI systems are restrained in some way to facilitate the user having fun. These restraints are modulated to provide human players with a challenging gameplay without completely obliterating and demoralizing them. This may explain why you can never really pull away from other racers in *Mario Kart* or why computer opponents can mount surprising last minute comebacks in *NBA Jam*. They might be cheating a little, but it is more likely they are just better than you. So you might want to learn to play a real guitar as well as being a *Guitar Hero*.

18.3 Embodied Autonomous Agents

An NPC or bot is just like any other animate creature, such as a human, animal, or robot. Each has a body of some physical form, or embodiment. Each makes decisions to move its body toward achieving its objectives. The decision making of each is affected by how its body interacts with physics. For example, one author's physical embodiment is reasonably strong, but it is slow and does not jump very high (a consequence of being in his thirties!). Such limitations restrict his abilities to properly function as a professional basketball player, regardless of his smarts as a basketball player. Thus, his basketball-related decisions try to maximize his capabilities such as emphasizing defense and rebounding, never attempting to dunk, and most important, not pursuing a career in professional basketball. In games, however, developers have the power to create virtual worlds to their specification, letting the second author vicariously enjoy life as a professional basketball player. In our exploration of NPCs as animate creatures, we will consider the simple example of controlling a pilot for a 1980s barnstorming game, where the player tries to fly through barns without hitting barn roofs or windmills.

NPCs, robots, humans, and other animate creatures are examples of an embodied autonomous agent—that is, an entity that automatically and independently (or autonomously) makes decisions to drive its embodiment. *Embodiment*, in this sense, refers to "physical form," defining how the character affects and is affected by the physics of the game. In the barnstorming example, the player is embodied as a plane that can increase and decrease both its altitude and speed within certain limits. Embodiment (Figure 18.3)

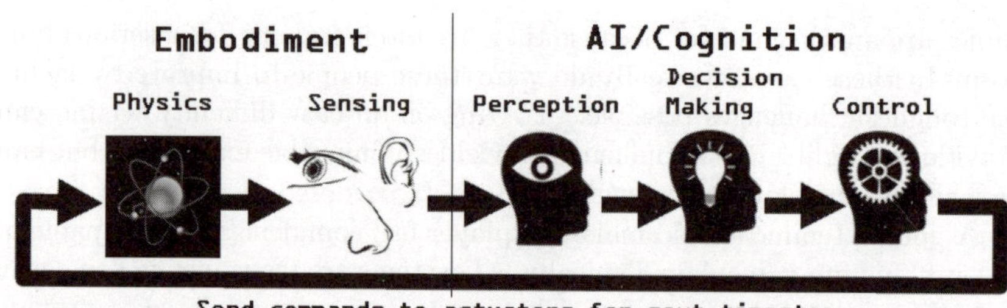

Figure 18.3. A nonplayer character is essentially an embodied autonomous agent, having a physical form (or embodiment) and "brains" (or cognition). AI is about cognition in the form of a character's perception of its world, making decisions toward some goal, and generating control commands based on these decisions. A feedback control describes the continual interaction between a character's cognition and a dynamic, constantly changing environment.

is the only property that separates a robot (with real-world hardware and subject to the true laws of physics) from an NPC (with virtual hardware and subject to programmer-defined physics).

An NPC's embodiment is affected by programmed rules of physics, as discussed in Chapter 15. An embodiment has state, describing its current physical status, and degrees of freedom (DOFs), variables the agent can control to affect the game. Typical state variables include pose (position and orientation), health, score, wealth, supplies, and so forth. Typical DOFs include forward, horizontal, and vertical movement, firing of weapons, casting spells, available moves in a board game, and so on. In our example, the barnstorming plane has two state variables that describe horizontal and vertical position on the screen and two DOFs that control vertical and horizontal speed. The plane's state can be reliably controlled through its DOFs. Although simple for the plane and most other cases, executing an action through a character's DOF can sometimes be a complex issue. For example, a reaching action for a humanoid character often requires inverse kinematics (IK) to convert a desired hand position into angular values for the rotational DOFs at the shoulder, elbow, and wrist joints. When physical simulation is applied to an embodiment (as described in Chapter 15), realizing the desired effects through the DOFs becomes much more complicated due to the uncertainty involved in making predictions about physics. This uncertainty arises because physical forces must be applied at the DOFs to produce movement, and predicting the outcome of forces applied at DOFs can be nontrivial. For this reason, many games use ragdoll physics, where the DOFs are passive and not controlled by an AI.

An agent in the general sense does not necessarily require embodiment. Any decision-making entity with the power to affect the game is an agent.

Examples of disembodied agents include a coach agent for a football game or a hint system for assisting a human player. Disembodied agents indirectly affect the game by provide advice and directions to embodied agents who directly act on the environment. As a minor philosophical point, the human player in games such as *SimCity* could be considered disembodied, unless the player actually represents the city and not its government.

18.3.1 Feedback Control

A *feedback control loop* is one model that allows us to describe the continual interaction between an embodied autonomous agent and a game environment. Embodied agents both affect and are affected by the game environment due to their direct and continual interaction. At any moment in time, an NPC receives information about its world, makes decisions based on this information toward some goal, and then performs an action according to its decisions. The character's action (in part) causes a change to the game state at the next moment of time. Thus, the character's actions have consequences that we call feedback. That is, actions taken by a character (and other characters in their world) directly affect future game states and, consequently, the character's future decisions. Thus, a game agent's behavior is influenced by both previous actions taken and the gameplay dynamics. For example, a first-person shooter agent who is low on health at the current moment might need to first open a door to access a health pack in the near future.

AI engines that use feedback are formally (in terms of control theory) called *closed-loop* systems due to the continual causality arising from agent-environment interaction. Shown in Figure 18.3, closed-loop systems model agent-environment interaction assuming that the characters modulate their behavior based on changes in the world. Many characters use *open-loop control* and act without regard to the state of the world, such as a man-eating plant, flying fish, or Bowser boss enemies in NES *Super Mario Bros.* In such cases, the control loop is broken by having no sensing or perception. Instead, a pipeline is formed starting from the decision maker, who acts only with respect to time, along to physics. A Koopa Troopa (turtle) enemy is mostly open-loop, except that it has a simple closed-loop behavior for reversing direction when bumping into an object. Each driver in *Super Mario Kart* has a closed-loop control system, continually acting in response to road conditions, other drivers, and their position in the race.

A feedback control loop has five primary components: physics, sensing, perception, decision making, and control. Physics and sensing are related to the character's embodiment and environment. Physics (or dynamics) updates the game state based on the character actions (and actions of other characters) and programmed rules of physics. Sensing describes the character's limitations to observe the complete game state. In the barnstorming example, the pilot AI has full observability of the plane's exact 2D screen location. However, the AI has only partial observability of the barnstorming course in that only nearby obstacles can be seen. In contrast, *Pac-Man* agents have full observability over the complete maze and the locations of other agents regardless of their position. In contrast, agents in *DOOM* fully observe information about their own body (health, weapons, ammo), but external information (location, map geometry, enemy locations) are not observed directly and must be inferred from visual perception. Just a side note: The distinction between sensing and perception can be a bit fuzzy. Characters in *The Sims* might have full observability in that they have access to information about all the other agents and entities (such as a toaster across town) in the game implementation. However, these characters choose to not use this information in making decisions, even though they could. It is then the responsibility of the player to tune out his or her inner conspiracy theorist and just have fun.

The AI engine is responsible for three components (perception, decision making, and control) in the control loop.

- **Perception.** The character's estimation of game-related information from sensing. If partial observability applies, perception attempts to "fill in" unobserved game-state information. Even for full observations, perception can guide the *attention* of the AI by eliminating irrelevant information. Perception also applies to estimating other factors that influence the game, such as detecting strategies used by other players.

- **Decision making.** The determination of a course of action from the perceived game state. Decision making is undoubtedly the core component of any game AI and often requires a tradeoff between the accuracy of decisions and the speed involved in their computation. In the barnstorming example, decision making will involve when to fly high and when to fly low. For example, an AI might decide to fly at 300 feet to avoid colliding into an oncoming windmill. Later, we discuss search and theorem-proving as methods for decision making.

- **Control.** The generation of values for the characters' DOFs to execute the decided course of action. Control is mostly an issue for driving of physically simulated characters (see Chapter 15), but techniques such as inverse kinematics (IK) also fit into this context. In the barnstorming example, control would adjust the vertical speed (through a virtual control stick) to move from the current height to 300 feet, the desired height.

- **Learning.** In the form of automatic adaptation by the character, this is typically not one of the components of a control loop. Instead, learning is used to refine and improve the performance of individual components with experience over time. For example, a learning algorithm could help perceive an opposing player's tendencies, evolve characters tailored to the style of a particular human player, or adapt old AI routines to new games. It should be further noted that learning is not a magic black box. The same rules of "garbage in, garbage out" still apply. Grand fantasies of Lt. Data, Kitt, Skynet, and learning not to play *Global Thermonuclear War* (one of the authors showing his age again!) are not coming anytime soon. However, careful application of learning could give your NPCs some interesting adaptive qualities.

18.3.2 The Barnstorming Example

Let's coalesce these notions into a barnstorming example, outlined in the following procedure and illustrated in Figure 18.4. In this example, our AI

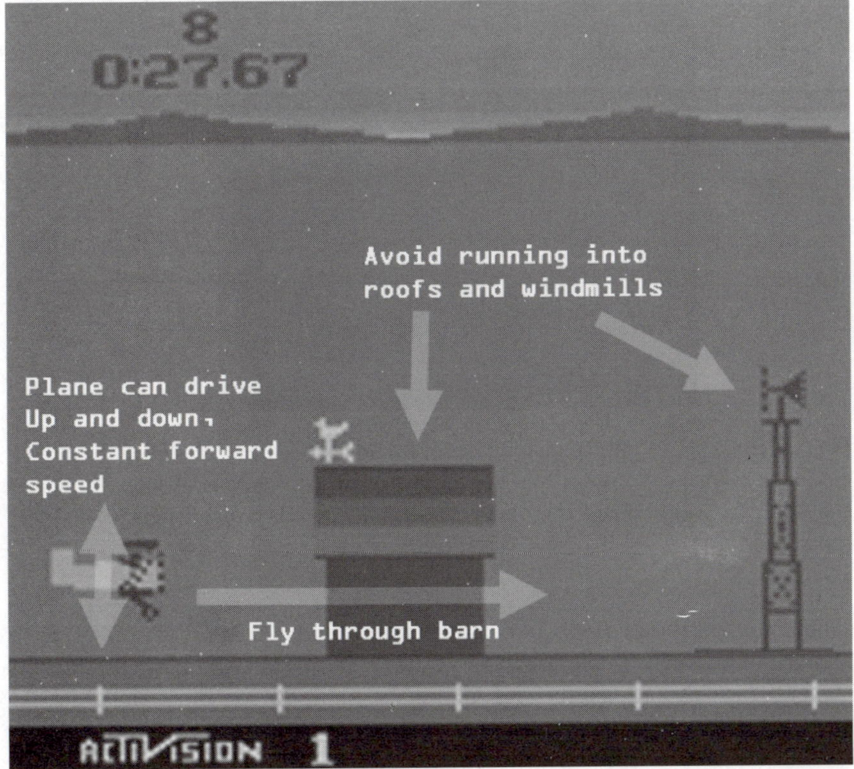

Figure 18.4. Barnstorming example: a player (or AI) tries to dive through barns without hitting windmills or barn roofs.

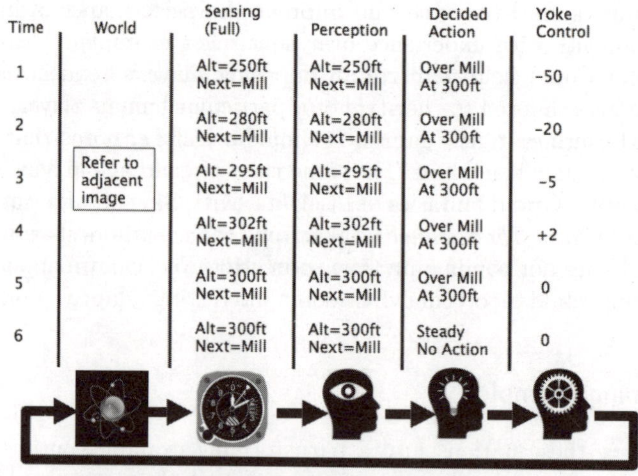

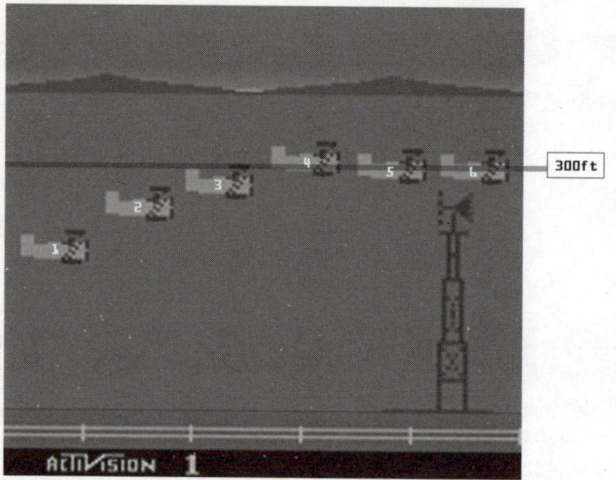

Figure 18.5. Feedback control in the barnstorming example for clearing a windmill. Six iterations shown in terms of variables in each step of the control loop (top) and the resultant trajectory of the plane converging to a clearance height of 300 feet (middle).

should control the plane to both go over windmills (at a height of 300 feet) and go under barns (at a height of 10 feet). Note that when crashes occur, the game assesses a penalty and allows the plane to continue; thus, our AI does not need to explicitly handle such exceptions.

Our AI takes as input an altimeter reading and a set of barns and windmills on the screen. Our perception system identifies the closest oncoming object, which demands our immediate attention. Our decision making is a simple if-else statement that reacts to the oncoming object by choosing one of three actions: diving under the barn, elevating over the windmill, or taking no action. Control acts to minimize the plane's distance with the action's desired height. This control is performed by moving the yolk to a position based on the distance to the desired height. For instance, consider when the windmill is the oncoming object and the plane's height is 250 feet. The "go over windmill" action will be taken, setting the desired height to 300 feet (see Figure 18.5). Over successive iterations, the control routine will move closer to the desired height until it is reached. The following pseudocode illustrates this closed-loop controller.

```
ACTION_TYPE * function AI_policy(STATE_TYPE *s)
  ACTION_TYPE *a = malloc(ACTION_TYPE);
  COMMENT: ... do something smart with s to set a ...
  AI_policy_procedure(s,a);
  return a;

AI_policy procedure(state is [objects,altimeter],
                    action is [throttle,yolk])
{
   LOCAL VARIABLES: oncoming_object, decided_action

   *** Perception ***
   set oncoming_object to nearest object ahead of the plane

   *** Decision Making ***
   if oncoming_object == barn
     then set decided_action to ``dive under barn''
   otherwise if oncoming_object == windmill
     then set decided_action to ``go over windmill''
   otherwise set decided_action to ``steady''

   *** Control ***
   if decided_action is ``dive under barn''
     then set yolk = 10ft-altimeter
     COMMENT: push yolk away to dive toward 10ft
   if decided_action is ``go over windmill''
     then set yolk = altimeter-300ft
     COMMENT: pull yolk closer to elevate toward 300ft
   if action is ``no action''
     then set yolk = 0.0
   set throttle to ``slow''
   COMMENT: assume constant forward speed
}
```

Note that this AI policy is functional but not the best possible choice. This policy considers only the closest oncoming object and thus will not work well with objects that are spaced close together. For instance, if a barn were immediately followed by a windmill, diving under the barn would most certainly lead to crashing into the windmill. It would be best to skip this barn because its positive benefits are outweighed by the negative ramifications of crashing into the windmill.

18.4 Decision Making: Reaction and Deliberation

Decision making is undoubtedly the most critical component of a game's AI. Every NPC must make decisions to play smartly, or at least to give the human player the illusion of competence. At the most abstract level, decision making involves crafting a policy, which is a function that takes as input the agent's belief about the current game state and outputs a course of action. We can state a policy D functionally as $a = D(s)$, where s is the perceived game state and a is an action. In the barnstorming example, s is the plane's height and the oncoming object, and a sets the plane's desired height based on the oncoming object.

The nuts and bolts of decision making revolve around picking appropriate algorithms and representations that will produce smart behavior. The spectrum of decision-making techniques vary from deliberation to reaction, each having respective benefits and shortcomings. This distinction can be roughly categorized as "Think hard, then act!" versus "React! Don't think!" Figure 18.6 illustrates this spectrum and related techniques. Note that this is not a hard distinction. Many techniques use some combination of deliberation and reaction.

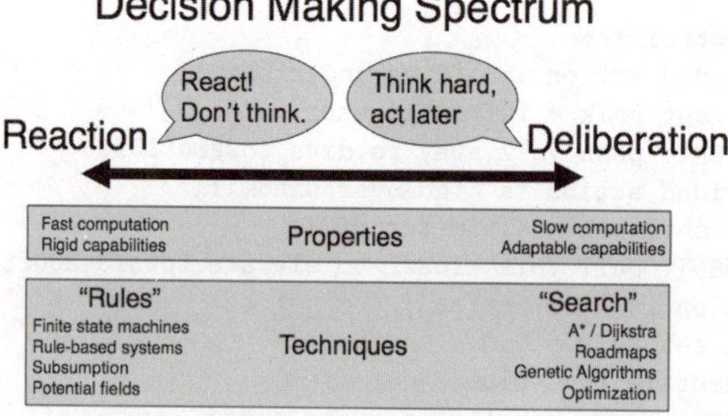

Figure 18.6. Feedback iterations for the barnstorming example.

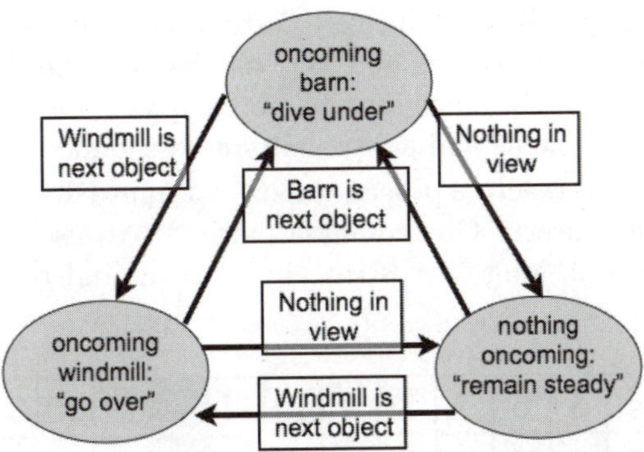

Figure 18.7. Our simple barnstorming controller could be stated as this reactive finite state machine.

Reactive techniques emphasize quick decision making, often using a structured set of rules. Such rules are often manually crafted with specific scenarios in mind. As a result, the quality of reactive decision making is typically rigid, working well mostly in situations envisioned by the programmer. Reactive policies are typically expressed as a finite state machine (FSM), although expert and rule-based systems are other means to express similar reactive behavior. An FSM is a model of discrete states and associated actions. FSM states are a categorization of situations the agent could encounter in the game world. FSM actions are the agent's response to being in a certain state and will result in a transition to the same or another state. Our barnstorming policy is a purely reactive example and can be stated as an FSM, as illustrated in Figure 18.7. The barnstorming FSM has states for each oncoming object (barn, windmill, none) and actions to respectively react to each state ("dive under barn," "go over windmill," "steady").

Reactive policies are typically well suited for highly scripted behavior, such as in executing a specific fighting strategy, athletic play, or car-driving task. Reaction also works well for background characters and group/crowd control with low computational overhead, such as flocking behaviors with birds, football offensive linemen, and pedestrians in cities.

In contrast, deliberative techniques emphasize making the best possible decisions by searching across all possibilities. Search algorithms are the main tool in the "sense-plan-act" loop for deliberation. Deliberative algorithms *sense/perceive* sufficiently complete models of the world, *plan* search over all possible future situations that would result from taking various sequences of actions, and *act* by executing the best course of action. Each possible outcome is evaluated with respect to some score, or metric of success, and the best outcome is selected. For example, *pathfinding* (Figure 18.8) is a common search task for navigating an NPC to a specific location in a level. Such search procedures can be prohibitively costly due to the large (exponential) number of potential outcomes and actions that can be taken. However, deliberation provides the flexibility to perform well for a large variety of decision-making problems and adaptability across games.

Deliberative and reactive procedures are not mutually exclusive and can often be used in concert. One common pairing is to use deliberative techniques for high-level, long-term strategic planning and reactive techniques

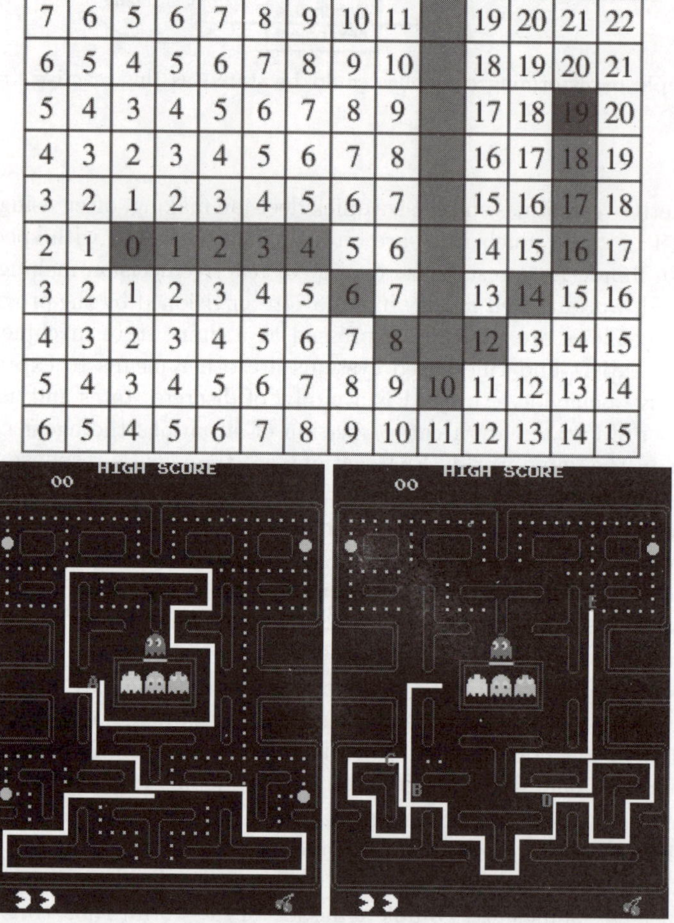

Figure 18.8. (Top) Pathfinding between a start and goal location on a 2D grid is a common example of deliberative decision making. (Bottom) The "cherry pattern" is an example of a planned path one could could follow to beat *Pac-Man*, with the caveat that the path is known ahead of time and not computed during the game. (Image courtesy of mameworld.net)

Figure 18.9. NPCs in *F.E.A.R.* combine FSMs and planning for highly adaptive enemies that leverage their environment and tactical elements. (Image courtesy of Vivendi Universal)

for responding to immediate, time-critical situations. Another deliberative-reactive strategy is to have multiple decision making working in parallel and then combine (through "arbitration" or "fusion") these decisions into a collective action. Monolith's *F.E.A.R.* (Figure 18.9) is widely acclaimed for using both FSMs and two forms of deliberative planning: STRIPS planning for problem solving and A* search for navigation (both of which are described later in this chapter). The result is that highly adaptive and inventive enemies take advantage of various facets of their environment (crawlspaces, windows, ladders, taking cover), as well as discovering tactics for surprise attacks.

Regardless of the technique used, two main aspects are involved in decision making.

- **Knowledge representation.** How do you represent knowledge about the task, the game environment, other characters, and so on? This aspect is about defining the space of possible states and integrating perceived information.

- **Action selection.** How do you find actions that will enable goals to be met? Some combination of deliberation and reaction is often used to perform action selection.

18.4.1 Knowledge Representation

Knowledge representation pertains to how your agent will store and structure information such that it can be appropriately processed. A knowledge representation defines an agent's *state space*, the set of all possible states the agent will consider. (An agent's state space may not necessarily be the same as the game's state space.) A good representation will allow for the agent's objectives to be expressed as goal states in its state space. Decision making is essentially about finding a way to get from the agent's current state to a goal state. The problem with knowledge representation is that devising a single definition to cover all tasks of interest is difficult and would probably be diving deeply into the philosophy of AI. However, several practical representations have been long established for specific tasks. In the barnstorming example, the knowledge representation is composed of two variables: the type of oncoming object and the plane's height. This representation is quite small, allowing for easy crafting of a set of reactive decision-making rules.

For deliberative search-based decision making, a *decision tree* is the typical knowledge representation of choice. Described in Section 7.5.1, the agent's current state is the root node of the decision tree and has a child for each action it could take from this state. From these children, actions can be taken to produce possible states for another level of children and so on. Once the decision tree has been constructed, the best course of action is prescribed by finding the path (or sequence of connected nodes) that connects the root node to the best outcome.

A situational calculus representation is suited for high-level problem solving using predicate logic. Expressing "situations" as mathematically logical expressions, how do we logically prove we get from our current situation to a goal situation? Two types of functions, fluents and actions, are used to model the game world as logical expressions. Fluents are "true or false" (or Boolean) statements about properties of the world in a given state. For example, $at(home, S)$ would return "true" if my agent is at home in a particular state S and "false" if not. If we want to have dinner at home, an additional fluent $have(food, S)$ with the logical AND operator $\wedge$ could be used to ask whether my agent both has food and is at home: $have(food, S) \wedge at(home, S)$.

Similarly, actions logically map current situations to future situations and allow us, using fluents, to state the consequences of certain actions. Actions are logical operators commonly expressed using the STRIPS (Stanford Research Institute Problem Solver) language as preconditions (expressions that must be true for the action to be performed) and postconditions (what will be true after the action is performed). Postconditions are often split into deletions (true conditions that will become false) and additions (false conditions that will become true). For example, "doing" dinner $do(dinner(food, home), S)$ in state S requires a dinner action with preconditions $have(food, S) \wedge at(home, S)$, deletion $have(food)$, and addition $\sim need(food)$. If the preconditions are met, then let's eat! Otherwise, a few other actions are needed, such as $move(end, start)$ and $buy(food)$, to have dinner, expressed as

$$do(dinner(food, home), do(move(home, do(buy(food, do(move(store, home), S)))))).$$

A waypoint graph is another popular knowledge representation, often used for pathfinding and navigation. Pathfinding is a common AI task for navigating in a game world. In pathfinding, such as in *Pac-Man* (Figure 18.8), the agent's objective is to navigate to a specific goal location (or a set of desirable locations) from its current position. (Note that we do not discuss how goal states are selected, as this highly depends on the nature of the game.) To navigate, an AI must find paths, preferably the shortest path, in the waypoint graph between its current and goal locations. Waypoints are specific locations in the game world, represented as nodes in the graph. A pair of waypoints are connected by edges if the character can directly travel between them. A path is found by chaining together a set of waypoints that form a connecting path for traveling to the goal.

18.4.2 Shortest-Path Search

Unlike a decision tree, a waypoint graph can contain cycles and thus requires different algorithms to find suitable paths for navigation—namely, the shortest-path search. When pathfinding, there may be many paths that will lead to the goal, with some paths being better than others. Simple search algorithms, such as breadth-first search or depth-first search, can easily find a valid but suboptimal waypoint path. For instance, depth-first search could return a path that visits all the other waypoints before reaching the goal. Defining *optimality* is one way to search for the "best" path rather than just a valid path. We typically define the optimal path as the shortest path to the goal. Assuming every pair of connected waypoints has an associated cost (e.g., distance), the shortest path will be the waypoint path that incurs the lowest cost.

Dijkstra's algorithm is useful for finding the shortest path between a location and all the other waypoints. Starting from the agent's current location, Dijkstra visits every waypoint by following their connections and tabulating the shortest path to each waypoint along the way. For each waypoint visited, the algorithm determines whether or not this waypoint offers a cheaper shortest path to each of its connected waypoints and accordingly adjusts their shortest path.

One problem with Dijkstra and the simpler search algorithms is that, at worst, every waypoint and its connections must be analyzed by the search algorithm. As the number of waypoints grows, the search time increases. If many waypoints are present, the search process may take too much processor time and resources to be interactive. These computational problems are further confounded in that whenever the world changes, the search must restart. Algorithms such as A* search address this speed issue by considering only paths that show promise for being good solutions. A* is essentially Dijkstra's algorithm that chooses which waypoints to explore by both the cost to the waypoint and guess/estimation about the waypoint's cost to the goal. The guess is usually based on the straight-line (Euclidean) distance between the waypoint and the goal. An example of A* pathfinding on a 2D grid is shown in Figure 18.8.

```
def A-star(start,goal):
    var closed := ``the empty set''
    var q := make_queue(path(start))
    while q ``is not empty''
        var p := remove_first(q)
        var x := ``the last node of p''
        if x in closed
            continue
        if x = goal
            return p
        ``add x to closed''
        foreach y in successors(x)
            enqueue(q, p, y)
    return failure
```

Listing 18.1. A* search pseudocode (from *Wikipedia*)

18.4.3 Potential Fields and Local Optimization

Shortest-path search is a good option when pathfinding a waypoint graph of reasonable size. However, other perfectly good methods for pathfinding do not require a waypoint graph, such as probabilistic road maps (which create new nodes and edges for a waypoint graph) and Voronoi planning (to map a space topologically). One method in particular, potential fields, lets us think of decision making as a reactive local optimization. Potential fields treat the world as a collection of attractors, which the agent wants to move toward, and repellors, from which the agent wants to stay away. Goal states are attractors; enemies, walls, and other obstacles are often repellors.

Each attractor/repellor exerts an influence on the agent as a gradient, or velocity vector, analogous to a force acting on a particle. (Newtonian models of physics for forces acting on particles is covered in Chapter 15.) The influence of each attractor/repellor can be visualized as a height field over locations in the environment. In this height landscape, repellors rise to high altitudes, attractors sink to low altitudes, and the goal state has the lowest altitude. If phrased appropriately, the collective attraction and repulsion potentials that are acting on the agent will, eventually, move it down the height field to the goal location. This height field interpretation casts potential fields as a gradient-descent technique.

Because they are reactive, potential fields are very fast decision makers but are susceptible to problems with local minima. Potential fields can be faster than shortest-path searches because their time complexity is a factor of the number of attractors and repellors rather than the number of waypoints and edges. However, shortest-path search probably guarantees the best global path will be found, whereas potential fields can be stuck in a suboptimal local minimum. This local minimum problem can be solved by performing wavefront planning before each movement along the potential fields. Using wavefront planning in this manner, however, will likely require much longer computation time than shortest-path search.

18.4.4 Problem Solving and Theorem Proving

Like navigation, general problem solving is about making decisions to get from a current to a goal state. Navigation is a specific case of problem solving, using cases where the knowledge representation (state space and operators) are naturally defined in terms of moving through the open space of an environment. More generally, knowledge could be represented using a situational calculus (described following), where logical expressions define situations and logical operators define actions and their consequences. In this scenario, we can treat a goal situation as a theorem to prove, given the current situation and provided action operators. Each step of the proof is a change in situation caused by a single-action operator. Using search procedures such as those just described, a valid course of action exists if the goal theorem can be proved.

The Towers of Hanoi (see Figure 18.10) is a canonical example of theorem proving for problem solving. In this game, the disks on the leftmost peg must all be moved to the rightmost peg. Only one disk can be moved to another peg at a single time, and a larger disk cannot be placed on top of a smaller disk. Objects in this domain are N disks ($d_1 \ldots d_N$) with increasing radius and 3 pegs ($p_1 \ldots p_3$). Fluents are $on(x, y)$ to ask whether object x is on object y, $smaller(x, y)$ for relative object proportions, and $clear(x)$ to ask if object x is the top object on its peg. A single action, $move(x, y, z)$, moves object x from a source object y on top of another object z. This action has preconditions as this logical expression: $clear(x) \wedge on(x, y) \wedge clear(z) \wedge smaller(x, z)$, with additions $on(x, z) \wedge clear(z)$ and deletions $on(x, y) \wedge clear(z)$. For the case with four disks, the initial condition is

Figure 18.10. *The Towers of Hanoi* is an example of using theorem proving to automatically solve a game.

$on(d_1, d_2) \wedge on(d_2, d_3) \wedge on(d_3, d_4) \wedge on(d_4, p_1) \wedge clear(p_2) \wedge clear(p_3)$, and the goal to be proved is $on(d_1, d_2) \wedge on(d_2, d_3) \wedge on(d_3, d_4) \wedge on(d_4, p_3)$. Given the problem stated in this logic, search routines such as depth-first searches (but hopefully something smarter) can continually try various sequences of actions until they reaching goal condition. We know it will reach the goal eventually because such puzzles have already been proven (by human mathematicians) to have solutions, but this is not the case for all logical problems.

Similar to other approaches to deliberation, theorem proving is equivalent to thinking of scenarios as nodes in a graph, thinking of actions as edges, and using a search to find a path to the goal. Using problem solving in this manner is not really an algorithmic challenge but rather a knowledge-representation issue. Search procedures are the engines that makes problem solving go, but knowledge representation is the fuel. Thus, one must be careful to craft representations that properly reflect the domain. For example, *The Towers of Hanoi* example will fail without a fluent for $smaller()$ and may have difficulty finding a solution with irrelevant actions, such as $spin\_on\_peg()$. Similarly for NPCs, they will not be able to reason on information not contained in fluents. Duck and cover makes no sense if your character does not have information about what can be used for projection or whether they are being fired upon.

18.5 Learning

How do AI systems learn from past experience and observable phenomenon? The answer to this question lies in the topic of *machine learning*, the extraction of rules and patterns from data. Despite common conceptions, learning is not a black-box solution that will just work. Instead, learning is about

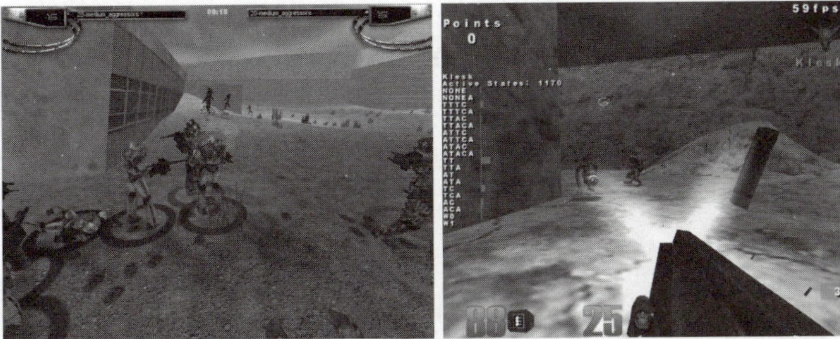

Figure 18.11. Screenshots of games using learning: (left) the *NERO* (Neuro Evolving Robotic Operatives) game using neural networks for training and evolving group combat behavior and (right) *Q-Boltz Millennium Wars*, a class project by Taylor and Lees that uses reinforcement learning with *Quake Bots*. (Left image courtesy of Ken Stanley)

statistical computation, using mathematical procedures to model, extract, and predict the properties in data. When used in the proper context, learning can be a valuable tool that allows your agents to refine their behavior over time and adapt to new constraints in the game world. In Figure 18.11, the Stanleys' *NERO* project and various projects with *Quake Bots* (using methods such as Soar and Q-learning) have demonstrated that careful application of learning and cognitive architectures can significantly improve game AI performance.

For many good reasons, machine-learning techniques are underutilized in current games, but they have the potential to bring a renaissance in game AI. Simple approaches to learning, such as nearest-neighbor algorithms, are trivial to implement and can yield reasonable accuracy. These algorithms, however, often produce erratic behavior when the amount of training data is insufficient and can require prohibitively long periods of time to properly train. Machine-learning research offers many mathematically sophisticated methods to improve learning performance but with computational costs that are too great for most games. In several cases where learning fails, it is not necessarily a problem with the learning algorithm itself but rather how the algorithm is used. Expecting a neural network to learn in the same manner as a human being will only lead to frustration. We have yet to develop algorithms that perform anywhere close to the accuracy and generalizability of humans. Further, the true nature of exact computations occurring in the human brain have yet to be clearly defined.

The three basic forms of learning algorithms are supervised learning, reinforcement learning, and unsupervised learning. Understanding their distinctions will help you to select the right tool for your purposes. Supervised learning is about learning functions $f(x) = y$ that map inputs x to outputs y from a collection of data pairs (X, Y). Unsupervised learning is for finding models that represent data X for compression, clustering, or frequency analysis. Reinforcement learning is used explicitly for learning decision-making policies based on receiving rewards, sort of like a continual game of "getting warmer, getting colder."

18.5.1 Supervised Learning

Supervised learning is probably the most important class of learning algorithms for games. These algorithms are suited to function approximation—that is, estimating the function $f(x) = y$ that generated a given set of input-output pairs (X, Y). Why is this useful? Once a function is learned, new inputs x' can be evaluated to predict a potential output $\hat{y}'$. For decision making, a policy D is a function $D(s) = a$, mapping input states s to output actions a. Consider the example of play calling for an American football game (see Figure 18.12). If we often compete against an opponent with relatively consistent play calling, a learned function could predict opponent

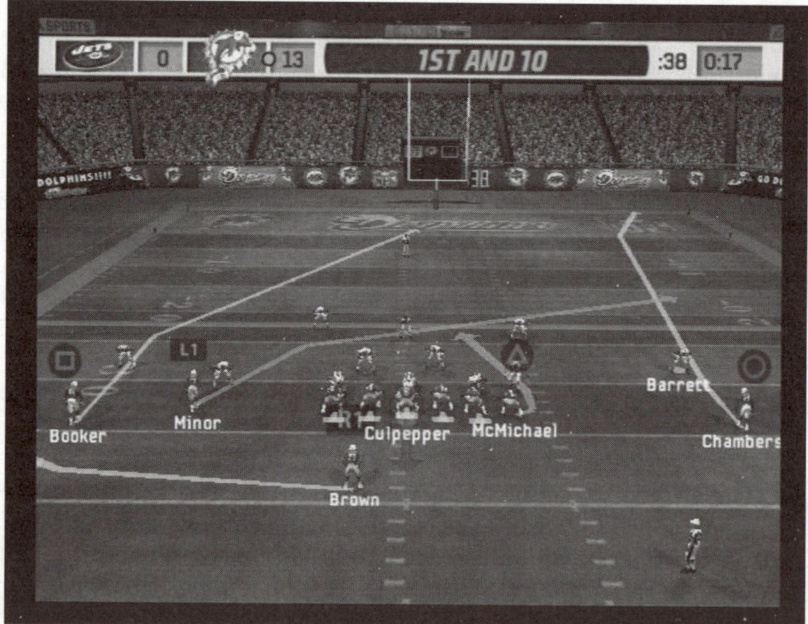

Figure 18.12. Play calling for American football games, such as EA's *Madden*, are an opportune place to learn what plays work in certain scenarios or the play-selection habits of certain opponents. (Image courtesy of Electronic Arts, Inc.)

play calls from game situations. For instance, we might be able to learn that a given player might always call a specific pass play on third downs with four yards to go, and thus our agent can choose an appropriate defense to counter. Such a predictive ability could be a considerable advantage and could also be applied to adversarial encounters for first-person shooters (such as in *Quake Bots*), tennis, and fighting games, as well as behavior cloning: copying the behavior of a player.

Supervised learning breaks down into classes of algorithms: *classification* into one of N output categories and *regression* with multidimensional real-valued outputs. Classification involves learning decision boundaries that partition input data into distinct sets. Regression can be performed by fitting known functions, such as linear $f(x) = ax + b$ or quadratic $f(x) = ax^2 + b$ functions, to all or various parts of the data. In this case, fitting refers to finding model parameters (e.g., a and b) that minimize the error in accurately predicting the output of each training pair.

Neural networks, in their standard formulation, are a form of supervised learning. A neural network is a collection of functions with a known form and parameterization. Each node in a neural network is functional, mapping its inputs into an output that can be used as an input by other nodes. Collectively, these nodes are working together to map training inputs into the network to match training targets. Learning occurs in neural networks, using algorithms such as backpropagation, by finding parameters for all nodes that minimize the prediction error of the network.

Nearest-neighbor methods perform classification and regression without a model by simply looking at the outputs of neighbors. k-nearest neighbor techniques predict the output of a new input point x' by finding the training points with the k most similar inputs and using these training outputs to predict the output $\hat{y}'$. Note that each training data point $x_i \in \Re^N$ has an integer label y_i and the same dimensionality as the test point $x' \in \Re^N$. When training data are plentiful, nearest-neighbor methods yield usable results but have noticeable discontinuities in their decision boundaries and approximated functions. Kernel methods, such as support vector machines (see Figure 18.13) and Gaussian processes, are more advanced versions of nearest neighbors that yield smoother (or *regularized*) and more accurate predictions at the cost of significant computation for optimization.

```
def nearest_neighbor_classify(X,Y,x'):
Compute Euclidean distance between x' and all points in X
Find k training points with the smallest distance to x'
Set y' as a the label most common among nearest neighbors
Return y'
```

Listing 18.2. Nearest-neighbor classifier pseudocode.

Figure 18.13. The support vector machine is a popular technique for supervised classification, as illustrated. This spiral data set consists of dark and light points in 2D that are separated into "dark" and "light" regions by a support vector machine. (Image courtesy of Jonathon C. Lau)

18.5.2 Reinforcement Learning

One limitation of supervised learning is the expectation that a single input will uniquely map to a single output. This limitation can be overly restrictive in many decision-making scenarios. In our football play–calling example, a given opponent might tend to call one of four plays in "third and four" scenarios. Obviously, it's good to know that four plays out of the (potentially) hundreds of plays are favored. However, if our predictions are wrong 75 percent of the time, learning will be detrimental to our agent's decision making. Further, if our predictions are consistently good, a human opponent will eventually adjust his or her play calling over time toward a new, more effective strategy. If the learned function does not correspondingly adapt, the agent will become easier to defeat over repeated play.

Reinforcement learning methods address both issues of nonfunctional mappings and adaptation over time for decision-making policies. Instead, learning a functional policy $D(s) = a$ directly, reinforcement learning can estimate a *value function* $Q(s, a) = v$. The value function states the *expected value* v of taking action a in state s. When in a particular state, an agent can examine the relative value of taking each action, which, when normalized, form a probability distribution. This distribution over actions allows the agent to account for multiple possible action outputs. Value functions can be instantiated into specific policies by selecting the "best" action in each state or selecting randomly weighted actions by the values in Q. In contrast to the offline batch processing of supervised learning, reinforcement learning is an *online* procedure, continually updating the value function based on rewards. Similar to scoring metrics in minimax, a reward function evaluates the immediate value of the agent's current state, yielding a scalar reward. Using algorithms such as *Q-learning* or *SARSA*, immediate rewards are used to update the expected value of the previous action just taken. In this respect, each decision made by the agent is a new piece of data that is autonomously generated and immediately incorporated into the learning process. Because reinforcement learning never ends, it is often faced with an "exploration versus exploitation" tradeoff—that is, should the agent make decisions to optimally exploit its current value function or make suboptimal decisions in the hope of finding a better value function.

```
def q_learning(p,g):
Enforce learning rate p is between 0 and 1
Enforce reward discount g is between 0 and 1
Initialize a 2D array for Q(s,a)
s = ''current character state''
while ''the character is active''
  Choose an action a from Q for the current state s
  Execute action a
  Observe the character's new state s' and reward r
  Update Q(s,a):
  Q(s,a) := Q(s,a) + p * (r + g max[a'](Q(s',a') - Q(s,a)))
end
return Q
```

Listing 18.3. Q-learning pseudocode.

Reinforcement learning is modeled formally as a Markov decision process (MDP). MDPs not only account for uncertainty in decision making (by learning value functions) but also uncertainty in executing actions by learning transition functions. A partially observable MDP (POMDP) additionally accounts for perceptual uncertainty in an agent's ability to estimate its current state. Although POMDPs provide a sound and general model for autonomous learning, it is often computationally intractable to apply.

Genetic algorithms, as used (potentially) by games like *Spore*, are often a specific instantiation of reinforcement learning. Genetic algorithms were popularized by the seminal *Evolving Virtual Creatures* work by Karl Sims in the 1990s [Sims 94]. In one aspect of this work, Sims evolved creatures both physically and mentally for playing competitive block capture, as shown in

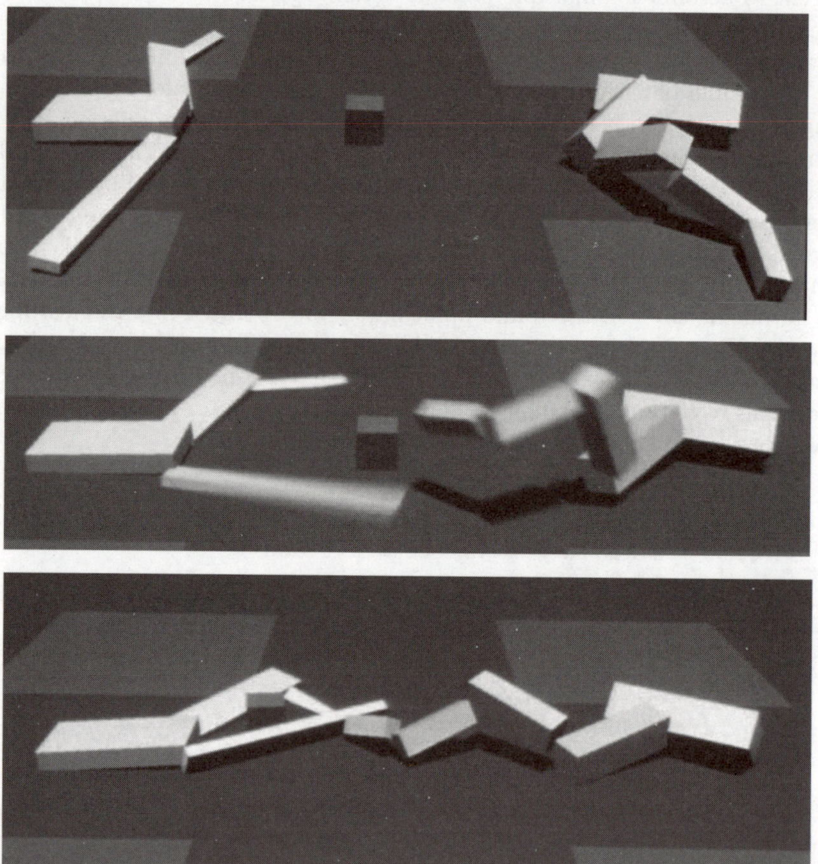

Figure 18.14. Snapshots for Karl Sims's *Evolving Virtual Creatures* work [Sims 94], where creatures would evolve their bodies and control algorithms toward the objective of taking a block from other creatures in competitions. The goal of each player in a match is to possess the block on his side of the environment when time elapses. (Images courtesy of Karl Sims)

Figure 18.14. The physical form and control algorithm of each creature is described by a string representing its DNA. A population of creatures was maintained and constantly competed against each other to determine their "fitness." Fit creatures would be kept and used to create future generations through genetic operators, such as mutation and crossovers (reproduction by combining strings from two separate creatures). Unfit creatures would die out in future generations. At its time of publication, this groundbreaking work utilized both (the now common) physical simulation to govern the character's motion during competitions and learning through genetic algorithms.

Genetic algorithms are related to policy gradient search procedures. Policy gradient methods iteratively search over the space of possible policies to find the most likely policy instead of estimating the expected value of actions. Genetic algorithms rephrase this search into an evolutionary framework, where a "fitness function" rewards better policies and evolutionary operations (such as mutation and crossover) to autonomously explore.

18.5.3 Unsupervised Learning

Unlike supervised and reinforcement learning, unsupervised learning algorithms are given training data consisting only of inputs X with unknown outputs Y from an unknown function $y = f(x)$. These algorithms must determine how to label each datum given data input with predicted functional output. A histogram is one of the simplest forms of unsupervised learning that models the frequency of encountering a given type of input data. For example, the table at the end of a stage in *Dance Dance Revolution* that lists the number of steps performed at different levels of accuracy is a histogram. A win-loss record is an even simpler type of histogram. A histogram is a specific instance of density estimation for estimating and predicting the probability of observing some event. If a histogram sufficiently represents data probabilities, this information could be used to adjust various properties of the game. For (infamous) computer assistance procedures, histograms can be used to identify situations where a player is having difficulty and could use a helping hand.

Clustering is the unsupervised classification of data points into different groups. It is often a preprocessing step to provide output labels for supervised classification procedures to learn decision boundaries.

Dimension reduction is another form of unsupervised learning that is useful for data compression. Dimension reduction is about finding outputs that accurately represent data (such as high-resolution textures and geometry) but with significantly lower dimensionality, thus allowing more data to be stored with less memory. Principal components analysis (PCA) is a standard method for linear-dimension reduction, which essentially fits a high-dimensional ellipsoid to a data set. The largest axes of the ellipsoid form the new lower-dimensional coordinates for the data.

18.6 Exercises

1. Create FSMs that describe existing NPC enemies. Pick five enemies that appear in first-person shooter games. For each of these NPCs, draw a graph that describes the basic states of the character and the transitions between these states.

2. Implement a pathfinding character. Create a program with a binary 2D array (or grid world), where a "0" is an open space and a "1" is a barrier, that takes as input start and goal locations. Write an A* routine to perform pathfinding on this grid. How does this compare to other search methods?

3. Using the *Quake Bots* engine, implement two NPCs: one that uses an FSM that you outlined previously and one that uses A* pathfinding. Let the NPCs fight up to 100 engagements. How well did the strategies work relative to each other? Can you create an NPC that uses both A* and an FSM?

4. Using your existing grid world program, implement a Q-learning procedure for navigation. Use the grid location as the state variable s and "up/down/left/right" as actions. Give the learner 200–1000 trials for finding a fixed goal location from random start locations. Does the navigation performance improve? What does the $Q(s, a)$ function look like?

5. Port your Q-learning routine to a *Quake Bots* NPC. How do you represent the NPCs state? What actions can the NPC take? Can an array representing this Q-function be stored in memory? Could this array be stored more efficiently? Let your learning NPC play against your FSM player for 250 engagements. Does the learner improve over time? What could you do to initialize the Q-function to make learning occur faster?

6. Watch your friends play an American football game over several hours. Record how many times they choose a specific play and formation for each down and yardage situation. Do you see a pattern? Try recording what pitches your friends tend to throw in a baseball game for certain ball-strike counts or what moves they tend to use in a fighter. Could you write a routine to predict their behavior?

18.7 Resources

- Russell and Norvig, *Artificial Intelligence: A Modern Approach* [Russell and Norvig 95].
- Laird and van Lent, "Machine Learning for Computer Games" [Laird and van Lent 05].
- Laird and Duchi, "Creating Human-like Synthetic Characters with Multiple Skill Levels: A Case Study using the Soar Quakebot" [Laird and Duchi 00].
- Bishop, *Pattern Recognition and Machine Learning* [Bishop 07].
- Duda, Hart, and Stork, *Pattern Classification* [Duda et al. 00].
- Stanley, Bryant, Karpov, and Miikkulainen, "Real-Time Evolution of Neural Networks in the NERO Video Game" [Stanley et al. 06].
- Orkin, "Three States and a Plan: The AI of F.E.A.R." [Orkin 06].
- Bourg and Seemann, *AI for Game Developers* [Bourg and Seemann 04].
- Buckland, *Programming Game AI By Example* [Buckland 04].
- Schwab, *AI Game Engine Programming* [Schwab 04].

CHAPTER 19

Social Issues

19.1 Ratings and Content

> Violence has always been and remains a central interest of humankind and a recurrent, even obsessive, theme of culture both high and low. It engages the interest of children from an early age, as anyone familiar with the classic fairy tales collected by Grimm, Andersen, and Perrault are aware. To shield children right up to the age of 18 from exposure to violent descriptions and images would not only be quixotic, but deforming; it would leave them unequipped to cope with the world as we know it.
>
> —Judge Posner, U.S. Court of Appeals [Schiesel 07]

Sex, violence, and the gender gap are the three most important and visible social issues relating to games today. These issues are not unique to games; people are and always have been concerned with the impact of *all* media on society, particularly how it affects children.

When discussing the psychological impact of content, it is important to realize that not all content is intended for or available to all audiences. Films, some printed materials (such as pornography), and most drug (e.g., alcohol, tobacco, and prescription medications) sales are restricted by state and national regulations to ensure that potentially inappropriate materials are not consumed by children. In most countries, games are also rated into age-appropriate categories based on violence, sex, and drug content. The rating systems and methods for preventing inappropriate sales to minors vary between countries. In the United States, ratings are by the independent Entertainment Software Rating Board (ESRB), based on information disclosed by developers, and sales are voluntarily restricted to those categories by stores. See Hyman's article [Hyman 05a] for a summary of the process in the U.S. and other countries.

19.1.1 Why Sex and Violence?

It is a common misperception that sexuality and violence are pervasive in video (if not board) games. This might be because these sensational and emotional issues create interesting material for newspaper articles and convenient rallying points in political debates. Although many games have themes implicitly drenched in sex and violence, protagonist Lara Croft's oversexed physique in *Tomb Raider* and the violence from *Grand Theft Auto III* are not representative of the level of sexual and violent content in games as a whole. In practice, most games have ratings and content roughly equivalent to the film PG rating, since child-safe content is more marketable (due to a broader audience) than mature content. Developers tend to intentionally tone down to have their games rated appropriately for everyone, or at least teens. Games with the ESRB Mature rating, like the MPAA NC-17 rating, are considered unmarketable by publishers and are not even stocked by most game stores.

True games (as opposed to sandbox experiences like *The Sims* and toys) are about conflict. Sex not only helps to advertise games and titillate the player, but it also creates a motivation for conflict—for example, with the Mario cliche of the captive princess. Violence is a method for resolving conflict. Juul [Juul 05] observes that violence and death are easy to quantify, and therefore are a good fit for game mechanisms that depend on quantitative interactions. Furthermore, most games are also descended from true military war games [Perla 90], so violence is unsurprisingly part of that provenance.

Advances in AI and physics technology should therefore enable more nonviolent games, since they increase the ways of interacting with the environment and characters beyond attacking them. We are seeing the beginning of this trend with increasing physics-based gameplay—for example, in *World of Goo*—and in social interaction—for example, in *Harvest Moon*.

19.1.2 Are Virtual Sex and Violence Harmful?

As parents of small children, as well as game developers and scientists, both of the authors of this book believe it is important for parents to control the play experiences of their children. Moreover, we see the discussion of the effects of virtual experiences on people as being separate from the discussion of whether those experiences should exist. It is natural to draw a connection between children, play, and games, since children spend much of their time playing games. However, the most interesting games produced by the industry and discussed in this book are not intended for children. So if games affect the psychological outlook of the player, that does not mean that games should not contain material that is inappropriate for children. It just means that parents need to exercise care (and receive help from the industry) in which games their children play, with whom, and when.

Many have argued for and against a causal relationship between real-world violence and in-game violence. The statistics are inconclusive. The *Economist* credibly claimed no significant relationship based on the fact that "in America, violent crime actually fell sharply in the 1990s, just as the use of video and computer games was taking off" [Economist 05], but we are also faced with frequent anecdotal evidence to the contrary. Many scientific studies have concluded one way or the other, but there is no general consensus. (Nonetheless, we think that most parents take a "common sense" view that five-year-olds should not be playing *God of War*'s bloodthirsty fight scenes or sex slave minigames). Thus, the issue remains undecided, and more research is needed on the impact of game content on both children and adults.

Stepping back from psychology to art, one can make a different argument. A game cannot be a meaningful art form and cultural relic *unless* it does affect the player significantly. The films most often considered the best, such as *The 400 Blows* and *Apocalypse Now*, contain sexual and violent themes that profoundly affect the viewer. So developers who are seeking to promote gaming as an art form should be arguing for and attempting to create a causal relationship between in-game experiences and out-of-game actions. Of course, that relationship should not be one where in-game violence and sexual acts lead players to increase out-of-game violence and dangerous promiscuity. Instead, it should be one where violence and sex, like other emotionally charged events, are used as tools to make the player think about his or her role in society and the implications of certain actions.

19.1.3 Women and Games

Most game developers are men, and most game players are women. The latter statistic is shocking to some because it goes against conventional wisdom. Overall, women tend to play more casual and free games such as *Scrabble*, *Bejeweled*, and *Minesweeper*. Because these games are rarely considered in the public consciousness that defines games as hardcore experiences like *Half-Life 2*, there is some reason for the conventional wisdom to be the opposite of the actual statistics.

Regarding the gender gap in players, why should we care that many hardcore action and strategy games appeal more to men than to women and that 75 to 85 percent of games sales are to male consumers [Cassell and Jenkins 00]? Cassell and Jenkins argue that because most games are designed primarily to appeal to young men, young women are less familiar with and less encouraged to explore the technology that in turn leads to a measurable technology literacy gap in technology-related fields. Do many hardcore games appeal to men because men are better at them? Shahade's [Shahade 04] history of women and chess suggests not. Shahade reports that among chess players, women are equally or disproportionally represented at all higher levels. That is, about 10 percent of all chess players are women, and about 10 percent of the serious tournament players are also women, so women seem to be as good at competitive chess as men, yet fewer women play. If women were not as good at serious strategy games, one would expect the upper levels to be dominated by men disproportionally to the total ratio of players at all levels. More work is needed to find out why games appeal more to men than women and whether the games or our attitudes toward them need to change to remedy this discrepancy.

Although many game-development companies would not consider themselves biased against women, in our experience many of them implicitly create an environment that makes women feel less welcome as employees. They are usually staffed by young men who are themselves hardcore gamers raised on male-targeted games, depend on heroic development schedules with crunch periods (that are harder on young mothers than young fathers), and engage with male-targeted marking at the developer and publisher levels. The standards in a game workplace are not those found in most professional environments today, especially at smaller and independent developers.

This implicit discrimination is not behind closed doors. At the industry's (now defunct) major press event, E^3, most booths were staffed by female models in skintight outfits. Although it is more from naivety of young developers and the adrenaline-fueled deadlines than maliciousness, the general atmosphere of game development is generally hostile to women and minorities. This hurts the industry's ability to produce games that appeal to everyone and is out of step with societal workplace standards.

Many game companies are male dominated not by choice but simply because few women apply for positions. Why is that so? Psychologist Janet Lever concluded that boys *like* to argue about the rules, but they do so in a way that does not terminate the game session and instead extends it into the metagame of rule development [Lever 76], whereas girls tend to avoid social conflict in game sessions. That result implies that boys (for whatever reason) are predisposed toward the act of game development and might, when they are adults, become game designers. The link is fragile, however, and it does not explain how this imbalance arises or why it persists. Undergraduate computer science departments across America have far fewer female students than male students, and the ratios have been *dropping* lately, in contrast to math and other sciences where ratios have climbed over decades to be nearly

50:50. Thus, one also expects fewer starting game programmers to be female. But this does not explain why most game artists and writers are male, when art and writing departments are often dominated by female students.

On the positive side of gender issues in games, it must be noted that many best-selling games such as *The Sims*, *Karaoke Revolution Party*, *Guitar Hero*, *Harvest Moon*, and most board games are at least as appealing to women as to men. In fact, most of the best-selling games of all time are those that appealed to both men and women; it is hard to become a best-selling game by turning off half of the market. The industry as a whole seeks to broaden its player base and does not intentionally ignore female players. *World of Warcraft*'s popularity is due in part to its success at attracting many female players, thus opening a larger market for itself than competing MMOs. Nintendo's recent efforts with the Wii and the DS to produce nonviolent games with alternative means of interaction have broadened both the age and gender demographic for players.

19.2 Industry Quality of Life

Working on games is incredibly satisfying. The development environments are relatively young, energetic, and liberal workplaces. The products have consumer appeal and grant their developers a modicum of fame. Although successful game development requires discipline and structure, it also requires creativity and ingenuity. Occasionally, a small development company scores a major hit and makes the founders wealthy.

Those are the positive aspects of professional game development. Compared to equivalent jobs outside the games industry, there are many negative aspects. Most game developers work a 60-hour week, with all-night sessions and working weekends being the standard when it gets close to shipping time. Few companies pay overtime or award comp time for these long hours. Developers are generally salaried, and this is part of the job description. Most programmers are paid about 70 percent of what they would make in other areas of the industry, and no one has much job security, since companies regularly lay off staff after a title ships.

In 2004, an anonymous blog post by "ea_spouse," a developer's fiancé, brought significant attention to the working conditions of game developers. The post [Hoffman 04] claimed that Electronic Arts made developers work regular 48-hour, six-day weeks and 85-hour, seven-day crunch weeks, with those who complained being encouraged to quit. The post was supported by hundreds of comments from game developers and spouses, and it led to the creation of many quality-of-life blogs. These agreed that similar conditions existed at their companies and particularly highlighted the salary disparities. For example, at the time, EA's CEO was paid $1.4 million and received millions of dollars in stock compensation, whereas entry-level programmers averaged about $40,000 a year.

In response to massive media attention and employee dissatisfaction, some companies revisited their policies. This included Electronic Arts, although the changes were not entirely voluntary there: employees won a $16 million lawsuit against EA, which also forced EA to reclassify 440 entry-level employees as hourly workers and pay them overtime during crunch sessions [Jenkins 06].

The ea_spouse post and related lawsuit do not mean that all EA studios were bad at the time. It also doesn't mean that after the suit, all are now good places to work. EA has many studios around the world and is one of the largest employers in the industry. At the time, EA was symbolic of a large part of the industry. However, it is a constantly changing company. In fact, some of EA's studios today provide exceptional benefits and quality of life for employees. For example, at the Redwood Shores headquarters, developers enjoy a sand volleyball court, basketball and tennis, and a state-of-the-art gym. They can receive on-site massage, laundry, car service, and some medical care, and are invited to many community events. Most developers are encouraged to work more efficiently, but not necessarily more hours. This isn't just because Redwood Shores is the headquarters studio. Many other EA studios sport equally lavish facilities, as shown in Figure 19.1.

Figure 19.1. Employee fitness room (back), kitchen (left), and gaming room (right) at Electronic Arts studios. In the center is the view out one developer's window. (Image courtesy of Electronic Arts)

Quality of life has become a persistent issue in the industry. The number of different employers is consistently decreasing as large publishers bring developers in-house. In many cases, this improves job security, since large companies, such as EA, Sony, and Activision, are better able to weather market downturns and failed products. These large conglomerates are also good for entry-level developers and recent college graduates, since most small companies cannot afford to train new developers and will hire only people with previous experience.

The downside of a large company is that it has many layers of management, which tends to reduce creative expression and make employers less sensitive to employee satisfaction. Across the industry, having only a few large employers also means fewer alternative employment options for developers. This means that if you like working on games but are unhappy with your current game development job, there aren't as many alternatives as there were a decade ago.

Developers today have several forms of organization that can address quality-of-life issues. The International Game Developers Association (IGDA) has a working group specifically devoted to quality-of-life issues and is associated with *Game Developer Magazine*, the industry's journal. The July 2007 issue specifically addressed continuing quality-of-life problems. *Game Developer Magazine* also publishes an annual review of salaries for various jobs across the industry and a list of the best and worst publishers and development houses. The independent GameWatch.org website (launched by "ea_spouse") has very active forums where developers can discuss their workplace and better understand conditions at a company before applying for a job there.

Conditions are probably better than they were in 2004, but most nongame developers would find development to be more work for less pay and fewer benefits compared to other jobs with the same skill set. Yet many developers find that the chance to work with a tight-knit team on an entertainment product in a creative role makes up for this labor disparity. Some companies treat their employees well and others treat them poorly, and those seeking jobs in the industry need to use available resources such as *Game Developer Magazine* and GameWatch.org to evaluate potential employers carefully.

ea_spouse's own story has a happy ending: she married her fiancé, who quit EA after receiving part of the $16M settlement. She became a game designer, and they are now happily working at another game company.

19.3 Real and Virtual Economies

Massive multiplayer online role-playing games (MMORPGs) are persistent virtual worlds where players gain inventory and abilities over time. In-game objects have in-game value because they increase a character's power. Most MMORPGs contain economies within the game world that allow players to buy and sell objects. Stabilizing these economies has become a major challenge of game design, and many development companies are now hiring professional economists to manage their virtual economies.

Before MMORPGs, in-game objects had little real-world value. After a game of checkers is over, you would not pay anything to have an additional checker. But MMORPGs are persistent, so the game is never over. And because in-game objects are scarce and require time (which costs money via subscriptions and opportunity cost) to acquire, they have real-world value.

A similar situation exists for cards and figurines in "collectible" games such as *Pokemon*, *Magic: The Gathering*, and *HeroClix*. These games have rules that allow players to bring in extra pieces they have purchased, thereby gaining more power. For the games to have some semblance of fairness, this increased power is primarily through access to novel strategies that are well suited to the player's own style, rather than a strict numerical advantage.

Not surprisingly, once virtual objects assume real value, the in-game and out-of-game economies interact. *World of Warcraft* is an online fantasy game with about 7 million subscribers. Players subscribe to the game for years and invest substantial time building individual characters. A huge out-of-game market exists for virtual objects such as characters and wealth. This has led to several social dilemmas.

Most game companies have traditionally banned buying and selling of in-game objects with real-world money for many reasons. Players are dissatisfied when their hard-won achievements are eclipsed by someone who simply bought their way into the game. The only value of an in-game achievement is what a player places on it, so this devalues the game and makes it less engaging. Developers fear the liability associated with theft and fraud of virtual objects, as well as accidental destruction in the event of a server crash. By banning real-world trading, they can claim that virtual assets have zero monetary value and therefore no damage is done when they are stolen or destroyed. Likewise, they can claim that no taxable assets change hands in the game. When in-game and real-world economies interact, the developer loses some control over the game's balance, since it will begin to adjust to the real-world economy.

It has become sufficiently profitable to sell in-game objects so playing games solely to acquire those objects is now a viable profession. This is known in the industry as gold farming, since it was most prominent early in *World of Warcraft* when players pursued mundane tasks repetitively to earn virtual gold to sell in a real-world secondary market. The only raw materials for gold farming are a game subscription, a computer, and (relatively unskilled) human labor. The labor requirement has led to the formation of sweatshops, primarily in African countries and China, where players continually produce in-game goods for minimal wages. This has a decidedly negative social impact that arises directly from the persistence aspect of the game.

Some game and game-like companies actively encourage real-world commerce. *Second Life* and *There* have built virtual worlds with an official currency exchange and produce most of their revenue by selling virtual objects. They also encourage players to create new game assets and sell them in the games. These virtual worlds are at the very fringe of games because they lack goals and balance. This is necessary; it would be impossible to balance a game where players can purchase arbitrarily powerful objects. The relative openness of the economies and, at this time, relative lack of popularity compared to big MMORPGs—these worlds have only tens of thousands of subscribers—have prevented the creation of sweatshops and allowed the developer to directly profit from game-related commerce. By assigning a real-world value to virtual objects, however, they are open to the liability and potential tax consequences. There is also some concern (albeit currently with little evidence) that organized crime and terrorists might use virtual economies to launder real-world funds.

Politicians are eager to tax the increasing stream of revenue from virtual objects. Games and subscriptions are currently taxed throughout most of the world, but in-game transactions are not. Now that players are trading objects and companies are essentially giving away objects in games that have real-world value, it is reasonable for legislatures to consider how those actions are affected by taxation policies. At this time, no country has its virtual assets taxed, but many countries are currently debating new laws that would tax such assets.

Legally assigning value to in-game objects will have a serious impact on games and game design. The most likely outcome will be increased banning (and ban enforcement) of trading and end-user license agreements that limit the liability of the game companies. For those companies that derive significant revenue from in-game sales, this will likely lead to increased prices and increased security and data retention.

19.4 Resources

- Cassell and Jenkins, *From Barbie to Mortal Kombat: Gender and Computer Games* [Cassell and Jenkins 00].
- Hyman, “Rated and Willing: Where Game Rating Boards Differ” [Hyman 05a].
- Hoffman (a.k.a. ea_spouse), “EA: The Human Story” [Hoffman 04].

- Gee, *What Video Games Have to Teach Us About Learning and Literacy* [Gee 03].

Appendices

Worksheets and exercises present a framework for producing a professional design document, and that document guides you through the process of development, helping to ensure that you stay on schedule and plan thoroughly to avoid surprises like "we forgot to budget for an animation tool!" The worksheets and exercises are not intended to reduce game development to filling out forms. Use the pieces that are appropriate for your project and disregard the rest. Leverage them as a channel to direct your creativity and enthusiasm.

APPENDIX A

Minigame Worksheet

See Chapter 1 for instructions on using this worksheet.

All worksheets are available on the book's website (http://www.akpeters.com/mcguirejenkins/).

____

Game Title

For ___-___ players, ages_____ to______. Requires approximately 6 minutes.

Winning Condition:

____

____

Playing Pieces:

______________________________ ______________________________

______________________________ ______________________________

______________________________ ______________________________

______________________________ ______________________________

______________________________ ______________________________

Game Setup:

____

____

____

____

Team Members:

______________________________ ______________________________

______________________________ ______________________________

Rules:

1. ____

____

____

2. ____

____

____

3. ____

____

____

4. ____

____

____

5. ____

____

____

6. ____

____

____

7. ____

____

____

APPENDIX **B**

Overview Worksheet

The overview worksheet is used for the initial proposal. In a classroom, it is also used for homework exercises leading up to critiques. We provide two versions of the worksheet. The first is more marketing oriented and closer to the industry version. The second removes some marketing information to make room for the executive summary and a mechanics diagram directly on the overview sheet. This favors design over marketing in the early stages, which is more appropriate for academia and indie developers.

This appendix includes one example of the second worksheet variation completed for a game called *Agents*. See Chapter 4 for full instructions and completed examples of the first worksheet variation.

All worksheets are available on the book's website (http://www.akpeters.com/mcguirejenkins/).

______________________ *Title*

______________________ *Your Name*

"______________________" *Tagline*

______________________ *Genre*

______________________ *Platform*

______________________ *Target Audience*

Picture

Plays like ______________________ meets ______________________
Popular Game A Popular Game B or twist

Goal: ______________________

Major Mechanics:

1. ______________________ 2. ______________________

Setting: ______________________

References

1. ______________________ 4. ______________________

2. ______________________ 5. ______________________

3. ______________________ **6.** ______________________

Key Experiences

1. ____________________

2. ____________________

3. ____________________

Selling Points

1. ____________________

2. ____________________

3. ____________________

Related Games:

1. ____________________

Title *Publisher or Developer* *Genre/Platform* *Year*

2. ____________________

Title *Publisher or Developer* *Genre/Platform* *Year*

3. ____________________

Title *Publisher or Developer* *Genre/Platform* *Year*

Title ______________________________

Tag line "______________________________"

Your name ______________________________

Genre ______________________________

Platform ______________________________

Market ______________________________

Setting ______________________________

Logo or Box Art

Plays like ____________________ meets ____________________

Popular Game A *Popular Game B or twist*

Summary ______________________________

Mechanics

1. ____________________ 3. ____________________

2. ____________________ 4. ____________________

Reference Art

1. ____________________ 4. ____________________

2. ____________________ 5. ____________________

Related Games:

1. ____

Title *Publisher or Developer* *Genre/Platform* *Year*

2. ____

Title *Publisher or Developer* *Genre/Platform* *Year*

3. ____

Title *Publisher or Developer* *Genre/Platform* *Year*

Supporting Screenshot or Mechanic Analysis Diagram

Title: Agents
Tag line: "No, I expect you to die."
Genre: Modern card game
Market: Techno-thriller movie audience
Setting: James Bond: Near future techno-spy vs. megalomaniac villains.
Plays like *Munchkin* **meets** *Shadows Over Camelot*

Summary: Secret agents from different countries cooperate on missions. **Missions** are random encounters ala *Munchkin*. Success increases the power of all agents who opt into the mission, but helps the current player disproportionably. An agent can subvert others and then turn **double agent** to attack the others and win solo.

Mechanics:

1. RPG
2. Statistical Combat
3. Cooperation/Traitor
4. Recharge time for abilities

References:

1. Robert Ludlum (e.g., *Bourne Identity*)
2. James Bond books & movies
3. *Miami Vice* TV show
4. *Remington Steel*, *Knight Rider*, etc.
5. Alistair McLean books
6. Tom Clancy
7. *T.S./S.I.* RPG
8. d20 Modern SRD

Related Games

Munchkin *Jackson / Steve Jackson Games* *Card* *2001*
Abstraction of RPG-style combat into a card game. Players compete, but can recruit others to aid in random encounters for a price. Combat is deterministic, with played cards determining attributes. Various themes, including fantasy and sci-fi; most self-referential and humorous. Agents uses a board to reduce math, has players deploying different cards each mission, and is more cooperative. Bestselling S.J. game to date.

Shadows Over Camelot *Laget & Cathala / Days of Wonder* *Board* *2005*
Cooperative Arthurian quests with a possible traitor. Each character has specific abilities and a small number of special objects can be acquired. The traitor is secretly determined before the game begins and has little freedom once revealed. Gameplay primarily through cards, with the board only for arranging them. Only effective co-op board game to date.

Top Secret (T.S./S.I.) *Rasmussen & Niles / TSR* *RPG* *1987*
Compact secret agent pen & paper RPG with a percentile-based combat system. Several versions published since 1980, with 1987 version definitive. Out of print since 1992.

APPENDIX C

Technology Plan Worksheet

This worksheet lists major areas you must address in your technology plan. See Chapter 6 for instructions and discussion. (The gray lines make it easier to read the table and have no significance.) Be sure to update your schedule with development time for any in-house technology and the budget for licensed technology. Note that the management tools exclude accounting software and other functions common to all companies and focus specifically on game-management issues; additional tools may be needed for non–game-specific functions.

All worksheets are available on the book's website (http://www.akpeters.com/mcguirejenkins/).

C.1 Common

C.1.1 Document Tools

	Editing Tool(s)	Storage Format	Export To	Export Tool/Format
Management tools				
Document Management				
Schedule system				
Bug Tracking System				
Design Document				
Revision Management System				
Text and Layout Tool				
Diagram Tool				
Chart / Graph Tool				
Internal Distribution Method				
Publish Distribution Method				
Tag database				
In-game help system				
Constants database				

C.2 Video Games

C.2.1 Art Pipeline

	Editing Tool(s)	Storage Format	Export To	Export Tool/Format
Asset Management				
Concept Art				
Texturing				
Animation				
3D Modeling				
UI & 2D Art				
Level Editing				

C.2.2 Audio Pipeline

	Editing Tool(s)	Storage Format	Export To	Export Tool/Format
Script writing tool				
Music Composition				
Physical Sound Damping				
Microphones				
Instruments				
Foley and Effects				
Mixing				
Dialog Recording				
Audio Editing				

C.2.3 Code-Development Tools

	Editing Tool(s)	Storage Format	Export To	Export Tool/Format
Revision Management Tool				
Compiler				
Debugger				
Build Tool				
CPU Profiler				
GPU Profiler				
Memory Leak Detector				
Code Coverage Testing				
API Documentation				
Automated Test Tool				
Automated ("nightly") Build				

C.2.4 Runtime Components

	Editing Tool(s)	Storage Format	Export To	Tool/Format
Engine				
Scripting Language				
Low-level Graphics API				
High-Level Graphics API				
Physics				
Audio				
Network				
Animation				
Copy Protect/Shareware Reg.				
Artificial Intelligence				
User Interface				

C.3 Board Games

C.3.1 Rulebook

	Editing Tool(s)	Storage Format	Export To	Tool/Format
Asset Management System				
Text / Layout				
Illustrations				
Cover Art				
Printing Method				
Binding Method				

C.3.2 Prototype

	Illustration & Layout Tool	Storage Format	Mounting Method		
			Size / Count	Printing Tech.	Mount Surf.
Board					
Cards					

	Vendor	Count	Specifications
Dice, Spinners, etc.			
Other Playing Pieces			
Storage Boxes & Bags			

APPENDIX D

Budget Worksheet

All worksheets are available on the book's website (http://www.akpeters.com/mcguirejenkins/).

Document Tools

	Tool	Each	Copies/Seats	Total
Document Management				
Schedule system				
Bug Tracking System				
Text and Layout Tool				
Diagram Tool				
Chart / Graph Tool				

Art Tools

	Tool	Each	Copies/Seats	Total
Asset Management				
Level Editing Tool				
Animation Tool				
Character Tool				
Texturing Tool				
2D Art Tool				

Audio Tools

	Tool	Each	Copies/Seats	Total
Script Writing Tool				
Effect Editing Tool				
Composition Tool				
Music Format License				

Code Tools

	Tool	Each	Copies/Seats	Total
Revision Management Tool				
Compiler				
Debugger				
Build Tool				
CPU Profiler				
GPU Profiler				
Memory Leak Detector				
Code Coverage Testing				
Documentation Tool				
Automated Test Tool				
Automated ("nightly") Build				

Licensed Engine Components

	Component	License	Cost
Engine			
Scripting Language			
Low-level Graphics API			
High-Level Graphics API			
Physics			
Audio			
Network			
Animation			
Copy Protect/Shareware Reg.			
Artificial Intelligence			
User Interface			

Licensed & Contracted Content

	Asset	License	Cost
Models			
Music			
Sound Effects			
Textures			
Levels			
Animation			
Cut-scene Video			
Audio Studio Time			
Motion Capture Studio Time			

Production Costs (Board Game)

	Method	Each	Num Prototypes	Total
Rule Book Printing				
Card Printing				
Board Printing				
Figurines/Pawns				
Box & Box Art				
Dice, Spinners, Etc.				
Counters				
Other				

Salaried Development Staff (Commercial)

	Monthly Salary	Hiring Cost & Equipment Ovhd.	Benefits & Recurring Ovhd.	Months	Total
Producer					
Assistant Producers					
Art Director					
Lead Artist					
Concept Artists					
Model Artists					
Texture Artists					
Animation Artists					
Audio Developer					
Lead Programmer					
Engine Programmers					
Tools Programmers					
Gameplay Programmers					
Lead Designer					
Designers					
Script Writer					
Q.A. Lead					
Q.A.					

Not Shown: non-development staff, administrative and facilities costs, sales and marketing costs, management and legal expenses, budget/time breakdown

APPENDIX E

Schedule Worksheet

This chapter presents a series of schedule templates that will give you an idea of the formatting and approximate time distribution for projects of varying sizes. Start with one of these, and adjust it to your actual team size and project scope. Try to keep the milestones in place, and change the features and tasks. Remember that as the team grows, the cost of communication and coordination increases.

Most projects require a follow-up presentation (e.g., for a corporate demo or student project) or distribution step (for an indie software release). That time is not factored into these schedules. As a rule of thumb, add another 20 percent to the end of the project for this.

All worksheets are available on the book's website (http://www.akpeters.com/mcguirejenkins/).

Team: One highly experienced programmer, one artist (optional; ignore the art path otherwise)
Hours Per Day: 16
Starting Position: Familiar game engine or series of libraries, temporary artwork

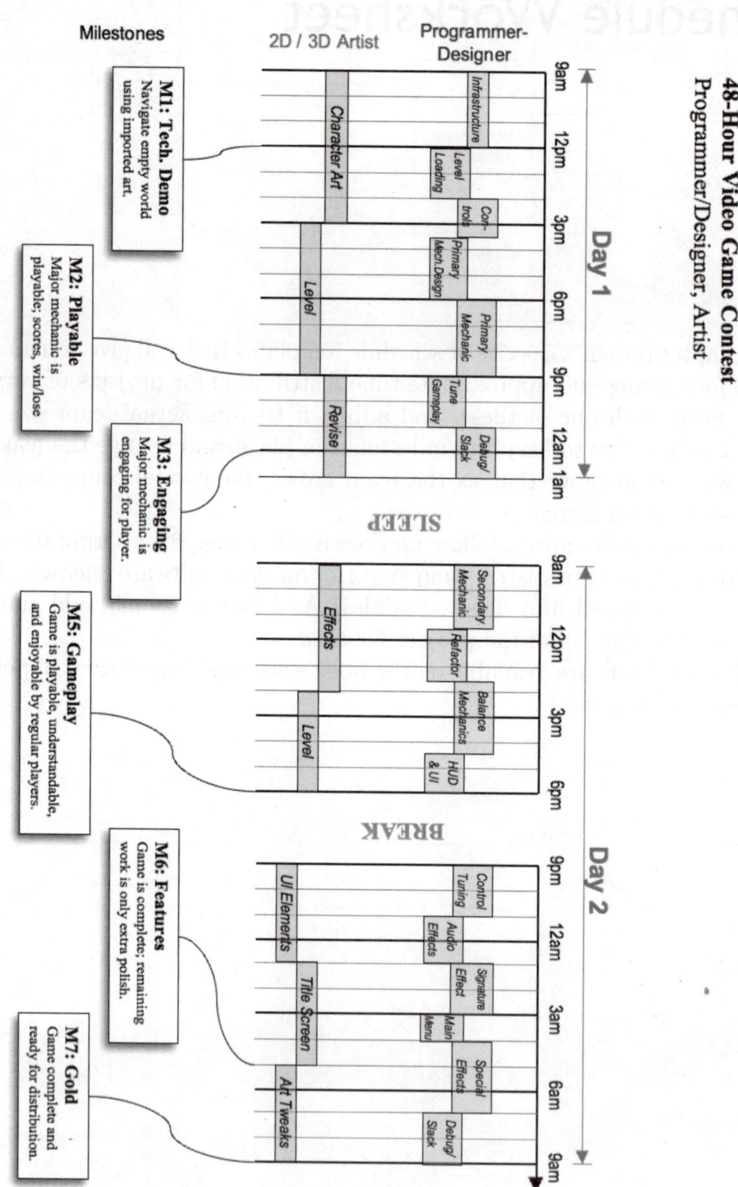

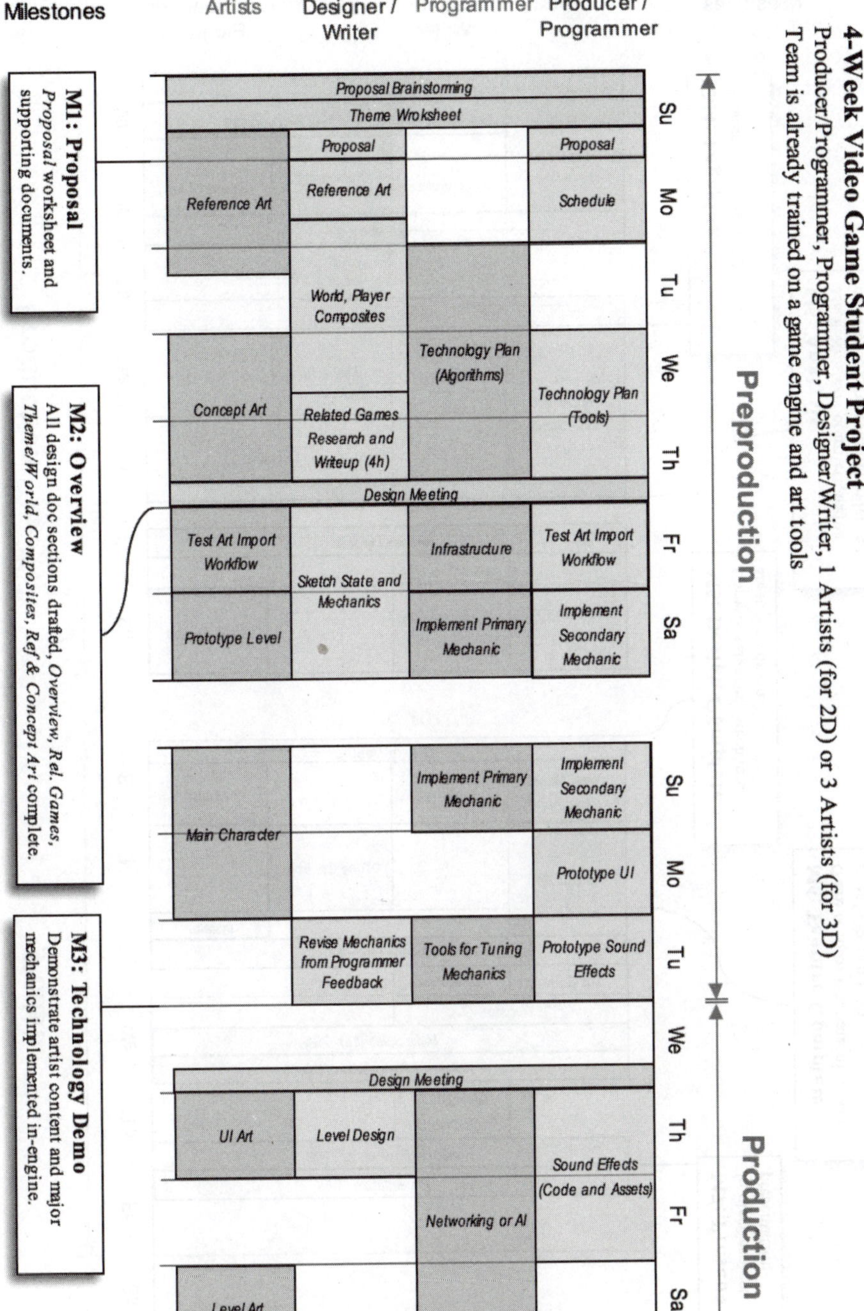
4-Week Video Game Student Project
Producer/Programmer, Programmer, Designer/Writer, 1 Artists (for 2D) or 3 Artists (for 3D)
Team is already trained on a game engine and art tools
Preproduction
Production
Milestones
Artists
Designer / Writer
Programmer
Producer / Programmer
Su
Mo
Tu
We
Th
Fr
Sa
Su
Mo
Tu
We
Th
Fr
Sa
Proposal Brainstorming
Theme Wroksheet
Proposal
Proposal
Reference Art
Reference Art
Schedule
World, Player Composites
Technology Plan (Algorithms)
Technology Plan (Tools)
Concept Art
Related Games Research and Writeup (4h)
Design Meeting
Test Art Import Workflow
Sketch State and Mechanics
Infrastructure
Test Art Import Workflow
Prototype Level
Implement Primary Mechanic
Implement Secondary Mechanic
Main Character
Implement Primary Mechanic
Implement Secondary Mechanic
Prototype UI
Revise Mechanics from Programmer Feedback
Tools for Tuning Mechanics
Prototype Sound Effects
Design Meeting
UI Art
Level Design
Networking or AI
Sound Effects (Code and Assets)
Level Art
M1: Proposal
Proposal worksheet and supporting documents.
M2: Overview
All design doc sections drafted, Overview, Rel. Games, Theme/World, Composites, Ref & Concept Art complete.
M3: Technology Demo
Demonstrate artist content and major mechanics implemented in-engine.

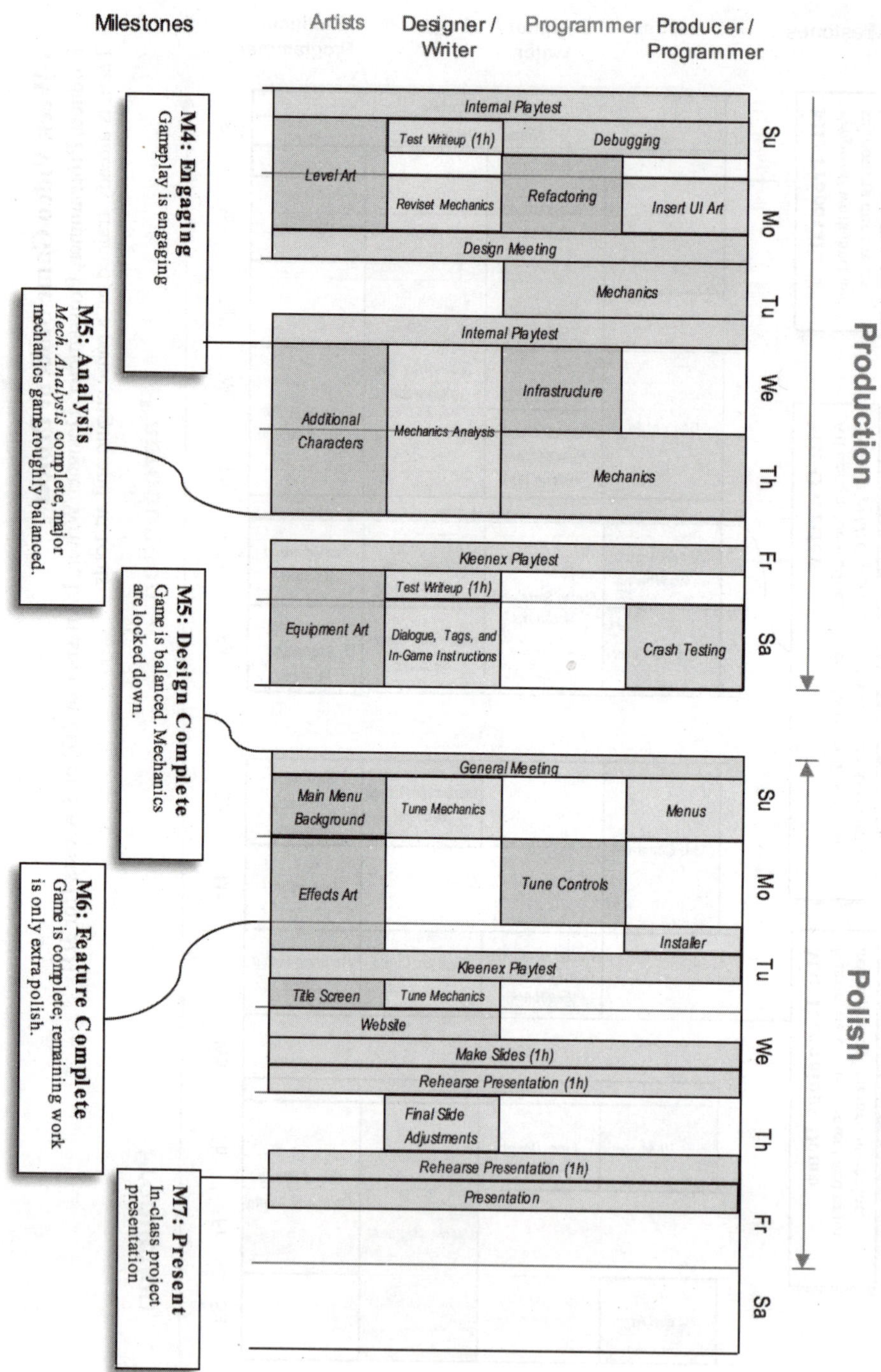
Milestones
Artists
Designer / Writer
Programmer
Producer / Programmer
Internal Playtest
Test Writeup (1h)
Debugging
Level Art
Reviset Mechanics
Refactoring
Insert UI Art
Design Meeting
Mechanics
Internal Playtest
Additional Characters
Mechanics Analysis
Infrastructure
Mechanics
Kleenex Playtest
Test Writeup (1h)
Equipment Art
Dialogue, Tags, and In-Game Instructions
Crash Testing
General Meeting
Main Menu Background
Tune Mechanics
Menus
Effects Art
Tune Controls
Installer
Kleenex Playtest
Title Screen
Tune Mechanics
Website
Make Slides (1h)
Rehearse Presentation (1h)
Final Slide Adjustments
Rehearse Presentation (1h)
Presentation
Su
Mo
Tu
We
Th
Fr
Sa
Su
Mo
Tu
We
Th
Fr
Sa
Production
Polish
M4: Engaging
Gameplay is engaging
M5: Analysis
Mech. Analysis complete, major mechanics game roughly balanced.
M5: Design Complete
Game is balanced. Mechanics are locked down.
M6: Feature Complete
Game is complete; remaining work is only extra polish.
M7: Present
In-class project presentation

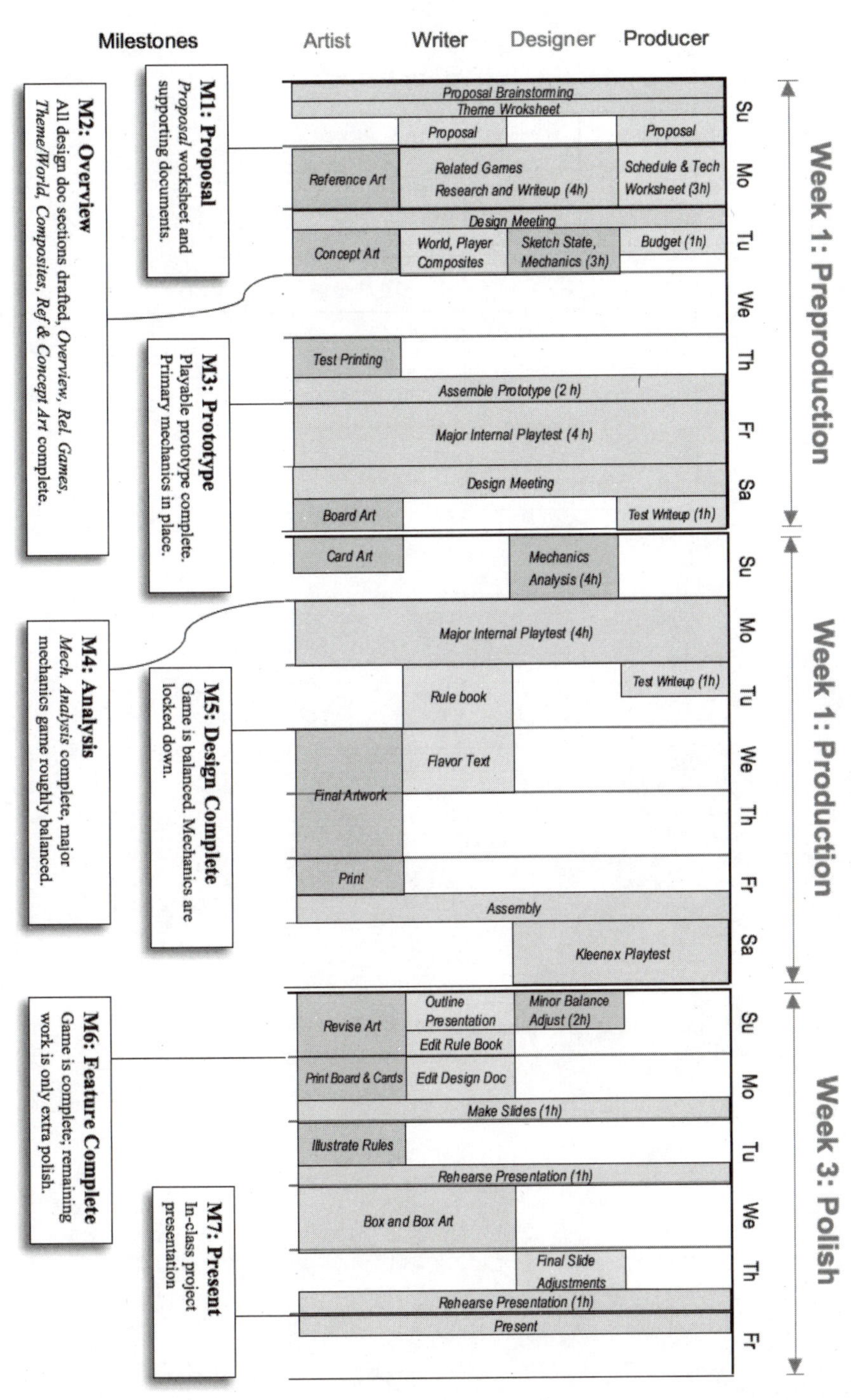
3-Week Board Game Student Project
Producer, Designer, Artist, Writer
Milestones
Artist
Writer
Designer
Producer
Week 1: Preproduction
Week 1: Production
Week 3: Polish
Su
Mo
Tu
We
Th
Fr
Sa
Proposal Brainstorming
Theme Wroksheet
Proposal
Proposal
Reference Art
Related Games Research and Writeup (4h)
Schedule & Tech Worksheet (3h)
Design Meeting
Concept Art
World, Player Composites
Sketch State, Mechanics (3h)
Budget (1h)
Test Printing
Assemble Prototype (2 h)
Major Internal Playtest (4 h)
Design Meeting
Board Art
Test Writeup (1h)
Card Art
Mechanics Analysis (4h)
Major Internal Playtest (4h)
Test Writeup (1h)
Rule book
Flavor Text
Final Artwork
Print
Assembly
Kleenex Playtest
Revise Art
Outline Presentation
Minor Balance Adjust (2h)
Edit Rule Book
Print Board & Cards
Edit Design Doc
Make Slides (1h)
Illustrate Rules
Rehearse Presentation (1h)
Box and Box Art
Final Slide Adjustments
Rehearse Presentation (1h)
Present
M1: Proposal
Proposal worksheet and supporting documents.
M2: Overview
All design doc sections drafted, Overview, Rel. Games, Theme/World, Composites, Ref & Concept Art complete.
M3: Prototype
Playable prototype complete. Primary mechanics in place.
M4: Analysis
Mech. Analysis complete, major mechanics game roughly balanced.
M5: Design Complete
Game is balanced. Mechanics are locked down.
M6: Feature Complete
Game is complete; remaining work is only extra polish.
M7: Present
In-class project presentation

APPENDIX **F**

The Games Canon

Famous, infamous, radically innovative, critically acclaimed, or blockbuster successes, these are games everyone in the field should know about. They form the base of prior art. In any field, professionals work within a mainstream culture that references important previous work. These form the critical jargon (e.g., "this painting references Van Gogh's *Starry Night*") and the cultural context for new ideas.

Research is important in any field. It is how we build on the successes of the past and avoid their failures. You wouldn't try to write a book or create a car without first learning about the ones that preceded yours. When creating a game, you should research previous games. This list summarizes some of the most important games. It is intended as a jumping-off point for further research if a game sounds like one you'd like to make. Read through it to familiarize yourself with the previous work. No game designer would be taken seriously without at least passing familiarity with these titles, and most designers have studied several of them in depth.

For brevity, only the most critically acclaimed (or derided) and popular games are listed. In many cases, a previous game introduced a concept (e.g., *Crystal Caverns* predated *Wolfenstein*) but had a minor impact. These also include the games that designers often list as their major influences.

For additional cannon lists, see Lowder's book [Lowder 07] for an excellent recent review of major board games by famous game designers, boardgamegeek.com for up-to-date Internet ratings, and Wikipedia's best-selling (if not best) video game list at http://en.wikipedia.org/wiki/List_of_best-selling_video_games.

F.1 Minicanon

The minicanon contains the bare minimum set of games that you should be familiar with to appreciate the examples in this book and start making your own games. A games course should offer these or equivalents to students at a minimum, and anyone serious about games should own them. Most of these games are explained in more depth in the following sections and referenced throughout the text (see the index for references). Note that these aren't necessarily the absolute *best* games in their class, according to one specific design criterion, but they are likely the most widely acclaimed, easiest to acquire, and successful.

- *Carcassonne* by Klaus-Juergen Wrede is a board game that features tile-laying and semicooperative mechanics. It has multiple ways of earning points, relatively low variance, and deep strategy and is supported by a series of expansions and alternative rule sets.

- *Settlers of Catan* by Klaus Teuber is a board game with trading and building mechanics. *Settlers* and *Carcassonne* cover most of the mechanics found in modern strategic German board games and clarify the differences in mechanics and business models that distinguish them from ancient games and twentieth-century American games. They have also both successfully been converted to Xbox 360 video games. *Puerto Rico* is a good substitute for *Settlers* and features similar mechanics and theme but more advanced play and better balance.

- Chess is representative of ancient strategy games. It is played internationally from casual to tournament levels and features rich emergent play. Almost everyone is immediately familiar with the basics of the game, and the knight and king playing pieces are challenged only by the six-sided die for the iconic status as the symbol of gaming in general.

- Go beats chess in complexity (due to the large board), age, and elegance (there are only two rules to the game!). Although less popular in America than chess, many classic mechanics and strategies arise directly from the rules of go, including encirclement, flanking, captures, and variable board size.

- Poker is a gambling card game that rivals all other games in terms of tournament popularity and purse size. It is exemplary as a classic card game and relies almost exclusively on bidding mechanics, which can be studied in depth through the many variants on this game. Poker is familiar to most gamers and requires only a standard deck of cards to play.

- **StarCraft**, or any other major RTS/TBS video game (e.g., *Warcraft*, *Civilization*, *Populous*, *Master of Orion*, *Empire Earth*), is a requirement for any game developer. We have a slight preference for the *Age of Empires* series, which combines some modern RTS UI conventions and elements of casual gameplay to make the games more accessible to new players (and also has a free demo of the latest version). These play like a board game but with mechanics so complex that you need a computer to resolve them, nicely showing the transition from strategy to tabletop wargame to computer game. The character-building RPG mechanics made famous by *Diablo* and *Dungeons & Dragons* all appear in RTS games, but the "character" is the army or civilization. Mechanics are at the forefront of RTS games, and these are a celebration of complexity.

- **Half-Life 2** stands out among FPS games. It is exemplary as a shooter, and the engine supports the other popular shooters *Counter-Strike* and *Team Fortress*, but *HL2* also pushes farther toward storytelling than any other FPS and is among the most technically sophisticated of its time in terms of technology and Internet distribution business model. We believe that the original *Half-Life* had a better quality balance (*HL2*'s graphics and physics advanced substantially, but the puzzles, mechanics, and story were at the same level as *HL1*) but believe that new gamers would appreciate *HL2* more because they are accustomed to modern graphics and audio.

- **Tetris** is iconic as a puzzle and casual game, and decades after its introduction is still considered the standard to meet. The elegant gameplay, tremendous commercial success, and geometric twist on dominoes meets *Connect Four* make this game a classic. *Bejeweled*, *Hexen*, *Maki*, and other popular arcade puzzle games are directly inspired by *Tetris*.

- **Guitar Hero** and its sequels were neither the first rhythm games nor the first guitar games, but they took the genre to perhaps its natural acme. *Guitar Hero 2* and *Rock Band* (by the same developer, Harmonix, and the moral sequel to *GH2*) are the best of the series. By combining a physical prop with popular music, these games offer broad casual gamer appeal and have consistently been among the best sellers every year since their introduction. Reasonable substitutes are *Dance Dance Revolution (DDR)*, *Karaoke Revolution*, *PaRappa the Rapper*, and *Guitar Freaks*, although these do not have the same mass appeal.

- **Super Mario Bros.** and its many sequels (e.g., *Mario 64*, *Super Mario 3*, *Super Mario Galaxy*) stand out as best-of-breed platformers. These have tight arcade controls for hardcore gamers combined with cartoony content for casual players. They are polished to a shine by Nintendo's development team and feature a Japanese experiential aesthetic that is still grounded enough for mainstream Western audiences. The Mario games are consistently among the best-selling games of all time, and Mario is probably the most recognizable (and longest lived) video game character—the video game equivalent of Mickey Mouse. As with most of Nintendo's most popular games, the Mario games were designed by Shigeru Miyamoto.

- **The Sims 2** and its sequels and expansions are the best of breed (and best-selling) of the god game/pet-raising genre games. These feature most of the mechanical complexity of an RTS, but that complexity is buried behind fiction so compelling that the player's mental model invariably aligns with the artificial characters and not the mechanics. *The Sims* series is often considered the best-selling video game of all time, taking sequels and expansion packs into account. The game was designed by industry veteran Will Wright, who dedicated it to the memory of Dan Bunten, author of *M.U.L.E.*

- **Indigo Prophecy** is deeply flawed in its action sequences, and the plot goes haywire halfway through the game, yet it is one of the best examples of the potential for interactive fiction. This arcane mystery game features characters that the player will really empathize with and scenes that inspire true anxiety, fear, desire, and awe. Although few narrative games can touch *Indigo Prophecy*, some other well-respected narrative games include *Dreamfall* and *Jade Empire*. The older Lucas Arts games (many by Tim Schafer and with writing by Orson Scott Card) feature rich characterization, humor, and fantastic scenes but only occasionally gripping narratives: *The Secret of Monkey Island*, *Grim Fandango*, *Full Throttle*, and *The Dig*.

F.2 Card

Blackjack (a.k.a. 21). Working from one or more copies of a standard 52-card deck, players draw cards and attempt to build a sum that is higher than the dealer's but does not exceed 21. Except for changes to the payoff ratios, this game has been unchanged since its introduction in French casinos around 1700. Blackjack has several properties that are unique among casino games: the house's advantage over the player is minimal; the players are independently opposed to the dealer, and not each other; and by tracking (counting) the cards that have been played and changing their bets as the odds shift, players can gain a statistical advantage over the house and reliably win.

Poker is a betting game with many variations; it seems to have been a primarily American game that spread up and down the Mississippi river in the mid-1800's. Players compete to build the best ranked hand. Hand rankings are designed to create a steep probability falloff, and the predominant strategy in the game regards the placing of bets. The *Texas Hold 'Em* variation has recently become extremely popular due to televised tournaments with multimillion-dollar pots and extensive Internet gambling sites.

Rummy games, including the most popular gin rummy and canasta variations, have players attempting to divide their hands into sets called "melds" that match by either number or suit. Rummy games seem to date to the eighteenth or nineteenth century and were developed across the Western hemisphere. They are similar to the independently created nineteenth-century Chinese mahjong game.

Bridge is played by four players who work in teams of two that sit opposite their partner. It is one of the classic trick-taking games, where each round is divided into several steps and players attempt to win the steps (tricks). Each trick involves players sequentially playing cards around the table. In straight bridge, players want to win as many tricks as possible. The popular contract bridge variation requires a team to make a contract declaring how many tricks they will win and then challenges them to meet that prediction to gain points.

F.2.1 Real-Time

Set (1991) is a real-time card game played with a custom deck of cards. Players race to identify sets of cards that are either all similar along a certain axis (e.g., color or symbol) or all different along that axis.

Pit (1904) is a real-time card game that simulates a stock exchange floor. The game uses a custom deck of cards that represents different commodities. Players make pairwise trades with each other, attempting to create a hand containing only one kind of commodity. Different commodities have different values, so when played for multiple hands, there is a tradeoff between completing a set quickly based on what is most popular in the hand you were dealt (low risk) and trying to switch to a more valuable commodity (high risk, high reward).

F.3 Racing

Daytona USA ushered in detailed 3D graphics and compelling multiplayer gameplay to arcade racing at its 1994 release. *Daytona USA* is a stock car–racing game that enabled up to eight players to simultaneously compete over an intracabinet network. This game used Sega's Model 2 system board that was capable of rendering large numbers of texture-mapped polygons, distinguishing *Daytona USA* from other flat-shaded 3D racers. *Daytona USA* is one of the highest-grossing arcade games of all time.

Burnout 3 was a critically acclaimed and commercially successful game for Xbox, Xbox 360, and PlayStation 2 that used road battles as a primary mechanic within a nominally racing game. Generic clones of real-life cars take and cause damage as they cover exotic road courses at high speed. Crashes are shown in slow motion with instant replay, whereas the other players' cars are driven by AI to avoid interrupting the game. In the innovative Takedown mode, players compete to maximize the damage caused by driving into intersections and oncoming traffic in short course setups.

Gran Turismo. The *Gran Turismo* series has led to the most accurate simulation of race car driving in commercial games. In addition to its spectacular graphics, *Gran Turismo* has a highly accurate model of driving physics for a large number of licensed vehicles. These physics provide both a uniquely immersive racing experience and a means for actual car manufacturers to plausibly test new design ideas. The original *Gran Turismo* was the best-selling game for the original PlayStation.

Mario Kart is a cartoony take on the racing genre, with Mario, Luigi, and other Nintendo characters piloting go-karts through short Mario-inspired courses. Gameplay is focused on controlling the kart's skid around corners, deploying power-ups, and exploiting shortcuts. Power-ups are randomly assigned, with the distribution favoring powerful offensive weapons for players near the back of the pack and weak defensive power-ups for leaders. The series originated as *Super Mario Kart* for the Super NES platform, where it used a series of 2D tricks to simulate a 3D third-person view. Later versions included true 3D graphics and more interesting courses enabled by them.

Wave Race 64 became one of the most memorable games for the Nintendo 64. Sponsored by Kawasaki, licensed jet skis raced on water through various obstacle courses and weather conditions. The motion of the water and its reaction to the jet ski in *Wave Race 64* were especially notable, given the difficulty in programming fluid dynamics at the time of its release.

Wipeout was one of the first 3D racing games for home console systems, released in 1995 for the original PlayStation. (*Virtua Racing* for the Sega Genesis came earlier but lacked the processing power to make a significant impact.) *Wipeout* featured antigravity racing that replaced standard cars with hovering vehicles with weapons. This new take on racing along with a stylized futuristic look greatly contributed to the success of the PS1. (*F-Zero* for the SNES originated the futuristic racing genre for consoles but did not become a 3D racer until *F-Zero X* for the N64.)

Track Mania is a racing game that allows players to create and share their own tracks in the style of the older Broderbund game *Stunts*.

F.4 Quest

F.4.1 Text

Colossal Cave Adventure was the text-based start of the entire adventure/quest genre by Crowther and Woods in 1977 in Fortran for the PDP-10. This fantasy adventure combined the real-world Mammoth Caves in Kentucky with Lord of the Rings–inspired fiction. Also, it was the origin of the gamer in-joke "xyzzy," which was a magic word from the game that in fact had no effect.

Hunt the Wumpus. Written in BASIC by Gregory Yob in 1972, the fantasy-themed game challenged players to deduce the location of the Wumpus monster within a dodecahedral grid.

Zork and its sequels, originally created by MIT graduate students as a follow-up to *Adventure*, also launched the game developer Infocom. *Zork* was distinguished from its peers by richer storytelling and a slightly more sophisticated command-line parser than similar early text games.

Multi-user dungeons (MUDs) were the extension of text quest games to multiplayer. Essentially the text predecessors of massive multiplayer online RPGs, MUDs are generally fantasy RPGs in the style of other text games but where the leading players frequently modified the source code of the game to craft new items and areas.

F.4.2 Point-and-Click

Point-and-click adventures are graphical quest adventures. LucasArts produced some of the most endearing and innovative hits in this genre on their

SCUMM engine. These include (many by designer Tim Schafer): *Loom*, creating spells from music; *Full Throttle*, Mad-Max world with action sequences; *Grim Fandango*, creatively set in the Mexican Day of the Dead; *Monkey Island*; and *The Dig*, written by sci-fi author Orson Scott Card.

King's Quest was the seminal series for Sierra On-Line. Designer Roberta Williams was one of the first female game developers. The series was built on cartoony graphics and Arthurian-style quests with occasional magic. The series is also notable for innovating the use of pseudo-3D, where predrawn scenes contained multiple depths and characters changed size appropriately as they moved into the distance.

Leisure Suit Larry and its sequels by Chuck Benton are sex-comedy adventures released by Sierra On-Line. These are among the most mainstream of the "adult" games ever published, in part because they aren't as racy as advertised.

Myst series introduced 3D rendering to point-and-click games by using prerendered images. Its photorealistic world, mixture of video and images, and puzzle-oriented gameplay made it one of the most popular games of all time and saw ports to many platforms. *Myst* has seen a number of less-popular sequels, as well as a reissue as a real-time 3D game *RealMyst*.

F.4.3 Adventure

Adventure-quest games are typically sandbox-like environments where the player has the option of pursuing a series of quests but can explore freely between them. Looked at another way, they are essentially RPGs with the advancement profile fixed. These have full graphical capabilities and generally feature real-time combat.

The Legend of Zelda games for the Nintendo platforms by Shigeru Miyamoto have sold over 50 million copies collectively. They chronicle the adventures of Link, an elflike hero who collects magic items and befriends strange creatures in his repeated quests to save Princess Zelda or their world. The series is known for playful interaction with the environment, allowing significant replay in areas—for example, traveling back and forth in time at the same location, changing the size of Link relative to the environment, or changing the time of day.

Grand Theft Auto III (GTA3), although the third in the *GTA* series, is really a distinct game from the previous incarnations. *GTA3* features a fully open world where the main character is a minor criminal who rises to be a major crime boss. The game is known for its smooth integration of vehicle and foot travel and combat, seamless travel through a large city, and crime-movie cliches. The game gained notoriety in the popular press due to specific mechanics for car-jacking, soliciting (and optionally killing) prostitutes, and the general crime-spree theme. This notoriety ultimately helped sales because it acted as free advertising. The game spawned a series of imitators, including *Mafia*, *Godfather*, and *Scarface*.

God of War combines rhythm-game mechanics for complex, cinematic interactions (a la *Dragon's Lair*) with standard fighting-game controls. Mature-rated game that pulls no punches: sex minigames, dark music and themes (suicide, betrayal, murder, punishment), and an Ancient Greece mythology setting that was novel at the time of its release. Massive set-piece battles and hundreds of custom animations create an epic feel. Followed up by sequel and imitator *Heavenly Sword*.

F.5 Educational

Despite studies and arguments for the educational potential of games, few games promoted as educational software have actually been very popular or interesting. Only two stand out as exceptionally successful.

Where in the World Is Carmen Sandiego? is a simple detective quest game released in 1985 for Apple II that was eventually ported to many other platforms and followed up with several sequels over the next two decades, as well as branching into other media, such as television. The primary mechanic in the original game is to use geocentric clues, such as currency and maps, left at a crime scene to predict the next destination of master spy Carmen Sandiego.

The Oregon Trail is an RPG that simulates a journey west from Missouri to Oregon in the nineteenth century. The game was designed by student teachers in 1971 as a classroom aid and eventually published by Broderbund as educational software. The simulation is fairly complex and historically accurate, and it has been updated and rereleased about once a decade.

F.6 Alternate Reality

Alternate reality games blur the line between game and reality by involving real-world locations and technology such as phones and websites. They are played collectively by thousands of people sharing information on the

Internet through forums. The primary creator of alternate reality games is 42 Entertainment, which uses them as parts of marketing campaigns.

The Beast was the first major game in this genre. Launched in 2001 by Microsoft to promote the film *A.I.: Artificial Intelligence*, the game was primarily played through clues buried in an artificial website that helped players track down a killer in a plot somewhat parallel to the movie.

I Love Bees was launched in 2004. Used by Microsoft as part of the advertising campaign for *Halo 2*, this game was integrated with major plot points of that game. Players entered the game through the website ilovebees.com, which purported to be about beekeeping but was actually the portal for the game.

F.7 Traditional Abstract Strategy

Backgammon evolved from ancient Roman and Egyptian games and has been played in a recognizable form for the last thousand years. In the early twentieth century, the addition of the doubling cube mechanic changed gameplay to its modern form by taking the expected value of winning from each position into account [Robertie 02].

Checkers (a.k.a. Draughts). American checkers/British draughts is played on the diagonals of a chessboard, international draughts is played on the diagonals of a 10×10 board, and Canadian checkers on a 12×12 board. Players move uniform pieces by sliding along diagonals or leapfrogging opponent's pieces, the latter option also being the capture mechanic. Pieces can only advance until they reach the opposite row, at which point they are promoted to kings and can move in both directions. The game dates to around 1500 B.C.E., although so many variations exist that it is hard to precisely date the origin or the introduction of alternate rules. The game is currently solved in the sense that computers are unbeatable at it because they can make perfect plays (due to the relatively low [Schaeffer et al. 07] tree size of 10^{20}); in solving for optimal play, it was discovered that checkers always ends in a draw between perfect players, and thus it *is* fair in some sense.

Chess is an abstract strategy game played on an 8×8 board with pieces that have varying movement capabilities. The objective is to capture the slow-moving king piece. Split from its ancestor, Chinese chess, around 600 C.E. and moved steadily west, it evolved a number of variations that reduce the play time and increase the tactical complexity. Today, it is one of the most significant board games in the West, ranked second only to poker in terms of the significance of board-game tournaments. The branch factor of the decision tree is about 37 [Keene and Levy 91], and computer programs with pruning and naive static evaluators are able to beat the best human players regularly.

Chinese checkers is relatively young compared to other games in this category (actually originated in Germany in 1893; "Chinese" was for marketing purposes). The game is played on a six-sided star covered in a hexagonal grid using marbles. The goal is to move your set of marbles to the opposite side of the board using leapfrogging.

Chinese chess is an early (circa 300 B.C.E.) variant of Western/Middle Eastern chess that features slower-moving and more restricted pieces. Games tend to involve more trading of pieces than chess. Not particularly popular in America but played seriously in Europe and Asia.

Dominoes is an ancient game of parallel independent origins (circa 1120 C.E.), with the modern variant derived from the Chinese version. Introduction to Europe circa 1700 C.E. Played by matching pieces to the existing board (i.e., tile-laying), with the goal of exhausting one's own set of pieces before the opponent.

Go is an ancient strategic board game of encirclement and territorial control. Originated in China, possibly around 2000 B.C.E., and moved through Japan and Korea around 400 C.E. Played on a 19×19 board by placing stones of alternating colors; shorter variations are played on 13×13 and 9×9 boards. The game is significantly harder in terms of computational complexity than chess and is one of the few abstract strategy games for which current computer algorithms are no match for skilled human players (the branching factor in the decision tree is estimated to be in the range 150–200 [Keene and Levy 91]). The most significant tournament game in Asia. Unlike most board games, players are very serious about the game materials, with the best sets constructed from nachiguro stone, clamshell, and Kaya wood.

Parcheesi is a nineteenth-century American version of the traditional Indian game pachisi (a.k.a. parchs in Spain). It uses dice, which some would argue makes it not an abstract strategy game.

Mancala is a family of traditional, primarily African and Asian, board games, including kalah, oware, and congklak, that involve placing seeds in a series of pits in the board game and capturing based on this process.

F.8 Stealth

These action video games favor deliberate, cautious movement to slip through overwhelming odds. Players must carefully manage both visibility and noise to avoid detection and strike quickly and lethally.

Metal Gear Solid is a series of games by Hideo Kojima across multiple platforms, released between 1987 and 2008. These are credited as the origin of the stealth genre. Kojima is famous for combining many disparate mechanics into his games. Some of these go so far as to lie outside the game world proper; for example, in the Psycho Mantis battle at the end of the first MGS game, the player must unplug the controller from slot 1 and move it to slot 2. Kojima's approach is a subject of debate among developers and critics. Although most agree that his games are epic and beautiful, many argue that they are also incoherent and therefore not engaging for many players.

Thief is a series of first-person stealth games in a medieval/steampunk setting by the famous Looking Glass studios. *Thief* is credited as introducing 3D and first person to the stealth genre and is notably one of the few stealth games not in a modern setting. The more recent *Assassin's Creed* title is a nominally sci-fi variation on *Thief*, where players are sent back in time to perform medieval assassinations. It is more combat-heavy than *Thief* and benefits from more recent character animation and rendering technology.

Splinter Cell is a series of highly successful stealth action games primarily for Xbox in a world created by novelist Tom Clancy. The games can be thought of as a US-based and more mass-market version of the *MGS* games. Players control Sam Fisher, a US secret agent who infiltrates various terrorist bases. The later games feature cooperative play and team-based multiplayer matches as well as a single-player storyline. The team matches are interesting because the mechanics and strategies for the terrorists and spies are asymmetric. The signature look of the character is his trifocal thermal/night vision glasses, which glow green.

F.9 Physics Games

Although many computer games incorporate physical simulation and even basic physics puzzles, these are games where the primary game mechanic is physics itself.

Jenga is a physical puzzle game where two players remove small wood planks from a large, stacked tower. The loser is the first to remove a structurally vital piece and bring the tower down.

Toribash is a turn-based fighting video game where players explicitly position the limbs of their character to land attacks. Character animation and physics are the primary mechanic.

Labyrinth is a physical puzzle to guide a ball bearing through a maze by tilting the roll and pitch of the maze floor. The maze path is relatively simple but is littered with holes that return the ball to the starting position.

Line Rider is a video game in which the player draws a 2D track for a sled rider, who is then physically simulated through the course. There is no explicit objective, but players often seek especially complicated or long courses that avoid crashing the sled.

Crayon Physics Deluxe is a video game in which players attempt to solve simple 2D physics puzzles by drawing new elements into the world. Rendered with a crayon-on-paper feel.

World of Goo is a construction video game in which the player builds mass-spring systems out of "goo" to travel through the game world and solve physics problems.

Khet is a chess-like abstract strategy board game where a special attack targets pieces hit by a real-world laser. Pieces are adorned with mirrors and beamsplitters to make basic optics part of the strategy.

The Incredible Machine uses limited 2D physical simulation to present brain-teaser puzzles involving Rube Goldberg–style machines.

F.10 German Board Games

Late twentieth and early twenty-first century strategy games, primarily produced in Germany and with Reiner Knizia and Klaus Teuber among the best-known designers.

Settlers of Catan is perhaps the most popular game in this genre. As a more sophisticated version of *Monopoly*, it bridges between causal players of American games and more hardcore German board-game enthusiasts. Gameplay involves trading resources and expanding one's own settlements to control more territory. Relatively high variance and a strong first-player advantage tend to turn off more-experienced gamers. Several expansion packs and a related card game are also available. Extremely popular as an Xbox Live game on Xbox 360, as well. It involves strong player interaction between the trading mechanic and competition for choice locations on the board.

Puerto Rico involves player-run plantations and associated buildings. Players do not directly interact with one another; instead, competition for limited resources and indirect effects of neighbors' actions create nuanced strategy. This popularized the multiple-role mechanic originally introduced in *Cosmic Encounter* (1977).

Ticket to Ride simulates a train network over America (or Europe, depending on the version). Players take turns building train routes, attempting to create paths between specific cities that are part of their secret agenda. Additional agendas can be purchased throughout the game, increasing risk and reward.

Cartagena weakly embodies its setting of a pirate jailbreak but provides interesting leapfrog mechanics. Players use cards to advance their pirates toward freedom but can only replenish their hand by moving the pirates backward toward the jail. Opponents' pirates can be jumped over at no cost, so each piece is a springboard for oneself as well as for the opponent. It works well as a two-player game.

Carcassonne is a board game in which players cannot move pieces but build a map in turns by placing tiles and optionally marking a newly placed tile with their control markers. Tile placement is constrained in a manner similar to dominoes, where tiles must match along their edges. *Carcassonne* is exemplary of the circa-2000 German board-game renaissance. It scales well with varying numbers of players, has essentially two game rules but complex strategy, and is published with several expansion packs that slightly alter rules and expand the available tile set. Tile placement is a widely used gaming mechanic (BoardGameGeek lists about 1,000 games with this as a primary mechanic). It is popular as an Xbox Live port for the Xbox 360 console as well as a board game.

Citadels is a card game that combines rotating roles with city-building RPG mechanics. It plays a little like a simplified *Puerto Rico* but with more direct interaction between players. Today the game is always packaged with its *Dark City* expansion. The expansion is particularly noteworthy because it provides additional cards that can selectively replace (but not augment) cards from the original game. Gameplay is based more on the interaction of roles than the roles themselves, so this produces a combinatorial explosion in the number of variations. This keeps the game fresh for veterans, and amazingly, the game is fairly well balanced despite its design complexity.

F.11 American

This includes early twentieth-century American board games, primarily published by Parker Brothers and Milton Bradley.

Sorry! was published in America by Parker Brothers in 1934, but it is based on an earlier English game. Up to four players move pawns forward or backward according to dice or cards (depending on the edition) in a race. The moves are proscribed by the dice; players only choose which pawn to move. The game is named after a rare roll, "Sorry!", that allows the player to move an opponent's pawn back to the start. The strategy is extremely limited, making this game popular with children.

Rook is a trick-taking card game introduced in 1906 by Parker Brothers that is similar to bridge. Supposedly, the motivation for the game was to leverage the popularity of bridge but to use a custom card deck that avoids the stigma of gambling associated with standard cards.

Scrabble is a crossword puzzle tile-laying game by Hasbro where players score points by constructing English words that intersect each other horizontally or vertically. Players with a large vocabulary, especially including obscure two- and three-letter words, have a distinct advantage. Strategy centers around placing tiles over multiplier squares and controlling such squares on the board as well as creating words.

Boggle is a word game where players race against time to find the most English words in a 4×4 grid of letters formed by simultaneously rolling special six-sided dice printed with letters. In a sense, this is the inverse of *Scrabble*, because players must recognize words instead of synthesizing them. The game easily admits a large number of players. It rewards obscure and long words by discounting words identified by multiple players and quadratically increasing the value of words with their length. The difficulty of the game is related to the letter distribution, which changes between editions.

Monopoly is often claimed to be the best-selling commercial board game. It is a relatively simple economic strategy game, where players purchase territory and charge each other rent for landing on spaces. The game has high variance and a single commodity (money), which limits strategy compared to later German board games in the same style, such as *Settlers of Catan* and *Puerto Rico*. *Monopoly* is highly regionalized, with special editions carrying the street and business names local to a particular city, country, or even college.

Chutes and Ladders (a.k.a. *Snakes and Ladders* in the United Kingdom) is a children's game with zero choices; players simply roll dice and move pawns according to the board. This is helpful for teaching counting and rules to small children.

Risk is a strategic conquest board game published in 1957 that presages the rise of German board games. It combines randomness with more strategy than other games in this section. The basic mechanics are positive feedback in the growth of units, statistically determined combat, and territorial control.

F.12 *n*-in-a-Row

Tic-tac-toe (a.k.a. naughts and crosses in the United Kingdom) is a game where two players take turns placing their mark on the squares of a 3×3 grid. The winner is the first to achieve a string of three marks in a row, in a column, or along a diagonal. It is a classic example of a children's game, where once players understand minimax strategy, the game is always a draw.

Connect Four is a game where players attempt to make strings of four marks on a 4×4 grid, with the constraint that marks must accumulate outward from one side of the board, as if they were physical objects fighting gravity. The game was proven to be a forced win for the first player [Allis 88].

Gomoku is played on a go board with go stones, and players attempt to make strings of five pieces.

Pente is a more interesting version of gomoku, where exactly two stones sandwiched by opponent's pieces because of an opponent's play are captured and removed from the board. In *Pente*, a player wins by making a string of five stones or by capturing five pairs. *Pente* is rare in that it is a simple (it has only two rules), abstract board game that is relatively young (circa 1978).

F.12.1 Artistic Rendering

Okami, rendered in the style of Japanese watercolor, uses character drawing as a gameplay element to allow players to summon objects.

Jet Grind Radio (a.k.a. *Jet Set Radio*) is a roller-skating simulator with rhythm-game graffiti sequences. It is rendered in an anime-cartoon style and was followed by and acceptable GameBoy port and a poorly received Xbox sequel.

Viewtiful Joe is a GameCube and PS2 side-scrolling brawler with a comic-book appearance. The feel of the fighting gameplay and the comic-book look were highly praised by critics. It launched a series of sequels for Nintendo and PlayStation platforms.

XVIII was a relatively stock FPS but was rendered in a comic-book style to match its namesake graphic novel. It used comic-book elements in some interesting ways, such as using a separate panel to show action taking place elsewhere in the scene simultaneously.

F.13 Games by Scientists

These games were created primarily to explore interesting mathematical or psychological properties, many of which have since become popular in their own right. Note that famous German board-game designer Reiner Knizia holds a PhD in mathematics, although his games are intended for general audiences and are not listed here.

Subway Shuffle, by Bob Hearn, is a puzzle game for OS X that involves sliding subway cars around specific graphs; each graph is a new level. The game grew out of his thesis that explored the computational complexity of board games.

Game of the Amazons is a chess variant created by Walter Zamkauskas. Players control four queens on a 10×10 chessboard. After moving, queens shoot arrows at an additional square to which they could move. Squares on which arrows land are removed from play. The winner is the last player to make a move. The game has become very popular for analysis among computer scientists.

Hex was created independently in the 1940s by John Nash and Piet Hein. It was later famously touted as an example of a game that is always won by the first player. Ironically, it has since been produced as a commercial game and is still played online today.

Façade, written as an experimental game by researchers, is an immersive computer role-playing game set at a dinner party. The player sees a 3D first-person, cartoon view and interacts using typed natural language in real time. The goal of the game is to prevent the breakup of the other characters' marriage. *Façade* received critical praise for its AI and nontraditional gameplay. It was originally released as freeware, and a commercial sequel is reportedly in production.

Werewolf. The original incarnation of this party game, known as *Mafia*, was created by a psychology student in the 1980s. It has since become both a popular party game and a subject of some fascination by computer scientists.

F.14 Game Books

These are single-player games that capture the essence of a pen-and-paper RPG in a book-form factor and novel-style story.

Tunnels and Trolls is a single-player, pen-and-paper RPG similar to first edition *D&D*; the books are adventures that require separate manuals to play. It was revised heavily between 1975 and 1979 and experienced limited popularity with occasional reissues. This was the series that created the game-book genre.

Choose Your Own Adventure was the most popular of the game-book series in America, with over 200 titles. Unlike other game books, these used a straight decision tree and avoided all other RPG mechanics. The writing style notably used the second person to avoid gender pronouns for the main character. The series was created by R. A. Montgomery and Edward Packard in 1979, who were also the primary authors for the remainder of the series.

Fighting Fantasy is a popular game-book series in the United Kingdom, with over 60 titles that existed as self-contained, single-player RPGs. It was created by Steve Jackson and Ian Livingstone in 1982, and it was played using a combination of RPG-like die rolls and player statistics, as well as explicit player decisions. It eventually expanded into a multiplayer RPG as well.

F.15 Unique

These games are so radically innovative that they have no companions in their categories and are therefore also important for game designers to follow because they represent new avenues for mechanism advancement. Part of this distinction is simply due to these being recent games. Older, innovative games spawned whole new genres or fit well within existing ones and are listed elsewhere in this chapter, but these games are so new or innovative that they have not had enough time for the industry to catch up.

Shadows Over Camelot is a cooperative board game, where players battle "evil" that the rules force on them and a potential traitor among their number.

Indigo Prophecy (a.k.a. Fahrenheit) is a point-and-click adventure that actually succeeds as an interactive movie and has players controlling *both* the cops and robbers in a horror-crime drama.

Dogs in the Vineyard is a pen-and-paper RPG that resolves conflict by bidding for control of the narrative rather than statistical combat. Thus, players compete to be the game master; it is slightly reminiscent of *Amber*.

Shadow of the Colossus and its effective predecesser, *Ico* (see http://www.dicesummit.org/speakers.php?sp_id=83), each took four years to develop into the full-blown works of art that took the gaming press by storm when released. The games are extremely cinematic and raise complex ethical questions through the player's and character's internal dialog, not external narrative. Both games focus on relationships between two characters and their environment in a dream-like fantasy world.

Katamari Damacy is a PlayStation 2 game by Namco in which the player effectively drives an ever-growing ball of junk through the world, collecting objects of about the same scale by adding them to the ball. The bizarre plot behind this game and innovative mechanic made the game first a cult hit and then a major success.

F.16 Pen-and-Paper Role-Playing (RPG)

Pen-and-paper RPGs involve multiple players battling through a freeform adventure moderated by a game master or "dungeon master." These games generally use statistical combat, polyhedral dice, and complex rules. Although originally associated with cults in popular culture due to the novel and 1982 made-for-TV movie *Mazes and Monsters*, these enjoyed tremendous popularity among gamers and laid the foundation for the rule systems and simulations in many of today's video games.

Dungeons & Dragons is the classic RPG game, which simulates a Tolkein-style world using detailed statistical mechanics. The basic *D&D* system has been revised and expanded continuously (to this day) and was recently generalized from fantasy into the d20 System, similar to *GURPS*. As computer games grew in popularity, *D&D* successfully incorporated business ideas from them, including versioned releases with minor ("point") and major releases corresponding to the scope of rule changes, expansion packs such as *Oriental*

Adventures, and the open-source d20 rule system/one-game engine, multiple games.

Paranoia is a black-humor sci-fi game, where a schizophrenic AI dictator named The Computer rules over a dystopian city. The primary appeal of the game is the wacky setting and items. The game is intended for lighthearted play. Players have substantial secret alliances and agendas, and paranoia arises from these and The Computer's semi-irrational actions. Player characters have clones and frequently die during missions.

Generic Universal RolePlaying System (GURPS) is a role-playing system by Steve Jackson that defined generic simulation rules instead of those specific to a setting (such as *D&D*'s fantasy world). This was the first instance of a generic system. Today, the most famous is the d20 System by Wizards of the Coast. Compared to other pen-and-paper RPGs, the character creation is deterministic, and the statistics are streamlined. All dice used are six-sided. In 1990, the Secret Service believed that the under-development *GURPS Cyberpunk* expansion was "a handbook for computer crime" and raided the offices of Steve Jackson Games, seizing much of their equipment. This raid and the subsequent lawsuit popularized both that game and the *Hacker* card game that Steve Jackson designed in response.

Amber is a diceless RPG by Erick Wujcik based on the fictional setting of Roger Zelazny's Amber universe in the 1980s. It emphasizes actual role-playing over statistics, although characters are described by a point system that is used to resolve certain situations. The game has long been out of print but can be downloaded as a PDF from the Internet.

F.17 Computer Role-Playing (cRPG)

Computer RPGs tend to focus more on statistical combat and character building than on actually playing a role.

Ultima and its nine sequels by Richard Gariott at Origin Systems were seminal fantasy cRPGs that contained large worlds and highly branching plots.

Diablo is perhaps the best-of-breed cRPG, fantastically polished with an elegant online multiplayer component. Essentially based on the classic role-playing game (e.g., *Dungeons & Dragons* character-building mechanics), it took the "role playing" out; players are more focused on inventory and points than on the story and character. *Diablo* spawned a series of similar fantasy hack-and-slash games (many quite well regarded), including direct sequels, *Baldur's Gate*, *Neverwinter Nights*, and *Titan Quest*.

Fallout moved from the traditional fantasy to a postnuclear holocaust setting and incorporated a stronger story than previous games in the genre. *Bioshock* is the moral sequel by the same development team.

Knights of the Old Republic (KotOR) is set in the *Star Wars* universe and uses a variant of the *D&D* rules. It was notably the first RPG in that setting. The game's production values, including story, are generally well regarded, and players can choose to act either for good or evil.

Nintendogs is really exemplary in the pet-raising genre and not traditionally considered an RPG, but such games feature the same kinds of character building and role-playing mechanics. Players raise a group of puppies on Nintendo DS, using the microphone and touch screen to interact with their pet. The puppies grow over time and require regular care. Players can purchase toys and other accessories in-game to use with their virtual pet.

Fable is an aggressive Xbox RPG by veteran designer Peter Molyneux that sought to give players complete freedom to develop their character's personality. The game was a critical success despite complaints that it failed to deliver on the total freedom promised by early advertising. In-game characters respond to a player based on his or her past actions, and the physical appearance of the player character alters to appear good or evil, strong or weak, and so on, based on those actions. It is notable as one of the first major games where the player's actions determine his or her in-game sexuality, with gay romance supported within the game.

Animal Crossing and **Harvest Moon** are casual anime RPGs for Nintendo platforms in which players gather resources and friends. Although *Harvest Moon* and its sequels have relatively complex farming simulations, both games stress social interaction with nonplayer characters over other mechanics. *Animal Crossing* is notable for allowing time to pass in the virtual world even when the game is not being played by tracking a real-world clock.

F.18 Computer Strategy

Strategy games are character-building games where the "character" is an entire civilization.

M.U.L.E. was the original economic computer game. It was written for Atari 400 in 1983 and featured multiple players, relatively complex simulation mechanics, and a science-fiction settler setting. *M.U.L.E.* was written by Dan Bunten, who later underwent sex reassignment surgery and became Danielle Berry and thereby became the first known transsexual game developer.

SimCity was the game that introduced the modern "tycoon" and "sim" types of games and launched Will Wright's career as one of the most prominent game designers. A *SimCity* player takes on the role of the mayor of a growing city. The mayor must balance the functional needs of the city with the happiness of its citizens by setting taxation levels and building new infrastructure and entertainment facilities. It led to a series of similar successful simulation games by Will Wright, including *SimAnt* and *The Sims*, as well as less significant games by other designers, including *Rollercoaster Tycoon*, *Railroad Tycoon*, and *Sim Theme Park*.

X-Com is a turn-based tactical combat game renowned for its atmosphere and combat micromanagement. A squadron of marines face off against invading aliens, upgrading technologies between missions based on discoveries from alien remains.

StarCraft was the genre-defining strategic combat game. It takes place in a science-fiction setting where different alien races with radically different technology trees battle over control of a planet. This introduced what is now called the "4X" combination of elements—eXplore, eXpand, eXploit, and eXterminate—that has come to define RTS games, although ironically *StarCraft* is typically not considered a 4X game because later entries allowed more subtlety of negotiation and trade. Other major series with similar mechanics include *Rise of Nations*, *Age of Empires*, *Empire Earth*, and *Warcraft*. *StarCraft* has aged particularly well; it is still played heavily and is one of the most respected RTS games despite being over a decade old and having very dated graphics and UI elements.

Civilization (Civ) and its sequels by Sid Meier are the best-known and most-respected of the turn-based strategy games. They simulate real-world civilizations throughout history, combining technology, economics, and warfare. The scope of the games is incredible: 4000 B.C.E. through near-term future.

Advance Wars. This series for handheld consoles (GB, GBA, DS) showed that the depth of a tactical turn-based strategy wargame could be implemented on a handheld. Innovative primarily for its simplifications: single resource (money; resource-gathering automatic through taxes), few different units, small maps, and discrete grid movement. Cartoony graphics and battle cutscenes increase the friendliness for nontraditional wargamers.

Populous and its sequels by Peter Molyneux introduced the notion of the player as god rather than leader of a civilization. As a god, the player has the ability to affect terrain as well as the civilization but can only influence the civilization instead of controlling it. Sequels expanded the gameplay and mechanics, and the effective sequel, *Black and White*, introduced gestural input and a physical incarnation of the god's power in the form of a giant animal that the player must care for like a pet.

F.19 Classic Arcade

Classic arcade games were 2D action games originally created for dedicated hardware (frequently by Atari and NAMCO) circa 1980. These established many of the major action mechanics that are in place in more-sophisticated games to this day. Most of the classic games were actually slight variations on previous ones dressed with new themes (see Koster's book [Koster 07] for a concise graphical etymology of these). Most of these games also never end but instead constantly ramp up the difficulty level.

Defender is a horizontal 2D scrolling game in which the player pilots a spaceship that must destroy incoming aliens to defend humans along the ground. If captured by aliens, humans can be rescued by catching them when they fall from destroyed alien ships. The game is known for the difficulty of its control scheme, which contains five buttons as well as a directional joystick control.

Pac-Man is a pie-shaped character that navigates a fixed maze, attempting to cover every square of the maze before being caught by four ghosts. The character can turn the tables and chase the ghosts for a limited time by eating a power pill. The game was followed up by an almost identical sequel, *Ms. Pac-Man* (introducing the first female game protagonist), and in 2007 the original designer Toru Iwatani created *Pac-Man Championship Edition* for Xbox Live Arcade, which critics consider a worthy sequel and extension of the basic gameplay. Other 3D and arcade sequels not involving Toru Iwatani have been released but are generally considered insignificant attempts to exploit the brand.

Missile Command was released in 1980 during the Cold War between America and the USSR, capitalizing on global fears of nuclear war. The player controls two gun batteries that must shoot down incoming nuclear missiles that threaten the player's cities.

Centipede is a vertical shooter game in which the player fires upward from the bottom of the screen at swarming insects. The player loses if hit by the centipede that continuously winds down the screen (as in *Space Invaders*). It was designed by Dona Bailey, the first female arcade game designer.

Asteroids is a free-direction space shooter where the player destroys asteroids that recursively fragment into smaller pieces. The playing field is toroidal, in that it wraps at both the top and bottom and left and right (as in *SpaceWar*).

Tempest is an abstract shooting game where the player moves around a closed or open set of vertices near the viewer while obstacles fly out at him or her from the distance. It introduced the notion of continuing a previous game when lives run out. The original arcade version was played with a dial instead of a joystick.

Frogger. In this game, players hop a frog across rivers on logs and across streets, trying to dodge incoming traffic.

Pong was one of the first commercial games, released in 1972. It is a simple table-tennis game where players move paddles to reflect a ball at each other. The original form was a hobby project by William Higinbotham at Brookhaven National Laboratory, called *Tennis for Two*, that was played on an oscilloscope and created in 1958, thus making Higinbotham the first video game author.

SpaceWar is a two-player space shooter created by Steve Russell, Martin Graetz, and Wayne Wiitanen in 1962 for the DEC PDP-1. The players fight in the presence of a gravity well, using it to slingshot themselves to conserve their limited fuel while battling with missiles.

Battlezone was the first first-person game, the first 3D game, and the first color game (using monochrome graphics behind a color film). The game was designed by Ed Rotberg. Players drive tanks around a planar battlefield filled with obstacles, attempting to shoot opposing tanks. A variation was commissioned by the U.S. military for use in actual tank training.

E.T. the Extra-Terrestrial was released for the Atari 2600 as a spin-off of the film of the same name. It is notable for being unplayably bad and a complete commercial failure despite sales of 1.5 million units, since 4 million units were produced. This was widely considered one of the biggest failures in gaming history and led to Atari's bankruptcy and contributed to the collapse of the games industry in 1983.

F.20 Rhythm Games

Simon is a physical electronic puzzle in which the player must press buttons in response to a proscribed sequence.

PaRappa the Rapper was one of the first rhythm games. It expanded the basic *Simon* gameplay to the PlayStation console and required the player to match both timing and sequence of button presses. The game responds to correct play with the main character singing a rap song rather than abstract sounds.

Dance Dance Revolution (DDR) popularized the rhythm game genre, taking it mainstream in America and introducing one of the first major "exercise" games that the Wii console later leveraged extensively in its marketing campaign. *DDR* players match a sequence of dance steps on an eight-button dance pad as popular music plays.

Karaoke Revolution expanded rhythm games to karaoke singing by requiring a player to actually sing the lyrics of the song and grading him or her by both pitch (effectively, sequence) and rhythm. The series is wildly popular and at this time contains six sequels as well as music-genre specific versions such as *Country Karaoke Revolution*. Although it has produced other innovative rhythm games in the past, this was the first real hit for developer Harmonix.

Guitar Hero was developed by Harmonix and later continued by various Activision studios in sequels. In the style of previous guitar game *Guitar Freaks*, it is a straightforward rhythm game played with a plastic guitar peripheral. Harmonix's attention to detail and inclusion of five fret buttons and a tremolo arm on the guitar polished the game to a shine, and it stood as the best-selling game for two years in America. After MTV purchased Harmonix, they lost the rights to the series but followed up with best-selling *Rock Band*, which merges *Karaoke Revolution* singing, *Guitar Hero* guitar and bass, and *PaRappa the Rapper* drumming.

F.21 Massive Multiplayer

These video games have thousands, or millions, of simultaneous players in huge, persistent worlds. Subscription numbers for these games can be found at http://www.mmogchart.com/.

Ultima Online was one of the first MMO games, released in 1997, and continues successfully to this day. The design team included major designers Richard Gariott ("Lord British") and Raph Koster ("Designer Dragon"). It is distinguished among most other MMOs in that players can build and buy persistent buildings within the game world and that skills are not based on experience points.

World of Warcraft by Blizzard is the largest and most successful MMO to date, with approximately 10 million subscribers as of 2007, dwarfing all its competition. The game does not stray far from the fantasy and *D&D* roots of the genre, but it is beautifully polished and is credited with bringing many female players into a previously male-dominated genre.

Lineage and *Lineage II* are second only to *World of Warcraft* in terms of raw popularity, although their player base is largely Korean as opposed to more international.

Star Wars Galaxies is a complex MMO by designer Raph Koster that is set within the *Star Wars* universe. Despite initial commercial success, the game experienced early controversy over the difficulty of becoming a Jedi and suffered huge commercial and critical losses over a series of major changes that reduced complexity in favor of real-time combat and altered winning strategies in the game.

RuneScape is unique among MMOs in that it is written in Java and runs in a web browser. The graphics and sound are extremely poor compared to other MMOs, yet it has a tremendous player base of about 6 million users and is growing at a substantial rate.

A Tale in the Desert is set in Ancient Egypt. It is unique among MMOs in that it has no combat system and has a distinct beginning and ending (after the ending, the game begins again). It contains proactive interaction between developers and players, with the actual game rules changing according to player petitions.

Second Life is a sandbox virtual world that is a source of great controversy; it has many press releases, branding, and licensing deals but perhaps few actual players. It has significant player building control, and because of the media popularity, it is also beloved by academics. It consists of entirely player-created content, in-game currency tied to real-world currency, sale of virtual property, companies with virtual presence, and no censorship. The lack of censorship has led to significant sales of in-game sex toys and prostitution.

Yohoho! Puzzle Pirates is a casual, puzzle-based MMO in which simple puzzle games substitute for typical RPG combat and resource gathering. Developer Three Rings has since followed up with the cowboy themed *Bang! Howdy* MMORPG.

Planetside This is a science-fiction MMO FPS where three factions fight massive battles for territory on different worlds. Player actions can lead to actual gains for a faction on the world scale, unlike most other MMOs. It combines vehicle and foot combat and is estimated to have 20,000 players, 60,000 at its peak.

Guild Wars is a critically acclaimed RPG series, also notable for allowing MMO play without subscription fees. It offers both adventures and PvP play. Adventures are run as instanced levels, where only the current party appears within the level. Thus, the world is MMO, but the actual adventures are effectively just multiplayer. Play is socially and mechanically focused around guilds and alliances between guilds.

F.22 Sports

Although sports can be considered games, they are generally well known and need less introduction (in part because there are many fewer sports than video and board games). This section lists games *about* sports.

Fantasy football blends the performance of real professional American football players with the personnel decisions of game participants. Players (or "owners") in a fantasy football league select a roster of real players through a draft process and subsequent trading and deals. The individual performance statistics of these players during real competition contributes to the score of an owner in a fantasy league. Fantasy leagues have become immensely popular, allowing football enthusiasts to enjoy the sport in a more interactive manner.

John Madden Football '92 was the first console release of this flagship American football series, appearing for the Sega Genesis in 1991 and setting the template for modern football games. Although it used 2D rendering and sprites, *Madden '92* featured 3D-like gameplay and physics, allowing for effects such as tipping of a pass, tacklers bouncing off ball carrier's, and more prominent weather effects. This 3D-like feeling also emerged from rendering the field about the ball carriers perspective, slightly elevated off the field and tilted downward, providing greater vision of the field. Quarterback vision was also improved by isolating each receiver in his own window on the screen, associated with a specific button. *Madden '92* featured an extensive offensive playbook and defensive schemes for each team based on what NFL teams actually used. Players, serving as their own coach, could seamlessly select various personnel, formations, and plays for each snap. Arguably, the greatest impact of *Madden* is its exclusive licensing of NFL players and teams and modeling of their abilities in the game, giving players a unique sense of immersion into NFL football. Electronic Arts has successfully followed this formula of exclusive licensing, immersive graphics, and compelling gameplay in its series for other sports, such as *NHL Hockey*, *FIFA Soccer*, and *Tiger Woods PGA Tour*.

Tony Hawk is a series of skateboarding games for both PC and portables. The series is named after famous skater Tony Hawk, who appears in the games both as a character and in video sequences. The series was inspired by the classic 1987 *Skate or Die!* title and heavily influenced by *Jet Grind Radio*. These combine racing, rhythm, and quest mechanics with a skateboarding simulation engine for emergent play. Later games in the series were commended for their punk-rock soundtracks featuring popular bands. The latest installment, *Tony Hawk's Proving Ground*, is a great example of portable game design. It can be played in two-minute sessions, yet combines RPG mechanics, about six different quest styles, and free-form exploration along the lines of *GTA3*. The reward cycles are tuned such that the player always has a sense of accomplishment on some quest that can be achieved yet is also always facing a set of new quests that he or she cannot yet beat.

NBA Jam brought about a new form of sports game focused on unrealistic gameplay with exaggerated physics that appears cartoonish. *NBA Jam* is a two-on-two basketball game featuring real NBA players. Although the rules of basketball are roughly followed, players can jump to superhuman heights and perform unbelievable dunks. Defense often involves shoving and pushing over of an offensive player. Midway successfully extended the action-over-rules approach into football with *NFL Blitz*, which featured seven-on-seven games, limited playbooks, and wild tackling.

Wii Sports is notable for its ability to integrate the movement-based Wiimote into six different sports games with plausible physics. The game also has been noted to improve the physical fitness and weight loss of its players. A fitness mode allows players to undergo training, where their performance is graded with an "age" and plotted over several months.

Tecmo Bowl was a highly popular American football game for the NES console. Unlike *Madden*, it featured highly limited gameplay with four plays per team and virtually no plausible notion of physics. Gameplay was driven mostly by simple deterministic triggers to generate game events such as tackles, receptions, and interceptions. However, these triggers were set up in such a way that gameplay was more like a highly compelling strategy game. At every snap, defenses can select one play of the four to shut down, forming something like a rock-paper-scissors dynamic.

Duck Hunt is the seminal gun-based shooting game, originally appearing in arcades and for the NES. *Duck Hunt* involved shooting ducks that randomly flew across the screen, using a physical light-gun technology. Although a simple gameplay mechanic, games such as *House of the Dead*, *Virtua Cop*, and *Time Crisis* use similar technology with a more involved story.

Baseball Stars is one of the author's favorite games of all time, released for the NES. *Baseball Stars* was one of the first games to have data memory. This allowed player, team, and season data to persist when the console was powered down, extending gameplay beyond a single sitting. Users could create teams of their own, improve player abilities based on money earned from winning games, and compete in six-team leagues with up to 125 games. For stat junkies, the game also featured tracking over individual player stats and statistical category leaders over the course of a season. *Baseball Stars* was the first to feature female baseball players. Although the basic gameplay mechanic was straightforward, *Baseball Stars* set itself apart with excellent fielder controls for diving, jumping, and climbing walls to catch balls. If you see one of the authors playing with his iPhone, he is mostly likely playing *Baseball Stars* on the iPhone NES emmulator.

F.23 Fighting

Karate Champ established the one-on-one, side-perspective style of fighting games during the mid-1980s. Gameplay followed the format of formal karate competitions in a dojo, unlike the street-based "knockout" style of current fighters. Two 2D characters wearing solid color uniforms sparred to land single blows to score a point or half-point toward winning a two-point match. Characters were controlled by a two-joystick system for selecting moves that had a high learning curve, which quickly distinguishes a player's skill level.

Street Fighter II set the standard for the 2D fighting genre in the early 1990s. Characters were given distinct stories and personalities, matched with special moves and stylistic appearance, allowing players to customize their fighting techniques. Graphically, the game provided a greater sense of immersion through animated backgrounds customized to locales around the world and large sprites for displaying characters. *Mortal Kombat* followed this template toward a darker theme, using images of real actors for sprites and fatality-inducing finishing moves.

Virtua Fighter was the first 3D fighting game. Moving away from the sprite-based models of 2D fighters, characters were modeled as articulated geometries. Each character had unique body parts represented as polygonal geometries that were kinematically connected by rotational joints. The motion and fighting moves for each character were hand-animated and adapted from actual martial arts disciplines. Characters were rendered with flat shading with Sega's Model 1 board.

F.24 First-Person Shooters

DOOM from id Software revolutionized the PC games industry. It could be considered the most significant game of all time, in part because of when it was released and the influence it had over subsequent games and the growth of the industry.

DOOM was the first major success of the shareware business model. It introduced first-person 3D perspective, the "looking over your gun" view, mouse-look, co-op and competitive network multiplayer, sci-fi marine versus demons/aliens storyline, and a moddable game engine. Every pure shooter since has been a minor refinement of this powerful set of elements. The game was created by the development dream-team of programmer John Carmack; level designers John Romero and Sandy Peterson; graphics by Adrian Carmack, Kevin Cloud, and Gregory Punchatz; and sound designer Bobby Prince. Most of these developers went on to create other successful games and movies at other companies.

Several sequels and games using the same engine (e.g., fantasy world *Heretic*) were later released. The original *DOOM I* and *II* engine used billboard characters and a ray-casting trick for 3D rendering that was only slightly more computationally intense than 2D rendering. The same technique was also used in id's *Castle Wolfenstein*, released prior to *DOOM* but with less cultural impact.

Notable contemporaries of *DOOM* include *Duke Nukem 3D*, which included innovative weapons such as a holographic decoy, laser trip mines, and shrinking gun, and *Dark Forces*, which immersed players in the universe of *Star Wars*. The *DOOM 3* game was technologically sophisticated but lacked the raw power and innovation of the original relative to its peers.

Quake and its sequels are the spiritual successors to *DOOM*, taking the core gameplay and enhancing the graphics with a fully polygonal real-time 3D world. The *Quake* engines were licensed to create hundreds of other first-person games, including *Half-Life*.

Half-Life is one of the most critically acclaimed shooters of all time. *Half-Life*'s only gameplay innovation was the use of crude physics to make "crate pushing" and "jumping" puzzles, but the carefully scripted world immersed players in the story. That story's interesting characters and captivating plot twists led to the game's massive success and several sequels. *Half-Life* extended *Quake*'s natural moddability, which led to the creation of *Counter-Strike* and other popular online games.

Counter-Strike (*CS*) is a terrorist/counterterrorist mod for *Half-Life* that has been the most popular online game for over a decade, combining light RPG elements, strongly strategic team play, and first-person shooting skills. *Team Fortress Classic* expands that recipe with RPG classes and was second in popularity only to *CS*.

Unreal and the **Unreal Tournament** series brought shareware developer Epic Megagames great success and introduced several FPS-game subtypes, including capture the flag and last man standing. These led to the technologically similar game *Gears of War* by Epic.

Halo was the game and the series that launched Microsoft's Xbox consoles and brought back co-op gameplay that had been absent in FPS games since *DOOM*. It offers little innovation over other titles but has impressively polished gameplay, providing an experience that delivers consistently and plays smoothly on the Xbox consoles.

Daikatana was designed by *DOOM* veteran John Romero. It is famous for gameplay (and resulting commercial) failure, largely because the nonplayer character sidekicks have such bad AI that they keep dying and thus making it impossible for the player to progress. As the first title by Ion Storm, it was also released three years late, which made it an expensive early mistake for the company, and the advertising campaign with the slogan "John Romero's about to make you his bitch" was poorly received.

Trespasser was an aggressive attempt to create a truly immersive FPS. Set in a *Jurrassic Park*–like world, it features full physical simulation for all elements and no on-screen display of statistics. Unfortunately, it is infamous in the industry as a massive control failure. The physics and poor controls simply made the game too hard to play, and most players simply stumbled around, accidentally knocking over crates.

Deus Ex and its sequel are adventure games with RPG and FPS mechanics. They are primarily notable for presenting at least two ways to complete each challenge—for example, stealth versus brawn. Designed by Warren Spector.

Bibliography

[Ahearn 02] Luke Ahearn. "The Game Proposal, Part One: The Basics." *Gamasutra.* Available online (http://gamasutra.com/features/20021220/ahearn_01.htm), 2002.

[Ahearn 06] Luke Ahearn. *3D Game Textures: Create Professional Game Art Using Photoshop.* Burlington, MA: Focal Press, 2006.

[Akenine-Möller et al. 08] Tomas Akenine-Möller, Eric Haines, and Naty Hoffman. *Real-Time Rendering, Third Edition.* Wellesley, MA: A K Peters, 2008.

[Allis 88] Victor Allis. "A Knowledge-Based Approach of Connect-Four." Master's thesis, Vrije Universiteit. Available online (ftp://ftp.cs.vu.nl/pub/victor/connect4.ps.Z), 1988.

[Baraff and Witkin 97] David Baraff and Andrew Witkin. "Physically Based Modeling: Principles and Practice." SIGGRAPH Course Notes. Available online (http://www.cs.cmu.edu/~baraff/sigcourse/), 1997.

[Baraff and Witkin 98] David Baraff and Andrew Witkin. "Large Steps in Cloth Simulation." In *Proceedings of SIGGRAPH 98, Computer Graphics Proceedings, Annual Conference Series,* edited by Michael Cohen, pp. 43–54. Reading, MA: Addison Wesley, 1998.

[Barron 01] Todd Barron. *Multiplayer Game Programming.* Roseville, CA: Prima Tech, 2001.

[Baty 04] Chris Baty. *No Plot? No Problem.* San Francisco, CA: Chronicle Books, 2004.

[Bishop 07] Christopher M. Bishop. *Pattern Recognition and Machine Learning.* New York: Springer, 2007.

[Bjork and Holopainen 04] Staffan Bjork and Jussi Holopainen. *Patterns in Game Design.* Hingham, MA: Charles River Media, 2004.

[Bleiweiss 05] Avi Bleiweiss. "GPU Shading and Rendering: Shading Compilers." In *ACM SIGGRAPH 2005 Courses.* New York: ACM Press, 2005.

[Bluth and Goldman 04] Don Bluth and Gary Goldman. *Don Bluth's The Art of Storyboard.* Milwaukie, OR: DH Press, 2004.

[Booker 05] Christopher Booker. *The Seven Basic Plots: Why We Tell Stories.* London: Continuum International Publishing Group, 2005.

[Bourg 01] David M. Bourg. *Physics for Game Developers.* Sebastopol, CA: O'Reilly & Associates, 2001.

[Bourg and Seemann 04] David M. Bourg and Glenn Seemann. *AI for Game Developers.* Sebastopol, CA: O'Reilly & Associates, 2004.

[Brooks 95] Frederick P. Brooks, Jr. *The Mythical Man-Month: Essays on Software Engineering, 20th Anniversary Edition.* Reading, MA: Addison Wesley, 1995.

[Buckland 04] Mat Buckland. *Programming Game AI By Example.* Plano, TX: Wordware Publishing, 2004.

[Capps 06] Michael Capps. "Capstone Talk." In *Symposium on Interactive 3D Graphics and Games.* Redwood City, CA, 2006.

[Carless 06] Simon Carless. "Marvelous Ideas." *Game Developer Magazine*, 2006.

[Cassell and Jenkins 00] Justine Cassell and Henry Jenkins. "Chess for Girls? Feminism and Computer Games." In *From Barbie to Mortal Kombat: Gender and Computer Games*, edited by Justine Cassell and Henry Jenkins, pp. 2–45. Cambridge, MA: MIT Press, 2000.

[Cieslak 07] Marc Cieslak. "Video games: The next generation." *BBC News.* Available online (http://news.bbc.co.uk/2/hi/programmes/click_online/7041086.stm), 2007.

[Craig 04] John J. Craig. *Introduction to Robotics: Mechanics and Control*, Third edition. Upper Saddle River, NJ: Prentice Hall, 2004.

[Crawford 84] Chris Crawford. *The Art of Computer Game Design.* New York: McGraw-Hill Osborne Media, 1984. Available online (http://www.vancouver.wsu.edu/fac/peabody/game-book/Coverpage.html).

[Crawford 03] Chris Crawford. *Chris Crawford on Game Design.* New York: New Riders Games, 2003.

[Csikszentmihalyi 90] Mihaly Csikszentmihalyi. *Flow: The Psychology of Optimal Experience.* New York: HarperCollins Publishers, 1990.

[Derakhshani 04] Dariush Derakhshani. *Introducing Maya 6: 3D for Beginners.* Alameda, CA: Sybex, 2004.

[Despain 08] Wendy Despain, editor. *Professional Techniques for Video Game Writing.* Wellesley, MA: A K Peters, 2008.

[Dornan 06] Cain Dornan. "Interview with John Carmack." *Gamer Within.* http://gamerwithin.com/?view=article\&article=1319, 2006.

[Drake 67] Alvin W. Drake. *Fundamentals of Applied Probability Theory.* New York: McGraw-Hill College, 1967.

[Duda et al. 00] Richard O. Duda, Peter E. Hart, and David G. Stork. *Pattern Classification, Second Edition.* New York: Wiley-Interscience, 2000.

[Eberly 00] David H. Eberly. *3D Game Engine Design: A Practical Approach to Real-Time Computer Graphics.* San Francisco, CA: Morgan Kaufmann, 2000.

[Eberly 03] David H. Eberly. *Game Physics.* San Francisco, CA: Morgan Kaufmann, 2003.

[Economist 05] "Video Gaming." *The Economist.* Available online (http://www.economist.com/science/displaystory.cfm?story_id=4246109), 2005.

[Foley et al. 96] James D. Foley, Andries van Dam, Steven K. Feiner, and John F. Hughes. *Computer Graphics (2nd ed. in C): Principles and Practice.* Reading, MA: Addison-Wesley Longman, 1996.

[Fisher et al. 92] Roger Fisher, William Ury, and Bruce Patton. *Getting to Yes: Negotiating Agreement Without Giving In, Second Edition.* Boston, MA: Houghton Mifflin, 1992.

[Fullerton et al. 04] Tracy Fullerton, Christopher Swain, and Steven Hoffman. *Game Design Workshop.* San Francisco, CA: CMP Books, 2004.

[Games Investor Consulting Ltd. 06] Games Investor Consulting Ltd. "The Standard Development Model." Available online (http://gamesinvestor.com/Business_models/Development/development.htm), 2006.

[Gee 03] James Paul Gee. *What Video Games Have to Teach Us About Learning and Literacy.* New York: Palgrave MacMillan, 2003.

[Glassner 04] Andrew Glassner. *Interactive Storytelling: Techniques for 21st Century Fiction.* Natick, MA: A K Peters, 2004.

[Gottschalk et al. 96] S. Gottschalk, M. C. Lin, and D. Manocha. "OBBTree: A Hierarchical Structure for Rapid Interference Detection." In *Proceedings of SIGGRAPH 96, Computer Graphics Proceedings, Annual Conference Series,* edited by Holly Rushmeier, pp. 171–180. Reading, MA: Addison Wesley, 1996.

[Gray 03] Kris Gray. *Microsoft DirectX 9 Programmable Graphics Pipeline.* Redmond, WA: Microsoft Press, 2003.

[Halliday et al. 07] David Halliday et al. *Fundamentals of Physics,* Eighth edition. New York: Wiley, 2007.

[Hecker 97] Chris Hecker. "Rigid Body Dynamics" series. *Game Developer Magazine,* October/November 1996–June 1997.

[Hoffman 04] Erin Hoffman. "EA: The Human Story." Available online (http://ea-spouse.livejournal.com/274.html), 2004.

[Hogg and Ledolter 91] Robert V. Hogg and Johannes Ledolter. *Applied Statistics for Engineers and Physical Scientists, Second Edition.* Upper Saddle River, NJ: Prentice Hall, 1991.

[Hyman 05a] Paul Hyman. "Rated and Willing: Where Game Rating Boards Differ." *Game Developer Magazine,* 2005.

[Hyman 05b] Paul Hyman. "Rated and Willing: Where Game Rating Boards Differ." *Game Developer Magazine.* Available online (http://www.gamasutra.com/features/20051215/hyman_01.shtml), 2005.

[IEEE 84] IEEE. *Annals of the History of Computing* 6:1 (1984).

[Isbister 06] Katherine Isbister. *Better Game Characters by Design: A Psychological Approach.* San Francisco, CA: Morgan Kaufmann, 2006.

[Jakobsen 01] Thomas Jakobsen. "Advanced Character Physics." In *Game Developers Conference*, 2001.

[Jenkins 06] David Jenkins. "Programmers Win EA Overtime Settlement, EA_Spouse Revealed." *Gamasutra.com.* Available online (http://www.gamasutra.com/php-bin/news_index.php?story=9051), 2006.

[Juul 05] Jesper Juul. *Half-Real: Video Games Between Real Rules and Fictional Worlds.* Cambridge, MA: MIT Press, 2005.

[Keene and Levy 91] Raymond Keene and David Levy. *How to Beat Your Chess Computer.* Batsford Books, 1991.

[Koster 04] Raph Koster. *A Theory of Fun for Game Design.* Phoenix, AZ: Paraglyph Press, 2004.

[Koster 07] Raph Koster. "Blog Post on Construction MMO." *Penny-Arcade Website.* Available online (http://www.penny-arcade.com/2007/10/10), 2007.

[Laird and Duchi 00] John E. Laird and John C. Duchi. "Creating Human-like Synthetic Characters with Multiple Skill Levels: A Case Study using the Soar Quakebot." In *AAAI 2000 Fall Symposium Series on Simulating Human Agents*, 2000.

[Laird and van Lent 05] John E. Laird and Michael van Lent. "Machine Learning for Computer Games." In *Proceedings of the Game Developers Conference*, 2005.

[Lengyel 02] Eric Lengyel. *Mathematics for 3D Game Programming & Computer Graphics.* Hingham, MA: Charles River Media, 2002.

[Lever 76] Janet Lever. "Sex Differences in the Games Children Play." *Social Problems* 23 (1976), 478–487.

[LoPiccolo and Sussman 06] Greg LoPiccolo and Daniel Sussman. "Postmortem: The Buzz on Harmonix's *Guitar Hero*." *Game Developer Magazine*, February, 2006.

[Lowder 07] James Lowder. *Hobby Games: The 100 Best.* Green Ronin Publishing, 2007.

[Luce and Raiffa 57] R. Duncan Luce and Howard Raiffa. *Games and Decisions: Introduction and Critical Survey.* New York: John Wiley & Sons, 1957.

[Maguire 94] Steve Maguire. *Debugging the Development Process: Practical Strategies for Staying Focused, Hitting Ship Dates, and Building Solid Teams.* Redmond, WA: Microsoft Press, 1994.

[McConnell 96] Steve McConnell. *Rapid Development: Taming Wild Software Schedules.* Redmond, WA: Microsoft Press, 1996.

[McGuire 05] Morgan McGuire. "The SuperShader." In *Shader X^4: Advanced Rendering Techniques*, edited by Wolfgang Engel, Chapter 8.1, pp. 485–498. Boston, MA: Charles River Media, 2005. Available online (http://www.cs.brown.edu/research/graphics/games/SuperShader/index.html).

[Moscovich 00] Ivan Moscovich. *Probability Games and Other Activities.* New York: Workman Publishing Company, 2000.

[Mosteller 65] Frederick Mosteller. *Fifty Challenging Problems in Probability with Solutions.* Reading, MA: Addison-Wesley, 1965.

[MTV Networks 08] MTV Networks. *Multiplayer* blog. "Reviews Week" category. Available online (http://multiplayerblog.mtv.com/category/reviews-week/), 2008.

[Mulholland and Hakala 04] Andrew Mulholland and Teijo Hakala. *Programming Multiplayer Games.* Plano, TX: Wordware Publishing, 2004.

[Myerson 97] Roger B. Myerson. *Game Theory: Analysis of Conflict.* Cambridge, MA: Harvard University Press, 1997.

[NPD Group 07] NPD Group. "2006 U.S. Video Game and PC Game Retail Sales...". Press Release. Available online (http://www.npd.com/press/releases/press_070119.html), 2007.

[Omerick 04] Matthew Omernick. *Creating the Art of the Game.* New York: New Riders Games, 2004.

[Perla 90] Peter P. Perla. *The Art of Wargaming.* Annapolis, MD: Naval Institute Press, 1990.

[Press et al. 92] William H. Press et al. *Numerical Recipes in C: The Art of Scientific Computing*, Second edition. Cambridge, UK: Cambridge University Press, 1992.

[Read 02] Robert L. Read. "How to be a Programmer: A Short, Comprehensive, and Personal Summary." Available online (http://samizdat.mines.edu/howto/HowToBeAProgrammer.html), 2002.

[Olson 06] Ryan Olson. "Indie Game Devs: Forget It." *Red Herring.* Available online (http://www.redherring.com/Home/16830), 2006.

[Orkin 06] Jeff Orkin. "Three States and a Plan: The AI of F.E.A.R." In *Proceedings of the Game Developers Conference*, 2006.

[Robertie 02] Bill Robertie. *501 Essential Backgammon Problems.* Las Vegas, NV: Cardoza, 2002.

[Rollings and Adams 03] Andrew Rollings and Ernest Adams. *Andrew Rollings and Ernest Adams on Game Design.* New York: New Riders Games, 2003.

[Rollings and Morris 99] Andrew Rollings and Dave Morris. *Game Architecture and Design.* Scottsdale, AZ: Coriolis Group Books, 1999.

[Rost 05] Randi J. Rost. *OpenGL(R) Shading Language (2nd Edition).* Reading, MA: Addison-Wesley Professional, 2005.

[Russell and Norvig 95] Stuart J. Russell and Peter Norvig. *Artificial Intelligence: A Modern Approach.* Upper Saddle River, NJ: Prentice Hall, 1995.

[Salen and Zimmerman 03] Katie Salen and Eric Zimmerman. *Rules of Play: Game Design Fundamentals.* Cambridge, MA: The MIT Press, 2003.

[Schaeffer et al. 07] Jonathan Schaeffer, Neil Burch, Yngvi Bjornsson, Akihiro Kishimoto, Martin Muller, Rob Lake, Paul Lu, and Steve Sutphen. "Checkers Is Solved." *Science.* Available online (http://www.cs.ualberta.ca/~chinook/project/), 2007.

[Schiesel 07] Seth Schiesel. "Courts Block Laws on Video Game Violence." *The New York Times.* Available online (http://www.nytimes.com/2007/08/21/arts/television/21vide.htmlex=1345435200&en=fcb3722b0fd4c6af&ei=5124&partner=permalink&exprod=permalink), 2007.

[Schneier 96] Bruce Schneier. *Applied Cryptography.* Bonn: Addison-Wesley, 1996.

[Schwab 04] Brian Schwab. *AI Game Engine Programming.* Hingham, MA: Charles River Media, 2004.

[Shreiner et al. 05] Dave Shreiner, Mason Woo, Jackie Neider, and Tom Davis. *OpenGL(R) Programming Guide : The Official Guide to Learning OpenGL(R), Version 2 (5th Edition).* Reading, MA: Addison-Wesley Professional, 2005.

[Schutyema 06] *Game Design: A Practical Approach.* Boston, MA: Charles River Media, 2006.

[Shahade 04] Jeniffer Shahade. *Chess Bitch.* Siles Press, 2004.

[Shirley et al. 05] Peter Shirley et al. *Fundamentals of Computer Graphics, Second Edition.* Wellesley, MA: A K Peters, 2005.

[Sims 94] Karl Sims. "Evolving Virtual Creatures." In Proceedings of SIGGRAPH 94, Computer Graphics Proceedings, Annual Conference Series, edited by Andrew Glassner, pp. 15–22. New York: ACM Press, 1994.

[Slavicsek et al. 04] Bill Slavicsek et al. *d20 Modern System Reference Document.* Wizards of the Coast. Available online (http://www.wizards.com/default.asp?x=d20/article/msrd), 2004.

[Snader 00] Jon C. Snader. *Effective TCP/IP Programming: 44 Tips to Improve your Network Programs.* Reading, MA: Addison-Wesley Professional, 2000.

[Spector 07] Warren Spector. "ACM SIGGRAPH Video Game Symposium Keynote," 2007.

[Spong et al. 05] Mark W. Spong. *Robot Modeling and Control.* New York: Wiley, 2005.

[Stam 03] Jos Stam. "Real-Time Fluid Dynamics for Games." In *Game Developers Conference*, 2003.

[Stanley et al. 06] Kenneth O. Stanley, Bobby D. Bryant, Igor Karpov, and Risto Miikkulainen. "Real-Time Evolution of Neural Networks in the NERO Video Game." In *Proceedings of National Conference on Artificial Intelligence*, 2006.

[Steed 01] Paul Steed. *Modeling a Character in 3DS Max.* Plano, TX: Wordware Publishing, 2002.

[Steed 02] Paul Steed. *Animating Real-Time Game Characters.* Hingham, MA: Charles River Media, 2002.

[Stevens 97] W. Richard Stevens. *UNIX Network Programming: Networking APIs: Sockets and XTI.* Upper Saddle River, NJ: Prentice Hall PTR, 1997.

[Stroustrup 00] Bjarne Stroustrup. *The C++ Programming Language.* Reading, MA: Addison-Wesley Longman, 2000.

[Terdiman 03] Pierre Terdiman. "OPCODE: Optimized Collision Detection." Available online (http://www.codercorner.com/Opcode.htm), 2003.

[Todd 07] Deborah Todd. *Game Design: From Blue Sky to Green Light.* Wellesley, MA: A K Peters, 2007.

[Turcan and Wasson 03] Peter Turcan and Mike Wasson. *Fundamentals of Audio and Video Programming for Games.* Redmond, WA: Microsoft Press, 2003.

[Viega et al. 02] Jon Viega, Pravir Chandra, and Matt Messier. *Network Security with OpenSSL.* Sebastopol, CA: O'Reilly & Associates, 2002.

[Viega et al. 03] John Viega, Matt Messier, and Genen Spafford. *Secure Programming Cookbook for C and C++.* Sebastopol, CA: O'Reilly & Associates, 2003.

[Walker and Walker 01] Chad Walker and Eric Walker. *Game Modeling Using Low Polygon Techniques.* Hingham, MA: Charles River Media, 2001.

[Wang 61] Hao Wang. "Proving Theorems by Pattern Recognition–II." *Bell System Tech. Journal* 40:1 (1961), 1–41.

[Wang 65] Hao Wang. "Games, Logic and Computers." *Scientific American.*

[Ward et al. 07] Kelly Ward et al. "A Survey on Hair Modeling: Styling, Simulation, and Rendering." *IEEE Trans. on Visualization and Computer Graphics* 13:2 (2007) 213–234.

[West 06] Mick West. "Using Verlet Physics to Simulate Blobs." *Game Developer Magazine*, May 2006.

[West 07] Mick West. "Practical Fluid Dynamics." *Game Developer Magazine*, March/April 2007.

Index